THE FALLS OF ROME

Over the course of the fourth through seventh centuries, Rome witnessed a succession of five significant political and military crises, including the Sack of Rome, the Vandal occupation, and the demise of the Senate. Historians have traditionally considered these crises as defining events, and thus critical to our understanding of the "decline and fall of Rome." In this volume, Michele Renee Salzman offers a fresh interpretation of the tumultuous events that occurred in Rome during Late Antiquity. Focusing on the resilience of successive generations of Roman men and women and their ability to reconstitute their city and society, Salzman demonstrates the central role that the senatorial aristocracy played, and the limited influence of the papacy during this period. Her provocative study provides a new explanation for the longevity of Rome and its ability, not merely to survive, but even to thrive over the last three centuries of the Western Roman Empire.

MICHELE RENEE SALZMAN is Professor of History at the University of California, Riverside. A recipient of fellowships from the National Endowment for the Humanities, the American Academy in Rome, the Institute for Advanced Study, Princeton, the American Philosophical Society, and the Institute for Advanced Study in Jerusalem. She is the author of *On Roman Time: The Codex Calendar of 354 and the Rhythms of Urban Life in Late Antiquity* (1990), and *The Making of a Christian Aristocracy* (2002). She has also published *The Letters of Symmachus. Book 1. Introduction, Text and Commentary. Translation with Michael Roberts* (2011). She is the General Editor of *The Cambridge History of Religions in the Ancient World* (Cambridge University Press, 2013). With Michael Roberts, she has also published *The Letters of Symmachus. Book 1* (2011), and coedited two books, *Pagans and Christians in Late Antique Rome: Conflict, Competition and Coexistence in the Fourth Century* (Cambridge University Press, 2016), with M. Sághy and R. Lizzi Testa, and *Violence in Late Antiquity: Perceptions and Practices* (2006), with E. Albu, H. Drake, M. Maas, and C. Rapp.

The Falls of Rome

Crises, Resilience, and Resurgence in Late Antiquity

MICHELE RENEE SALZMAN

University of California, Riverside

CAMBRIDGE UNIVERSITY PRESS

Shaftesbury Road, Cambridge CB2 8EA, United Kingdom

One Liberty Plaza, 20th Floor, New York, NY 10006, USA

477 Williamstown Road, Port Melbourne, VIC 3207, Australia

314–321, 3rd Floor, Plot 3, Splendor Forum, Jasola District Centre, New Delhi – 110025, India

103 Penang Road, #05–06/07, Visioncrest Commercial, Singapore 238467

Cambridge University Press is part of Cambridge University Press & Assessment, a department of the University of Cambridge.

We share the University's mission to contribute to society through the pursuit of education, learning and research at the highest international levels of excellence.

www.cambridge.org
Information on this title: www.cambridge.org/9781107529090

DOI: 10.1017/9781316275924

First published 2021
First paperback edition 2024

A catalogue record for this publication is available from the British Library

Library of Congress Cataloging-in-Publication data
NAMES: Salzman, Michele Renee, author.
TITLE: The Falls of Rome: Crises, Resilience and Resurgence in Late Antiquity / Michele Renee Salzman, University of California, Riverside.
DESCRIPTION: Cambridge, United Kingdom ; New York, NY : Cambridge University Press, [2021] | Includes bibliographical references and index.
IDENTIFIERS: LCCN 2021008470 | ISBN 9781107111424 (hardback) | ISBN 9781316275924 (ebook)
SUBJECTS: LCSH: Rome – History – Empire, 284–476. | Rome (Italy) – History – 476–1420. | Rome – History – Germanic Invasions, 3rd-6th centuries. | Rome – Politics and government – 284–476. | Rome (Italy) – Politics and government.
CLASSIFICATION: LCC DG311 .S315 2019 | DDC 937/.09–dc23
LC record available at https://lccn.loc.gov/2021008470

ISBN   978-1-107-11142-4   Hardback
ISBN   978-1-107-52909-0   Paperback

Contents

Maps

Figures

Acknowledgments

I want to thank the many students whom I have taught, especially on-site in Rome and Italy, for their curiosity. When teaching about the monuments and topography of the city of Rome, I asked them to consider the fate of these sites after their initial construction – not just the physical spaces, but the people who made the institutions that existed in these places and that changed over the *longue durée*. This question invariably led to other issues. Over the years, I realized that there was nothing easily available in English that satisfied my students about even such a fundamental Roman institution as the Senate, whose central building still stands in the Roman Forum. Student questions about the fate of the city of Rome provided the genesis of this book, which has led me to focus, more and more, on its leaders – its senatorial aristocracy, its emperors, and its bishops – who, in confronting crises, managed to restore and rebuild Rome, time and again. I have been deeply inspired by their resilience.

This book covers more than three centuries. I have relied on and learned much from the scholarship of my predecessors and my contemporaries. There has been an explosion of historical and archaeological research, much of it in Italian, French, and German. I have tried to utilize as much of it as was relevant. I have incorporated revised versions of three earlier articles into this book, but I have added to each of these articles. And I reference my other publications in the notes as well.

I want to acknowledge my debt to my many colleagues with whom I have shared ideas and words over the years of this book's gestation: Ryan Albrecht, Emily Albu, M. Shane Bjornlie, Ra'anan Boustan, Kim Bowes, Peter Brown, Sarah Bühler, Giovanni Cecconi, Angelos Chaniotis, Guido Clemente, Sam Cohen, Nicola Denzey Lewis, Elizabeth Digeser, Hal Drake, Susanna Elm, Paula Fredriksen, Patrick Geary, Caroline Goodson, Piotr Gorecki, Monica Hellström, David Hunter, Kristina Iara, Oded Irshai, Gregor Kalas, Jacob

Latham, Noel Lenski, Helmut Leppin, Mark Letteney, Paolo Liverani, Rita Lizzi Testa, Carlos Machado, Muriel Moser, James O'Donnell, Fabrizio Oppedisano, Silvia Orlandi, Pierfrancesco Porena, Claudia Rapp, Helmut Reimitz, Sebastian Schmidt-Hoffner, Ed Schoolman, Kristina Sessa, Brent Shaw, Karen Torjesen, Dennis Trout, Andrew Wallace-Hadrill, Edward Watts, Zeev Weiss, John Weisweiler, and Ann Marie Yasin.

A grant from the Center for Ideas and Society from the University of California, Riverside allowed me to hold a workshop on my book in September 2020. I owe a large debt of thanks to the participants of that seminar, including M. Shane Bjornlie, Nicola Denzey Lewis, Piotr Gorecki, Kristina Sessa, and Edward Watts. Their comments were extremely helpful in shaping and correcting the final manuscript.

Various friends and colleagues have happily read and commented on different chapters. I want to thank especially Brent Shaw for his careful reading of an earlier version of Chapter 2, which I delivered at the 2020 Annual Meeting of the Society for Classical Studies, Seminar on *State Elites: Senators, Emperors and Roman Political Culture 25 BCE–400 CE*. And a special thanks to Rita Lizzi Testa, who generously shared her ideas and read a version of Chapter 6. Ned Schoolman and Samuel Cohen were generous in their time and made helpful suggestions on Chapters 6 and 7.

In addition, I have benefited greatly from the editorial help that I have received from Beatrice Rehl, Vici Casano, Katherine Tengco Barbaro, and Bret Workman. Over the years, I have had able research assistance from talented graduate students, many of whom are now professors, including Moyses Marcos, Richard Rush, and Colin Whiting. I greatly appreciate Ian Mladjov's willingness to realize the maps for this book; they are a glorious addition. Richard Rush has been invaluable in preparing the index.

There are many institutions that have supported my work, and I am most grateful to each of them. Special thanks go to the American Academy in Rome and its library staff. The head librarian, Sebastian Hierl, along with Paolo Brozzi, Denise Gavio, Kristine Iara, and Paolo Imperatore have offered me a second research home over many years. My desk there on the lower level has been a scholar's dream. A residency at the American Academy in Rome offered me the time and space to research and think, and I have returned often to this community. A Fellowship at the Institute for Advanced Study in Princeton opened up a tremendous opportunity to work on the final two chapters of this book, with the benefit of conversations with Peter Brown, Angelos Chaniotis, Patrick Geary, and Helmut Reimitz. I appreciated my two months as a visiting scholar at Tübingen University where I profited from sharing my work with Sarah Bühler, Sebastian

Schmidt-Hofner, and John Weisweiler. A weeklong visit to Cambridge University allowed me to discuss the last two chapters with audiences, thanks to the support of Caroline Goodson and Andrew Wallace-Hadrill. I am grateful to the Institute for Advanced Study in Jerusalem, where I participated in two research groups that helped focus on different aspects related to my book, the first with Oded Irshai and Brouria Britton-Ashkelony, the second with Oren Tal, Rina Talgam, and Zeev Weiss. A fellowship from the Bogliasco Foundation offered me the opportunity to research Chapter 2 at a critical time in my thinking.

The California Consortium for Late Antiquity, funded by the University of California, has been a constant source of stimulation and support. It has allowed me to work through various aspects of this book among wonderful friends and colleagues: Emily Albu, Diliana Angelova, Ra'anan Boustan, Mike Chin, Elisabeth Digeser, Hal Drake, Susanna Elm, Claudia Rapp, Ed Watts, and Ann Marie Yasin.

This book represents a journey that has been made possible only because of the constant love, sustenance, and caring of my family and friends. I want to send my love to my brother Kelvin Salzman and his wife Marsha Salzman, and their children Harrison, Russell, and Beth Salzman, and Harrison's husband, Mark; and to my brothers-in-law, Michael and Armand Brint, and Michael's wife, Sue Brint; and to my inspiring mother and father-in-law, Shirl and Wally Grayson. My special thanks to my wonderful children, Juliana and Ben Brint, and to my son-in-law, William Sommer IV. They have patiently endured visiting far too many Roman "rocks" on family trips over the year. Finally, this book is dedicated to my husband Steven Brint, whose ability to support and find joy in things small and large still amazes me. Through the years of my talking and working on this book, reading and responding to my ideas, and enduring through and well before these pandemic times, my husband, Steven Brint, has been a constant source of love.

Abbreviations for Frequently Cited Works

All abbreviations in the notes follow standard format in the Chicago Manual of Style. *Here I list the abbreviations used for frequently cited works in the notes for easy reference.*

Anon. Val. = Anonymus Valesianus, in J. C. Rolfe (transl.), *Ammianus Marcellinus*, vol. 3, Loeb Classical Library, Cambridge, MA, 1982, pp. 508–69.

PCBE. Italiae = *Prosopographie Chrétienne du Bas-Empire Part 2. Italie (313–604)*, 2 vols., Rome, 1999–2000.

Blockley 1983 = *The Fragmentary Classicizing Historians of the Later Roman Empire: Eunapius, Olympiodorus, Priscus and Malchus*, ed. R. C. Blockley, 2 vols.: Text, Translation and Historiographical Notes (ARCA 10), Liverpool, 1983.

CA = *Collectio Avellana, Epistulae imperatorum pontificum aliorum inde ab a. CCCLXVII usque ad a. DLIII datae Avellana quae dicitur collectio*, ed. O. Guenther (= *CSEL* 35). Part I, Prolegomena. Epistulae I–CIV. Vienna, 1895. Pars II, Epistulae CV–CCXXXXIIII, Vienna 1898.

Cass. *Var.* = *Cassiodori Senatoris Variae*, ed. T. Mommsen (*Monumenta Germaniae Historica*). Auctores Antiquissimi 12, Berlin, 1894. Translation by M. S. Bjornlie, *The Variae. The Complete Translation*, Oakland, CA, 2019.

CBCR = *Corpus Basilicarum Christianarum Romae*, ed. R. Krautheimer, R.V. Frankl and S. Corbett, 5 vols. Vatican City, 1937–77.

CCSL = *Corpus Christianorum, Series latina.* Turnhout.

CIL = *Corpus Inscriptionum Latinarum*

CSEL = *Corpus Scriptorum Ecclesiasticorum Latinorum*, 104 vols. Vienna.

C. *Iust.* = *Codex Justinianus*, in P. Krüger (ed.), *Corpus iuris civilis*, 2 vols. Berlin 1887. Translation by B. W. Frier, ed. *The Codex of Justinian: a new annotated translation*, 3 vols., Cambridge, 2016.

C.Th. = *Codex Theodosianus*, in T. Mommsen and P. Meyer et al. (eds.), *Theodosiani Libri XVI cum Constitutionibus Sirmondianis,* Berlin, 1905. Translation by C. Pharr, *The Theodosian Code and Novels and the Sirmondian Constitutions*, Philadelphia, 1969.

EDR = *Epigraphic Database Roma* (http://www.edr.-edr.it/default/index.php).

Frag. = *Fragmenta*, Fragments

Gregory, Ep. = *S. Gregorii Magni Registrum Epistularum, Corpus Christianorum Series Latina 140, Libri I–VII: 140A, Libri VIII–XIV, Appendix*, ed. D. Norberg, Turnhout, 1982. Translation by J. R. C. Martyn, *The Letters of Gregory the Great,* 3 vols., Toronto, 2004.

HE = *Ecclesiastical History*

Hist. Aug. = *Scriptores Historiae Augustae,* text and translation by D. Magie, 3 vols., *LCL*, Cambridge, MA and London, UK, 1982–91.

ICUR = *Inscriptiones Christianae urbis Romae septimo saeculo antiquiores*, 3 vols., ed. G. B. De Rossi, Rome, 1857–1915.

IG = *Inscriptiones Graecae*

ILCV = *Inscriptiones Latinae Christianae veteres,* ed. E. Diehl, Berlin, 1925–31.

ILS = *Inscriptiones Latinae selectae,* ed. H. Dessau, Berlin, 1892–1916.

Just *Nov.* = Justinian, *Novellae, Corpus Iuris Civilis*, vol. 3: eds. R. Schoell and W. Kroll, Berlin, 1954 rept. of 1895 edition. Translation in *The Novels of Justinian*, by D.M.D. Miller and P. Sarris, Cambridge, 2018, 2 vols.

Lib. Pont. = *Liber pontificalis*, ed. L. Duchesne, *Le Liber Pontificalis: Texte, introduction et commentaire*, BEFAR, vol. 1, Paris, 1981 reprint of 2nd ed. of L. Duchesne (Paris, 1955–57; original edition, 2 vols. 1886–92). Translation by R. Davis, *The Book of Popes*, Liverpool, 2010 reprint.

Lib. Pont. Eccl. Rav. = Agnellus Ravennatis, *Liber Pontificalis Ecclesiae Ravennatis*, ed. D. Deliyannis, Turnhout, 2006.

LCL = *Loeb Classical Library*

LSA = *Last Statues of Antiquity* (http://laststatues.classics.ox.ac.uk)

LTUR = *Lexicon topographicum urbis Romae*, 6 vols., ed. E. M. Steinby, Rome, 1993–2000.

LTUR Suburbium = *Lexicon topographicum urbis Romae: Suburbium,* 5 vols., ed. A. La Regina, Rome, 2001–8.

MGH.AA = *Monumenta Germaniae Historica. Auctores Antiquissimi*, Berlin.

N. Anth. = Anthemius, *Novellae*, in T. Mommsen and P. Meyer, eds., *Theodosiani Libri XVI cum Constitutionibus Sirmondianis et Leges novellae ad Theodosianum pertinentes*, vol. 2, Berlin, 1905.

N. Maj. = Majorian, *Novellae,* in T. Mommsen and P. Meyer eds., *Theodosiani Libri XVI cum Constitutionibus Sirmondianis et Leges novellae ad Theodoscianum pertinentes*, vol.2, Berlin 1905.

N. Val. = Valentinian III, *Novellae*, in T. Mommsen and P. Meyer eds., *Theodosiani Libri XVI cum Constitutionibus Sirmondianis et Leges novellae ad Theodosianum pertinentes*, vol.2, Berlin, 1905.

PL = *Patrologia Latina*

PLRE = J. R. Martindale, A.H.M. Jones, and J. Morris, eds. *The Prosopography of the Later Roman Empire.* 3 vols.: Volume 1 (260–294); Volume 2 (395–527); Volumes 3A and 3B (527–641). Cambridge, UK, 1971–1992.

Prosper, *Chron.* = Prosper, *Epitoma chronicon*, ed. T. Mommsen, *Chronica Minora* 1, *MGH AA* 9, 1892, pp.385–485.

PS = *Pragmatic Sanction*. Included as Appendix VII in *Corpus Iuris Civilis* iii: *Novellae*, R. Schoell and W. Kroll, eds., Berlin, 1954 rept., pp. 799–802; also at *Iuliani Epitome Latina Novellarum Iustiniani*, G. Hänel, (ed.), Leipzig, 1873, pp. 185–91. Translation in *The Novels of Justinian*, D. J. D. Miller and P. Sarris, Cambridge, UK, 2018 pp. 1116–30.

Procop. *Wars* = Procopius, *The Wars*, 5 vols. Translation by H. B. Dewing; revised and updated by Anthony Kaldellis, Indianapolis/Cambridge, 2014 based on the original edition in the Loeb Classical Library, Cambridge, MA, 1959.

RIC = *The Roman Imperial Coinage*, London, 1984–94.

SC = *Sources Chrétiennes*

Thiel = *Epistolae romanorum pontificum genuinae et quae ad eos scriptae sunt a S. Hilario usque ad Pelagium II*, A. Thiel ed., 2nd ed., Braunsberg, 1868.

VC = *Vita Constantini* in F. Winkelmann (ed.), *Über das Leben des Kaisers Konstantins,* Berlin, 1975. Translated by A. Cameron and S. G. Hall, *Eusebius. Life of Constantine*, Oxford, 1999.

Zos. = Zosimus, in F. Paschoud, ed. and translation, *Zosime. Histoire Nouvelle*, 5 vols., Paris, 1971–89, first edition; 2003, second edition.

Abbreviations for Imperial Offices in Late Antiquity

com.	*comes* (count/ a senior military/civilian official)
com. dom.	*comes domesticorum* (commander in charge of the imperial bodyguard)
com. Or.	*comes Orientis* (count/official in charge of the diocese of the East)
cons.	*consularis* (consular, title of governor of certain provinces, of the lowest senatorial rank of *clarissimus*)
cos.	*consul* (highest magistrate in the Roman Republic, two designated every year. By the late third century, it was an honor with no function.)
CRP	*comes rei privatae* (count/official in charge of the private estates of the emperor)
CSL	*comes sacrarum largitionum* (count/official in charge of the sacred largesses or imperial treasury, oversees taxes and revenues)
iud.	*iudex* (judge or title for a high official)
mag. equ.	*magister equitum* (master of the horse, commander in chief of the cavalry)
mag. mil.	*magister militum* (master of the military, commander in chief of the army.)
mag. off.	*magister officiorum* (master of offices, head of the bureaucracy of the court and communications)
mag. ped.	*magister peditum* (master of the soldiers, commander in chief of the infantry)
MUM	*magister utriusque militium* (master of the army and cavalry, commander in chief of all armed forces. They commanded regional armies. For example, MUM Africae

	= *magister utriusque militiae Africae*, the commander in chief of Africa.)
pat.	*patricius* (patrician, honorific title of great distinction revived by Constantine)
PPO	*praefectus praetorio* (praetorian prefect. In late antiquity, the most important civil official, linked to regions. So, for example, the PPO Ital. was the praetorian prefect of Italy; PPO Gall. was the praetorian prefect of Gaul.)
praep.	*praepositus* (title for the official in charge, used for various posts in the imperial military or civil administration)
proc.	*proconsul* (title of the highest-ranking governors of certain provinces)
PSC	*praepositus sacri cubiculi* (grand chamberlain, normally the highest-ranking eunuch in the imperial service. Responsible for the imperial family's security and their palace.)
PUC	*praefectus urbis Constantinopolitanae* (prefect of the city of Constantinople, principal civilian authority who responds directly to the imperial court)
PUR	*praefectus urbis Romae* (prefect of the city of Rome, principal civilian authority for replaces in Rome, Ostia and Portus who responds directly to the imperial court)
QSP	*quaestor sacri palatii* (quaestor of the sacred palace, the emperor's chief legal advisor and drafter of laws)
quaest.	*quaestor* (civic official, traditionally the first step in the career of a senatorial aristocrat)
trib. et not.	*tribunus et notarius* (imperial notary/clerk)
v.c.	*vir clarissimus* (literally, "most outstanding man," title for the lowest of the three senatorial ranks)
v.glor.	*vir gloriossimus* (literally, "most glorious man," a senatorial honorific title)
vic.	*vicarius* (vicar who, by late antiquity, was the deputy of the praetorian prefect and supervised the provincial governors, located in dioceses)
v.inl. or v.ill.	*vir inlustris/illustris* (literally, "most illustrious man," title for the highest of the three senatorial ranks)
v. sp.	*vir spectabilis* (literally, "admirable man," the middle of three senatorial ranks)

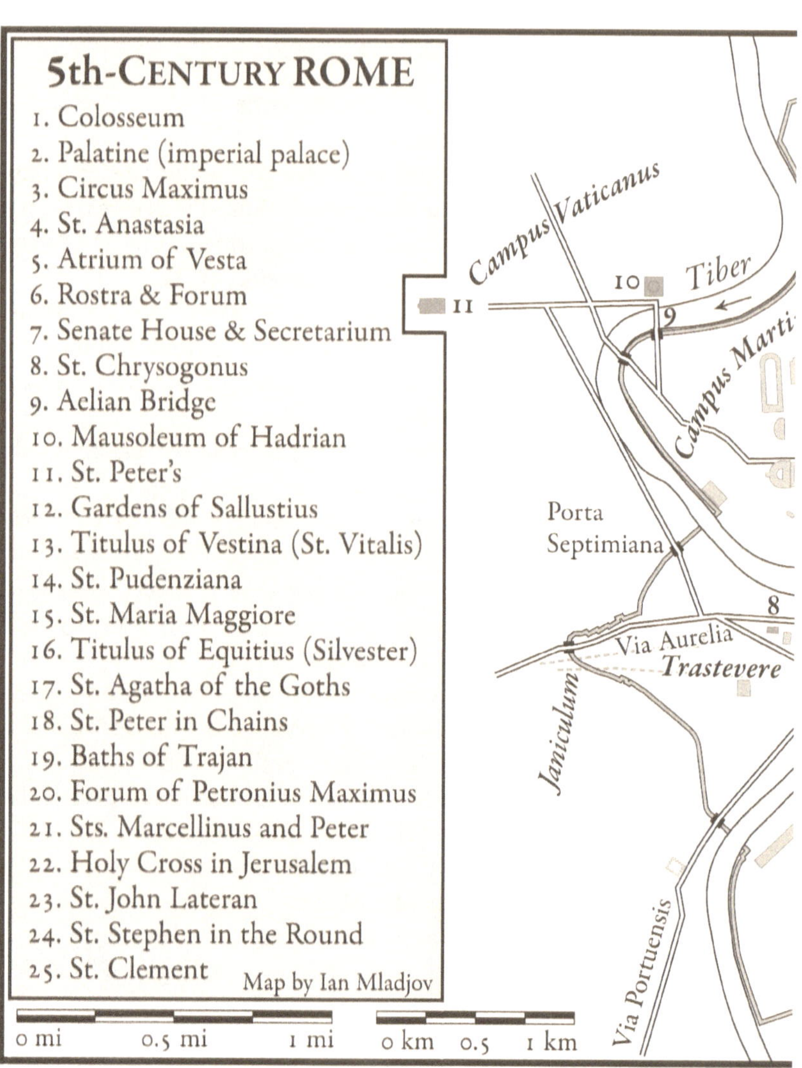

Map 1 Fifth-century Rome.

Via Flaminia
Porta Pinciana
Porta Salaria
Via Nomentana
Castra Praetoria
12
Campus Agrippae
us
Porta "Clausa"
St. Laurence outside the walls
Quirinal
13
14
15
Via Tiburtina
17
16
Via Labicana
18
7
6
19
Esquiline
Capitoline
5
21
20 Via Praenestina
1
22
4
2
25
3
Caelius
23
Porta Asinaria
24
Aventine
Via Ostiensis
Porta Metrovia
Via Appia
Via Latina
Porta Ardeatina
St. Paul's outside the walls
Cemetery of St. Callixtus

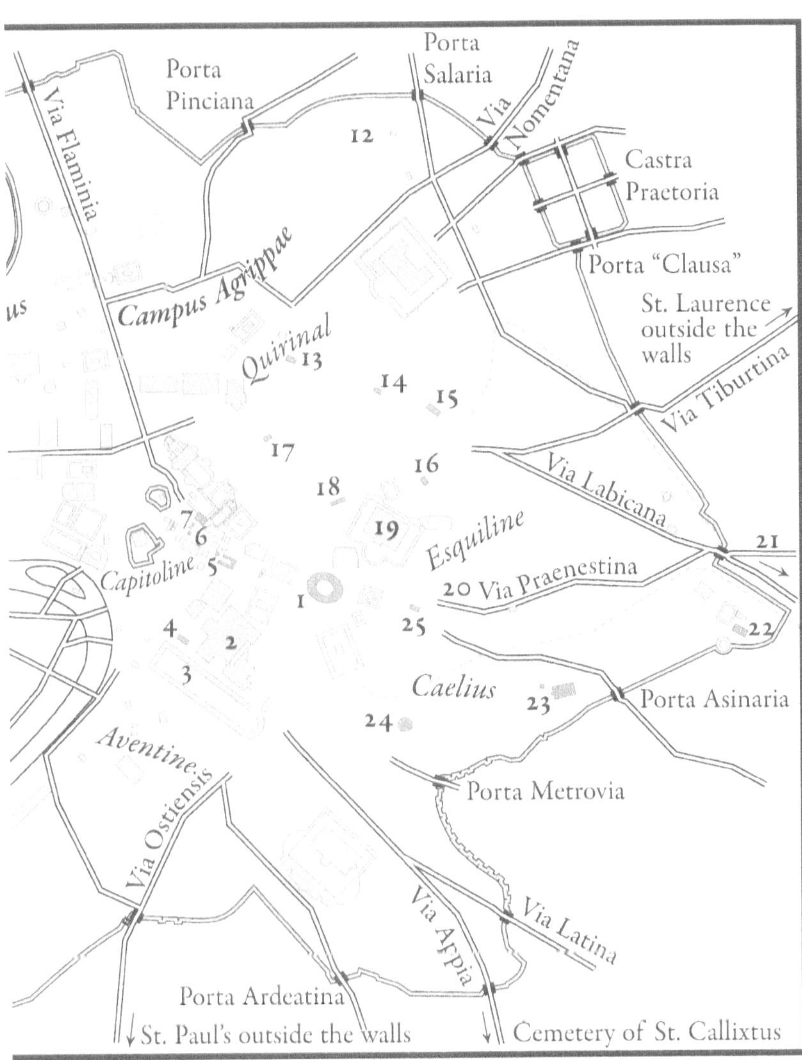

Map 1 (cont.)

1

Approaches to the Fate of the Late Antique City

> Experience is not what happens to a man; it's what a man does with what happens to him.
>
> —Aldous Huxley[1]

> My heart is moved by all I cannot save
> So much has been destroyed
> I have to cast my lot with those, who, age after age,
> Perversely, with no extraordinary
> Power, reconstitute the world.
> —Adrienne Rich, Excerpt from *Natural Resources.*[2]

This book is about what generations of men and women experienced and did in the wake of political and military crises that overtook the city of Rome from the late third through the early seventh centuries. Rome was still the largest city in the western Mediterranean and an imperial capital, with a resident aristocracy and prestigious institutions that had enabled Romans to rule an empire since the third century BCE. The five political and military crises that I analyze are the ones that historians have considered critical for understanding the "decline and fall of Rome." By focusing on how these crises led Romans to act to rebuild their city, I offer an alternative perspective for understanding the last three centuries of the western Roman Empire, its imperial city, and its senatorial aristocracy. Although the fortunes of Rome's leaders – senators, emperors, generals, and bishops – ebbed and flowed in a city which suffered population loss and reduced resources, the senatorial aristocracy remained at the center of the city's recovery. The resilience of Roman senatorial aristocrats who, time and again, used their resources to fuel the city's resurgence in the midst of loss, is significant and moving.

---

[1] Huxley 1933, p. 5.   [2] Rich 1978, p. 67.

Yet the resilience and power of Roman senatorial aristocrats in relation to other elites is often understated by those who write the history of the city in the final centuries of the western Roman Empire. I begin with a paradigmatic example of that oversight which is also relevant to Rome's most important physical defense – the wall that encircled the city built under the emperor Aurelian (270–75) for a barbarian invasion that never happened. Soon enough, in the coming centuries, Rome would be under attack and Aurelian's Wall, along with his reorganization of the city's food supply, were critical to the city's survival. But the wall and the food supply are also emblematic of how Romans were able to restore the city after each military and political crisis.

Waiting for the Barbarians: Aurelian's Wall and the Defense of Rome

> Since all that [had] happened [the war with various Germanic tribes] made it seem possible that some such thing might occur again, as had happened under Gallienus, after asking advice from the Senate, he [Aurelian] extended the walls of the city of Rome.[3]

In the uncertain times of the late third century, Italy faced a series of invaders. In 259, Germans had penetrated as far south as the city of Rome. The Senate, with the emperor and military away, armed soldiers and citizens to ward off the attack.[4] In 270, the Iuthungi invaded northern Italy. The newly acclaimed emperor, Aurelian, defeated them in autumn of 270 and then fought the Vandals. But the Iuthungi returned to Italy and surprised Aurelian in a wood near Placentia (modern Piacenza), where the emperor faced a disastrous rout.[5] The news of his defeat spread terror, especially since the inhabitants of Rome remembered the all-too-recent attack on their city under the emperor Gallienus (253–68), as noted in the epigraph at the

---

[3] *Hist. Aug. Aur.* 21.9: trans. Magie, vol. 3, pp. 235–37: *His actis cum videret posse fieri ut aliquid tale iterum, quale sub Gallieno evenerat, proveniret, adhibito consilio senatus muros Urbis Romae dilatavit.* Cf. *Hist. Aug. Aur.* 39.2: *muros Urbis Romae sic ampliavit, ut quinquaginta prope milia murorum eius ambitus teneant.* ("He so extended the wall of the city of Rome that its circuit was nearly fifty miles long.") The actual wall was only twelve miles long, so either the word *milia* refers to 50,000 feet, not miles, or this is a gross exaggeration.

[4] Zos. 1.37.2 specifies the Senate at Rome: ἡ γερουσία. See too Zonaras 12.24.

[5] Aurelian's defeat in 270 is noted by the *Hist. Aug. Aur.* 18.3; 21.1–3; Aur. Vict. *Epit.* 35.2; Zos. 1.37.1–2. The *Hist. Aug. Aur.* 18.3–.4 refers to wars with the Marcomanni. Zos. 1.49.1 identified the Germans whom Aurelian confronted in Italy as Alamanni, but they were accompanied by their neighbors, identified correctly as Iuthungi by Dexippus *Frag.* 6 [Jacoby]. See too Potter 2004, pp. 269–70; Paschoud, 1996, pp. 118–20 and on Zosimus, Paschoud 2003, pp. 168–69.

beginning of this section.[6] The Iuthungi made their way as far south as Umbria before being defeated there and again near Ticinum (modern Pavia). The proximity of the enemy led to rioting in the streets.[7] The Senate tried to restore calm. According to the unverified account in the anonymous fourth-century *Augustan History*, some senators turned to the famous Sibylline Books, the set of oracles in Greek verse that were consulted on how to avert the anger of the gods in a crisis. If this account is true – an issue that scholars still debate because of the unreliability of the *Augustan History* – the Senate undertook ceremonies of purification on behalf of the populace.[8]

When the victorious Aurelian entered Rome in 271, he found a city in open revolt. The mint workers, fearful of reprisals for their manipulation of the currency, took up arms against him. Some senators supported their revolt in what the author of the *Augustan History*, the fourth-century historian Aurelius Victor, and the early sixth-century historian Zosimus allege was a plot against the emperor by those senators unhappy that the army had chosen Aurelian as ruler and perhaps concerned that they would be implicated in the currency manipulation.[9] Fighting between Roman soldiers and the rebels broke out in the city. The mint workers and their supporters retreated to the Caelian Hill in Rome, where in the struggle that followed, thousands of Aurelian's soldiers died in hand-to-hand combat.[10] Aurelian had faced insurrections before, and perhaps now he repeated what would become a signature claim for the legitimation of his regime, that "God had

---

[6] See note 3 above and *Hist. Aug. Aur.* 18.4: *In illo autem timore, quo Marcomanni cuncta vastabant, ingentes Romae seditiones motae sunt paventibus cunctis, ne eadem quae sub Gallieno fuerant provenirent.* For confusion about the Marcomanni, see note 5 above.

[7] Aur. Vict. *De Caes.* 35.2; *Epit. de Caes.* 35.2 and Zos. 1.49.1 and Paschoud 1971, vol. 1, p. 163. For the rebellion in Rome, see Zos. 1.49.1–2; *Hist. Aug. Aur.* 18.4–6; 20.3; 21.5–6; 38.2–4; Aur. Vict. *De Caes.* 35.6; Eutrop. *Brev.* 9.14 and commentary by Paschoud 1996, pp. 118–20.

[8] For the consultation of the Sibylline books and the Senate's religious response with the celebration of the *ambarvalia* and *amburbium*, the sole narrative is *Hist. Aug. Aur.* 18.4–6; 20.3–8. Although Aurelian's letter berating the Senate's belated response is fictional and we cannot be certain that the purificatory rites were practiced, it is plausible that the Senate consulted the Sibylline Books now, as they had under the previous emperor Claudius II (268–70); see Aur. Vict. *Caes.* 34.3; and the *Epit. de Caes.* 34.3. For this account, see Paschoud 1996, vol. 5.1, pp. 121–23.

[9] For the mintworkers' rebellion and the senators involved, see *Hist. Aug. Aur.* 21.5 and 38.2–4; Aur. Vict. *De Caes.* 35.6; and Zos. 1.49.2, ed. Paschoud 2003, who, on pp. 168–69, includes the names of the senators later executed as Septimius, Urbanus, and Domitian. We know little about these men. See Watson 1999, pp. 52–53, on the complicity of the senators; Dey 2011, p. 112. On the mintworkers, Turcan (1969), pp. 948–59.

[10] Aur. Vict. *De Caes.* 35.6 cites 7,000 soldiers killed, as does *Hist. Aug. Aur.* 38.2. Malalas, *Chron.* 12, incorrectly identifies this revolt as taking place in Antioch. Doubts about the number of men killed are expressed by Dey 2011, p. 112, note 7.

given him the purple," for he had been "born to rule."[11] Aurelian's seasoned troops quashed the revolt. The insurgents were executed as well as some senators who had supported them.[12] Some later sources recalled this move as a vindictive act against senators motivated by the new emperor's need for money, but it was also a stark reminder that it was better to cooperate than to rebel.[13]

Although in 271 Rome had not fallen to the Germanic Iuthungi, the inhabitants along with their new emperor faced the task of rebuilding the city along with their relationship. They did so with remarkable speed and resourcefulness. The most visible sign of this act of restoration of the city, noticeable even to a visitor to Rome today, is the construction of a city wall, the first since the fourth century BCE. Aurelian's Wall extended for twelve miles, reaching eight meters high and 3.5 meters thick, and was reinforced at intervals of 100 Roman feet (29.6 meters) with square towers.[14] The Wall was clearly intended for defense, and it quickly took on a number of other functions such as tax collection. But I want to underscore how much Aurelian's Wall quickly redefined the city and the relationships of its inhabitants to it and to one another. As Robert Coates-Stephens aptly observed based on an archaeological case study of the Sessorium Palace in Rome (see Map 2), construction in this region now took place within the confines of Aurelian's Wall, and there is no evidence of continued civic building outside the wall.[15] Only burial sites with churches were the kinds of communal structures that we find outside the walls in the coming centuries.

The Wall concentrated human interactions within newly established confines, and developed new relations beginning with its very construction. Building the Wall required not only imperial financing but also the support of a large number of the city's inhabitants. The Senate, which had been responsible for the protection of the city a decade earlier, would have supported this fortification to protect its members and

---

[11] *FHG* 4.197, ed. Müller at 10.6 in Latin reads: *Aurelianus seditione militari aliquando appetitus dixit falli milites, qui regum fata in sua se potestate habere putarent. Quippe deum, qui dator sit purpurae (quam utique dextera praetendebat), etiam annos regni definire.* Although we cannot date this military insurrection, the notion that Aurelian was chosen by the gods and hence born to rule emerges from his coins and inscriptions more widely; see especially Wienand 2015, pp. 63–99.

[12] *Hist. Aug. Aur.* 38.2–4; Aur. Vict. *De Caes.* 35.6; Zos. 1.49.2; and Malalas, *Chron.* 12.

[13] Amm. Marc. 30.8.8 underscores the tradition that this was motivated by money, as does the *Hist. Aug. Aur.* 21.5–9.

[14] Dimensions from Dey 2011, p. 19.

[15] Coates-Stephens 2012, pp. 83–110. For its impact on trade, see Malmberg 2015, pp. 196–98.

their homes.[16] Senatorial aristocrats would also have seen the advantage of a public works project that, as Hendrik Dey observed, served to "divert the energies of the masses away from more destructive avenues" by employing several thousand workers.[17] Building the Wall was a mutually beneficial decision that simultaneously restored Rome's security, boosted relations between Aurelian and the city's inhabitants, and defined how residents interacted with one another.

Aurelian's reorganization of the food supply of the city also promoted good relations with the city's residents. Since the late republic, a number of citizens living in Rome had been granted the right, chosen by lot, of free grain. In the early empire these recipients, male adult citizens, numbered between approximately 160,000 and 180,000. They received tickets (*tesserae frumentariae*) that they and then later their heirs exchanged for monthly rations at the *Porticus Minucia Frumentaria* in the Campus Martius in Rome (see Map 2).[18] Since the recipients of the grain dole are estimated to have made up between one-fifth and one-quarter of the city's population, this public dole could not have fed the entire city, which in the first century CE is widely estimated to have reached between 700,000 and 1,000,000 inhabitants and to have continued at roughly that size into the fourth century.[19] Although the rest of Rome's inhabitants bought their grain on the private market, state-subsidized grain stabilized food prices for the residents of Rome. This reduced the potential for food shortages and rioting while also demonstrating the state's generosity. Aurelian's efforts at improving the food supply thus won him popularity while at the same time gaining greater control over suppliers and administrators. Changes in the system benefitted some of the new corporations such as the bakers, for now Aurelian distributed free bread instead of grain. Under his rule a decentralized system for the bread's distribution occurred in a variety of locations (steps or banks) across

---

[16] *Hist. Aug. Aur.* 21.9, a not entirely reliable source, underscored that Aurelian's construction occurred after his having consulted with the Senate (*adhibito consilio senatus*). For the building of the wall, see also Aur. Vict. *Epit.* 35.7–9. Although the actual construction of the wall negatively affected some private estates, as can be documented, for example, for the Esquiline Hill gardens, the advantages to the propertied classes must have outweighed the concerns of those few. We do not know if the owners of affected estates were compensated for their losses.

[17] Dey 2011, p. 113.   [18] For the grain dole and its recipients, see Virlouvet 1995 and 2000.

[19] Estimates about the size of the population are based on the grain dole. See Lo Cascio 2000, pp. 57–59, and Lo Cascio 1999, pp. 178–82 for estimates of 650,000–700,000. For the assumption that the grain supply and hence the population was relatively stable into the fourth century, see Vaccaro 2013, pp. 262–65, and Virlouvet 2000, p. 103 with bibliography. These numbers are widely but not uniformly accepted. For a succinct discussion of population estimates, see Morley 2013, pp. 29–44, and Sessa 2018, p. 54.

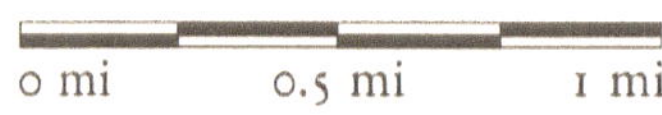

Map 2 Rome in 275.

the city. This also facilitated crowd control. Finally, Aurelian added free pork for those on the dole and sold wine at subsidized prices to the population at large.[20]

---

[20] For Aurelian's reorganization, see *Hist. Aug. Aur.* 48.1; Aur. Vict. *Caes.* 35.7; and *Chronographus a. 354*, ed Mommsen, 1892, MGH AA 9, p. 148. For the "steps" or banks, see *Th. Cod.* 14.17.2, 364 CE, and 14.17.3, 368 CE. It seems unlikely that the bread and pork were provided for the entire population. On this see too Machado 2019, pp. 45–61.

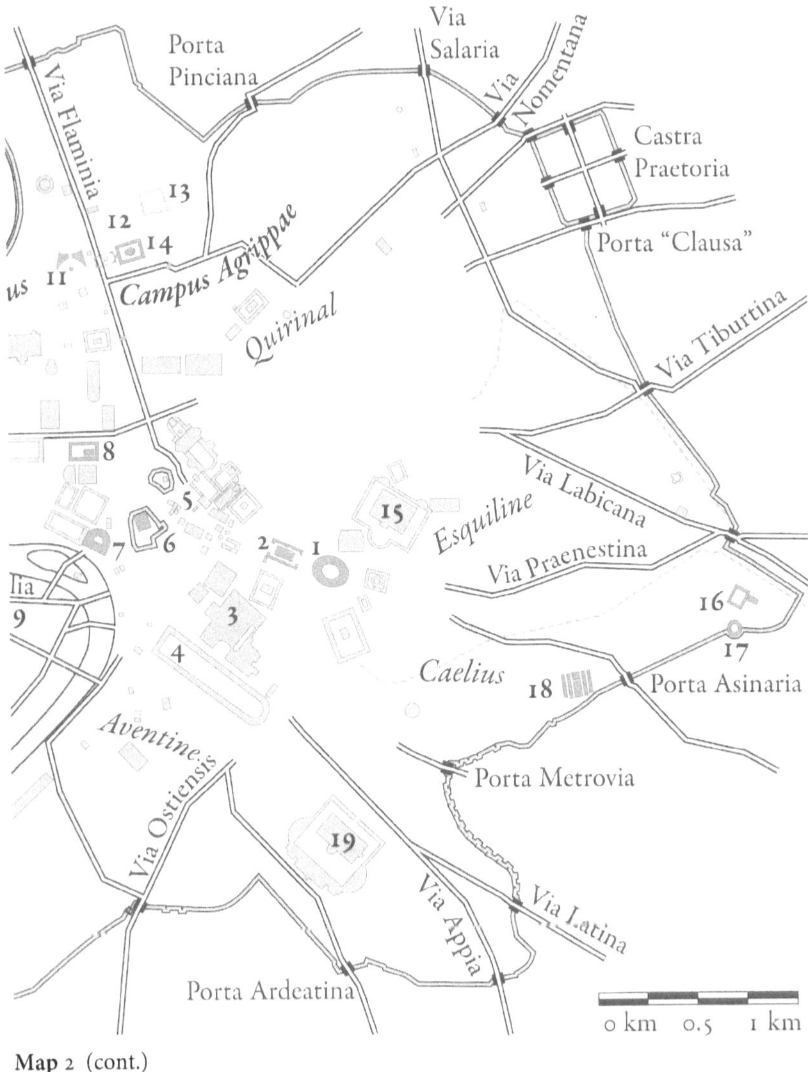

Map 2 (cont.)

The administration of this restructured and expanded food dole fell to a large degree upon Roman senatorial aristocrats, whose oversight of aspects of the supply system opened up exceptional avenues for their own economic and political gain. This reorganization resulted in a consolidation of power among the praetorian prefects, the provincial governors, and the urban prefects of Rome, all of whom were senators whose appointments were approved by the emperor.[21] But the urban prefect was the key official in Rome held responsible for the food supply. When the price of wine was too high or the grain ships did not arrive on time in Rome's port, he faced murderously angry crowds who could burn down his home or do real bodily harm.[22] Despite these potential dangers, senatorial involvement in this reorganized system offered unmatched opportunities to augment their wealth and political prestige. Dedicatory inscriptions survive that underscore the patron–client networks that developed between urban prefects and the guilds of Rome's food suppliers, such as the bakers, pork suppliers, and wholesale dealers.[23] These ties offered real financial rewards as well since senatorial urban prefects were often also the owners of estates in Italy and North Africa that supplied the grain, pork, and wine for the city, either to the private markets or to the state.[24]

Aurelian also strove to secure the loyalty of senators through his religious patronage. Aurelian attributed his success to a deity associated with military victory, *Sol Invictus* (The Unconquered Sun), for whom he built a new and magnificent temple in the Campus Agrippae (where he also conveniently stored the wine that he now distributed at reduced prices).[25] Once more, senators took a leading role, accepting appointments as *pontifices Solis*.[26]

---

[21] Machado 2019, pp. 30–61.

[22] The urban prefect was blamed for famines or food or wine shortages; see Amm. Marc. 14.6.1; and 19.10.1–4 for the prefect Tertullus who during a food shortage in 359 calmed the angry crowd by showing his young boys; see Cracco Ruggini 1961, pp. 152–76 for a full list of food shortages. In 409, a hungry mob murdered the urban prefect, Pompeianus 2, *PLRE* 2, p. 897–98.

[23] Honorary inscriptions of corporations to the twice urban prefect, L. Aradius Valerius Proculus and the urban prefect Attius Insteius Tertullus survive; see *CIL* 6.1690, *CIL* 6.1692, and *CIL* 6.1693. For the career of Proculus, see Salzman and Roberts 2015, p. 16 on Symm. *Ep.* 1.3.4 and Populonius 11, *PLRE* 1, pp. 747–49, urban prefect 337–38 and 351–52. For Attius Insteius Tertullus, urban prefect in 307–08, see Tertullus 6, *PLRE* 1, pp. 883–84. For more on these networks, see Machado 2019, p. 47 especially.

[24] For more on the ties between private sales and the food supply, see Vaccaro 2013, pp. 262–65 with bibliography. See too my discussion in Chapters 2 and 3. For the estates of senators in Italy and Southern Italy, see Vera 2005, pp. 26–30; for Sicily, see Vaccaro 2013, pp. 265–72; in North Africa, see Salzman 2002, pp. 93–96 for the fourth century and Conant 2012, pp. 135–42, for Romano-African estate owners who flourished into the fifth-century Vandal period.

[25] The Temple of *Sol* is well attested: see *Chron* of 354, ed. Mommsen 1892, 1981 rept., p. 148: *templum Solis et castra in campo Agrippae dedicavit [Aurelian]*; Aur. Vict. 35.7: *His tot tantisque prospere gestis fanum Romae Soli magnificum constituit donariis ornans opulenti*; Hist. Aug. Aur. 25.6: *templum Solis fundavit*; 48.4: *in porticibus templi Solis fiscalia vina ponuntur*. See *LTUR s.v. Sol, Templum*, pp. 331–32 and Salzman 2020A, pp. 149–67, for its identification as the Temple of *Sol Invictus*.

[26] So, for example, he appointed the senator Iunius Gallienus, *CIL* 14.2082, from Lavinium (Latium), as *pontifex dei Solis invicti*. See Rüpke 2008, 65, p. 386; Salzman 2020A, pp. 149–67; and more broadly, Hijmans 2010, pp. 381–427.

Under Aurelian and afterward, the new priestly college of *Sol Invictus* and the new solar temple to this deity became a focus of senatorial aristocratic activity. As one more sign of his outreach, Aurelian chose a western senatorial aristocrat to share the consulship with him in 271 and allowed two others to hold the office in 272.[27] The consulship was still the highest magistracy in the empire, although this still-prestigious honor, bestowed by the emperor, had lost any real political or military function. Its recipients, however, gained significant prestige and influence.[28]

Given the ways in which Aurelian restored his ties to Rome and its senatorial aristocracy, it is not surprising that Aurelian or his supporters could find no better reward for his defeated enemy Tetricus than to make him a senator, and some later accounts claim that he married the vanquished queen Zenobia to a Roman senator.[29] For his respect for senators as well as his critical role in the fortification of the city, Aurelian was remembered with some admiration by the pro-senatorial fourth-century author of the *Augustan History* despite his harsh repression of the insurgents who had greeted his arrival in the city at the beginning of his regime.[30]

We should also appreciate how Roman elites – senators and the military in the urban cohorts – along with non-elites, worked with Aurelian to restore the city. Aurelian offered incentives, material – wall, temple, food – and metaphysical – honor and priesthoods – to support an emperor who was divinely legitimated as one "born to rule." Senators seized upon these new opportunities for honor and office, undertaking civic patronage roles along with making real economic gains. Religion was especially relevant for this relationship. The emperor, elites, and non-elites used religion to create a new "topography of devotion" for Sol Invictus in the city.[31]

Yet the resilience of Roman senators at this critical juncture and the building of a wall with long-term implications for the survival of the city have not received enough attention. This situation is due, in part, to the brevity of Aurelian's reign, less than five years. But it also is true because the

---

[27] Potter 2004, pp. 265 and 270.

[28] For the consulship in late antiquity, see Bagnall, Cameron, Schwartz, and Worp 1987, pp. 1–6.

[29] For Tetricus receiving senatorial status and an office after his surrender, see Aur. Vict. 35.5; Eutr. *Brev.* 9.13. *Hist. Aug. Aurelian* 39.1 claims he held the office of *corrector Lucaniae*, while the *Hist. Aug. Tyr. Trig.* 24.5 says that Tetricus received the office of *corrector totius Italiae*. Doubts about the veracity of this account as the result of Aurelianic propaganda do not diminish the fact that senatorial status was offered as a means of bribing this rebel emperor. For Zenobia wed to a Roman senator, see Zon. 12.27 [607], ed. Banchich and Lane, 2009, p. 60.

[30] *Hist. Aug. Aur.* 42.4 notes that he was deified; and 50.5: *populus eum Romanus amavit, senatus et timuit.*

[31] "Topography of devotion" is a phrase used by Moralee 2018, p. 42.

resurgence of Rome even before Constantine does not fit easily into narratives of "decline and fall." Nor do many modern historians fully appreciate that the city of Rome remained central to the material and political survival of the Roman Empire. That is where this book begins, for newer work on the city of Rome requires rethinking its position in the Mediterranean in late antiquity.

The Influence of the City of Rome on Its Mediterranean Empire

This book focuses on the city of Rome and not on a subset of cities or on the western Roman Empire writ large because the city's influence had shaped the outlines of its Mediterranean empire. The city of Rome was a nexus of political, cultural, and social networks that the Romans had developed to assert their control of the Mediterranean. Importantly, the "city" – as Rome was called – remained into late antiquity, in the words of Robert Markus, "the head, centre and sum of the world; the world was only the expanded version of the city."[32] This equivalency was possible because, as Lucy Grig trenchantly observed:

> Where "Roma" is involved there is always a certain ambivalence: Rome is not just an *urbs* [city], even the *urbs* ([the city,] as she was for so many of her inhabitants): there is always slippage between the city and the idea, *urbs* and *imperium, urbs* and *orbis.* The city of Rome was both symbol and society, material and immaterial, its topography both symbolically redolent and endlessly polyvalent.[33]

This situation was also true in late antiquity. Aurelian's Wall was both a material and immaterial statement of the city's centrality as an urban as well as a Mediterranean-wide imperial hub into the late Roman period down though the late sixth century CE.

The city of Rome continued to exercise a centripetal attraction for elites and non-elites alike. In large part because of Rome's role as the capital of the empire, "the ruling elite invested the spoils of imperialism in the urban environment, and migrants flocked to service their needs and gain a share of the empire's wealth; but the elite made this investment precisely because of the importance of the city in establishing and maintaining their power. Rome's greatness was itself a crucial element of the ideology that sustained Roman rule."[34] The migration of men and women to Rome that replenished the city's population provided labor for the building projects that elites and the state initiated. The city – with its monuments and topography, its "free

---

[32] Markus 1970, p. 26.   [33] Grig 2012, p. 127.   [34] Morley 2013, p. 29.

bread and circuses" – provided the empire's inhabitants "a template for a new way of life that the Romans eagerly put before the eyes of their subjects, current and prospective."[35]

To meet the demands of its capital city with its exceptionally large population, the Romans had developed an economy and trade network as well as social and political structures that extended across the Mediterranean.[36] In a pretechnological age, meeting the demands for resources as well as for labor to support a city of this size was an impressive feat. Feeding Rome required tremendous organizational skills as well. The public grain dole, the reorganization of which I discussed as part of Aurelian's response to crisis, provides a good example of how much the Roman state and its elites invested not just money and manpower but also prestige in the special status and size of the city of Rome. There is a strong note of pride in this accomplishment, evidenced when, for example, the first-century senator Pliny the Elder concluded that "no city in the whole world . . . could be compared to Rome in magnitude."[37] Although the public grain dole fed fewer than a quarter or a fifth of its inhabitants, the networks of state-supported trade that coexisted with private merchants drew on grain from Egypt, North Africa, and Italy to supply the city allowed the population to grow to this unprecedented size.

Rome's complex food supply system continued into late antiquity, making Rome still, from the fourth through the sixth century of this study, the largest city in the western Mediterranean. Rome's unique status continued even after Constantine established Constantinople as an imperial capital, to which he channeled Egyptian grain after 332.[38] The Roman market compensated for this change with a marked growth in the agricultural output from Sicily and other Italian regions. Thus, as has become increasingly clear from recent archaeological studies of Sicily, Apulia, Campania, and Sardinia, a newly established corn belt in these areas in the fourth century, thriving alongside trade from Carthage and North Africa, maintained the overall features of the food supply of Rome and its public grain dole that had developed in the early empire and in the late third century.[39] Moreover, there is evidence, such as the improvement of Sicily's road network, that the

---

[35] Dey 2015, p. 2. For Rome's fame as a source of "bread and circuses," see succinct accounts in Erdkamp 2013, pp. 262–77 and Virlouvet 2000, pp. 103–35; and on games, see Purcell 2013, pp. 441–60.

[36] Morley 1996, pp. 33–39.   [37] Pliny the Elder, *Hist. Nat.* 3.5.67.

[38] Vaccaro 2013, p. 267. On Constantinople and the channeling of Egyptian grain to the eastern city, see Socr. *HE* 2.13.

[39] Vaccaro 2013, p. 267; Panella et al. 2010, p. 58.

Roman aristocracy "made increasing financial investments in southern Italy and Sicily from the late second and third [centuries CE], which accelerated in the fourth."[40] This late Roman development continued into the fifth century, allowing Roman aristocrats to feed Rome and grow wealthier still as they invested in estates in Sicily as well as in urban properties in and around the city of Rome.

Given that Rome was so deeply embedded in economic, political, and social networks around the Mediterranean, what happened there made a difference across the empire. That is one reason why I focus on the city in this book. Though its monopolistic and privileged assertion of being "the" capital of the empire no longer stood unchallenged, given the rise of Constantinople and the reality that emperors no longer resided for long periods in Rome, the city and its aristocracy continued to shape the political, economic, social, and religious life of Mediterranean society. The eastern court and emperor were aware of their influence and resources. Indeed, the notion that the empire had simply split into two halves beginning with Constantine's establishment of Constantinople cannot be sustained: Politics, then as now, went beyond the local. On the contrary, the reemergence of strong ties between the eastern and western emperors and elites was especially critical in the sixth century. Even after the Gothic War when eastern Romans (i.e. Byzantines) ruled in Italy and the city declined as an urban center that attracted wealthy elites, the memory of Rome as an imperial capital remained.[41]

Given the ongoing significance of the city of Rome from the fourth through the sixth centuries, it is understandable that emperors, generals, and senators, along with bishops, continued to demonstrate their concern for the city as well as to manifest their own power and prestige by taking action in response to the crises faced by the inhabitants of Rome. The good ruler was expected to invest in the city both materially – as Aurelian had done by building his wall and temple to Sol Invictus – and also on a human level by establishing personal ties with Roman senatorial aristocrats. Consequently, non-elites returned to the city as well. Tradespeople, laborers, and migrants came back to Rome in search of opportunities and sources of support that were not available in other cities. However, these recovery efforts have not attracted adequate attention.

---

[40] Vaccaro 2013, p. 268; Vera 2005, pp. 206–9.
[41] For the use of the term Byzantine to distinguish eastern Roman forces from Italo-Roman ones in Italy, see Chapter 6, note 23.

Paradigms for Rome: Catastrophists, Transformationalists, and World Historians

To better appreciate why the resilience of Rome's civic elites and their continuing role in the recovery of the city have been underappreciated, I will briefly discuss the historiography on the "decline and fall" of Rome paradigm and its most important modern alternatives. I then turn to my approach to the study of Rome and its elites.

As I argue, to fully understand the resilience of Rome, we have to consider the role of its senatorial aristocracy, who were the products of a culture in which competition for influence and prestige acted as a stimulant. Crises brought about changes in the late Roman world that rendered politics in the late antique city more diffuse and variable. Personal relations played an even greater role than they had previously in winning power and building social networks that enabled material and political advancement. This competition energized rather than enervated senatorial aristocrats during the last three centuries of the western empire. At times, it is true, their actions led to downturns and failure. But their intervention also allowed for the recovery of urban life and society, both of which have been overshadowed by the assumptions that come with alternative paradigms for understanding the end of late antique Rome.

The Shadow of Edward Gibbon. Since the publication of Gibbon's history in the late eighteenth century, historians have engaged in a lively debate about the utility of his paradigm of "decline and fall" to describe the last centuries of the western Roman Empire, from the early fourth through the late sixth centuries. Although Gibbon decided to extend his history into the fifteenth century and to include the fall of Byzantium, his view of the fall of the western Roman Empire has remained influential. As he said in the conclusion to his seven-volume work, his history describes the "triumph of barbarism and Christianity."[42] Indeed, to his mind, these external factors acted on Rome with the force of biological necessity: "The decline of Rome was the natural and inevitable effect of immoderate greatness. Prosperity ripened the principle of decay: the causes of destruction multiplied with the extent of conquest."[43] Few, if any, modern historians would agree with Gibbon that Christianity sapped the spirit and resources the empire needed to face its challenges, for, as N. H. Baynes and A. H. M. Jones observed long ago, Christianity thrived alongside the eastern Roman Empire for centuries after the end of the western imperial system.[44] But Gibbon's ghost lives on.

---

[42] Gibbon, ed. Bury, vol. 7, 1897, p. 321.   [43] Gibbon, ed. Bury, vol. 4, 1897, p. 161.
[44] Baynes 1943, pp. 29–35. Jones 1964, chapter 25.

Bryan Ward-Perkins, in his provocatively titled book *The Fall of Rome and the End of Civilization*, and Peter Heather, in *The Fall of Rome*, are among the most influential historians who have revived Edward Gibbon's paradigm insofar as both emphasize the external impact of the "barbarians" – the Germanic incursions in the case of Ward-Perkins, and the Hunnic invasions in the case of Heather – as the primary cause of the "end of civilization."[45] A popular strain in Anglophone scholarship has continued to focus on the weakness of the Roman military in confronting German invaders.[46] More recently, some scholars have incorporated the impact of climate change and disease to explain the decline of Rome's western empire without fully considering their impact on the eastern empire.[47] None of these narratives has moved away from a view of an empire more or less "fated" to decline and fall; differing emphases highlight and even add new elements to an old paradigm. Scholars have sometimes used the term *catastrophist* to describe what I regard as a neo-Gibbonian viewpoint insofar as they see the fall of the western Roman Empire as the result of catastrophic, destructive, and disruptive forces that brought about an end to Roman "civilization."

This "decline and fall" perspective is famously at odds with an alternative understanding of this period proposed by historians influenced especially by the work of the historian Peter Brown. These *transformationalists* have argued for the ongoing vitality of Rome's culture and institutions by stressing "change, continuity, and transformation over collapse."[48] Brown's work has inspired a generation of scholars who particularly emphasize innovations and continuities in religion and culture that gave new life to the society and institutions in the Roman Empire, West and East. The rise of Christianity in Europe and of Islam in the Near East are perhaps the primary positive developments of this era.[49] So, for example, Peter Brown sees the bishop's role in caring for the poor and the development of an ideal of Christian charity as revolutionary advancements quite distinct from traditional forms of civic patronage or euergetism (elite gift-giving or civic philanthropy).[50] Other scholars have emphasized continuities that led to innovation. So, for example, Alan Cameron has brilliantly considered how Christian writers continued to use classical education and rhetoric to craft new Christian literary works such as the mid fourth-century traditional epico-panegyrical

---

[45] Ward-Perkins 2005; Heather 2006, especially pp. 443–59.

[46] See, for example, Goldsworthy 2009, p. 149.   [47] Harper 2017, p. 33.   [48] Dey 2015, p. 5.

[49] Brown 1971, p. 7. This book has been widely influential in developing the transformationalist view.

[50] Brown 2002, p. 11; and 2012, pp. 79–81.

poem of the aristocratic woman Proba, which is stitched together with lines from Vergil's *Aeneid* to praise Christ.[51]

An alternative to these perspectives has been taken more recently by what I call proponents of a world-historical paradigm. Mark Humphries, inspired by the work of the anthropologist Jack Goody, has proposed that we should dismiss both the "decline and fall" paradigm and the "transformationalist" one as the "western theft" of history. Relying on Goody's arguments that historians have "taken the experiences of Europe as the central framework within which the totality of history is interpreted" and that there is an implicit western bias that history progresses in an essentially upward curve, Humphries proposes that we consider developments in late antiquity against a world-historical background. Hence, we should, for example, study barbarian invasions or geopolitical politics across Eurasia from the third through the eighth centuries and not restrict ourselves to the Mediterranean world.[52] Taking a similarly broad view of time and geography, Walter Scheidel has argued that the fall of Rome was "the best thing that ever happened, clearing the path for Europe's economic rise and the making of the modern age" by the sheer fact of the Empire's "going away and never coming back."[53] Scheidel's work ranges from Roman times down through the Napoleonic era and is broadly comparative, making connections, for example, between Rome, Byzantium, and China.

These three paradigms have shaped studies of other late antique cities as well, from Antioch and Constantinople to Ravenna and Rome. Indeed, this development is understandable since scholars of late antiquity generally agree that late Roman cities are not just mirrors of ancient society but are also a "valuable gauge of broader patterns of cultural evolution."[54] So for catastrophists like J. H. W. G. Liebeschuetz, the demise of key elements of Roman urban life – be it the decline of civic councils, the private patronage of amphitheaters and baths, or the disappearance of high-quality imported pottery – is a valid indicator of the end of the Roman city.[55] The demise of these institutions reflects the fracturing of networks of trade and communication that had made urban life possible and profitable. Gian Pietro Brogiolo and Bryan Ward-Perkins, catastrophists as well, argue that changes in urban life, except for the late antique Christianization of the city, are best described as the "dissolution of a sophisticated and impressive experiment in how to order society – an experiment developed by the Greeks and Romans."[56]

---

[51] Cameron 2011, pp. 327–37 of late antiquity.
[52] Humphries 2017, pp. 18–19, citing Goody 2006, pp. 13–25 and Goody 2010, especially pp. 115–26.
[53] Scheidel 2019, blurb and p. 503 for quote.   [54] Dey 2015, p. 7.
[55] See Liebeschuetz 2003, pp. 104–36 especially; and Christie 2011, for example, on baths, pp. 112–40.
[56] Brogiolo and Ward-Perkins 1999, pp. XV–XVI.

In opposition to this view, transformationalists emphasize innovation and continuity in urban phenomena. Although these scholars acknowledge a decline in population or the fracturing of trade networks, along with losses of material wealth overtaking a city that had fallen in a siege, transformationalists focus instead on the maintenance of urban life such as the continued use and repair of infrastructures like aqueducts or the presence of circuit-walls. As art historian Hendrik Dey observed, "many of the leading urban nuclei of the Roman period continued to be characterized in late antiquity and the early Middle Ages by a relative concentration of population, by new kinds of monumental and domestic architecture, by continued signs of political, economic, and cult activity, and also by the continuing presence of the most prominent members of society."[57] For Dey, the building of monumental colonnades, as can still be seen in cities like Antioch or as existed in Milan, represents distinctive innovations characteristic of late antique cities.[58] The construction of monumental churches across the Mediterranean in connection with the veneration of saints, as analyzed by Ann Marie Yasin, provides another example of an innovative transformation in the late antique city with important implications for the patterns of social life.[59] While admitting that there is tremendous variation in the survival of particular cities and regions in late antiquity, transformationalists like Dey and Yasin nonetheless emphasize innovations and continuities as indicators of the vitality of urban life in late antiquity, in the West as well as in the East.[60]

The third paradigm for understanding the Roman Empire within a world-historical context has also been applied to cities in late antiquity. So, for example, Neil Christie for Italy and Adam Rogers for Britain have suggested that we see the city in the late antique period within a longer arc of history as but one stage in settlement patterns that go back to pre-Roman times.[61] If we consider the late Roman phase of a city like London over this longer time frame, its late antique phase would be but one in a long arc of time, a perspective that would encourage London's comparison with cities across the Eurasian continent. To focus on a particular period is to admit a subjective choice that does not address the full history of a city.[62] The notion that late antique cities can be studied in a global and comparative framework is also recognized by Mark Humphries in his 2019 survey on the late Roman city.[63]

---

[57] Dey 2015, p. 8.   [58] Dey 2015, pp. 65–126.   [59] Yasin 2009, especially pp. 14–97.
[60] Dey 2015, pp. 9–10 and note 28 for bibliography.
[61] N. Christie 2006, p. 185; on Britain, Adam Rogers 2011, pp. 47–72; 177–79.
[62] Humphries 2019, pp. 86–87 makes this point.   [63] Humphries 2019, pp. 86–88 and note 382.

Resilience and Resurgence in the Face of Crisis: An Alternative Perspective

I offer this schematic summary of the dominant paradigms in modern historiography on the "falls" of Rome – the city and its western empire – to provide context for my own perspective on the evidence from the city of Rome. I have learned much from them and from the writings of other scholars. But I have been moved to write this book because no one of these approaches captures the contingencies, choices, and resourcefulness with which individuals and groups faced the political and military crises that they encountered in late antique Rome.

The alternative paradigm that I offer sees the recovery and rebuilding of Rome after crisis as the response of elites – emperors, senators, generals, and bishops. Admittedly, the resurgence of Rome in the fifth century took place within the context of diminished horizons, with fewer people and less wealth. Nonetheless, the actions of Roman elites in relation to one another shaped the city's recovery, for better or for worse. Although the power of different elites fluctuated, the senatorial aristocracy remained at the center of the city's resurgence, and as a group, senators and the Senate increased their power over the course of these centuries. So, too, did the influence of the bishops grow, but their role in the resurgence of the city was far less than many have suggested. The most destructive transformation of the city of Rome, in terms of public life, occurred only after the disappearance of the senatorial aristocracy and its focalizing institution, the Senate, in the late sixth and early seventh centuries.

Although I focus on the resilience of elites in response to crisis, I am keenly aware that it is not enough to simply narrate what happened in Rome over these centuries. As Aldous Huxley observed in the opening epigram to this chapter, not just the event but also the process by which we make meaning of the event and then act on this experience is relevant. At times, the ways in which Romans experienced and understood a crisis led them to make new relationships or to engage in structural change. So, for example, when the senator Petronius Maximus, one of the wealthiest and most honored of men in mid fifth-century Rome, chose to compete for power by plotting the murders of the general Aetius and then of the emperor Valentinian III, he brought about the fall of the last successful imperial dynasty in the West and the sack of Rome three months later. Petronius's political power was great. However, he miscalculated when he chose to betroth his son to Valentinian's daughter, a girl already engaged to the son of the Vandal King Geiseric.[64] Geiseric used these

---

[64] For the career of Petronius Maximus, see *PLRE* 2, pp. 749–51. For the plot, see Priscus, *Frag.* 30.1 = John of Antioch, Frag. 201, ed. Blockley 1983, pp. 326–32. See also Marcellinus *comes*, s.a. 455 (3);

actions as a pretext for attacking Rome in 455. The Vandal occupation of the city for fourteen days was one of the most ruinous events that Romans had faced.[65] Thus Petronius's interpretation of his position led him to take actions that led to the fall of Rome in 455, a crisis that ultimately strengthened the ties between Roman senators and the German general Ricimer (see Chapters 4 and 5).

If we view the world as the Romans at the time did and consider how individuals and groups reacted to these and other events that they themselves regarded as crises, we can see that senators, emperors, bishops, and generals also interpreted these events as opportunities to advance their own positions or viewpoints. Roman elites in these centuries demonstrated what social scientists call *resilience*, defined as the marshalling of resources to reorganize and restore social formations even in the face of fractures and swerves. Although social scientists have developed this model to analyze environmental shocks on societies or to consider state-level interventions to mitigate the consequences of catastrophic events like plagues or earthquakes, I use the term *resilience* to consider how Roman elites adapted to the shocks from political and military crises that overtook the city of Rome during the last three centuries of its existence. Thus I follow those scholars who study how the "resilience of a society affects other groups and institutions within the same society", and acknowledge that the burden of recovery and its costs are not shared equally.[66]

Part of society's resilience, I would add, is making meaning of events to initiate action. Hence, my history of the last centuries of the city of Rome emphasizes the humans who led the city's responses. I consider their efforts as social resilience. This view makes the history of Rome more dependent on human actors, and therefore the "falls" of Rome are more circuitous and circumstantial than the catastrophist paradigm suggests. Rome depended upon leaders who could absorb shocks and marshal resources to bring about

---

and my discussion in Chapter 4. By forcing Valentinian's widow to marry him and engaging his son to Valentinian's daughter, Petronius gave reasons for the Vandal King Gaiseric to attack.

[65] See my discussion in Chapter 4.

[66] Izdebski, Mordechai, and White 2018, p. 291. There is a vast and growing bibliography on resilience that traces its origins in environmental history into the social sciences. But I am using the term resilience as a historian to focus on the social responses to political and military shocks. For discussion of the ways in which this term has been used, see, for example, Izdebski, Mordechai, and White 2018, pp. 291–303; Folke 2006, pp. 253–367; and for sound criticism of how historians should apply resilience as a concept, see especially Sessa 2019, pp. 211–55. I thank Kristina Sessa for bringing to my attention the associations of this term for social scientists involved in assessing environmental catastrophes. That is not, however, how I am using this term.

the city's recovery. Over these centuries, the senatorial aristocrats remained in this position, as did the bishops of the city to varying degrees.

While I emphasize the resilience of Roman elites in response to crises, the catastrophist paradigm focuses on these same political and military events and sees them as setting the city and its inhabitants on an ever-downward, virtually unavoidable spiral. This approach has thus underestimated the political and economic strength of Romans and their institutions, including the Senate, over the *longue durée*. So, for example, rather than dismiss the delegation sent in 476 from the Senate of Rome to the eastern emperor Zeno that asserted that one emperor in the East was enough as merely the ineffectual actions of a weak institution manipulated by a strong general, Odoacer, I argue that the embassy was an expression of the changed political goals of still powerful and wealthy western senators.[67]

Certainly, the textual and archaeological evidence indicates that the city of Rome suffered periodic losses and disruptions in both population and trade over the centuries I cover in this book. However, we are, at best, able to only estimate the extent of loss of any crisis on a human scale. Even such basic information as the population of Rome, as I noted earlier, is approximated primarily on the basis of textual references to the grain dole. If we accept these calculations, then the population of the city of Rome declined from its high of between 700,000 and 1,000,000 residents in the early fourth century to between 300,000 and 500,000 in the mid fifth century.[68] Yet how much the city decreased in size after this can only be estimated.[69]

Even in a city that faced a sharply declining population, there is ample evidence of rebuilding and restoration after crisis. Although ongoing political and military crises in the second half of the fifth century hampered recovery, the city of Rome remained at the center of late Roman political and aristocratic society. And it was also the home of the bishop of Rome.

No one of the crises discussed in this book brought about the catastrophic end of Rome. An important set of papers that tried to assess the damages of the sack of Rome in 410 showed, in place after place in the city, the limited impact of this attack despite the fact that it had radically shocked contemporaries since it had been the first time in more than eight hundred years that the city had "fallen to barbarians."[70] Hence, in opposition to the neo-Gibbonian perspective, I see ample evidence that

[67] Malchus *Frag.* 14., ed. Blockley 1983, pp. 418–21.

[68] For the calculations for the mid fifth century, see my discussion in Chapters 3 and 4.

[69] The sixth-century city lacks the information for the grain dole that we have for the mid fifth century. See my discussion in Chapters 4, 5 and 6, note 121; cf. Sessa 2018, p. 54.

[70] See the essays in Lipps, Machado, and von Rummel 2013.

losses in population and trade after this occupation of the city did not destroy urban life. Even the disruptions to the grain supply of the city after the Vandal sack of 455 were met with new sources of food, as more recent work on agricultural production in Sicily and southern Italy, along with Sardinia, has indicated.[71] These sources of food continued to feed Rome's smaller urban population in the ensuing decades.

At the same time, the loss of control of the western Roman provinces of Gaul, Spain, Africa, and Britain over the course of the first half of the fifth century brought significant changes in society and politics. Evidence from excavations of elite housing in Rome, as that on the Esquiline Hill, as well as from texts that document charitable gifts to the church indicate that by the late fifth century, a number of large urban homes had been broken up into smaller housing units, reused for commercial purposes, or donated to the church.[72] These are significant transformations that reflect changed dynamics in the economic, political, and social life of the city. Some of these changes were the result of the ruptures created by the political and military crises that we hear about from late Roman writers.

Because I want to take into account the harsh breaks created by certain crises, I cannot fully align with the transformation paradigm. Not all changes led to new or positive developments. The abandonment of certain villas or apartment buildings, for instance, is evidence that their owners either had died or had deemed rebuilding as not a viable option. The owners of the Esquiline Treasury never returned to their home to reclaim their wealth and social position.[73] People did die and suffer when Rome was taken captive; I can well believe that the enslavement of Romans brought tears to the eyes of the bishop Deogratias when he saw them in Carthage after the Vandal capture of the city in 455.[74] If we focus only on developments in religion and culture, as many scholars who fall under what is generally described as the transformation paradigm tend to do, we miss sight of critically important economic, military, and political as well as institutional changes.

Nonetheless, my approach aligns more with that of scholars who focus on change over rupture. And like scholars associated with the transformation paradigm, I see the responses to crisis by Romans over these centuries as leading to the recovery and resurgence of Rome, even if this meant the loss, for example, of freedom of movement for men and women in certain professions,

---

[71] Vaccaro 2013, pp. 259–313 for analysis with bibliography.

[72] Machado 2012B, pp. 120–21; Salzman 2017, p. 251; and Machado 2019, pp. 261–69.

[73] On the owners of the Esquiline Treasure likely buried in the early fifth century, see Cameron 1985, pp. 135–45.

[74] Vict. Vit. *Hist.* 1.25, *MGH AA* 3, p. 7. Trans. by Moorhead 1992.

or the increasing insistence on forced religious orthodoxy.[75] Nor do I think we can easily assess the history of Rome in simple terms of upward or downward progress over these centuries, as is implied by these paradigms. So, for example, the civic ideals that justified free food for certain Roman citizens as their right were in a dialectical relationship with the Christian idea of distributing food to those in need as the embodiment of the virtue of charity. This complex of justifications for the continuation of Rome's grain dole is emblematic of the limitations of approaching this period through either the lens of Christian innovation or through one of catastrophic administrative rupture.[76] The Romans who maintained the city's free food supply based their actions on a combination of motivating factors.

The third paradigm for Rome, one that locates the city within a world-historical framework, cannot explain the resilience of the city in terms of individuals and groups. There is value in this macro-historical approach, but the loss of granularity obscures the agency of individual men and women whose actions in response to crises were based on specific circumstances and decisions. So, too, this macro-historical approach is not adequate for considering how different segments of society, such as the bishops, interacted with one another. Hence, this third paradigm will not provide insight into the ways in which these specific Romans demonstrated resilience in late antiquity, nor will it explain how they were able reshape urban life in the face of events that our sources regarded as crises.

The Senatorial Aristocracy of Rome

Key to the resilience of the city was the senatorial aristocracy of Rome. As legitimators of political authority and as wealthy landed estate owners, their power increased from the late third century onward. Emperors as well as military commanders sought to integrate them in support of their rule. Indeed, to comprehend this dynamic, it is essential to appreciate the economic resources, social prestige, political power, and cultural values of Roman senatorial aristocrats.

These individuals owed their social status in no small part to their wealth. Senatorial wealth was based, in general in the Roman Empire, on extensive landownership. But importantly, senators reinforced their economic and social standing in society by holding high office. These offices allowed

---

[75] For growing limits on certain professions, such as bakers and pork suppliers in the third and fourth centuries, see Bond 2016, pp. 160–61.

[76] For this dialectic, see Salzman 2017B, pp. 65–85.

them to protect and transmit from generation to generation both their inherited landed wealth and certain senatorial status distinctions that elevated the members of senatorial families above the rest of society. From the second century on, ambitious sons of senators who had attained the requisite high political office held the title of *clarissimus* ("most outstanding").[77] Their wives and daughters also held this title, but, of course, women could not attend meetings of the Senate.[78] Thus, central to senatorial status since the late republic and continuing into the early imperial period was the attainment of a political office that allowed one the full benefits of senatorial rank, such as the right to sit in the Senate in Rome.[79]

Certain families took great pride in continuing a tradition of public service. Those families that had attained the consulship were distinguished as "noble" (*nobiles*) into the fourth century.[80] Aristocrats not only boasted of their ancestors who had been consuls; they also proudly displayed painted portraits of their ancestors in their homes and traced their family trees back for centuries.[81] The pervasive concern for senatorial status continued to motivate members of established senatorial families to seek high office even though we see under Constantine and in the fourth century that the sons of senators in Rome inherited the title of *clarissimus* and, once approved by the Senate, became senators in Rome. Nonetheless, to realize the full benefits of senatorial status and to fulfill aristocratic expectations, aristocratic families strove to have their members attain a senatorial office; the higher the office, the higher the senatorial standing of the man and his family. Roman senatorial aristocrats passed this distinction on to their heirs and sought to establish ties with members in collateral family lines. These distinctions were formalized with higher senatorial rank by the later fourth century (see Chapter 2).

Based on senatorial status, a senatorial aristocrat could claim not just material wealth and a high office but also more general social prestige.

---

[77] If Weisweiler 2020, pp. 29–56, is correct, only sons who were going to engage in a civic career were given the honor of being called either "most outstanding youths" (*clarissimi iuvenes*) or "most outstanding boys" (*clarissimi pueri*).

[78] Women were called *clarissimae feminae* from the second century on; see also Weisweiler 2020, pp. 42–44 with bibliography.

[79] Salzman 2020, pp. 251–94 for an overview; and see also Weisweiler 2020, pp. 29–56, for full bibliography on the early empire.

[80] On the definition of the term "noble" (*nobilis*) based on this and a narrow range of high offices in the fourth century, see Barnes 1974, p. 446, and for counterarguments, see Salzman 2002, p. 22.

[81] For his proud presentation of family busts in the atrium of his wife's house, see Symm. *Ep.* 1.2. For ancestral portraits considered part of a Roman house according to earlier law, see Flower 1996, pp. 40–47.

Senators were assumed to possess good noble birth, high moral character, and a good education. As Symmachus said, the members of the senatorial aristocracy comprised "the better part of the human race."[82] And this continued to be the widely shared view. Similarly, the sixth-century senator Cassiodorus connected a noble family and other superior personal qualities or characteristics, such as education, to public service: "Ancestry itself is already glorious: praise has its origins in noble birth. For you, the advent of life is likewise the beginning of public office."[83] To a Roman, at the root of public service was the honor it bestowed. Indeed, public office was called, in Latin, *honor* or *honos*. Concern about achieving such public honor, as well as being recognized as possessing it, was a pervasive preoccupation of the late Roman aristocrat and the status culture that he inhabited.

Indeed, senatorial status was desirable also for its material benefits. Individual senators and their families enjoyed certain fiscal and legal privileges associated with senatorial status.[84] So, for example, senators were exempt by Roman law from the duty of financing acts of munificence in their cities of origin, were protected from physical torture, and participated in the meetings of the Senate in Rome.[85] Roman senatorial families took pride even in their distinct obligations, including residency in the city of Rome, which was officially required for senators, as was the sponsoring of games associated with certain senatorial offices.[86]

However, being a member of the senatorial aristocracy was not the same as being a senator by virtue of holding a high office at the imperial court or in the state bureaucracy. In the early empire, men in these positions had a lower social rank, being mostly equestrians. But the rank of many holders of these positions changed under the reign of Constantine. Thus, the emperor opened up new avenues for formerly equestrian imperial administrators to attain senatorial, that is, *clarissimate*, rank. After 312, civic officials who had arisen through office were found holding senatorial rank alongside men who were senators by birth. So, too, certain military officers were given senatorial rank.

---

[82] Symm. *Ep.* 1.52: *pars melior humani generis*.

[83] Cass. *Var.* 3.6.1: *origo ipsa iam gloria est: laus nobilitati connascitur. Idem vobis est gignitur quod vitae principium*. Modified translation of that offered by Bjornlie 2019, p. 125.

[84] This view of elites is similar to, but not the same as that of Haldon 2004, pp. 184–85.

[85] For these privileges in the early empire, see Mommsen 1887, pp. 466–75 and Weisweiler 2020, pp. 29–35. For exemption from torture, see *C. Th.* 9.35.3, 377 CE. For the exemption from curial duties, see Jones 1964, p. 741; La Rocca and Oppedisano 2016, pp. 23–24; and Chapter 2.

[86] For the required profession of residence, see *C. Th.* 6.2.13; Chastagnol 1992, pp. 298–99; and for the fourth century, La Rocca and Oppedisano 2016, pp. 185–6, and Chapter 2 note 239. The offices of quaestor or praetor still required the giving of games in Rome; see Symm. *Or.* 8; and Moser 2018, pp. 37–39 for a succinct discussion.

At the same time and in the aftermath of the civil war in 312, Constantine made certain key adjustments that opened up new opportunities to hold high office to men from the senatorial aristocracy. (See Chapter 2.)

To accentuate differences in the career paths and social origins of these men who all were now called the "most outstanding" (*clarissimi*) and held senatorial rank, I use the term *senatorial aristocrat* to mean those senators who were from established Italian or Rome-based families, who were tied to the city of Rome in particular, and who pursued civic careers. I am well aware that this usage is somewhat problematic since the term *aristocracy* is used by modern historians to describe a legally privileged class of interconnected families whose position is based on the inheritance of large landed estates. In contrast, the late Roman senatorial aristocracy combined inherited wealth with political office, a powerful conjunction that allowed for the accumulation of intergenerational resources.[87] Thus, the term senatorial aristocracy in this book refers to a narrower group than all men of senatorial rank. Those who attained senatorial rank through their positions in the imperial court or in service to the emperor, or high-ranking military officers also attained senatorial rank and are among the senatorial elite, but I refer to them as the imperial or military elite. Senators in Constantinople with civic office are noted as such.

As I demonstrate in Chapter 2, Constantine and his successors turned to members of the senatorial aristocracy to supplement the civic administration of the fourth-century empire. His innovations brought unprecedented opportunities for political influence for senatorial aristocrats. Certainly, those senatorial families that benefitted most from these changes did so in no small part because they were able to retain a large portion of their income from agriculture and business. Thus, their political and economic influence augmented their social and cultural positions in the fourth century and after.

In the absence of a resident emperor in the city of Rome, a reality true from Constantine's time until the mid fifth-century reign of Valentinian III, senatorial aristocrats became increasingly central to the running of the state. Consequently, the Senate as an institution grew in influence and prestige. The loss of large areas of Gaul, Africa, and Britain over the course of the first half of the fifth century meant that the senators and Senate of Rome and Italy gained greater political prominence in the city and region. Territorial losses brought more limited horizons and reduced the number of senators over the

---

[87] For fuller justification of the use of this term, see Salzman 2002, pp. 20–24. For the problems with this view as applied to the early empire, see Weisweiler 2020, pp. 29–56.

course of the fifth century as elites from the provinces chose to make Rome their residency less frequently. However, the attraction of the city of Rome, especially to certain powerful families that competed for office, remained and even increased as the stage on which they could assert and accrue power grew smaller.[88]

The political influence of Roman senatorial aristocrats cannot on its own explain the decisions of scores of men and women – both elites and non-elites – to return with their families to the city of Rome after each political and military crisis, especially during the second half of the fifth century after a series of increasingly violent attacks had undermined urban life. To understand this dynamic and the reasons why senatorial aristocrats were able to absorb shocks and repeatedly marshal their resources – the definition of *resilience* used by some scholars – to rebuild the city of Rome, we need also to consider the enduring institutions, values, and social networks that compelled senators to reinvest in the city even after the losses they had suffered during the assaults on the city in the years 312, 410, 455, and 472 and in the sixth century after the Gothic War.[89]

Based on my study of Rome in late antiquity, I argue that the processes of competition for influence among senators – those from established aristocratic families as well as those new to senatorial status through either civic, imperial, or military careers – were central to the recovery of Rome in the aftermath of a series of major political and military crises. The extensive economic resources that senatorial aristocrats had accrued over centuries provided the means for them to participate in this competition. Wealth was a key factor, to be sure. But the choice made by Rome's senators, conditioned by previous resolutions to crises, to return to Rome to rebuild their city – materially, ideologically, and institutionally – was also based on a competitive prestige culture and values that had been present in Roman society for centuries. For these men and women, and those who emulated their positions in society, service to the state either in the city of Rome or in the empire at large remained the key source of their status. High civic office – *honor* – continued to be central to senatorial aristocratic identity, even in the face of an increasingly weakened state.

The social dynamics of competition among senators for political advantage did, however, shift in relation to events and developments over the period of this study. In the fourth century, senators primarily competed for political favor among themselves and from the emperor. However, after the

<hr>

[88] Machado 2013, pp. 62–63; and on this I agree also with Machado 2019, pp. 13–14.
[89] For this definition, see Harper 2017, p. 20 and note 27. See my discussion in note 66 above.

crisis of 410 and continuing into the fifth century, political influence was more diffuse. Senators strove for political advantage from the imperial court, either in Ravenna or Constantinople; from fellow senators in Rome; or from military men powerful in Gaul and Italy. Senatorial competition for political favor – from a variety of sources – was a stimulant to recovery after crisis. Under weak and absent emperors, senatorial competition was dispersed in ways that made political life in Rome in the fifth century CE sound a lot more like what it must have been in the last decades of the Roman republic in the first century BCE, when senators vied for influence with each other without a strong, central figure in control.[90] When Valentinian III returned to Rome in the 440s and permanently after 450, his presence led to increased competition from senators, as the usurpation of Petronius Maximus attests (see Chapter 4). By the late fifth century, and continuing into the sixth century, these dynamics shifted again under Germanic kings who controlled Italy but relied greatly on senators to legitimate their positions and administer Rome and Italy (see Chapters 5 and 6).

The resilience of Roman senators also depended on the maintenance of their social networks – friends, family, clients. These ties had political repercussions. By the late fourth century, senators could and did at times ally themselves with the "barbarian" – that is, Germanic – military leaders. Rather than seeing senatorial aristocrats as the puppets of these strong generals, I stress the active engagement of senators with military elites. Although the generals Ricimer and Odoacer had control of their military forces, both commanders sought alliances with senatorial aristocrats.[91] Senatorial aristocrats not only provided legitimacy and stability, they also served in key positions in the state, as magistrates, patrons, and ambassadors. Thus, the political influence that Rome's senatorial aristocrats exercised through their social and political networks made them increasingly important to the military through the early sixth century.

It is not that surprising, then, that many senators had come to rely on these military figures and no longer saw the need for a resident western emperor. So, unlike those scholars who think that in the fifth-century senators managed to establish themselves (once more) at the center of imperial power as the means to their survival, I emphasize senatorial willingness to turn away from an imperial presence in either Rome or Ravenna (see Chapter 5).[92] Their influence increased over this century, I argue, because they of their

[90] Matthews 1981, p. 19.   [91] On these men, see my discussion in Chapters 4 and 5.

[92] Stein 1959, I, pp. 380 ff; Clover 1978, pp. 169–75; Humphries 2003, p. 44. Here I also part company from Matthews' groundbreaking 1975 study of western aristocracies. My view of the rising political power of the Senate and viewing it as a protagonist in the late antiquity owes much to

autonomy and leadership in Rome and Italy. Senatorial aristocrats had grown increasingly comfortable using their political and economic resources in support of their friends, be they aspiring courtiers, kings, emperors, or generals. So, for example, when the Gothic king Alaric besieged Rome between 408 and 410, senators took on greater leadership roles in negotiations and in the recovery of the city (see Chapter 3).

Although provincial aristocrats developed their own regional networks and identities over the fifth century, Rome nonetheless continued to attract newcomers, including upwardly mobile men and women from the provinces and from the East who recognized the power and influence to be gained by making friendship ties with or becoming part of Rome's senatorial aristocracy.[93] This had been the case for the mid fifth-century Gallic senator Sidonius Apollinaris.[94] Others came to Rome for financial or educational opportunities. Consequently, the city continued to attract new men and women even as severe political and military crises forced migrations at times. Senatorial aristocratic networks were diminished but not disrupted by these crises in the fourth through the sixth centuries. With the loss of western provinces, the city of Rome became increasingly important as the stage upon which Italo-Roman senatorial aristocrats could still compete for status and high office. Thus, we can better understand their willingness to reinvest their resources in reconstituting the city.

Christianizing Rome: The Influence of the Bishop of Rome

The spread of Christianity did not mitigate the competition for prestige among Roman senatorial aristocrats and elites in general. The teaching of Christian virtues like humility and piety by bishops and the clergy did not diminish the appeal of senatorial status and high political office. Nor did most senatorial aristocrats turn away from secular careers. The notion that senators simply traded their togas for the bishop's mitre does not fit well the trajectories of the majority of senatorial aristocrats in Rome.[95] Gibbon's assumption that the church merely stepped in where the state had been is not viable.[96]

the work of Mazzarino, as articulated, for instance, in his important 1974 article. See too on his view Oppedisano 2020B, pp. 27–39.

[93] On this I agree with Machado 2019, p. 14; and Wormald 1976, pp. 221–22. See too Barnish 1988, pp. 130–34.

[94] On his career, see especially Harries 1994.

[95] For a nuanced analysis of aristocrats as bishops in Gaul, see Brown 2012, pp. 494–95; and in southern Gaul, see Esders 1997, p. 185.

[96] On this widespread view held by Gibbon and his contemporaries, see Pocock 1999, p. 3.

On the contrary, in Rome senatorial aristocrats played an important role in influencing the city's religious life. Wealthy Christian senators with large incomes at their disposal funded their favorite Christian communities and used their houses as well as their patronage to advance their ideas about proper Christian worship in the city. We can see the impact of their influence, for example, in the building of neighborhood churches (the titular churches) or in their funding of funeral celebrations, which fed the poor in the great churches of the city.[97] They patronized certain deacons and priests whose presence at banquets and religious services in their great homes in Rome was a source of friction among the clergy.[98] Even Leo (440–61), one of the most influential bishops of Rome, faced competing aristocratic senatorial traditions of worship when he strove to craft liturgies centered on St. Peter's.[99]

Certainly, the bishop of Rome claimed control of religious life in the city over lay senators as well as the clergy. The bishops of Rome traced their authority to their apostolic succession from Peter, the first bishop of the city. They asserted authority over the consecration, discipline, and doctrine of a large number of clergy in the city, and over those in the suburbicarian churches (i.e., those literally "under the city"), which were located in that part of Italy that lay south of a line roughly from the gulf of modern Ancona to Genoa, including as well Sicily, Sardinia, and Corsica. As Kristina Sessa observed, by ca. 500 there would be around 200 bishops under their authority, far more than other bishops in the western Roman Empire.[100]

The bishops of Rome faced ongoing challenges to their authority not just from lay senatorial aristocrats, but also from other Christians. Rome was teeming with a variety of Christian sects. The church had only in the early third century managed to have centralized Christian leadership.[101] Many sects in the fourth- and fifth-century city, such as Arians and Novatians, had their own bishops.[102] Even the bishops and clerics who recognized the authority of the Christian bishop of Rome were not forced to follow his

---

[97] For the use of houses by aristocrats as religious centers, see Bowes 2008; and Machado 2019, pp. 162–97. For the titular churches, see my discussion in Chapter 2, and Sessa 2012, pp. 127–73. For aristocrats feeding the poor at parties in the great churches in Rome, see Grig 2006, pp. 146–61.

[98] Hunter 2017, p. 505.   [99] For Leo's use of liturgy, see Salzman 2013, pp. 208–32.

[100] On Petrine primacy, see Demacopoulos 2013. For the growth of the papacy and area under his authority, see Sessa 2012, pp. 25–27. For the suburbicarian churches and their organization, see Moorhead 2015, pp. 12–13.

[101] For the evidence from Rome as centralizing authority relatively late, see Brent 1995, pp. 458–580.

[102] For a discussion of the limits on the later fourth-century Bishop Damasus (366–84), see Trout 2015, pp. 9–10.

advice, and those bishops outside of the city were especially able to selectively apply his opinions to match their own views.[103]

Tensions with clergy within the Christian church at Rome also undermined the authority of the bishop of Rome, and these emerged openly, most often over the issue of episcopal succession. We see some of these strains in one well-known conflict over succession, when two men, Ursinus and Damasus, were both elected bishop in Rome in 366 by competing groups of Christians within the Church in Rome. The dispute could not be resolved, leading to violence in the streets of the city. The civic magistrate in charge of Rome, the urban prefect Praetextatus, a pagan senatorial aristocrat, put an end to the rioting, but skirmishes persisted. With the backing of the emperor, Praetextatus supported Damasus over Ursinus, thereby essentially defining the correct – that is, orthodox – notion of Christianity, in this case that of Damasus (366–84).[104] Yet Damasus's position over his own clergy and in society was weakened by this fight. Moreover, as Carlos Machado has well argued, the senatorial aristocratic officials, in this case the urban prefect, by resolving such disputes thereby exercised great influence over the "life and history of the Christian community" in Rome.[105]

The bishops of Rome also faced challenges to their authority from emperors and the imperial court, East and West. Certainly, following Constantine, the emperors (with the exception of Julian, 361–63) supported the spread of Christianity in the city and empire. Constantine set the precedent for elite patronage with his lavish donations and church building.[106] Yet imperial donations to the church were considered private gifts, and thus keeping imperial favor was critical for keeping the financial support that bishops used for their own purposes.[107] Being dependent on an imperial or senatorial patron for financial support did, however, place certain limits on the public role that the bishops of Rome would have, as we shall see. And from the early fourth century, imperial intervention in Christian controversies led to tensions with the bishops of Rome, as in other cities, that at times similarly undermined the authority of the bishop (see Chapters 2 and 4 especially).

---

[103] On Rome as a court of appeals in disciplinary cases for the metropolitan sees of Arles and Thessalonica, see Sessa 2012, p. 27. On Rome's assertion of authority over Gaul, for example, see Mathisen 1989, pp. 44–68.

[104] In this interpretation of these events, I am in agreement with Machado 2019, pp. 171–72.

[105] Machado 2019, p. 171.

[106] For the standard emphasis on the role of the emperor on the Christianization of Rome's physical spaces, see especially Krautheimer 1980, pp. 59–87; see too Chapter 2.

[107] Pietri 1976, 1, pp. 79–83; and Neil 2017, p. 56 and note 30.

For these and other reasons that I explore subsequently, my work supports those scholars who see the bishops of Rome as structurally, relatively weak civic leaders despite the rhetoric in texts such as the *Book of the Popes*, a sixth-century collection of papal biographies modeled on Suetonius's *Lives of the Caesars* (discussed below).[108] Because the bishops were part of a Christian church that was not nearly as developed as its medieval counterpart, in this book I favor the term bishop of Rome instead of pope for the fourth and fifth centuries. The Latin word *"papa,"* or pope, meaning father, was used for many other bishops around the Mediterranean, and only in the sixth century, as John Moorhead has proposed, do we see a shift to using the word pope as a title with the implication of office only for the bishop of Rome.[109] Hence I use the term pope as well as bishop only for the sixth-century holders of this office and their successors.

Although the bishops of Rome did act on behalf of the city to feed the poor or to ransom prisoners at specific moments, the emperors, the kings, and the senators were the dominant civic leaders in Rome for the centuries covered in this book. Nor was the removal of the western emperor in 476, in my view, the pivotal moment that created a powerful papacy in Rome, in the medieval sense of the term as an institution with complete civic authority.[110] On the contrary, only after the Gothic War did the rhetoric concerning the civic authority of the bishops of Rome as expressed by Gelasius (bishop of Rome 492–96) come closer to matching their public role.

The Five Falls of Rome: Method and Evidence

This book is structured around five military and political episodes and responses to what the Romans themselves saw as crises that overtook the inhabitants of the city of Rome in the period between 312 and 604. Modern historians follow the views of the ancients in seeing these five events as crises. This period covers the changes associated with the new empire of Constantine and extends through the "decline and fall" of the western Roman Empire. My aim, however, is to better understand Roman resilience over this *longue durée*.

I focus on the political elites active in the city of Rome – senatorial aristocrats, emperors, kings, generals and bishops. Rome's senatorial aristocratic leaders emerge as singularly important because they were the ones who so frequently led Rome's recovery and because Rome was a hegemonic society in which wealth brought power – political, social, religious, and military.

---

[108] See, for example, Sessa 2012, pp. 25–30; and Chapter 2.   [109] Moorhead 1986, pp. 337–50.
[110] See, for example, the arguments of Meier 2015, pp. 15–68.

Thus, when I use the term *elite*, I mean it as John Haldon so well defined it: as "the leading element of this ruling, or dominant, social-economic class, those who shared a situation in respect of access to political/ideological power and influence."[111] In Rome, as elsewhere, members with senatorial rank may or may not have been born into their positions. In fact, the senatorial elite was not one single block. As noted earlier, the senatorial aristocracy of Rome, tied to the city of Rome and its environs, was distinct from those senators who, often new to senatorial rank, had attained their status through service at the imperial court or in the administration of the state. Even within the senatorial aristocratic families of Rome, marriages and adoptions brought new men into this group as well. But all elites – senatorial, imperial, and military – competed to preserve and advance their interests, bringing them at times to work together and at other times to contest with one another for positions, status, wealth, and personal satisfactions.

It is worth underscoring, however, that all elites – senatorial, imperial, and military – could not function without the support and work of non-elite Romans. On a domestic level, as the masters of large urban households, Roman senatorial aristocratic elite men and women relied on laborers, often slaves, for the maintenance of their lifestyles. It is well known, for example, that educated slaves often managed the financial records and performed domestic tasks such as cooking, cleaning, and educating children in the houses of wealthy senatorial elites. In rebuilding Rome after a crisis, elites would naturally also seek to replace not just their domestic workers but also those who could rebuild the city, from its walls to its food supply. Understanding this human dynamic is important for explaining the ability of elites to recover Rome after each crisis. So, for instance, in the years following the sack of Rome in 410, the urban prefect wrote to the emperor to increase the grain supply as people were returning more quickly than anticipated to the city.[112] The urban prefect also needed to have professional bakers return. As well, he needed his staff to help in the distribution of the bread. Even the restoration of order required non-elite assistance. While wealthy aristocrats employed their own private bodyguards, the urban prefect Flavius Leontius employed lightly armed forces to quell urban riots in 355 and 356.[113]

---

[111] Haldon 2004, p. 181.   [112] See my discussion in Chapter 3.

[113] Amm. Marc. 15.7.2. In the early third century, the urban prefect had soldiers at his disposal, but the military urban cohorts disappeared over the course of the fourth century and were replaced by a limited police force under the urban prefect. For the early third century, see Ulpian (*Digesta* 1.12.1.12) and Kelly 2012, pp. 410–24; for the fourth century, see Chastagnol 1964, pp. 254–56.

The performance of elite status also required public recognition by non-elites. Restoring a part of the Colosseum or a statue in the Roman Forum or funding circus games remained an integral component of elite senatorial status that relied on acknowledgment by non-elites.[114] Similarly, elites strove for public recognition of their acts of Christian virtue, be it almsgiving or building churches. However, the competition for influence on and honor from elite peers or the emperor was probably, for most Roman senators, an even greater stimulant for action than the adulation of the crowd.[115]

The pattern of crisis and reconstruction that I trace over the three hundred years of this study resulted in a city far smaller in population, wealth, and resources. Yet the responses of the still-dominant leading groups in Rome – senatorial aristocrats, the emperor and imperial courtiers, the military, the Germanic kings, and the bishops – to the political and military crises that came to the city, beginning with the civil war of Constantine and Maxentius in 312 and ending with the post–Gothic War period, demonstrate how its inhabitants recovered Rome. Roman senatorial aristocrats were convinced that this was a city worth renewing time and again.

I focus on responses to military and political crises because these events allow me to consider one other key element in assessing the role of elite leadership – time. As much as possible, I look at the first decade or two after an event to gauge the recovery of the city and its inhabitants. I concentrate on the immediate responses because, as the work of certain social scientists has underscored, processes of change are highly sensitive to events that take place in the early stages of an overall historical sequence.[116] Analysis of historical causality has led scholars to appreciate that not only what one does but when one does it has a larger than expected impact on the outcome of events and the ability of a society to recover. By restricting my time frame, I can better discern patterns to recovery.

The five crises that I analyze were also the ones that were highlighted by our ancient sources. In addition to what ancient histories and chroniclers tell us about what they saw as critical inflection points, I have incorporated the evidence of individual lives as pieced together from inscriptions, letters, and allusions in a wide variety of ancient documents and literary texts. I focus on those senatorial aristocrats who lived in Rome, owned property there, or held office there. I reconstruct the lives of individual actors, notably those who took on leadership roles by holding high office, in the moments after a crisis.

---

[114] For the work of urban prefects after 410, see my discussion in Chapter 3.

[115] On the critical importance of peer recognition, see Salzman 2002, pp. 43–56.

[116] Mahoney 2000, pp. 507–48, for the classic formulation of this idea. For its application, see, for instance, Pierson 2000, pp. 251–67.

Of particular importance for this study are the private letters and letter collections of individuals who visited Rome or lived there over the centuries. Scholars have come to appreciate the complex nature of these letters and have sought to interpret them within their historical, literary, and social contexts. The letters of the Gallo-Roman senator and urban prefect, and later bishop of Clermont, Sidonius Apollinaris are a good example of how much scholars have come to see these writings as literary works that were carefully curated for publication. Additionally, this collection of letters provides vivid descriptions of this man's interactions with Roman senators, emperors, and clergy in the mid fifth century.[117]

This heightened sensitivity of scholars to our sources has also been applied to the study of material culture. For individuals, the thousands of inscriptions that have survived from Rome are a critical source of untapped and ever-increasing information. But for these, too, scholars have become increasingly aware of the need to be sensitive to context. So, as Silvia Orlandi has shown, the monumental inscription that she has recently interpreted as evidence of a restoration of the Colosseum by the urban prefect identified as Iunius Valerius Bellicius befitted an imperial celebration, thus narrowing the date of his actions to either 417 or 422 (see Figure 6 in Chapter 3).[118] Hence the context, here public honorific, supplies important clues. And, as is well known, Rome is extraordinarily well supplied with personal inscriptions, including those not only from public honorific monuments but also from private dedications, funerary sites, and official records.[119] I rely on these to reconstitute the lives of many of the men and some women whose responses to crisis I focus on in this study.

I also incorporate what I regard as underutilized evidence as new sources for this book. One area that I have found particularly rich for this study is the laws, letters, and documents that shed light on the actions of the bishop and clergy of Rome. For example, the letters of bishops Leo and Pelagius and documents like the *Scriptura of 483* of Pope Simplicius, preserved within the documentary record of a Church Council of 502, can convey important information not only about internal church controversies and differing theological positions but also about the role of senatorial aristocrats and bishops.[120] Of particular import for this book are the collections of

---

[117] For a good introduction to the letters of Sidonius Apollinaris and other late antique letter collections, see the essays in Sogno, Storin, and Watts 2017.

[118] Orlandi 2017, pp. 212–14.

[119] I refer to some of these collections of inscriptions in my list of abbreviations. For a succinct discussion of late antique epigraphy, see Salway 2015A, pp. 364–93.

[120] For the letters of Leo and Pelagius, and the *Scriptura of 483* that survives in the record of the Church Council of 502, see my discussion in Chapter 5. The collections of papal letters appear in several different modern editions, which are usefully described by Neil 2017, pp. 449–66.

documents pertaining to the church in Rome. The one today known from the monastery that preserved it, the *Avellana Collection*, dated to sixth-century Rome, has been the object of much recent study.[121]

Another important collation of the biographies of the *Lives of the Popes* is also dated to sixth-century Rome. Its first edition is generally viewed as finalized in the 530s based on a fundamental study of the manuscripts by Louis Duchesne, which has been augmented by Herman Geertman who argued that this first edition was completed in 535.[122] A second edition (now standard) of the *Lives of the Popes* was produced soon afterward, in the 540s, under Pope Vigilius (537–55). It reworked the lives of the first edition to reflect contemporary concerns and was itself extended into the ninth century by anonymous compilers who had access to church archives in Rome.[123] (In this book, I follow the text of Duchesne's second edition, but I note where the text is suspect due to later additions.) Most importantly for this study, however, is the need to determine the reliability of the information in the *Lives of the Popes*. Not all scholars agree on the historical value of particular *Lives*.[124] Some of the *Lives* were finalized to reflect the views of the second edition's sixth-century compilers. So, for example, the *Life of Pope Silvester*, bishop at the time of the emperor Constantine, asserts that Silvester baptized Constantine. This goes against all contemporary sources but reflects fifth-century and later legends about the bishop.[125] Similarly, the *Life of Pope Symmachus* (498–514) includes details to justify his office that conflict with other documents pertaining to this controversial pope and his disputed

---

[121] For the *Avellana Collection*, see the important collections of essays in Lizzi Testa and Marconi 2019; and Blair-Dixon 2007, pp. 59–76.

[122] For the text of the *Book of the Popes* (*Liber Pontificalis*), I use the revised edition of Duchesne 1981, with observations on the publication at pp. xlvii–xlviii and ccxxx–ccxxxi. Duchesne suspected that the *Lives* of Vigilius, Pelagius I (556–61), John III (561–74), and Benedict I (575–79) were added during the pontificate of Pelagius II (579–90); see Duchesne 1981, pp. ccxxxi–ccxxxii. For the English translation, I modify that of Davis 2010, who also summarizes these details, xiii–xiv, xlvi–xlviii. For an excellent discussion of these developments, see Trout 2015, pp. 58–60. For modification of this publication scheme based on a reassessment of the manuscripts, see Geertman 2003, pp. 267–72.

[123] Davis 2010, p. xiv, sees the *Book of the Popes* as the work of "low level officials in the papal bureaucracy, whether laymen or, more probably, lower clerics." Others see this book as more literary and of dubious historicity, but still largely the work of clerics. See notes 124 and 125 below.

[124] For doubts about the historicity of information in the *Lives*, see, for instance, McKitterick 2011, pp. 19–34, McKitterick 2020, pp. 203–09; and Blair-Dixon 2007, pp. 59–76.

[125] For the *Life of Silvester*, see *Lib. Pont.* 33, ed. Duchesne 1981, pp. 170–201. For further discussion of the image of Silvester as a later construction, see Chapter 2.

election.[126] Nor do all scholars agree that even the information in the *Lives* that was likely derived from church archives, like the donation and ordination lists, is fully reliable.[127] Clearly, each *Life* presents particular challenges that require careful historical contextualization and consideration of the manuscript evidence before we assume that it is reliable. Nonetheless, the *Lives of the Popes*, along with the other collections pertaining to the Church in Rome offer still underappreciated sources of evidence for Roman responses to crisis, not only the reactions of bishops and clergy, but those of lay Romans and senatorial aristocrats as well.

I am not the first scholar to use many of these sources, nor am I the first to recognize the resources at the disposal of bishops and senators. But new information about the city in late antiquity, new scholarly work on relevant sources, and the new perspective I develop focusing on resilience and resurgence have led me to write on what many would consider a very old topic, the "Decline and Fall of Rome." I hope that the reader will gain from considering, as I have, how Roman elites, in the face of great losses, were able to, in Adrienne Rich's words, "reconstitute the world." I turn in Chapter 2 to their first major challenge, to what many historians see as the truly pivotal crisis for Rome – the civil war that culminated with the victory in 312 by Constantine, Rome's first Christian emperor (306–37). The interactions between senators, bishops, emperor, and the military in the aftermath of 312 set the foundations for the resurgence of the city and its aristocracy in the coming centuries.

---

[126] For the *Life of Symmachus*, see *Lib. Pont.* 53, ed. Duchesne 1981, pp. 260–68. For the controversies surrounding his papacy and the slanted information in the *Lives of the Popes*, see my discussion in Chapter 5.

[127] For a strong argument for the veracity of the donation lists in the *Lives*, see Liverani 2019, pp. 169–218; and Trout 2015, pp. 59–60, summarizing Geertman's views on this aspect of the text.

2

The Constantinian Compromise

After that is the province of Campania, not indeed exceedingly large, but however possessing wealthy men, a region sufficient for itself and a food supply for one ruling in Rome. . . . Italy, abundant thus in all ways, possesses also this greatest good: the greatest city, most eminent and most regal, that shows its virtue in its name and is called Rome [. . .] It [Rome] moreover has also the greatest Senate of wealthy men, whom, if you would wish to examine one by one, you would find that all have been made powerful magistrates [*iudices*] or will be powerful ones; or indeed could be powerful magistrates but are unwilling to be on account of their desire to enjoy their own [properties] free from care.

—A Description of the World and its Peoples 54–55,
Anonymous, composed aroud 350 CE.[1]

The battle between Constantine and Maxentius at the Milvian Bridge outside of Rome has taken on mythic proportions in the imaginations of writers and artists from 312 on. In the influential version of events promulgated by Bishop Eusebius in his *Life of Constantine*, this was an epic confrontation that pitted the force of the Christian god, wielded by the newly converted Constantine, against the pagan-inspired troops of Maxentius. This triumphalist narrative permeated fourth-century society and was famously promulgated by later Christians who knew that his victory would usher in major

---

[1] *Expositio totius mundi et gentium* 54–55: *Post eam Campania provincia, non valde quidem magna, divites autem viros possidens et ipsa sibi sufficiens et cellarium regnanti Roma[e]. . . Italia ergo omnibus abundans insuper et hoc maximum bonum possidet: civitatem maximam et eminentissimam et regalem, quae de nomine virtutem ostentat et vocatur Roma. [. . .] Habet autem et senatum maximum virorum divitum: quos si per singulos probare volueris, invenies omnes iudices aut factos aut futuros esse; aut potentes quidem, nolentes autem propter suorum frui cum securitate velle.* This work is generally dated to the age of Constantius II, after 350. Text from Porena 2013, p. 335. Translation by author.

religious changes, even as the city and its elites remained predominantly pagan into the late fourth century.[2]

I begin this chapter with the battle of the Milvian Bridge not for its religious implications, however, but because this civil war presented the first major political and military crisis for the fourth-century city. Although the battle took place six kilometers outside the city walls, Constantine's victory brought the government of Maxentius to a violent end, with a great loss of human life and property. In the recovery effort that followed this crisis, the senatorial aristocracy played a leading role, as they would do in the next two centuries. They were, after all, among the wealthiest men in Italy, as the epigraph to this chapter asserted. They used their considerable resources to rebuild Rome and their place in it. Senatorial aristocratic support for the new regime, I argue, was critical for Constantine's success.

After 312, senatorial aristocrats took on key civic leadership positions. Constantine turned to western senators to administer the areas of the empire under his control, even as he expanded the number of positions that offered senatorial, that is, *clarissimate*, standing, and as he redefined the ways in which senatorial status was attained.[3] Senatorial aristocrats thrived even as Constantine continued certain administrative changes that made Italy more similar to other provinces. The emperor also divided the peninsula into two districts for administrative purposes, the northern *Italia Annonaria* and the southern *Italia Suburbicaria*, divided by the Arno and Esine Rivers.[4] Under this administrative system, senators rose to positions of power. So, for example, when Constantine removed a strong military presence from Rome after 312, he left a senatorial civic official, the urban prefect, in charge of what was essentially its police guard, the urban cohorts.[5]

In the face of such wide-ranging administrative, social and religious changes, Roman senatorial aristocrats demonstrated their resilience as they recovered Rome. Indeed, holding high office under Constantine had enabled western senatorial elites not just to retain but also to *expand* their political and social influence in Rome and the empire, a change all the more significant in

---

[2] For the pace of the conversion of the Roman senatorial aristocracy, even the most expansive view would not see the majority of senators as Christian until the middle, and as I have argued, in the last quarter of the fourth century; see Salzman 2002, pp. 13–20; 161–77. For earlier dates, see Cameron 2011, pp. 173–205, 783–891 with bibliography.

[3] Garbarino 1988, pp. 65–66; Heather 1988, pp. 184–210; Salzman 2002, pp. 31–35 and ibid., 2020, pp. 251–94; Dillon 2015, pp. 42–66.

[4] For the provincialization of Italy and the development of dioceses by Diocletian, see Aur. Vict. 39.30–32; the changes under Constantine are discussed more fully by Porena 2013, pp. 329–49.

[5] Chastagnol 1960, pp. 225–27.

the absence of a resident emperor. Since the empire was partitioned between Constantine and his co-augustus, Licinius after 312, only after the defeat of Licinius in 324 and the return to one-man rule did new opportunities in the East open up for western senators. Western senators extended their patronage and social networks, securing their bonds with provincial elites and clients in the East as well as with those in the West.[6] Indeed, the clients of some senators numbered into the hundreds, one manifestation of their growing influence.

No wonder, then, that Constantine sought to make alliances and marriages with a number of senatorial families. The senators, or at least those who took up high office under Constantine, were motivated by a variety of reasons. Some sought to compete for honor and to win praise for their service. Admittedly, not all were so motivated, nor were they all spinelessly self-regarding, as some have argued.[7] Their willingness to work with the new regime represents, to a certain extent, their desire to compromise. Thus senators, who were predominantly pagan, did not engage in open conflict over religious differences, as was once argued.[8] In return, in the decade after 312, senatorial aristocrats became increasingly influential in "shaping the distribution of resources and life chances on the ground."[9] The foundation by Constantine of a new capital city in the East, Constantinople, in 324 with its own set of institutions, elites, and opportunities was little cause for concern to powerful contemporary western senatorial aristocrats.[10]

Given the historic role played by Constantine in spreading Christianity, it is ironic that senatorial aristocrats were more cooperative with Constantine than were the early fourth-century bishops of the city. Indeed, the bishop of Rome and the clergy, along with other Christians in the city, benefitted greatly from the restoration of their property and the recognition of their legal standing after 312. Constantine openly patronized Christianity, building basilicas even as he appointed Christians to high political office.[11] But contrary to the view presented by such pro-papal

---

[6] For the building of patronage networks through the holding of office first in the West and then, after 324, in the East, see Moser 2018, pp. 48–54; and my discussion below.

[7] For negative views of senators as political influencers, see Cameron 2011, pp. 783–801 and Cameron 2012, pp. 133–71. See also the mostly negative view by Wickham 2005, pp. 154–56.

[8] For open pagan–Christian conflict, see Alföldi 1948; with arguments against it by Salzman 2016, pp. 11–45; and Lizzi Testa, Salzman, and Sághy 2016, pp. 1–8.

[9] Weisweiler 2019, SCS Abstract. Weisweiler 2015B, pp. 17–41 has emphasized senatorial subservience.

[10] Ramskold and Lenski 2012, pp. 31–58 on Constantinople as another Rome. However, Moser 2018, pp. 214–76, has raised doubts about a second Senate in Constantinople under Constantine; see my discussion below about the status of Rome-based elites.

[11] For his church building in Rome, see my discussion below. For imperial appointments, see Salzman 2016, pp. 2016, pp. 11–45; Moser 2018, pp. 214–76, and my discussion below. The tables

sources as the sixth-century *Book of the Popes* or by eminent scholars like Charles Pietri, the bishops of Rome under Constantine – Miltiades (311–14) and then Silvester (314–35) – were relatively weak partners. They failed to cooperate with Constantine as he had desired in the first major controversy after 312 involving the African bishops, the so-called Donatist schism that I discuss later in this chapter.[12]

We can certainly understand the distrust of Constantine on the part of the bishops of Rome. The persecution of Christians immediately preceding the Constantinian settlement and Galerius's 311 Edict of Toleration had, no doubt, planted feelings of suspicion and fear. Trusting a recently converted emperor whose language and acts were bluntly intended to terrorize subjects into submission was another matter.[13] Thus, Constantine's legal threats that any Jews trying to stop conversion to Christianity "be delivered immediately to the flames" or that any who attack Christians be "beaten with clubs, in public, provided their status allows" show how easily this emperor could turn force against any who opposed him.[14]

Given these suspicions, we can better understand why, in their interactions with Constantine after 312, the bishops of Rome did not develop a good working relationship with this emperor, as had certain Gallic bishops and the Spanish bishop Ossius of Cordoba.[15] Nor do we have evidence that the bishops of Rome developed close ties to members of Constantine's family, who remained in the city as imperial representatives. Finally, there is little evidence that these bishops developed strong senatorial aristocratic patrons under Constantine either. The responses of the bishops of Rome after 312 set a pattern that limited their influence for decades to come. Thus, unlike the senatorial aristocrats whose power increased greatly as they recovered the city in the post 312 decade, the bishops of Rome were relatively weak public figures, especially compared to bishops in other cities. How the Romans got to 312 is critical for understanding these foundational developments.

---

for urban prefects published in this chapter are adapted from the ones that I published in Salzman 2016, pp. 243–62. Sections of that chapter have been excerpted here or revised with permission of Cambridge University Press.

[12] Pietri 1976, pp. 160–87.

[13] I owe this point to Brent Shaw. His characterization of the "profound sense of unease" felt by Christians in North Africa is apt, also, for the clergy in Rome. On this dynamic, see Shaw 2011, pp. 490–505 especially.

[14] For Constantine's law against Jewish molestation of Christians in 315, see C. *Th.* 16.8.1; for the 323 law protecting clergy, see C. *Th.* 16.2.5.

[15] The Gallic bishops, being relatively very few in number and drawn from a higher social local elite for the most part, were in a different position, but their support was vital. On these bishops, see especially Eck 2007, pp. 69–94 and note 170 below.

Civil War in Rome: The Battle of the Milvian Bridge

It was not at all clear who would win the civil war that had brought Constantine to Rome in October 312. The contestants were well matched. Both contenders had been disappointed by the succession plans of the departing emperors. Maxentius, son of the former western augustus, Maximian, and Constantine, the son of the western augustus Constantius Chlorus, had both been denied office when the augusti Diocletian and Maximian had simultaneously stepped down from power in 305.[16] Instead, the emperors had advanced Galerius as senior augustus in the East. At the death of Constantius Chlorus in 306, Galerius designated Severus augustus in the West. But dynastic sentiment remained strong. Maxentius in Rome and Constantine in York were proclaimed augusti by the soldiers who had supported their fathers.[17] Both men were ambitious for power. Galerius chose to accept Constantine as a caesar rather than face civil war on two fronts. Moreover, as Mark Humphries has suggested, Galerius perhaps realized that Constantine's accession filled a vacuum in the imperial system, for Constantine's assumption of control over the lands of his father – Gaul, Spain, and Britain – could coexist with Severus's position as augustus in control of Italy and North Africa. With Constantine as caesar, the basic structure of the tetrarchy left by Diocletian and Maximian could continue.[18]

However, that was not the case with the accession of Maxentius, who, with the support of the praetorian guard in Rome in October 306, took over the territory of Severus, Italy and North Africa. Like Constantine, Maxentius had the support of the local forces (i.e., the *praetoriani, legio II Parthica,* and *equites singulares*), who were said to have been angered by Galerius's attempts to reduce their numbers and influence.[19] But unlike Constantine, Maxentius also counted among his supporters several senators in Rome who held high office, especially in the latter years of his regime; some likely resented Galerius's newly proposed land tax on Italy and Rome and welcomed the opportunity for political advancement.[20] Maxentius's focus on Rome and his reliance on pagan aristocratic senators are apparent if we

---

[16] Humphries 2008, pp. 89–92.

[17] Zos. 2.9.2, calls Constantine, the "illegitimate son" of Constantius. Zosimus suggests that the soldiers were manipulated by Constantine. The praetorians who supported Maxentius had also been under the authority of Maximian. For a hostile view of Maxentius's elevation, see Lact. *De mort. pers.* 26.1–3; 44.4.

[18] Humphries 2008, p. 92. Lact. *De mort. pers.* 26.4, asserts that Galerius hated Maxentius and he could not allow three Caesars.

[19] Lact. *De mort. pers.* 26.4.

[20] For Galerius's tax on Italy and Rome, see Aur. Vict. *Caes.* 39.31; Lact. *De mort. pers.* 23.1–6, 26.2. For Maxentius's reliance on senators in his government, especially in the later years of his regime, see Wienand 2017, p. 47; Lenski 2008, pp. 204–57.

consider the number of men who served in his regime and continued to serve his successor (for examples, see Table 2.1). When Galerius refused to recognize Maxentius and sent the augustus Severus to Italy to put down his usurpation, senators and praetorians continued to support Maxentius. Severus's troops deserted him. Severus was then captured and imprisoned, left to die, as our sources tell us, in either Rome or Ravenna in 307.[21]

Severus's death gave Constantine the opportunity to gain recognition, moving from caesar to *filius augustorum* in late 308 or 309, and finally being recognized as augustus in 310.[22] Constantine's marriage to Fausta, daughter of the former western augustus Maximian, in 307 was an effort to gain legitimacy through his connection to the imperial college. In contrast, Maxentius styled himself as a more traditional emperor, focusing on Rome and Italy. When an uprising in Africa in 308 by the deputy of the praetorian prefect Lucius Domitius Alexander disrupted the shipment of grain to the city, Maxentius raised taxes to provide food for the urban population, in part to demonstrate his concern as "good" emperors customarily did.[23] He also sent an army against Alexander in Africa under the control of the senator Rufius Volusianus and a general.[24] Taking advantage of Maxentius's difficulties in Africa and aware of Severus's earlier failed assault on Italy as well as Galerius's unwillingness to intervene, Constantine marched his troops south from Gaul over the Alps, first taking Milan, then Verona, before turning toward Rome. Like Caesar who came from Gaul intent upon taking power in Rome, Constantine's successes preceded him, striking fear in the civilian population.[25]

As Constantine camped just north of the city, Maxentius consulted the gods and his advisors. Maxentius was encouraged by divine signs and the Sibylline Books, which senatorial priests consulted on his behalf; according to Zosimus, Maxentius also could count on the fact that his troops had numerical superiority.[26] What Maxentius could not count on was the urban population. Although Rome had been protected since the early 270s by a wall that encircled the city with twelve miles of twenty-five-foot-high protection, to which Maxentius had added a ditch, Maxentius would have been hard-pressed to

---

[21] Humphries 2008, p. 88.   [22] Humphries 2008, p. 92.

[23] Van Dam 2018, p. 15; Aur. Vict. *Caes.* 40.24; *Chronica urbis Romae, MGH* AA 9, p. 148, states that he levied a tax of gold on all Romans, not just senators and farmers, contra Van Dam 2018, p. 15. Zos. 2.14 follows the senatorial view of Maxentius as a cruel and rapacious tyrant.

[24] For Volusianus, see Volusianus 4, *PLRE* 1, pp. 976–78.

[25] For Severus's failed attack, see Zos. 2.10.1–2. For Galerius's decision to send Licinius against Maxentius and his own aborted assault on Italy, see Zos. 2.10.3–7. For Constantine's movements, see Zos. 2.15.1.

[26] Zos. 2.16.1.

feed all the inhabitants and maintain their loyalty through a long siege. If Constantine were to impede the grain supply from Ostia by closing off the Tiber River, a demoralized and hungry population could easily riot. According to Lactantius, jeering and fearful spectators in the circus had already shouted to Maxentius that Constantine could not be defeated. True or not, the size of the urban population and the concern to maintain civic order worked against the alternative strategy of having the population resist by remaining inside the city walls.[27]

Faced with a potentially violent urban population and encouraged by his troops' numerical superiority, as well as by alleged reports of divine favor, Maxentius decided to march his men out of the city on the Flaminian Way. He crossed over the Tiber River to fight in a flat, open plain by means of a pontoon bridge near the Milvian Bridge.[28] The fighting was fierce; Zosimus acknowledged that an "immense number of other soldiers were killed."[29] It is worth underscoring the obvious: contrary to the later tradition that would paint Maxentius as a cruel tyrant, Maxentius's soldiers did not abandon him. He also had senatorial aristocrats who sided with him against Constantine. Only after Maxentius had ordered a retreat back to the city over the pontoon bridge did the troops turn back. Unfortunately for them, the bridge unexpectedly collapsed under the weight of men and animals. Disaster followed; Maxentius drowned in the Tiber, along with an unknown number of his followers.[30]

Constantine was now the senior augustus in the West. He had built up a power base in Gaul during his six years in residence there, and his victories in Italy demonstrated his military prowess to Italo-Romans. He would enter Rome at the head of a victorious army after a battle that had taken place outside the walls of the city. But nothing in his experience in government in Gaul had been like what he would encounter when he entered Rome, a city with a far more complex social, religious, and political landscape; with a large population, a Senate proud of its traditions, and a bishop whose clergy, although numbered in the hundreds, faced a number of dissident Christian groups.

---

[27] Lact. *De mort. pers.* 44.7.

[28] Zos. 2.15 for the numerical superiority of Maxentius; 80,000 Romans and Italians, along with a number of allies equaling a force of 170,000 foot and 18,000 horse. Constantine, according to Zosimus, had come to Britain with 90,000 infantry and 8,000 cavalry, a number that has been questioned, suggesting to Ridley 1982, p. 153, note 33, that the numbers in *Pan. lat.* 9 are more likely, that is 100,000 for Maxentius (*Pan. lat.* 9.3.3) versus 40,000 for Constantine (*Pan. lat.* 9.5.1).

[29] Zos. 2.16.2–3.   [30] Zos. 2.16.4.

The Resilience of Rome's Senatorial Aristocracy

Though Constantine had defeated Maxentius on October 28, 312, he delayed his entry into Rome until the following day. It must have been a tense night for the senators and soldiers who had been loyal supporters of the Maxentian regime. Some senators feared retribution, for they had been among the inner circle who had urged Maxentius to exit the city to engage in fatal combat.[31] It was in everyone's interests to show enthusiasm for the new ruler. That was the official version of events expressed by the anonymous panegyrist of 313, who admitted that he had not been present for the event but described it nonetheless: there was "so numerous a throng of people, so numerous an entourage of senators [who] carried you along and at the same time detained you... Thereafter, crowding through all the roads, they [the people] awaited, watched for, wished and hoped for your appearance, so that they seemed to besiege the man by whose siege they had been liberated."[32] The panegyrist expresses the view that we see was soon adopted by the Senate: Constantine was liberating Rome from a tyrant and his faction. The arch to honor Constantine's 312 victory, dedicated by the Senate, similarly echoes the notion that it was a faction that had supported Maxentius.[33] The official celebration of this day in the *Codex-Calendar of 354* recorded the event as "Removal of the Tyrant" (*Evictio tyranni*) and celebrated the triumph as the "Arrival" (*Adventus*) of Constantine, with three full days of games, October 29 through 31.[34] By turning this civil war into a liberation movement against a faction, the orator obscured the senators' fears of reprisal for their support of Maxentius. Constantine acted quickly to reinforce his control of the city; he destroyed the camps of the Horse Guard (*equites singulares*) and the Praetorian Guard, as well as obliterating the burial grounds of the former, and he made sure there would be no resistance by parading the head of Maxentius on a pole through the streets of Rome.[35]

---

[31] For the senators who urged Maxentius to face Constantine in combat outside the walls, see especially Lenski 2008, pp. 204–57.

[32] *Pan. lat.* 12 (9) 19.1: *tanta te populi densitas, tanta senatus stipatio provehebat simul et detinebat. ... [4]: Inde omnibus circumfuse viis, dum excederes, opperiri prospicere optare sperare, ut viderentur eum a quo obsidione liberati fuerant obsidere.*

[33] This suggests a senatorial writer who is aware of the idea that "evicting a faction" recalls the language of Augustus and the Augustan revolution; see Koortbojian 2020, pp. 123–68.

[34] In language that echoed Augustus's *Res Gestae*, coins proclaimed Constantine *liberator urbis suae*; see E. Marlowe 2010, pp. 217–18. For the *Codex-Calendar of 354*, see Salzman 1990, pp. 131 and 135.

[35] Aur. Vict., *Caes.* 40.25; garrisons noted by Zos. 2.17.2. For punishment of the *equites* of Maxentius, see Speidel 1986, 253–62. For the destruction of the Praetorian's camp as well, see Zos. 2.17; Aur. Vict. *Caes.* 40.25; Lact. *De mort. pers.* 26.

As a recently victorious emperor, Constantine came to the Senate for support. According to the panegyrist of 313, the emperor, by his deeds and actions, "restored the Senate [to] its former authority [*senatui auctoritatem pristinam reddidisti*]," even as he "refrained from boasting of the salvation" that he offered and promised clemency.[36] The panegyrist claimed that Rome was fortunate to have had this "civic victory" (*civilis victoria*).[37] This play on words masked the reality of a civil war. More than merely making promises, Constantine reappointed Maxentius's urban prefect, Anullinus, for a month-long tenure to help ensure the transition. This office, in charge of the city of Rome (see below), was critical to the functioning of the city and to building ties to the Roman senatorial elite. It mattered little to Constantine that Anullinus had earlier, under the emperor Diocletian, prosecuted Christians.[38] Continuity with the previous government was signaled, also, by Constantine's next two appointments to urban prefect, both of whom were respected Roman senators who had held this office under Maxentius.[39] To reassure senators of his clemency, Constantine also passed an edict against informers and stated that he would not seek revenge through prosecutions.[40]

The panegyrist depicts a Senate and populace seeking to demonstrate their support for the victor. He does not acknowledge the real fear of retribution that many felt, and the hope that Constantine would indeed live up to his

---

[36] *Pan. lat.* 12 (9).20.1: *Nam quid ego de tuis in cura sententiis atque actis loquar, quibus senatui auctoritatem pristinam reddidisti, salute quam per te receperant non imputasti, memoriam eius in pectore tuo sempiternam fore spopondisti? .... tamen qualia fuerint clementiae tuae gloria nuntiavit.* And clemency is emphasized again at: 20.4: *gladios ne in eorum quidem sanguine distringi passus est quos ad supplicia poscebat.* (He allowed swords to be drawn not even against those whom you demanded for punishment.) The panegyrist of 313 reflects imperial policy when remarking the emperor's clemency. Eusebius, *VC* 1.41.3, noted an imperial letter recalling to their homes "those subjected to the tyrant's savagery," a formula that would apply to political opponents of Maxentius as well as Christians.

[37] *Pan. lat.* 12(9).20.2–3. Nixon and Rodgers, eds. 1994, p. 325, note 127, remark on the novelty of the claim in Latin panegyric.

[38] For Anullinus 3, see *PLRE* 1, p. 79; he was proconsul of Africa 303–04, urban prefect in 306–07 under Maxentius, then urban prefect for a second time from October 27 to November 29, 312. However, the Anullinus who was proconsul of Africa in 313 is likely a different man, perhaps his son; see Anullinus 2, *PLRE* 1, pp. 78–79, and Barnes 1982, pp. 116–17. Anullinus 3 was only in office for one month, however, contra to Barnes 2011, p. 83, who asserts he was in office for thirteen months and redates the subsequent consulship of Aradius Rufinus a year later.

[39] Aradius Rufinus, urban prefect for the third time according to *PLRE* 1, p. 775 from November 29, 312 to December 8, 313; and then C. C(a)eionius Rufius Volusianus, urban prefect for the second time *PLRE* 1, pp. 976–78 from December 8, 313 to August 20, 315; and see my discussion of these men below and Table 2.1.

[40] *C. Th.* 10.10.2, dated December 1, 312 or 319; but also 10.10.1, dated January 18, 312. See too Grubbs 1995, pp. 113–14. Zos. 2.17.2 notes some punishments for close Maxentian supporters, along with the elimination of Maxentius's horse guard and the destruction of their cemetery.

well-advertised clemency. Not surprisingly, the Senate granted Constantine the right of listing his name first in the imperial college, recognizing him as the senior augustus (though this action allegedly infuriated Constantine's rival in the East, augustus Maximin Daia).[41] The Senate also rededicated Maxentius's buildings in Constantine's name.[42] The recovery of the city was made easier by the renaming of these structures. To show their fidelity, the panegyrist of 313 tells us that the Senate also dedicated a statue:

> For just cause, Constantine, the Senate has recently dedicated to you a statue of a god, and Italy shortly before that a shield and crown, all of gold, to lessen in some part the debt of their conscience. There is and often will be due a likeness to divinity, a shield to valor, and a crown to dutifulness (*pietati*).[43]

The orator lets slip the tension and fear of reprisal by alluding to the Senate's and Italians' guilty "conscience." This statue was one of a number that appeared as part of the rebuilding of the city; the emperor himself erected many in "the most crowded places" in Rome.[44]

The panegyrist of 313 added that the Senate's statue made Constantine divine in some way, although we cannot say if Constantine's statue had the attributes of a particular deity – such as Sol or Jupiter – as some scholars have proposed.[45] But this statue, along with the acts of the Senate, validated Constantine's dynastic claims to rule using traditional pagan religious symbols. The Senate also approved as an honor to the Flavian family a priesthood, which would flourish in Africa and Italy in the coming century.[46]

---

[41] Lact. *De mort. pers.* 44.11: *primi nominis titulum.*

[42] Aur. Vict. *De. Caes.* 40.25–26: *Quorum odio praetoriae legiones ac subsidia factionibus aptiora quam urbi Romae sublata penitus, simul arma atque usus indumenti militaris. Adhuc cuncta opera, quae magnifice construxerat, urbis fanum atque basilicam Flavii meritis patres sacravere.*

[43] It was recent because, as the Panegyrist of 313 says, it was *nuper*; see *Pan. lat.* 12(9).25.4, as noted by Nixon and Rodgers, eds. 1994, pp. 331, note 157. For the Latin text, p. 607: *Merito igitur tibi, Constantine, et nuper senatus signum dei et paulo ante Italia scutum et coronam, cuncta aurea, dedicarunt, ut conscientiae debitum aliqua ex parte relevarent. Debetur enim et saepe debebitur et divinitati simulacrum* [mss. *aureum*] *et virtuti scutum et corona pietati.* There are manuscript problems that make *dei* problematic. I translate *pietas* as dutifulness rather than as Nixon and Rodgers do, patriotism, to get at the ethical and religious element that is often associated with the Roman notion of this word; see *OLD*, s.v. *pietas*, 1–3.

[44] Aur. Vict., *De Caes.* 40.28, *statuae locis quam celeberrimis, quarum plures ex auro aut argenteae sunt.*

[45] Alföldi 1948, p. 69, for the identification with *Sol*. See Bardill 2012, pp. 212–15. For this colossal statue and its identification as Jupiter, see Presicce 2007, pp. 117–31, and Presicce 2005, pp. 138–55.

[46] Aur. Vict. *Caes.* 40.28: *tum per Africam sacerdotium decretum Flaviae gentis.* Victor only mentions the Flavian cult in Africa, but it is clear that the imperial cult was also practiced in Italy, as evidenced by the request for a cult temple in Hispellum, dated variously to 333, 335, or 337; see *ILS* 1:158–59, no. 705, and Van Dam 2007, pp. 19–34, 53–57, 363–67. Constantine's last urban prefect, L. Aradius Valerius Proculus *signo* Populonius, proudly held the title of *pontifex flavialis*, imperial priest of the cult, in an inscription dedicated in Italy. Because Proculus'

In the eyes of certain Christian bishops, however, Constantine's entry into Rome also supplied the opportunity for him to assert his new faith in public. In the edition of his *Church History* published before 316, Eusebius tells us that soon after Constantine had entered Rome, he ordered that a statue of himself be dedicated in public with an inscription:

> And straightway he gave orders that a memorial of the Saviour's Passion should be set up in the hand of his own statue; and indeed, when they set him in the most public place in Rome holding the Savior's sign in his right hand, he bade them engrave this very inscription in these words in the tongue: "By this salutary sign, the true proof of bravery, I saved and delivered your city from the yoke of the tyrant; and moreover, I freed and restored to their ancient fame and splendor both the Senate and the People of Rome."[47]

The inscription does not exist, but most historians follow Eusebius and see the salutary sign alluded to in the inscription as a distinctly Christian symbol.[48] Indeed, that is the way it is explained in the earliest reference to this inscription and statue in a speech Eusebius delivered for the dedication of the new cathedral in Tyre in 314 or 315.[49] Eusebius's source for his information about Constantine's entry into Rome may well have been a lost panegyric, but his explanation of the emperor's actions as Constantine's public profession of Christianity was also included in his 314 or 315 oration.[50] Eusebius's statement in his speech in Tyre and in his *Ecclesiastical History* indicates that by this early date, some Christians

inscription was put up after his return from Africa, he may have held this position in Italy. Constantine had made sure to honor his father as a *divus* and had promulgated his worship; see MacCormack 1981, pp. 110–13. The *natalis* of Constantius is noted in the *Codex-Calendar of 354* on March 31; see Salzman 1990, pp. 139–42.

[47] Eusebius *HE* 9.9.9–11; and *VC* 1.39–40. For the date of the *HE*, see Van Dam 2011, pp. 82–100. For the words of the arch echoing Augustus's *Res Gestae*, see Koortbojian 2020, pp. 123–68.

[48] Eus. *VC* 1.41.2 and *HE* 9.9; and Ruf. *HE* 9.9.10–11: *in hoc singulari signo, quod est verae virtutis insigne, urbem Romam senatumque et populum Romanum iugo tyrannicae dominationis erep-tam pristinae libertati nobilitatique restitui.* Most scholars see this as a Christian sign; see the discussion by Lenski 2014, pp. 155–96. For a different interpretation of this sign, see Van Dam 2011, pp. 191–200, who favors Rufinus's text and argues that the sign did not have any Christian significance. In fact, there is no reason to trust Rufinus's interpretation. Rufinus had been in Rome some decades earlier, so his memory was faint. Moreover, Rufinus simply assumed that Constantine was a Christian in 312.

[49] Eus. *HE* 10.4.16. For dating the oration to 315, see Barnes 1981, p. 162.

[50] Van Dam 2019, 211–40 on the "lost oration." Moreover, the statue mentioned by Eusebius matches the standing male type who holds a spear or *vexillum*. On this, see Girardet 2010, pp. 89–95; and Lenski 2014, pp. 155–96.

regarded the statue as an open display of the emperor's faith, as was the symbol that the emperor had painted on the shields of his soldiers before the 312 battle, which was, according to both Lactantius and Eusebius, a reference to the Christian god.[51]

Constantine also began manifesting his support for Christianity in his official dealings with the people and Senate of Rome very soon after 312. So, for example, when granting exemptions from liturgies to Christian clergy in his letter of 313 to the Roman senator Anullinus, proconsul of Africa and son of the urban prefect who had just changed sides to support the emperor, Constantine criticized traditional religion: "Christian priests should not be drawn away by error or sacrilegious fault from the worship which they owe to the Divinity."[52] In addition, Constantine's building projects made an impressive physical statement about his personal support for Christianity. We do not have a certain beginning date, but soon after 312, work began on building a platform over the destroyed camps of the horse guard on the Caelian Hill to make way for the first imperially sponsored Christian basilica in Rome. Named in late Roman sources as the Basilica Lateranensis after its location, as the Basilica Constantiniana after its founder, or as the Basilica Salvatoris according to the saint honored at its consecration, this vast structure, underneath modern St. John Lateran, made manifest imperial patronage for Christianity on a level far beyond mere tolerance.[53]

Constantine's support for bishops and priests elevated the status of the clergy in society. Soon after his victory over Maxentius, in a letter of 313 with his coemperor Licinius referred to today as the Edict of Milan, Constantine guaranteed freedom of worship to Christians and restored church property at the expense of the imperial treasury in order to maintain divine favor for the emperor and the Roman state.[54] I mention these public actions to demonstrate that Romans were made aware of Constantine's religious proclivities soon after 312. Nonetheless, the senatorial aristocracy, who were largely pagan, supported Constantine and willingly participated in celebrating the new regime. Whatever

---

[51] Lact. *De mort. pers.* 44.5; Eus. *VC* 1.37.1. For the Christogram as a Christian symbol, see especially Girardet 2010, pp. 52–62. However, not all would agree that the Christogram was only a Christian symbol; see Bardill 2012, pp. 159–78.

[52] Eus. *HE* 10.7.2. See Anullinus 2, *PLRE* 1, pp. 78–79. For his activity in Africa, see also Lizzi Testa 2014, pp. 254–57.

[53] See Johnson 2012, pp. 282–85. The beginning date of this work is uncertain, however; see my discussion below. For the various names for the basilica, see *Lib. Pont.* 34, ed. Duchesne 1981, p. 172, and Brandenburg 2005, p. 20.

[54] The joint policy agreed upon in 313 in Milan is attested not by an edict but by a letter of 313 issued by Licinius to eastern provincial governors; see Lact. *De mort. Pers.* 48.2–12 for a Latin version, and Eus. *HE* 10.5.2–14 for a Greek version. See too Lenski 2012, pp. 70–72.

concerns they felt about the emperor's support for Christianity, they were not great enough to deter them from continuing to serve in office. Indeed, Constantine's reforms, to be discussed below, benefitted senatorial aristocrats and went far to ensure good relations with this emperor, regardless of any religious differences. Compromise on this, as on other matters, allowed for cooperation in a restored Rome.

Perhaps the most permanent sign of senatorial support is the still-standing Arch of Constantine on the Via Triumphalis that the Senate dedicated to celebrate his *decennalia* at some time after July of 315 (see Figures 1 to 5).[55] This monument made visible the senatorial view of recent events and depicted the attributes they expected of a good emperor; the re-used reliefs that were recut for this arch focus on two imperial virtues, *virtus* and *pietas*.[56] Two of the six newly carved fourth-century reliefs on the north side (see Figures 2, 4, and 5) of the arch facing the city include the role of senators alongside the emperor. The scene of address, *oratio*, depicts the emperor in military dress, surrounded by bearded senators in togas, some of whom raise their right hand in acclamation, in front of recognizable monuments in the

Figure 1 Arch of Constantine, general view of south side. Jeff Bondono. IMG_7186–20141006 (www.jeffbondono.com).

---

[55] For the argument that the Arch of Constantine was begun only after the July 315 visit, see Rose JRA 2021, DOI: https://doi.org/10.1017/S1047759421000015, pp. 1–36.

[56] Faust 2011, pp. 377–408.

Figure 2 Arch of Constantine, general view of north side. Jeff Bondono, IMG_3273-(www.jeffbondono.com).

Figure 3 Arch of Constantine, Battle of Milvian Bridge, south side. Photo by Lynne Lancaster.

Forum, including the five-column Monument of the Tetrarchs and the Arch of Septimius Severus (recognizable by its triple arches; see Figure 4). This scene also links this victorious emperor with "good emperors" from the past.

Figure 4 Arch of Constantine, *Oratio,* north side. Jeff Bondono, IMG_8363 (www
.jeffbondono.com).

Statues identified with Hadrian and Marcus Aurelius are depicted on the
rostra in the relief.[57] In the matching relief, the emperor, this time in
a *contabulatio* toga, is counting out gifts of money (the *congiaria*). He
demonstrates his liberality (*liberalitas*) by pouring coins into the toga folds
of the senator positioned next to him, and is surrounded by togate senators
and officials on the same platform (see Figure 5). Their presence indicates
their supporting role in the state when they, as administrators, received and
helped distribute imperial largesse to the populace at large. On each side of
the relief are two-storied structures with two accounting offices where the
liberalitas continues.

The imagery on the arch and the absence of Christian symbols or language
advances a traditional senatorial view of the senators' role of working
alongside the emperor to bring prosperity and peace to Rome. Indeed, one
would expect that message in a monument that was, as its inscription
proclaimed, set up by the "Senate and People of Rome."[58] This assertion of
a traditional, pagan senatorial interpretation of recent events including the
battle of the Milvian Bridge (see Figure 3) articulated the ongoing influence
of senators in service to the Roman emperor and state.[59] In this regard,
Constantine demonstrated a striking willingness to incorporate senators
from established Italo-Roman aristocratic families into his new empire
after 312 and to use them in roles that had not been available to senatorial
aristocrats prior to his accession. Indeed, in the late third and early fourth
centuries, senators had seen that men with equestrian status, often from the
provinces, had become administrators and governors not just of the provinces but also of Italy. This situation, coupled with the fact that senators
rarely served in the military in the later third century, meant that there had

---

[57] Bardill 2012, pp. 95–97.

[58] *CIL* 6.1139=*ILS* 694.4–5. For the role of the Senate in dedicating arches, see Lenski 2014,
pp. 155–96, who notes that the honor of dedicating triumphal arches had fallen to the Senate
in the early empire.

[59] Salzman 2016, pp. 11–45.

been a net loss of civic positions available to traditional Roman senatorial aristocrats in the early fourth century. Constantine's rule changed this trend, even as he ushered in important reforms in the administration of Italy and in the modes of attaining senatorial rank.

Constantine's Reforms and the Resilience of the Senatorial Class, 312–25

Scholars agree that Constantine reformed the basis for attaining senatorial rank and that he expanded the number of men who held senatorial status. But debate continues over how and when Constantine did these things, how much resistance he incurred by making these changes, and what impact they had on the political power and influence of the senatorial aristocracy. As I argue based on the evidence at hand, Constantine's reforms concerning senatorial standing likely did, at times, lead to internal tensions, but they did not undermine the hegemony of the western senatorial aristocracy.

The idea that Constantine's reforms had these negative impacts on the senatorial aristocracy arises, in part, because Constantine also changed some of the administrative reforms previously undertaken by Diocletian (284–305). Diocletian had divided the diocese of Italy into provinces governed by equestrian or military governors (*correctores* or *praesides*) and had established a tribute system for Italy analogous to that of other provinces, a step decried by some ancient sources.[60] This administrative system began to change under Constantine. The chief civic office, that of the praetorian prefect, reported to the emperor and by 326 held the title of praetorian prefect of Italy (see my discussion below). In Italy, after 313, we find two officials, called vicars (*vicarii*), assisting the praetorian prefects and thus responsible for fiscal matters, including the collection of grain (*annona*), taxes, military supplies, and who also had oversight of some courts. The vicar of Italy (*vicarius Italiae*) was responsible for northern Italy (*Italia Annonaria*) and resided in Milan. The vicar in the city of Rome (*vicarius in urbe Roma*, later the *vicarius urbis*) was responsible for the provinces south of the Arno-Esino Rivers (*Italia Suburbicaria*) including Rome, and he resided in the city of Rome.[61] This equestrian position would, over time, be assumed by senators and would also carry with it senatorial status. These civic positions allowed for greater fiscal control of Italy by the emperor. At the same time, Constantine resumed the

---

[60] See Lact. *De mort. pers.* 7.4; and note 20 above.

[61] See Porena 2013, pp. 336–39. The *vicarius Italiae* would be responsible for Italy north of the Arno-Esino river: Emilia and Liguria, Venezia and Istria, Alps Cottia, Recia. The *vicarius Urbis* controlled Tuscia and Umbria, Flaminia and Picenum Campania, Apulia and Calabria, Lucania and Bruzzi, Sicily, Sardinia and Corsica.

Figure 5 Arch of Constantine, *Liberalitas*, north side. Photo by Lynne Lancaster.

practice of appointing members of the existing senatorial aristocracy to administer Italy.[62] Finally, Constantine expanded the powers of the senator responsible for Rome, the urban prefect (see my discussion below). These reforms are fundamental for understanding the political influence and loyalty of western senators to Constantine in the decade after 312.

The Expansion of the Senatorial Order and Senate. The influential scholar André Chastagnol argued that the expansion of the senatorial order and of the Senate in Rome to two thousand men occurred quickly in the decade between 312 and 326. Chastagnol based his view on his idea that the absorption of the equestrian class into the senatorial order and the reorganization of career paths had happened by then, including changing the responsibilities of the praetorian prefect to become those of chief financial officers and developing their administrators, the *vicarii*, who, as noted above, collected the bread and supplies (*annona*) for the military along with the taxes.[63] For Chastagnol, these were attempts to diminish the influence of western senators. But these assumptions are flawed.

First, we now know that the equestrian class did not disappear entirely; equestrians continued to be recorded into the fifth century, although their role in the state diminished under Constantine and his successors.[64] Many equestrian positions were upgraded to senatorial status, as we shall discuss below. Second, although it is true that Constantine disbanded the elite

---

[62] For fuller discussion of these changes, see Cecconi 1994, pp. 21–84; Salzman 2002, pp. 31–33; Dillon 2015, pp. 45–53.

[63] We know about these changes from a later law of 367, *C. Th.* 6.35.7. However, it must have begun earlier, as argued by Porena 2013, pp. 340–41. For the process, see especially Garbarino 1988, pp. 347–62; La Rocca and Oppedisano 2016, pp. 64–66.

[64] Lepelley 1986, p. 237, numbers 44–49; p. 238, numbers 50–51; and p. 239, numbers 59–60. Dillon 2015, pp. 44–49.

Figure 5 (cont.)

praetorian guard of the city, his reform of the office of praetorian prefect is not well attested until 325 or 326, with the prefecture of Fl. Constantius.[65] Therefore, it seems unlikely that these reforms had a negative impact on the career paths of senators in the decade after 312. And most importantly, reforms of the praetorian prefecture after 326 did not mean the loss of high office and prestige for western senatorial aristocrats. On the contrary, Constantine tweaked the preexisting system and established a comprehensive senatorial *cursus honorum* that incorporated all senatorial posts in the empire in the wake of his victory over Licinius in 324 and a dramatically increased need for loyal administrators, as we shall see.[66]

Constantine's reforms in the administration of Italy and the West after 312 expanded the number of new senatorial positions. So, for example, he converted a number of equestrian governorships to senatorial status with the title of *consularis* or *praeses*, thereby making them more attractive to senators.[67] In particular, in the provinces of the diocese of Italy, he turned to senators from established aristocratic families, who used their positions to revitalize their patronage ties to the cities and territories under their control.

These changes did, over time, augment the number of men in senatorial positions. By 400, there were an estimated three thousand men in each half of the empire every year who, upon retiring from office, possessed senatorial rank at any one time.[68] But this gain was gradual. Under Constantine, the number of new senators did certainly increase, but Constantine continued to appoint men from established senatorial aristocratic families alongside men

---

[65] Porena 2003, p. 391; 2006, pp. 325–56; 2013, pp. 340–43.

[66] For these reforms, see Porena 2013, pp. 340–41; Porena 2006, pp. 325–26; Moser 2018, p. 23.

[67] Moser 2018, p. 23; Cecconi 1994, pp. 210–23; Salzman 2002, pp. 31–32.

[68] Heather 1998, p. 195.

new to senatorial status. Nor did he flood the Senate with hundreds of men new to senatorial rank in the decade after 312, or later, for that matter. The notion that his appointments had led to a greatly expanded Senate in Rome, increasing from around six hundred to two thousand men, comes from a 385 *Oration* of Themistius referring to an increase that was not even complete by the year 359.[69] There is no reason to think that such a large number of senators existed earlier under Constantine.

A second development under Constantine also affected entry into the senatorial class. The son of a senator inherited senatorial status, that of *clarissimate* or "most outstanding," from his father.[70] Women could attain senatorial standing as well, through either their husbands or fathers.[71] But boys and girls inherited only the title of *clarissimus* or *clarissima*. To attain the full benefits of this standing and to ensure that their children would be able to pass on senatorial standing, members of wealthy senatorial families were incentivized to advance their sons to high office as early as possible. Constantine's reforms also made it easier for them to do so. For example, a law of 329 removed the financial penalties for sons of senators under the age of sixteen who were away from Rome when they were proposed for the requisite lower offices of quaestor and praetor that served as important stepping-stones in a traditional civic senatorial career. Young men of senatorial birth took up the office of quaestor, a job without administrative responsibilities but entailing the financing of games, so that they could be formally enrolled in the Senate at as young an age as possible. The office of praetor also allowed a young senator to hold an office in the provinces, a position that facilitated building more social networks and raising funds. Both offices required the financing of public entertainments, a costly matter. The removal of the fees paid by underage boys who had been named to these offices but who were absent from Rome during the requisite games meant that wealthy senatorial families could, with less expense, more easily enroll their sons in the Senate at the earliest possible age in order to have them begin their civic careers.[72]

Another Constantinian reform dated to the end of his rule offers additional evidence for a rise in senatorial autonomy along with these

---

[69] For the 2000 men in the senate in Constantinople, see Them. *Or.* 34.13; see also Jones 1964, p. 527. Chastagnol 1992, pp. 236–38, who cited *C. Th.* 12.1.13 (326), dated the expansion of the Senate then based on his idea that it coincided with the demise of the curial class; neither idea can be accepted now.

[70] Garbarino 1988, pp. 73–181 and 363–74; Weisweiler 2020, pp. 29–56, and pp. 42–44 for the early empire.

[71] Salzman 2002, p. 20; Garbarino 1988, pp. 366–68; *Dig.* 1.9.8; *C. Th.* 2.1.7, 392 CE.

[72] Moser 2018, p. 38.

reforms. I follow the view that the emperors proposed candidates for some of the quaestor positions (*quaestores candidati*) while other candidates who received financial assistance for their games from imperial funds were likely nominated by the Senate (*quaestores arcarii*). An inscription from between 335 and 337 suggests that under Constantine, the Senate gained the freedom to co-opt men whom it saw as having the necessary financial and moral qualifications to take on the duties attached to the offices of praetor and quaestor without the interference of the emperor.[73] By 359, laws indicate that the Senate was fully responsible for the designation of the magistracies of praetor and quaestor.[74] These administrative reforms did not undermine the status of senators but instead gave them greater control over their membership and aided candidates in attaining high office.

After 312, senators by birth could enter a clearly defined and expanded civic career path and could take up any number of state positions not only in Italy but also in other western provinces; after 326, they could also hold senatorial civic offices that had been closed to them after 306 in the East, such as the proconsulship of Asia or Achaia.[75] After 312, western senators could attain the prestigious offices of urban prefect of Rome or the ordinary consulship as well as provincial governorships.[76] At the same time, offices that had once been only equestrian, including a number of provincial governorships, now provided their holders with senatorial standing, thus attracting senators from aristocratic families as well as upwardly mobile new men from imperial service or local curiae to serve the new regime of Constantine. It is a sign of how high a status senatorial rank was that Constantine also bestowed senatorial standing (the *clarissimate*), especially later in his reign, on some military generals, such as Ursinus, dux of Mesopotamia in 325–37, and Ursacius, the *dux* Africae in 320–21.[77]

The expansion of senatorial offices initiated by Constantine did increase the size of the senatorial elite so that by the mid fourth century, new

---

[73] Salzman 2002, p. 34; Lizzi Testa 2013, pp. 359–60; Moser 2018, p. 38; but not, as Chastagnol 1992, pp. 254–58 suggested, the right to vote on imperial *adlecti*. For the evidence for this development, see *CIL* 6.1708 = *ILS* 1222. Contra, see Del Chicca 2017, pp. 280–86.

[74] *C. Th.* 6.4.12 and 6.4.13, 361 CE; and 6.4.14–15, 359 CE.

[75] For the office of proconsul of Asia closed to senators from 306 to 325, see Moser 2018, pp. 20–25 and my discussion below.

[76] Porena 2013, pp. 340–48 for a succinct discussion; but see also Moser 2018, pp. 36–41.

[77] For Ursacius, see Ursacius 1, *PLRE* 1, p. 984; for Senecio, see Senecio 3, *PLRE* 1, p. 920. Cf. Ursinus 2, *dux* Mesopotamia, 325/337, *PLRE* 1, p. 987. We know this about his giving senatorial standing to military *duces* and *comites* from the alleged reversal of this generosity by his son, Constantius II; see Amm. Mar. 21.16.1–2.

distinctions had evolved into a precisely formulated system of ranking of these offices under the emperors Valentinian I and Valens (see this chapter's conclusion). These distinctions preserved the status and prestige of established senatorial aristocrats. But in the immediate decade after 312, the question arises as to why Constantine decided to turn to western senatorial aristocrats and expand the administrative positions open to them. The idea that he was simply trying to placate a hostile pagan aristocracy of Rome is not particularly compelling given the interactions discussed earlier.[78] Nor can the view that during the immediate decade, senatorial aristocrats lost more than they gained by Constantine's expansion of the senatorial elite with *clarissimi* who had been imperial administrators or upwardly mobile provincials from local curias.[79] Rather, this expanded system of offices served well the interests of wealthy senatorial aristocrats who were more than willing to compete among themselves or with new men to gain high offices and benefit from the new opportunities for office holding. Constantine, for his part, was eager to secure their much-needed loyalty and resources during a turbulent decade following a bloody battle for control of Rome. And if Constantine had hopes of better controlling aristocrats through this competition for office, he was certainly building on a preexisting status culture that encouraged these efforts.[80]

Officeholders 312–24

We can show the extent to which Constantine rewarded venerable pagan senatorial families by examining the lineage of high office holders during his rule when he controlled the West. They were central to the functioning of the city of Rome and the western empire, as Constantine was well aware.

Urban Prefects from 312 to 324. The office of urban prefect was a pinnacle of a senatorial career. No wonder the surviving senators in Rome were eager to take this office if offered. Indeed, the office of urban prefect had grown in prestige and power under Maxentius, whose reliance on senators for this and other high offices had increased later in his rule.[81] Under Constantine, urban prefects oversaw the civic and judicial administration of Rome and were

---

[78] For this view, see Arnhiem 1972, p. 51; Löhken 1982, p. 118.

[79] Dillon 2015, p. 50 for this view.

[80] Dillon 2015, p. 51 cites approvingly the view that Constantine aimed in part to control senators, but he does not credit, as I think is key, the preexisting status culture to which Constantine appealed.

[81] Wienand 2017, p. 147, note 84, for further documentation on this point.

granted new powers to take on these tasks. For the first time, Constantine gave the urban prefect the right to issue sentences in place of the emperor (*cognitio vice sacra*) in a tribunal that was likely held in the newly renamed Basilica of Constantine in Rome. The prefect's court thus became the locus for civic suits for senators and remained so through the late sixth century.[82] And in a symbolic break with republican traditions, Constantine gave the urban prefect (and not the consuls) the right to call the Senate to order.[83] In addition, the urban prefect was charged with the maintenance of the city – especially with the provisioning and distribution of food for its citizens, a task that required considerable skills, given an estimated population still ranging from 700,000 to 1,000,000 citizens.[84] Although the newly appointed *vicarius urbis* exacted the funds from the province of *Italia Suburbicaria* within which Rome was located, to pay for these benefits, the officials who distributed the grain and pork in the city reported to the urban prefect.[85]

These responsibilities augmented the honor of the office of urban prefect, which from 312 on remained the preserve of western senatorial aristocrats. These men saw it as the crown of a senatorial career, an expression of their own power as well as a means of strengthening their individual and familial social networks.[86] It was an especially important position to the emperor as well, for its holder mediated between the wealthy senators in the Senate in Rome and the emperor, who was absent from Rome and Italy for long periods. Indeed, Constantine reverted to the pattern that had been in place since the late second century, since emperors, with the exceptions of Gallienus (253–68) and Maxentius (306–12), had not resided permanently in Rome since then.

Chosen by the emperor, the urban prefect was critical for maintaining civil order. After the removal of the praetorian cohorts by Constantine in 312–13, the urban prefect could still use the urban cohorts as a security force. The newly named head of the remaining three urban cohorts, the *tribunus fori*

---

[82] Coarelli 1986, p. 29, attributes the augmented powers in large measure to Maxentius but supplies no evidence. More likely, as Chastagnol 1976, pp. 51–69, argued, this was a gradual process that also saw moments of rapid acceleration, especially after 312, when we see the innovative concession of *cognitio vice sacra* to the urban prefect, and the selection of a series of functionaries at the discretion of the urban prefect; on this see Porena 2005, pp. 218, note 61 and p. 224, note 94; Porena 2013, p. 339, for the location of the tribunal. See too Chastagnol 1960, pp. 180–83.

[83] Porena 2013, p. 339.   [84] For discussion of the population estimates, see Chapter 1, note 19.

[85] For the *tribunus fori suarii* who was in charge of the forum for the distribution of pork, see Chastagnol 1960, pp. 224–27. For duties in connection with the grain dole, see Chastagnol 1960, pp. 312–16; Machado 2019, pp. 45–47.

[86] On offices as critical for strengthening social networks of individuals and families, see Matthews 1990, p. 17.

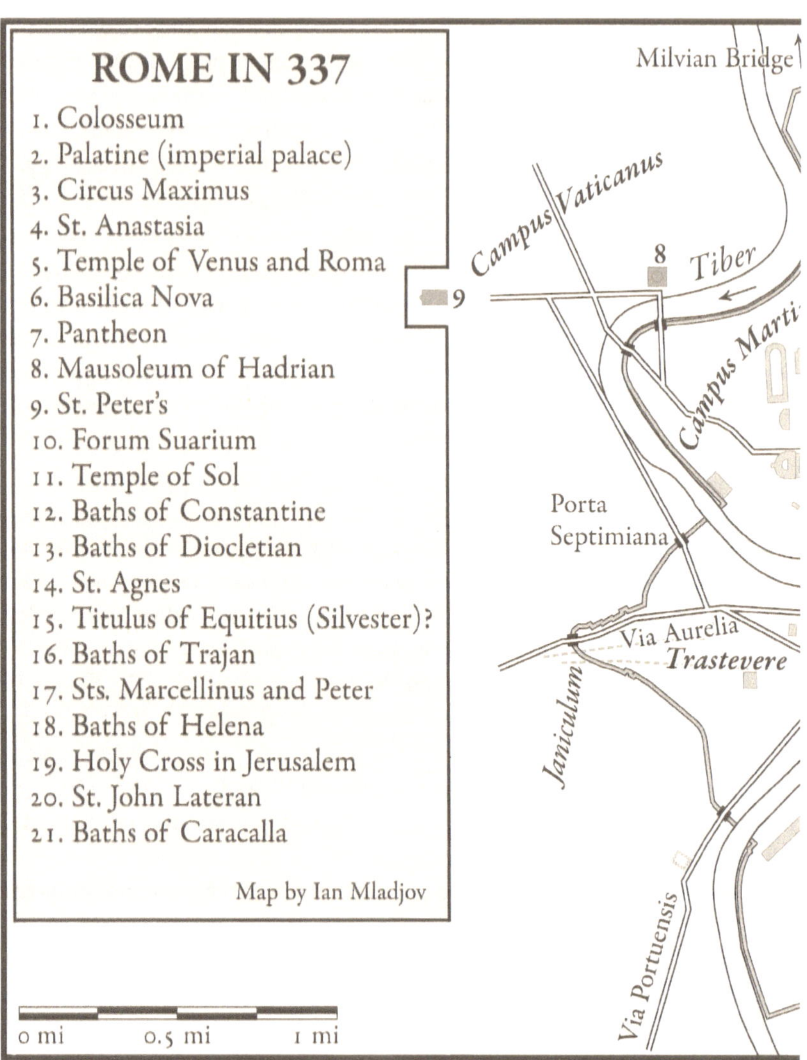

Map 3 Rome in 337.

suarii, reported to the urban prefect and oversaw the distribution of pork supplies for the city in the Pork Forum (*Forum Suarium*) near the Temple of Sol (see Map 3). In addition to the estimated lightly armed 4,500 men of the urban cohorts, the urban prefect had at his disposal attendants from the state bureaucracy.[87] He used these to police the city, a power that was especially

---

[87] Chastagnol 1960, pp. 224–26.

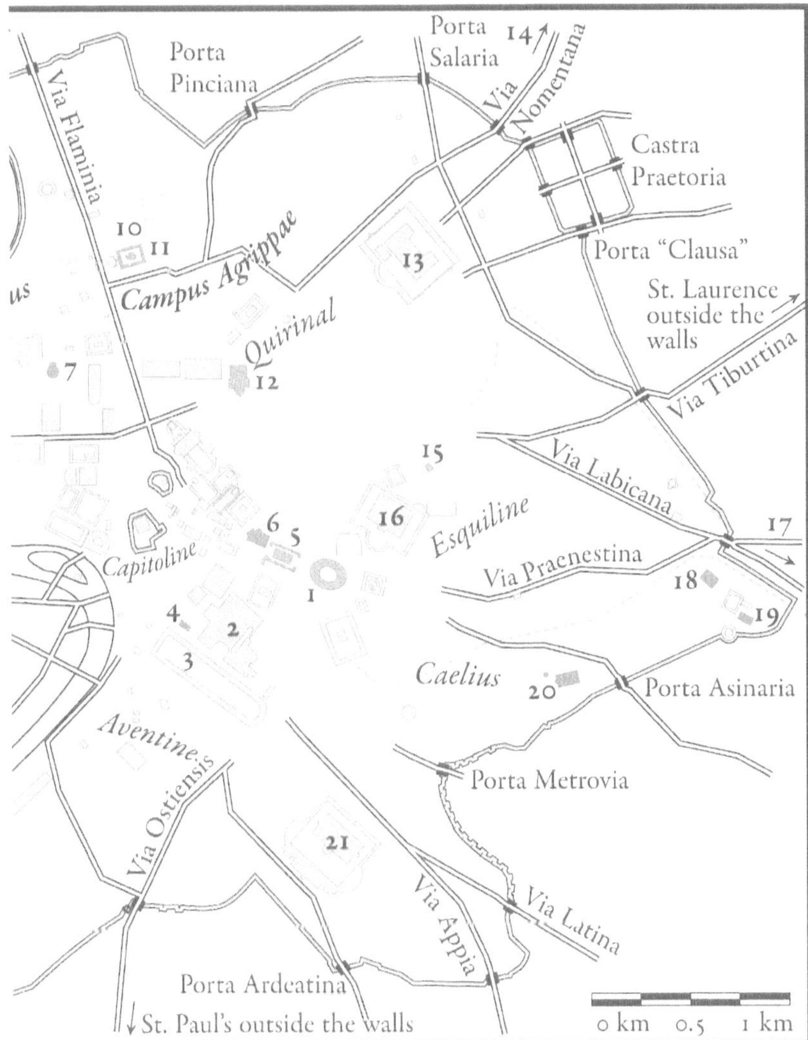

Map 3 (cont.)

necessary to stop rioting crowds, as happened most frequently at the games in the Colosseum and Circus Maximus (see Map 3) during food shortages or later during contested papal elections.

Although the offices and duties of the urban prefects were carefully regulated by the imperial court, there was ample room for them and their friends to use the opportunities offered by their oversight of these functions to augment their own political and economic influence. Indeed, we see this ability, for example, in the urban prefect's role in the distribution of Rome's food supply because, as Machado noted, "the very complexity and the number of resources and personnel involved . . . offered a variety of opportunities for aristocrats to further their social and political networks."[88] No wonder that Constantine and his court were careful to choose men whose influence would not threaten his position but would augment the prestige of his rule. It is a sign of Constantine's views on the prestige and utility of Roman aristocrats that the majority of the men he appointed to this key office were from wealthy, established Italian or African aristocratic families. Most were pagans as well, although some Christians appear in the 320s (see Table 2.1).

Families of Urban Prefects, 312–24. Of the eight men appointed by Constantine in the period from 312 to 324, from Anullinus through Locrius Verinus, all but two are attested as being from established Italo-Roman or African families. Five of the eight also held the consulship, although as bespeaks this period of transition, three of these men had held the consulship under Maxentius (see Table 2.1). This pattern is noteworthy, for it underscores how greatly Constantine tried, especially during his first decade in control of Italy and Africa, to reward and incorporate established, wealthy aristocratic families with deep ties to the communities in these areas. Constantine was keenly aware of the social landscape. Thus, for example, he not only prolonged the praefecture of C. Annius Anullinus, who had been consul in 295, but aware of this man's African roots, he also chose this man's son, Anullinus, to take on the mission of quelling the conflicts within Christian communities in North Africa (see my discussion of the Donatist controversy below) and made him proconsul of Africa in 313.[89]

Religious Choices of Urban Prefects. Although some urban prefects were Christian in the mid-320s, the majority were pagans from 312 through to the final years of the reign of Constantine. Of the eight men appointed by Constantine in the period 312–24, five were pagans or probably pagans, two were not attested, and only one was possibly a Christian. Ovinius Gallicanus, urban prefect in 316–17, has been identified as the donor of a Christian basilica, but it is not clear if it was he or his relative, Flavius Gallicanus, consul in 330, who paid for the church.[90] The first likely Christian falls in the

---

[88] Machado 2019, p. 47.   [89] On the son and father, both named Anullinus, see note 38 above.

[90] Champlin 1983, pp. 71–76, suggests he is to be identified with the Gallicanus noted in *Lib. Pont.* 34, ed. Duchesne 1981, p. 184, as donor of gifts to a church in Ostia. This is possible, but not certain. It is equally plausible that the donor called Gallicanus was Flavius Gallicanus, consul of 330.

period after the defeat of Licinius, Acilius Severus, urban prefect in 325–27.[91] This Acilius Severus may also be identified with the consul of 323 and with the Severus who corresponded with the Christian rhetorician Lactantius; certainly Jerome considered both Acilius and Acilius's son, who was a writer, Christian.[92] However, we do not know if the father was a Christian when he held office in 325–27, and we have some evidence to suggest that he was not; the name *Acilius* is included on a fragmentary inscription that has been plausibly identified on a list of senatorial members of a priestly college that must be dated prior to 315.[93] This inscription lends some support to the notion that this prefect was from an old senatorial family, the *gens* Acilia, which had been noble since the first century CE rather than, as some have argued, from a new senatorial family from Spain.[94] Although we cannot trace the earlier history of the family much before Constantine, it is clear that Acilius Severus continued to loyally serve the emperor. For his 326 imperial visit, Constantine disseminated gold plates that depicted Severus by his side.[95] It is perhaps worth remarking that though fragmentary, this plate has no Christian symbols.

The Anicii. A discussion of urban prefects in this first decade raises the issue of the Anicii, a family that rose to prominence in the third century.[96] Because of this family's nobility, the poet Prudentius in his *Contra Symmachum* boasted that one family member had the distinction of having converted to Christianity before all the other Roman aristocrats had done so.[97] Based on this poem, some scholars have asserted that Amnius Anicius Iulianus was that early fourth-century Christian, even though there is nothing specific to support this identification. Moreover, there were two other Anicii who were urban prefects a decade later under Constantine to whom Prudentius might be referring, namely, Sextus Anicius Paulinus, urban prefect in 331–33, or

[91] For a different view of the evidence that assumes religious affiliation without demonstrating it of a number of these urban prefects, see Barnes 1995, pp. 135–47.

[92] Jer. *De vir. ill.* 111: *Acilius Severus in Hispania: de genere illius Severi ad quem Lactantii duo epistularum scribuntur.* See Acilius Severus 16 and 17, *PLRE* 1, pp. 834–35, which suggests that he is perhaps Severus 3, *PLRE* 1, p. 831. Salway 2015, pp. 209–10 lays out the evidence. However, Severus 3 was more likely a vicar than a praetorian prefect in 322–23; see note 107 below.

[93] See Groag 1924–27, pp. 102–09. The inscription cites an Acilius seventh on a list of prominent senators of the early fourth century, who was likely the father, Acilius Severus, of the urban prefect of 325–26 (of the same name). Wienand 2017, pp. 141–48, makes a cogent argument for dating this inscription just prior to 315.

[94] Jacques 1986, pp. 152–55. For the argument, see Porena 2005, p. 237. For doubts about this identification, see Salway 2015, p. 210.

[95] Fuhrmann 1939, pp. 161–75; and Leader-Newby 2004, pp. 44–45.

[96] Novak 1979A, pp. 119–65; and additional bibliography in Cameron 2012, p. 134 and note 3.

[97] Translation by Cameron 2011, p. 180, of Prudentius, *Contra Symmachum* I.552–53: *Fertur enim ante alios generosos Anicius urbis / Inlustrasse caput: sic se Roma incluta iactat.* ("For it is said that a noble Anician before all others shed luster on the city's head (so glorious Rome herself boasts).")

Amnius Manius Caesonius Nicomachus Anicius Paulinus, urban prefect in 334–35.[98] As Alan Cameron has argued, the formula in an inscription for Sextus Anicius Paulinus that calls him *benignus* and *sanctus* was also used for pagans.[99] And Amnius Manius Caesonius Nicomachus Anicius Paulinus left no evidence of his religious affiliation either.[100] If Prudentius is right about the Anicii having converted early – which is assuming that this Spanish poet accurately knew the histories of these Roman families – we cannot say which of these early Anicii were Christian or whether they were Christian at the time they held the office of urban prefect. The earliest securely attested Christian male member of the Anicii was Sextus Petronius Probus, consul in 371.[101] References to the Anicii family by later authors remark its members' wealth and office holding, not their religiosity.[102] Indeed, even as Christians began to emerge in high office, key to their promotion by the emperor and their acceptance by their peers was that they, too, belonged to venerable and established, wealthy families.

Consuls under Constantine, 314–24. One official act that Constantine used to recognize the prestige of senators was his appointment of ordinary consuls. This position was a greatly sought-after honor, for the ordinary consuls gave their names to the year, attaining immortality of a particularly Roman kind. Constantine's appointment of senators from old Roman aristocratic families to this office marks a distinct change from the practices of the late third century, when the office had increasingly been reserved for emperors and their mostly equestrian administrators.[103] But after his victory and reforms, Constantine's appointments of ordinary consuls from 314 through 324 underscore his desire to reintegrate traditionally Roman senatorial families into his government. Senators by birth from old noble families attained this honor with great regularity; by a conservative estimate of the evidence, senators retained eight of the ten ordinary consulships allocated to

---

[98] Sex. Anicius Paulinus 15, *PLRE* 1, pp. 679–70, and Amnius Manius Caesonius Nicomachus Anicius Paulinus 14, *PLRE* 1, pp. 679.

[99] Cameron 2011, p. 180; Novak 1979A, pp. 119–65 points to a Vestal Virgin (*CIL* 6.2131). Alan Cameron adds that *sanctus* was never used for an "ordinary" Christian in our sources.

[100] I agree with Cameron 2011, p. 180, that the omission of pagan priesthoods on an inscription to this prefect is not evidence that he was a Christian because this had become normative. The inclusion of this man on a list of senators from the early fourth century, with a name restored as [Am]nius Anicius P[aulinus] is not proof he held a pagan priesthood either because we cannot be certain if the list was that of a priestly college, as was suggested by Groag 1924–7, pp. 102–9.

[101] Sex. Claudius Petronius Probus 5, *PLRE* 1, pp. 736–40.

[102] Ammianus Marcellinus, 16.8.13, writing in the late fourth century, subverts praise for this family's success by ascribing to them greed greater than the generation that served Constantine; see Zos. 6.7.4 on this family's wealth in the fifth century.

[103] Porena 2013, p. 348; see too Davenport 2019, pp. 586–91.

men outside the imperial family or the emperor himself from 314 until 324.[104] This trend continued for Constantine's entire reign. Down through 337, the majority of ordinary consulships allocated for men other than the emperor or imperial family members went to senators from old Roman families.[105] The increase in the number of formerly equestrian officials or imperial courtiers as consuls attested only during the last five years of Constantine's rule (i.e., 332, 334, and 337) does not overturn the marked restoration of the ordinary consulship to the senatorial aristocratic families of Rome.

The Praetorian Prefects, 312–24. In contrast to the social profile of his urban prefects, the five praetorian prefects appointed by Constantine in the years 312–24 in the West were mainly upwardly mobile new men, mostly equestrian in rank. Nonetheless, their advancement into senatorial aristocratic society and their attaining senatorial standing does not appear to have occasioned the kind of tension that one would expect if older senatorial aristocrats had felt threatened by their elevation. On the contrary, a number of these former praetorian prefects adopted traditional senatorial aristocratic lifestyles and focused their attentions on Rome. This practice had been traditional for upwardly mobile provincials and equestrians for centuries. Not surprisingly, we hear the panegyrist Naziarius praise the Senate's willingness to ensure its dignity by its inclusion of "the best men out of every province."[106]

The praetorian prefects in this first decade who were newcomers to senatorial society had gained status through imperial service.[107] For example, Petronius Annianus, praetorian prefect from 315 to 317, had no known origin, making it most likely that he arose through equestrian

---

[104] Salway 2015, pp. 199–220 calls into question the origins of some of these men, but even his less certain view leads to a clear majority of western senators. Salway, p. 218, identifies a changed pattern where an ex-equestrian official or imperial courtier is paired with a senator pursuing a traditional career primarily in the last five years of Constantine's rule, i.e., 332, 334, and 337; this also took place in 314. If this is a sign of changed priorities, as Salway argues, it is one that did not diminish the continuing success of western senatorial aristocrats who now also took up several new positions.

[105] Porena 2013, p. 348, note 38, identified eighteen of the thirty possible positions for the entirety of Constantine's reign as being from old Roman senators. Porena counted thirty out of the fifty consuls open for men outside the imperial family or the emperor himself during Constantine's twenty-five years (excluding nine imperial consular couples and two consuls belonging to the family of Constantine). Salway's numbers are slightly different.

[106] Nazarius, *Pan. Lat* IV (X).35.2: *cum ex omnibus provinciis optimates viros curiae tuae pignerareris, ut senatus dignitas non nomine quam re esset inlustrior, cum ex totius orbis flore constaret.*

[107] I do not include as a praetorian prefect in Table 2.2 Severus 3, *PLRE* 1, p. 83, for he was most likely a vicar, not praetorian prefect in 322–23. If so, he would be the same man as Acilius Severus 16. *PLRE* 1, p. 834. Not all agree: see Moser 2018, pp. 71–72.

service to consul in 314 prior to his prefecture.[108] Iunius Bassus, praetorian prefect from 317/18 to 322, and again later from 326 to 333/334, is not attested as coming from an aristocratic family. Like Petronius Annianus, Iunius Bassus rose to senatorial rank through this office and imperial service. But Iunius Bassus travelled in aristocratic Roman social circles, if he was the recipient of Optatian's poem 21, dated to 324. He built at his own expense an impressive home in the elite residential area on the Esquiline Hill in Rome (see Table 2.2).[109]

Some aristocratic senators no doubt viewed these new senators in their midst as rough and socially backward. Nevertheless, their advancement and, in time, acceptance by the likes of established aristocrats such as the late fourth-century senator Symmachus suggest that this elevation was a desirable outcome with benefits for all involved. Symmachus's father, in fact, wrote poems of praise for several new senators under Constantine – like Petronius Probianus, identified as praetorian prefect of 321 and certainly urban prefect in 329–31. Petronius's acceptance in later fourth-century aristocratic society is emblematic of the fluidity that fueled elite society in Rome.[110] He, like Iunius Bassus, had sons active in elite aristocratic circles through the fourth century (see Tables 2.1 and 2.2).

Family Ties and Patronage

Marriage alliances between aristocrats and the imperial family are also important indicators of the resilience of senatorial aristocrats in the immediate decade after 312. Three notable senatorial–imperial marriages all date to this first decade after the Milvian Bridge battle. They indicate the desire of emperors and aristocrats to join forces, on a personal level, to affirm the close ties between the aristocracy and the emperor's family.

Anastasia, the sister of Constantine, married the Roman aristocrat Bassianus, brother of the Senecio who was a supporter of Licinius.[111] This marriage shows the immediacy of Constantine's desire to incorporate

---

[108] See Porena 2003, pp. 295–96 on this man. For Petronius Annianus 2, *PLRE* 1, p. 68, see also Salway 2015, p. 207.

[109] Iunius Bassus = Bassus 14, *PLRE* 1: 154: Moser 2018, pp. 296–97; Porena 2006, pp. 337–42. For his house, see Guidobaldi, *LTUR* 2, 1995, pp. 69 ff.

[110] Petronius Probianus = Probianus 3, *PLRE* 1, p. 733. For his possible praetorian prefecture in 321, see Moser 2018, pp. 26, 71; since he is not securely attested, he is not included in Table 2.2.

[111] Moser 2018, pp. 32–34 discusses these marriages, but fails to note that they all cluster in the first period of Constantine's reign. For these women, see too Hillner 2017, pp. 75–94. For Anastasia 1, see *PLRE* 1, p. 58; for Bassianus, see Bassianus 1, *PLRE* 1, p. 150; for Senecio, see Senecio 1, *PLRE* 1, p. 820.

senatorial aristocrats right after his 312 victory. Constantine was eager to win over important senators to his cause when he was aligned with Licinius. But after Constantine had fallen out with Licinius, he used the marriage of Eutropia, another of his sisters, in 320, to the senator Virius Nepotianus, consul of 336 and a member of an old aristocratic family with roots going back to the second century, to ensure ties with the senatorial aristocracy as he competed for influence more openly with Licinius.[112]

In the early 320s, Constantine's half-brother Julius Constantius wed a daughter of one of the oldest senatorial families of the city, the Neratii; this family traced its roots to the time of the emperor Septimius Severus. This marriage produced the future caesar Gallus, who had been born around 325 or 326.[113] Again, this alliance ensured that the imperial family would bind another senatorial family to its fortunes in the immediate aftermath of the fall of Licinius, when Constantine needed the loyalty of western elites in order to better control his newly acquired eastern empire. In recognition of these western senatorial traditions, Constantine also distinguished Julius Constantius with a title, *patrician*, that harkened back to earliest Roman times.[114] These instances of honoring Rome's senatorial families underscore the importance to Constantine of establishing dynastic ties with these elites immediately after 312.

Iulia Hillner has argued that Constantine's desire to do so was also manifested by his leaving female members of the imperial family as placeholders in Rome.[115] Unfortunately, the archaeological evidence that Hillner used for these women's presence in the city is not secure.[116] Textual evidence only suggests that Constantine's wife, Fausta, was in Rome in 326 and that she had perhaps returned there earlier while Constantine traveled to Gaul and Illyricum to deal with a range of issues, most notably his co-ruler, Licinius.[117] However Constantine's mother, Helena, is attested in Rome earlier, perhaps soon after 312, and she continued to live there until her burial in 330.[118] Given this

---

[112] See Eutropia 1, *PLRE* 1, p. 316; see Virius Nepotianus 7, *PLRE* 1, p. 625.

[113] For Julius Constantius, see Constantius 7, *PLRE* 1, p. 226; for his wife Galla, see Galla 1, *PLRE* 1, p. 382. It is not known where Gallus was born.

[114] For the use of *patricius* or patrician not as a hereditary distinction but as bestowed by Constantine and denoting a dynastic distinction, see Moser 2018, pp. 80–81.

[115] Hillner 2017, pp. 78–85.

[116] The fresco and inscription that Hillner reads as evidence for the presence of imperial women in Rome have been challenged by Liverani 1993, pp. 134–52.

[117] For Fausta possibly in Rome, see Zos. 2.29.3–4. For Constantine's movements, see Barnes 1982, pp. 68–80.

[118] For Helena in Rome, see Zos. 2.29.23–4. Helena restored baths in Rome, *CIL* 6.1136, dated to 317?– 324; see Map 3. She was buried in Rome on the Via Labicana: Eus. *VC* 3.46–47; and *Lib. Pont.* 34, ed. Duchesne 1981, p. 182. For her presence in Rome, Moser 2018, p. 35.

emperor's efforts to build personal ties with Roman aristocratic families, it is reasonable to think that Constantine's mother had remained in Rome to remind senatorial aristocrats of their allegiance to the absent emperor.

The Reunification of Empire: Constantine and the Senatorial Elite after 324

The close ties between the absent emperor Constantine and the senatorial elite of Rome that I have identified took a new turn after the final defeat of Licinius in 324. Some of Constantine's most controversial actions unfolded once he controlled the entire empire. Indeed, perhaps the most discussed event in their relationship, in terms of an overt conflict with the senators and people, is an incident that took place during Constantine's visit to Rome in July 326.

Constantine's Vicennalia Celebration in Rome, July 326. Constantine chose to begin his vicennalia celebrations in Nicomedia, but he traveled to Rome to celebrate the end of his anniversary year in the appropriate seat of empire, arriving in the city between July 18 and 21, 326. This visit was in itself an important statement of the willingness of this emperor to live up to traditional expectations for Roman rulers. But something happened that led to a popular outburst. The early sixth-century pagan historian Zosimus asserts that Constantine's refusal to participate in traditional pagan rites was the cause of the outpouring of the crowd's anger:

> When an ancient festival fell due, and it was necessary for the army to go up to the Capitol to carry out the rites, for fear of the soldiers he [Constantine] took part in the festival, but when the Egyptian sent him an apparition that unrestrainedly abused the rite of ascending to the Capitol, he stood aloof from the holy worship and thus incurred the hatred of the Senate and people. Unable to endure the curses of almost everyone, he sought out a city as a counterbalance to Rome, where he had to build a palace.[119]

Zosimus likely had taken this anecdote from the lost history of the fourth-century historian Eunapius, and it has fueled the notion in modern

[119] Zos. 2.29.5–30.1: Τῆς δὲ πατρίου καταλαβούσης ἑορτῆς, καθ' ἣν ἀνάγκη τὸ στρατόπεδον ἦν εἰς τὸ Καπιτώλιον ἀνιέναι καὶ τὰ νενομισμένα πληροῦν, δεδιὼς τοὺς στρατιώτας ὁ Κωνσταντῖνος ἐκοινώνησε τῆς ἑορτῆς· ἐπιπέμψαντος δὲ αὐτῷ φάσμα τοῦ Αἰγυπτίου τὴν εἰς τὸ Καπιτώλιον ἄνοδον ὀνειδίζον ἀνέδην, τῆς ἱερᾶς ἁγιστείας ἀποστατήσας, εἰς μῖσος τὴν γερουσίαν καὶ τὸν δῆμον ἀνέστησεν. 2.30 Οὐκ ἐνεγκὼν δὲ τὰς παρὰ πάντων ὡς εἰπεῖν βλασφημίας πόλιν ἀντίρροπον τῆς Ῥώμης ἐζήτει, καθ' ἣν αὐτὸν ἔδει βασίλεια καταστήσασθαι. Paschoud 1971, pp. 334–53, argues for the authenticity of this event but dates it to 315, as had Straub 1972, pp. 100–18. Wiemer 1994, pp. 469–94 similarly reads it as pagan–Christian conflict, as does Fraschetti 1999, pp. 96–108.

scholarship that Constantine fled Rome and then founded Constantinople as a rival to Rome.[120] However, closer study of this incident does not, in my mind, support Zosimus's use of it to demonstrate overt pagan–Christian conflict. Rather, given that the evidence from the only other source to mention it was the eastern professor of rhetoric Libanius, it seems that the populace – not the Senate and people – expressed their discontent in ways that offended Constantine. I argue this for several reasons.

Zosimus's text is the sole authority that asserts that popular dissatisfaction occurred in the context of a religious sacrifice. Augusto Fraschetti identifies this incident as having occurred at the games to Jupiter in September 315, but there is no indication of that festival in our second source for this event.[121] First, as Hans-Ulrich Wiemer has observed, Libanius describes this incident and records the presence of his brothers, details that allow us to date the visit securely to Rome in 326 for this emperor's vicennalia.[122] Second, when Libanius gives us details about the 326 incident in two speeches that he delivered to Theodosius in the 380s, he uses them in both texts to praise imperial tolerance for popular expressions by the people in the Hippodrome.[123] In fact, it is unlikely that Libanius would have raised this incident if it had been the result of religious intolerance, since the rhetorician was eager to portray Theodosius's predecessor, Constantine, as a ruler tolerant of his people in all matters, especially including religion.[124]

Libanius does indicate that Constantine had been disturbed by the "calls" (βοαῖς) of the crowd. He then asked his brothers how to handle the "skittishness" (σκιρτημάτων) of the assemblage. Libanius does not tell us what aroused the outburst of the crowd. In *Oration* 20, he underscores that these responses were only catcalls directed at the emperor and thus were not similar to the riot against the statues of the emperor Theodosius.[125] This is a key detail, for it suggests that whatever happened to Constantine in

---

[120] Zosimus's allegation that Constantine's founding of a new capitol in response to this event cannot be accurate for Constantinople was initiated before his 326 visit to Rome; Grig 2013, pp. 3–30. See, for this assumption, for example, Novak 1979, p. 277.

[121] Fraschetti 1999, pp. 96–108. Fraschetti identified the rites described by Zosimus as the popular *Ludi Romani* celebrated in honor of Jupiter, September 12–15.

[122] Wiemer 1994, pp. 469–94, made this argument for this dating, pointing to the evidence from Libanius, *Oration* 19.19 and *Oration* 20.24. For the celebration of the beginning of his *vicennalia* on July 25, 325 and its conclusion in Rome on July 25, 326 see Jer. *Chron.* s.a.a. 326: *Vicennali Constantini Nicomediae acta et sequenti anno Romae edita.* Because I disagree with Van Dam's dating of this incident, I also do not agree with his analysis of Constantine's relations with the Senate; see Van Dam 2018, p. 34.

[123] Lib. *Orat.* 19.19–20 and 20.24.

[124] I thank Raffaella Cribiore for this suggestion about Libanius's motivation.

[125] Lib. *Orat.* 20.24.

Rome was not so hostile as to be the occasion of a riot but was more like the shouts and movements of unruly crowds seen drunkenly dancing. Hence, if Libanius's use of the word *skittishness* (σκιρτημάτων) here is similar to his use of the word elsewhere, he is describing drunken dancing.[126] Libanius concludes with Constantine's decision to tolerate such practices by issuing an *edictum ad populum* in which he asserted that emperors should laugh at rather than punish popular outbursts.[127]

The reason for this popular outburst directed against Constantine is simply not known. And it is striking that despite the anti-Constantinian pagan tradition that arose soon after the end of the Constantinian dynasty, in the account narrated by Aurelius Victor, one of the earliest pagan writers to critique this emperor's reforms, this popular outburst and Constantine's unwillingness to perform an animal sacrifice in Rome are not noted.[128] In 326 one can imagine a number of reasons why the crowd "catcalled" Constantine, as we will see.[129] His murders of his son and of his wife were recent acts that could well have incurred popular disapproval. Contrary to Zosimus's view, Libanius concluded that Constantine's actions "put him on good terms with Rome."[130]

Moreover, there are several indicators that Constantine's 326 visit was intended to build strong ties with western senatorial aristocrats and that his actions contributed to the growing prestige of the Senate. The emperor minted a series of gold medallions, including one of quite significant weight, 4.5 solidi. On its reverse, it depicts a laureate figure in a toga holding a globe, the symbol of the world, and a scepter, the symbol of rule. The figure is surrounded by the legend *SENATUS*, and the obverse shows the diademed bust of Constantine with the legend *CONSTANTINUS AUG[USTUS]*.[131] These medallions were gifts to the wealthy and influential senators of Rome. A second issue of silver coins shows the celebration of the Senate and the People of Rome as part of

---

[126] Lib. *Orat.* 19.19 uses the word σκιρτημάτων, meaning the leapings of dancers. This is a word that Libanius uses in reference to dancers at festivals, and so it evokes a similarly frenzied motion and atmosphere. For his other usages, see *Or.* 12.46, 15.19, and 64.119bis.

[127] Lib. *Orat.* 19.19; Wiemer 1994, pp. 470–72; 488–92.

[128] See Neri 2017, pp. 13–35. At pp. 28–30 Neri makes the excellent point that this association of the murders as relating to post-326 reforms is found only after the rebellion of Magnentius, an action against the Constantinian dynasty in which several Roman senators were implicated. However, many of the other criticisms of Constantine's anti-traditional reforms are found in Aur. Vict. *Caes.* 33.34.

[129] Here I part company with Wiemer 1994. Zosimus's assertion that pagans attacked Constantine for not sacrificing has no support from Libanius's account of this same episode.

[130] Lib. *Orat.* 19.19.

[131] Alföldi 1948, p. 99. For the coin, see *RIC* 7: 326, no. 272. For the argument that this coin was not issued for Constantine's consulship, see Moser 2018, pp. 17–18.

this special Rome series.[132] As I have argued before, the circus games to honor the Senate, the *Victoria Senati*, were likely first celebrated in connection with this visit. This day is attested for the first time in the *Codex-Calendar of 354* on August 4, just nine days after the vicennalia games on July 25, thus fitting the pattern for such games under Constantine.[133]

Clearly, there were tensions between emperor and elite, as the events indicate. However, the evidence for their relationship's having fractured over Constantine's support for Christianity is not demonstrable. Nor did the emperor's absence from Rome and the establishment of Constantinople as his residence in the last decade of his rule mean the demise of the political, economic, and social dominance that Roman senators had assumed after 312 and that, as I will discuss, they continued to play throughout his reign.

Dynastic Upheaval and Senatorial Rivalry. Constantine's visit to Rome in 326 coincided with a series of events that demonstrate this emperor's intent to secure good relations with western senatorial elites at a critical juncture in his rule. Although he had finally defeated Licinius and was now in control of the eastern provinces of his former co-augustus, this victory came at the same time that he was suffering some personal losses. Earlier, in 316, Constantine had elevated his brother-in-law Bassianus, whose wife was the emperor's sister Anastasia, as caesar with authority over Italy as a means of countering Licinius's son's claim to that role.[134] As noted, Bassianus was from an old established Roman family.[135] Yet Bassianus was soon executed for treason in what seems to have been a conspiracy orchestrated by his brother Senecio, also a member of the senatorial aristocracy but a supporter of Licinius. Other scholars assume that Bassianus's death had to do with Constantine's concern about a potential rival to his son's succession, for his first son had been born in 315.[136] In either case, Bassianus was caught up in the revenge that Constantine took against those senators whom he perceived had turned against him in this civil war. Bassianus's demise also underscores how closely Constantine tracked the political activities of western Roman senators, and especially those who had any potential political influence through their ties to his family.

Constantine's immediate family also suffered in the political upheavals that unfolded after the victory over Licinius. At some point shortly before his entry into Rome in 326, Constantine had condemned his son, the caesar Crispus, to death. The reasons for and date of his death are not certain, but

---

[132] For example, see the *Genium PR* silver coin from Rome, *RIC* VII: 327, no. 276 and Alföldi 1948, with Moser 2018, p. 18.

[133] Salzman 2016, p. 38; Salzman 1990, pp. 185–86.

[134] *Anon. Val.* 5 (15). See too Potter 2013, p. 169.   [135] See Bassianus 1, *PLRE* 1, p. 150.

[136] Hillner 2017, p. 79.

Constantine's dissatisfaction with Crispus on some level is clear. Perhaps he had decided to remove Crispus, the eldest son of his first marriage, to avoid dynastic rivalry, especially in light of later writers' allegations of an adulterous affair between Crispus and his current wife, Fausta, whose murder, it was said, had also been approved by the emperor during this period.[137] The loss of Fausta, who had ties to the Roman senatorial aristocracy, helps explain the presence of Helena, Constantine's mother, in Rome.[138] Helena's burial in Rome after her death in 330 secured the family a permanent place in the memory of the city's inhabitants.[139] With the loss of Crispus, Constantine returned his brothers to public life, perhaps as part of the general amnesty of these vicennalia celebrations and to demonstrate the strength of his family dynasty after the execution of his son Crispus.[140]

Optatian's Recall. Constantine's awareness of the desirability of maintaining loyalty among western senators in July 326 may also shed light on his treatment of Optatian, a senator and poet whose illustrious future was abruptly cut short at some point before 326. He had been forced into exile, most likely on an accusation of adultery, but senatorial infighting and resentment were probably the underlying motivations.[141] From exile, Optatian wrote to the emperor begging for clemency in a poem dated soon after the defeat of Licinius in 324: "Just ruler, look at me, afflicted by the punishment of exile because of a false accusation."[142] The false accusation is not specified, nor are the reasons for Optatian's recall. But since Optatian's request was accompanied by a book that brilliantly used figured poetry to praise the emperor and advance a Christian message, we can easily assume that Constantine recalled him in recognition of this gift.[143] In poem 8, Optatian praises Christ and emperor: "You, son of god, sole salvation, sacred, you justly are the god of the good; you offer grace for the faithful." The poet interweaves a Christogram into this poem and

---

[137] On Crispus' death, see Aur. Vict. *Caes.* 41.11; Eutrop. 6; Zos. 2.29. Different explanations have been proposed. See Potter 2013, pp. 243–47, and Wienand 2017, p. 128, note 27. Fausta's involvement is suggested, but not demonstrated, by her death in this period. On her death, see Zos. 2.29.3–4; and Hillner 2017, pp. 75–94.

[138] *Pan. Lat.* 4 (10), 35.4–5 with Moser 2018, p. 35.

[139] For her burial, see Eus. *VC* 3.46–47; *Lib. Pont.* 34, ed. Duchesne 1981, p. 182.

[140] Wiemer 1994, p. 516 on the recall of the brothers.

[141] Wienand 2017, pp. 124–32 for the charge of adultery; Moser 2018, pp. 36–37 on senatorial infighting.

[142] Optatian, *Carm.* 2.3: *Respice me falso de crimine, maxime rector, exulis afflictum poena.* For a reconstruction of his career, see Wienand 2012, p. 397.

[143] Optatian, *Carm.* 1.15 for the book.

praises the emperor as one whose acts and rewards were "approved under the law of Christ."[144]

But the book did not stand on its own. Senators had likely advanced Optatian's recall as well, even perhaps, as Johannes Wienand has imagined, by presenting the book in conjunction with Constantine's 326 visit to Rome. The noble C(a)eionius Iulianus (signo Kamenius) may well have taken the lead since he may have had family ties to Optatian.[145] But the politics of the moment are also relevant; an imperial pardon in response to such a personal senatorial request would be in keeping with the spirit of the day and sheds light on the efforts of Constantine to reinforce senatorial loyalty before returning to rule in the East.[146] After his recall, Optatian's career reflected some of the new honors that opened up for western elites after 326. It is striking that, his appointment as proconsul of the province of Achaia between 326 and 329 was followed by two largely honorific turns as urban prefect for no more than a month at a time – September 8–October 8, 329; and April 7–May 10, 333.[147] His exceptionally dramatic return and his literary skills, along with his professed religious choice, explain why Jerome mentioned Optatian's pardon in his *Chronicle*, although listing the wrong year.[148]

Constantine's Departure for Constantinople. It may have been remorse at the demise of Fausta in Rome that led Constantine to depart the city so quickly after his vicennalia in 326. Any role he had played in the death of his wife, the daughter of the former tetrarch with ties to Rome, could have

[144] Optatian, *Carm.* 8: *nate deo, solus salvator, sancte, bonorum/tu deus iusti, gratia tu fidei.* A Chi Rho is interwoven into the text; see Mueller, ed. 1877, *Publilii Optatiani Porfyrii, Carmina*, p. 45, for the visualization of the text. See too Wienand 2012, p. 397; Optatian, *Carm.* 8.3–5: *Summe, fave! Te tota rogat plebs gaudia rite, / Et meritam credit, cum servat iussa timore/ Augusto et fidei, Christi sub lege probata.*

[145] For the recall, see Washburn 2013, pp. 144–60. Wienand 2017, pp. 130–31, makes the argument for a family tie based on the survival of Optatian's name Publilius in the family of the Ceionii, and hence identifies as a plausible supporter M. Ceionius Iulianus (*signo* Kamenius) = Iulianus 26, *PLRE* 1 p. 476. Another supporter is perhaps Iunius Bassus, if he is the Bassus to whom Optation, *Carm.* 21 is dedicated; see Table 2.2.

[146] Wienand 2017, pp. 132–35 for the 326 dating. For the conjunction of imperial ceremonies with pardons, see Diocletian's general pardon on his *vicennalia*, Eusebius *Mart. Pal.* 2.4; Washburn 2013, pp. 149–50; and Wienand 2017, p. 131.

[147] On Optatian's career, I follow much of what Wienand 2017, pp. 121–65, has proposed, including his recall in 326. But I do not see clear evidence to date his exile nor to believe that Optatian was exiled by the emperor and not the Senate. And we do not know if Optatian's family was new to senatorial status; see Table 2.1. This career path is at odds in key details with the career outlined for Optatianus 3, *PLRE* 1, p. 649.

[148] Jer. *Chron.* s.a. 329: ed. Helm: *Porphyrius misso ad Constantinum insigni volumine exilio liberatus.* For the likely misdating to 329 instead of 326, see Wienand 2017, pp. 124–35.

created hostility. Constantine left the city very soon after the conclusion of the games, and he did not return to celebrate his tricennalia games there in 336. Instead, he held those in Constantinople, the "altera Roma" that he had founded with its newly minted set of elites, the *clari* – as the *Origo Constantini* stated – who formed a new council, or *Senatus*, in the eastern counterpart to Rome.[149] The absence of the emperor from Rome during this last decade increasingly left senators to their own devices, a reality that was not, however, all that undesirable or new. Emperors had been absent from Rome since the third century. More importantly, Constantine did not undermine the hegemony of senatorial elites in the West or curtail their holding of appointments in the East. On the contrary, Constantine's administrative reforms and appointments in this decade demonstrate his continuing reliance on Roman western senatorial elites even as he promoted a number of new men to senatorial standing in the West and East during the last decade of his rule.

The career of Optatian, with his appointment as proconsul of Achaia (326–29), and that of Ceionius Rufius Albinus, proconsul of Asia, are good indicators of the new possibilities for office for westerners in eastern administrative positions after 324. (For Achaia, see Tables 2.3.2.)[150] And they were not the only western senators to benefit from these new possibilities. For example, the proconsuls of Asia included several Roman senators – Domitius Zenophilus, Anicius Paulinus, Ceionius Rufius Albinus, and Fabius Ttitanus.[151] Other posts, previously equestrian, were also opened up to westerners; the newly named *comes Orientis*, the administrator of this eastern province and resident in Antioch, went to western senators, beginning in 335 with Lollianus signo Mavortius.[152]

Holders of High Office: Urban Prefects, 325–37. Constantine's preference for members of established elite families is also seen in the ten appointments for nine different men in the final decade of his rule after the defeat of Licinius. Seven of the nine men (excluding Optatian and Probianus) were from well known and established aristocratic families. Again, the prefecture was a reward given at the end of most men's careers: Four of the nine urban prefects had held consulships before they held urban prefectures, and three

---

[149] Moser 2018, pp. 58–63, argues against there being a second Senate in Constantinople under Constantine. That remains an open question. However, Constantine clearly intended his capital to be "another Rome" and that its elites would attain senatorial standing by holding office, even if the laws are slow to indicate this.

[150] Moser 2018, p. 24, cites these examples, along with Valerius Proculus (*consularis* in the province of Europe and Thrace). Albinus was *proconsul Asiae sortitus*, implying that he had been allotted that province but had not officially taken it up; see Albinus 14, *PLRE* 1, p. 37.

[151] See Moser 2018, Appendix B.   [152] Moser 2018, p. 21.

had held a consulship soon after holding an urban prefecture. However, there was some sign of change in terms of religion. Two of the nine men in this decade were Christian or probably Christian while two were pagan or probably pagan; the religious proclivities of the remaining five men are not clearly attested (see Table 2.1). But the key to their appointments was that they were established senators: Both Acilius Severus and Optatian were prominent senators during the decade before they were appointed to office.[153]

It was possible, nonetheless, for upwardly mobile new to attain the urban prefecture as had Lucer(ius), or Locrius, Verinus; he was one of five urban prefects whom Avianius Symmachus eulogized in epigrams written in the late fourth century. Verinus's military career and then administrative service as *vicarius* in Africa led Symmachus to praise his time in office, a sign that Verinus had by then been regarded by some members as an accepted member of the senatorial aristocracy.[154] This kind of upward mobility fit with that of new provincial men who were the traditional "seedbeds" of the aristocracy, and they were welcomed into its midst as such. That there were tensions at times with these new men is clear, but the praise for one such successful new man suggests the ways in which senatorial elites replenished their families. The necessity of protecting their financial resources lies in part behind the senatorial aristocracy's openness to certain wealthy, upwardly mobile new men. Certainly, wealth was a key concern for senators and emperor, and it helps to explain the willingness of Constantine to turn to western senatorial elites throughout his reign.

Consuls, 325–37. Constantine's upgrading of senior equestrian civic offices to senatorial status circa 324/5 is evidenced in the men who became consuls. In 327, the consul of that year, Flavius Constantius was likely of nonsenatorial origin.[155] At this time there was a noticeable increase in the number of men from the equestrian rank who had been in imperial service and now were appointed consuls. However, Roman senatorial elites from the West were still honored with this office slightly more often than these men were. Of the twenty-one times that consuls who were not members of the imperial family or emperors were appointed in the years between 324 and 337, eleven have been securely identified as coming from old established Roman elite families.[156] The precedence of

---

[153] See Salzman 2016, pp. 11–45.

[154] On Verinus in Symmachus's epigrams, see Salzman and Roberts 2015 ed., pp. 13–17, and Moser 2018, pp. 26–27.

[155] For the reforms in 325, see Chastagnol 1992, pp. 238–39 and Porena 2012, p. 306. Salway 2015, p. 213 rejects identifying *PLRE* 1 Maximus 49, with Maximus 48, urban prefect in 319–23 but he did hold a prior senatorial post; see Moser 2018, p. 21.

[156] I used Salway 2015, pp. 189–220 for these calculations. Porena 2013, p. 348, note 38, identified eighteen of the thirty possible positions as being from old Roman senators.

appointing ex-equestrian affairs or imperial courtiers over traditional senatorial elites to the consulship identified during the last five years of Constantine's rule (i.e., 332, 334, and 337) illustrates the rising status of new elites and may well have created a certain resentment toward them among older senatorial families, another sign of tensions at the end of Constantine's reign but not a threat to the already achieved hegemony over western society by this date. But by this late date, some of these families could also take on once firmly equestrian offices, like that of the praetorian prefect.

Praetorian Prefects, 325–37. As Pierfrancesco Porena has demonstrated, the changes undertaken by Constantine that had made the praetorian prefecture also a pinnacle of a senatorial career only emerged after 324/25, and only by 326/28 do we see this office attract men born into senatorial aristocratic families. Indeed, some prefects of senatorial families are attested at the very end of Constantine's reign, but most senators by birth were not securely attested until the reigns of the sons of Constantine.[157] It is worth noting here, too, that the praetorian prefects of Constantine had been deprived of their military duties, so the appointment of senators thereafter into what had become a civic office with oversight of the administration or regions is more easily understood.[158]

Of all thirteen named men who can be identified as serving under Constantine and his family as praetorian prefects, only three are possibly from established Roman senatorial families (see Table 2.2). As befit this equestrian office until the reforms of 325 noted above, even after this date, most were new men who had arisen from equestrian standing through imperial service in the provincial administration or at court. However, this office seems to have risen in status, for the last two praetorian prefects, C. Annius Tiberianus, in office from 336 until 337, may have been born into a senatorial family, as Felix, praetorian prefect of Africa from 333 to 336, may have been.[159] Another praetorian prefect, Valerius Maximus, also serving toward the end of Constantine's rule, may also have been from a senatorial family (see Table 2.2). Like the Constantinian praetorian prefects in the first decade after 312, these men appear to have been well integrated into fourth-century Roman senatorial society. Six of the eleven new men had children who are attested among the senatorial order in the next generation (see Table 2.2). Whatever initial resentment their elevations may have caused, they and their families were incorporated into Roman society over the course of fourth century.

---

[157] Porena 2003; 2006, pp. 325–56; and 2007, pp. 237–62.

[158] For the praetorian prefect's loss of military responsibilities other than provisioning the troops, see Porena 2006, passim, who suggests that this change likely was initiated in the late third century under Diocletian.

[159] Felix = Felix 2, *PLRE* 1, pp. 331–32.

The Wealth of Rome's Senators: Resources for Elite Resilience

As the reforms of Constantine and his actions show, the emperor courted western senatorial aristocrats for his government and established reforms to allow wealthy senators to work for his regime. Since wealth was one necessary criterion for senatorial status, it is worth considering, albeit briefly, the arguments for Constantine's threats to senatorial economic well-being, factors that would have created tensions.

Taxes. For this discussion, I highlight the new economic developments that allegedly threatened the financial health of the senatorial aristocracy. The first is the assumption that the taxes under Constantine threatened elites. Indeed, new taxes had been levied on Italy before Constantine's rule when it had become a province under Diocletian; Aurelius Victor decried this change as destructive for those working on the land.[160] But as Andrea Giardina has demonstrated, senatorial aristocrats were aware that levying taxes on farmers (*coloni*) made them rely more and more on powerful landowners (*domini*) for protection and aid. Hence, these taxes augmented the landlord's control of their *coloni* and increased elite control over their clients.[161] Provincial taxation worked to the benefit of large landowners who found ways to use their influence to protect their properties and their farmers from this land taxation.

Even the *follis senatorius* or *collatio glebalis* (tax on senators) did not have a destructive effect on the wealth of senators. This tax was likely initiated in 326 in conjunction with reforms of the senatorial class. It is usually explained as a tax or assessment of one's wealth that indicated that a person had the right property qualifications to be a member of the senatorial class.[162] As such, it served to keep the hierarchy within the senatorial order. The wealthier senators were known as such through this tax, which also demonstrated their prestigious positions in the state and the Senate. As a sign of one's status and as a means to disqualify men from senatorial entry, this tax assured the maintenance of the status quo for the richest senators under Constantine. It did not, however, undermine wealthy senators' financial resources in any way, nor was it necessarily due to passivity that they accepted the imposition of the tax.[163]

In general, the ability of senators to become governors of provinces and to hold positions both in the West and in the East enabled senators to protect their

---

[160] Aur. Victor, *Caes.* 39.23.   [161] Giardina 1993, pp. 51–68.

[162] Giardina 1993, pp. 51–68. For the tax, see Zos. 2.38.4.

[163] See Moser 2018, pp. 40–41 and Potter 2004, pp. 397–98 for taxes to justify status. Jones 1964, pp. 431–32, also sees this tax as not financially burdensome in the early fourth century. Senators complained about the *collatio glebalis* only later in the fourth century, and these taxes were removed in the early fifth century; see Barnish 1989, p. 256.

wealth.[164] The return of peace allowed western senators to maintain and even increase their wealth since so much of it was tied to agriculture and shipping interests. Finally, the capability of senators to make effective marriage alliances to protect their wealth was another strategy that contributed to senatorial resilience.

In sum, the senatorial aristocracy was still the wealthiest, most powerful elite group in Italy and Africa. This view was also expressed in the epigraph to this chapter, a text written in the second half of the fourth-century. The aristocracy's financial and political strength lie in Campania and Italy, and was manifested in the institution that allowed them status, the Senate in Rome.[165] As Rita Lizzi Testa has observed, the "amalgamation of assets along coherent territorial lines ... [benefited senators whose] economic interests could be protected, consolidated, and even expanded on a local basis through forms of semiofficial patronage and the official instrument of a small but essential number of governorships."[166] No wonder, then, that Constantine sought to incorporate senatorial aristocrats into his empire. Once assured of their fidelity in the decade after 312, he turned to them to govern newly acquired territories, as reflected in his eastern appointments. His reforms for attaining senatorial status did not undermine the hegemony of the senatorial aristocracy in the west.

Finally, Constantine's religious policy was not, by and large, seen as a threat to western senatorial interests. Although senators were predominantly pagan in and after 312, Constantine's support for Christianity did not undermine their own priestly positions. As they gradually adopted Christianity over the course of the later fourth century, they found that Christianity opened up new patronage options.[167] Thus Constantine's embrace of Christianity did not remove senators from taking a leading role in Rome's religious life, though it did bring a new group onto the urban stage, namely the bishops and clergy. However, the bishops did not cooperate with the new emperor in as positive

---

[164] This had also been the case even in the later third century. Although senators no longer held high positions in the military, they still held high office and provincial governorships in peaceful areas which allowed them to protect their properties; see Mennen 2011, pp. 69–70, and 143–44.

[165] *Expositio totius mundi et gentium* 54–55. The text is cited in the epigraph to this chapter.

[166] Lizzi Testa (forthcoming). See especially Lo Cascio 2009, pp. 19–70, and Vera 2012, pp. 115–22. Although Lizzi Testa notes that this has been best studied in areas of northern Italy, it is typical of Sicily and central Italy as well.

[167] For senatorial aristocrats and wealthy non-elite donors of churches, especially titular churches, see especially Hillner 2007, pp. 225–62. Wealthy Christian aristocrats could also donate sarcophagi that decorated basilicas, such as that of the consul Junius Bassus; on that, see Machado 2019, pp. 148–49.

and relatively straightforward manner as the senators of Rome had. We can see this pattern emerge very early in their relationship.

Constantine and the Bishops of Rome

In the aftermath of his 312 victory, Constantine set about restoring the status of Christians and returning property to them; in taking these steps, he was following the practices of earlier emperors. But he went far beyond his predecessors' actions when he gave the bishops of Rome, Italy, Gaul, and Africa wealth and unprecedented privileges. For example, he granted Christian clergy, for the first time, exemption from curial duties and financial obligations.[168] In early 314, Constantine signaled his personal involvement in Christian affairs by calling bishops to a meeting that had quasi-official status since he offered clergy the free use of the public post.[169]

A closer examination of the interactions between Constantine and the bishops of Rome in matters having to do with the African church in what came to be known as the Donatist Controversy shows how tensions developed that weakened the bishops of Rome as compared to bishops in other areas. In the series of negotiations revolving around the Donatists in the aftermath of 312, the bishops of Rome exercised their autonomy and yet marginalized themselves from the emperor and other clergy. The misunderstandings and failures to resolve this conflict, I argue, help to explain the limited influence and relative weakness of the bishop of Rome under Constantine, a pattern that would be long-lasting. At the same time, this dispute highlights the roles that senatorial aristocrats also played that enabled their ongoing influence on the religious life of the city.

Constantine's Turn toward the Bishops of Rome in the Donatist Controversy

It was natural for Constantine to turn to the bishops of Rome for assistance in restoring order to the West after his victory of 312. When he had governed in Gaul from 306 on, Constantine had interacted with bishops there, including the Spanish bishop Ossius of Corduba and the Gallic bishops Reticius of

---

[168] Eus. *HE* 105.15–17; 6.1–5; 7.1–2; and on clerical immunity, see also *C. Th.* 16.2.7; 16.5.1.

[169] Eus. *HE* 10.5.18; and Drake 2012, pp. 117–19 on the radical departure that Constantine's summoning of the Council of Arles represented in terms of imperial engagement.

Autun, Marinus of Arles, and Maternus of Cologne.[170] After defeating Maxentius and, along with Licinius, proclaiming toleration in what is today called "The Edict of Milan," dated to February 313, Constantine instructed the proconsul Anullinus to restore church property – "whether gardens, or buildings, or whatsoever" – to Caecilian, bishop of the group identified as "Catholic Christians" in Carthage.[171] By mid-April of 313, however, Anullinus had relayed a petition to Constantine from the supporters of an alternative Christian faction in Carthage under their own bishop, Majorian, accusing Caecilian of crimes, civic or criminal or both (*crimina*).[172]

This complaint led Constantine to turn the matter over to the then-bishop of Rome, Miltiades, along with three bishops from Gaul whom Constantine knew already, Reticius, Maternus, and Marinus. The emperor's directive is worth quoting at some length, preserved in the Greek translation by Eusebius:

> It seemed good to me that Caecilian himself, with ten bishops, who seem to call him to account, and such ten others as he may deem necessary to his suit, should set sail for Rome [so] that there a hearing may be granted him in the presence of yourselves, and moreover of Reticius and Maternus and Marinus also, your colleagues (whom I have ordered to hasten to Rome for this purpose), in such a manner as you may perceive to be in accordance with the most sacred law. Nevertheless, that you may have the fullest knowledge of all these same matters, I have subjoined to my letter copies of the documents that were sent to me by Anullinus, and have dispatched them to your aforesaid colleagues. Which when your Firmness reads, he will gauge by what method the most careful investigation can be made of the above-mentioned suit, and a just decision arrived at; since it does not escape the notice of your Carefulness that the respect which I pay to the lawful Catholic Church is so great, that it is my wish that ye should leave no schism whatsoever or division in any place.[173]

---

[170] Eck 2007, pp. 69–94 has argued strongly for his familiarity with the three Gallic bishops after he went to Gaul in 306. See now Digeser 2019, pp. 103–24. For Ossius, see also Lizzi Testa 2016, pp. 183–96. For Constantine ending the persecutions by 306 in Gaul, an area where they were only feebly enforced, see Lact. *De mort. pers.* 24.9; *Div. inst.* 1.1.13, and Lenski 2016, p. 102.

[171] For the so-called Edict of Milan issued likely in February 313, see Eus. *HE* 10. 5.2–14; Lact. *De mort. pers.* 48.2–12. For the dating, see Barnes 1982, p. 71. For Constantine's letter to Anullinus issued soon after, see Eus. *HE* 10. 5.15–17.

[172] The letter of Anullinus transmitting to Constantine the Donatists' petition against Caecilianus is quoted by Aug. *Ep.* 88.2 and dated to April 15, 313.

[173] Eus. *HE* 10.5.18–20 for the full letter. I cite sections 19–20, translation by Kirsopp Lake, pp. 455–57, *LCL* vol. 265: ἔδοξέ μοι ἵν' αὐτὸς ὁ Καικιλιανὸς μετὰ δέκα19 ἐπισκόπων τῶν αὐτὸν εὐθύνειν δοκούντων καὶ δέκα ἑτέρων οὓς αὐτὸς τῇ ἑαυτοῦ δίκῃ ἀναγκαίους ὑπολάβοι, εἰς τὴν

By turning this dispute over to the bishop of Rome, Constantine seems to be following a third-century imperial precedent. The third-century emperor Aurelian had referred a dispute about possession of a church in Antioch to the then-bishop of Rome and Italian bishops.[174] Although in 260 the emperor Gallienus had returned property to Christians directly after he had ended a persecution of Christians, in 313 Constantine preferred to let the bishops resolve disputed claims.[175] Nor was Miltiades unfamiliar with the problems involved; Maxentius's orders to restore the property of Christians in Africa (under his control again after a civil war) had been relayed through Miltiades, who had been bishop of Rome since July 2, 311.[176] Thus, when confronted with this controversy that hinged in part on the restoration of church property, it made sense that Constantine sought to resolve this contested issue by turning it over to the current bishop of Rome, Miltiades, and the three Gallic bishops.[177]

In Constantine's letter (as Eusebius had preserved it) there is only a vague reference to the precise nature of the other accusations against Caecilian. Their substance only emerges from later documents.[178] Caecilian's election to the bishopric had not been accepted by the alternative faction of Christians led by Bishop Majorian in Carthage because, they alleged, his

---

Ῥώμην πλῷ ἀπιέναι, ἵν' ἐκεῖσε ὑμῶν παρόντων, ἀλλὰ μὴν καὶ Ῥετικίου καὶ Ματέρνου καὶ Μαρίνου, τῶν κολλήγων ὑμῶν, οὓς τούτου ἔνεκεν εἰς τὴν Ῥώμην προσέταξα ἐπισπεῦσαι, δυνηθῇ ἀκουσθῆναι, ὡς ἂν καταμάθοιτε τῷ σεβασμιωτάτῳ νόμῳ ἁρμόττειν, ἵνα μέντοι καὶ περὶ πάντων αὐτῶν τούτων πληρεστάτην δυνηθῆτε ἔχειν γνῶσιν, τὰ ἀντίτυπα τῶν ἐγγράφων τῶν πρός με παρὰ Ἀνυλίνου ἀποσταλέντων γράμμασιν ἐμοῖς ὑποτάξας, πρὸς τοὺς προειρημένους κολλήγας ὑμῶν ἐξέπεμψα· οἷς ἐντυχοῦσα ἡ ὑμετέρα στερρότης δοκιμάσει ὅντινα χρὴ τρόπον τὴν προειρημένην δίκην ἐπιμελέστατα διευκρινῆσαι καὶ κατὰ τὸ δίκαιον τερματίσαι, ὁπότε μηδὲ τὴν ὑμετέραν ἐπιμέλειαν λανθάνει τοσαύτην με αἰδῶ τῇ ἐνθέσμῳ καθολικῇ ἐκκλησίᾳ ἀπονέμειν, ὡς μηδὲν καθόλου σχίσμα ἢ διχοστασίαν ἔν τινι τόπῳ βούλεσθαί με ὑμᾶς καταλιπεῖν.

[174] For Aurelian, see Eus. *HE* 7.30.19, and the discussions by Eck 2007; Lenski 2016A, p. 69; and Digeser 2019, p. 116.

[175] Eus. *HE* 7.13 for Gallienus's rescript to the bishops administered through a civic official. Constantine's policy is discussed at length by Lenski 2016, pp. 102–3; 123–37.

[176] Aug. *Brev. Coll. C. Donat.* 3,18,34 (*CCSL* 149A, 299): *Miltiades misisse diaconos cum litteris Maxentii imperatoris et litteris praefecti praetorio ad praefectum urbi, ut ea reciperent quae tempore persecutionis ablata memoratus imperator chirstianis iusserat redd*; Aug. *ad Donat. post. Coll.* 13 (17) (*PL* 43, 662 = *CSEL* 53.113–114). Cf. *Conl. Carth. Capit. Gest.* 3.498–500 (*CCHR. SL* 149A.47). As Lenski 2016, p. 102, note 9 notes, all three sources indicate that the order was forwarded through Miltiades of Rome. For discussion of the politics of Maxentius, see Kriegbaum 1992, pp. 7, 54, and especially at 26; and von Schoenebeck 1939, pp. 5–6.

[177] Eus. *HE* 10.5.15–20.

[178] This charge was investigated at the Council of Arles in 314 and it was pronounced groundless; on this see Aiello 2013, pp. 203–18. For a reconstruction of these charges based on the anti-Donatist documents preserved by Augustine, which he used in the early fifth century, see Calderone 1962, pp. 171–73.

consecration as a bishop had been performed in 311–12 by the "traitorous" bishop Felix of Aptunga. Felix, they asserted, had lost his right to do this because he had betrayed the faith during the recent persecutions of Christians and had turned over scriptures to the authorities to avoid martyrdom.[179] As such, he was one of those "traitors" (*traditores*) who had, according to this rigorist view, to undergo rebaptism in order to reclaim their standing as Christians and clergy. Since Caecilian's elevation was not valid, the faction maintained, property should not go to him and his followers. To resolve these matters, as Eusebius's letter cited above indicates, Constantine ordered Caecilian to go to Rome with ten of his accusers and ten of his defenders so that Bishop Miltiades and the three Gallic bishops could make their determination.

Miltiades failed to resolve this controversy. And more damaging, he also did not follow imperial instructions. Although Constantine's directive, preserved in the letter to him, left it to Miltiades to determine how to best investigate this matter to arrive at a just decision (ὄντινα χρὴ τρόπον τὴν προειρημένην δίκην ἐπιμελέστατα διευκρινῆσαι καὶ κατὰ τὸ δίκαιον τερματίσαι), Miltiades made sure that he would not face the possibility of being outvoted by the Gallic bishops, one of whom was known to have had a lenient position on the lapsed.[180] Instead, Miltiades called for a synod in Rome with fifteen Italian bishops over which he would preside as *iudex vice Caesaris* (judge in the place of Caesar). In October 313, nineteen bishops in all met at the *Domus Faustae*, part of the imperial palace in the area of Rome "at the Lateran" on the Caelian Hill, near the site of the new church that Constantine was likely already building on the barracks of the defeated horse guard (see Map 3).[181] Although calling synods was one way for bishops to mediate matters, it is also clear that using this procedure allowed Miltiades to pack the tribunal with Italian bishops under his authority.[182]

---

[179] On this first phase of the controversy, see also Barnes 1982, pp. 238–47.

[180] Eus. *HE* 10.5.20. Reticius of Autun wrote *Adversum Novatianum*, a work that was more open toward the lapsed. See Jer., *De Vir. Ill.* 82; and Aiello 2013, p. 207.

[181] The beginning date of the work on Constantine's Basilica is still open to debate, but the extensive remodeling of the Caelian Hill and the massive nature of the undertaking reinforces the arguments from ancient sources that the project began very soon after the defeat of Maxentius, in late 312. Curran 2000, pp. 94–95, argues for late 312 or early 313. Lenski 2016A, p. 181, sees the numismatic evidence as reinforcing this dating. Recent excavations of the site have not resolved the dating, although it has shed light on the extensive nature of the work involved in demolishing the preexisting camps of the defeated imperial horse guard; see Haynes et al. 2017–18, pp. 320–25. On the *Domus Faustae*, I follow the arguments of Nash 1976, pp. 191–206; Liverani 2004, pp. 17–49; and Liverani 2020, pp. 6–24, that this was part of imperial property and not the home of Constantine's wife, Fausta.

[182] For church councils or synods before 314, beginning as early as 253, see MacMullen 2006, pp. 2–4.

Constantine must have been disappointed in the result of Miltiades's intervention and more than a little irritated by the bishop. The council held in Rome in October 313 did not restore unity to the church in Africa, the very reason that he had asked for Miltiades's mediation so as to "leave no schism whatsoever or division in any place."[183] As Constantine had said in his earlier letter in the spring of 313 to Anullinus, Proconsul of Africa, unity in the church was vital to the well-being of the state: "when they [Christians] show greatest reverence to the Deity, the greatest benefits accrue to the state."[184] Moreover, the emperor's intercession, along with his beginning construction of a Christian basilica, the present-day St. John Lateran, likely in early 313, was intended to demonstrate his personal engagement with Christianity (see Map 3).[185]

Miltiades, himself of African origin and only recently elevated to the papacy in July 311, had used the imperial request to assert his dominance over the clergy in Rome and Italy along with an assertion of his autonomy. As one who had come to the papacy in a city facing similar divisions over how to treat lapsed Christians and the restoration of property, he had faced similar conflicts within the city's clergy and Christian community.[186]

Miltiades's council ruled in favor of the claim of Caecilian as the rightful bishop of Carthage and against his opponents, led now by a bishop named Donatus (consecrated by the opposing bishop between April 15 and October 2, 313). This opposing faction, now called the Donatists, were also angered by the ruling because it stipulated that in a city where there were two contesting bishops, the eldest bishop would remain, and the other would be assigned to another community. And more specifically, it excluded their bishop, Donatus, from any position.[187] No wonder that what was later known as "the judgment of Miltiades" (*iudicium Miltiadis*) so angered the supporters of Donatus that their subsequent documents accused Miltiades of

---

[183] Eus. *HE* 10.5.20.

[184] Eus. *HE* 10.7 can be dated to April 313, along with his other letter to Anullinus in Eus. *HE* 5.15–17 and at 6.1–5. For discussion of the dating of these letters beginning likely in late 312, see Lenski 2016, p. 105, and Lizzi Testa 2014, pp. 87–97.

[185] This intervention, along with his imperial donations for churches, which likely commenced by 313 with his personal funding for the modern church of St. John Lateran, demonstrated publicly his personal support for Christianity in the immediate aftermath of his 312 victory. For further bibliography in support of Constantine's public adoption of Christianity after 312, see Salzman 2016, pp. 11–45. For a counterview that sees his conversion in 324, see Nagy 2016, pp. 377–98.

[186] Divisions within the Christian community in Rome during the persecution had harmed the community; see Damasus, *Carm.* 18.3 and Aiello 2013, p. 204.

[187] For Donatus's election, see Maier 1987, 1.129–32; *PCBE* 1.293–94, Donatus 5; and Lenski 2016, p. 105. For this decision, see Aug. *Ep.* 43.5.16; 185.10.47; and Di Berardino 2000, p. 317, citing the *Ep. ad Aelafium* (*CSEL* 26, pp. 204–6).

being a *traditor* – that is, of handing over sacred scripture in the recent persecution and hence being a faithless arbiter.[188] Supporters of Donatus also complained, with justification, it seems, that at the last minute Miltiades had insisted that Bishop Donatus provide actual evidence in accord with Roman legal procedure.[189] In essence, Miltiades had hijacked the council to bring charges of violating canon law without any warning.[190] According to a later Christian tradition, Miltiades had wanted to assert episcopal control over judgments concerning other bishops and not leave this matter open to imperial influence.[191]

Realizing that Miltiades had fueled rather than silenced this escalating conflict and responding to further entreaties from the Donatists, Constantine convened a second council to hear additional charges against the pro-Caecilian faction in Carthage brought by supporters of Donatus.[192] The emperor ordered a number of bishops from Italy as well as from Gaul to travel to Arles for this August 1, 314, council; he even put the public post at the bishops' disposal, itself an important statement of the esteem of this meeting and its participants.[193] As presiding bishop, Constantine chose Marinus, Bishop of Arles, who had been one of the three Gallic bishops present at the 313 Rome council. Constantine had apparently lost faith in Rome's bishops to resolve this matter. Indeed, he could have referred the Donatists' complaints to the new bishop of Rome, Silvester, who had been in office since late January 314.[194] Constantine did not do that. Perhaps he had heard the allegation that Augustine reports that Silvester himself was also a *traditor* who had cowardly handed over sacred books during the persecution.[195] Instead, Constantine acceded to a request by the Donatists for a change of venue and personally intervened to choose the new judge.

---

[188] Aug. *Ep.* 43.2.4; and Di Berardino 2000, p. 317.

[189] Aug. *Ep.* 43.7.16 for Miltiades' actions. For the Donatists' charge against Miltiades, see Aug. *C. Parm. Don.* 1.5.10. For the conclusion, see Optatus *Tract.* App. 3 = Maier 1987, no. 18, ll. 34–36 with Eck 2007, p. 75.

[190] On this issue, I agree with Calderone 1962, pp. 180–81 and 231–39.

[191] Aiello 2013, p. 209 and note 68. The full council was read out in the full assembly in 411 in Carthage but was later lost and so can only be partially reconstructed; see the Carthage Council, *Capitula gestorum* III, 322, 325, p. 509; Optatian, *Contra Parm. Don.* I.23; and Di Berardino 2000, p. 317.

[192] Eus. *HE* 10.5.21–24. For further discussion, see Drake 2000, pp. 218–19. See also Optatian App. 3 (*CSEL* 26.204-6) = Maier 1987, no. 18. On this act by Constantine, see also his *Ep. ad Aelafium* (CSEL 26, pp. 204–06).

[193] See note 169.

[194] For a good discussion of the administrative issues involved, see Potter 2013, pp. 193–203.

[195] Aug. *Un. bapt.* 27.30; and Canella 2013, p. 241 on the rumor that may have been circulated by the Donatists that he had been a *traditor* under the bishop of Rome, Marcellinus.

Scholars dispute it, but I am inclined to believe that Constantine did not attend the Council at Arles because his presence is not mentioned in Eusebius's account of these events in his *Ecclesiastical History*.[196] We are quite certain, however, that the bishop of Rome, Silvester, did not attend the Council of Arles. Instead, he sent his deacons, Eugenius and Cyriacus, and two priests to represent him. As the newly elected bishop of Rome, Silvester decided it was advantageous to distance himself from this imperially mandated council; but many did attend – between twenty-six and forty-four bishops, priests, and deacons.[197] I underscore here that Silvester's choice to not attend the council went against an imperial request. Letters like the one Constantine had sent to Bishop Chrestus of Syracuse had not persuaded Silvester. Moreover, there is no precedent controlling Silvester's decision.[198] The Council of Arles was the first time an emperor had called bishops together for a synod. His decision was not simple adherence to tradition.[199] But in 324, Silvester could claim that he was now following a precedent set in 314 when he again chose to not attend a council called by the emperor, the first worldwide Council of Bishops at Nicaea.[200] Silvester's nonattendance at the Council of Arles set a pattern that would be useful for future bishops of Rome.

Silvester's absence was noted by the other bishops. Assuming the veracity of the *Letter* written by the Council of Arles that has come down to us after the meeting to inform Silvester of its decisions, his failure to attend had influenced the outcome of the meeting:

> Dearest brother, oh that you were present when this great spectacle took place; indeed, we believe since the decision rendered against them was very

---

[196] This is the argument of Girardet 1989, pp. 151–74. For an opposing position, see Aiello 2013, pp. 211–12. For the account, see Eusebius, *HE* 10.5.18–24.

[197] Numbers of attendants vary depending on the manuscript; see Munier 1963, pp. 1–7. Constantine had called the bishop of Syracuse, one Chrestus, to attend and gave the public post to him according to Eus. *HE* 10.5.21–24. For the canons issued after that council, see *C Chr SL* 148.9–23. See also on this council, Optat. *App.* 4 (*CSEL* 26.204–06) = Maier 1987, no. 18.

[198] After Silvester, the bishops of Rome did not travel to other cities for church Councils generally. However, they did travel to other cities at times to consult with the emperor on matters; see note 199 below.

[199] Pietri 1976, p. 168, argues that there was a precedent that the bishop of Rome only participated in assemblies in his own city, thus preserving the "Seat of the Apostles." There is no explicit precedent, however. And the bishop of Rome could leave the city when he desired; so, for example, Innocent went to Ravenna to negotiate with the emperor and hence was absent from Alaric's 410 sack of Rome; see Chapter 3.

[200] Theodoret, *HE* 1.7.3; Eus. *VC* 3.7.2. And for discussion of the absence of Silvester from the Council of Nicaea, see Pietri 1976, 172–78.

severe, that, had you joined us in judgment, our assembly would have rejoiced with greater gladness.[201]

Moreover, the bishops made decisions on a host of matters without Silvester's guidance. They conveyed their decisions to Silvester so that he could introduce these to his clergy:

> Be it resolved, therefore, in the presence of the Holy Spirit and his angels, that we would also give judgments concerning those things which stir up any individual and you, as if you were present; it is further resolved, with the assent of one who occupies the greater diocese, that this be introduced to all through you especially. What therefore it is that we have decided, we have subjoined in our brief written statement.[202]

How Silvester responded to this letter telling him what to do is not attested. But it is clear that by not attending, Silvester also lost the opportunity to directly influence other bishops.

In light of these frustrations, we can better appreciate why Constantine effectively limited the role of the bishop of Rome in resolving conflicts. In particular, Constantine allowed plaintiffs to move their hearings to avoid the oversight of the bishop of Rome as the Donatists had done when seeking a second hearing outside his jurisdiction. As a result of Constantine's moving the Donatists' complaint to a council in Arles, bishops of other regions (such as Gaul) had greater influence since dissident Christians could shift disputes away from the bishops of their own city or from the "courts of pagans" to bishops and councils in areas more favorably disposed to their complaints.[203] By 318, the right of bishops to determine disputes, the *episcopale iudicium*, was an important extension of episcopal authority, especially since the bishops' judgments were not eligible for appeal.[204] Yet the flexibility that Constantine had established when he allowed disputants to move their cases undercut the authority of the bishops of Rome. Not surprisingly, later bishops of Rome sought to reverse

---

[201] *The Letter to Sylvester from the Council of Arles* (AD 314). Translation here by author. See *Conciles Gaulois du IVe Siècles*, ed. Gaudemet 1977 (SC 241), pp. 37–39: *Et utinam, frater dilectissime, ad hoc tantum spectaculum interesses tanti fecisse, profecto credimus quia in eos severior fuisset sententia prolata, et te pariter nobiscum iudicante coetus noster maiori laetitia exultasset.*

[202] *Conciles Gaulois du IVe Siècles*, ed. Gaudemet 1977, (SC 241), p. 42: *Placuit ergo, praesente Spiritu sancto et angelis eiusdem, ut et de his quae singulos uosque movebant iudica proferremus, <quasi> te consistente; placuit etiam, annuente qui maiores dioeceses tenet, per te potissimum omnibus insinuari. Quid autem sit quod senserimus, scriptis nostrae mediocritatis subiunximus.*

[203] Lenski 2016A, p. 251. Bishops could resolve disputes between Christians as Paul had admonished in his *First Epistle to the Corinthians* (6:1–6).

[204] Lenski 2016A, p. 251.

this precedent.[205] But the pattern had been set by Constantine's interactions with these early bishops of Rome.[206]

How Silvester felt about Constantine's intervention in the Donatist matter is not attested. But Constantine's actions may well have reinforced the bishop's suspicions about the motivations of this emperor. By February 315, Constantine gave in to a request to hear charges brought by Donatists against Caecilian's consecrator, who was then acquitted. In the spring of 315, after returning from Rome and his *decennalia* celebrations described earlier, Constantine began to organize to hold a hearing of charges brought by the Donatists against Caecilian. He personally heard the case of the Donatists in Milan in the summer of 316. At that time, Constantine ordered the confiscation of church property in Donatist control and demanded that the Donatists reunite with the church of Caecilian.[207]

Donatist resistance to Constantine's decision did not end there, and conflict continued. Widespread persecution of Donatists did not take place, but the emperor or his governors did send an unspecified number of Donatists into exile to try to keep peace in Africa. But after 321, Constantine changed course and called for open toleration of Donatists and ordered that all efforts to seize Donatist churches stop.[208] This was a useful position now when his primary focus was his war with Licinius in the East. He may have hoped to return to the Donatist controversy after he controlled the empire, but there is no evidence of further action. Rather, as Noel Lenski observed, Constantine's last letter to a Catholic bishop in North Africa in 330 urged acceptance of the Donatists' control of an imperial church in Cirta. The emperor had more pressing controversies in the East to attend to. But Constantine's personal intervention in the Donatist controversy and his exile of certain Donatists were strong reminders that the power of the

---

[205] Rescript of Gratian and Valentinian II, *CSEL* 35.54–57 in reply to a petition of the bishop of Rome, PL 13.575–84. A rescript of the emperors Gratian and Valentinian II dated to 378–79 indicates that the bishop of Rome sought imperial permission for ecclesiastical jurisdiction over recalcitrant bishops and metropolitans by forcing them to appear in Rome or before judges named by the bishop of Rome.

[206] On this point, I agree with Aiello 2013, pp. 213–314.

[207] For the insistence of the Donatists on a hearing from the emperor himself in 315, see Optat.us *App.* 5 (*CSEL* 26.208–12); Optatus 1.25.1 (*SC* 412.226); Aug. *Ep.* 43.7 [20] (*CSEL* 34.101–02). For the hearing in the summer of 316, see Aug. *Ep.* 43.7 [20] (*CSEL* 34.101–02); Aug. *C. Cresc.* 3.71[82] (*CSEL* 52.487); Aug. *Ad Don. p. coll.* 33 [56] (*CSEL* 53.158). For the decree by Constantine on the Donatists in 316, see Aug. *Ep.* 99.3 (*CSEL* 34.409); *Ep.* 93.14 (*CSEL* 34.458); *Ep.* 195.9 (*CSEL* 34.601); and *C. Th.* 16.6.2. For discussion of the rhetoric of unity, see too Lenski 2016A, p. 197.

[208] For Donatists in exile, see Aug. *Ep.* 149.9 (*CSEL* 44.243); Lenski 2016, p. 108, note 32, and Shaw 2011, pp. 433–35. For the call for toleration of Donatists, see Optatus *App.* 9 (*CSEL* 26.212–13); Aug. *Ad Don. P. coll.* 33[56] (*CSEL* 53.158).

emperor could be turned against Christians at any time. This only confirmed the suspicions of some bishops about imperial intentions.

Fraught Relations between Silvester and Constantine

Constantine's intervention in the Donatist controversy and the absence of information about any further interaction with the bishop of Rome, Silvester, in contemporary sources are significant because Eusebius and other fourth-century Christians were intent on attesting to Constantine's faith as a loyal servant of Christ. This silence suggests a distant and somewhat fraught relationship between emperor and bishop. The one fourth-century source, a sentence by the Bishop Damasus, speaking in a Roman synod of 378, offers little to counter this image of their relationship. Damasus tells us that Silvester argued his own case when accused by "sacrilegious men" before the emperor Constantine.[209] The charge is not known. Presumably, Constantine pardoned Silvester. As noted above, Silvester faced opposition in Rome from other Christians, some of whom had already accused him of being a *traditor* in the past. But there is no suggestion of a personal contact, or of closer ties. Nor do we hear of personal interactions between Silvester and other members of the imperial family – notably Fausta or Helena, or Constantine's sister Constantia – all of whom were living in Rome at various points throughout the bishop's reign.[210]

In fact, not until the fifth and early sixth centuries does Silvester emerge as a leading figure of the church with a major role in the city or in the life of Constantine and his family. So, for example, the sixth-century *Life of Silvester* in the *Book of the Popes* asserts that he was the first bishop to be a donor of a neighborhood church, the so-called *titulus Equitii*; but this *titulus* is not evidenced archaeologically until the late fifth–early sixth century.[211] (See Maps 1 and 3.) Similarly, we cannot trust the assertion in the *Book of the*

---

[209] The Roman Synod of 378, Mansi 3, p. 627: *Nam Silvester papa a sacrilegis accusatus, apud parentum vestrum, Constantinum causam proprium consecutus est.* See *CA* 13, Guenther Pt. I, p. 191 for the reply. Gratian does not reply to this request that popes be judged only by the emperor's council, as Girardet 2009, pp. 466–75 has argued.

[210] Hillner 2017, pp. 75–94 sees a constant presence for Fausta and Helena. However, the evidence for Fausta being in Rome is not as certain until 326, in contrast with the evidence for Helena's presence; see notes 116–18 above and Moser 2018, p. 35. For Constantia, see Constantia I, *PLRE* 1, p. 221.

[211] For the fifth-century cult of Silvester, see *Lib. Pont.* ed. Duchesne 1981, p. 201; Pietri 1976, pp. 17–21; and Canella 2013, pp. 241–58, who makes the case for this legend dating to the second half of the fifth century in conjunction with the Churches of St. Silvester and St. Martino ai Monti, the former identified with the *titulus Equitii*. For the post-Constantinian dating of these churches, see Angelelli and Guidobaldi 2016, pp. 353–60, and Guidobaldi 2003, pp. 5–12.

Popes that Silvester converted Constantine and baptized him. Only in this later document and late fifth-century hagiographical texts do we even hear, for the first time, of the miraculous cure of Constantine's leprosy by the bishop to explain the emperor's conversion to Christianity in 324 and his baptism by the bishop.[212]

The donations by Constantine were gifts that he, as imperial patron, gave to the Church of Rome and its bishop. Although Constantine is credited in certain versions of the sixth-century *Life of Silvester* with donating St. Peter's in the Vatican at the request of the bishop, Silvester's role in initiating this gift is not at all certain.[213] And if Monica Hellström and Nicola Denzey Lewis are right – as I think they are – that St. Peter's was built in the 330s not as a church but as a giant covered cemetery for Christian burial, then the emperor was building a public monument that provided a public service, notably protected space for Christian burial and commemoration of the dead.[214] Silvester's role is diminished. Indeed, even the assertion in the *Book of the Popes* that Silvester had asked Constantine to build the church of Paul's outside the Walls is likely a much later addition, inserted, it would seem, to explain the lacunae in our sources about this imperial–episcopal relationship.[215]

Certainly, Constantine's patronage of Christianity and donations when Silvester was bishop is supported by archaeological as well as textual evidence. The sixth-century *Book of the Popes* cites the gifts and churches funded by this emperor or his family that were built on imperial land in and around the city of Rome (see Map 3): the Constantinian Basilica (or the Basilica of St. Salvator, the modern St. John Lateran), the Basilica of St. Laurence on the Via Tiburtina, that of Sts. Marcellinus and Peter outside the walls, St. Agnes on the Via Nomentana, the Basilica of the Holy Cross in Jerusalem in the Sessorian Palace, St. Peter's in the Vatican, St. Paul's outside the Walls, and Sts. Peter, Paul, and John the Baptist at Ostia, Rome's port. Modern scholars dispute the accuracy of the donations[216] and Constantine's role in building some five of these churches – St. Agnes, St. Laurence, St. Paul outside the Walls, Sts. Marcellinus and Peter, and even St. Peter's – but the Constantinian foundations of the remaining churches and his support for

---

[212] See *Lib. Pont.* 34, ed. Duchesne 1981, p. 201; Pietri 1976, pp. 17–21; and Canella 2013, pp. 241–58.

[213] *Lib. Pont.* 34, ed. Duchesne 1981, p. 182.

[214] Hellström 2016, pp. 291–313; Denzey Lewis 2020, pp. 182–86, 315–19.

[215] See Bardill 2012, p. 248. On the silence about Silvester, see also Sessa 2017, pp. 77–91 and Aiello 2013, pp. 203–18.

[216] For the veracity of the Constantinian donation lists in the *Book of the Popes,* see Liverani 2019, pp. 169–218; and Pietri 1978, pp. 319–21. For skepticism on the Constantinian donations in the *Book of the Popes*; and the *Life of Silvester* in particular, see McKitterick 2011, pp. 19–34; 2020, p. 203.

Christianity are certain. Taken together, imperial patronage represents a significant investment in the Christian community in Rome.[217]

The bishops Miltiades and then Silvester benefitted from Constantine's patronage, as did the priests and deacons under them. These sites of Christian memory offered the clergy new ceremonial possibilities and announced their new status. Eusebius tells us, for instance, the bishops consecrated with a mass the church in Tyre in 314 or 315, and the Church of the Holy Cross in Jerusalem in 335.[218] When Silvester presumably consecrated the basilicas and churches built by Constantine in Rome is not attested, nor can we be certain he did so in the presence of the emperor.[219]

Silvester certainly gained in status from Constantine's support, but he also had many other responsibilities as he ministered to the community of the faithful in Rome; the consecration and conduct of all clergy within the city of Rome fell to the bishop of Rome and his seven deacons. There must have been a few hundred clergy under his direction, for one account of third-century Rome lists over 140 clergy.[220] Pastoral care for Christian communities, directing liturgical worship, as well as managing church properties and disciplining the clergy were the general tasks of any bishop. Silvester devoted his energies to these and many other tasks. But it is unlikely that in the course of his duties, he also presided over the emperor at any church services attended by Constantine when he came to Rome in 315 and 326; as Neil McLynn observed, only on the eve of his death in Constantinople did the emperor attend services in church. Rather the emperor, like many aristocrats, developed private worship practices within his own home, or rather palace.[221]

Silvester, like the other bishops, was dependent on wealthy patrons. It is noteworthy that aside from Constantine and Helena, the sole patron attested

[217] Hellström 2016, pp. 291–313 for doubts about the Constantinian dating of St. Agnes, St. Laurence, and Sts. Marcellinus and Peter. See too Denzey Lewis 2020, pp. 315–31. Not all scholars agree on this list. Bardill 2012, p. 248 with bibliography, sees St. Peter's as the work of Constantine's son, Constantius II, though I am not convinced and support the Constantinian date.

[218] For the church in Tyre, see Eus. *HE* 10.3–4. For the Church of the Holy Cross in Jerusalem, see Eus. *VC* 4.43–47. Bishops reserved the right to consecrate churches, as the extant sermons on such occasions indicate at the end of the fourth century; see, for example, Gaudentius, *Sermones* 17 (*CSEL* 68).

[219] The role of Silvester in consecrating the Lateran Basilica is often assumed, but the particulars attributed to him in the *Book of the Popes* reflect sixth-century practice; see McKitterick 2020, pp. 197–220.

[220] Eus. *HE* 6.42 for third-century Rome.

[221] McLynn 2004, pp. 236–42. For priests and deacons at the banquets and private services in the homes of the elite, see Ambrosiaster, *Question 101*, and Hunter 2017, p. 505.

under Silvester, again mentioned in the *Book of the Popes*, is one Gallicanus, who donated a church in Ostia.[222] In the coming decades, patronage by Christian aristocrats, like the sons of Junius Bassus, would enrich the church, even as these same patrons left a large imprint on the city, attaching their names and those of their families to the churches, chapels and charities they endowed. Thus wealthy lay aristocrats shaped Christian practices and the Church in Rome over the course of the fourth and fifth centuries.

The Legacy of Constantine and the Power of Public Ceremony

Constantine adopted similar strategies to win the allegiance of senatorial and ecclesiastical elites. He bestowed honors and wealth in exchange for loyalty and service. But ironically, the senators and the Senate were more willing to cooperate with the emperor than the bishops of Rome were. We see this same attitudinal difference in the ways in which our sources report the reactions of senators and bishops to the death of Constantine.

Eusebius asserts that at the news of Constantine's demise, the Senate and people of Rome "begged that the remains of their Emperor should be kept by them and laid in the Imperial city."[223] Indeed, Eusebius ascribes to Romans the traditional senatorial view that Rome was the proper place for an emperor's entombment; honorable burial in the city, the "home of the empire and of the virtues" (*lar imperii virtutumque*), was widely held as the proper reward for a good emperor.[224] To the senators and people of the city, Constantine had been just that. Consequently, the inhabitants of the city wanted the son, like his mother, Helena, to be buried in Rome.[225] However, this act did not happen, for, as Eusebius informs us, Constantine had left instructions for his entombment in Constantinople. Nevertheless, despite the absence of a body in Rome, the Senate found ways to adapt its ceremonial to honor this emperor and to take a leading role in his public mourning, sending representatives to the funeral in Constantinople.[226] The Roman Senate consecrated this good emperor with whom they had had such

---

[222] Whether we identify Gallicanus as the urban prefect in 316–17 or consul in 330, his patronage falls under the reign of Constantine; see note 90 above. For the attribution of titular churches to wealthy clergy along with lay elites, see Hillner 2006, pp. 59–68 and 2007, pp. 225–61.

[223] Eus. *VC* 4.69.2.

[224] MacCormack 1981, p. 134, citing Amm. Marc. 25.10.5. For Rome as the *Lar imperii virtutumque*, see Amm. Marc. 16.10.3.

[225] For Helena's burial in the mausoleum built near a villa after her death ca. 330, see Curran 2000, p. 102.

[226] For a good discussion of the funeral with bibliography, see Averil Cameron and Hall 1999, pp. 331–50.

a mutually beneficial relationship. The senators honored Constantine as a *divus* (deified god) with certain traditional rites, like the ceremonial display of images showing his elevation to heaven, and the Senate subsequently recognized Constantine's sons as heirs of a god.[227] Constantine was also the last emperor to have coins issued to commemorate his deification and consecration, an action that happened with senatorial decree, although these coins omitted signs of the imperial cult that were distinctly pagan such as an altar, temple, and funeral pyre.[228] Such acts of devotion continued even in Constantinople, if Philostorgius can be believed; the imperial statues there received incense and candle lightings, as was likely the case in Rome as well.[229]

In contrast, we hear of nothing similar from the bishop of Rome or his clergy in honor of Constantine. Only in Constantinople, as Eusebius tells us, was there a funeral. The emperor's sarcophagus was placed in the Church of the Holy Apostles, surrounded by the caskets of the Twelve Apostles so that he might share in their honor and receive devotions with them.[230] Constantine's final resting place would make him into an *isapostolos* ("equal of the Apostles") or a "thirteenth Apostle," like St. Paul.[231] The challenge that this burial implied for the authority of the bishops of Rome and the veneration of Saints Peter and Paul in their city must not have escaped the bishops' notice. As in his life, so in death, the absence of any role for the bishop of Rome in this important ceremonial moment emerges from the silence. Once more, the bishop of Rome marginalized himself from the final events of the Constantinian dynasty.

After Constantine: Rome in the Later Fourth Century

The regime of Constantine was supported by a newly influential senatorial order composed of established aristocratic senatorial families alongside new men from Italy or the provinces. Emperors after Constantine continued to rely on senators to administer the state and turned to them to support their rule as holders of high office. Unlike the later third century, when the military so dominated that civic elites were largely removed from positions of influence, the fourth century saw a rise in the real political power and prestige of senators

---

[227] Eus. *VC* 4.69.2.

[228] Van Dam 2007, p. 59 and note 31. For the coins, see Bruun 1954, pp. 19–31; and Bonamente 2011, p. 344, note 19.

[229] Phil. *HE* 2.17.   [230] Eus. *VC* 4.60.

[231] For this reasonable view, see O'Dahl 2013, pp. 199–203.

and especially of senatorial aristocrats from Rome and Italy, who retained their predominance in society into the late fourth century.

The composition of the senatorial order did, however, change. The number of men of senatorial rank reached an unprecedented number – an estimated three thousand men in the western Roman Empire by the end of the fourth century.[232] In this greatly increased pool of talented men, competition for honor – made manifest by the holding of office – led to the evolution of new status distinctions. By the middle of the fourth century, ordinary senators, the "most outstanding" (*clarissimi*) were being distinguished from those at the upper rungs of senatorial rank – that is, those of "admirable" (*spectabilis*) and then ultimately "illustrious" (*illustris*) standing.[233] By the time of the emperors Valentinian I and Valens (364–78), these distinctions had been formalized in laws that associated these titles with the order of precedence of all officeholders of senatorial rank, including those in civic and imperial service as well as those who served in the military.[234]

The ordering of these honors demonstrates the concern that emperors and senators had to be recognized with the correct degree of senatorial distinction. The highest honor remained the ordinary consulship, an office without any duties that bestowed the title of *illustris* on those who attained it. Former consuls took precedence over all other senators as well.[235] After them came senators with *patrician* status, an honorific senatorial distinction revived by Constantine but, again, one with no duties.[236] Below them but still at the *illustris* rank were the praetorian or urban prefectures and the generals, either the commanders in chief of both infantry and cavalry (*magister utriusque militae*) or the generals who were in command of infantry or cavalry (*magister militum* or *magister equitum*). *Illustris* was also the title for the principal ministers serving the emperor at court, including those who were responsible for financial matters (*comites rei privatae* or *comites sacrarum largitionum*). After them were the proconsuls and vicars, now

---

[232] Heather 1998, pp. 184–210, although some of the men in the imperial bureaucracy attained senatorial rank only upon retirement.

[233] Dillon 2015, pp. 56–63 for detailed discussion of this process and the laws that responded to these struggles. See especially *C.Th.* 6.5.2, under Valentinian, to punish those who strove to claim rank higher than what they deserved.

[234] For the gradual development of these grades, see Salzman 2002, pp. 40–43; Garbarino 1988, pp. 65–66; Dillon 2015, pp. 53–63.

[235] *C. Th.* 6.6.1 stresses the "evident authority" (*evidenti auctoritate*) of the tradition that gave the consul precedence.

[236] On Constantine's revival of the title of *patricius* or patrician, see Moser 2018, pp. 80–81; *C. Th.* 6.6.1 and Dillon 2015, p. 60.

generally possessing "admirable" (*spectabilis*) rank, with whom were equated some military officers, the "counts of the soldiers" and "dukes" (*comites rei militaris* and *duces*). At the bottom senatorial rank of "most outstanding" (*clarissimi*) were the consulars of provinces or lower-level military officers such as tribunes.[237]

Senatorial rank mattered not just for honorific purposes; one's rank also determined legal and economic privileges. For instance, only the highest ranked senators, the *illustres*, had exemption from service in their local town assemblies. Such privileges made real how the most prestigious senators, the *illustres*, accrued the greatest benefits from their rank. In this way, emperors encouraged senators by birth to hold high office. At the same time, laws from the 380s on placed restrictions on the lower ranks of senators, the *clarissimi* and *spectabiles*, that made it increasingly difficult financially for them to enter the Senate in Rome or Constantinople.[238]

Tensions between men new to senatorial status and men from established aristocratic families did at times emerge, but the senatorial aristocracy of Rome and Italy had long been in the habit of absorbing talented newcomers. This situation was also the case in the later fourth century. Thus, despite changes in status distinctions, Rome-based senatorial aristocrats maintained the economic and political resources that enabled them to retain their predominance in late Roman society and to make ties with elites across the empire. In fact, the later fourth century was a time of great prosperity for senatorial aristocrats. Senators like Symmachus, who cultivated classical values that allowed for a life of leisure to read, write, and visit with friends and family, punctuated by periods of service to the state, represented an idealized, albeit viable, civic senatorial tradition that was the goal of many senatorial aristocrats. He, like his peers, was easily able to meet the financial demands and the fiscal residency requirement of life in the city of Rome.[239]

At the same time, the later fourth century saw the growing influence of the military and of imperial officials and courtiers on civic society. These new senators included not only Romans of provincial background but also Goths, Huns, Sueves, Vandals, and other barbarians who had fought for the Romans or were engaged with the imperial court. By virtue of his military office, for instance, the general Fravitta (*magister militum*, 400) held the highest

---

[237] *C. Th.* esp. 6.5.2, 384; 6.6.1, 382, 6.7.1, 372, and 6.7.2, 380; for an overview, Jones 1964, p. 143.

[238] See Jones 1964, pp. 741–43. See laws beginning with *C.Th.* 12.1.111, 386 CE; Garbarino 1988, pp. 270–73; and La Rocca and Oppedisano 2016, pp. 24–30.

[239] See Salzman and Roberts 2015, pp. xliv–liii. For residency requirements and senatorial census, see La Rocca and Oppedisano 2016, pp. 30–32 and pp. 185–86: Jones 1964, pp. 536–37.

senatorial rank, *illustris*, with the relevant legal and fiscal privileges.[240] Indeed, Fravitta is an interesting example of how some military commanders adapted to Roman society. The historian Zosimus described Fravitta as "by birth a barbarian, but otherwise a Greek, not only in habits, but also in character and religion."[241] Zosimus was singling this general out for his adherence to paganism in the year 400. As a pagan himself, Zosimus emphasized that there were still pagans, not just in the military but also in society at large. Nonetheless, it had become increasingly difficult for men at the highest levels of senatorial society, inside or outside the military, to be pagan.

The most obvious change in late Roman society was the spread of Christianity through all levels of society. By the late fourth century, Christians were a majority of the population of senators and of the senatorial aristocracy of Rome.[242] But the senators – like the population at large – were not uniform in their adherence to one Christian theological formulation. Many – notably the barbarians – the name Romans used for non-Romans, including Germanic peoples – were adherents of a version of Christianity that other Christians and modern scholars today label as Arianism. Simply put, Arians were Christians who viewed Christ, the son of God, as being a later creation with a similar essence, that is as *homoiousios*. Some Arians who believed this nonetheless refused the term *homoiousios* as unbiblical and used the word *homoios*, and hence were called *homoians*. Others believed God and Christ was of different substances, and hence were called *anomoians*. The Council of Nicaea, convened by Constantine in 325, had aimed for theological unity and promulgated a formulation of Christianity, what is today called the Nicene Creed, that asserted that God the father and Christ the son were of the same substance, *homoousios*. The Nicene formulation did not succeed in ending the controversy. Constantine himself reversed his views toward the end of his life, and Church councils and emperors continued to condemn Arianism over the course of the fourth century.[243] Although Nicene Christianity was dominant in the West, barbarians who were *homoians* were legally tolerated, as argued cogently by Ralph Mathisen.[244] Thus, the spread of Christianity – with its various sects – mitigated social differences and allowed for the accommodation of barbarians and others into Roman society at all levels

---

[240] For the career of Fravitta, see *PLRE* 1, pp. 372–73.   [241] Zos. 5.20.   [242] See note 2 above.

[243] For the changing positions of emperors on Arianism over the course of the fourth and fifth centuries, see Drake 2012, pp. 123–30.

[244] For Roman legal tolerance, see Mathisen 2014, p. 146.

From the perspective of an inhabitant of the city of Rome, the late fourth century was a good time to enjoy the benefits of Roman rule. The changes in the senatorial order that unfolded over the course of the fourth century encouraged senatorial aristocrats to manifest their status and prestige in the city of Rome, spending their money and that of the state on games and circuses along with donating to their preferred religious groups as they traditionally had. No external forces threatened the walls of Rome. The major upheavals created by civil war in Italy did not damage the city's infrastructure or threaten its survival. The trade networks and food supply (*annona*), secured by a functioning state bureaucracy, protected by an expanded military presence, and overseen by senatorial administrators, worked well enough. As noted earlier, the grain from Egypt that was diverted from Rome to Constantinople was more than made up by Roman land-owners in Italy and North Africa who supplied Rome's population.

The increasing status of Constantinople in the late fourth century did not threaten Rome and western senatorial aristocratic society, nor did it provide an alternative model for the inhabitants of Rome to follow. Constantinople, with an estimated population of perhaps half a million people and with a Senate similarly made up of wealthy men, was quite different from Rome, being far more dependent on and defined by its resident emperor and imperial court. The senatorial and ecclesiastical leadership of that city had a different status and mode of interaction than Rome did. Indeed, an eastern bishop writing at the end of the fourth century boastfully claimed, "Prefects and city magistrates do not enjoy such honor as the magistrate of the church, for if he enters the palace, who ranks the highest, or among the matrons, or among the houses of the great? No one is honored before him."[245] But in Rome, where the emperor did not permanently reside and where senatorial aristocrats retained their traditions of social and political predominance, the bishop could not exercise such influence without facing lay competition for control over the religious life of the city.

Though the fourth century saw the rising status of the bishop and clergy in Rome, more recent scholarship has rightly emphasized not only the persist-ence of pagan senatorial traditions but also the ways in which these senatorial patronage traditions competed with the influence of the bishops of Rome in society.[246] Even the charismatic Bishop of Rome, Damasus (366–82), who left an impressive mark on the city's Christian martyria through his classicizing

---

[245] John Chrys. *In acta apost.* 3.5 (*PG* 60.40).
[246] Machado 2019, p. 30; Krautheimer 1980, pp. 59–87; Denzey Lewis 2020, pp. 182–86 on funerary feasts and almsgiving by aristocrats.

inscriptions, had far less impact on Rome's religious life than scholars had previously thought, as Nicola Denzey Lewis has well argued.[247] In Rome in the later fourth century, where the emperor did not permanently reside and where senatorial aristocrats retained their social and political leadership of civic life, which extended to the religious life of their families and dependents, the clergy faced a society that claimed the right to determine their own patterns of worship. So, as Kimberly Bowes has shown, we also find aristocratic families worshipping in private chapels in their homes or villas, removed from the oversight of the bishops.[248]

When the Emperor Theodosius died in 395, leaving behind two sons, Honorius in the West and Arcadius in the East, the ideal of two imperial courts working in harmony and coordinating their efforts to secure the borders was regarded as an effective solution to the challenges of controlling the Roman Empire. One law and one religion – Christianity – embraced by one imperial family epitomized the ideal, even if in reality tensions and conflicts arose between the two imperial courts and the senatorial, military, and imperial elites who revolved around them. Few could have predicted the crises of the early fifth century. The incursion of Germanic forces across the Rhine frontier in 405 and 406 was a rude awakening. These attacks in the early fifth century presented challenges that forced senators and bishops to renegotiate their relations with each other, with the emperor, and with Rome's generals. In the fifth-century crises that overtook the city, the resilience of senatorial aristocrats and the Senate in recovering Rome opened up new avenues for ensuring their own power and prestige even at the expense of the imperial state.

---

[247] Denzey Lewis 2020, pp. 71–125. Even the famous quip by the Roman senator Praetextatus, "Make me bishop of the city of Rome and I will straightaway be a Christian," has been contextualized by scholars who underscore the sarcasm in this comment, recorded by Jer., *c. Joh. Hieros.* 8: *facite me Romanae Urbis episcopum et ero protinus Christianus.* On the relative weakness of the bishops of Rome, see too Sessa 2012, pp. 28–29; Demacopoulos 2013, pp. 35–38; and my discussion in Chapter 3.

[248] Bowes 2008, pp. 75–102. See too Hunter 2017, pp. 505–9.

3

Responses to the Sack of Rome in 410

My voice sticks in my throat: and, as I dictate, sobs choke my utterance. The city that captured the whole world is captured.

—Jerome, *Letter* 127, 412 CE[1]

Although the memory of the event is still fresh, anyone who saw the numbers of the Romans themselves and listened to their talk would think that nothing had happened, as they themselves admit, unless perhaps he were to notice some charred ruins still remaining.

–Orosius, *History Against the Pagans*, 417 CE[2]

After three years of intermittent sieges and failed negotiations, someone opened the Salarian Gate of Rome to the Gothic general Alaric on August 24, 410. Alaric, infuriated by his failed negotiations with the western emperor Honorius, allowed his Gothic and Germanic soldiers to plunder at will. They set on fire parts of the city, including the Gardens of Sallustius, a lavish green park between the Quirinal and Pincian Hills.[3] (See Map 1 at the beginning of the book.) The Goths targeted wealthy private homes as well as churches and public buildings in search of portable wealth. Slaves and nobles alike were seized, the former to provide labor, the latter for ransom. After terrorizing the inhabitants from August 24 to August 27, 410, the Goths departed for southern Italy to try to pass by sea to North Africa.[4] News of these events reverberated around the Mediterranean. Jerome, nestled in his monastery in

---

[1] Jer. *Ep.* 127: *Haeret vox, et singultus intercipiunt verba dictantis. Capitur urbs, quae totum cepit orbem.* On the exaggeration in Jerome's statements about 410, see Salzman 2009, pp. 175–92.

[2] Oros. *Hist.* 7.40.2: *Cuius rei quamvis recens memoria sit, tamen si quis ipsius populi Romani et multitudinem videat et vocem audiat, nihil factum, sicut etiam ipsi fatentur, arbitrabitur, nisi aliquantis adhuc existentibus ex incendio ruinis forte doceatur.*

[3] Procop. *Wars* 3.2.24. For the opening of the gate by treachery or by a woman, see note 70 below.

[4] See notes 77–78 below. The year 2010 saw a host of books and articles on this event. For the impact on the city of Rome, see articles in Lipps, Machado and von Rummel (edds.) 2013.

96

far-off Bethlehem, bemoaned the "fall" of Rome as the end of the world, as the epigraph to this chapter underscores. From his retreat in Palestine, the ascetic Pelagius saw this as the apocalypse and blamed it on the failure of "the order of the nobles."[5]

But by 417, other Romans, like Orosius and Olympiodorus, would write that the city had fully recovered and that apart from a few charred remains, it was as if the sack had never happened.[6] However, neither perspective captures the reality of life in Rome after 410. As I will demonstrate, the responses of Roman elites to 410 did bring about the recovery and resurgence of the city. Nonetheless, the trauma of 410 had long-lasting effects not only on the city and its inhabitants, but also on the political trajectory of Italy and the West.

To appreciate the complex landscape that Roman elites faced in the decade after 410, I begin with a brief outline of what led to the city's fall. The prolonged negotiations that had preceded that event and the elevation of a senator to be emperor changed the balance of power among Roman senators, imperial officials, the military, and the bishops. The material, social, and political interventions undertaken by these men and women brought about a new equilibrium. Regardless of how one sees the increasing political power claimed by senatorial aristocrats, their efforts – at times in competition with one another and at other times working together with generals and the imperial court – were key to the resurgence of the city. In contrast, the influence of Rome's bishop on the restoration of the city was diminished in the post-410 decade and only recovered slowly, most notably with the coming of the emperor Valentinian III and his family to the city in the 440s. But by the 420s, due to the contestation for influence among elites and the successful settling of the Goths in Gaul and Spain, the senators of Rome could boast of living in the *caput mundi* (the head of the world), still the largest city in the western Roman Empire.

The Failure of Honorius and the Imperial Administration, 408–10

Most historians – modern and ancient – blame the western emperor Honorius and the intrigues of the imperial courtiers for the failed negotiations that led to

---

[5] Pelagius, *Ep. ad Demet.* 30.1: *Recens factum est, et quod ipsa audisti, cum ad stridulae buccinae sonum, Gothorumque clamorem, lugubri oppressa metu domina orbis Roma contremuit. Ubi tunc nobilitatis ordo? Ubi certi et distincti illius dignitatis gradus?* ("It [the apocalypse] came to pass recently, as you yourself heard, when to the shrill sound of the war-trumpet and the shouts of the Goths Rome, the mistress of the world, crushed with dismal fear, shuddered. Where was the order of nobles then? Where were the occupiers of those fixed, distinct grades of their hierarchy?") Trans. by Rees 1998, p. 69.

[6] Oros. *Hist.* 7.40.2 in the epigraph to this chapter; Olymp. *Frag.* 25, ed. Blockley 1983, p. 188.

Alaric's sack of Rome in 410. The sixth-century Greek writer Procopius brilliantly captured the critique. He described how, when the information about the final fall of Rome was relayed to Honorius by his eunuch cook, the emperor was upset only because he thought his pet cock, named Rome, had died; even when the cook corrected him, the emperor expressed merely relief that his cock was still alive. Honorius's stupidity (*amathes*), his complete lack of concern for his citizens, along with his foolish reliance on his courtiers convey how unfit for rule Honorius was.[7]

This image reflected a literary tradition hostile to this emperor, but the reality of the situation in Italy and the western Mediterranean was more complex. It cannot be explained simply due to the foolishness or detachment of the emperor. In fact, Honorius and his courtiers had been in negotiations with Alaric, a Gothic general, for at least three years prior to the sack, but the emperor had not been able to set a consistent policy in response to his demands. Alaric claimed payment for himself and his followers – fighters, refugees, women, and children. He had fought for the Romans since 395. The breaking of the Rhine frontier in 405–6 by large bands of Germanic troops and an uprising in Britain and Gaul by the usurper Constantine III in 407 had made his service critical.[8] Most recently, Alaric had fought in Illyricum in 406 upon orders from Honorius. But the western emperor changed course and no longer needed Alaric's services there.[9] Honorius's commander in chief, the powerful general Stilicho, had persuaded Alaric to move to Gaul to fight for Honorius to suppress the usurper Constantine III.[10] Yet Honorius balked at what was represented as Alaric's changing and excessive demands for payment.

As negotiations with Alaric continued, Roman senatorial aristocrats and the Senate, as a decision-making body, were involved in what was, as Matthews well observed, "a dramatic extension in the range of its political experiences."[11] At times, the Senate negotiated with the emperor, with

---

[7] Procop. *Wars* 3.2.25–26: "So great, they say, was the the stupidity of this emperor." Trans. here and throughout by Kaldellis 2014, p. 147. This scene is depicted by the famous Waterhouse painting of Honorius; see the discussion by Dunn 2010, pp. 243–62.

[8] For the crossing of the Rhine frontier by Sueves, Vandals, Alans, Burgundians, and their allies as a key break of the Roman defenses, see especially Heather 2006, pp. 192–211. For the uprising in Britain that led to the rise of the general Constantine, who gained control of Gaul early in 407; Zos. 5.27.2, 31.4, 6.3–4.

[9] Zos. 5.26.2 reports Stilicho's plans to seize control of the provinces of eastern Illyricum for the western government of Honorius. See Soz. 9.4.3 for Honorius's appointment of Iovius as prefect of Illyricum. For Honorius's change of mind, see Zos. 5. 29.7–8.

[10] See Stilicho, *PLRE* 1, pp. 853–58. For Stilicho's persuasion, see Doyle 2019, pp. 136–37.

[11] Matthews 1990, p. 302.

Stilicho, and with Alaric independently. It came together to debate foreign affairs, financial policy, and diplomatic missions. This activity brought real responsibility and power, as well as danger to senators and the city.[12] This emerged clearly early in 408, when Alaric moved to Noricum from Epirus on the way to Gaul and, stopping just north of the Alpine passes to Italy, threatened to attack if he was not paid for his recent services to Honorius.[13] The demand for gold was conveyed to Honorius and the Senate by the general Stilicho, commander in chief of the western army who had negotiated with Alaric for Honorius. Stilicho, the son of a Vandal father and a Roman mother, was quite familiar with the late Roman senatorial aristocracy for he had been the beneficiary of Rome's willingness to incorporate Germans into the highest levels of society. Stilicho had married a Roman aristocratic woman, Serena, cousin of Honorius. Their eldest daughter, Maria, had married Honorius in 398, and after Maria's death in 407 or 408, their second daughter, Thermantia, also wed Honorius in 408.[14]

The debate about the Roman response to Alaric's demands that took place in a Senate meeting held at the imperial palace in Rome was a long and heated one, and accounts of it underscore the decisive role of getting the senators to support Stilicho's arrangements. Although the first vote of the Senate favored war and no recompense to Alaric, Stilicho persuaded the senators that the payment was justified. A majority of the senators reversed course and provided some 4,000 pounds of gold from their own funds to pay the price demanded for peace.[15] This was not, after all, an overwhelming sum since a wealthy senator had a yearly income of about 4,000 pounds of gold.[16] Not all senators were happy with this resolution. The aristocrat Lampadius famously decried this action: "This is not a peace but a promise of slavery."[17] Stilicho's enemies later used this intervention to convince Honorius that the general wanted Rome's wealth to incite barbarians against the empire.[18] Indeed, the wealth of the senators at this juncture is striking, especially in contrast to the financial

---

[12] See Matthews 1990, pp. 296–305. But senatorial political influence can only partially be attributed to the presence of the court in northern Italy, a point that Matthews, p. 303, emphasized.

[13] Zos. 5.29.4–8. See too Matthews 1990, p. 276.

[14] For these women, see Serena I, *PLRE* 1, p. 824; Maria 3, *PLRE* 2, p. 720; Aelia Materna Thermanita, *PLRE* 2, pp. 408–9. For fuller discussion of the dynastic implications, see Doyle 2019, pp. 103–40.

[15] Zos. 5.29.9, dating likely to early 408; and Olymp. *Frag.* 7.2, ed Blockley 1983, pp. 158–59.

[16] Olymp. *Frag.* 41.2, ed. Blockley 1983, pp. 204–5.

[17] Zos. 5.29.5, using the Latin from Cicero. Lizzi Testa (unpublished manuscript), identifies this Lampadius not with Postumius Lampadius, who was *PPO* under Attalus, but with the Lampadius who was brother of Fl. Mallius Theodorus, Lampadius 2, *PLRE* 2, p. 655, following Paschoud 2011, p. 221. If so, then his was a powerful opposing voice.

[18] Oros. 7.38; Jer. *Ep.* 123.16.

constraints allegedly faced by Honorius. Soon after this vote, Stilicho convinced Honorius not to travel to Constantinople for the funeral of his brother, the eastern emperor Arcadius, arguing in part, that the trip was too costly.[19]

Tensions between emperor and general escalated when Honorius left Rome for the relative safety of Pavia, near Ravenna, in May 408.[20] For his part, Stilicho was said to be unhappy with the emperor's presence near the army, allegedly concerned that the Roman soldiers would rebel against his leadership.[21] Yet Ravenna was a more secure place to reside, and Honorius was allegedly swayed by this argument by his mother-in-law, Stilicho's wife, Serena.[22] Certainly, the emperor's departure and continued absence from Rome opened new opportunities for misunderstanding between him and the senators, even as it encouraged their independent political action. It is worth underscoring here that the emperor's sojourn in Ravenna was not intended to be permanent. After 402, Ravenna was another *sedes imperii* – seat of empire – with the ability to strike coins, but Rome was still viewed as the *caput mundi* (head of the world), which is why I follow Andrew Gillett and others who argue that Honorius resided there for long intervals from 401 or 402 to 408.[23]

With Stilicho alive and in control of the military In Italy, Honorius must have felt that the city of Rome was relatively safe. Between 401 and 403, Honorius had substantially restored and extended the wall that Aurelian had built.[24] (See Map 1.) Rome's wall did, in fact, withstand sieges twice in 409. But Honorius's departure, with his body guard, reduced the number of active troops in the city. And the city only had a limited number of armed defenders. After 312, Constantine had eliminated the resident imperial horse guard (*equites singulares*), and the urban cohorts disappeared over the course of the fourth century, leaving the urban prefect only a limited police force of lightly armed men under his control.[25] The small number of experienced soldiers in the city was known to Alaric, who, when told that the citizens were trained and ready to fight, mockingly dismissed them by saying that thicker grass was easier to mow than thinner.[26]

---

[19] Zos. 5. 31. On the wealth of Roman elites in their houses, see Olymp. *Frag.* 41, Blockley 1983, pp. 204–6.

[20] Gillett 2001, pp. 140–41 for the movements of Honorius.   [21] Zos. 5.30; 5.32.2–7.

[22] Zos. 5.30.2.

[23] Deliyannis 2010, pp. 49–51; Gillett 2001, pp. 140–41. However, Doyle 2019, p. 130 argues the view that Honorius had transferred his court to Ravenna in 402 as a result of Alaric's siege of Milan.

[24] Dey 2011, pp. 32–47.

[25] Chastagnol 1960, pp. 254–95. On Constantine's disbanding of the *equites singulares*, see Chapter 2, note 35.

[26] Zos. 5.40.3.

The fall of Stilicho in August 408 changed everything. His death led to a significant weakening of the state and its defense. Stilicho, powerful as he was, had created enemies at court. Indeed, our sources blame Honorius for being manipulated by his courtiers, especially the head of the imperial bureau of secretaries, the eunuch, Olympius.[27] Olympius spread the rumor that Stilicho intended to place his own son, Eucherius, on the eastern throne in place of the son of Honorius's deceased brother, the eastern emperor Arcadius. This led to a mutiny of the soldiers at Ticinum.[28] In the purge that followed, Stilicho was executed at Honorius's command, as were many of the Gothic soldiers who had supported him. Those who could escape fled to Alaric's army.[29] At this juncture, in autumn of 408, the Senate followed Honorius's lead and voted to put Stilicho's widow, Serena, to death. She, too, was charged with colluding with her husband and their son, Eucherius, who was also hunted down and killed.[30]

The demise of Stilicho unleashed even greater political intrigue at the court in Ravenna, and the upheavals that followed hampered any efforts to protect Rome from attack. Honorius, who must have been aware of and had some hand in Stilicho's execution, now faced factions jockeying for power. The eunuch Olympius who had engineered Stilicho's fall, now in charge of the imperial bureaucracy as *magister officiorum*, soon fell from power, attacked by other eunuchs as being disloyal.[31] By the end of February or March 409, his replacement, the praetorian prefect Jovius, who had started advocating for a policy of conciliation with Alaric, also was removed from office for being "a friend and client of Alaric."[32] The eunuch Olympius was recalled from exile only to be removed again from office and finally murdered, ironically, for his part in the murder of Stilicho.[33]

In these uncertain times, with constant political turnover in Ravenna, the defense of Rome and a negotiated settlement with Alaric was left increasingly to the Senate. Some inhabitants, fearing attack, fled Rome.[34] But many stayed

---

[27] Zos. 5.34.1–5. Olympius was *magister scriniorum* then for his career, see Olympius 2, *PLRE* 2, pp. 801–2.

[28] Zos. 5.32.1–4.   [29] Zos. 5.34–35.

[30] Zos. 5.38.1–4. Paschoud 2011, pp. 257–66 alleges that the Senate was angry at Serena's role in the sale of the property of the senatorial ascetic couple Melania the Younger and Eucherius. For the murder of Eucherius, see Zos. 5.35.3.

[31] Zos. 5.46.1; Olymp. *Frag.* 8.2 ed. Blockley 1983, pp. 162–63. Lizzi Testa dates this to 409; see Lizzi Testa 2012, 1–32.

[32] For a full discussion of the twists and turns of these negotiations, see Matthews 1990, pp. 284–306; quote on p. 293; and Lizzi Testa (unpublished manuscript). For Jovius's appointment, see *C. Th.* 2, 8, 25 (April 409). For Jovius's connection with Alaric, see Zos. 5.48.2 and Matthews 1990, p. 293, note 4.

[33] Zos. 5.46.1; Olymp. *Frag.* 8.2, ed. Blockley 1983, pp. 162–63.

[34] Gerontius, *Life of Melania the Younger*, 19–20 = *Vie de Sainte Mélanie*, SC 90, ed. Gorce, 1962.

behind, trusting in the city's military and civic leadership to protect them. The Senate sent several embassies to Honorius and to Alaric to press for a settlement.[35] According to Zosimus, Alaric wanted only a "moderate" sum of money, an exchange of hostages, and the concession of land in Pannonia for his people to inhabit.[36] Encouraged by additional Hunnic and Gothic soldiers, and having summoned his brother-in-law, Athaulf, from Pannonia, Alaric marched through northern Italy to the walls of Rome unopposed. This first siege of the city in 408–9 brought starvation and suffering for the inhabitants.[37] The Senate took action on its own. It sent an embassy to negotiate with Alaric, headed by a prestigious senator, the former urban prefect Basilius, and a certain tribune, a friend of Alaric named Ioannes.[38] At the same time, the then-urban prefect and senator Pompeianus turned to traditional religion to try to restore civic confidence; pagan priests from Etruria, who happened to be in Rome, offered to perform public rites on behalf of the city.[39] According to the Greek historian Zosimus, the bishop of Rome, Innocent I, would have allowed the rite if it was performed in private. The priests, however, refused this stipulation, so, of course, when the city fell, this vignette provided further justification for the sack among pagans.[40] Lizzi Testa, for one, takes this episode as evidence for how great were the religious and social tensions that the siege unearthed.[41]

But it is worth again emphasizing the role that the Senate took at this juncture. In response to his demands, the Senate sent a second embassy to Alaric, who now was demanding 5,000 pounds of gold, 30,000 pounds of silver, and large quantities of spices and clothing. The Senate then voted to approve this amount and to raise this money based on a census of their own property undertaken by Palladius, the chief financial officer.[42] Although Palladius's failure to collect the full amount was attributed to greed or sudden poverty by Zosimus, the Senate determined to raise the money by despoiling the statues of the pagan gods, an act that later pagan writers saw as contributing to the fall of the city.[43]

The payment to Alaric gave the Romans a brief respite to get food from the port city nearby. Now more citizens fled the city and Gothic slaves bolted to join Alaric's forces, swelling their number, allegedly, to more than 40,000.[44] After this payment, the Senate again tried to get the Emperor Honorius to negotiate with Alaric. Indeed, throughout this period, we hear of several

---

[35] Zos. 5.36. [36] Zos. 5.36.
[37] Zos. 5.39–40. For Basilius, urban prefect in 395, see *PLRE* 1, Basilius 3, p. 149. [38] Zos. 5.40.
[39] Zos. 5.41.1. For another source that verifies this incident, see Soz. 9.6.1–7.
[40] Salzman 2015, pp. 346–59. [41] Lizzi Testa 2013, 81–112.
[42] Zos. 5.41.4–5. See Palladius 19, *PLRE* 2, pp. 822–24. [43] Zos. 5.41.4–6. [44] Zos. 5.42.2–3.

embassies undertaken by the Senate to resolve the standoff.[45] And although Honorius was supposed to finally ratify an agreement to release Gothic hostages, he and his courtiers kept delaying their approval. Zosimus reports another senatorial embassy to Ravenna, one including the senators Priscus Attalus, Caecilianus, and Maximianus, which again tried to convince the imperial court to accept their prearranged settlement.[46] The senators even took with them the bishop of Rome, Innocent I, trying to reinforce their position by appealing to Honorius's piety.[47] Still, Honorius would not act, caught up in shifting internal court politics. But in an attempt to assuage the worsening finances of the senators, Honorius made Priscus Attalus the new chief financial officer (*comes sacrarum largitionum*), and then soon after, he appointed him as urban prefect of Rome.[48]

The career of Priscus Attalus shows the political possibilities for a Roman senator – and for the Senate – in the polyglot capital. Attalus was regarded as one of the leading members in the Senate, although his father had likely come from Antioch and had established himself in Rome in the late fourth century, rising to the office of urban prefect in 371–72 under the emperor Valentinian I. By the turn of the fifth century, Priscus Attalus was well positioned to lead, inheriting status along with property in Sardinia and Rome as well as in the East.[49] As early as 398, he had represented the Senate on an embassy to Honorius that had successfully argued that senators not provide recruits to the army.[50] His status, education, and experience made him a natural choice to represent the Senate on embassies in 409 and gave him a key role in the events that followed.[51]

The situation in the city turned desperate in the winter of 409 when Alaric seized the city's port, Portus, and its granaries. Faced with starvation and potential food riots, the Senate accepted all of Alaric's demands. In a direct challenge to Honorius, the Senate, with the support of Alaric, recognized as emperor Priscus Attalus, one of their own.[52] According to Philostorgius, the

---

[45] Zos. 5.40; 5.41.4; 5.42; and 5.45.5.   [46] Zos. 5.42–44.   [47] Zos. 5.45.5.

[48] Zos. 5.44; urban prefect under Honorius in 409, Zos. 5.46.1; Philost. *HE* 12.3; Soz. *HE* 9.8.1. He was prefect by March, after the death of Pompeianus; see Priscus Attalus 2, *PLRE* 2, pp. 180–81.

[49] Matthews 1990, pp. 42, 303, note 2. His father is most likely Publius Ampelius, Ampelius 3, *PLRE* 1, pp. 56–57. Attalus corresponded with Symmachus; see note 50 below and Cecconi 2013, pp. 141–56.

[50] Symm. *Ep.* 6.58, 6.62, 7.54, 113, 114 for the 398 embassy. Cecconi 2013, pp. 143–44 doubts Attalus's eastern origins, but Philostorgius *HE* 12.3 asserts this, and most scholars agree. His career underscores the possibilities for upward mobility in Rome for provincials.

[51] See Zos. 5.44.1 and note 45 above for the embassy in 409. For Attalus's interest in literature, see Symm. *Ep.* 7.18. For his studies with Himerius, see Him. *Or.* 29.

[52] Zosimus 6.7.1–2

Romans – that is, the Senate and citizens – chose Attalus as emperor, and Attalus then appointed Alaric general, the post that he had sought from Honorius.[53] Attalus, upon his accession, delivered an oration promising to restore the Senate to its "ancient honor."[54] He also minted coins with a legend that harkened back to Roman traditions – namely, "Invicta Roma Aeterna."[55] The legend emphasized Rome as the seat of power. His appeal to tradition likely included an openness to paganism; that attitude would explain why Priscus was called a pagan by later writers, although he subsequently was baptized by an Arian bishop, an event that may explain Sozomen's remark that pagans and Arians were upset by his death.[56]

A strand of modern scholarship influenced by hostile ancient writers, sees Priscus Attalus as no more than a "puppet emperor" of Alaric, intended to challenge the authority of the emperor Honorius.[57] But this interpretation does not hold up on closer inspection, as Giovanni Cecconi has demonstrated.[58] Rather, the events show that Attalus was a powerful senator in his own right. Frustrated by a weak and ineffective imperial court, he took the opportunity offered by Alaric to take the throne – with the support of a number of senators. Indeed, for two years, Attalus and the Senate had tried to mediate a compromise between Honorius and Attalus.[59] Attalus's political experience and prestige, along with his ambition, led to his elevation, but he was not the only senator who saw rebellion as the best means to protect senatorial interests.

The role of the Senate is often overlooked in the events leading up to 410, especially by modern historians who assume this institution was no more than a relic.[60] But throughout these years, the Senate had been deeply involved in the political developments of the day. For this and other reasons, Attalus promised to revive senatorial traditions. He also turned to fellow senators to hold office under his regime. The eminent senators Lampadius and Marcianus accepted positions as praetorian prefect of Italy and urban

[53] Philost. *HE* 12.3.4; Cecconi 2013, p. 150. Cecconi follows the sequence of events in Philost. *HE* 12.3.4, though this sequence is reversed in Zos. 6.6.3; 7.1.1 and Soz. *HE* 9.8.1. Sozomen has Alaric compel Roman acceptance of Attalus as emperor. Alaric wanted to be *magister militum*; see Socr. *HE* 9.7.1–2; Zos. 5.48.1–3.

[54] Zos. 6.7.3; Soz. *HE* 9.8.2.   [55] *RIC* X, Priscus Attalus, 1403–08; 1411–12.

[56] For Priscus Attalus as a pagan, see Philost. 12.3.4. For his baptism by the Gothic bishop Sigishar, see Soz. *HE* 9.9.1.

[57] For the view that Alaric forced the Senate to vote on Attalus, see Soz. *HE* 9.81.1 and Zos. 6.6.3; 7.1.1. For this as a "puppet government," see for example Mathews 1990, p. 295.

[58] Cecconi 2013, pp. 141–56.   [59] Zos. 5.44.1.

[60] On this point, I agree with Lizzi Testa (unpublished manuscript), who discusses the historiographic tradition. Even Cecconi 2013, p. 148, who provides a pathbreaking assessment of Priscus Attalus, still fails to give enough credit to the Senate as an institution with relevance and political influence.

prefect of Rome, respectively.[61] Another senator, Tertullus, accepted the honor of the consulship from the emperor Attalus.[62] Certainly, some senators did not join the new regime. Zosimus relates that the Anicii, one of the most powerful of the established Roman families, were resentful of the "general good fortune" of Rome under Alaric's control.[63] Still, enough of the senators approved of their new emperor and this new government to confirm Attalus as emperor and Alaric as his new general.

Priscus Attalus recognized that the survival of his regime and of Rome depended on maintaining the city's grain supply from Africa. To do that, he would have to remove Africa from Honorius's control. Attalus appointed a Roman general, Constans, to undertake the assault, even though Alaric had urged employing a Gothic general, Druma, as commander instead.[64] Attalus's independence as demonstrated by his appointment of a Roman general lends further support for viewing him not as a mere "puppet" of the Gothic general. He also helped Alaric in the negotiations with Honorius, likely seeking to persuade Honorius to repeat his own example since, earlier in 409, Honorius had recognized another rival usurper in Gaul, Constantine III.[65] According to Zosimus, a fearful Honorius was willing to accept this arrangement, and only the arrival of reinforcements from the eastern court changed his mind about making this concession.[66]

The failure of Constans, Attalus's general, to take Africa and ongoing resistance on the part of Attalus and the senators to sending a Gothic general to Africa changed Alaric's mind about his support for Attalus. Later in the year, Alaric forced Attalus to renounce his office and to return to private life, even as Alaric recommenced what were his final negotiations with Honorius.[67] The blame for the breakdown in this last set of talks varies, depending on the source. But there is a general consensus that the unexpected appearance of Alaric's enemy, the Goth Sarus, disrupted them.[68]

---

[61] Zos. 6.7.2; for Lampadius, see note 17 above. The identity of Marcianus is not certain. Matthews 1990, pp. 303–4, would identify him as Marcianus 14, *PLRE* 1, pp. 555–56, but this identification is questioned because it assumes a later date for the *Carmen Contra Paganos*, which is more likely dated to 384. On this, see Cameron 2011, p. 194. Matthews would see him as tied to the future senator Tarrutenius Maximilianus 3, *PLRE* 2, p. 741.

[62] Tertullus's consulship is mentioned by Zos. 6.7.4 and Oros. 7.42.8. See Tertullus 1, *PLRE* 2, p. 1059.

[63] Zos. 6.7.4.   [64] Zos. 6.7.5–6; Soz. *HE* 9.8.3.

[65] Olymp. *Frags.* 13–14, ed. Blockley 1983, pp. 170–75; Zos. 5.43.1–2 for Heraclian, and McEvoy 2013, p. 196, note 44. Zos. 6.8.1–2 indicates that Honorius was willing to accept this, but was deterred by the arrival of new forces from the East.

[66] Zos. 6.8.1–2.

[67] Zos. 6.12.3; Soz. *HE* 9.8.10; with discussion by Matthews 1990, p. 299; Cecconi 2013, pp. 144–45.

[68] Zos. 6.13; Soz. *HE* 9.9.3; and Philost. *HE* 12.3.

Honorius's failure to concede led Alaric, in anger and frustration at not receiving an agreement on even a modified request for land for his followers, to turn against Rome.[69]

For the third time, Alaric laid siege to the city, but this time someone opened a gate. Procopius attributed this betrayal either to a treacherous woman of the Anician family who had taken pity on the starving urban dwellers or, in an inventive, Homeric-inspired incident, to the treachery of some handsome young barbarians who had been taken into the city as a warranty of peace.[70] Regardless of the culprit, the city fell. Frustration at yet another set of failed negotiations had led Alaric to the walls of Rome again, but if the gate had not been opened, the city could have held out, as Honorius and his couriers had likely believed. It was certainly safer to blame the treachery of one individual or the "barbarians" for the fall of the city than to acknowledge the failed leadership of the emperor Honorius. In any case, on the evening of August 24, 410. Alaric's men entered unopposed, plundering the city for three days before leaving for greener pastures in southern Italy.[71]

If we look at the path of Alaric's men through the city, anger at Roman institutions is visible. His men targeted imperial buildings as well as the homes of senatorial aristocrats, which were also, obviously, rich sites to plunder. As noted earlier, after Alaric's entrance into the city by the Salarian Gate, the Goths set fire to the Gardens of Sallustius, which were now part of the imperial properties. (See Map 1.)[72] They then went into the center of the city, directing their attention to public buildings in the Forum, notably the Senate House. Churches were also plundered, although, according to Orosius, the Goths (who were Arian Christians) were under orders from Alaric to not burn the city and to respect Christian places of worship.[73] Orosius describes Alaric's men leading Christians to safety in St. Peter's, singing hymns together as they walked.[74] But the evidence, to be discussed concerning Rome's restoration, shows that Alaric's men did not entirely respect these commands. They also sacked private houses on the Caelian and Aventine Hills and in Trastevere before departing through the Appian Gate. (See Map 1.)

---

[69] Zos. 6.13; Soz. *HE* 9.9.2–5; and Philost. *HE* 12.3–4.

[70] Procop., *Wars* 3.2.14–27. The woman was Anicia Faltonia Proba, allegedly. For the Anicii as philobarbarian, see notes 106 and 107 below.

[71] For full discussion of the event, see the essays in Lipps, Machado, and von Rummel (eds.) 2013.

[72] Procop. *Wars* 3.2.24.   [73] Jord. *Get.* 30, 156.

[74] Oros. *Hist.* 7.39.3–14. And for a merciful barbarian treatment of another Nicene Christian woman, see Sozomon *HE* 9.10.

The terror of these days and some sense of the trauma of these events pervade our sources, which were, by and large, written by witnesses at a distance from the violence.[75] Yet Jerome vividly describes the beating with sticks and the whipping that the elderly virgin Marcella faced at the hands of Gothic invaders who broke into her home looking for gold and treasures. No wonder, then, that she died soon after.[76] The relief felt by Romans that the Goths had gone further south so soon is palpable in a later sermon of the bishop of Rome Leo I (discussed later in this chapter). Alaric had evidently planned to cross to Sicily but was prevented from doing so, likely by a dearth of ships.[77] Alaric's unexpected death at Cosenza (ancient Cosentia) in Bruttium led to the elevation of his successor and brother-in-law, Athaulf, who in early 411 led the Goths from southern Italy to Gaul. Their departure greatly eased Roman fears of a second attack.[78] However, by late 410 or early 411, a new general had emerged at the court of Honorius, Flavius Constantius, a Roman from the Danubian provinces. He would lead the restoration of political and military stability in the West.[79] He quieted the political intrigue at court and took up the fight against usurpers in Gaul – notably Constantine III in 411 – with the aid of the Goths under Athaulf, who were now paid for their services in 412.[80]

It is indicative of the degree of dissatisfaction with Honorius's rule and fear of punishment that some Romans who had aligned themselves with the Goths followed them from Italy to Gaul; Priscus Attalus left for Gaul, along with his son Ampelius.[81] Athaulf tried once more to negotiate a position for himself and food for his people before settling near Narbonne in late 413. Honorius, now faced with another revolt, this one by the general Heraclian who had attacked Ravenna in 413, would not agree to the demands of Athaulf at this date. Fortunately for Honorius, Constantius quickly defeated Heraclian in Italy.[82] But the Goths were not happy with their treatment.

---

[75] On the silence of writers in geographical proximity to Rome, see Bjornlie 2020, pp. 260–62.

[76] Jer. *Ep.* 127.13–14.   [77] Olymp. *Frag.* 16, ed. Blockley 1983, pp. 176–77.

[78] Jordanes, *Get.* 158; Philost. *HE* 12.4; Oros. *Hist.* 7.43.2; Prosper *Chron.* s.a. 412; Procop. *Wars* 3.2.37.

[79] Olymp. *Frags.* 33 and 37, ed. Blockley 1983, pp. 196–99; 201. Constantius is from Naissus, a city in Dacia. For his career, see Constantius 17, *PLRE* 2, pp. 321–25.

[80] Olymp. *Frags.* 8; 14, ed. Blockley 1983, pp. 160–63 and pp. 172–75, respectively. Matthews 1990, p. 302 for the murder of the courtier Olympius. For the murder of the general Allobichus in another court upheaval, Olymp. *Frag.* 15, and Soz. *HE* 9.12.5, ed. Blockley 1983, pp. 174–77, following Matthews 1990, p. 312, note 2. On the dating of the beginning of Constantius's ascendancy, see McEvoy 2013, p. 196, note 48. For the defeat and murder of Constantine III, see Olymp. *Frag.* 17 and Sozomen *HE* 9.15.1, ed. Blockley 1983, pp. 174–81; and Matthews 1990, pp. 312–13.

[81] Cecconi 2013, p. 145, emphasizing Prosper, *Chron.* s.a. 409: *Attalus Romae imperator factus, qui mox privatus regno Gothis cohaesit.* See too Olymp. *Frag.* 14. ed. Blockley 1983, pp. 172–75.

[82] For Heraclian's attack on Ravenna and his defeat by Constantius, see Oros. *Hist.* 7.42; Philost. *HE* 12.6. Heraclian, *comes Africae*, had been loyal to Honorius during the usurpation of Alaric

Hence, in January 414, Athaulf married Galla Placidia, the uterine sister of Honorius, and Attalus rose to be emperor once more. Attalus even composed a wedding song at the marriage, which took place in the home of a Gallo-Roman aristocrat, accompanied by a number of other Roman and Gallic nobles. Their presence is further proof of the willingness of some Roman aristocrats to align with the Visigoths against an ineffective and distant imperial court in Ravenna.[83]

Only after the murder of Athaulf by one of his slaves in 415 did Honorius find a resolution to the Gothic problem. The new Gothic king Vallia swore allegiance to Honorius and signed a treaty with the Romans in 416. Vallia returned Galla Placidia to Honorius's court in Ravenna. Attalus, still alive, was also sent back to Rome to be paraded in the triumphal games that Honorius celebrated there in 416. The display of this defeated usurper was intended as a lesson for other Roman aristocrats of the dangers of independent action. In a show of Honorius's clemency, he cut off only two of Attalus's fingers and exiled him.[84] By 416, however, the rebuilding of Rome was well under way.

Rome Restored: The Competition for Power after 410

In the three years during which Rome had been under siege, the balance of power had shifted significantly. The emperor Honorius had been vilified as ineffective and uncaring, but he had survived and was now supported by the eminent general, Flavius Constantius. The emperor also sought to rebuild ties with the senators and to reassert his influence and that of the imperial court from Ravenna. Constantius, too, established ties with the senators with whom he could work to restore Roman rule. Indeed, it was in the best interest of the emperor and the general to overlook the collusion of those senators who had supported the usurpation of Attalus and Alaric in an effort to encourage them to remain in or to return to Rome soon after 410. All involved were eager to blame Alaric and his "puppet emperor" Attalus rather than publicize the degree to which senators had conspired with the Gothic general. And aside from Attalus, no other senator is known to have suffered punishment.

and Attalus, but in April 413, as consul, he withheld grain shipments to Rome; see McEvoy 2013, p. 188, note 64.

[83] Cecconi 2013, p. 146. McEvoy 2013, p. 201; and see Olymp. *Frag.* 24.1–6, ed. Blockley 1983, p. 187, for the wedding, at which the nobles, Candidianus, Phoebadius, and Rusticius were present.

[84] Oros. *Hist.* 7.43.12 for Valila's decision to restore Galla Placidia to Ravenna and to become an ally of Rome. See too Hydatius, s.a. 417. Kulikowski 2007, pp. 178–84. For Priscus Attalus's fate and exile to the Isles of Lipari, see Olymp. *Frag.* 14, ed. Blockley 1983, pp. 174–75; and Olymp. *Frag.* 26.2 = Philost. *HE* 12.5, ed. Blockley 1983, pp. 190–91.

As Honorius and Constantius sought to reassert their authority over Rome and to secure senatorial support for their government, they faced a politically active senatorial aristocracy newly engaged in the running of government who had experience in foreign affairs and financial policy. Many of these men saw the possibilities for independent action in a senate that had taken on greater diplomatic importance. Significantly, senatorial aristocrats saw it as incumbent on themselves to retain what Matthews has described as "the tradition of participation in public and political life."[85] The three years leading up to the fall of the city had allowed, or some would say forced, the Senate and individual senators to make an unusually large number of political and financial decisions independent of the emperor and the court in Ravenna. Senatorial aristocrats returned to rule under Honorius with even greater awareness of their positions in the empire, and they used this new appreciation of their value to rebuild not only the material city but also their own relationships and those with other elites on more equal footing.

Before 410, as Carlos Machado has rightly observed, "political collaboration between Rome and Milan (later Ravenna) was based on a fragile arrangement involving two power-blocks with interests and agendas that did not always coincide."[86] Machado is referring to the senators active as high officeholders, many from established aristocratic families, who were primarily focused on Rome and Italy. This bloc collaborated with imperial courtiers and bureaucrats who, ever since the reforms of Constantine, were also holders of senatorial rank. The third elite bloc that also was a factor was the military, who also had gained senatorial rank by holding military office, the highest being the illustrious (*illustris*) rank of master of soldiers (*magister militum*) or master of the cavalry (*magister equitum*).[87] There can be no doubt that the importance of the military had increased in light of recent invasions from a host of Gothic, Hunnic, and Vandal armies arriving on the northern frontiers after 405–06. After 411, the general Flavius Constantius led the military response that restored stability in the West.[88] As a reward for his service, Constantius was wed to Galla Placidia, the sister of the emperor Honorius, in January of 417.[89] Constantius was proclaimed augustus by Honorius in February 421.[90]

---

[85] Matthews 1990, p. 398.   [86] Machado 2013, p. 64.

[87] See my discussion of the senatorial ranks at the end of Chapter 2.

[88] Olymp. *Frags.* 33–34; 37, ed. Blockley 1983, pp. 196–201.

[89] For Constantius's marriage to Galla Placidia in 417, see Olymp. *Frag.* 33, ed. Blockley 1983, pp. 196–99 = Philost. *HE* 12.12.

[90] Olymp. *Frag.* 33, ed. Blockley 1983, pp. 196–97; and for discussion, see Constantius 17, *PLRE* 2, p. 324.

This pattern – one in which power was triangulated among the military generals, imperial courtiers, and senatorial aristocrats – would remain throughout the balance of Honorius's rule and that of his successor, Valentinian III.[91] Importantly, the possibility of attaining power led to greater contestation for influence among elites, whose leadership was critical in restoring Roman rule to what was left of the western empire. And most importantly, in my view, the city of Rome revived as quickly as it did in large part due to this same competition on the part of elites – military, imperial, and senatorial.

My focus in this section of the chapter is on reconstructing the role of senatorial aristocrats because, in my view, they were the essential actors fueling the resurgence of the city of Rome in the decade following 410. Senatorial aristocrats demonstrated remarkable resilience, will, and creativity. They were motivated, in no small part, by their desire for personal advancement, namely, the very traditional desire for honor and power to protect themselves and their family, friends, and clients. Nonetheless, because senatorial aristocrats viewed the city of Rome as the stage on which they acted out their lives and their status, they worked with the support of the emperor and the military to rebuild the city, marshalling their resources to speed up the city's recovery. Certainly, not all aristocrats were able to return and thrive after 410. But enough did, relying on their properties and rents from estates across Italy, Sicily, Sardinia, Gaul, and until the 440s, North Africa, to revive the city of Rome in the decade after 410. They benefitted, too, from an imperial court and a military eager to support these efforts.

The elite contestation for influence that restored the city of Rome also extended to the religious life of the city. The bishop of Rome and the estimated fifty to one hundred priests as well as seven deacons and their subdeacons made up another elite component of late Roman society.[92] As bishop during the sieges and after the sack, Innocent I (401–17) oversaw this new elite as well as a good number of lower clergy (readers, acolytes, exorcists, doorkeepers). Although the bishop of Rome claimed to be the single authoritative leader of the Roman church and hence should play a key role in restoring the city's community of faithful, Innocent, unlike a modern pope, did not command a highly developed and consolidated monarchic episcopate and structure. Rather, Innocent oversaw a rudimentary bureaucracy and had but limited

---

[91] See McEvoy 2013, pp. 1–22, and 305–29 for the implications of the child emperor; and see too McEvoy 2010, pp. 151–92.

[92] This is the estimate for the clergy based on clergy in attendance in the later fifth centuries; for further discussion see Thompson 2015, pp. 22–25 with reference to the synods.

power to enforce his views on Christian communities in the city or abroad.[93] Moreover, in the city of Rome, Innocent oversaw a church with ongoing internal divisions. A fiercely contested episcopal election in which clergy and deacons along with a number of secular elites had brawled in the streets had only been resolved to allow the church to come together under Damasus (366–84). But tensions between priests and the bishop's central assistants, the seven deacons, persisted, a situation that came out into the open in the subsequent papacies of Innocent's successors Zosimus (417–18) and Boniface (418–22). In addition, in a city as large as Rome, Innocent and his successors faced a number of competing Christian sects; we hear of actions against Manichaeans, Montanists, Priscillianists, and Novatians, the latter of whose churches Innocent seized.[94] These religious realities and competing sects further undermined attempts by the bishops of Rome to claim hegemonic control over all Christians in the city in the early fifth century.

The sack of Rome called the bishop of Rome's authority further into question, for it was also a crisis of faith, as the *Sermons* of Augustine delivered in North Africa to refugees from the city in the two years immediately after 410 make vividly clear.[95] Pagans, newly emboldened, blamed the "fall" of Rome on the emperor's chosen religion; Christians questioned the god who had brought such suffering on the city and its Christian faithful and had allowed the martyria and churches to be plundered. The bishop of Rome, Innocent, who had been part of a failed embassy to Ravenna when the city had fallen, had to face his task of rebuilding Rome while encountering these and other challenges to his authority from within the Christian community of the city.[96] Among those who challenged episcopal authority were the Christian senatorial aristocrats. With their tradition of religious patronage, they continued to sponsor their favored titular churches and clergy in neighborhoods across the city as well as in their private homes. In light of these challenges, the bishops of Rome in the decade after 410 – Innocent, Zosimus, and Boniface – often turned to liturgy to assert their authority and to restore the Christian communities of Rome, foregoing a more public role in restoring the city.

The year 410 dealt a serious blow to Rome's urban fabric – not only to its population, infrastructure, and wealth – but also to the trust that the inhabitants of the city had in the institutions associated with the imperial state,

---

[93] So, for instance, when Spanish bishops came to Rome for assistance on what to do about readmitting repentant followers of the Spanish bishop Priscillian, Innocent offered an opinion but had no means to enforce it. For Innocent's letter, see Innocent I, *Ep.* 3 (*PL* 20.486–94). For the limits of his authority within Rome as well, see especially Dunn 2015, pp. 89–107.

[94] Socr. *HE* 7.2. For the law of Honorius, which had Innocent's support, see *C. Th.* 16.5.40.

[95] Salzman 2015, pp. 346–59.　　[96] See notes 193 and 194, and my discussion below.

including the episcopate. In the decade that followed, the restoration of the city fell largely to secular elites. Indeed, there was a notable activism on the part of the senatorial aristocrats and the imperial state that was manifested in the maintenance and repair of the ancient buildings and monuments dear to their identities, like the Senate house; this same activism is discernible in the politics of the period during which senators took on office and new leadership roles in the wake of this attack. Senatorial activism, in my view, grew out of a natural desire for influence as elites strove to reassert themselves in the reviving city in the face of a weakened imperial court. And by the 420s, Rome was enjoying a resurgence, judging by modern measures such as the returning population, housing repairs and constructions, jobs, infrastructure, and quality of life – notably, bread, pork, and games. Thus, although the urban population had not returned to the same levels as existed before 410, the city was certainly growing again. If we use the estimates based on pig bones in southern Italy, there were around 120,000 recipients of the pork dole in Rome in 419 and around 140,000 in 452, statistics that imply a speedy recovery by 419 and a total population numbering between 300,000 and 500,000 residents.[97] This number is a decrease from the estimates of between 700,000 and 1,000,000 residents at the end of the fourth century, but it still made Rome the largest city in the western Mediterranean.[98] To explain this resurgence and the important role that contestation among elites – senatorial aristocrats working along with military and imperial elites – played in bringing Rome back to life, I begin with the key civic leader on the ground, the urban prefect.

The Importance of the Urban Prefect of Rome

Since the changes in the age of Constantine, the office of urban prefect oversaw the preservation of Rome's infrastructure as well as a host of vital services ranging from law and order, the food supply, building repairs, and maintenance to public games and circuses. The urban prefect, much like the mayor of a great city today, held political and social power that made it a highly influential but demanding post. He did have a bureaucracy in Rome to help with his tasks. By the early fifth century, even the prefect of the food supply was under his authority.[99] The position of urban prefect was most

---

[97] Barnish 1987, p. 166. The key texts for these numbers are *C. Th.* 14.4.10 and the *Nov. Val.* 36. Barnish estimated that in 452 Rome had a total population between 300,000 and 500,000.

[98] See too population estimates in Chapter 1, note 19.

[99] For the office of urban prefect, see Chastagnol 1960, passim, and especially pp. 54–63; Machado 2019, pp. 46–47; and for the prefect of the food supply (*praefectus annonae*), see *Not. Dig. Occ.* 4.

often held by members of established Roman aristocratic families and was seen as a peak in the career of many an Italo-Roman senator. Indeed, these senators had a long tradition of serving the city and the government, using – if it was to their advantage – their own funds to support games, circuses, food, and buildings for the populace of Rome in exchange for honor, status, and economic advantages. Appointed by the emperor, the urban prefect mediated between the emperor and the Senate, as evidenced by his role in calling the Senate into meetings. The holders of this position were therefore, in the decade after 410, especially critical for rebuilding the city and keeping the peace. They were increasingly aware of their import-ance and used the opportunities of office presented by their management of a large number of necessary repairs to the city, for instance, to augment their status and power under a regime that was struggling to reassert its authority.

Honorius and Constantius were keenly aware of the need for men of high status to fill the office of urban prefect in order to ensure the support of Rome's senators. But they were aware as well of the influence of the holder of this office. Indeed, emperors had kept a close eye on the urban prefects lest those who were too ambitious, like Priscus Attalus, undermine their rule.[100] Emperors had also selected urban prefects with awareness of polit-ical conditions in the city, as their attention to the religion of their appoint-ees had demonstrated.[101] Of the twelve men attested as urban prefects in the period 410–23, six were certainly or at least probably from Italian and Roman noble families, and even those whose family origins are uncertain, like Petronius Maximus, were from wealthy and high-status families. (See Table 3.1.) Typical is the urban prefect of 414; Caecina Decius Acinatius Albinus was likely part of the Ceionii and the Decii family; his son, Basilius, would go on to hold high office later in the century (see Table 3.1). These men were wealthy landowners with a stake in the city. Palmatus, urban prefect in 412, was a wealthy Christian aristocrat whose beneficence to the church did not preclude him or one of his family members from dedicating an ancient Egyptian statue of Jupiter in their ancestral house.[102] Even the brief appointment of the Gallic poet Namatianus in the summer of 414

---

[100] Machado 2019, p. 32 makes this point, as does Chastagnol 1960, pp. 392–462.

[101] See Chapter 2, and Salzman 2016, pp. 29–35.

[102] His family later donated a house of theirs in Rome, with bath and bakery, to support St. Maria Maggiore, a church built at the time of Bishop Sixtus III (432–40): see *Lib. Pont.* 46, ed. Duchesne 1981, p. 233. For the statue of the Egyptian Jove rededicated by the urban prefect Neratius Palmatus, see *LSA* 2538.

speaks to respect for Roman traditions; Namatianus's father had also likely been urban prefect as well as consular in Italy.[103]

Honorius, along with Constantius, was determined to bring men into this sensitive but powerful office who had been untouched by close involvement with the recent usurpation of Alaric and Attalus. In this effort they followed a policy quite different from that of Constantine (discussed in Chapter 2), who had tried to convey continuity in society by continuing the urban prefects of Maxentius in office. In contrast, Honorius chose new faces, a move presenting further evidence of his awareness of the danger that had been presented by Attalus's attempted usurpation. Of the twelve men attested as urban prefects in the period 410–23, only six are attested as having held any civic office prior to that point.[104] The first urban prefect appointed by Honorius in 410, Bonosianus, is otherwise unattested before or after attaining this position, but he must have been a trusted official whose loyalty to the emperor and general would not have been in doubt.[105] Although these appointments affirm the desires of Constantius and Honorius to work with Italo-Roman senatorial aristocrats, the recently attempted coup also had had an impact.

The omission of some important families from this office during this decade speaks to some tensions both within the senatorial aristocracy and with the emperor and his court. Indeed, some new men appear to have been more successful than others, leading some scholars to argue that the absence of the powerful Anician family from this office through most of this decade was the result of this family's philo-barbarian sentiment; this attachment had allegedly led an Anician woman to open the gates of Rome to Alaric's Goths.[106] However, I am not the first to find this view problematic. It assumes that the Anicii were one clan united behind a consistent political position on the issue of barbarians; however, the Anicii, as Alan Cameron has demonstrated, were much more loosely tied together and, like other elites, formed alliances as the politics of the moment demanded.[107] Nor were all members of the Anicii out of favor in this decade if the Probus who held the position in

---

[103] See Table 3.1. His father was Lachanius; see *PLRE* 1, p. 491. Rut. Nam. *De red. suo* 1.579–80 attests his father's prefecture, which is likely that of urban prefect. I see no evidence of a trend to bring in Gallo-Roman aristocrats here as suggested by McEvoy 2013, pp. 198–203.

[104] Gracchus, urban prefect in 415, was likely consular of Campania in 397. He was likely from a Roman senatorial aristocratic family as were four of the others; see Table 3.1.

[105] Although Chastagnol 1962, p. 269 suggests that Bonosianus was already in office during the sack, there is no evidence for this.

[106] This was proposed by Cracco Ruggini 1988, pp. 79–81, with bibliography; and most recently by Roberto 2012, p. 212, following the views of Zecchini 1981, pp. 123–40.

[107] Cameron 2012, pp. 133–71.

charge of the state finances, the count of the sacred largesses (CSL, or *comes sacrarum largitionum*), from 412 to 414 is identified as the son of a member of the Anician family (see Table 3.2). And the 418 appointment as urban prefect of a member of the Symmachi family who had married into the Anicii, Aurelius Anicius Symmachus, goes against the idea that all with ties to the Anicii had one political view, although by then, it is worth noting, the Visigoths had been settled in Gaul by the general Constantius.[108]

The Restoration of Rome. The act of constructing and repairing Rome's infrastructure and buildings was a traditional avenue for senatorial aristocrats and emperors to demonstrate their status and beneficence in Rome. As Gregor Kalas well observed:

> Senators frequently paid for building projects while honoring emperors, since aristocrats in Rome felt obliged to share patronage credit with imperial sponsors, who garnered most of the credit. Yet … inscriptions usually masked the degree to which imperial authorities competed with local senators in establishing pre-eminence over the urban fabric of Rome. Such struggles motivated Valentinian I (364–75) to address a letter to Rome's urban prefect prohibiting the construction of new buildings and encouraging the restoration of extant historic structures, effectively preventing senators from using new building projects to assert their local agendas.[109]

The evolution in the language of late antique building inscriptions from the fourth century on, as Carlos Machado has demonstrated, with the increasing use of formulae that emphasized that the urban prefect was dedicating the work *to* emperors but that the work was *not by* the emperors who paid for it, points to the ways in which urban prefects seized "every opportunity available for advertising their status and power."[110] Similarly, the inscriptions that advertise repairs on buildings after 410 by senators or by urban prefects offer their efforts as an act of munificence to the emperor but emphasize the status and power of the official overseeing this work. And the late fourth-century stipulations that senators not undertake new construction – a restriction aimed at reducing their influence and conserving the traditional façade of cities – was reiterated in November 411 when Honorius said that although some claimed the "pretense of any emergency" to try to build new structures, this reason was not allowed and was expressly prohibited in a rescript to the

---

[108] For the ongoing debate about the terms of this treaty, see McEvoy 2013, p. 202, note 84.
[109] Kalas 2010, p. 26, cites *C. Th.* 15.1.11 (May 25, 364).
[110] Machado 2019, p. 67. This too was noted by Löhken 1982, pp. 75–76.

prefect of Rome, Bonosianus, concerning a city in Suburbicarian Italy, an area that was under his supervision.[111]

It is in this spirit of competitive building that we can appreciate the ways in which Rome after 410 opened up possibilities for Rome's urban prefects, along with their senatorial peers, to compete for influence by repairing or adorning edifices in Rome, albeit to honor the emperor and/or his general, the master of soldiers. Their competitive reconstruction efforts also help explain the uptick in the statuary habit in Rome, especially in the later part of the decade, as new statues were dedicated or old ones repaired and/or resited.[112]

Repairs in the Area of the Senate in the Roman Forum. The efforts of Rome's urban prefects are recorded most clearly in areas that traditionally had ideological and political importance to senatorial and imperial identity, namely, in the area of the Senate House in the Roman Forum. Repairs near the Senate House are recorded fairly quickly.[113] (See Map 1.) Epiphanius, urban prefect of Rome from October 15, 412, to May 27, 414, is attested as having made an important repair here:[114]

> *Salvis dominis nostris Honorio et Theodosio victoriosissimis principibus, secretarium amplissimi senatus, quod vir inlustris Flavianus instituerat et fatalis ignis absumpsit, Flavius Annius Eurcharius Epifanius v.c., praef. urb., vice sacr. iud., reparavit et ad pristinam faciem reduxit.*

> With our lords, the most victorious princes, Honorius and Theodosius, being safe, Flavius Annius Eucharius Epifanius, a *vir clarissiumus*, prefect of the city, [and] judge of appeal, repaired the *secretarium* of the most distinguished Senate, [a building that] Flavianus, a man of *illustris* rank, had erected and an inescapable fire had consumed, and he [Epifanius] returned it to its original appearance.[115]

Several aspects of this inscription contribute to an understanding of the contestation for influence by elites that fueled the restoration of the city.

---

[111] *C. Th.* 15.1.48 to Bonosianus, PUR November 28, 411. The restrictions on new building were also aimed at conserving ancient buildings, as articulated in laws from the fourth century; see Lizzi Testa 2001, pp. 685–91.

[112] For a full discussion, see Ward-Perkins and Machado 2013, pp. 353–63.

[113] Chastagnol 1962, pp. 270–72, attributed the repairs of the Senate house to Neratius Palmatus, PUR in 412, based on his reconstruction of *CIL* 6.37128, revising *Neratius Iu* to read Neratius P and positing his name as Neratius Iunius Palmatus. Orlandi 2013, p. 341, has reexamined the inscription and sees no room for this wording. Orlandi dates the inscription to the fourth century based on the style of the lettering and the cutting of the block. Finally, there is no indication of the office of urban prefect. Hence, I agree with Orlandi that this repair cannot be securely dated to 412.

[114] Epiphanius, in *PLRE* 2, p. 399, s.v. Epiphanius 7.   [115] *CIL* 6.1718 = *ILS* 5522.

First, although the inscription commences with the standard dedication under secure emperors, it also honors the prestigious senator Nicomachus Flavianus the Younger, who had built this monument (*instituerat*) only a decade earlier when he was urban prefect in 392–94. Flavianus's family had fallen from favor because Flavianus the Elder had participated in the failed usurpation under Magnus Maximus and Eugenius. The father had committed suicide, and his name had been condemned by Theodosius I, who had, however, cleared Flavianus the Younger of any crime.[116] Theodosius II later reversed this decision on the father so that by the time that Epiphanius restored this building, the family was again in good standing. Epiphanius's inscription thus has a double honorific function – to praise its senatorial founder as well as the emperors named.

Second, this restoration should be read within the charged political circumstances after 410. Ernst Nash had shown that the *Secretarium Senatus* was where senators conducted trials of their peers accused of capital crimes.[117] This senatorial duty was asserted in the late fourth century by a law of 376 and is either a fourth-century innovation or a fourth-century reiteration of the right of senators to sit in judgement of each other.[118] Although it may seem odd to a modern audience that "augmenting senatorial authority necessarily occurred in conjunction with an expression of concord with the ruling emperors," to a senatorial audience this inscription augmented their status in proper formulaic language.[119] Epiphanius was asserting the senatorial right to sit in judgment of one's peers during a period when some senators who had aligned themselves with the usurper Alaric would likely have been brought up on charges. This occurrence was a real possibility. In 416, when Honorius celebrated his triumph over the Goths in Rome, he made a point of very publicly punishing Priscus Attalus in front of the Senate and people of Rome, as noted above.[120]

And third, acknowledging that the destruction of the *Secretarium Senatus* had been "inescapable" (*fatalis*) can be seen as a step toward healing. By adopting this view of the recent destruction, Epiphanius avoids assigning any guilt to human – that is, senatorial – agency. Epiphanius's dedication thus encouraged Romans to accept the past destruction as having been divinely sanctioned and to move forward by reestablishing senatorial traditions in Rome.[121] This notion of the "inescapable" fate that had led to the rebuilding

---

[116] Nicomachus Flavianus, *PLRE* 1, p. 347, s.v. Flavianus 14. See too Hedrick 2000, pp. 25–28. For a good discussion of this monument and argument, see Kalas 2015, pp. 158–60.

[117] Nash 1976, p. 194.   [118] *C. Th.* 9.1.13.   [119] Kalas 2015, p. 159.   [120] See note 84 above.

[121] Orlandi 2013, p. 342 discusses the intent of *fatalis* but does not make the associations suggested here.

or relocating of statues mentioned in the post-410 inscriptions recurred and was a characteristic Roman aristocratic perspective that supported efforts to restore the city and aristocrats' role in them. We see it in a restoration from an inscription from the Circus Flaminius on an architrave, now lost, dated to the first prefecture of Glabrio Faustus, 421–23, that mentions a building *fatali casu subversam* ("destroyed by an inescapable event") and in a law that refers to the attack of Alaric as *fatalem hostium ruinam* (inescapable disaster caused by the enemy).[122]

Before leaving the area of the Senate, we should note that, in addition to the inscription acknowledging Epiphanius's repair of the *Secretarium Senatus*, there are other inscriptions that date to this same period and area. A richly decorated architrave with an inscription dedicated to Honorius and Theodosius was part of this post-410 restoration, but another refurbishment that speaks of the gilded room in the Senate house (*cameram auro fulgentem*) dedicated on behalf of the "Genius of this most abundant Senate" (*pro genio senatus amplissimi*) by the urban prefect Flavius Ianuarius, or Ianuarianus, cannot be securely dated.[123]

Repairs across the City by Urban Prefects. There are other reports of restorations across Rome associated with the activity of the urban prefect in the aftermath of 410, even if we cannot know in all cases that the repairs were caused by the sack of the city. The repairs and resiting of statues in the Decian (Aventine) Baths by the urban prefect Caecina Decius Acinatius Albinus in 414–15 describes the work on the steam room (*cellam tepidariam*) that had to be repaired due to a collapsed wall, and another inscription on a marble base in this area records the addition of statues (now lost), presumably from some other building that had been moved to ornament this work.[124] The statues were most likely moved from an unstated location to this more frequented area, a practice that had developed in the fourth-century city.[125] We cannot know the cause of the collapsed wall, but the insertion of Albinus's name for the repair at this early date is indicative of the competitive process of restoration that I want to underscore.

Another instance of restoration occurred when, as urban prefect from 418 to 420, the eminent senator Aurelius Anicius Symmachus proudly

---

[122] For the building identified as perhaps the Porticus Minucia, see *CIL* 6.1676, and Orlandi 2013, p. 342. For the law, see the *N. Val.* 32.6, 451 CE, and Orlandi 2013, p. 342, note 66.

[123] For the richly decorated architrave, see *CIL* 6.41386–41387. For the restoration of the *cameram auro fulgentem* by the urban prefect named Flavius Ianuarius or Ianuarianus whose prefecture is not securely dated, see *CIL* 6.41378 with discussion by Orlandi 2013, p. 341; and Spera 2012, pp. 127–42.

[124] *CIL* 6. 1703; and 1659 for the prefect who "added [the statue] for ornamentation" (*facto a se adjecit ornatui*). On this, see Orlandi 2013, p. 339; Chastagnol 1962, p. 274. This man was also prefect in 426, but this dedication can be dated to his first turn of that office.

[125] Orlandi 2013, p. 342.

proclaimed his work in the Roman Forum. Another inscription records that he repaired a marketplace in Ostia, Rome's port city, for "the ornamentation and the benefit of the citizens."[126] Another urban prefect, Glabrio Faustus (421–23), is attested by an inscription on a fragment of an architrave in the Circus Flaminius, noted earlier, now lost but known from manuscripts. The architrave was part of a building or portico that had been "overturned by an inescapable fall," an event that was traditionally associated with the sack of 410 but that may refer to an earlier earthquake on what was, as Orlandi has argued, a reused block.[127] Hence, we cannot know if the repair was directly tied to the sack of 410, but the work was undertaken by this urban prefect.

However, some restorations cannot be so well dated. The restoration of statues in front of the Basilica Julia in the Roman Forum (see Map 1), is generally attributed to the urban prefect of 416, identified with, Gabinius Vettius Probianus. But based on the writing, this identification has been questioned and may instead be the work of a late fourth- rather than an early fifth-century urban prefect.[128] Nonetheless, the enthusiasm of urban prefects to be identified with reconstruction efforts after 410 speaks to a reinvestment in the city that augmented aristocratic status at the same time. That there were other repairs to buildings by urban prefects in the decade after 410 is certain, but not all inscriptions have survived.

Trends in Honorific Statues in Rome. Another sign of the growing prestige of senators and the Senate after 410 emerges from a consideration of the number and locations of honorific statues. Indeed, as Bryan Ward-Perkins and Carlos Machado have observed, the events of 410 "did not kill the statue habit in Rome." The contestation for honor that drove Roman elites continued to feed the statuary habit there in a way that contrasts markedly with its prevalence in other cities in Italy. Although these scholars observed a gap – or, as they put it, a dent – between 407 and 416 in new statue dedications, the urban prefects were repairing and relocating statues as early as the period 412–14.[129] However, in the fifth century, new statue dedications emerged that support my view of the increased authority of senatorial and military elites in Rome.

---

[126] For the works in the Roman Forum, see *CIL* 6.36962. For Ostia, see *CIL* 14.4719, and the reconstruction of the text by Chastagnol 1962, p. 281: . . . *r]eparatu[m ad ornatum] Urbis et i[n usum civium]*. For a discussion of reconstruction efforts, see Vannesse 2010, pp. 508–10; and Spera 2012, pp. 113–55.

[127] *CIL* 6.1676: *fatali casu subversam*. On this block, see note 122 above.

[128] *CIL* 6 3864a=31883; and *CIL* 6.3864b=31884. For fuller discussion see Orlandi 2013, pp. 341–42, who proposes a late fourth-century date for the relocation of these statues. For Probianus as urban prefect, see Table 3.1.

[129] Ward-Perkins and Machado 2013, pp. 353–55. Quote on page 354.

Carlos Machado identified sixty-nine statue bases dedicated in the Roman Forum between 284 and 476. Thirty-four of these were dedicated to emperors; seven were dedicated to senatorial aristocrats; and four, to generals. At first sight, this area appears to be an imperial space, but the distribution changed greatly over time. Between 337 and 410, emperors received the majority of identifiable dedications (thirteen of twenty-one). But after 410, not a single freestanding statue dedicated to an emperor in the Forum has been identified, while aristocrats and aristocratic generals received three – Petronius Maximus, Flavius Constantius, and Aetius.[130] This decline in the imperial presence and rise of the political prominence of aristocrats and generals are all the more striking since during the second quarter of the fifth century, the emperor Valentinian III often came back to reside in Rome.

These dedicatory patterns underscore that the competition for honor among elites in Rome had tilted in favor of senators and generals. And it is worth noting that this group had developed ties to one another as well. Generals, like Stilicho, had developed friendship networks with Roman senators as a means of securing political advantages. Indicative of the value of such a tie between senators and generals is the honorific statue by the urban prefect Aurelius Anicius Symmachus to the commander in chief Flavius Constantius dated to 420.[131]

A similar trend emerges from the area of the Forum of Trajan, which, as Robert Chenault has convincingly shown, was the locus of senatorial honorific statues from the early fourth into the late fifth century. Seven of twenty statues dedicated to senators from the Forum of Trajan date to after 410, according to Chenault, and only four imperial statue dedications out of a total of twenty-nine are attested.[132] Only one from the Forum of Trajan was a fifth-century imperial dedication, in 417–18, nominally from the "Senate and People of Rome" (*SPQR*), under the direction of (*curante*) the urban prefect Rufius Antonius Agrypnius Volusianus: "Under our lord Honorius, most flourishing, most invincible prince."[133] Whether the emperor is honoring the senators by his presence or the emperor is being honored by the presence of other senators, it is clear that Honorius is being incorporated into a space, the

---

[130] Machado 2006A, pp. 157–92.

[131] For this urban prefect, see Table 3.1. For the dedication in 420, see *CIL* 6.1719. Constantius also received another honorific statue by an unknown dedicator, *CIL* 6.1720. Both date before his elevation to Augustus in 421. For the dedication to Stilicho from the rostra in the Forum, see *CIL* 6. 1195, 406/407.

[132] Chenault 2012, pp. 103–32. For the dedication in 417/418, see *CIL* 6.1194.

[133] *CIL* 6.1194: *D.n. Honorio florentissimo invictissimoq. Principi, s.p.q.r., curante Rufiio Antonio Agrypnio Volusiano, v.c., praef. Urb. Iterum vice sacra iudicante.* The adjective used for Honorius, *invictissimo* ("most invincible"), is taken up by him only after the victory over the Goths in 416.

Forum of Trajan, devoted to senators as if he were one of them. The second statue to Honorius was dedicated between 418 and 420 by the urban prefect Aurelius Anicius Symmachus in the *porticus* of the theater of Pompey, a building that apparently had been damaged in 410.[134]

Senatorial Fora. In Rome, traditional dedicators – emperors and the Senate as well as aristocratic family members – are attested throughout the fifth century. But there is one other development that also speaks of the growth of senatorial prestige in the city of Rome. We have evidence that senators also started installing statues in their family *fora* – squares associated at times with the *domus* of their families or simply areas that they developed for daily interaction among people of different social standing. This intrusion on public spaces by senatorial families is a physical manifestation of their growing encroachment on the urban fabric of the city, a privilege that was once jealously restricted to members of the imperial family.[135] For example, the aristocrat Sibidius dedicated a forum in the Campus Marius when he was urban prefect in 421–23; his heirs and relatives in the 430s dedicated new statues in this forum that was likely tied to the workings of the pork supply as well.[136] Petronius Maximus and Fl. Eurycles Epityncanus, urban prefect in 450, both built *fora* near their houses or in prime residential areas. The former was built on the Caelian Hill near the modern St. Clement, the latter on the slopes of the Esquiline on the site of the earlier Esquiline Forum, and both are first attested only in the fifth century (see Map 1).[137]

Feeding Rome: The Honor and Burden. After 410 Honorius sought to act once more as imperial patron of Rome and to take up his traditional role as the provider of "bread and circuses." As discussed in Chapter 1, emperors provided free bread to a certain proportion of the population – the *plebs frumentaria* – who, from the time of the late third-century emperor Aurelian, were also the recipients of pork and state-subsidized oil and wine.[138] Indeed, one of the signs of the revival of Rome is a law from 419

---

[134] *CIL* 6. 1193, cf. 1191.

[135] On laws controlling new building, see Lizzi Testa 2001, pp. 671–707.

[136] Ward-Perkins and Machado 2013, pp. 354 and 358. See s.v. Forum Sibidius, *LTUR*, p. 346 (Pap); and Santangeli Valenzani 2007, pp. 63–82. Anicius Acilius Glabrio Faustus, who dedicated these statues in 438, was urban prefect under Honorius; see Table 3.1. For the inscriptions, see *CIL* 6.1678, 413891, 1767.

[137] For the forum of Petronius Maximus, see *CIL* 6.1198=ILS 807–8. For the forum of Epityncanus, see *CIL* 6.1662 = *ILS* 5357; and *CIL* 6.31888. For further discussion, see Machado 2019, pp. 266–67.

[138] A subset of citizens who received bread sufficient for one individual (not a family) for a month as the hereditary right of citizenship in Rome, the qualifications of which by the late fourth and early fifth centuries were hereditary citizenship and, in some categories, service to the state; see Chapter 1, notes 18 and 20.

in which the emperor Honorius stipulated that five pounds of pork be distributed per individual citizen recipient for five months of the year.[139] This would come to roughly three million pounds of pork, an amount somewhat smaller than the 3.6 million pounds noted in a law of Valentinian III in 452 and half as much as the amount issued in a constitution in 367.[140] Based on the assumption that pork and grain distributions fed the same percentages of the populace as they had done in the early empire, Elio Lo Cascio calculated that in 419 the number of people who benefitted from the distribution of pork was 120,000 and the city's population was almost 500,000 as compared with the approximately 700,000 to 1,000,000 estimated in Rome before the sack.[141]

Although the emperor paid for food for Rome with state funds, the distribution was administered by senators in their position of urban prefect, who also by the early fifth century directed the efforts of the prefect of the *annona*.[142] This bureaucratic development gave the urban prefect more power since he now oversaw, we think, the prefect of the food supply (*praefectus annonae*), who was the official in control of the fund for foodstuffs (the *arca frumentaria*) and was in charge of everyday operations in Ostia, Portus, and Rome.[143] Now there were increased opportunities for senators to accrue honor and blame for the functioning of Rome's food supply for a population that appears to have grown soon after 410. Indeed, a fragment of Olympiodorus alludes to this development. In 414 or 415, the urban prefect Caecina Decius Acinatius Albinus (September 414 to July 415) wrote to the emperor that the food ration provided for the people was inadequate because of the increase in the city's population. The prefect claimed that he had enrolled 14,000 new inhabitants of Rome in a single - day.[144] New births and the return of refugees make this a plausible figure for some historians.[145] In opposition is the view of Nicholas Purcell, who has regarded this request as "grandiloquent over-provisioning" by an emperor eager to blot out the memory of his past inactivity.[146] However, it seems unlikely that this would be the case; no evidence to support such imperial posturing around the food supply exists. Moreover, Philostorgios suggests that this population growth happened with imperial support since after

---

[139] *C. Th.* 14.4.3; 419 CE.

[140] *N. Val.* 36.1–2, 452 CE; *C. Th.* 15.4.4, 367 CE under Valentinian I.

[141] Lo Cascio 1999, pp. 163–82; 2000, pp. 60–61.

[142] Jones 1964, pp. 698–99 and note 143 below.

[143] For this development by the early fifth century, see *Not. Dig. Occ.* 4 and the discussion by Machado 2019, pp. 46–47. For the fund for the food supply, see Chastagnol 1960, pp. 176–77.

[144] Olymp. *Frag.* 25 with note 56, ed. Blockley 1983, pp. 188–89.

[145] Lo Cascio 1999, pp. 163–82; 2000, p. 60–61; Barnish 1987, p. 166.   [146] Purcell 1999, p. 139.

signing the treaty with the Goths in 416, Honorius had come to Rome and allegedly put in place a *synoikismos*. According to Purcell, *synoikismos* here means "the deployment of imperial authority to gather from whatever source was available a new population."[147] It was clearly part of Honorius's propaganda of imperial refoundation, a message that was aimed in no small part at the senatorial elite.

The actual size of the grain supply (*annona*) at this juncture is unknowable, but the dynamic of its logistics is worth discussing. The urban prefect is presented as both facilitating food distribution and increasing the supply for Rome to meet the needs of a rapidly growing population. Honorius was eager to comply since he wanted to erase the memory of the sack through this act of imperial beneficence. The resulting prestige for augmenting Rome's food supplies would also go to the urban prefect, whose handling of his duty would ingratiate him with the city. Thus, this vignette illustrates how a senatorial urban prefect gained influence by generously feeding the people of Rome. But the emperor felt the need to assert his generosity in person. Honorius returned to Rome to celebrate his triumph over Alaric by hosting games and making generous gifts.[148]

Financial Responsibilities and Resources

Controlling the finances related to the feeding and functioning of Rome naturally made the office of the urban prefect, along with that of the emperor, singularly important in restoring the city after 410. Not only did the urban prefect oversee the food supply, he also controlled the funds from the *arca vinaria*, the treasury responsible for the supply of wine and meat, which was also traditionally used for building repairs. But urban prefects, like modern administrators, always needed more money. Indeed, the urban prefects regularly turned to the emperor's administrators, specifically to the chief financial officer of the imperial treasury (*comes sacrarum largitionum*) for additional money. Alternatively, the urban prefect could seek money from the Senate, as did the urban prefect of 376.[149] Of course, urban prefects could – and did in 414–15 – directly ask the emperor for additional funding. In times of need, they also could use their own monies to avoid food shortages or to

---

[147] Philost. *HE* 12.5 = Olymp. *Frag.* 26.2, ed. Blockley 1983, p. 191. See Purcell 1999, p. 149.

[148] Prosper *Chron.* s.a. 417, Philost. *HE* 12.5 = Olymp. *Frag.* 26.2, ed. Blockley 1983, p. 191. Honorius's 416 victory celebration took place at some time after May 3 and before July 4 when he is attested in Ravenna, according to Gillett 2001, p. 138. McCormick 1986, pp. 57–58 proposed June 28, 416, for the triumph in Rome and Constantinople.

[149] Ambr. *De offic.* 43.45–51 for a case in 376 where the urban prefect turned to the Senate for funds.

supplement the entertainments paid for by the emperor. Certainly, during the siege of 408, the empress Laeta, Gratian's widow, was not the only aristocrat who shared her supplies with people in need, particularly her clients.[150]

Count of the Imperial Treasury (*comes sacrarum largitionum or CSL*). The office of the count of the imperial treasury was of particular importance to the revival of the aristocracy. This high-ranking financial officer collected the *chrysargyron*, the taxes on senators, customs duties, and other voluntary payments, and also was in control of mines, state mills, dye works, and minting.[151] Because this official determined the taxes on individual senators, the choice of a Roman senatorial aristocrat installed in this position under- lines the desire on the part of Honorius and his general, Constantius, to work with senators to restore their well-being and to incorporate them in their government. The *comes sacrarum largitionum* was also a member of the imperial council, or consistory, that advised the emperor (*consistorium*), a situation that explains why this office was also a springboard for an ambitious senator to reach other high offices and honors.

Honorius appointed members of powerful Roman senatorial families to this office after 410; in 412–14 he appointed a Probus who has been identified as possibly belonging to the senatorial Anicii (see Table 3.2).[152] Another man, whose date of service is uncertain but whose office fell before 417, was Lucillus, father of Decius, whose appointment as consular of Tusciae and Umbriae suggests that he too was a member of the Italian senatorial aristoc- racy (see Table 3.2). Between 415 and 416–19, the noble Petronius Maximus held this post; he was one of the most influential senators of the fifth century. His family was among the high elites of the city, although his uncertain origin has suggested to some scholars how upwardly mobile provincial elites were absorbed into senatorial circles in Rome.[153] In any case, these ties would be helpful to senatorial aristocrats as they sought tax relief in this time of recovery.

Laws and Financial Assistance. In addition to choosing Roman senatorial aristocrats for key civic offices, Honorius and Constantius passed laws to relieve the tax burdens on this group of landowners as part of their efforts to help the recovery of Italy after 410. In 413 a major tax concession reduced the

---

[150] Zos. 5.39.4; see also Brown 1992, pp. 82–83.

[151] Kahzdan and Cutler, eds. s.v. *comes sacrarorum largitionum*, 2005, oxfordreference.com/view/ 10.1093

[152] This assumes the Probus chosen was Probus 1, *PLRE* 2, p. 910, and possibly identical with Probus 11, *PLRE* 2, pp. 913–14. See Table 3.2.

[153] For Petronius Maximus as urban prefect in 415, see Chastagnol 1962, pp. 281–82, followed by Delmaire 1989, p. 197 and Machado 2013, p. 65. For his family and social ties, see note 208 below and Chapter 4, note 17.

liability of taxpayers in a number of areas in Campania, Tuscany, Picenum, Samnium Apulia, Calabria, Bruttium, and Lucania; the emperor made this a five-year remission to one-fifth of their former tax assessments. A second law of 418 further reduced the liability of Campania to one-ninth and that of Picenum and Tuscany to one-seventh of their previous levels, with no time limit; the intent was to remove complaints about taxes on abandoned lands as well as to reduce the burdens on those who had returned.[154] Clearly, Italy had suffered greatly from the wars fought on its soil. Tax relief would help revive its agriculture to levels of production that could sustain its population. Most of the large landowners in these areas were senatorial aristocrats; hence, these concessions speak to the very real pressure the elites put on the government to heal the damage to Italy's economy as a result of the Gothic presence. That said, the aristocracy perhaps benefitted most from these tax reductions as these taxpayers returned to rebuild their estates and homes in Italy and in Rome.[155]

Praetorian Prefects of Italy, Africa, and Gaul. The need for experienced men led Honorius and Constantius to appoint some men who had already held office in the government of Alaric and Attalus to the position of praetorian prefect in the post-410 decade. But since these men would be tied to the court now in Ravenna, they would have been more easily controlled. Certainly, in the praetorian prefects in the decade after 410, we find men who had made their way up to this position by holding offices both at the court and through the traditional civic offices in the run-up to Attalus's usurpation. For example, from 416 to 421, the office of praetorian prefect was occupied by a Roman senatorial aristocrat, Palladius, who had also served as chief financial officer (CSL) earlier and who had also been tied to the imperial court (see Table 3.4). Ioannes, praetorian prefect from June 412 to June 413 and again in 422, is another interesting case. He had been a high-ranking civic official who had served on the senatorial embassy that had gone to Alaric in 409. Ioannes's earlier experience in government is, as Carlos Machado rightly notes, "a good illustration of the degree to which court and senators were forced to compromise in order to rebuild the political settlement that had broken with the fall of Stilicho in 408."[156]

Circus Races and the Games. An inhabitant of early fifth-century Rome would probably have said that life had returned to normal when the circus

---

[154] *C. Th.* 11.28.7, May 413; 11.28.12, May 418. See also *C. Th.* 15.14.14, March 416. For abandoned lands, see *C. Th.* 11.1.31, Jan. 412. If an area could meet some of their tax demands, they were given tax reductions; see *C. Th.* 13.11.13, June 412. For this issue, see McEvoy 2013, p. 202.

[155] McEvoy 2013, p. 202.

[156] Machado 2013, p. 63. For Ioannes, see Table 3.4, and Ioannes 4, *PLRE* 2, p. 594 = Ioannes 2, *PLRE* 1, p. 459.

races and the games in the amphitheater had returned. The animal combats, gladiatorial contests, and theatrical performances of pantomimes that constituted the traditional games, along with the circus races, had long been the locus for wealthy senatorial aristocrats to display their status as part of their office-holding duties as well as being the site for imperial munificence. When exactly the circus races and games began again is hard to know, but the circus races and some games were held at the latest in 414 for the visit of Honorius for his *vicennalia*.[157] The celebration was far less elaborate than it had been in the past. When Constantius celebrated his consulship in this same year in Ravenna, he had had to use monies, less than expected, from the seized estates of the usurper Heraclian; only 2,000 pounds of gold emerged.[158] The relative poverty of the general contrasts with that of the senators, who although having suffered from the Gothic presence, were recovering financially over this decade. By early 423 to 425, a senator of the Anician family (Probus, son of Olybrius) easily spent 1,200 pounds of gold on his praetorian games.[159]

Archaeologists support these textual references to the return of the games. One of the central spaces for senatorial elite activity after 410 was the Flavian Amphitheater, or Colosseum, where gladiatorial combats and animal hunts were held. (See Map 1.) A series of inscriptions from the Colosseum through the fifth and well into the early sixth century shows the importance of this space for elite displays of status and accruing honor on the part of senatorial aristocrats, generals, and emperors. The first restoration of the Colosseum after the sack is recorded in an inscription by Iunius Valerius Bellicius, urban prefect between 417 and 423 (see Figure 6). Although not enough of the inscription survives to allow us to know the full nature of the restoration, scholars have hypothesized that these inscriptions can be associated with the reopening of the Colosseum and its purification.[160] This connection would have been necessary because archaeologists have found bodies buried next to the Colosseum in contravention of the laws against intramural burials; these internments have been dated to the early fifth century and interpreted as a sign of the desperate nature of the sieges before 410. Hence, Silvia Orlandi posits that one of the first tasks the Romans would have had to do would have been to exhume the bodies and purify the area of the amphitheater under the direction of the urban prefect with the approval of the Senate.

---

[157] Gillett 2001, p. 138 notes that Honorius is attested there by a law dated to August 30, 414 CE, *C. Th.* 16.5.55.

[158] Olymp. *Frag.* 23, ed. Blockley 1983, pp. 186–87.

[159] Olymp. *Frag.* 41.2, ed. Blockley 1983, pp. 204–7.

[160] Orlandi 2004, pp. 42–46; 67–81; and 86–159; and 2013, p. 340; Rea 2002, pp. 126–39.

Figure 6 Photo of fragments of the Bellicius inscription from the restoration in the Colosseum. *Source* Figure 4 from Orlandi 2013, p. 340.

The return of games to the amphitheater underscores the survival not just of animal hunts but also of gladiatorial combats. Indeed, images of these also appear, as Orlandi has observed, on one of the medallions known as *contorniates*, which were minted in conjunction with Roman games dated to 413 or 423 that show on one side a bust of *Dea Roma* with the acclamation "Rome Unconquered, a Fortunate Senate" (*Invicta Roma, felix Senatus*); the other side displays a scene of gladiatorial combat with the legend "Let the Renewal of the Spectacle/Gladiatorial Game Be Fortunate" (*Reparatio muneris feliciter*).[161] These artifacts point to the restoration of gladiatorial games and circuses in Rome by the end of the decade, accomplished with the support of Roman elites and a Christian emperor. Indeed, the earlier 399 law of Honorius that had tried to prevent gladiators from going into the service of senators had not at all closed off this form of entertainment, which arguably continued in the city until 438. Animal hunts and circus games were held long after that, into the sixth century, because senators and emperors wanted to continue them as a means of asserting their own status and power.[162]

Rebuilding Relationships: Senators, Emperors, and Generals in Rome

Senatorial, imperial, and military elites took active steps to restore the city in the immediate decade after the Gothic capture of the city. Their focus on

---

[161] The date of this *contorniate* series falls in this period, either to 413, according to Alföldi, or a decade later under Valentinian III, according to Chastagnol; see the discussion by Orlandi 2004, pp. 42 ff.

[162] See Ville 1960, pp. 320–35; and Salzman 1990, p. 227. For the games in 523, see Cass. *Var.* 5.42.

Rome may have grown out of necessity; Rome was of renewed importance to the western empire in light of lost territories in Africa, Gaul, Britain, and Spain. Rome – the *caput mundi* still – could rise again through the efforts of Rome's leadership. The key figure directing the restoration on the ground, as the evidence indicates, was the holder of the office of urban prefect. This position was consistently filled with members of Roman and Italian elite senatorial families, most of whom had not held high office before 410. With these urban prefects, we see a new generation of senators emerging and lending their talents and considerable resources to the city as they competed for influence. The emperor Honorius encouraged new senators, appointing them in the hope of restoring his relationship with Rome's aristocracy because he deemed their support critical for the stability of his government. At the same time, Honorius's government was heavily reliant on the general Constantius. And Roman senators were equally aware of the need to build ties to the general. Not surprisingly, then, the urban prefect in 420, Aurelius Anicius Symmachus, dedicated a statue to honor Constantius, praising him as a "repairer of the state and the father of the most invincible of princes."[163] This award shows the development of ties between senators and the military, part of the triangulation of power that was the hallmark of Rome in the decades after 410.

After 416, Honorius returned to Ravenna; his authority having been reasserted, he did not contest for power in Rome again in person. His final return was in 423, when his body was laid to rest in the mausoleum of the Theodosian dynasty south of the transept of St. Peter's.[164] His burial in Rome reasserted his family's support for the city and its ties to Roman imperial traditions of rulership, even as he offered imperial support for the bishop and church of Rome. Indeed, the bishop and the clergy welcomed imperial support because the decade after 410 had been challenging. The bishop of Rome, as we shall see, had to contest to reassert his authority in the face of other elites and non-elites who had been newly empowered by the events of 410. There were competing Christian bishops and sects in Rome who vied for followers with the bishop of Rome. As well, there were internal divisions within the clergy that contributed to the turmoil within the church during this decade, even as other lay elites – senators, emperors, and generals – sought to assert their influence using, as they always had, religion to further their positions in Rome. The ongoing contestation for influence with

---

[163] *CIL* 6.1719 = *ILS* 801. The inscription begins: *reparatori rei publicae [et] parenti invictissimo[rum] principum.*
[164] *LTUR Suburbium* IV, s.v. *S. Petri basilica, coemeterium, episcopia, cubicula, habitacula, porticus, fons, atrium,* pp. 185–95: p. 193 (H. Brandenburg). Johnson 1991, pp. 330–38.

lay and religious elites thus weakened the bishop of the city and hampered his efforts at recovery until the arrival of new imperial patrons in the later 420s who could help finance rebuilding the Church in Rome.

Bishops and the Clergy after 410

Many Christians saw the fall of Rome in 410 as a crisis of faith. In North Africa, Augustine vividly recreated the doubts expressed by ordinary Christians: "Look, it's during Christian times that Rome is being afflicted, or rather has been afflicted and burnt. Why in Christian times?"[165] Augustine delivered a series of sermons in the years 410 and 411 to an audience of refugees and worshippers before arriving at a new definition of Roman – that is, Christian – faith based on the dismissal of the physical *Urbs Roma:* "Perhaps Rome isn't destroyed; perhaps it has been scourged, not put to death, chastised perhaps, not obliterated. Perhaps Rome isn't perishing . . . if Romans aren't perishing. I mean, they won't perish if they praise God; they will if they blaspheme him. What is Rome, after all, but Romans?"[166]

However, the inhabitants of Rome were less convinced by this argument. For those who had remained as well as those who had returned, the physical restoration of their communities by their bishop was of urgent importance. Indeed, the faithful needed immediate pastoral care. Yet when the city had been taken, the bishop at the time, Innocent I (410–17), had been in Ravenna as part of a senatorial embassy to Honorius's court.[167] After the sack, Innocent remained at court for many months, not returning to the city until 412.[168] His absence had been problematic, leading some to turn to God for justification.[169] In the face of such doubts in a church that was suffering from physical losses, Innocent turned to the importation of liturgy to revive Christian communities across the city.

[165] Aug. *Sermon* 296.9 (=*serm.* Casin. 1,133): *Ecce temporibus christianis Roma affligitur, aut afflicta est, et incensa est: quare temporibus christianis?* For the sermons on the fall of Rome, see De Bruyn 1993, pp. 405–21; and Salzman 2015, pp. 346–59.

[166] Aug. *Sermon* 81 (*PL* 38. 505): *Forte Roma non perit, si Romani non pereant. Non enim peribunt, si Deum laudabunt: peribunt, si blasphemabunt. Roma enim quid est, nisi Romani?*

[167] Zos. 5.45; Oros. *Hist.* 7.39; and Sozomen, *HE* 9.7.

[168] Demougeot 1954, p. 32, note 3. From Ravenna, Innocent wrote to the bishop of Nich (*Ep.* 299, ed. Jaffé-Wattenbach, *Regesta I*, p. 46) stating that he stayed at Ravenna: *propter Romani populi necessitates creberrimas.* For Innocent's activities, see Dunn 2009, pp. 319–33.

[169] Oros. *Hist.* 7.39.

Liturgy and Topography: Contestation for Influence after 410

The Church of Rome incorporated a day to do penance and give thanks to God for the liberation of the city after the departure of Alaric in 410.[170] The best evidence for this day of commemoration is an important but little appreciated sermon, *Sermon* 84, preached by a later bishop of Rome, Leo (440–460), in the years 441–45.[171] Because this sermon was once thought to refer to the 455 sack of the city, it has not been fully appreciated for the evidence it provides for the ways in which the bishop and his clergy had responded to the events of 410.[172] But there are good reasons to associate this sermon and the annual day of penance and liberation with an earlier liturgical innovation taken by Innocent (410–17) soon after 410. The content of Leo's sermon certainly fits the sack of 410, and the likelihood of this day being an annual event is further suggested by its comparison with other such celebrations across the early fifth-century empire.

Leo *Sermon* 84. Leo's *Sermon* begins by lamenting the sparse church attendance on this day of thanksgiving prayer for surviving the sack:

> The religious devotion with which the whole congregation of the faithful used to come together to give thanks to God . . . on account of the day of our penance and our liberation (*ob diem castigationis et liberationis nostrae*) has lately been neglected by almost everyone, as the rare few who are present demonstrate. . . . For it is great danger when men are ungrateful to God, and through forgetfulness of his benefits feel no remorse for their chastisement, nor rejoice in their pardon.[173]

Leo explains that the city survived because God "softened the hearts of the raging barbarians," a reference to the liberation of the city when the Goths

---

[170] For some of these arguments, see Salzman 2014, pp. 183–201; and 2013, pp. 208–32.

[171] Chavasse's work on the manuscripts of Leo demonstrated that there was an initial publication of some fifty-four Sermons of Leo from the first five years of his pontificate and hence this sermon must refer to the 410 sack of the city; see Chavasse 1973, pp. 523–24 and pp. CXCI–CXCII, with discussion in vol. 138, pp. XIVXLV and CLXXV–CXCIII. See, too, Montanari 1997, vol. I. pp. 171–214. For dating this sermon to August 30 or September 6, but not precisely to the year 442 CE as Chavasse (p. 523) proposed, see my discussion above and Salzman 2014, pp. 183–201.

[172] Courcelle 1964, p. 184, note 2 is one of the few to identify Leo's remark as a reference to Alaric's departure from Rome, but he was arguing against the views of most scholars who saw it as a reference to the Vandal attack on Rome in 455.

[173] Leo, *Sermon* 84.1 (*CCSL* 138A, p. 525): *Religiosam devotionem, dilectissimi, qua ob diem castigationis et liberationis nostrae, cunctus fidelium populus ad agenda Deo gratias confluebat, pene ab omnibus proxime fuisse neglectam, ipsa paucorum qui adfuerunt raritas demonstravit, et cordi meo multum tristiae intulit, et plurimum pavoris incussit . . .. Magnum enim periculum est esse homines ingratos Deo, et per oblivionem beneficiorum eius nec de correptione conpungi, nec de remissione laetari.*

departed.[174] But he is emphatic that the Christians understand the true reason for their survival:

> Who restored this city to safety? Who snatched it from captivity? Who rebuilt this city for health? Who protected it from slaughter? Was it the circus games, or the watchful care of the saints? And by whose prayers was the divine decision to punish altered so that we who deserved wrath were saved for pardon?[175]

Leo is pained because less attention is paid to "veneration of the saints" (*cura sanctorum*) in church than to the "circus games" (*ludi Circensium*):

> It shames me to say it, but one must not keep silent. More effort is spent on demons than on the apostles, and the wild entertainments draw greater crowds than the blessed shrines of martyrs.[176]

The bishop argues that those Romans who believe that liberation was owed to the stars – that is, to fate or astrology – or to the gods are mistaken; he labels these people as "impious" and puts them in the same category as those who mistakenly trust in games, like the senatorial elites who fund them.[177]

But if it was God who had softened the barbarians' hearts, it was the bishop in church who had to convey thanks and lead the community on this day of "penance and liberation." In essence, Leo is asserting the symbolic role once held by the emperor who, as *pontifex maximus*, maintained the good will of God. For the bishop, however, the good will of God is maintained through the prayers of thanks mediated by the bishop's intersession in church, not in the circus.

This same conjunction of ideas – of a crisis as a sort of punishment with gratitude to God for survival – was certainly familiar to Christians living in Rome. So, for example, Romans still celebrated annually the Theodosian victory over the usurper Maximus, overthrown in 388.[178] In 425 a thanksgiving procession in Antioch with prayers in church was organized

---

[174] Leo, *Sermon* 84.2 (*CCSL* 138A), p. 525: *corda furentium barbarorum mitigare dignatus est.*

[175] Leo, *Sermon* 84.1 (*CCSL* 138A), p. 525: *Quis hanc urbem reformavit saluti? Quis a captivitate eruit? Quis a caede defendit? Ludus Circensium, an cura sanctorum, quorum utique precibus divinae censurae flexa sententia est, ut qui merebamur iram servaremur ad veniam?* Trans. adapted from Neil 2009, p. 120.

[176] Leo, *Sermon* 84.1 (*CCSL* 138A), p. 525: *Pudet dicere, sed necesse est non tacere: plus impenditur daemoniis quam apostolis, et maiorem obtinent frequentiam insana spectacula quam beata martyria.*

[177] Leo's concern with demons and the effects of the stars also led to his attacks on Manichees and heretics; see especially Maier 1996, pp. 440–61.

[178] Procop. *Wars* 3.4.16. After Theodosius, we hear of annual thanksgiving masses to celebrate other imperial victories; see Salzman 2014, pp. 190–91.

to celebrate Theodosius II's defeat of the usurper John.[179] Also, a day was added to the Christian Calendar of Constantinople to thank God for the survival of the city after the earthquake of November 6, 447; this day was commemorated annually with a procession and special liturgy, including thanksgiving prayers.[180] Such thanksgiving celebrations were annual events in the fifth century, allowing the bishop to organize the community to come together to commemorate their survival and to give thanks to God for the restoration of life under the direction of the bishop.

The Anniversary of 410 under Innocent. Leo's description of his service suggests that such a date had become part of the annual calendar of the city of Rome by the time that he was preaching in the early 440s. But the initial day of penance and liberation – which was once much more popularly attended, he complains – would have most likely been developed earlier in the fifth century, most reasonably under the papacy of Innocent. It may have begun in conjunction with Honorius's visits to Rome, either in August 414 for his *vicennalia* or in 416 for celebrations of his victory over the Goths.[181] Both of these were moments of thanksgiving, the former to celebrate the *vicennalia* and probably also the defeat of the usurper Heraclianus; the latter, to celebrate the defeat of Attalus; such imperial victory celebrations were often turned into annual events. If the original day of thanksgiving for liberation and penance had been a spontaneous event soon after 410, it may have become an annual event in association with the commemoration of Honorius's visit to Rome in 414 or 416. The manuscript evidence for the date of delivery for Leo's *Sermon* 84 lends some support connect it to Honorius's 414 stay.[182]

If this is the case, the thanksgiving service described by Leo's *Sermon* 84, held on either the last Sunday in August or the first Sunday in September in the years 441–45, hearkens back to a ritual instituted some thirty years earlier that had become an annual event. In the 440s, as Rome faced the threat of the

[179] Socr. *HE* 7.24; John of Antioch, *De insidiis*, Frag. 82, De Boor *Excerpta historica* 3.27–29. See McCormick 1986, p. 60.

[180] Baldovin 1987, p. 186, notes 117 and 118. The *Chronicon Paschale*, compiled during the reign of Heraclius, ca. 629, Baldovin, p. 586, indicates that this was a contemporary celebration at the Church of the Triconch in Constantinople. If the liberation of Rome was an annual thanksgiving ritual, it would seem that Rome preceded Constantinople in this regard. This commemoration appears to have lasted for at least 200 years, for it is recorded in a *Chronicle* dated to the year 629 CE as a contemporary celebration.

[181] For the August 414 and 416 visits, see Gillett 2001, pp. 137–41, and for the 414 visit, see *C. Th.* 16.5.55.

[182] For discussion of the manuscript evidence leading to the likelihood that the celebration was held in conjunction with the 414 visit of Honorius, see Salzman 2017B, pp. 65–85.

Vandals, Leo preached a message similar to that of his predecessor Innocent: Survival depends on divine aid, for which the bishop leads the city in doing penance and giving thanks in church.

But in Rome, unlike in Constantinople, where we hear of thanksgiving for imperial victories often including public processions, no such processions were recorded. As Jacob Latham has shown, there were no Christian processions in Rome until 556, when we find the first papal processions due to Byzantine interventions in episcopal politics; their absence from Rome contrasts with their occurrence in other late antique cities.[183] This late date for a processional liturgy in Rome and the relative slowness of the church in Rome in developing a stational liturgy are indicative, as I have also argued elsewhere, of the limited authority of Rome's bishop, literally unable to take control of the city's streets.[184] We see these same limits as well in the early decade after the sack as evidenced by the limited rebuilding efforts of the papacy.

Rebuilding Churches, 410–23. In the aftermath of the damage done to the churches and martyria in 410, the bishops of Rome did not undertake a major rebuilding campaign during the first decade of the city's restoration. In fact, as Manuela Gianandrea has observed, there is not a single act of artistic patronage that we can attribute to Innocent (401–17) throughout his tenure.[185] Not until Celestine (422–32) do we hear of an episcopal dedication of a church in the wake of damages done by the Goths; the *Liber Pontificalis* records that the Basilica of Julius was dedicated – not built – after the Gothic conflagration under this bishop of Rome and that silver liturgical vessels were presented upon its dedication without recording the funding source for either.[186] We know of one additional site that was damaged in the events of 410 because Bishop Sixtus of Rome (432–40) later requested that the emperor Valentinian construct a silver *fastigium* (a lintel or colonnade) in the Constantinian basilica, the modern St. John Lateran, because "it had been removed by the barbarians."[187]

The modesty of these early fifth-century efforts on the part of Rome's bishops can be explained by a number of factors. First, the fifth-century bishops of Rome were not aristocrats, nor did they have access to the kinds of financial resources that many of their senatorial parishioners had. To build churches, they relied on wealthy Roman aristocrats, clergy, or emperors. The only building attributed to the bishop of Rome, Innocent, in the

---

[183] Latham 2012, pp. 298–327.   [184] Salzman 2013, pp. 208–32.   [185] Gianandrea 2017, p. 183.

[186] *Lib. Pont.* 45, ed. Duchesne 1981, vol. 1, p. 230. Gianandrea 2017, p. 186 makes the important distinction between *dedicare* and *facere*.

[187] *Lib. Pont.* 45, Duchesne 1981, p. 233. For the *fastigium* as a lintel or colonnade within the church, see the discussion by Davis 2010, p. 115.

sixth-century *Liber Pontificalis* was funded by a senatorial aristocratic woman, Vestina. In her will, she had left instructions to sell off her jewelry and pearls and to use the money to build a church, with the help of some priests; Innocent carried out her wishes and thus established a titular – that is, a neighborhood – church in Rome (see my discussion of this term below).[188] In post-410 Rome, bishops remained dependent on wealthy donors – be they Christian senatorial aristocrats, non-elite clerics, or emperors – for their major building projects, as we shall see shortly under Valentinian III.[189] Thus where some scholars see the gradual widening of episcopal power in the fifth-century city, the building evidence suggests that its leadership was too concerned with internal reconstitution and caring for its dependents to play a significant civic role in this decade.

The Bishop of Rome Innocent and the Treatment of Captive Romans. Given what seem like limited episcopal resources, we can perhaps better understand why we do not hear that Innocent ransomed Christian prisoners who had been abducted by the Goths, a reality of siege warfare. Rather, Innocent aimed to restore the Christian communities of Rome primarily through liturgical innovations and his pastoral care. Yet here, too, we see the limits of his authority, as exemplified in the case of the abduction of a Roman woman named Ursa at some time in his papacy, perhaps due to the siege or capture of Rome in 410. Her husband, Fortunius, no doubt mourned his loss, but rather than wait for her to return, he had remarried. To his surprise, Ursa later returned. Finding that he had remarried happily, she went to the bishop, Innocent, for assistance in getting her husband back. Innocent agreed to help, but he could only do so through the intervention of a powerful senatorial aristocrat named Probus, whom Innocent called "deservedly illustrious lord, my son" (*domine fili merito illustris*).[190] Innocent wrote to Probus to try to persuade him to get Fortunius to put aside his second wife. This indirect method of providing pastoral care demonstrates the limits of Innocent's authority.

On the one hand, as Kristina Sessa has cogently observed, the bishop had no legal leg to stand on; according to Roman law, if the enemy captures

---

[188] *Lib. Pont.* 42, Duchesne 1981, p. 220 cited the church donated by Vestina as the *basilica sanctorum Gervasi et Protasi*. However, the church is called the *Titulus of Vestina* in the Council of 499 (*MGH. AA* 12 p. 11). Its name reflects its donor.

[189] Hillner 2007, pp. 225–61. See too Bowes 2008, pp. 65–67; Salzman 2013, pp. 208–32.

[190] Innocent *Ep.* 36 (*PL* 20, 602). For Probus identified with Flavius Anicius Petronius Probus, consul of 406, see Probus 11, *PLRE* 2, pp. 913–14. For an excellent discussion of this case, see Sessa 2012, pp. 140–44.

a spouse, one can remarry without incurring penalties, although there may have been an accustomed waiting period.[191] Yet Innocent was promoting the Christian view of marriage as a permanent bond, so, as Sessa emphasized, the only option for Innocent was to work through preexisting social networks, which is why he had written to Probus, a high-ranking senator, to persuade Fortunius to change his mind. Probus was likely the patron of Ursa and Fortunius, who were either members of his household or his tenants, clients, or freedmen/freedwomen. The success or failure of Innocent's intervention is not known, but it points to the kind of indirect, limited influence the bishop of Rome had in helping to resolve some of the personal domestic issues that emerged in the wake of this "fall" of Rome. To do so, he had to involve the illustrious senator Probus in a domestic dispute; this scenario must have played out across the city as captured folks returned to Rome after 410.

Internal Conflicts. Innocent, like his immediate successors, faced challenges to his authority from clergy within the church, a situation that also deterred him from taking a larger role in the restoration of the city. Tensions persisted between the powerful seven deacons who worked closely with the bishop. The deacons had financial responsibilities that gave them power and influence, and they came into conflict at time with the city's priests who served in the more than twenty neighborhood churches across the city.[192] The bishop also faced challenges to his authority from rival Christian sects, which, we know, still thrived in the fifth century.

We can see some of these tensions emerge as Innocent was forced to take a stand on the views of the ascetic Pelagius, who had resided in Rome. Pelagius had spread views on sin and free will that were counter to those of some powerful contemporary Christian bishops, most notably Augustine. After living through the events of 410 – which Pelagius described as the apocalypse – he departed for North Africa and then traveled to Palestine, but his followers remained in the West. Toward the end of his reign in 417,

---

[191] Sessa 2012, p. 141, pointing to the *C. Th.* 5.7.1, dated to 366 CE. Justinian would change this law in 536, *Nov.* 22.7, and reaffirmed in 117.12 in 542, to put in place a waiting period of five years before remarriage if the captured spouse was not known to be alive; if the captured spouse was alive, remarriage was not possible.

[192] For the seven deacons with their duties, see *Lib. Pont.* 21, ed. Duchesne 1981, p. 148. For the number of priests, see note 92 above. For structural tensions with priests in the more than twenty titular churches in the early fifth century, see Hunter 2017, pp. 496–510, and note 195 below.

Innocent openly condemned Pelagius and his followers.[193] But Innocent's successor, Zosimus, failed to satisfy the clergy in his handling of Pelagius and his followers. Hence, a number of them complained about their treatment in person at the court of the emperor Honorius in Ravenna.[194]

After the untimely death of Zosimus in 418, divisions within Rome's clergy emerged openly on the question of a successor. Eulalius was supported by his fellow deacons as well as a few priests and the population at large, while his rival, Boniface, drew support largely from his fellow priests, some seventy of whom wrote to Honorius to dispute the events as relayed to the emperor by the then urban prefect Anicius Symmachus.[195] The disputed election led to fighting in the streets of Rome. In what we will see as a recurrent pattern, the emperor, the general Constantius, and the senatorial aristocratic urban prefect Anicius Symmachus were all involved in trying to put an end to the violence.[196] But rather than go into the political and theological differences, I emphasize here that the continuing tensions within the church between deacons and priests that emerged full-blown in the disputed election of 418 limited the ability of the bishops to engage as fully as possible in the restoration of the city in the decade after the sack. These internal challenges from his own clergy as well as from other Christian groups in the city, as represented, for instance, by the Pelagians, diminished the influence of these bishops through the end of Honorius's reign, even as the city was regaining its economic, political, and social footing.

Rome Resurgent: The City under Valentinian III (425–55)

The resurgence of Rome helps to explain the return of Emperor Valentinian III and his court to the city in the second quarter of the fifth century. It is worth considering these decades under Valentinian III to fully appreciate the

[193] The twists and turns of this well-documented controversy survive; see Wermelinger 1975; and Marcos 2013, pp. 145–66. Innocent condemned (*damnavit*) Pelagius and his supporter Caelestius; see *Lib. Pont.* 21, ed. Duchesne 1981, p. 220. For Pelagius on 410, see note 5 above.

[194] For the view that Zosimus's actions divided the clergy, see Wermelinger 1975, p. 137, and Marcos 2013, p. 159.

[195] See *Lib. Pont.* 43 and 44, ed. Duchesne 1981, pp. 223–29. For the deacons backing their fellow deacon Eulalius who also had the support of the population at large, see Honorius, *Exemplum sacrarum litterarum (Gestis omnibus)* = CA 15 (*CSEL* 35, pp. 60–61); and *Precum ad Honorium (Petimus clementiam)* = CA 17 (*CSEL* 35, pp. 63–64). For the seventy presbyters who contested the events, see *Precum ad Honorium (Petimus clementiam)* = CA Ep. 17 (*CSEL* 35, pp. 63–65).

[196] See *CA*, 16, 19, 29, 34 (*CSEL* 35, pp. 59–60, 61–63, 66–67, 74–76, 80–81), for correspondence between Symmachus and the emperor Honorius; CA 29, 30, and 32 (*CSEL* 35, pp. 74–76, 78–79) for correspondence between Symmachus and Constantius.

revival of Rome so soon after the 410 capture and before moving to Chapter 4 on the crisis of 455.

Because Rome was central to the stability of the empire, the death of Honorius and the usurpation in Rome in 423 by John, a high court official, the former chief of the notaries (*primicerius notariorum*), were seen as a serious threat to the eastern court and the Theodosian dynasty.[197] The eastern emperor, Theodosius II, the nephew of Honorius, refused to acknowledge John and sought to restore legitimate Roman rule. In Constantinople in late 424, Theodosius II thus proclaimed as caesar – junior ruler, as it were – the six-year-old boy Placidus Valentinian, son of Honorius's sister Galla Placidia and the now deceased general and (briefly) western emperor Flavius Constantius.[198] To signal his support, Theodosius II betrothed his one-year-old daughter, Licinia Eudoxia, to Placidus Valentinian, now Valentinian III.[199] He also sent a military expedition to Italy. Support for John's rule fell apart. The Senate reversed its allegiance, and by mid-425 the then urban prefect, Anicius Acilus Glabrio Faustus, made manifest his support for the new regime by dedicating a statue honoring Valentinian III as caesar.[200]

Faustus was likely again urban prefect when in Rome on October 23, 425, Valentinian III was elevated to the position of emperor in a public ceremony, which the city's mints commemorated by issuing gold coins as gifts to certain supporters and senators.[201] Since he was a child, Valentinian's mother, Galla Placidia, and the officials in his court took control of administering the state. Thus, for instance, as Mark Humphries underscores, the western court issued laws in the name of Valentinian III and Theodosius II to assert imperial control over Italy and Africa.[202] The court, located mostly in Ravenna, also passed laws to gain the support of senators and the Senate in Rome. In 426, Valentinian III partially remitted the gold, a virtual tax, traditionally paid to the emperor by the senators, and passed laws dealing with inheritance and

---

[197] For the usurpation by John, see Ioannes 6, *PLRE* 2, pp. 594–95. See the discussions by McEvoy 2013, pp. 229–31; Humphries 2012, p. 164.

[198] See Humphries 2012, p. 164 and notes 15–16 for bibliography. For Galla Placidia and Constantius, see notes 89 and 90 above.

[199] For Licinia Eudoxia, born in 422, see Marcell. com. *Chron.* s.a. 422, and Licinia Eudoxia 2, *PLRE* 2, pp. 410–12. The marriage took place in Constantinople in 437.

[200] *CIL* 6.1676. For Valentinian as Caesar, see Olymp. *Frag.* 43.1, ed. Blockley 1983, pp. 206–7.

[201] See Kent, *RIC* 10.363 (nos. 2001–2002) for the gold solidi. On this event, see Humphries 2012, pp. 164–65.

[202] Humphries 2012, p. 165.

succession that would have appealed to wealthy elites.[203] Valentinian's court relied on the military to maintain control. Soon after 425, two powerful but competing Roman generals emerged, Flavius Aetius and Boniface. Indeed, Flavius Aetius, who had originally supported the usurper, had gathered a force of Huns that he later disbanded, but the Romans had continued to rely on a range of Germanic paid soldiers to fight for them now as they had since the late fourth century. Aetius had disbanded the Huns with the fall of John and then changed his allegiance to support Valentinian III.[204]

Valentinian III made an early ceremonial visit to Rome in 425–26 to assert his control, but we cannot track his return visits there with certainty until the 440s, when he was recorded as being there often – between January and March 440, in August 442, from March to December 443, and between 445 and 447 – before taking up permanent residence in 450 until his death on March 16, 455.[205] The continual presence of the emperor and his court has to be appreciated against the background of recent history. With the exception of Maxentius (306–12), Valentinian III was the first emperor to reside in Rome since the mid third-century Gallienus. The prolonged presence of Valentinian and his court in the city brought new possibilities for advancement and influence, which further fueled the ambitions of Rome's senatorial aristocratic, ecclesiastical, and military elites alongside their imperial peers.

In this reviving city, all but one of the attested urban prefects under Valentinian III (425–55) were senators from Rome. In the early years, Valentinian sought continuity with the regime of Honorius and reappointed men who had held this office before, such as Faustus and Petronius Maximus. And there continued to be a number of urban prefects drawn from the great senatorial families such as the Petronii, the Acilii, the Glabriones, and the Nicomachi.[206] Importantly, the majority of Valentinian's praetorian prefects of Italy also came from distinguished Italo-Roman senatorial families, another indication of the close ties between this emperor and the aristocracy.[207]

---

[203] For the remission of the gold given to the emperor (*aurum oblaticium*) in 426, see *C. Th.* 6.2.25. For the laws, see Honoré 1998, pp. 249–51.

[204] For Flavius Aetius, see Aetius 7, *PLRE* 2, pp. 21–29. For Boniface, general since 423, see Bonifatius 3, *PLRE* 2, pp. 237–40.

[205] Humphries 2012, pp. 161–82, with references to travels at p. 166, citing the important study by Gillett 2001, p. 145.

[206] Humphries 2012, pp. 161–82. Grossi 2019 provides important new dates for the urban prefects under Valentinian, while reinforcing their important senatorial families. I do not, however, see evidence for a strong political division between the Anicii and the Caeionii-Decentii as Grossi (pp. 160–61) proposes. However, the inclusion of Gallo-Roman names is an important observation.

[207] Twyman 1987, pp. 480–503.

Emblematic of the resurging influence of senatorial aristocrats working in close conjunction with the imperial court is the career of Petronius Maximus. His father had spent lavishly on his son's praetorian games after 410; Olympiodorus claims that Petronius Maximus's father spent 40 *centenaria* (which equaled 300,000 solidi, or 4,000 pounds) of gold on these games, dating to approximately 411, an amount twice as much as what Symmachus spent on his son's games in 402.[208] This expenditure in the period soon after the 410 capture should be seen as an important reinvestment on the part of this family in a traditional form of civic euergetism intended to gain political influence in a time-honored way. It worked. Petronius was tapped to serve as the key financial figure, the count of the imperial fund, in this critical period of recovery, 416–19, before attaining the position of urban prefect (420–21), an office he held again, likely before his two praetorian prefectures (421?–39, 439–41). He was twice honored as consul (433, 443) as well as named *patricius* by 445.[209]

Petronius Maximus's career evidences the status that a wealthy senatorial aristocrat could achieve by holding a combination of traditional senatorial civic offices along with providing service to the imperial court. His life embodied the values that raised him, at least according to the Gallo-Roman aristocrat Sidonius Apollinaris: "His hospitality and character, his wealth and his display, his literary reputation and his magistracies, his estate, and his roll of clients were splendid indeed; the very division of his time was so carefully looked after that it was measured and arranged by the hourly periods of the clock."[210] Nor was Petronius Maximus alone in gaining power and status through office and patronage. The Roman aristocrat Anicius Acilius Glabrio Faustus, who as urban prefect restored part of the Colosseum, attained the position of praetorian prefect of Italy, Illyria, and Africa, where he worked closely with the imperial administration before attaining his consulship in 438.[211]

Roman senatorial aristocrats, along with the emperor and his family, also manifested their restored positions in society through their patronage of the church. A prominent fifth-century family that could claim an urban prefect in 412, passed on a house (*domus Palmati*) to the church of Rome.[212] We do not know the exact circumstances of the donation, but the Bishop of Rome,

---

[208] Olymp. *Frag.* 41.2, ed. Blockley 1983, pp. 204–5.   [209] See Maximus 22, *PLRE* 2, pp. 749–50.

[210] Sid. Apoll. *Ep.* 2.1.4: *igitur ille, epulae mores, pecuniae pompae, litterae fasces, patrimonia patrocinia florebant, cuius ipsa sic denique spatia vitae custodiebant ut per horarum disposita clepsydras explicarentur.* Transl. by Anderson, *LCL*, 1996, p. 477.

[211] See Faustus 8, *PLRE* 2, pp. 452–54. For the restorations, see *CIL* 6.32090.

[212] For the prefect of 412, see Palmatus 2, *PLRE* 2, p. 824; and Table 3.1.

Sixtus III (432–40) used it as part of the patrimony when building the church of modern St. Maria Maggiore.[213] Indeed, a decline in population after 410 reduced pressures on Rome's housing market, a factor that also contributed to making donations of urban houses, along with public baths and bakeries, a more attractive avenue for aristocratic patrons to enhance their status among their fellow worshippers as well as their influence in the church.[214]

The donations of Roman aristocrats like Palmatus certainly augmented the wealth of the church of Rome, but such gifts also emphasized the role of elites as religious patrons. As has been well studied, wealthy aristocrats frequently donated private properties, either houses (*domus*) or apartment blocks (*insulae*) that became the foundations of a number of Rome's neighborhood churches – the *tituli*, or titular churches – whose name refers to the fact that the donors legally owned the properties that they were now giving to the church. Indeed, many of these titular churches continued to bear the names of their private founders or were associated through foundation legends with aristocratic owners. The question persists among scholars as to how much control donors exercised over the titular churches that were donated.[215] Some tensions over this issue do emerge (see Chapter 4). Nonetheless, the donation of elite urban properties after 410 led to the growing wealth of the church and gave more resources to the bishop of Rome to use at his discretion.

The return of the emperor Valentinian III to the city for extended periods of time fueled a construction boom for the church in Rome. Valentinian III and his family were generous benefactors. As Andrew Gillett observed, in the *Book of the Popes* the donations by Valentinian III represent the largest imperial investment in the Roman church since the time of Constantine.[216] Even if one does not fully accept the accuracy of the

---

[213] The *domus* furnished a rent of 155 solidi and 3 *siliqua* (*Lib. Pont.* 38, ed. Duchesne 1981, p. 233), an amount comparable to the 155 solidi rent from one *domus* under Bishop Damasus. See too Spera 2012, pp. 219–27, esp. 224–27 for wealthy Roman aristocrats active in Rome after the 410 sack.

[214] The *Liber Pontificalis* records a large number of such donations to the fifth-century church; on their impact, see Machado 2019, pp. 192–94.

[215] See Salzman 2013, pp. 229–30. See also Hillner 2006, pp. 56–65, who adds that a number of the titular churches were donated by wealthy clergy. For the division among scholars on how much control the lay patron had on these titular churches once donated, see Machado 2019, p. 193, who suggests, with reason, that episcopal control increased over time. Hillner 2006, pp. 61–62 points to evidence for the bishop's complete control from a letter of Bishop Pelagius dating to 558 (*Ep.* 17, ed. Gasso). That fits with my view of the increased civic authority of the bishop of Rome in post Gothic War Italy. (see Chapter 6), For the definition of the *titulus* as the legal right of possession of the owner, see Pietri 1978, p. 328. For more on the titular churches in fifth-century Rome, see Chapter 4.

[216] Gillett 2001, p. 145.

amounts listed in the *Book of the Popes*, the construction projects are impressive: the imperial family (re)built St. Peter in Chains; restored the mosaics and decoration of the Church of the Holy Cross in Jerusalem; and rebuilt St. Paul Outside the Walls as a monumental church and decorated its triumphal arch, donating gold and silver as well as sculptures, structures, and liturgical furnishings to this last church along with doing the same to St. Peter's in the Vatican and St. John Lateran.[217]

Bishop Leo of Rome (440–61), even more than his predecessors Celestine I (422–32) and Sixtus III (432–40), was able to benefit from Valentinian's support, and he used it to contest for influence with Rome's senatorial elites not only through church building and decoration but also through the visual manifestation of episcopal authority demonstrated by his control of topography and liturgy. In Leo's *Sermons* – which were edited and circulated during his lifetime – we see the bishop of Rome congregating the faithful at St. Peter's in the Vatican on a regular basis and at new times of the year in a period when most Christians were not yet expected to attend church every Sunday and when there was not yet a set church or place that the bishop of Rome would return to every year for his sermons on the feasts of the martyrs of Rome.[218] Indeed, through the fourth and into the early fifth century, St. Peter's was used only infrequently for liturgical purposes, mostly at Christmas or for the Feast of Saints Peter and Paul, and was most often a site for commemoration of the dead.[219] But Leo's sermons highlight St. Peter's as the focus of episcopal liturgy. Hence Leo's efforts at centralizing ritual at St. Peter's – what I call his use of liturgical topography – aimed to make the Vatican sanctuary, not St. John Lateran, as some have proposed, "the religious center ... and the symbol of the papacy" in the middle of the fifth century.[220]

[217] For sources, see Ward-Perkins 1984, p. 237 and Humphries 2012, p. 167. Gianandrea 2017, pp. 208–12 suggests that Valentinian III also started the construction of St. Stephen in the Round.

[218] See Green 2008, pp. 3–4; MacMullen 2009, pp. 81–89. Masses might be held on a weekly basis in the urban *tituli*, but that does not mean weekly attendance. On weekly services, see Saxer 1989, II, p. 928.

[219] See Pietri 1976, pp. 575–95; Krautheimer 1983, pp. 112–16; Bauer 2012, pp. 155–70; and de Blaauw 1994, pp. 496–511. I agree with de Blaauw that the "sleepless priest" performing rites at St Peter's on the Feast of Saints Peter and Paul should be identified with the bishop of Rome; Paulinus, *Perist.* 12, 61–64.

[220] Krautheimer 1983, pp. 112–16 acknowledges the competition between St. John Lateran and St. Peter's, but proposes that St John Lateran was the seat of the papacy based largely on physical changes to the area, as does Thacker 2007, p. 43, who sees the emergence of St. Peter's only under Pope Symmachus (498–514). However, the archaeological evidence to support this view, like the bishop's palace, does not exist for the early fifth century and the textual evidence is open to interpretation. For a different point of view, see Liverani 2004, pp. 17–49.

Leo's use of topography within Christian liturgy should thus be seen as one of the earliest episcopal attempts to contest for space – physically and symbolically – in Rome. Leo encouraged Christians to forego games on civic holidays and to participate instead in communal public worship, most often at St. Peter's in the Vatican. Since the fourth century, this site had been a locus for conspicuous aristocratic munificence – private burial monuments, funerary banquets, and charity. Drunken feasts "far from the bishop's conversation" suggest that the rites at St. Peter's had been hard for the bishop to control, especially since Rome's aristocrats spent lavishly there into the fifth century.[221] For example, a senatorial woman named Anastasia and her husband decorated an unidentified structure in the basilica, perhaps the baptistery, in the late fourth century, while another Anastasia, who was married to the consul of 423, paid for the decoration on the façade of the basilica at the request of the bishop Leo.[222]

By centralizing episcopal liturgy, including public vigils and fasts, at St. Peter's, Leo was openly asserting his authority and control in competition with Rome's aristocracy. Simultaneously, Leo's use of liturgy at the Vatican site offered a stage to demonstrate his authority in the same space as the imperial family. When Valentinian III and his family came to Rome in 450, they visited St. Peter's on the day after their arrival to attend a vigil, probably the feast known as the Chair of Peter (*cathedra Petri*).[223] A little later that year, Valentinian III's mother, Galla Placidia, along with the assembled Senate, presided over the reburial of Placidia's long-dead son, Theodosius, in a chapel in St. Peter's.[224] Leo benefitted from the presence of the imperial family as he asserted his religious role also in front of Roman elites.

---

[221] For criticism of drunken feasting at St. Peter's, see Aug. *Ep.* 29.9–10 (*CSEL* 30.1), 119–20 (*remotus . . . ab episcopi conversatione*). For the failure of the bishop of Rome's control there, see Thacker 2007, p. 43. For one aristocratic funeral in St. Peter's, that of Pammachius' wife, see Paulinus of Nola, *Ep.* 13.11 (*CSEL* 29), pp. 92–95. For aristocratic charity to the poor in the Vatican area, see Amm. Marc. 27.3.6; Bauer 2012, pp. 156–59.

[222] For the senatorial Anastasia and Damasus, see *CIL* 6.41331a = *ICUR* n.s. II, 4097. For the Anastasia married to the consul of 423, see CIL 6.41397a= *ICUR* n.s. II, 4102. And see the discussion by Machado 2019, pp. 190–91. Her son, the wealthy Rufius Viventius Gallus, also donated to a construction in St. Peter's; see Gallus 3, *PLRE* 2, p. 492, and *ILCV* 1759.

[223] Leo, *Epp.* 55–58.

[224] Continuation to Prosper in the Codex Reichenaviensis, c. 12, ed. Mommsen 1892, p. 489 *Theodosius cum magna pompa a Placidia et Leone et omni senator deductus et in mauseoleo ad apostolum Petrum depositus est.* See the discussion by Humphries 2012, p. 170.

Rome and the Coming of the Huns and the Vandals

The resurgence of Rome and the growing influence of its elites – senatorial, ecclesiastical, imperial, and military – in a revived capital were threatened by Rome's conflicts with the Vandals and Huns. After the Vandals had seized Carthage in 439, Valentinian III signed a second, very important treaty with the Vandal king Geiseric in 442, which from the Roman imperial perspective was very advantageous. It ended Vandal attacks and divided the wealthy North African provinces between Vandals and Romans.[225] Imperial lands in the fertile provinces of Africa Proconsularis and Byzacena as well as eastern Numidia and western Tripolitania were lost to the Vandals, but the emperor regained control of the less fertile provinces of Mauretania Caesariensis, Stifensis, and western Numidia.[226] (See Map 4.)

Valentinian III's government worked to reduce the impact of the losses on those affected, especially the aristocrats; he remitted taxes for those landholders who had suffered losses in the recent war and even gave portions of the imperial estates to those who had lost lands to the Vandals and to those involved in supplying bread for Rome, even as he tried to control the military situation on the Numidian frontiers.[227] The impact of these territorial losses on Rome's aristocracy thus varied greatly. But it surely is a sign of financial stress that by the mid fifth century, the less wealthy provincial aristocrats of the two lower senatorial grades (*clarissimi* and *spectabiles*) were no longer required to come to Rome to give games and no longer required special permission to reside in the provinces; only the men with the highest rank, the "illustrious" senators (*illustres*), came to the city to sponsor the games – in essence a tax on their wealth – and had to establish fiscal residency in Rome.[228] These changes show that the bifurcation of the senatorial elites continued. (For these differences, see the last section of Chapter 2.) Indeed,

---

[225] Prosper, *Chron.* s.a. 442.

[226] Conant 2012, p. 22 and note 9, citing Vict. *Vit.* 1.13, p. 7 and *N. Val.* 13 and 34.

[227] *N. Val.* 12; 13; 34.3–4. Compare Leo, *Ep.* 12 to the bishops of Mauretania; and see Merrills and Miles 2010, pp. 64–65.

[228] For these senatorial requirements, see Chapter 2 note 239. *C. Iust.* 12.2.1, 450 CE, states that *clarissimi* and *spectabiles* were not required to undertake the office of praetor. *C. Iust.* 12.1.15 abolished the need for permission to reside in the provinces, between 426 and 442 CE. Jones 1964, p. 529, observed that: "Marcian by excusing provincial *spectabiles* and *clarissimi* from the praetorship, cut their last effective link with the senate. The *illustres* thus came to form the inner aristocracy . . ." The lower ranks of senators contributed money for the games to a special treasury, the *arca quaestoria*; see Zuckerman 1998, p. 129. However, residency in Rome was required for all active in the Senate there, which could include the lower senatorial ranks of *spectabiles* and *clarissimi*. Thus residency further distinguished provincial *clarissimi* and *spectabiles* from senators of those ranks in either Rome or Constantinople. On this, see Cass. *Var.* 7.37; Cracco Ruggini 1998, p. 347; La Rocca and Oppedisano 2016, pp. 30–31 and 185–86.

these distinctions in senatorial rank had only sharpened in the fifth century, enabling the wealthier senators to be able to withstand financial losses in Africa.

The treaty was confirmed by what some have seen as a "massive break" with Roman tradition.[229] Emperor Valentinian III, now wed to Licinia Eudoxia, agreed to a future marriage of the Vandal king Geiseric's eldest son, Huneric, to his four-year-old daughter, Eudocia.[230] Traditionalists, if they were upset, are not recorded as being such. Most Romans, and certainly those in Rome, must have breathed a collective sigh of relief. Of key import was the treaty's stabilization of the grain supply for Rome, which was now paid as part of the Vandals' yearly tribute to Rome.[231] Moreover, it is clear, from a variety of sources, that this treaty allowed for trade to continue between North Africa and the western Mediterranean. Only now, Vandal landlords, alongside Roman ones, sold their goods from Africa across the Mediterranean; a considerable number of amphorae filled with African olive oil shipped abroad date from the Vandal period, and African goods continued to travel to Rome and Italy after the enactment of the treaty.[232]

Although it used to be said that the Vandal seizure of Africa irrevocably weakened the Italian senatorial aristocracy, that idea is no longer viable. Indeed, landowners in Africa had faced significant losses, but the wealthiest senators weathered these changes and even saw increased revenues resulting from increased demands for their produce from Italy and Sicily. As scholars have noted, by the 450s, the loss of African territories alongside the losses of Britain and large parts of Gaul and Spain meant that the western empire was far smaller than it had been in the early fifth century. This reduction in its western provinces, conversely, made Italy and the city of Rome, along with the senatorial aristocrats who resided there, more influential.[233] This was one factor in Valentinian III's decision to reside in Rome rather than in Ravenna after 450.

Yet 450 was also the year that the eastern emperor, Marcian, feeling secure and in need of funds, stopped paying the customary tribute to the Hunnic forces that had become increasingly powerful under the direction of their then king, Attila.[234] The Huns had been pressuring the Roman frontiers

---

[229] Heather 2006, p. 292.
[230] Merobaudes, *Panegyricus* II, ed. Vollmer, *MGH AA* 14, pp. 22–18, esp. p. 12, lines 24–29 and Merobaudes, *Carmen* 1.17–1.8, ed. Vollmer, *MGH AA* 14.3 with commentary by Clover 1971, pp. 24, 51–54; and Conant 2012, p. 23. For Eudocia, see Eudocia 1, *PLRE* 2, pp. 407–8.
[231] Procop. *Wars* 3.4.13, and Conant 2012, p. 23, note 13.
[232] Conant 2012, pp. 51–52 and note 153; pp. 48–49 and note 141.
[233] Humphries 2007, p. 40. McEvoy 2017, pp. 95–97 and note 2.
[234] For a good discussion of these events, see Maas 2015, pp. 1–25.

along the Rhine and the Danube since the late fourth century, but payments had managed to keep this group in the Balkans. Angered and in search of an easier target, Attila and his forces moved westward into Gaul. The Huns suffered a defeat there at the hands of the Roman general Aetius, who had led a coalition of Romans, Franks, Burgundians, and Visigoths against Attila in 451 on the Catalaunian Plains.[235] However, Attila retreated with his followers, a mix of Hunnic and other Germanic soldiers, wives, and children, into northern Italy in 452. Allegedly, he had been asked to come by Iusta Grata Honoria, the daughter of the previous emperor Constantius and the empress Galla Placidia.[236]

When Attila was encamped in the area of Venetia (near Mantua), the emperor, Senate, and people of Rome sent an embassy, which included Leo, to deter his attack. Money exchanged hands, and a famine in Italy along with the outbreak of the plague made Attila withdraw to the Great Hungarian Plain.[237] As he celebrated his new marriage to a Gothic princess, Attila went to bed drunk and somehow hemorrhaged, choking to death in his own blood.[238] After Attila's demise in 453, disunity overtook the Hunnic leaders and their confederation disintegrated.[239] The emperor Valentinian III and the inhabitants of Rome in 454 could look forward to a world without any immediate Hunnic threat. Indeed, with the accretion of power and wealth increasingly centered on a smaller group of aristocratic families in Rome, with a resident imperial family, the future of the fifth-century city and its aristocracy once more looked secure.

Elite Contestations after 410: Some Interim Conclusions

The sack of Rome in 410 was a crisis in the eyes of contemporaries, but it also offered new opportunities for Roman elites. The Roman senatorial aristocracy, along with the military elite, may have gained the most in terms of power and influence as they rebuilt their relationships with one another,

---

[235] This battle is discussed along with changes in the military by Elton 2015, pp. 193–95.

[236] For Honoria's life, see *PLRE* 2, pp. 568–69. Honoria had unhappily embraced the life of a virgin, but after breaking her vows, was forced into an engagement to a senator in Constantinople whom she despised. In an attempt to avoid this lackluster marriage, Honoria wrote to Attila in search of assistance and sent her signet ring. Attila saw this as a marriage proposal and demanded half of the western Empire as her dowry. Only the intervention of her mother, Galla Placidia, saved her from execution by her brother. See Priscus, *Frag.* 17 = John of Antioch, *Frag.* 199.2, ed. Blockley 1983, pp. 300–4.

[237] Priscus, *Frag.* 22 = Jord. *Get.* 42.219–24, ed. Blockley 1983, pp. 310–13.

[238] Priscus, *Frag.* 24 = Jord. *Get.* 49.254–55, ed. Blockley 1983, pp. 316–19.

[239] For a succinct summary of Attila's demise and its impact, see Maas 2015, pp. 16–18.

with imperial courtiers, and with the emperor Honorius. The proliferation of statues to honor senators and generals in public spaces of the city once monopolized by the emperor and the imperial family – in the Forum, the Forum of Trajan, and the Colosseum – was one way of demonstrating their enlarged influence. (See Map 1.) After 410 we see the emperor Honorius reasserting his authority in Rome even as he ceded the active role of defending the city to the military and of administering it to the senatorial aristocracy.

Another indication of the intrusion of senators and generals into the civic life of the city, and a good example of their close ties, is afforded by their interactions as they tried to put a halt to the fighting that overtook Rome over episcopal succession after the death of the Bishop of Rome Zosimus in 418. The then urban prefect, Symmachus, wrote letters to inform the emperor, but he also wrote to the general Constantius for advice about how to proceed. It is fitting that Symmachus addressed his letter to the general as "Lord, forever illustrious and magnificent in all ways, and deservedly sublime and outstanding patron, Constantius."[240] Similarly gracious was the general's reply to the urban prefect, whom he addresses as "your eminence" (*tua eximietas*).[241] Both the prefect and the general referenced the emperor in their responses, but his consultation of the general is a sign not only of Constantius's importance but also of his ties to senatorial aristocrats. It is eminently fitting that in addition to the statue to honor Honorius dedicated by this urban prefect in the Theater of Pompey, a statue to Constantius as "the repairer of the republic and parent of the most unconquered princes" was also installed in Rome in 420 by this same urban prefect.[242]

The year 410 and its aftermath had a significant impact on the church and the bishop of Rome. Although much modern scholarship has traditionally argued that "already by the fifth century the popes had taken over the role of emperors within the city of Rome in authority, patronage, and church benefaction," the evidence from 410 and the bishops' responses in the decade following go against that simple transformation.[243] Rather, this

---

[240] *CA* 29 (*CSEL* 35, p. 74): *Domino semper illustri et cuncta magnifico meritoque sublimi ac praecelso patrono Constantio.*

[241] *CA* 30 (*CSEL* 35, p. 76).

[242] For the dedication of a statue by the urban prefect Symmachus to Constantius see note 163 above. For the statue by Symmachus to Honorius, see *CIL* 6.1193.

[243] McEvoy 2013, p. 277, referring to the traditional view of Rome in which the bishop had a large civic role. In support of this perspective of the bishop as civil leader, see, for example, Neil 2009, pp. 4–8; and the influential work by Krautheimer 1983, pp. 99, 121, discussed by Gianandrea 2017, pp. 183–216. For a counterview, see Humphries 2007, pp. 25, 46–47, 54–57; and 2012, pp. 161–82.

chapter has shown that especially in the post-410 period, Rome was very much still beholden to secular elites – senatorial, imperial, and military – for patronage, rebuilding, and security. The transition from an imperial to a papal city had clearly not yet happened. On the contrary, Bishop Innocent, while playing a role in the embassy to Honorius and being consulted by the urban prefect on a pagan sacrifice, was an ineffective protector of the city; his responses after 410 focused on liturgy and pastoral care. Conflicts with other Christian sects in the city, such as the followers of Pelagius, as well as the internal divisions within the church clergy took up his attention and limited the civic influence of the bishop in the decade after 410. In contrast, the rebuilding of relationships among senators, emperors, and the military fueled the city's restoration efforts and allowed these elites to provide strong leadership.

The memories of 410 and elite responses to it shaped the ways in which later senators reacted to subsequent crises, influencing as well, as we shall see, their willingness to work with new leaders in Rome, be they chosen by the eastern emperor or by Ostrogothic kings. Rather than seeing the events of 410 as trapping Rome in a downward spiral, I suggest that we adopt the view of late fifth-century senatorial aristocrats who saw 410 as an opportunity to use this crisis to further their influence. In their eyes, 410 had been a disaster, but over the decade that followed, the damages and losses were viewed against the background of a resurgent Rome, a city in which individuals and groups contested for influence, honor, and wealth. Indeed, part of the difficulties for modern readers seeking to understand what happened to the city and how it recovered comes from the shifting memories of those whose descriptions of 410 were shaped by their own rhetorical goals.[244]

It is not surprising that in a city experiencing growing aristocratic influence, a rising military force, and a resident imperial court open to ecclesiastical elites, one of the most successful of Rome's senators emerged to seek imperial office – with destructive consequences. Petronius Maximus, as we shall see in Chapter 4, acted, as ambitious senators had done for centuries, by removing his competition. The political crisis that ensued led to the second "fall" of the city during the fifth century, this time to the Vandals in 455. It would be a different set of elites who would have to respond to this new crisis.

---

[244] For the role of memory in recreating the events of 410, see Bjornlie 2020, pp. 248–79.

4

Rome after the 455 Vandal Occupation

> After this death of Maximus, there followed immediately – and fittingly – a Roman captivity worth of much lamentation. Geiseric found the City bare of all defences. He encountered the holy bishop Leo, who rushed outside the city gates; his pleading, with the intervention of God, so softened him [Geiseric] that after the surrender of the city, he undertook, so far as was in his power, to refrain from fire, slaughter, and punishments. Then for fourteen days, through an untroubled and open search, Rome was emptied of all its wealth, and many thousands of captives – all who were satisfactory in terms of age or occupation – along with the queen [Licinia Eudoxia] and her daughters [Eudocia and Placidia] – were led back to Carthage.
>
> —Prosper, *Chronicle* for the year 455 CE[1]

The Vandal sack of Rome in 455 is often described in our sources as devastating to the city of Rome and to the Roman senatorial aristocracy. The Vandals arrived at a moment when the city, due to a series of political upheavals, lacked leadership. Rome was recovering from the murder of the Emperor Valentinian III by Gothic soldiers (March 16, 455). Two months later, his successor, Petronius Maximus, was killed by fellow Romans (May 31, 455) in panic at the news that the Vandals were at the walls of the city. The Romans did not even try to defend themselves. They simply opened the gates and submitted to the occupation and plundering of the city that

---

[1] Prosper, *Chron.* s.a. 455: *Post hunc Maximi exitium confestim secuta est multis digna lacrymis Romana captivitas, et urbem omni praesidio vacuam Gisiricus optinuit, occurrente sibi extra portas sancto Leone episcopo, cuius supplicatio ita cum Deo agente lenivit, ut, cum omnia potestati ipsius essent tradita, sibi civitate, ab igni tamen et caede atque suppliciis abstineretur. Per quattuordecim igitur dies, secura et libera scrutatione, omnibus opibus suis Roma vacuata est, multaque milia captivorum, prout quique aut aetate aut arte placuerunt, cum regina et filiabus eius Cartaginem abducta sunt.*

lasted fourteen days.[2] The contemporary Gallic writer Prosper (in the epigraph above) chose to conclude his *Chronicle* with this event, as if 455 marked the end of Roman history. Then, as Prosper simply stated, Rome was "emptied out of its wealth."[3] The sixth-century Gothic writer Jordanes, looking back, also emphasized the losses at the hands of the Vandal king Geiseric, who "despoiled the city of everything."[4]

Such responses have led modern scholars to proclaim that the city of Rome and its elites never fully recovered after 455; rather, the aristocracy was in "retreat." Impoverished by disruptions to their economic networks, they had fled to safer havens in Ravenna or Constantinople or to their provincial estates.[5] Some scholars have stated that as a result of this downturn, aristocrats simply gave their houses (*domus*) in Rome to the church.[6] The Vandal seizure of the city in 455 and the flight of impoverished senators to their rural properties to become a "subregional elite" thus become an important harbinger of the transition from the ancient to the medieval world.[7]

This dramatic narrative of a decimated city and an eviscerated senatorial aristocracy after 455 does not, however, fit the evidence on the ground. The way the Vandals captured Rome and the responses of Rome's elites – senators, generals, and emperors – restored Rome to its central position in the western empire in the decade after its fall. The bishops of Rome had

---

[2] Prosper, *Chron.* s.a. 455. For arguments about the dating of the sack, see Roberto 2012, pp. 149–54.

[3] Prosper, *Chron.* s.a. 455: *omnibus opibus suis Roma vacuata est.*

[4] Jord. *Rom.* 334: *Gizericus tunc rex Vandalorum ab Eudoxia Valentiniani uxore invitatus ex Africa Romana ingressus eamque urbem rebus omnibus expolitam eandam Eudoxiam cum duabus filiabus secum in Africa rediens duxit,* ed. Blockley 1983, Frag. 30.3, p. 332.

[5] See bibliography and arguments by Cracco Ruggini 2002, pp. 820–50. Cracco Ruggini is emblematic of the view that the Vandal sack was "un momento di autentica cesura," pp. 843–45. For the lure of their provincial estates, see for example Clover 1978, p. 170 note 3 for bibliography.

[6] Roberto 2012, p. 153, note 49, cites a number of archaeologists who date the decline of housing on the Aventine and the Caelian hills to this period, including Pavolini 2001, pp. 616–18. Typical is the report of the excavation of a *domus* on the Vicus Caprarius that was destroyed by fire, which the excavator relates to the Vandal sack of 455, although the pottery dates from the late fourth through the early fifth century; see Insalco 2002, p. 46. Santangeli Valenzani 2012, pp. 219–27, sees housing decline in the second half of the fifth century On elite housing, as a measure of decline and donations to the Church, see too Machado 2006, pp. 111–38, and Machado 2019 pp. 259–69.

[7] Wickham 2005, p. 204, and pp. 203–19, although he admits that even after the Gothic War there were some wealthy senators. Matthews 1990 (Post-script, pp. 391–92) saw this migration as the result of the fragmentation of regional elites under Honorius. This theme was developed by Wormald 1976, pp. 221–22 and reiterated by Machado 2013, pp. 49–50.

a limited role in this recovery. As I argue in this chapter, elites and non-elites returned to Rome almost immediately after the Vandals had departed. Senatorial aristocrats took key leadership roles at this critical moment, taking action and holding high civic offices in the decade after 455.[8] I focus on the senatorial aristocrats at the uppermost levels of late Roman society for they were the most powerful men in Rome at the time. Senators worked with generals and emperors, and also with the bishops of Rome, to reconstitute society, even as they strove to ensure their own positions at the center of power.[9]

In my view, senatorial aristocrats took on these high civic offices not out of some vague sentimentality but because post-455 Rome offered them the political, economic, religious, and social means to advance their own interests and compete for power.[10] Some aristocrats may well have been prompted to action after the Vandal departure because they or their fathers recalled how important it had been to take on leadership roles in the wake of 410. After Alaric's sack, as discussed in Chapter 3, Roman aristocrats had returned to active political life by holding high civic offices and built strong relationships with the emperor and the military.[11] The return of the emperor Valentinian III to reside in Rome throughout the 440s and to ceremonially move his family there in 450 was, among other things, an indicator of how important Rome and its senatorial aristocracy had become to imperial rule.[12]

Senatorial aristocrats took a leading role in rebuilding Rome in the post-455 period of reconstruction, just as they had in the post-410 period. As Roman senatorial aristocrats repaired their city, they focused in particular on their relationships with the military. The generals – Avitus, Majorian, and Ricimer – were key to protecting the city and the empire, and Roman aristocrats were aware of the importance of the army in securing the reestablishment of urban life. Given their importance, it is not surprising that the military provided two emperors – Avitus and Majorian – in this decade,

---

[8] I have adapted for this chapter the tables for high civic office holders that first appeared in my article, Salzman 2017 C, pp. 243–62 = 2017 C. Sections of that article have been adapted and excerpted here with permission of Brepols Press.

[9] Machado 2013, pp. 50–51, observed in his study of senatorial aristocrats through 440 that the predominance of male office holders is an expression of a hierarchical society dominated by a few powerful men.

[10] For vague sentimentality about Roman traditions, see, for example, Clover 1973, pp. 168–73. For the importance of senators, see Matthews 1990.

[11] See Chapter 3 and Machado 2013, pp. 49–76.

[12] Gillett 2001, pp. 137–67; Humphries 2007, pp. 21–58; and McEvoy 2010, pp. 151–92.

though the general who emerged as the most powerful throughout this period was Ricimer, who was not himself an imperial contender.[13]

Senatorial aristocrats were newly empowered political players in the aftermath of 455 alongside military and imperial elites. As the Gallo-Roman aristocrat Sidonius Apollinaris observed in a letter written in 468, these senators were so powerful that apart from the military generals, they "stood easily next to the Emperor in purple."[14] So it is not surprising that two emperors in this decade were senatorial aristocrats – Petronius Maximus and Libius Severus – and a third, Anicius Olybrius, would briefly become emperor soon after in 472.[15]

However, as I discuss in this chapter, senatorial aristocrats were able to rise to political prominence in no small part because they had retained important financial and social resources that they used to rebuild Rome, the locus of their pre-455 identities. Again, the urban prefect played the central role in the recovery of the city. Yet even as the senatorial aristocracy increased their influence and power by working with military and imperial leaders, the civic sway of the bishop of Rome declined. After 455, the papacy had far fewer resources at its disposal. Prior to 455, the Bishop of Rome Leo I (440–61) had relied heavily on support from the resident emperor, Valentinian III, and his family.[16] After 455, a weakened imperial court also meant a less generous patron for the church in Rome. Yet the bishops still faced competition for influence not just from various Christian sects in the city, but also from lay aristocrats. This view of a weakened papacy after 455 is reinforced by the silence of the bishops of Rome on the Vandal captivity and on Vandal threats to the city and empire. Although Bishops Leo and Hilary (461–68) continued to assert the special status of Rome in letters and tracts, their silence points to their limited civic role in two decades of declining influence.

The 455 Sack of Rome

Many ancients – and many moderns – have blamed the capture of Rome in 455 on the actions of the then-emperor, Petronius Maximus, who had been

---

[13] McEvoy 2017, p. 110 emphasizes the military as a source of emperors in this period.

[14] Sidonius Apollinaris, *Ep.* 1.9.2. Trans. by Anderson 1956, p. 385: *Hi in amplissimo ordine seposita praerogativa partis armatae facile post purpuratum principem principes erant.* "In the most elevated rank, if we leave out of account the privileged military class, they [the senators Gennadius Avienus and Caecina Basilius] stood easily next to the Emperor in [royal] purple."

[15] See notes 17 and 24 below.

[16] *Lib. Pont.* 47, ed. Duchesne 1981, pp. 238–41. For private funding for the bishop of Rome's projects, see Pietri 1978, pp. 317–37; Pietri 1981, pp. 435–53; Hillner 2006, pp. 59–68; Hillner 2007, pp. 225–61; and Gianandrea 2017, p. 212.

one of the most distinguished members of the Senate and was tied to powerful Roman families, including both the Anicii and Petronii. He had been praetorian prefect of Italy two or three times, urban prefect of Rome two times, and consul two times, having earned the status of *patrician* by 445.[17] He had been a close advisor of the previous emperor, Valentinian III, and perhaps even been his tutor.[18] Valentinian III had come to the throne at age six in 425, and he had ruled under the regency of his mother, Galla Placidia, sister of the emperor Honorius.[19]

By 454, with the dissipation of the Hunnic forces after the death of Attila in 453 and with the quieting of relations with the Vandals after the settlement of 442 that had recognized their hold on large sections of North Africa, Valentinian III, now a mature ruler of thirty-five, sought to confirm his control of the remainder of his empire. In what is strikingly similar to the actions taken by the emperor Honorius against his commander in chief Stilicho, a young emperor Valentinian III was once more said to have been manipulated by court advisors and murdered his strongest general, Aetius, on September 21, 454. Most ancient sources point to Petronius Maximus as the one who had incited Valentinian to act, playing on his fear that he would lose his throne to the general.[20] Modern scholars, however, also point to the failure of Aetius's efforts to protect Italy from the Huns who had, in 452, marched into Italy and plundered its towns.[21] Only Attila's unexpected death in 453 had reduced the Hunnic threat, but Aetius's botched military response was apparent at court.

After Aetius's murder, Petronius Maximus is again cited in our sources as encouraging Aetius's disgruntled military officers to retaliate for the murder of their beloved general. In Rome, the latter murdered Valentinian III, the last male member of the Theodosian family, on March 16, 455.[22] In the upheaval that followed, Maximus seized power, winning the support of the Senate and the army and overcoming potential rivals, including the then–resident head of

---

[17] For the scholarly consensus, see Oppedisano 2013, pp. 58–70; and Henning 1999, pp. 16–27. For Petronius Maximus's career, see Maximus 22, *PLRE* 2, pp. 740–51. For Maximus as a member of the *gens Anicia*, see Chastagnol 1962, pp. 281–86, and Oppedisano 2013, pp. 61–62 and note 2. The political importance of the Anicii as a group has been accepted by Roberto 2012, pp. 142–44, but rightfully critiqued by Cameron (Alan) 2012, p. 147. For the ties of Petronius also to the family of the Petronii, see Grossi 2019, pp. 58–60.

[18] For Petronius as that anonymous "tutor" (*praeceptor*) of Valentinian III, see Panciera 1996, pp. 277–97; Henning 1999, pp. 28–32; and Grossi 2019, p. 56.

[19] McEvoy 2013, pp. 223–304 on Valentinian III and see also my discussion in Chapter 3.

[20] Oppedisano 2013, p. 55 for discussion and notes 33–34 for a wide range of sources, including those in notes 22 and 23 below.

[21] Maas 2015, p. 17.

[22] Priscus, *Frag.* 30 = John of Antioch, *Frag.* 201, ed. Blockley 1983, pp. 326–33; and *Frag.* 30.3 = Jord. *Rom.* 334, ed. Blockley 1983, pp. 332–33 with text in note 4 above.

the imperial bodyguard, Majorian.[23] On March 17, 455, Maximus thus became the second of four senatorial emperors in the fifth-century city, a sign that senatorial aristocrats were able to access imperial power during that century.[24]

Maximus's rule disrupted the status quo in the West. Most immediately, he upended the 442 treaty that Valentinian III had established with the Vandals who controlled large portions of North Africa and the grain supply critical to the people in Rome. The tribute paid in grain provided a good part of the food supply of Rome.[25] To ensure the continuity of this relationship, Valentinian III had engaged one of his daughters, Eudocia, to Huneric, the son of the Vandal king Geiseric, and he had kept the boy in Rome as a guarantee to this arrangement.[26] Maximus certainly knew of this prior engagement, but he had calculated that legitimating his rule by forming family ties with the remnants of the Theodosian dynasty was worth the risk of strained relations with the Vandal king. So Maximus instead betrothed his son, Palladius, to Eudocia, the daughter of Valentinian III, and he also forced Licinia Eudoxia, the widow of Valentinian III, to marry him immediately.[27] Eastern sources uniformly preserve the rumor that it was the appeal of the widowed empress Eudoxia to Geiseric "out of distress at the murder of her husband and her forced marriage" that had brought the Vandal king to the gates of Rome.[28] But blaming the Vandal attack on a wronged queen is a *topos* that even some eastern writers found inadequate.[29] They, instead,

---

[23] Priscus, *Frag.* 30 = John of Antioch, *Frag.* 201, ed. Blockley 1983, pp. 330–31, lines 78–80, states that Eudoxia, Valentinian's wife, supported Majorian who had been the head of the imperial bodyguard (*comes domesticorum*) under Valentinian III; this reading follows the emendation of the text by Blockley.

[24] Priscus Attalus was the first senatorial emperor in the fifth century city; see Chapter 3 and Priscus Attalus 2, *PLRE* 2, pp. 180–81. Libius Severus was the third, as discussed below. Anicius Olybrius was the fourth; see Olybrius 6, *PLRE* 2, pp. 796–98, and Chapter 5. In Gaul, Iovinus 2, *PLRE* 2, pp. 621–22, a senator became emperor 411–13.

[25] On this treaty, see Chapter 3 and note 225.

[26] On the engagement of Huneric and Valentinian III's daughter in 442 and its implications for Geiseric, see Conant 2012, pp. 23–29; Barnes 1983, pp. 266–67. For Huneric as a hostage in Rome, see Procop. *Wars* 3.14.13, and Hunericus, *PLRE* 2, p. 573. The girl is likely the eldest daughter of Valentinian III, Eudocia. See also Chapter 3.

[27] Hydatius, *Chron.* 155 (455), p. 104 notes the engagement of Maximus's son to a daughter of Valentinian III.

[28] Roberto 2012, pp. 145–46. Priscus, *Frag.* 30 = John of Antioch, *Frag.* 201, ed. Blockley 1983, lines 86–89, pp. 330–31, includes Eudoxia's summons as reason for the attack. Priscus's rumor is repeated as fact by Marcellinus *comes*, *Chron.* s.a. 455.3, ed. Mommsen, *MGH AA* 11, p. 86. Procop. *Wars* 3.4.37–39 also cites the invitation of Eudoxia. Hydatius, *Chron.* 160 [167], s.a. 455, ed. Burgess 1993, pp. 104–5, is the only western source to note the *fama*.

[29] For the literary trope of women causing war by their invitation to an enemy, see Mazzarino 1946, pp. 18–23, note 8. Honorius's sister, Iusta Grata Honoria, also allegedly wrote to Attila to bring his Huns to Italy in 449; see Honoria, *PLRE* 2, p. 568.

underscored the opportunistic greed of Geiseric who, now freed from restraints, could plunder Rome at will since the city, weakened by a recent usurpation and uncertainty about Maximus as emperor, was unprotected.[30]

The Vandals arrived in the area near Rome in late May. Their presence caught Maximus unaware. All the sources agree that the citizens and military were so terrified that they did not put up any armed resistance. Many tried to flee instead, including the recently elevated Emperor Maximus. But he was discovered, albeit in disguise, by his fellow citizens who, angered at his cowardice and usurpation, stoned him to death and then tore him apart, limb by limb, on May 31, 455.[31] His death did not, however, appease the Vandal king. Geiseric sought more than merely a salve to his honor.

In the dramatic description included as the epigraph of this chapter, the fifth-century Gallic chronicler Prosper relates that after the city had been taken, the bishop Leo went outside the city walls to address Geiseric. Prosper paints Leo as a courageous savior who warded off the worst. There are echoes of how Prosper credits Leo for having successfully led a senatorial embassy that had negotiated with Attila in Venetia and deterred him from allowing his Huns to attack Rome in 452.[32] In contrast, this intervention in 455 failed to stop the occupation of the city. The Bishop of Rome, Leo, did win a concession from Geiseric, according to Prosper, to abstain from "fire, slaughter, and punishments."[33] Geiseric, after all, was a Christian, albeit an Arian one. Deemed heretical by Nicene Christian bishops, Arians had survived and lived side by side with their Nicene neighbors in Italy and elsewhere. Indeed, most of the Germans serving in the Roman army or as mercenaries, including the Goths, were Arians.[34] Perhaps in recognition of their shared faith as well as for financial reasons, Geiseric systematically pillaged Rome for fourteen days, from June 2 to June 16, and seized those deemed desirable for ransom instead of murdering the city's inhabitants.[35]

---

[30] Priscus, *Frag.* 30 = John of Antioch, *Frag.* 201, ed. Blockley 1983, pp. 330–31, lines 82–86; Procop. *Wars* 3.5.

[31] Priscus, *Frag.* 30 = John of Antioch, *Frag.* 201, ed. Blockley 1983, pp. 330–33, lines 90–100. Mathisen 1981, pp. 232–47, and note 3.

[32] Jord. *Get.* 42,223 = Priscus, *Frag.* 22, ed. Blockley 1983, pp. 310–11.

[33] Prosper, *Chron.* s.a. 455, in note 1 above, is the sole fifth-century source to give Leo a role in persuading Geiseric to desist from violence. The *Gallic Chronicle of 511*, s.a. 454/455, ed. Burgess 2001, p. 98, similarly emphasized Geiseric's restraint: *Valentinianus interficitur foris Romae; post quem Maximus diebus LXX adeptus imperium. Nam terrore Vandalorum tumultu vulgi occisus est et mox ingresso Genserico sine ferro et igne Roma praedata est et post Avitus imperatur.*

[34] See my discussion of the different views deemed Arian at the end of Chapter 2.

[35] Procop. *Wars* 3.5; Prosper, *Chron.* s.a. 455, with the text in note 1 above.

Fifth- and sixth-century writers describe the loss of property from buildings, private houses, and churches, but no intentional burning of the city is recorded in a reliable source.[36] Procopius asserted that Geiseric resided on the Palatine, but his residence there had not stopped him from plundering the imperial palaces.[37] Indeed, the imperial palaces had been recently improved since, as discussed in Chapter 3, Valentinian III had lived there since the 440s and had ceremonially moved his family to Rome for the last five years of his rule.[38] Valentinian III had lavished much attention on his residence, judging from a recently excavated large semicircular pavilion expensively decorated in cut marble on the Pincian Hill that has been attributed to him.[39] Procopius, who had been in a position to access accounts we lack when he wrote in 535, and who witnessed the 534 victory celebration of Justinian which displayed Roman spoils seized by the Vandals in this attack, is quite specific about the damage to certain parts of the city:

> Geiseric, for no other reason than that he suspected that he would gain much money, set sail for Italy with a great fleet. Going up to Rome, as no one stood in his way, he took possession of the palace … and, placing a huge amount of gold and other imperial treasures in his ships, he sailed to Carthage, having spared neither the bronze nor anything else whatever in the palace. He plundered also the temple of Jupiter Capitolinus and tore off half the roof. The roof was of bronze of the finest quality and, as a thick layer of gold had been poured over it, it shone as a magnificent and wonderful spectacle. But one of the ships with Geiseric, which was bearing the statues, was lost, they say, yet the Vandals reached port in the harbor of Carthage with all the others.[40]

The statues, along with the gold, silver, and bronze objects seized in the city, including the treasures of the Jews which Titus had brought to Rome, were intended to embellish the residences of Geiseric and his Vandal followers who had settled in Carthage and in North Africa on estates that had once belonged to Romans.[41]

---

[36] Malalas, *Chron.* 14.26; Procop. *Wars* 3.5.1, and 4.9.5. On Vandal pillaging, see Victor Tonn. *Chron.* 455; Cass. *Chron.* 1263; Marcell. *comes Chron.* s.a. 455, 3; and Theophanes *a.m.* 5947 who emphasizes the wealth seized from houses as well as from churches, as does Zonaras 13.25.25. Only Evagrius *HE* 2.7 talks of fire damage to the city. For a vivid description of the sack, see Roberto 2012, pp. 147–56.

[37] Procop. *Wars* 3.5.1, and 4.9.5; Malalas, *Chron.* 14.26; Roberto 2012, p. 149 and note 43.

[38] Humphries 2012, pp. 161–82, with the dates and times based on Gillett, as noted by Humphries at p. 162.

[39] For this attribution, see Humphries 2012, pp. 173–74.

[40] Procop. *Wars* 3.5; 4.9.4-.5. On the sixth-century display of these images to justify Justinian's war on the Vandals and the reshaping of this event, see Moralee 2019, 313–17.

[41] On statues from Rome, see especially Ambrogi 2012, pp. 157–218.

When the Vandals departed, they also took with them a large number of hostages, including a certain number of aristocrats and most notably Valentinian's elder daughter, Eudocia, who had not yet married; her sister, Placidia; and the now twice-widowed empress, Licinia Eudoxia.[42] When some Roman captives arrived in Carthage, the bishop there, Deogratias, was so moved by their plight that he sold "all of the gold and silver vessels used in worship and freed the freeborn people from being slaves of the barbarians."[43] How many people fled or were taken captive by the Vandals and the impact of these events on the population of Rome are significant questions.

Population. If we use the population estimates for Rome that were based in large part on the laws stipulating an increase in the pork dole from approximately 120,000 recipients in Rome in 419 to around 140,000 in 452 (see Chapter 3), then there is reason to accept the scholarly estimate that the total population of the city prior to the 455 Vandal attack would have been between 300,000 and 500,000.[44] This number is a decrease from the estimates of between 700,000 and 1,000,000 residents at the end of the fourth century, but it is still a large urban population by ancient standards.[45]

How much the population decreased after 455 and how long it remained at a reduced level is impossible to assess quantitatively with certainty. We know that a large number of people were taken hostage; Prosper lamented about the "many thousands" taken to be slaves or ransomed, an inexact number cited for rhetorical purposes.[46] In Carthage the Catholic bishop, Deogratias, ransomed off captives and housed them in two sizable basilicas.[47] If these were very large basilicas, then Deogratias perhaps ransomed between 3,000 and 4,000 people at a time.[48] The survivors who were not returned for ransom, including Roman citizens and an unknown number of slaves and non-Romans, would have otherwise been sold into

---

[42] For the seizure of Eudoxia and her two daughters, see Hydatius, Lem. 167 (s.a. 455), Marcell. com. *Chron.* s.a. 455, Jord. *Rom.* 334 (note 4 above), Procop. *Wars* 3.5.3, and Licinia Eudoxia 2, *PLRE* 2 p. 411. For the large numbers taken captive, see Prosper, *Chron.* s.a. 455.

[43] Vict. Vit. *Hist.* 1.25, *MGH AA* 3. 7. Trans. by Moorhead (1992).

[44] Barnish 1987, pp. 160–61, following Whitehead and Lo Cascio. All are using Valentinian's *Novel* of 452 that indicates 3,629,000 lbs. of pork was distributed (*N. Val.* 36) with the 419 edict of Honorius that indicated that pork recipients numbered 120,000 with 3,000,000 pounds of pork distributed each year (*C. Th.* 14.4.10); like Jones (1964, rept. 1986, p. 702), Barnish believes that the recipients of the pork dole were equal to those on the grain dole; in favor of this is also Rickman 1980.

[45] See my discussion of population estimates in Chapter 1, note 19.

[46] See note 1 above for the Prosper citation. The Latin is: *multaque milia captivorum.*

[47] Vict. Vit. *Hist.* 1,25, *MGH AA* 3.7.   [48] This number is based on estimated basilica capacity.

slavery.[49] Based on such scant allusions, we can only guess at the numbers of people involved; perhaps 20,000 to 40,000 people could have been taken back to Carthage as hostages. Some died from the journey or in captivity. Given the complete surrender of Rome and the suddenness of the Vandal occupation, the number who had fled the city or died in Vandal captivity was far less than would have been the case had the city suffered a long siege or if the Romans had fought a long, defensive war. The circumstances of the city's surrender may help explain why, soon after the Vandals departed, by 458, the food supply for Rome was functioning again; when the emperor Majorian granted a remission of tax arrears in 458, he excepted the pork levy from reductions and did not mention any decrease in the levy.[50] By then we hear that some fugitives as well as captives had returned to Rome and Italy from Africa.[51]

Scholarly estimates about the population of Rome after 455 once more rely on the grain and pork supplies of the city. Unfortunately, the textual attestations for the food supplies in Rome are much later, between fifty and ninety years after the Vandal occupation. But scholars continue to use them to argue for a steep population decline in the late fifth-century city. The texts are worth considering here. First is the description of the visit to Rome in 500 by the Ostrogothic king of Italy, Theoderic; according to the sixth-century *Anonymus Valesianus*, the king donated to the "Roman people and to the poor 120,000 modii of grain."[52] This number is so low that it has raised doubts about its accuracy; in addition, as S.J.B. Barnish has pointed out, "it corresponds remarkably with the 120,000 recipients of the pork dole in 419." Moreover, this passage cites annual distributions when traditionally grain and pork had been distributed on a monthly basis.[53] Finally, the *Anonymus Valesianus* conflates the charity the emperor extended to the poor with the grain dole distributed to Rome citizens. This conjunction suggests that what we have here is an act of charity, not an official account of the grain supply.[54]

The other evidence that is adduced to analyze Rome's population in the late fifth century is also from the sixth-century reign of King Theoderic. In

---

[49] Vict. Vit. *Hist.* 1,25, *MGH AA* 3.7.   [50] *N. Maj.* 2.1.

[51] Leo, *Ep.* 197, response 18 to the bishop of Narbonne in 458 concerning the treatment of prisoners returning to Italy from Africa.

[52] Anon. Val. *Pars Posterior* 12.67: *Per tricennalem triumphans populo ingressus palatium, exhibens Romanis ludos circensium. Donavit populo Romano et pauperibus annonas singulis annis, centum viginti milia modios, et ad restaurationem palatii, seu ad recuperationem moeniae civitatis singulis annis libras ducentas de arca vinaria dari praecepit.* Translation by J. C. Rolfe, LCL, 1986, pp. 550–51.

[53] Barnish 1987, pp. 160–61.

[54] For the continuation of the *annona* by Theoderic, see Cass. *Var.* 6.18.

535 he reduced the annual mandatory contribution of estate owners of the southern Italian provinces of Lucania and Bruttium to Rome's supply of pork and beef from 12,000 solidi to 1,000 solidi.[55] Using this lower number to estimate pork rations at the rate that was used in 452 – that is, 240 pounds of pork to the solidus – Lo Cascio has estimated 20,000 portions providing 40 percent of the meat supply, which would result in a population now between 50,000 and 60,000.[56] If we credit the pork theorists and assume a reduced population in 535 of between 50,000 and 60,000 residents – 250,000–450,000 down from approximately 300,000–500,000 in 452 – then a fifth of the population or less would have lived in the early sixth-century city.

If this population decrease is accepted for the year 535 – and not all scholars agree – we still do not know when or how much exactly the population of Rome had declined in the aftermath of 455.[57] The other evidence for the population comes from texts from early sixth-century Rome that present conflicting images of the city to suit their own rhetorical ends.[58] Nor can the reuse or subdivision of private housing (discussed below) give us reliable population numbers in the decade after 455. Even the respected Italian archaeologist Riccardo Santangeli Valenzani, who used the information from private houses to propose a 90 percent decline in the population of Rome by the end of the fifth century – a percentage that not all scholars accept – acknowledged that this decline was the result of a gradual change in living patterns that took place over the course of the fifth century.[59]

Although we cannot quantify the exact population loss of the city with certainty, the upheavals of 455 had a negative impact on the inhabitants of Rome. Many people fled, and a number died in captivity or were sold into

---

[55] Cass. *Var.* 11.39.

[56] Lo Cascio 2013, p. 418. This is also the view of Meneghini and Santangeli Valenzani 2004, p. 21.

[57] This number depends on several assumptions, such as the presumed continuation of how the pork ratios are assessed, how much these areas contributed, and even that the percentage of citizens and dole recipients remained the same over an 80-year period. For those who support this lower view, see Lo Cascio 2013 and Santangeli Valenzani 2004, pp. 21 and 41. For scholars who support a higher population, see Barnish 1987, pp. 160–61; and Brown 2012, p. 459, who thinks that a decline of 60 percent of the population after 410 seems too high. Giovannini 2010, pp. 431–54, proposed a decrease in the population due to high mortality rates, but she does not quantify the decline.

[58] Procop. *Wars* 6.7.38; 21.39 depicts a thriving Rome that he said was larger than Milan, which had suffered the massacre of 300,000 male inhabitants in 539. On this number as an exaggeration, see Barnish 1987, p. 161. Cass. *Var.* 11.39.1, written 533–35, speaks of how great the population in Rome was before his time. Brown 2012, p. 459 and note 24 incisively discusses the differing conclusions historians have reached based on these highly rhetorical texts.

[59] Santangeli Valenzani 2004, p. 41, and note 6 above.

slavery. How many returned is unknown. However, the evidence I discuss below indicates that within the decade after 455, a good number of the political, social, and religious leaders had returned to the city in order to reconstitute their society, albeit in a Rome with a reduced population.

Political and Military Responses to Crisis, 455–65

There can be no doubt that the Vandal occupation of the city shattered the sense of security of its citizens. This attack, along with the sudden end of the Theodosian dynasty with the death of Valentinian III, led to a series of ongoing political and military crises in the West that continued throughout the decade. As new sets of would-be emperors and generals took on the challenges of restoring order, they sought to make ties to Rome's senatorial aristocrats whom they viewed as increasingly important partners in recovering the city and legitimating rule. Senatorial aristocrats – at times working with and at other times against would-be emperors and generals – strove to revive Rome and to return themselves to positions of influence and prestige.

The Reign of Avitus (455–56)

After the Vandals departed from Rome, it took less than a month for a new emperor to emerge. By July 9 or 10, 455, Eparchius Avitus, the commander in chief (*magister utriusque militiae*) under Petronius Maximus, was acclaimed emperor by his army in Arles with the military and financial support of Gallic nobles and the Visigoth king Theoderic II (453–66).[60] In Rome, reaction to the news was positive, if we trust the Spanish chronicler Hydatius. Soon after Avitus's accession, the Romans, now including those in charge of the city – that is, the senators – "summoned" him to return to protect the city. By early October of that year, Avitus arrived in the city with a coalition of his Roman soldiers and those of the Visigothic king.[61] By quickly coming to Rome, he made it known that this city, its Senate, and its aristocracy were essential to his rule. His army also provided protection from future Vandal attacks. In an attempt to win the approval of its citizens, Avitus followed traditional Roman ceremonial expectations and

---

[60] On Avitus, see Eparchius Avitus 5, *PLRE* 2, pp. 196–98. See also Henning 1999, pp. 32–36; and for his rise to power, see Oppedisano 2013, pp. 71–81. For Theoderic 2, see Theodericus 3, *PLRE* 2, pp. 1071–73.

[61] Hydatius, *Chron.* 159 [166], s.a. 455, ed. Burgess, pp. 104–5, *a Romanis et evocatus et susceptus fuerat imperator.*

stayed to celebrate his consulship in the city on January 1, 456, against the proper backdrop of the Capitoline Hill.[62] He was acknowledged by the Senate in Rome, and he sent an embassy to the eastern emperor Marcian seeking official recognition of his rule.[63]

Avitus – a Gallic-raised emperor – was aware of his need to win the support of Italian and Rome-based senatorial aristocrats. An important appointment toward this end would be the man he designated urban prefect. For this consequential post, Avitus selected Iunius [Va]lentin[u]s, as attested by two inscriptions that cite his restoration efforts after a hostile attack (*hostili impetu sublata*).[64] A third inscription, reconstructed by Dirk Henning, tells us that Valentinus held this office in 455–56.[65] As I have argued elsewhere, Valentinus probably was from an important Italo-Roman aristocratic family – the Symmachi. Working with the epigrapher Ilaria Grossi, we proposed that his first name was Avitus – not Vettius – Iunius Valentinus.[66] Avitus as a *nomen* also appears among Roman elites, and these families are tied to the family of the Symmachi.[67] If this identification is accepted, this appointment was an important attempt on the part of Avitus to incorporate Italo-Roman senatorial aristocrats into his new government at the beginning of his regime.

Avitus also needed to recognize his supporters – namely, the Gallic elites. He advanced a number of Gallic aristocrats to high secular offices that in the past had been filled by Italo-Romans. Seven of Avitus's nine named civic appointments to high office were Gallic aristocrats, a striking assertion of the

---

[62] Sid. Ap. *Pan. Avito* VII. ed. For Avitus's remaining in Rome, see Roberto 2012, p. 159.

[63] Hydatius, *Chron.* 156 [163] and 159 [166], s.a. 455 ed. Burgess 1993, pp. 104–5.

[64] Valentinus 5, *PLRE* 2, p. 1140. The inscriptions that assert that Valentinus as urban prefect repaired something that had been overturned by an enemy attack (*hostili impetu sublata*) are *CIL* VI, 1788 = 31891= 41404 = EDR093627; and *CIL* VI, 31890 = 37106 = 41403 = EDR093626. For discussion of his identity, see Salzman 2017 C, pp. 243–62, and Grossi 2017, pp. 256–59. His name is also on two bronze weights. This hostile attack is identified with the Vandal sack by Henning 1996, and also by Modéran 2014, pp. 201–4. Modéran follows the reconstruction of the Rostra's extension, which he dates to Diocletian, but dates the inscription noting the repair to the time of the emperor Anthemius because he does not accept the testimony of Hydatius, *Chron.* 169 [176], ed. Burgess 1993, pp. 108–9, that dates the naval victory of Ricimer over the Vandals to the spring of 456. I see no reason to disagree with Hydatius and hence agree with Henning's arguments for dating the inscription, which postdates the extension of the Rostra.

[65] The inscriptions to date his urban prefecture are *CIL* VI, 32005, with additions *CIL* VI, 3793 (fr. f) (1) *CIL* VI, 20746 (fr. d) (2) *CIL* VI, 32005 (fragments a–e) (3) *CIL* VI, 41405 (frr. a–f) = EDR093628 cites Valentinus as urban prefect, but the dating is emended by Henning 1996, pp. 259–64: *Salv [is d] d.n.[n.] Marciano [et Avito p]p. Aug[g.] [. . .]us Iunius [Va]lentin[u]s, [praef(ectus)] urb[i –]*.

[66] Salzman 2017C, pp. 243–62, with Grossi 2017, pp. 256–59.

[67] For the full argument, see Salzman 2017C, pp. 243–62, and Grossi 2017, pp. 256–59.

centrality of this group to his regime (see Table 4.1).[68] Not only the praetorian prefects of Gaul, who were normally Gallo-Roman aristocrats, but such imperial offices as the head of the imperial offices (*magister officiorum*) as well as a number of tribunes were of Gallic origin (see Table 4.1). Avitus even chose to send the Gallic aristocrat Consentius to negotiate on his behalf with the eastern emperor in Constantinople.[69]

From the perspective of an Italian senator, however, Avitus's appointments were an unwelcome source of competition that challenged their status.[70] High civic office, after all, had ensured Italo-Roman senators the influence that they used to protect their political and economic position. Not surprisingly, some senators seem to have made a more advantageous alliance with another powerful general, Ricimer, the commander in chief of the Roman military in Italy. Indeed, Ricimer was a familiar presence since he had spent his entire life within Roman elite circles.[71] And he had just shown himself successful against the Vandals in Sicily and Corsica in a battle in late spring or early summer of 456.[72]

We have no way of knowing precisely when the conspiracy to remove Avitus began, but by the summer of 456, according to the seventh-century Gregory of Tours, Avitus had lost senatorial support. Gregory focuses on Avitus's moral failure. Because Avitus "chose to pursue excess," he was overthrown by the senators.[73] The seventh-century writer John of Antioch points to other tensions with Romans, arising from his failure to feed the city and protect its patrimony. It is worth quoting John's text in full:

> When Avitus was emperor of Rome, and there was famine at that time, the people blamed Avitus and forced him to send away from the city of Rome those whom he had brought with him from Gaul. He also dismissed the Goths whom he had brought as his own guard, and gave them a money payment raised from public works, through the sale of the bronze in them to the merchants, for there was no gold in the imperial treasuries. This roused the Romans to revolt since they were robbed of the adornment of

---

[68] This number omits Paeonius since he was not an aristocrat. Henning 1999, pp. 74–79 includes military appointments, which would add more Gauls to his count of eleven of fifteen appointments being men of Gallic extraction.

[69] See Consentius 2, *PLRE* 2, pp. 308–9; and Henning 1999, p. 76, note 27.

[70] Mathisen 1981, pp. 232–47 makes a similar argument.

[71] On Ricimer's career, see Anders 2010. See notes 77 and 80 below.

[72] Mathisen 1981, p. 244; Hydatius, *Chron.* 169 and 170 [176 and 177], s.a. 456–7, ed. Burgess, pp. 108–9. Oppedisano 2013, p. 90, also supports this date.

[73] Greg. Tur. *Historiae* 11.11: *ambisset imperium, luxoriosae agere volens, a senatoribus projectus.* Gregory added that Avitus lived in such fear of the senators even after his departure from the city that he had sought sanctuary in the church.

their city. Majorian and Ricimer also broke into open revolt now that they were freed from fear of the Goths. As a result, Avitus, afraid both of these internal disturbances and of the attacks of the Vandals, withdrew from Rome and began to make his way to Gaul.[74]

Avitus – with no military, fearful of the angry urban crowd and remembering perhaps the fate of Petronius Maximus – left Rome in late summer or early fall of 456.[75] In October of that year, Avitus fell at the hands of Ricimer and another powerful general, Majorian.[76]

The Reign of Majorian (457–61)

The western throne was empty for several months while senators, generals, and would-be emperors negotiated. The sources are not consistent about the length of the interregnum nor can we easily trace the negotiations. The two most powerful generals – Ricimer and Majorian – were in contention. Some think that Ricimer's "barbarian" origins may have been a hindrance to his accession; he was of Suevian and Visigothic royal lineage.[77] In the end, it was a Roman, Majorian, a general and head of the imperial bodyguard (*comes domesticorum*) under Valentinian III, who was proclaimed emperor, perhaps as early as April 1, 457, by the military.[78] (Majorian's reign likely officially began when the Senate acclaimed him and when he was formally installed as emperor some eight months later at Ravenna on December 28, 457.[79]) However, it seems more likely that Ricimer, who had held patrician status since February 457 and was commander in chief and count, preferred to remain Majorian's principal

---

[74] Priscus, *Frag.* 32 = John of Antioch, *Frag.* 202, ed., Blockley 1983, pp. 334–35.

[75] Roberto 2012, pp. 158–60.

[76] Priscus, *Frag.* 32 = John of Antioch, *Frag.* 202, ed., Blockley 1983, pp. 334–35. There is a scholarly debate about the movements of Avitus after he left Rome and the date of his death. I date his deposition to when he was at Placentia in October 456, a view also proposed by Oppedisano 2013, pp. 81–90.

[77] Sid. Ap. *Carm.* 2.361–62 speaks of Ricimer's royal descent. Ennod. *Vita Epiph.* 64, abuses him as a *ferocissimus Geta* and Malalas, *Chron.* 373 also called him a Goth. For more on his background, see Anders 2010.

[78] MacGeorge 2002, pp. 192–200, suggested the military acclamation of Majorian in *Fasti Vindobonenses priores*, s.a. 457 is the source for confusion about Majorian's accession date. If Majorian was waiting for the blessing of the eastern emperor Leo, his delayed elevation would make sense. Scholarship on the exact legal position of Ricimer at this time and negotiations with the eastern court are discussed by Oppedisano 2013, pp. 108–14, who also notes that Majorian had been favored over Avitus by the empress Licinia Eudoxia.

[79] *Auctarium epitomae Vaticanae*, one of the *Additamenta* to Prosper, ed. Mommsen 1892, rept. 1981, p. 492, gives the December 28, 457 date: *moritur Marcianus. Levatur Leo et Ravennae Maiorianus V. Kal. Ian.* On this, see also Marc. comes, *Chron.* s.a. 457; Jord. *Getica* 236. Sid. Apoll. *Carm.* 5.387–38; and Oppedisano 2013, p. 107.

military aide.[80] As we will see, Ricimer consistently chose to retain control of the military and to allow others to take on the role of emperor, *princeps*, not only at this juncture but in subsequent transitions as well.[81]

At the beginning of his rule, Majorian demonstrated that he sought not just the support of the army, but that he was intent on building good relations with the Senate and the Italo-Roman aristocracy. We see this effort in his open appeal to senators in a law of January 11, 458, two weeks after his formal installation. This first piece of legislation was delivered as a speech that was sent to the Senate of Rome:

> Emperor Majorian Augustus to the Senate of Rome: Know, O Conscript Fathers, that I have been made emperor by the decision of your election and by the ordination of our very gallant army. ... Also, on the Kalends consecrated to Janus, we raised aloft the fasces of the consulship. ... Grant now your favor to the Emperor whom you have made, and share with Us the responsibility for matters that must be considered. No person shall fear the practices of informers... No one shall fear calumnies except those that he himself had originated.[82]

This last reference to informers addressed a concern that would have been felt in particular by senatorial aristocrats, who were notoriously concerned about attacks on their persons or properties; such lawsuits could create economic havoc, especially in the wake of recent political events.[83] Another of Majorian's novels, which has not survived in full, was similarly addressed to the concerns of senators; its extant title indicates that no senator of the city of Rome, nor the church, would be compelled to give over to the imperial treasury anything that had been left to them in a will.[84]

---

[80] For Ricimer as patrician see *Fast. Vind. Prior.* s.a. 457, hence in the period between the fall of Avitus and the accession of Majorian. *PLRE* 2, p. 943, s.v. Fl. Ricimer 2 surmises that his appointment was made by the eastern emperor, either Marcian or his successor Leo. Ricimer was thus commander of the army, count, and patrician from 457–72. For the assertion of his status to the Senate, see *N. Maj.* 1.1: *erit apud nos cum parenti patricioque nostro Ricimere rei militaris pervigil cura.* For the official investiture of Majorian, Oppedisano 2013, pp. 105–8.

[81] Ricimer acted similarly after the death of Majorian; see note 80 above for his life.

[82] *N. Maj.* 1.1, trans. from Pharr 1969, p. 55, adapted by the author. The speech is *N. Maj.* 1.1; *Imperatorem me factam, Patres conscripti, vestrae electionis arbitrio et fortissimi exercitus ordinatione cognoscite ... Dicatis quoque Iano Kalendis suscepti feliciter consulatus ereximus fasces ... Favete nunc principi, quem fecistis, et tractandarum rerum curam participate nobiscum, ut imperium, quod mihi vobis annitentibus datam est, studiis communibus augeatur .... Nemo delationes metuat ... nullus calumnias reformidet, nisi quas ipse commoverit.*

[83] Kalas 2015, p. 157.   [84] *N. Maj.* 10.

Majorian also departed from Avitus's civic appointment patterns by choosing several Italian senators to serve in his administration (see Table 4.2). Most significant was the elevation of Fl. Caecina Decius Basilius, from one of the great families of the fifth century, the Decian family, as praetorian prefect of Italy in 458.[85] But Majorian also recognized the need to reconcile a number of Gallo-Roman elites, especially the former supporters of Avitus. Aside from the praetorian prefects of Gaul, posts now regularly held by Gallo-Roman aristocrats, he also appointed Ennodius as count of the private estates of the emperor (*comes rei privatae*, or *CRP*), a man probably associated with the bishop of Pavia and with strong ties to Arles.[86] Of the fourteen named civic appointments certainly or highly likely to have been appointed by Majorian (excluding military appointments; see Table 4.2), three were likely Italian, and five were probably Gallic in origin or residents in Gaul. Their regional ties suggest that Majorian had tried to put together a central administration that would better balance Italian and Gallic interests.[87]

Majorian went to great lengths to win over Rome's senatorial aristocrats and to show his determination to revive Rome. That was the message of the first extant law addressed to the urban prefect of Rome, Aemilianus, dated to July 11, 458, the first part of which I cite here:

> While We rule the State, it is Our will to correct the practice whose commission We have long detested, whereby the appearance of the venerable City is marred. Indeed, it is manifest that the public buildings, in which the adornment of the entire City of Rome consists, are being destroyed everywhere by the punishable recommendation of the office of the prefect of the City.[88]

Majorian's concern for preserving Rome's adornments (*ornamenta*) and public buildings was a marked contrast to his predecessor's decision to melt down bronze from public buildings to pay the troops. It was precisely his lack of respect for Rome's appearance (*kosmos*) that had incensed the populace against Avitus, according to John of Antioch.[89] No wonder, perhaps, that Majorian

---

[85] Fl. Caecina Decius Basilius 11, *PLRE* 2, pp. 216–17, and Henning 1999, p. 79, note 42. See Table 4.2.

[86] For Ennodius, see Ennodius 1, *PLRE* 2, pp. 392–93.

[87] Mathisen 1979, pp. 597–627. See also Mathisen 1991, pp. 163–66.

[88] *N. Maj.* 4.1, adapted translation from Pharr 1969, pp. 553–54. *N. Maj.* 4.1: *Impp. Leo et Maiorianus aa. Aemiliano praefecto urbi. Nobis rem publicam moderantibus volumus emendari, quod iam dudum ad decolorandam urbis venerabilis faciem detestabamur admitti. Aedes si quidem publicas, in quibus omnis Romanae civitatis consistit ornatus, passim dirui plectenda urbani officii suggestione manifestum est.*

[89] See note 74 above. Ambrogi 2012, pp. 157–218, at p. 172 and notes 50–51, records such efforts, such as when, in 407, the Emperor Honorius had stipulated that temples and statuary that were in good shape could be used for public buildings or even churches, and that imperial laws protected them.

took on the traditional imperial role of restorer and guarantor of this "venerable" city.

Although Majorian had endeavored to build good relations with Rome's senatorial aristocracy, he failed to retain their support. An embarrassing loss of a fleet of ships in Spain even before it sailed against the Vandals forced Majorian to settle for a "shameful" peace.[90] This treaty likely entailed further property losses for senators in North Africa as well as in the Balearic Islands, Sicily, and Corsica at the same time that the loss of the fleet also brought increased taxation.[91] Moreover, Majorian's decision to rule from Ravenna, not Rome, opened the way for senators to seek alternatives who could better protect their interests.[92] They seem to have found common cause with the general Ricimer, who was similarly dissatisfied with Majorian's rule and who already had a good working relationship with certain Roman aristocrats.[93] We can perhaps see a reference to this conjunction of interests in our best contemporary source for the end of Majorian's rule, the chronicler Hydatius:

> While returning to Rome from Gaul and arranging business essential for the empire and prestige of Rome, Majorian was treacherously ensnared and murdered by Ricimer, who was driven by spite and supported by the counsel of jealous men.[94]

Stewart Oost identified among the "jealous men" who aligned themselves with Ricimer were Italo-Roman aristocrats.[95] They gained the most from the

---

[90] For the military defeats, see MacGeorge 2002, pp. 207–08. She relies on the testimony of Hydatius, *Chron.* 195 [200], s.a. 460, ed. Burgess 1993, pp. 112–13. This accords with the testimony of the Gallic Chronicle of 511, 65,634 ed. Burgess 2001, p. 98. For the "shameful" treaty, likely referring to the cession of lands in North Africa and/or of islands, see John of Antioch *Frag.* 203 = Priscus 6.36.1–2, Blockley 1983, p. 339. John of Antioch, *Frag.* 203 = Priscus, *Exc.* = Priscus 6.1, Blockley 1983, p. 339 states that Geiseric had first tried to resolve the matter with negotiations, but Majorian did not agree. Geiseric then proceeded to ravage North Africa.

[91] For this view of the treaty, see Caliri 2012, p. 77.

[92] Majorian's accession ceremony was held in Ravenna, and it is clear that he stayed there, issuing *Novels* 1–6, 458–59 from Ravenna; *Novels* 9 and 11, 459–60 were issued from Arles. No extant novel of the ten that survive was issued in Rome.

[93] See Fl. Ricimer 2, *PLRE* 2, p. 943. Ricimer had been involved with the Senate of Rome in a law case earlier in 461. Ricimer and the Senate had acted in tandem to condemn the Gallic commander of the infantry, Agrippinus, or so it was believed; see V. Lupicini 11 = *MGH* (*Scr. Rer. Mer.*) III 149.

[94] Hydatius, *Chron.* 205 [210], s.a. 461, ed. and translation by Burgess 1993, pp. 114–15: *Maiorianum de Galliis Romam redeuntem et Romano imperio vel nomine res necessarias ordinantem Rechimer livore percitus et invidorum consilio fultus fraude interfecit circumventum.*

[95] Oost 1970, pp. 231–33 identified sections of the Italian aristocracy, the Church, and the civil service as included. I see little evidence of the latter two elites, but it is possible that they too resented the increased taxes for the Vandal war.

removal of Majorian in 461, and they were the ones who, along with Ricimer, recognized as the next emperor one of their own.

The Reign of Libius (or Livius) Severus (461–65)

Libius (or Livius) Severus, a senator from Lucania in southwest Italy, became emperor from November 19, 461, until his death in 465.[96] Known for having lived dutifully (*religiose*), Severus was a good choice to restore the city after the crisis of Majorian's death. Moreover, his rule returned to the Valentinian III model of government by ruling from Rome and filling mostly the ceremonial role of emperor. Severus relied on his commander in chief, Ricimer, to direct military affairs. The senators would be happy to return to Rome since Ricimer conducted embassies and undertook military action in response to their concerns. For example, senatorial landowners in Sicily were angered by continuing raids by the Vandal King Geiseric on their agricultural estates. To put an end to these, Ricimer sent an embassy to Gaiseric, which, unfortunately failed because the King demanded Eudocia's inheritance, for she was now married to his son Huneric.[97] In reality, Geiseric was extending his control to areas in Sicily and Sardinia, Corsica, and the Balearic Islands. (See Map 4.)[98]

Although the Vandals continued to be a problem to landowners in Sicily especially, senatorial aristocrats had much to be pleased with under this new emperor. Not only was Ricimer actively advancing the protection of senat-orial properties, Libius Severus also had made sure to appoint Italo-Romans to high civic office (see Table 4.3). The praetorian prefects of Italy – Caelius Aconius Probianus and Flavius Caecina Decius Basilius – were both from important Roman families, the former from the Aconii and the latter from the Decii.[99] Libius's urban prefects (461–65) were similarly names familiar to Roman aristocrats: Macrobius Plotinus Eustathius was likely a member of the family of the Macrobius who authored the *Saturnalia* with ties to the

---

[96] Stein 1959, pp. 380–81, is typical in seeing Libius Severus as a puppet only and ignores the political value of senatorial support for Ricimer.

[97] Mathisen 2003, 2009, p. 308. In 461, Ricimer sent an embassy to the Vandal King Geiseric; see Priscus, *Frag.* 38.1= *Exc. de leg. Rom.* 10, ed. Blockley 1983, pp. 340–41; Priscus, *Frag.* 38.2 = John of Antioch, *Frag.* 404, ed. Blockley 1983, pp. 341–42; and Priscus, *Frag.* 39, ed. Blockley 1983, p. 342.

[98] Priscus, *Frag.* 39, ed. Blockley 1983, p. 342; Conant 2012, p. 31. In addition to holding parts of Sicily, Geiseric also annexed Sardinia, Corsica, and the Balearic Islands, as noted by Blockley 1983, note 155, p. 395.

[99] Henning 1999, p. 85, note 77 and see Caelius Aconius Probianus 4, *PLRE* 2, p. 908, and Fl. Caecina Decius Basilius 11, *PLRE* 2, pp. 216–17.

well-known aristocratic family of the Symmachi; and Fl. Synesius Gennadius
Paulus, whose urban prefecture likely can be dated to this period, was also
probably a Roman aristocrat, a member of the Corvii or the Rufii of Rome.[100]

Ricimer had been the de facto ruler of Rome throughout the reign of
Libius, an arrangement that had worked well to allow Roman senatorial
aristocrats to return to positions of power and to rebuild their lives. It also
worked well for Ricimer.[101] Hence, there is thus little reason to suspect
Ricimer in the death of Libius Severus, as Cassiodorus claimed was the
rumor that he heard some fifty years later. More likely, as Sidonius
Apollinaris in 468 declared, Libius Severus died of natural causes.[102]
Indeed, additional proof of Ricimer's satisfaction at remaining in charge of
the military with another man as emperor, preferably a senator, was his
willingness to repeat this arrangement with Anthemius in 468, and with the
senator Olybrius in 472.[103]

The Increasing Influence of Senators and Generals

As this overview of political and military responses in the decade after 455
indicates, generals and would-be emperors worked with senatorial aristocrats
to restore Rome in the immediate aftermath of the Vandal occupation. Two
emperors, Avitus and Majorian, had risen through the support of the military
during this decade; two others were senatorial aristocrats – Petronius Maximus
and Libius Severus, and in 472, a third senator, Olybrius, was emperor. As
many scholars have observed, the most powerful figure remained the commander in chief, Ricimer, who made it a priority to maintain good relations
with senatorial aristocrats and to retain strong control of the army. Like the
other aspirants to power in this decade, Ricimer relied on Roman senators not
only because they lent legitimacy but also because they still controlled and were
willing to use their economic and social resources to rebuild Rome. To better
understand senatorial influence in the restoration of Rome, therefore, some
appreciation of their resources in the decade after 455 is necessary.

---

[100] Henning 1999, p. 85, note 75, and see Macrobius Plotinus Eustathius, *PLRE* 2, pp. 436–37 and Fl.
Synesius Gennadius Paulus 36, *PLRE* 2, p. 855.

[101] Mathisen 2009, p. 322 argues, based on some bronze coins of Libius Severus with a monogram
on the obverse, that Ricimer had been claiming an emperor's right, thus undermining Severus's
position. But Woods 2002, pp. 5–23, rightfully demonstrates that a more accurate reading of the
monogram would be that of the name *Severus*.

[102] Cass. *Chron.* 1280 s.a. 465: *ut dicitur Ricimeris fraude, Severus Romae in Palatio veneno
peremptus est.* Contra is Sid. Apoll. *Carm.* 2.317–18. I agree with those scholars who do not
give it much credence; for a fuller discussion, see Anders 2010, pp. 191–93.

[103] Priscus *Frag.* 38.2 = John of Antioch, *Frag.* 204, ed. Blockley 1983, pp. 340–41.

Map 4 Vandal Africa.

Senatorial Aristocrats: Economic Influence after 455. The 455 Vandal attack had upset preexisting arrangements. After Geiseric's seizure of Carthage and the treaty of 442 under Valentinian III, a number of Italo-Roman aristocrats had lost their estates in Africa Proconsularis and Byzacena as well as in eastern Numidia and western Tripolitania; those who stayed had had to negotiate with Vandal rulers over lost or shared

Map 4 (cont.)

properties and rents.[104] (See Map 4.) Imperial control now focused on the provinces of Mauretania Caesariensis, Sitifensis, and western Numidia,

---

[104] Prosper, *Chron.* s.a. 442. Roman lands in these fertile provinces were lost to the Vandals, but the emperor regained control of certain areas that, though less fertile, were used for the grain supply for Rome, along with the tribute paid by the Vandals until 455; Conant 2012, p. 22 and note 9, citing Vict. *Vit.* 1.13, p. 7 and *N. Val.* 13 and 34.

and aristocrats benefitted from the support of the Roman government, which helped to also reduce disruptions to the grain supply of Rome. (See Map 4.)[105]

The Roman government made certain arrangements that provided some compensation for senatorial aristocrats who had lost properties in the 440s, as discussed in Chapter 3. There can be no doubt that the ruptured treaty and the breakdown of the Vandal–Roman peace after the 455 attack was a financial blow to a number of senators; some lost more of their lands, and the continuing attacks of the Vandals along the southern shores of Italy as well as the Vandal raids on Sicily prevented a complete recovery. This situation is why Ricimer's efforts to negotiate an end to the Vandal attacks were so important to senators.[106] However, the textual evidence also indicates that most aristocrats – and certainly the wealthiest of the *illustris* rank – were able to weather the disruptions of trade after 455. Not only did wealthy senators own properties in several areas from which they drew rents and monies from the sale of their goods; they also could benefit from the ongoing trade with the East and the continuing influx of Mediterranean goods into the city.[107] The most powerful families survived this decade with their financial resources mostly intact; the Anicii, Decii, Corvii, and Symmachi are especially well attested. These families – along with a number of others of Italian or Roman origin – continued to dominate certain high civic offices and to also recoup their losses after 455.

Senatorial Estates and the Food Supply of Rome. Senatorial aristocrats may also have benefitted from the increased demand for food for Rome and Italy. After 455, Rome's leaders were under immediate pressure to secure the city's food supply in addition to dealing with the disruptions to trade caused by ongoing Vandal blockades and coastal raids on Sicily and Italy.[108] Against this background we can better understand why the second of Majorian's *Novels* (new laws), dated to 458 and directed to the praetorian prefect Basilius, concerned the remission of taxes for landholders and local elites (*decurions*). Majorian's law assuring that these landowners would not be too harshly treated by "ruinous tax collectors" benefitted Rome's landed

---

[105] Conant 2012, p. 22.   [106] On his efforts, see note 97 above.

[107] Brogiolo 2010, p. 222, note 19 citing the important ceramic studies by Saguì, especially 2002, pp. 7–42. And see De Salvo 2014, note 108 below.

[108] De Salvo 2014, pp. 73–84, demonstrates through analysis of the archaeology that the goods continued to be shipped from North African to the East and the West, though there were periodic disruptions. On this, see Mazza 1997–98, pp. 107–38.

senatorial aristocracy.[109] The protection of Rome's food supply speaks to the reality of the need to ensure the urban population's well-being, for regardless of a general tax amnesty, the requirements for the pork dole did not change.[110]

The continuing Vandal attacks on Italy throughout this decade led the state to seek new avenues to secure food for Rome and Italy. Archaeological evidence indicates that large property holders of Italian and Sicilian estates benefitted because their estates also supplied some of the *annona* for Rome and Italy. The grain fields of the Middle Tiber Valley, in common with much of the Italian peninsula, had been turned into large estates in the early to middle fourth century, and many of these continued to function into the late fifth century, as the pottery evidence indicates.[111] Other areas in central Italy, in Apulia, in Sicily, and in parts of Gaul also supplied food for Rome and Ravenna, making good some of the losses caused by the forfeiture of the African grain tribute.[112] It is probable – if not demonstrable – that a good number of these estates that supplied the *annona* belonged to senatorial aristocrats.[113] These estates benefitted from the increased demand not just for grain but also for oil and meat. As S.J.B. Barnish observed, Italian sites like St. Vincenzo al Volturno near Venafrum in Samnium and St. Giovanni di Ruoti in Lucania increased pig farming, evidence of the ways in which central Italian areas met the demands for food for Rome and Italy. The remains from these sites show extended use into the late fifth and early sixth centuries.[114]

This interpretation of the relative economic vitality of Rome and Italy, especially that of southern Italy and Sicily, follows the work of more recent scholars who have demonstrated that the Vandals had not cut off all trade and

---

[109] *N. Maj.* 2.2–2.3. Typical is the justification expressed for this action in 2.3: trans. Pharr 1969, p. 552: "Our Serenity has established this entire regulation as a remedy for the landholder, since it is Our will that he may sell his produce at a favorable opportunity for the purpose of paying his tribute and shall thus be revived by the grant of intervals of time." See too the discussion by Oppedisano 2013, pp. 133–44.

[110] *N. Maj.* 2.1; Oppedisano 2013, pp. 137–38.

[111] Patterson 2008, pp. 499–532, at p. 516, and also discussion on p. 508–09 asserts that the primary moment for diverging pottery usage in Rome and the countryside is increasingly marked after the fifth century. Patterson's figure 3 shows that there is no real drop in the settlements in the Middle Tiber Valley until ca. 525 CE, though the dating is not precise. However, this date is consistent with the South Etruria survey, which similarly shows sustained areas of inhabitation throughout 450–550, with a drop in the next period. See too Patterson 2006, pp. 93–117.

[112] Linn 2013, pp. 315–21, on the North African grain supplies arriving in Rome until 455 at least. For discussion of the archaeology that supports this view, see Brown 2012, pp. 470–72.

[113] Patterson 2008, pp. 508–10 cites the work of Tim Potter.

[114] Barnish 1987, pp. 157–86, and especially p. 161.

foodstuffs to the western Roman Empire after 455.[115] Now, however, the Roman state had to buy grain outright from Vandal merchants. Given this change in the food supply, the state also put pressure on Italian producers – that is, on holders of properties in Roman Italy that produced foodstuffs that could be transported over land or by river to Rome in a more secure manner than by sea. Although Simon Malmberg may be right in maintaining that river trade declined over the course of the fifth century, there is no reason to think that it had stopped suddenly after 455. A passage in Procopius's *Wars* describing the disuse of the towpath for hauling goods along the left bank of the Tiber in 537 is evidence for that period in the midst of the war and not a "rapid decrease in the volume of river traffic in the course of the fifth century."[116] Although there was a general decline in trade over the course of the fifth century, the return of elites and non-elites to Rome in the immediate decade after 455 and the state's continuing role in importing food for Rome from the Tiber Valley and central Italy, as well as by sea from Apulia and Sicily, must have mitigated the decreases in river trade caused by political upheavals and population decline.[117]

The political disruptions in the decade after 455 did, however, affect Italo-Roman producers. Until a new peace treaty was made with the Vandals, the provisioning of Rome by sea was challenging. This situation placed greater demand on estates in central and southern Italy to supply foodstuffs. The owners of these estates who benefitted the most from the increased demand for foodstuffs were, by and large, Roman senatorial aristocrats. As the state worked to secure the food supply of Rome, some aristocrats benefited from the higher demand for the food and goods produced on their Italian estates.

Rebuilding a City and Its Population

From the perspective of Roman senatorial aristocrats, working with generals and emperors to restore the city opened up new opportunities to accrue power, wealth, and prestige even as they competed among themselves and with other elites. There was much to do to rebuild Rome. The Vandals not only had reduced the city's population but also had damaged its physical fabric – its buildings and imperial monuments, its churches and pagan

---

[115] De Salvo 2014, pp. 73–84. Vaccaro 2013, pp. 271–79 for the ongoing vitality of Sicily and the western market, although some excavated sites did decline in the mid fifth century while many did not.

[116] Malmberg 2015, p. 192, cites Procop. *Wars* 5.26.9–12 as part of his argument. This is unlikely, as has also been argued by Aguilera Martin 2002, pp. 34–43.

[117] For the pressure on Sicily to supply grain, see especially the analysis of the archaeological evidence by Vaccaro 2013, pp. 259–313. For the state's ongoing role in feeding Rome, see notes 121 and 123 below.

temples, as well as its domestic housing. Once more, the official appointed by the emperor to undertake the task of overseeing the physical restoration of the city and its services was the urban prefect. This office, along with the office of praetorian prefect of Italy and consul, still stood at the pinnacle of a senatorial civic career. Its holders were key to successful relations between Italo-Roman senators and any would-be emperor; hence, it is worth underscoring that each of the emperors in this period appointed as urban prefect of Rome men from established, prestigious Italo-Roman aristocratic families. These men were of critical importance in restoring the city.

The Role of the Urban Prefect in Feeding Rome

Urban prefects, senatorial aristocrats, emperors, and generals all knew that the key to the restoration of urban life was securing the city's food supply. John of Antioch has already provided evidence for how dire the political consequences of food shortages in Rome were; a food shortage had led Avitus to dismiss his Gothic troops from the city and ultimately cost him the support of the people and the Senate.[118] The lesson had been learned; rulers who did not fulfill this task would be held accountable. So, too, would be the high civic magistrate who oversaw this system – namely, the urban prefect, a position that generally came to Italo-Roman senatorial aristocrats. Food distribution was both the responsibility *of* and the means by which to accrue honor *for* late Roman elites who held the office of urban prefect.

The task of the urban prefect in feeding Rome until this point had been far easier. Rome had enjoyed several decades of a secured food supply, even after the loss of large parts of the African grain fields to the Vandals in 428, because Valentinian III had negotiated a treaty in 442 that had secured land in some of the North African provinces to supply Rome.[119] In addition, Geiseric had been giving annual tribute (*dasmos*) to the western empire for the continuation of the state grain, the *annona*.[120] It may well be that a desire to stop making such payments factored into Geiseric's decision to attack the city in 455. But the grain supply for Rome resumed, and its oversight was of continuing political importance to the successful urban prefect, as is vividly attested by a *Letter* of

---

[118] See note 74 above.   [119] See note 112 above and note 120 below.

[120] Procop. *Wars* 3.4.13. See too Linn 2013, pp. 298–321. The terms of the 442 treaty are disputed; Sirks 1991, pp. 162–64, argues that the *annona* continued gratis as part of the treaty, while Wickham 2005, pp. 87–88, thinks this was done to profit the Vandals. There is little evidence for Wickham's view. The tax shortfalls that he cites on p. 88, note 84, can be the result of any number of factors.

Sidonius Apollinaris, urban prefect of Rome in 468. In it he describes his concern for his reputation (*fama*) should there be a food shortage under his watch and his great joy over the news that the grain ships from Brundisium had reached the port of Ostia.[121] The fact that the ships came from Brundisium on Italy's eastern coast suggests that the grain had come from Apulia or Sicily. The arrival of the grain ships to the port of Rome had long been cause to celebrate, so the event was recorded in the city's civic calendars in the mid fourth century.[122] The urban prefect who undertook this job and performed it well still accrued honor (*honorabilis*) and influence (*gratia*) before his fellow citizens, rewards still emphasized by the early sixth-century senator Cassiodorus.[123]

Emperors and would-be emperors as well as Rome's generals were happy to see the Italo-Roman senatorial aristocracy take on these responsibilities again, as the legislation of Majorian makes clear. Roman senatorial aristocrats still vied for the prestigious office of urban prefect after 455.

Repairing the Physical Fabric of Rome

The urban prefect was also the official responsible for restoring to Rome the "appearance of the venerable city."[124] This was not an empty phrase. The Vandals had targeted certain civic spaces – the Palatine Palace, the Temple of Jupiter Capitolinus, and the Roman Forum – among others. (See Map 1.) Hence, there was a certain amount of repair and rebuilding that the urban prefects had to oversee with state money, although some prefects accrued greater prestige and demonstrated their personal involvement in the city by noting that they were using their own money on repairs after 455 as they had also done at times before.

The Statuary Habit. Inscriptions attest to the efforts of a number of urban prefects who restored statues or moved them to remove evidence of damage in the decade or so after 455. The standard formulation indicates that the urban prefects moved statuary into more "frequented" areas – that is, more appropriate public areas or buildings. Iulius Felix Campanianus, likely urban prefect

---

[121] Sid. Ap. *Ep.* 1.10.2.

[122] Salzman 1990, p. 129. The *natalis annonis* fell on May 18 in the mid fourth-century civic calendar.

[123] Cass. *Var.* 6.18.1: *Si ad hanc mensuram censendae sunt dignitates, ut tanto quis honorabilis habeatur, quanto civibus profuisse, ad copiam populi romani, ut sacratissimae urbi praeparetur annona tam magnus populus.* And 6.18.3: *Quid habes melius quod optes quam illius populi gratiam quaerere, quam nos etiam constat optare?* Cass. *Var.* 11.5 notes that the *annona* was a constant preoccupation of the Ostrogothic king; see Durliat 1990, pp. 126–33. For more on this under the Ostrogoths, see too Marazzi 2007, pp. 279–316, especially pp. 292–96, for evidence of trade.

[124] *N. Maj.* 4.1.

between 465 and 467 and active in Rome in the 460s, moved statues from some unknown site "to improve the appearance of the Baths of Trajan" (*ad augendam Thermarum Traianarum gratiam*) on the Oppian Hill, as the reused bases indicate.[125] (See Map 1.) Attention to restoring statuary demonstrated reverence for Rome's traditions as well as aided the refurbishing of civic spaces. The urban prefect probably in office between 461 and 465, Macrobius Plotinus Eustathius, now identified as the son of the writer Macrobius, moved a statue into the Roman Forum "from hidden places" (*[ex ab]strusis lo[cis]*) at his own expense.[126] Although we have no way of knowing what this statue represented or if the statue had been hidden due to the sack, funding this move with personal money speaks to the personal engagement of senatorial urban prefects in renewing the city's public spaces. One urban prefect, Audax, holder of this office in 474–75, is attested as having restored a damaged statue near the Roman Forum "after a barbarian invasion had been ended," a phrase that some have interpreted as a direct allusion to the Vandal captivity of 455.[127] Certainly, the focus on repairing the Forum area offers a means of redefining the priorities of the city by restoring its public political spaces.

The Task of Urban Prefects in Rebuilding Rome's Infrastructure. Urban prefects oversaw all sorts of construction in the mid fifth century, some of which may have been necessary after the Vandal occupation, while other projects may have been the routine work of maintaining Rome's many monuments and buildings. Iunius [Va]lentin[u]s as urban prefect repaired something after the Vandal assault (*hostili impetu sublata*).[128] Campanianus, urban prefect likely between 465 and 467, is not attested for any specific task, but he had experience repairing Rome's aqueducts from his earlier office (count of the aqueducts).[129] The urban prefect now was in charge of this office directly.[130]

---

[125] *CIL* VI 1679 = *ILS* 5716. For Iulius Felix Campanianus, see Campanianus 4, *PLRE* 2, p. 256. He can be identified with Campanianus 1, *PLRE* 2, p. 255. For his urban prefectureship, see Scharf 1992, p. 278; and on his inscriptions, see Orlandi 2020, pp. 193–95. Her suggestion that his prefecture be dated to 469 is only hypothetical.

[126] Plotinus Eustathius 13, *PLRE* 2, p. 436 and Table 4.3. This urban prefect is likely identical with Eustathius (7), *PLRE* 2, p. 435, son of the author Macrobius; see Cameron 2011, p. 238, who suggests these dates for his urban prefecture.

[127] *CIL* 6 1663 = *ILS* 814 (before S. Maria Nova): *barbarica incursione/sublata restitutit*. Wheeler 1988, p. 82, defines *incursio* as a "sudden and unexpected assault" in official documents.

[128] See note 64 above.

[129] See Iulius Felix Campanianus 4, *PLRE* 2, p. 256. For his colleague, see Tarpeius Anneius Faustus 5, *PLRE* 2, p. 452. For identification, see Orlandi 2020, p. 194.

[130] Chastagnol 1960, pp. 47–8, citing the evidence of the *Notitia Dignitatum* for the fifth century. The office of Count of the Aqueducts (*comes formarum*) is attested in Rome at least through the time of Theoderic: see Cass. *Var.* 7.6.

Of more obvious political relevance is the public commemoration of the victories of emperors and rulers with inscribed commemorations on monuments or statues. I discussed earlier the honorific inscription citing the victory of Ricimer on the Rostra in the Roman Forum, which had been carried out by the urban prefect Valentinus.[131] As I noted in Chapter 3, the urban prefect had access to funding and materials provided by the state to use for this purpose, as well as for repairs to public buildings.

It is most likely a sign of the financial and political difficulties that Roman elites confronted in the decade after 455 that we have little evidence of the repair or construction of public monuments or buildings in Rome by urban prefects. This suggests that the recovery of Rome's public areas was not as vigorous after 455 as it had been after 410. However, we do have evidence of rebuilding private homes. In his first extant law of 458, the emperor Majorian criticized the urban prefect for allowing the re-use of materials from public buildings for private use:

> While it is pretended that the stones are necessary for public works, the beautiful structures of the ancient buildings are being scattered, and in order that something small may be repaired, great things are being destroyed. Hence the occasion now arises that also each and every person is constructing a private edifice, through the favoritism of the high administrative officials who are situated in the City, [and each person] does not hesitate to take presumptuously and to transfer the necessary material from the public places, although those things which belong to the splendor of the cities ought to be preserved by civic affection, even under the necessity of repair.[132]

The emperor warned the urban prefect that allowing this was a punishable offense (*plectanda urbani officii suggestione*).[133] In the next section of this law,

---

[131] See note 64 above.

[132] *N. Maj.* 4.1, adapted translation from Pharr 1969, pp. 553–54. *N. Maj.* 4.1: *Impp. Leo et Maiorianus aa. Aemiliano praefecto urbi. … Dum necessaria publico operi saxa finguntur, antiquarum aedium dissipatur speciosa constructio et ut parvum aliquid reparetur, magna diruuntur. Hinc iam occasio nascitur, ut etiam unusquisque privatum aedificium construens per gratiam iudicum in urbe positorum praesumere de publicis locis necessaria et transferre non dubitet, cum haec, quae ad splendorem urbium pertinent, adfectione civica debeant etiam sub reparatione servari.*

[133] *C. Th.* 15.1.19 (376): *nemo praefectorum Urbis aliorumve iudicorum, apud aliquod novum in urbe incluta …* These *iudices* were "appointed by the emperor": *quos potestas in excelso locat.* Hence, Oppedisano 2013 p. 152, note 88 rightly argues that these are high government officials, not ordinary judges, whom the emperor put in charge of preserving buildings in Rome by preventing private individuals from appropriating materials from public ones. Cf. *C.Th.* 11.7.8, 356, which stipulates: *exactione provinciarum, quas rectores aut praefecti annonae aut rationales per Africam sustinent, a maioribus iudicibus usurpari non debent. C. Th.* 11.7.8, 356,

Majorian specifically stipulates that temples established by "the ancients" be protected against private despoliation.[134] Certainly the beneficiaries of these building materials as well as the urban prefect and the high administrative officials (*iudices*) who derived influence and likely money from this trafficking would not have been happy at this injunction. They now faced a stiff fine of fifty pounds of gold. The punishment for non-elite officials was far worse; the public secretaries (*apparitores*) and accountants involved in this trafficking faced the prospect of having their hands cut off if they were found guilty.[135] To control this graft, Majorian delegated decisions about reusing materials to the Senate as a body, and then final approval rested with the emperor.[136]

How well Majorian's law was enforced is not known. Although injunctions against spoliation can be found in earlier laws, the specificity of this law suggests it was indeed, a contemporary problem. Indeed, Majorian's law fits well with the evidence, textual as well as material, that shows that individual Romans were rebuilding private homes, if not public structures. The efforts of individuals in the domestic sphere show a different, more limited side to the resurgence of Rome's elites after 455.

Restoring the Rhythms of Senatorial Social and Political Life: The Role of the Aristocratic Domus in Rome

The homes of rich Roman aristocrats were notorious for their wealth; Jerome's vignette describing the ascetic Marcella confronting a gold-

---

also uses *iudex* to reference a high official above the prefect of the *annona*. I translate *iudices* in Majorian's *N. Maj. 4.1* as high administrative officials.

[134] *N. Maj.* 4.1.11: *Idcirco generali lege sancimus cuncta aedificia quaeve in templis aliisque monumentis a veteribus condita propter usum vel amoenitatem publicam subrexerunt, ita a nullo destrui atque contingi, ut iudex, qui hoc fieri statuerit, quinquaginta librarum auri inlatione feriatur; adparitores vero atque numerarios, qui iubenti obtemperaverint et sua neutiquam suggestione restiterint, fustuario supplicio subditos manuum quoque amissione truncandos, per quas servanda veterum monumenta temerantu.* For an adapted translation see Pharr 1969, pp. 553–54: "Therefore, by this general law We sanction that all the buildings that have been founded by the ancients as temples and as other monuments and that were constructed for the public use of pleasure shall not be destroyed by any person, and that it shall transpire that a judge who should decree that this be done shall be punished by the payment of fifty pounds of gold. If his *apparitores* and accountants should obey him when he so orders and should not resist him in any way by their own recommendation, they shall be subjected to the punishment of cudgeling, and they shall also be mutilated by the loss of their hands, through which the monuments of the ancients that should be preserved are desecrated."

[135] *N. Maj.* 4.1. This harsh punishment is usually found for military deserters, as in Val. Max. 2.7.22; *HA Cass.* 4.5.

[136] *N. Maj. Nov.* 4.3.

seeking Goth in her house in 410 conveyed a well-known stereotype about Roman *domus* (houses of the wealthy) and their attraction for plunderers.[137] That these houses were meant to advertise the wealth and status of their owners was certain. And the *Fourth Novel* of Majorian (discussed above) provides evidence that some elites had returned to Rome and by 458 were busy reconstructing their damaged houses, albeit with materials from public buildings. The importance of such activity goes beyond the individual household, for, as Carlos Machado aptly observed, aristocratic *domus* were central for late antique Rome's topography of power:

> Domestic spaces played a fundamental role in the social and political strategies of the city's elite, being the place where they received their friends and clients, extending their personal networks to different parts of the Empire and through different segments of late Roman society. *Domus* were also the places where aristocrats exercised their power and influence, holding meetings and distributing favors and resources.[138]

Hence, the fate of the aristocratic *domus* after 455 would play a part in the restoration of senatorial society.

Ideally, we would like to know how many houses had been destroyed and abandoned and how many had been rebuilt after the Vandal captivity. Unfortunately, a clear quantitative answer based on an archaeological assessment and a precise chronology of restoration or abandonment for all the elite *domus* in Rome is not possible.[139] Indeed, even before 455, references to the houses of elites, *domus*, covered a wide range of types and sizes, ranging from richly decorated grand palaces to more modest abodes.[140] Nonetheless, our archaeological evidence and our textual sources suggest that the Vandals plundered widely in the houses of the wealthy elite especially, even if they did not wantonly torch them, and that some houses were abandoned by their owners in the second half of the fifth century. But this evidence does not cluster around 455 and thus does not suggest a sudden collapse in the housing market in the city in the subsequent decade.[141] Rather, the textual and archaeological evidence, thin as it is, points to the same situation that the law and the political developments outlined above do. In general, we see that a number of wealthy Romans, along with immigrants and new elites, returned to Rome, but they were no longer building new *domus*, nor were

---

[137] Jer. *Ep.* 127.13.   [138] Machado 2012B, p. 111.

[139] Guidobaldi 1986, pp. 165–237 is a good beginning, but it is now outdated, as is Guidobaldi, s.v. *domus* in *LTUR*. But this view is also accepted by Machado 2019, pp. 233–35.

[140] Machado 2019, p. 233.

[141] Machado 2012B pp. 111–38; Santangeli Valenzani 2012, pp. 219–27.

they restoring their houses to be quite as large and luxurious as before. A number of houses were partitioned for reuse in new ways, either for smaller living quarters or for the production of food or goods of some sort.

A good example is the large *domus* on the Esquiline Hill, located underneath the modern-day Piazza dei Cinquecento, which was inhabited from the second century into the late fifth or early sixth century, when it was partially abandoned. (See Map 1.)[142] In the late period of its use, some changes were made, as indicated by the presence of dividing walls; the largest room of the house had been despoiled of its marble, and a new residential area, partially decorated with frescoes, was arranged around a courtyard.[143] The upper story was also rearranged, suggesting to Carlos Machado and other scholars that the owners were still investing in this building.[144] Though the inhabitants of this house now lived in a smaller, less luxuriously decorated space, they continued to use it. We cannot tell if the inhabitants of the rebuilt house were among those considered elites, but if they were, they were living in a less grand circumstance. The structure was only abandoned in the later sixth century.[145]

This same pattern is seen elsewhere in Rome; for example, the house of Gaudentius on the Caelian Hill had been enlarged to incorporate two *insulae* (apartment buildings) and refurbished in the boom years of the fourth century. According to the excavator, in the mid fifth century the reception rooms on the lower level had been abandoned and buried, but the service areas below remained in use into the sixth and seventh centuries. It is possible, but not certain, that the upper floors were used for living quarters until the *domus* was abandoned at some time between the late fifth and mid sixth centuries.[146] Unfortunately, we cannot know for certain if this house reflects a possible movement to two-storied buildings that "allowed for greater specialization of space," a development associated with early medieval houses in Rome.[147] Nonetheless, the fate of this house is similar to that of

---

[142] Santangeli Valenzani 2012, pp. 219–227; Meneghini and Santangeli Valenzani 1996, pp. 172–77; see too Machado 2012B, pp. 120–22.

[143] Machado 2012B, pp. 120–22.

[144] Machado 2019, p. 259; Meneghini and Santangeli Valenzani 1996, pp. 173–75.

[145] Machado 2019, p. 261. See too Fig. 7.8, p. 260.

[146] The evidence for this date is relevant for this chapter since most of the material that was discarded dates to the period 480–550, hence indicating that the house was abandoned only after 480 at the earliest. See Machado 2012B, pp. 121–23, note 59. For the house, see Spinola 2000, pp. 152–56, discussed by Machado 2012B, pp. 121–22, and note 58. Broglio 2010, p. 219 sees the other parts of this house in use through the sixth to seventh centuries. For a discussion of the political implications of Gaudentius as a neighbor of Symmachus, see Machado 2019, pp. 246–48.

[147] Machado 2012B, pp. 121–22 and note 65 for the Houses in the Forum of Nerva.

the Esquiline Hill house, for adaptation indicates continued habitation in reduced circumstances.

Another, more recently excavated *domus* under Palazzo Valentini in the area of the Capitoline, *Domus* B, provides an additional example of this same pattern. In the late third or early fourth century, two houses had been joined together to build a large *domus*, which was decorated with expensive cut marble decoration (*opus sectile*).[148] This *domus* continued to be used into the fifth century, when a small bath was adapted to the site. A break in the marble socle, according to the current excavator, was likely caused by a fire. *Domus* B was abandoned in the late fifth or early sixth century.[149] The excavator identified this fire damage with one of two earthquakes, that of either 498 or 523, a dating also confirmed by the sequence of floors after the addition of the small bath as well as by mosaic and ceramic evidence.[150] If this was the house of the late Roman senatorial aristocrat Flavius Asterius, consul of 494 (since his name was found on water pipes in this area by nineteenth-century excavators),[151] *Domus* B indicates that the abandonment occurred here at the end of the fifth or in the early sixth century and that this house was not reinhabited, even though it was located in a central part of Rome, where elite housing was concentrated.[152]

There is, as far as I know, only one house in Rome, on the Vicus Caprarius on the Quirinal Hill, that has been identified by its excavator as having been destroyed and abandoned after the 455 sack. (See Map 1 for the Quirinal Hill.) But this destruction date is not securely tied to this event; in truth, the evidence for inhabitation disappeared after the first quarter of the fifth century, opening up several reasons for the abandonment of this *domus*, none of which are necessarily the 455 sack.[153] Rather, there are several long-term trends that may have led to the decision not to rebuild this house. As Carlos Machado has observed, although there had been a boom in elite housing in the fourth-century city, the lack of attestation for major renewals after the early fifth century suggests that the expansion of the housing market had ended.[154] And the instances of

---

[148] For the most recent discussion, see Baldassari 2008–9, pp. 343–84.

[149] In private conversation, Baldassari indicated on July 7, 2017, that a seismologist had examined the break and had made this estimation. See Baldassari 2008–9, and 2011.

[150] Baldassari 2008–9, p. 356.   [151] Baldassari 2011, p. 63.

[152] Machado 2019, p. 233, following the work of Jean-Pierre Guilhembet, who analyses the fourth-century *Regionary Catalogues* of the city, shows that elite houses were concentrated in Regions 8 (Roman Forum) and 10 (the Palatine), but also in the southeastern parts of the city, on the Caelian and Aventine hills.

[153] Insalco 2002, p. 46. The pottery evidence ends in the early fifth century, opening up the likelihood that a fire destroyed this site in the first half of the fifth century CE.

[154] Machado 2019, pp. 259–61.

excavated houses discussed above suggest that a number of elite *domus* had been abandoned over the course of the late fifth and early sixth centuries. The Caelian Hill, for example, lost a number of elite houses over the course of the fifth century after the destruction of the camps for the provincial troops (*castra peregrinorum*) in the early decades of that century. (See Map 1 for the Caelian Hill.)[155] Abandonment reinforces the impression of a population decline over the century. And the reuse of these buildings for more modest housing suggests the reduced economic circumstances of their former inhabitants, whoever they may be.

Nonetheless, Rome still attracted immigrants and a number of upwardly mobile new elites. For example, the commander in chief of the army and cavalry (MUM), Flavius Valila, who was called Theodovius (*qui et Theodovius*), came to Rome to live, serving there under the Emperor Anthemius in 471; he adopted what appears to have been a very traditionally Roman senatorial lifestyle, including owning his own inscribed seat in the Colosseum.[156] Theodovius had acquired the house and basilica of the fourth-century aristocrat Iunius Bassus, which he bequeathed in his will to the Bishop of Rome Simplicius (468–83) to be adapted into a church to honor the apostle Andrew.[157]

But Valila was not the only new man to come to Rome to seek his fortune. Provincials like Sidonius Apollonaris, who had come to Rome along with the emperor Avitus, sought to make their way in the houses of senatorial elites, which Sidonius described with admiration. When Sidonius returned to Rome during the reign of Anthemius, he stayed in the house of the aristocratic urban prefect Paulus, whose *domus* and owner were praised, respectively, for their hospitality and learning.[158] Like Rutilius Namatianus earlier in the century, Sidonius emulated senatorial aristocratic traditions, excelling in rhetoric as a means of advancing to high office.[159] Thus, after 455 the city remained a magnet for talent, attracting men who would seek to compete with the older elite families in a traditional senatorial aristocratic society, albeit one that was, judging from the archaeological evidence, less opulent.[160]

---

[155] Broglio 2010, p. 219 and note 9. For the Caelian Hill, the evidence suggests the destruction of the *castra peregrinorum* happened before the Vandal occupation, i.e., in the first decades of the fifth century; see Pavolini 2013, pp. 164–65.

[156] *CIL* 6.32169 + 32221. See Fl. Valila qui et Theodovius, *PLRE* 2, p. 1147. See the discussion by Orlandi 2020, pp. 188–89.

[157] See CIL 6.41402 = *ILCV* 1785 for the dedication. For the suggestion that the house had been tied to the church through an imperial donation, see Orlandi 2020, pp. 190–91 and note 34.

[158] Sid. Ap. *Ep.* 1.9.1.   [159] Rut. Nam. *De red. suo* 1, 13–14.

[160] Broglio 2010, p. 220–24 on the importance of immigration for fifth-century Rome.

There were changes in the habitation patterns taking place in the city over the course of the fifth and early sixth centuries. In Rome, the adaptation of certain buildings for food production or for such artisanal purposes as dyeing, metallurgy, and glassblowing, as evidenced on the ground floors of elite houses, has been noted.[161] The abandonment of houses meant that certain areas had been left in disuse; hence, their materials had been available for reuse in other parts of the city. However, during the late fifth and early sixth centuries, these urban workers lived next door to a small but still wealthy number of illustrious senators who still maintained traditional *domus*-centered lifestyles and whose conservative culture encouraged values based on high civic office, literary culture, and patronage. So, as noted above, when Sidonius Apollinaris was in Rome he openly discussed with his friend, the aristocratic Paulus, his plans to be welcomed into the homes of the two most important senators at the time, Gennadius Avienus, consul in 450, and Flavius Caecina Decius Maximus Basilius, praetorian prefect for Majorian and Severus and consul in 463. Both men still had splendid *domus*, although we cannot identify their houses based on archaeological evidence.[162] Especially after peace had returned in the late fifth and the sixth centuries, this *domus*-centered lifestyle, such as that described by the early sixth-century senator Cassiodorus, which included the enjoyment of "apsed halls and monumental *nymphaea* [water displays], can only be attributed to the highest echelons of society, interpreted as the residences of *viri illustres*."[163]

The house of Valila mentioned earlier raises a second important issue – namely, the willingness of elites to donate their houses with their rents and furnishings to the church. In 471, Valila had already donated funding for one church, today lost, in the town of Tivoli.[164] In Rome, Valila's donation followed elite patronage patterns that had existed since the time of Constantine. Federico Guidobaldi noted that eleven of twenty-nine titular churches that had arisen in the neighborhoods across the city over the early

---

[161] For a house on the Aventine in which an oil press was added in the fifth century, see Broglio 2010, p. 221 note 17.

[162] Sid. Ap. *Ep.* 1.9.2–6, and refers to his frequent visits to the *domus* of Gennadius but favors Basilius.

[163] Cass. *Variae* 4.51. Quote from Ellis, 2006, pp. 413–40.

[164] Valila's devotion to Christianity had led him to build a church in 471 on property near Tibur earlier; on this church, see the *Carta Cornutiana*, discussed by Orlandi 2020, pp. 189–90, with text in *Lib. Pont.* ed. Duchesne 1981, p. cxlvii. Since the Bishop of Rome, Simplicius, accepted his donation, Machado 2019, p. 195, assumes that Valila was a Nicene Christian.

fourth through the fifth centuries had previously been elite *domus*.[165] Based on Guidobaldi, Carlos Machado observes that "eighteen of the nineteen titular churches archaeologically attested in the late fifth century for which we have evidence (out of a total of twenty-nine known) were built reusing or adapting private properties, either *domus* or apartment blocks."[166] (See my discussion of titular churches in Chapter 3.) These bequests are clear signs of the willingness of aristocrats along with wealthy clerics to become patrons of the church of Rome.[167] Indeed, church leaders encouraged donations of property as signs of piety, as we see from the fictional accounts of the fifth- and sixth-century *Gesta Martyrum* (Accounts of the Martyrs).[168] To encourage such gifts, the names of donors had been read aloud in churches in Rome since the late fourth century.[169] But it is worth underscoring that the donations of *domus* did not indicate that these properties had lost their value. Nor did such gifts result in the impoverishment of their wealthy donors.[170]

Nonetheless, donations of houses like that of Valila do reflect the changing topography of Rome, where fewer wealthy elites now lived. As noted, the archaeological evidence suggests a gradual downturn in the population size as well as a decline in the number and size of several elite *domus*. But the dating of this archaeological evidence suggests not a sudden downturn in the housing and rental market in response to the crisis of 455 but rather a gradual loss of value over the century.[171] At the same time, the donations of elite houses to the church augmented the wealth at the disposal of the bishop of Rome, whose voice in the restoration of life in the city post-455 was strangely silent.

---

[165] Guidobaldi 1999, p. 65 cites these statistics and numbers. There is no radical increase in donations of houses cited by Guidobaldi, nor by Machado 2012B, pp. 111–38.

[166] Machado 2019, pp. 192–93, citing Guidobaldi 1989, pp. 386–91.

[167] Hillner 2006, pp. 59–68, and 2008, pp. 225–61. Salzman 2013, 209 note 4 for bibliography on the *tituli*, and 229–30 on the connection between titular churches and elite donors and local priests.

[168] The *Gesta of SS. Praxedis and Pudentiana*, the only one of the *Gesta* to use the actual label *titulus* for a church, relates that a priest named Pastor tells how a certain man, conveniently named Pudens, founded a titular church that he gave to Pastor. The daughter of Pudens, Praxedis, with this same priest Pastor, founded a second church, inside a bath of her house, which a bishop named Pius consecrated. For another donated house, see the *Passio S. Marcelli papae et. Soc.*, 12, 15, 23; and see Hillner 2006, p. 64.

[169] Jer. *In Jerem.* 11.15 (*PL* 24.755); Jer. *In Ezech.* 18.5 (*PL* 25.175); Innocent, *Ep.* 25.2 (*PL* 20,553–54 = ed. Cabié 1973); and see Brown 2012, pp. 39–42 for this practice.

[170] Machado 2019, p. 261 suggests that the transfer of properties to the Church threatened the survival of families. However, the number of elites who totally renounced their properties is small. On the tendency to privilege the rare ascetic donation as normative for women, see Salzman 2002, pp. 164–77: Sessa, 2012, pp. 54–61.

[171] Santangeli Valenzani 2011, p. 23 makes a similar statement, with bibliography cited. See too Machado 2019, pp. 268–69.

The Response of the Bishop of Rome to the Vandal Crisis of 455

Given the crises of 455, there was need for pastoral care and spiritual leadership as well as the military and political interventions previously discussed. The Vandal captivity of the city raised a host of problems that bishops typically faced after the falls of cities, including population displacement, prisoners of war, exile, flight, asylum seekers, refugees, food shortages, resettlement, and rape.[172] How the bishops of Rome in this decade dealt with many of these issues in Rome has to be discovered through external sources because Bishop Leo (440–61) does not directly address the crisis of 455 in extant texts, nor did his successor, Hilary (461–68). Indeed, although there were many "strategies of crisis management" catalogued by Pauline Allen and Bronwen Neil in their insightful study of episcopal letters, including, among others, petitioning, violent coercion, and diplomatic embassies, the bishops of Rome, Leo and Hilary, evidenced only three: liturgical responses, material aid, and social exclusion.[173] Their attested efforts indicate their desire to rebuild their communities in the face of a number of competing forces.

The omission of any direct reference by Leo or Hilary to the Vandal fourteen-day captivity and its aftermath, and their limited responses to these events also, in my view, signs of how precarious the bishop of Rome's position was after 455 and how much caution was required of these bishops in this uncertain decade. There was no Christian emperor like Valentinian III and no wealthy imperial family patron like Galla Placidia to support Leo's rebuilding efforts. Rome's senatorial elites, who had donated to the bishop as well as to their neighborhood churches, still exerted a counterforce to the efforts of the bishops.[174] Indeed, senatorial aristocrats still exercised influence in the titular churches – and over the priests in them – to which their families had donated so generously. But the bishop of Rome had to deal with a growing influx of German military elite who openly embraced a version of Christianity that was viewed by the papacy as heretical: Arianism, described in Chapter 2, was embraced by the most important general of the day, Ricimer. His public dedication of the ornamentation of

---

[172] Allen and Neil 2013, pp. 37–52.

[173] Allen and Neil 2013, pp. 193–200 lists strategies including: Petitioning, Dogmatic Instruction, Discipline and Administration, Containment, Social Exclusion, Diplomatic Embassies, Synods and Councils, Proscriptions, Violent Coercion, Liturgical Responses, and Material Aid.

[174] See my discussion in Chapter 3 of titular churches. For the contestation for influence between the bishop and the aristocratic patrons under Leo's papacy, see too Salzman 2013, pp. 208–32; and more generally, Bowes 2008, pp. 225–61; and Sessa 2012, pp. 54–62.

a church to St. Agatha of the Goths openly offered a place of worship in the center of the city for Arian Christians.[175]

The Arians were not the only group in Rome to challenge the Nicene views of the bishop of Rome. Leo opposed views of the nature of Christ associated with eastern church leaders, regarding such views as insufficiently embracing both the divinity and the human suffering of Christ. These alternative Christological formulations associated with Eutyches, leader of the monastery in Constantinople, and Nestorius, patriarch of Constantinople (428–31), also had followers in Rome. Since the beginning of his papacy, Leo had been involved in resisting these ideas and did so with greater force in the wake of the 451 Ecumenical Council of Chalcedon. This interpretation of the nature of Christ, which had been embraced by the eastern emperors Marcian and Leo and the church leaders in Constantinople, came to be known as the Chalcedonian formulation. In light of these political developments and, as Susan Wessel has argued, in response to the suffering of the population in the West, Leo tried to extend this formulation, which matched his views well, so as to unify regional churches under his jurisdiction.[176] He thus attempted to extend his authority beyond Rome, basing his position in part on his being head of the Church of Peter in Rome. The twists and turns of Leo's theological and political maneuvers in relation to the eastern court will not detain us now, but it was an ongoing issue that was the focus of Leo's and Hilary's energies after 455 as it had been before.

Liturgical Changes and Material Aid

The turmoil in 455 disrupted the annual sermon cycle preached by the bishop in Rome for a two-year hiatus, between March 455 and early 457. When Leo returned to the pulpit, his sermons expressed a new note of pessimism, including a unique reference to Job's trials.[177] Leo's dismissal of the value of possessions and his reiteration of the need to forgive debts in two *Sermons*

---

[175] On this church, see note 204 below. Even if Ricimer was a "homoian" in his beliefs and his position legal, his patronage of an Arian church was not desirable from the position of a Nicene bishop of Rome. On the status of Arianism in the state, see Chapter 2, note 244.

[176] For a good introduction to these controversies, see Wessel 2015, pp. 327–43; and Maas 2015, pp. 20–25.

[177] *CCSL* 138, ed. Chavasse CXIX. *Sermons* 49 and 50, for Lent, and *Sermons* 93 and 94, for the September fast are dated to the period from the end of March 455 to the beginning of 457/458, with a hiatus in this period, as argued by Chavasse, the modern editor of Leo's ninety-six preserved sermons. The quotation is from Job 7.1 in *Sermon* 50.2: "None are so holy, none so upright that, in this time 'In this life, which is wholly a trial' they should not need remission of some sin."

that are likely dated soon after 455 are pregnant with contemporary meaning.[178] And in the only certainly dated post-455 *Sermon*, 96, delivered on Christmas Eve 457, Leo strove to rebuild the community of the faithful by turning to once more excluding those who had been deemed heretical; this sermon does so by attacking followers of the discredited monk Eutyches of Constantinople.[179]

Leo's silence about the Vandal captivity in his sermons even after 457 is not an accident of preservation, for Leo also omits mention of these events from the 143 extant letters attributed to him and accepted as genuine. Not one of these makes specific mention of the Vandal captivity or of Leo's efforts to mitigate the suffering of those in Rome after the city's capture.[180] Moreover, Leo's *Letters* and *Sermons* were kept as church documents, preserved by and circulated to clergy for guidance and imitation.[181] We might think that silence about the Vandals befits Leo's view of his role as bishop since Leo does not note his other diplomatic efforts – neither his participation in the senatorial embassy in 452 that successfully negotiated with Attila to dissuade him from attacking the city nor his failed attempt to forestall Geiseric's onslaught in 455.[182] And it is also true that this silence was politic. The Vandal king Geiseric had taken the wife and daughters of Valentinian III hostage. The Romans were negotiating with the Vandals periodically throughout this decade. But such political concerns do not explain Leo's unwillingness to directly address the immediate needs of Rome's congregations after the Vandal occupation, given that earlier bishops such as Augustine did address these concerns in sermons to his congregation in Hippo after 410 (see Chapter 3).

Bronwen Neil attributed Leo's silence on the Vandal captivity and his lack of responsiveness to Leo's "unwillingness to admit the dire straits of the papacy in this period."[183] Part of Leo's challenge was clearly economic; the Church of Rome, like the city at large, had lost significant material wealth. Leo did not have the financial resources easily at hand to ransom "many thousands of captives."[184] Most importantly, the Bishop of Rome had lost his patrons; Leo and his successor Hilary could not presume a similar level of

---

[178] *CCSL* 138, *Sermons* 49.5 and 50.2.

[179] *CCSL* 138, ed. Chavasse CXIX. *Sermon* 96 is securely dated to Christmas 457, based on allusions to the murder of bishop Proterius in Alexandria in 457 by Eutyches's followers.

[180] *PL* 54 includes Leo's *Letters*. On his works and their acceptance, see Neil 2009, 13–15.

[181] Leo certainly must have written private letters, but these are not preserved, as observed by Neil 2009, p. 9.

[182] Jord. *Get.* 42,223 = Priscus *Frag.* 22, ed. Blockley 1983, pp. 310–11 on the Huns; Prosper, *Chron.* s.a. 455, on the Vandals.

[183] Neil 2009, p. 9.   [184] Prosper, *Chron.* s.a. 455.

financial support from Avitus, Majorian, and Libius Severus. The novels decreed by Majorian that promised that the imperial treasury would not seize any inheritance left to the church and that recognized the bishop of Rome's authority to decide contested cases involving the forced entry of individuals into the clergy evidence Majorian's recognition of the church's claims to adjudications concerning clergy, but Majorian is not on record as having provided any other financial assistance.[185] Nor did Majorian return to Rome to rule, depriving the bishop of Rome of the emperor's immediate presence as well.

We can see the impact of 455 if we briefly look at the building projects associated with Bishop Leo cited in the sixth century *Book of the Popes*. For these, Leo had relied heavily on the financial resources of the imperial family as well as those of private patrons. The *Book of the Popes* records for his pontificate the building (*fecit*) of a basilica to the bishop and martyr St. Cornelius near the cemetery of Callistus on the Appian Road and the establishment (*constituit*) of a monastery near St. Peter's. (See Map 1.) Otherwise, Leo is cited only for renovations (*renovavit*) over the twenty-one years of his papacy. Leo is recorded as having renovated the basilica and apse-vault ceiling (*cameram*) of St. Peter's; he did the same at St. Paul's Outside the Walls "after the divine fire," and reconstructed an apse vault at the Lateran Basilica. (See Map 1.)[186] His renovations at St. Paul's are tied to the patronage of Galla Placidia, who died in 450, and so fell prior to the 455 occupation. Similarly, the other renovations noted above also fit more comfortably in the time period before the death of his imperial patrons, Valentinian III (who died in 455) and Galla Placidia, since both had been fundamental donors for these projects.[187]

---

[185] *N. Maj.* 10, is not extant except for the title: "Neither a senator of the city of Rome nor the church shall be compelled to deliver to the Fisc anything that has been left to them in a testament by certain persons," not dated; *N. Maj.* 11, 460 CE, stipulates that no person shall be ordained a cleric against his will, and in 11.1, stipulates that bishops found guilty of this offense be sent to the bishop in Rome for trial. For a translation, see Pharr 1969, pp. 560–61.

[186] *Lib. Pont.* 47, ed. Duchesne 1981, p. 239: *Hic renovavit basilicam beati Petri apsotoli [et cameram] et beati Pauli post ignem divinum renovavit. Fecit vero cameram in basilica Costantiniana. Fecit autem basilicam beato Cornelio epsicopo et martyri, iuxta cymiterium Calisti, via Appia.* "Renovavit" in the *Lib. Pont.* has a specific meaning of repair, as opposed to building (*fecit*) or establishing (*constituit*). This work is dated prior to 455; see Duchesne 1981, p. 240 for the epigraphic evidence.

[187] Leo's effort at St. Paul's "after the divine fire" has no specific referent. But his renovation work there is associated with the patronage of the empress Galla Placidia who died in 450; see *Chron. Gall.* 452, no. 136 (s.a. 450) ed. Mommsen 1892, rept.1981, MGH AA 9, p. 662. For the lost inscription indicating her support, see *Lib. Pont.* 47, ed. Duchesne 1981, p. 240, note 6, and Gianandrea 2017, p. 196, note 82: *Placidiae pia mens operis decus omne paterni/gaudet pontifices studio splendere Leonis.*

The *Book of the Popes* does, however, mention one specific material action taken by Leo in direct response to 455:

> After the Vandal disaster, he [Leo] replaced all the consecrated silver services throughout all the titular churches . . . by melting down six water jars, two at the Constantinian basilica; two at the basilica of St. Peter; [and] two at St. Paul's, which the emperor Constantine had presented, each weighing 100 pounds; from these he replaced all the consecrated vessels.[188]

Leo's decision to replenish all the silver liturgical vessels in all the titular churches led him to take an unusual step: he melted down six hundred pounds of "Constantinian" water jars – items recorded as having been donated to the Lateran by the first Christian emperor when he had founded the first churches in Rome. How these water jars escaped the Vandal sack is an intriguing question; no doubt they had been hidden. Leo's melting of these jugs was memorable enough to be commemorated in the records of the Church of Rome, identified as a source for the *Book of the Popes*.[189] These objects' association with the first Christian emperor made them all the more precious, and this fact, too, points to Leo's desperate need for funds.

The replacement of liturgical silver had multiple contemporary meanings. In my study of fifth-century episcopal responses to the military and political crises that overtook Rome – based in large part on the *Book of the Popes* and on papal letters – the first sign of recovery was the provisioning of liturgical vessels. Indeed, Leo's decision to replenish liturgical plate is part of a typical pattern for episcopal crisis management that has been largely overlooked by scholars primarily intent on examining repairs to buildings.[190] Such vessels served as significant visual markers for the congregation of the power of the bishop in restoring the community. After the sack of 410, the restoration of liturgical vessels would have been the concern of the bishop of Rome at the time, Innocent (401–17), whose absence from Rome both during and after the sack may partially explain the lacunae in the *Book of the Popes* about his post-410 activities. Nonetheless, at some date during his papacy, perhaps after 410, Innocent was praised for giving (*obtulit*) silver plate to the *titulus* of

---

[188] Translation by Davis 2010, *Life of Leo*, 47.6, p. 37. For the text, see *Lib. Pont.* 47.6, ed. Duchesne 1981, p. 239: *Hic renovavit post cladem Wandalicam omnia ministeria sacrata argentea per omnes titulos, conflatas hydrias VI basilicae Constantinianae, duas basilicae beati Petri apostoli, duas beati Pauli apostoli, quas Constantinus Augustus obtulit, qui pens. sing. libl centenas; de quas omnia vasa renovavit sacrata.*

[189] See my discussion in Chapter 1.

[190] This is a point that is not explored by Allen and Neil 2013, who focus on pastoral care. Nor is it addressed in detail by Leader Newby 2004, pp. 61–122.

Vestina.[191] Soon after, Bishop Sixtus III (432–40) was praised for asking Emperor Valentinian III to replace the silver *fastigium* – the gabled colonnaded screen inside the chancel between apse and altar – in St. Peter's that Alaric and the Goths had removed.[192] And again, after the civil wars in Rome in the early 470s, the then bishop of Rome, Simplicius, was praised for donating a gold drinking vessel (*scyphus*) weighing five pounds and sixteen silver chandeliers weighing twelve pounds each for St. Peter's.[193]

After 455 Leo's decision to melt down the six Constantinian water jugs to replenish the silver liturgical vessels in the titular churches in Rome demonstrated his immediate economic need. Although the Vandal king Geiseric, an Arian, had agreed to refrain from setting the churches on fire during the sack, his men had helped themselves to the portable wealth of the churches. In addition to the mostly silver but also some gold liturgical vessels, the Vandals had no doubt taken votive offerings, lighting apparatus, and building ornaments since all of these could have been found in the churches of the city. As Philip Grierson memorably observed, churches after Constantine were veritable treasure houses.[194] This fact was well known. In his *History against the Pagans* written between 412 and 418, Orosius recounts how, during the 410 sack of Rome, a Goth had entered a church and found an elderly virgin whom he frightened into bringing out the silver and gold plate from St. Peter's that had been hidden there; "the size, weight, and beauty of the riches displayed" and the knowledge of their sacred devotion to St. Peter reportedly had so overwhelmed the Goth that he restored them to St. Peter's.[195] This story was comforting to the Christian faithful, but not all plunderers had been dissuaded this easily.

As Orosius's vignette also demonstrates, Christians believed that liturgical vessels were filled with sacred power. Indeed, these objects were part of the foundation of the community that used them. Whenever a church was established, liturgical equipment used in the performance of the Eucharistic and other rites was presented to the congregation, having been consecrated by the

---

[191] *Lib. Pont.* 42, ed. Duchesne 1981, p. 220. The funding for that plate was likely also from Vestina.

[192] *Lib. Pont.* 46, ed. Duchesne 1981, p. 233. This definition of *fastigium* is preferred with good reason by Davis 1989, p. 115.

[193] *Lib. Pont.* 49, ed. Duchesne 1981, p. 249. This *scyphus* was lighter than the usual ten pounds for such vessels recorded by the *Book of the Popes*, perhaps a sign of this bishop's limited resources as he tried to demonstrate his liberality. The *scyphus* was used for the additional wine that was placed on the altar when it was foreseen that the main chalice would not hold all the consecrated wine that was required for distribution to the congregation at mass.

[194] Grierson's remarks are noted by Marlia Mundell Mango, 1986, p. 1, and see her discussion on pp. 1–4.

[195] Oros. *Hist.* 7.39.8.

bishop. For example, the *Book of the Popes* records that when Bishop Celestine (422–32) dedicated the Basilica of Julius "after the Gothic conflagration" (i.e., after the Gothic sack of 410), he presented the community with silver liturgical vessels.[196] The bishop's recognition of the community to be formed was expressed materially. Leo's decision to replenish the liturgical silver of the titular churches of Rome by melting down Constantine's donations was an act of refoundation necessary after recent events.

Leo's focus on replenishing the silver plate in titular churches after 455 is also significant in light of his efforts to assert his authority over Roman aristocratic society. Indeed, silver plate had long been a status marker. Our knowledge of its real and symbolic importance comes from numerous silver hordes such as the one from the Esquiline Hill in Rome that had been buried by the eminent Turcii family in the fourth century.[197] Hence, the bishop's replenishing of silver liturgical plate was also an important means to assert his status as a patron by using the material language that other elites recognized. The compilers of the *Book of the Popes* showed the value of this act of patronage by recording the precise notations of weight for the liturgical vessels and other movable objects in a document that was itself composed to assert the importance of the papacy.

The focus on liturgical silver as a means of asserting episcopal authority especially over the titular churches in Rome emerges also at the time of Leo's successor, Hilary (461–68). Apparently, Leo's six hundred pounds of silver for Rome's twenty-nine titular churches was not adequate, a determination that explains why the *Book of the Popes* records that Hilary later made an additional donation of twenty-five silver drinking vessels (*scyphi*) for the titular churches, along with several other objects, all of which he kept "in safety" in the Lateran and at St. Mary Maggiore.[198] Hilary feared for the security of these luxury items, even inside Rome, but his efforts here were part of an ongoing attempt to draw the titular churches closer to the bishop, an effort demonstrated as well by his extension of the stational liturgy of Leo – that is, moving the bishop and worshippers between churches in set ceremonial moments.[199] In the sixth century, Cassiodorus mentions that the

---

[196] *Lib. Pont.* 45, ed. Duchesne 1981, p. 230. *The Liber Pontificalis* is quite specific about his donations, noting that it included a silver paten weighing twenty-five pounds; two silver *scyphi* each weighing eight pounds; two silver *amae* (drinking vessels) each weighing ten pounds; and five smaller silver chalices each weighing three pounds.

[197] On the Esquiline hoard, see especially Shelton 1981, and Al. Cameron 1985, pp. 135–45.

[198] *Lib. Pont.* 48.11, ed. Duchesne 1981, p. 244.

[199] On the stational liturgy in Rome beginning with Leo, not Hilary, see Salzman 2013, pp. 208–32.

vessels used by the deacons of Rome were so lavish that they were spoken of throughout the world.[200]

The finances of the papacy seem to have rebounded somewhat under Hilary, whose office began with the removal of the emperor Majorian in 461. The *Book of the Popes* records that Hilary built three new oratories in the Lateran Baptistery, all of which were decorated with "silver and precious stones."[201] These small chapels, similar to those in Ravenna, were not the major church constructions that earlier emperors had undertaken or that bishops had developed with the patronage of emperors or private supporters.[202] We are not certain who paid for Hilary's oratories and liturgical vessels, but given the general omission of information in papal sources about private donors, it may well be that the funding came from individual patrons. One example of private patronage survives from a now lost inscription that recorded that the Church of St. Anastasia on the Palatine Hill had been built through the efforts of the bishop of Rome and two lay persons, Severus and Cassia, perhaps a couple; these two benefactors are not otherwise known, but their funding was most likely used on the mosaic decoration of the apse.[203]

It was likely under Hilary's bishopric, or perhaps that of his successor, Simplicius, that we see a surprising example of episcopal tolerance for the elaborate decoration of an Arian church in Rome. The general Ricimer paid for a mosaic that he installed in the apse of the church that was later called St. Agatha of the Goths.[204] (See Map 1.) We cannot tell if the church was constructed new in the Subura area in Rome, a place long filled with "barbarians," as a place of worship for Arians or if it had been a preexisting church; nor is it clear that only Arians used it at the time that Ricimer donated the mosaic for the church.[205] By the late sixth century, however, Pope Gregory had rededicated the church to Catholic use and had ridden it of what he regarded as "Arian, demonic forces."[206] However, as John Moorhead observed, the donation of such a church for Arian Goths

---

[200] Cass. *Var.* 12. 20.3.   [201] *Lib. Pont.* 48.2–4, ed. Duchesne 1981, pp. 242–43 and p. 245 note 3.

[202] On the oratories imitating those of Ravenna, see Kinney 2017, pp. 82–84.

[203] Gianandrea 2017, pp. 206–7. The six-line verse text reads in part: *papae Hilari meritis olim devota Severi/nec non Cassiae mens dedit ista Deo.*

[204] The donation by Ricimer is dated by Mathisen 2009, p. 309 to any time between 459 and 471. Kinney 2017, p. 86 sees affinities in the use of impost blocks here and at St Stephen in the Round, in imitation of developments in Ravenna, and hence accepts a date around 470. But Kinney interestingly suggests a different set of builders were involved because the impost blocks over the columns in Ricimer's church were far more refined. It would seem reasonable to date Ricimer's patronage to the period between the death of Majorian and the accession of Anthemius, from 461 to 467, when Ricimer was in control of the city. Certainty is not possible.

[205] Kinney 2017, p. 86.

[206] Gregory *Ep.* 4.19 and *Dial.* 3.30. See too Mathisen 2009, pp. 307–25.

points to "surprising weakness in the leadership of the church in Rome, for elsewhere strong bishops, such as Ambrose in Milan … had been able to prevent opponents of the Council of Nicaea from obtaining the use of churches."[207] Hilary's letters and decretals articulated his ongoing support for Nicene Christianity and underscore that the acceptance of this lavishly decorated Arian church in Rome spoke to episcopal weakness.[208]

Some scholars have suggested that Hilary also began the Church of St. Stephen in the Round, a major construction, with the support of the emperor Libius Severus. (See Map 1.) However, the only evidence for the dating of this church's origins are the coins of the emperors Libius Severus and Majorian found in the foundation of this massive church. These provide no more than a *terminus post quem*. Nevertheless, because the size of this large basilica suggests imperial patronage, Manuela Gianandrea has posited that this church was begun by Valentinian III but was delayed by the events of 455. Indeed, that scenario would explain why the building was finished and dedicated by Hilary's successor, Simplicius (468–83).[209]

Hilary's construction of oratories suggests that he had found patrons, likely private wealthy lay elites or clergy.[210] Nonetheless, the limited nature of his work suggests that he, like Leo, had been facing financial constraints. Bishops Leo and Hilary focused on modest repairs to the apostolic churches in Rome, with no attention paid to the city's titular churches other than to replace the liturgical silver. But by this latter action, Leo and Hilary were striving to assert their presence in the neighborhood churches in Rome in the face of the ongoing competition for influence in Rome offered by lay secular elites and other Christian groups in the city in the wake of 455.

Advice as a Strategy of Crisis Management.

Leo did offer advice to bishops in Gaul and northern Italy about how best to deal with some of the kinds of problems raised by the Vandal invasions. If we assume that Leo had adopted similar policies when dealing with such cases in Rome, we can get some insight into how he handled pastoral demands after 455.

---

[207] Moorhead 2015, p. 34 makes this point, with which I concur.

[208] For his support for Leo, see the succinct summary in Allen and Neil 2013, p. 217.

[209] Gianandrea 2017, p. 208, posited this beginning rather than under Majorian or Libius Severus as had been suggested by Brandenburg 2005, pp. 480–510.

[210] For the argument that many of the builders of churches or basilicas, or founders of titular churches in Rome were wealthy clerics, along with a number of senatorial aristocrats, see Hillner 2006, pp. 66–67.

The fullest statement of Leo's administrative advice is found in his responses to some nineteen queries about various problems in his *Letter* 167 to Rusticus, the bishop of Narbonne in southeast Gaul, dated to 458–59.[211] Leo offered similar advice to two other bishops, Nicetas, bishop of Aquileia in northeast Italy, *Letter* 159.6–8; and Neo, bishop of Ravenna, *Letter* 166, thus suggesting that he had a consistent response to such problems. Leo advised about such issues as, what should a bishop do with captives who return and find that their spouses (mostly women) have remarried? What should a bishop do about those returning captives who do not remember if they had been baptized? What should be done with those returning captives who, in a pagan home, eat sacrificial meat?[212] His answers reveal an essentially conservative approach. For instance, Leo followed the precedent of Rome's Bishop Innocent, who, in the wake of 410, had upheld as a rightful marriage that of a captured woman named Ursa who had returned to find that her husband had remarried.[213] Innocent had asserted that the sacred nature of the marriage tie took priority, so Leo advised Bishop Rusticus to do the same. However, neither bishop's ruling had the force of law.[214] We have no way of knowing if Leo's advice had any weight, a fact that reenforces the limits of his authority.

One area that Leo does not often address again implies the financial constraints the church now faced. Leo's *Letters* and *Sermons* make occasional general remarks about the need to ransom prisoners, usually in the context of asking for donations, but his advice to bishops extends only to the treatment off returning prisoners, not to ransoming them.[215] Similarly suggestive of the papacy's limited resources is the fact that neither Leo nor his successor Hilary is praised in the *Book of the Popes* for having ransomed captives, although other bishops of Rome were, as, for example Symmachus (498–14).[216]

As Leo confronted these difficult human problems in the aftermath of 455, he must have found comfort in the advice he gave to a fellow bishop. To encourage Rusticus to remain in office, Leo cited *Matthew* 10:22: "Blessed is the one who perseveres to the end."[217] Leo did that, though his position after 455 was weaker than it had been before the Vandal capture. His financial

[211] Leo *Ep.* 167 (*PL* 54, 1197–1209). See Neil 2009, pp. 138–46 and Response answer 18 for advice about the return of captives from Africa.

[212] Leo, *Ep.* 159 (*PL* 54, 1138–40, March 21, 458) on married spouses; *Ep.* 166 (*PL* 54, 1191–96) to the bishop in Narbonensis Gaul; and *Ep.* 167 to the bishop in Ravenna, 458 CE (note 211 above). See also Neil 2009, pp. 139–40.

[213] Innocent, *Ep.* 36 (*PL* 20, 602–3), to Probus.   [214] See Chapter 3, note 191.

[215] Typical is Leo, *Sermon* 78.4, dated prior to 455. Leo refers to ransomed captives returning to Italy; see notes 212 and 213 above.

[216] *Lib. Pont.* 53, ed. Duchesne 1981, p. 263.   [217] Leo, *Ep.* 167 (*PL* 54, 1199).

resources had been greatly reduced. His imperial patrons had departed. He had to contend with aristocrats whose patronage of the church and clergy in Rome continued to give them real religious influence after the Vandal captivity, as it had before. But the financial and political supports of the papacy had been badly shaken, and this limited the efforts of the bishops in taking a leadership role in Rome's recovery.

The Wider Impact of 455

In the decade after 455, Italo-Roman aristocrats returned to Rome and actively intervened in the political events of the day. By allying themselves with powerful military figures and emperors, they ensured their return to their high status in society and to their positions as high civic officeholders. (See Tables 4.1, 4.2, and 4.3.) These strategies also guaranteed the continuity of established aristocratic families that emerged consistently as leaders during this decade, including the Decii, Anicii, and Aconii. However, despite their continuity, these families did not form set political blocks, as certain scholars have previously argued.[218] Their loyalty to family did not preclude their willingness to create ties with other elites, including upwardly mobile provincials such as the Gallo-Roman poet Sidonius Apollinaris. At other times, they aligned themselves with military elites, some of whom, such as Avitus and Majorian, were contenders for the imperial throne in this period. Roman aristocrats and generals also worked with bishops and priests as had Severus and Cassia; at other times, they patronized their neighborhood titular churches.[219]

Based on my analysis of the decade after the capture of Rome by the Vandals, I cannot agree with those scholars who see this event as a turning point in the decline of the Roman senatorial aristocracy and of the city in which they resided.[220] The speed with which Italo-Roman aristocrats returned to Rome, competed for influence, protected their interests – social, political, and economic – and maintained social networks empowered this group after 455. They were in a position to contest for power with a new set of actors, making alliances also with military generals and, most importantly, the patrician and commander in chief Ricimer.

The events of 455 and elite responses to them did, however, contribute in three important ways to the structural changes that led to the demise of the

---

[218] I do not see consistent positions taken by individual families, as is argued by Roberto 2012, p. 133, note 33, based on Zecchini 1981, pp. 125–27, and 2011, pp. 185–99. On this point, I agree with Cameron 2012, pp. 133–71. See too Chapter 4, notes 62 and 66.

[219] See notes 168 and 203 above.   [220] See, notes 5, 6 and 7 above.

western emperor. First, in this world of shifting alliances, Italo-Roman senators played an increasingly prominent political as well as religious and economic role. They quickly returned to Rome and reassumed their civic and social leadership roles. As holders of high civic office, primarily as urban prefect, they led the recovery that also preserved their political, economic, and social hegemony. Aspiring emperors, military leaders, and bishops still sought senatorial support for financial and political reasons. This was the dominant pattern in the decade after 455, and it continued after the fall of the Emperor Libius Severus in 465. In this world, Rome's senatorial aristocrats took on greater political influence, which they used to support or undermine the reign of the western emperor, be it the eastern Anthemius or the barbarian general Odoacer.

The political influence of senatorial aristocrats also contributed to the growing importance of Rome's Senate. This is a second important development that we saw in this period when, for example, Majorian gave to the Senate the charge to protect public buildings in Rome.[221] When Odoacer and Theoderic came to power later, they gave the Senate even more responsibilities. A reflection of these changes was the rise of a new position, the *caput Senatus* – whose holder took precedence in the Senate and was designated by the western rulers – a position that was removed from the reach of the eastern emperor.[222] As the oldest surviving institutional legitimator of Roman rule, the Senate could claim unparalleled prestige. Indeed, over the course of the fifth century, the standing of the Senate grew as the hold of the western emperor weakened. This dynamic contributes to our understanding why the idea of the loss of a western emperor became increasingly acceptable to senatorial aristocrats.

Third, the opportunities for office and power that opened up after 455 continued to attract elites to secular careers. This situation explains why in Rome we do not find bishops from old wealthy aristocratic families at this time. They had been the pipeline in areas in Gaul, where the nobility entered the church with regularity in the late fourth and the fifth centuries.[223] But this was not the trend in Rome, where the bishops advanced primarily through clerical networks, most often after holding the office of one of the seven deacons of Rome.[224] There was no aristocratic bishop in Rome in the fifth

---

[221] The Senate's role had been evolving. Valentinian III had granted to the Senate the right to contribute to imperial legislative activity, which they had not held since the early empire (*C. Iust.* 1.14.8). But, as Radtki 2016, p. 124 observed, we cannot be certain if they exercised this right.

[222] The *caput Senatus* is first attested securely under Odoacer and Theoderic; see Salzman 2019A, pp. 465–89; and Porena 2019, pp. 25–50.

[223] Mathisen 1993, pp. 89–104.   [224] Moorhead 2006, pp. 279–93.

century; not until Vigilius in 536 can we find a securely attested aristocratic holder of this office.[225] Because Roman senatorial aristocrats remained focused on civic offices, not ecclesiastical ones, the bishops of Rome did not come from families of wealth and prestige as did some bishops in other cities. And having lost their imperial patrons after the death of Valentinian III in 455, the bishops became increasingly reliant on secular elites in Rome. As a result, papal enthusiasm for a western emperor also waned.

Given the nature of elite responses to 455, we can better understand why Italo-Roman senatorial aristocrats returned to Rome, a city in which they could continue to play a dominant role. The loss of a western emperor, when it happened, would not have been devastating. But the civil war that played out in Rome in 472 and preceded the removal of the last western emperor was a far more challenging crisis for the city and its senatorial aristocracy.

---

[225] Salzman 2019A, pp. 465–89.

5

Why Gibbon Was Wrong

Thus the Western Empire of the Roman people perished with Augustulus. . . . Henceforth, Gothic kings held Rome.

—Marcellinus *comes*, Latin chronicler in Constantinople,
writing after 518 CE[1]

The conventional date for the fall of the western Empire, 476, is based on the exile of the last western emperor to reside in Rome, the fourteen-year-old boy Romulus, nicknamed "Augustulus," as in the epigraph to this chapter.[2] Modern historians have amply demonstrated that this idea about the dating of the "fall of Rome" was created by sixth-century eastern writers, with the earliest being Marcellinus *comes*, the Latin chronicler writing in Constantinople after 518. This date emerged among writers who at the time of Justinian sought to explain the relationship of the Ostrogothic kingdom to Constantinople and justify the reconquest of Italy.[3] To a Roman living in the

---

[1] Marcell. *comes, Chron.* s.a. 476: *Hesperium Romanae gentis imperium . . . cum hoc Augustulo periit . . . Gothorum dehinc regibus Romam tenentibus.* For the dating of the *Chronicle* of Marcellinus *comes*, see Croke 1983, pp. 87–90; and the excellent discussion in Arnold 2017, p. 115, note 2. For the text, see the edition by Mommsen, *MGH AA* 11, pp. 39–108.

[2] This view has been influential. At one time Gibbon had thought to stop in 476 with the fall of the empire in the West, i.e. at the end of his third volume, chapter 38. But after a year-long vacation, he returned to his original intention of writing a continuous history from the Antonine rulers through to the capture of Byzantium by the Ottoman Turks in 1453; see Trevor-Roper 1994, vol. 4, p. iv. For the use of the term Augustulus, see, for example, Procop. *Wars* 5.1.2.

[3] Croke 1983, pp. 81–119, first argued this in his brilliant article. For this eastern view articulated by Marcellinus *comes, Chron.* copied verbatim by Jordanes, see Croke 2001, pp. 190–95. Croke's arguments have been accepted widely; see, for example, Heather 1993, pp. 332–34, and Cameron 2012, p. 168 with additional bibliography in notes 169–170. Croke is right to emphasize that the eastern origin of 476 is also supported by the fact that it was used by later Byzantine chroniclers, first attested by Evagrius who wrote, ca. 592. However, 476 was used by earlier writers, including the early sixth-century Eustathius of Epihaneia. Some scholars have argued for the importance of

West, however, the crisis that emerged in 470 and culminated with the civil war of 472 was arguably the most devastating "fall of Rome" in the fifth century. Unfortunately, it is also the one that is least well documented.

Nonetheless, in the face of human loss and physical devastation, senatorial aristocrats decided to return to Rome soon after the fighting had stopped. By late 472, or early 473 at the latest, senators were again in leadership roles in alliance with German military elites. By 476 they had been back at work for almost four years, busy with their civic offices and continuing their traditional way of life as they revived Roman social, political, and cultural institutions.- The decision of Roman elites – and especially senatorial aristocrats – to return to Rome after 472 was not an inevitable choice. It does, however, reflect the growing political influence of senators and of Rome in an admittedly smaller western empire.

The shrinking of the western Roman Empire in the fifth century, with its renewed focus on Italy (discussed in Chapters 3 and 4), had given Italo-Roman senators new political power. The return to Rome of Valentinian III's imperial court in the mid fifth century had opened up opportunities to augment their social and political positions, as the career of the senator Petronius Maximus, who seized the throne in 455, demonstrated. Certainly, territorial losses and the ongoing Vandal attacks on Italy had reduced the financial resources of many of Rome's senatorial aristocrats as they contemplated returning to Rome after the civil war of 472. He or she would have fewer means with which to rebuild ties with would-be emperors, senators, generals, and bishops.

Yet senatorial aristocrats did return once more to Rome after 472. A number – but not all – allied themselves in support of the patrician commander in chief (*magister militum*) Ricimer and his military successors Gundobad and later Odoacer. Senatorial aristocratic support for these German generals laid the groundwork for the end of a resident western emperor. Indeed, it had become increasingly clear that the existing model of western imperial rule – a weak or young emperor with ceremonial and legal authority who was reliant on a strong general – had led to two decades of frequent political turnover.[4] But unlike those scholars who see the loss of an imperial presence in the West as a factor undermining the viability of Rome and its senatorial aristocracy, I consider the willingness of senators to cast aside this political model and to work in alliance with these German military

476, as for instance Meier 2015, pp. 15–68, based on a perceived shift in church/state relations. Others probe its meaning for historical memory; see Kruse 2019, pp. 148–84.

[4] McEvoy 2013 pp. 223–329 focuses on child emperors at the court of Valentinian III.

elites as positive developments that demonstrate, again, the creative resilience that enabled senators to remain dominant in Rome and Italy into the last decades of the fifth century.[5]

Since senatorial responses to 472 are key to understanding not just the removal of a resident western emperor but also the beginnings of the "barbarian" kingdoms in Italy, I begin by considering how the civil war broke out and its impact on the city and its elites. I focus on the senatorial aristocrats who helped restore Rome and reestablished the government alongside the generals Ricimer, Gundobad, and finally, Odoacer. Odoacer's rule over Italy (476–89/93) allowed for the reconstitution of Roman senatorial aristocratic society and fueled its growing political influence. Senatorial aristocrats also played an increasingly important role in ecclesiastical politics. Aristocratic patronage and support helped the papacy assert its independence from eastern imperial as well as patriarchal doctrine, a development with long-term implications for the religious contours of the church in the West in the coming centuries.

The Ties That Bind: The General Ricimer and the Emperor Anthemius

Given the unexpected death of Emperor Libius Severus in Rome in November 465, we can see why some of our sources suspected that Ricimer, the German commander in chief, was responsible for it; he had taken over the government after Severus's demise.[6] Ricimer was at the height of his power and prestige. In addition to his control of the military, he had already received the prestigious status of patrician (*patricius*), an honor bestowed sparingly since Constantine had revived it for senators and military commanders (and their wives).[7] Throughout the seventeen-month interregnum that followed, from November 465 to April 467, Ricimer controlled the western army as well as the administration of the state.[8] Yet he did not in those months, nor at any other time in his long career, try to be acclaimed as emperor. Nonetheless, the efficiency of his rule demonstrated that the West

---

[5] For this view, see, for example, See McEvoy 2017, p. 110.

[6] For the rumor, found only in Cassiodorus: *Chron.* 1280 s.a. 465 see Chapter 4, note 102, and especially Anders 2010, pp. 191–93. The date of Libius Severus's death in the *Pascale Campanum* is more likely correct than is the date August 15, 465 in the *Fasti Vind. Prior.* This is the views of most scholars, including MacGeorge 2002, p. 231 note 88.

[7] For patrician status renewed by Constantine, see Chapter 2, note 114. See also Mathisen 1991, pp. 173–90.

[8] *RIC* 2517–2350; noted by R.W. Burgess in an unpublished study of the coinage under Anthemius.

could operate quite well without a resident emperor, a lesson that was not lost on contemporaries.

The eastern emperor, Leo (457–74), did not immediately intervene. This lack of action was entirely consistent with his earlier practice, for he had not acted previously, even though he had refused to recognize Libius Severus (461–65) as Roman coemperor. Nor had Emperor Leo responded to Rome's request for military assistance against the Vandals made by a senatorial embassy in Constantinople, probably dated to 464. But like other fifth-century eastern emperors, Leo certainly had not forgotten the West. In response to the senatorial envoy, Leo had sent an ambassador to the Vandal king Geiseric to try to use diplomatic pressure to stop raids on Italy.[9] Although there were two separate imperial courts, two separate military forces, and two separate sets of elites, the idea of one unified Roman Empire remained. So, for example, laws were often issued under both emperors. But Leo resisted providing military intervention until the Vandals began attacking eastern territories in 467. Then, after yet another western senatorial delegation asking for something that is not quite clear, the eastern emperor Leo determined that he would respond by attacking the Vandals.[10] He also decided to send a coemperor to Rome.[11] This act reflected Leo's acknowledgment of the value of dynastic ties as a means of drawing the two halves of the empire together behind one imperial dynasty.[12] Moreover, by sending Anthemius, son-in-law of the previous eastern emperor Marcian,

[9] For the senatorial embassy to Leo dated after that of 461 and likely in 464, see Priscus, *Frag.* 51.1, ed. Blockley 1983, p. 360; and his warning through his ambassador Phylarchus to Gaiseric, Priscus, *Frag.* 52, ed. Blockley 1983, p. 360. Priscus, *Frag.* 41, ed. and trans. Blockley 1983, p. 345: "While the fugitive peoples were at odds with the eastern Romans, an embassy came from the Italians saying that they could not continue to resist unless the eastern Romans reconciled them with the Vandals." This is reiterated in Priscus *Frag.* 41.2, ed. Blockley 1983, p. 346, and assuming this is the same embassy, we are now told that Tatian, the ambassador, accomplished nothing.

[10] The Vandal attack on the East can be dated to 467; they alleged that the Eastern Romans had broken the treaty of 462, a treaty that Leo had signed; see Clover 1966, p. 193 note 2 who cites the evidence of Procop. *Wars* 3.5.22–.26, and a rumor from Daniel the Stylite 56 (ed. Delahaye, p. 175) that Geiseric was about to capture Alexandria, See Clover 1966, pp. 186–91 for the treaty.

[11] Evagrius, *HE* 2.16 = Priscus, *Frag.* 50, ed. Blockley 1983, p. 358.: "As a result of an embassy of the western Romans, Anthemius was sent as king (*basileus*) of Rome. To him Marcian, the previous one who had been Emperor (*bebasileukos*), had betrothed his daughter." There is no statement about what precisely the embassy wanted from Leo. Leo's appointment of Anthemius follows, in Epiphanius *H.E.* 2.15, the discussion of the elevation of Zeno, married to Leo's daughter, as *magister militum* to help with military matters in Thrace. Similarly, Anthemius was given a military task in the West. For the appointment of Anthemius, see Nicephorus Callistus, *HE* 15.11; Procop. *Wars* 3.6.5 = Priscus, *Frag.* 53.3, ed. Blockley 1983, pp. 362–66.

[12] For this as a persistent dynamic, see Croke 2015, pp. 98–124. For more general analysis of the division between the East and West, see the essays in Maas 2015, and especially pp. 12–25.

an experienced general and eastern senator to Rome, Leo also removed a potential rival from Constantinople.[13]

Leo assembled what our sources report as a record-sized fleet to send against Geiseric in 468.[14] To secure the Italian peninsula, he sent a military force under the direction of Anthemius over land during the winter of 466–67.[15] Anthemius's arrival brought much-needed money and military aid to fight off the Vandals, including several experienced eastern generals.[16] In late March or April 467, Anthemius arrived at Brontotas, a site near the eighth mile from Rome. There the army acclaimed him emperor, as the Senate later did.[17] Ricimer, still holding the title of commander in chief, accepted his accession.

Scholars marvel at Ricimer's endorsement of this eastern emperor and still ponder his motivations, as well as those of the Roman senatorial aristocracy, for doing so. But his choice seems clear to me. Ricimer understood that he had much to gain by accepting this arrangement. His authority in Italy had been acclaimed as second only to the emperor Anthemius.[18] Most importantly, Ricimer retained control of his troops in Italy, even though eastern generals had been chosen for the campaign against the Vandals.[19] Finally, Ricimer was bound to this new regime though his marriage to Anthemius's daughter, Alypia, in late 467 in Rome.[20] Ricimer had previously not had an attested wife or children. He must have welcomed the prospect of a close personal alliance with the ruling dynasty, following the examples of earlier German generals like Stilicho who had fought for the Romans. It is noteworthy, too, that the desirability of this political marriage outweighed the

---

[13] Anthemius had held the titles of *magister militum* and patrician, and had been consul in 455; Marc. *comes*, *Chron*. s.a. 467; Jordanes, *Get*. 236, *Rom*. 336. For his being the son-in-law of Marcian, see Evagrius, *HE* 2.16 = Priscus, *Frag*. 50, ed. Blockley 1983, p. 358.

[14] Theophanes, *Chron*. a.m. 5961 = Priscus, *Frag*. 53, ed. Blockley 1983, p. 360, and Procop. *Wars* 3.6.1–.2 and .5–.25 = Priscus, *Frag*. 53.3, ed. Blockley 1983, pp. 363–67.

[15] Sid. Ap. *Pan*. 2.199–201 and note 11 above.

[16] Anthemius was accompanied by the military count Marcellinus of Dalmatia; see Marcellinus 9, *PLRE* 2, pp. 710–11; and note 11 above.

[17] Cass. *Chron*. 1283 s.a. 467: *qui tertio ab urbe miliario in loco Brontotas suscepit imperium*. Hydatius, 231 (235) s.a. 467 says that his acclamation took place there, some eight miles from Rome; *Fasti Vind. Prior* s.a. 467 gives the date but not the location. Sid. Ap. *Pan*. 2.212–15 refers to the *ordo* seeking Anthemius's succession, which may perhaps be a reference to the senatorial acceptance. See also Marcellinus *comes*, *Chron*. s.a. 467 note 1 above; and MacGeorge 2002, pp. 234–35. See Roberto 2020, p. 141 note 1 for the possible dates and locations of these events.

[18] Ennod. *Vita Epiph*. 51 = p. 343: *qui tunc secundis ab Anthemio principe habenis rempublicam gubernabat*.

[19] MacGeorge 2002, pp. 56–60.

[20] Sid. Ap. *Carm*. 2.484–86, *Ep*. 1.5.10, 9.1. For full bibliography, see also MacGeorge 2002, p. 235, note 103.

religious differences between the Arian Ricimer and the Nicene Christian Alypia.[21]

A New Age of Hope: The Reign of Anthemius
(467–72)

In late 467 the marriage of Ricimer and Alypia was an occasion to celebrate. Sidonius Apollinaris, a Gallo-Roman aristocrat and gifted poet, had somehow survived the fall of his father-in-law, the deposed emperor Avitus. Apollinaris was now back in Rome as part of a delegation from his native Gaul.[22] He arrived just in time to witness the celebrations and wrote about them in letters that date sometime before 469 or 470.[23] Sidonius describes a city that had stopped to celebrate this event with the hope that this union of the "eternal Emperor's daughter [with the patrician Ricimer] would ensure the future security of the state."[24] In this time of transition, it would ill suit a Gallic visitor on a political mission to express any reservations. If Sidonius had had any doubts, he kept them well hidden; nor did he express any when he later circulated his letters among Gallic friends.[25]

Sidonius stayed on and delivered a celebratory panegyric on the new emperor on January 1, 468. Sidonius's panegyric provides a fascinating window into how Anthemius's accession was represented to contemporaries by one who wanted to show his support for the new ruler. Sidonius emphasized Anthemius's noble character, not just his familial ties.[26] In Sidonius's view, Rome had chosen Anthemius with "eagerness and affection," following

---

[21] On dynastic marriage in general, see Croke 2015, pp. 98–124.

[22] Sid. Ap. *Ep.* 1.5 and 1.9 does not reveal the reason for his mission. Sivan 1989, pp. 85–94 argues that the delegation was there to support Arvandus and his policy of cooperation with the Goths and Burgundians.

[23] Sid. Ap. *Ep.* 1.5.10: *cum hoc ipso tempore, quo haec mihi exarabantur* (at the very moment when these comments were being written by me). Hanaghan 2018, p. 634 rightly observes that this is a literary conceit, but a useful one for Sidonius. For the circulation of this letter dated prior to late 469 or 470 when Sidonius became bishop of Clermont, see Hanaghan 2018, p. 635. Sid. Ap. *Ep.* 1.9 is also dated to 467.

[24] Sid. Ap. *Ep.* 1.5.10: *filia Augusti perennis in spem publicae securitatis copulabatur.*

[25] Hanaghan 2018, pp. 631–49 proposes that the letter conveys latent criticism of the union of Ricimer and Anthemius, but that seems unlikely even in 469–70, when such criticism could be dangerous. Hanaghan's argument is based on retrospective reasoning; even his best evidence, Sidonius's use of the epithet *Graecus* in *Ep.* 1.7, was not necessarily an intentional dig, for Sidonius is reporting what the letter allegedly said, not what he himself thought. Nor can we know if the use of the epithet *Graecus* was derogatory.

[26] Sid. Ap. *Carm.* 2.218–19; *nam iuris habenis non generum legit respublica, sed generosum* (for when the state chose thee to wield the reins of government, it was for your noble soul, not for your noble family). Translation of Sidonius Apollinaris here and throughout by Anderson, *LCL.*

an ancient best tradition of selecting their own ruler.[27] Sidonius's praise of Ricimer's military acumen – "Unconquered [*invictus*] Ricimer" – and his royal lineage, albeit of Suevian and Gothic parents, tactfully attests to an obvious rise in the status of German military elites in Roman aristocratic society.[28]

Several Roman aristocrats supported Anthemius's position in part because they still ascribed to the ideal of a resident western emperor who shared power with his eastern counterpart. Certainly, they also welcomed the infusion of financial and military resources with which Anthemius had paved the way for his accession. Moreover, many western aristocrats had strong ties to their counterparts in the East. Several western aristocrats had family, friends, and clients in Constantinople. A branch of the wealthy Anicii, for instance, had moved East. One of its most prominent male members, Anicius Olybrius, had gone east after 455, and his daughter Anicia Juliana had descendants who flourished in Constantinople throughout the reign of Justinian.[29]

Although later writers criticized Anthemius as antibarbarian and used these epithets to explain tensions between the emperor and Roman senators as well as between the emperor and Ricimer, there is little contemporary evidence to support this view.[30] Anthemius had arrived with a military force that included a number of non-Roman – that is, barbarian – soldiers.[31] Malalas, an eastern Christian chronicler hostile to Anthemius, alleged anti-Gothic sentiments – that is, implying that Anthemius "feared Ricimer as he was a Goth." This ethnic slur was derived from the two men's subsequent falling out. However, Anthemius had given his daughter to Ricimer in marriage.[32] But it is also true that Anthemius did bring to Rome a number

---

[27] Sid. Ap. *Carm.* 2.524–26: *nunc aliquos voto simili vel amore, vetustas, te legisse crepa, numquam non invida summis emeritisque viris.* ("And now, Antiquity, thou who art ever jealous of the greatest men and greatest benefactors, prate if thou wilt of choices made by thee with like eagerness and affection!")

[28] Sid. Ap. *Carm.* 2.484–86: *sit socer Augustus genero Ricimere geatus; micant nobilitate: esto vobis regia virgo, regius ille mihi.* ("Let a parent who is Emperor be blessed by having his daughter wedded to Ricimer; both shine with the luster of nobility: in her you have a royal lady, in him a man of royal blood.")

[29] For the move of the Anicii toward the East, see Cameron 2012, pp. 160–68, and at p. 166, notes 158–59; for this Anicius Olybrius as emperor, see note 60 below.

[30] For Anthemius as anti-barbarian, see Vassili 1938, pp. 38–45.

[31] See, for example, Bilimer, *PLRE* 2, p. 230. His name recalls other Ostrogothic names, and so he is likely Ostrogothic. He was MUM per Gallias in 472, replacing Gundobad when the latter started supporting Ricimer, his uncle, in the conflict.

[32] Malalas, *Chron.* 14.45: "He [Anthemius] had aroused the enmity of his son-in-law Ricimer the *magister militum* and was afraid of him as he was a Goth." Translation by Jeffreys, Jeffreys, and Scott 1986.

of easterners as well as certain Hellenistic attitudes toward religion and culture. Our sources comment on Anthemius's cultivation of Greek literature and philosophy in Rome. The Roman aristocrat Fl. Messius Phoebus Severus had left Rome for Alexandria, a center for a number of Neoplatonists. Encouraged by Anthemius's patronage, Severus had returned to the city and risen to prominence. Indeed, Anthemius made Fl. Messius Phoebus Severus consul in 470 and also urban prefect in that same year, a rare accomplishment.[33] So, too, the Gallo-Roman senator Sidonius Apollinaris, who had appealed to Anthemius's love of Greek myth and learned allusions throughout his panegyric in this emperor's honor, was rewarded with the office of urban prefect.[34]

However, Anthemius's embrace of classicizing Hellenic culture and philosophy created some tensions with more conservative Romans, especially orthodox Christians. A hostile contemporary, Damascius, in his *Life of Isidore*, alleged that Anthemius's engagement with literary culture was part of the emperor's plan to restore idolatry in Rome, pointing to an appointee who was:

> by religious persuasion a Hellene, holding the same conviction as Severus, the devotee of idols, whom [Anthemius had] made consul. Together they had a secret plan to restore the abomination of idolatry.[35]

It is unlikely that this allegation is true or that the devout eastern emperor Leo would have appointed Anthemius if he had been a pagan. In fact, Anthemius had dedicated a church in Constantinople before his departure for Rome.[36]

Nevertheless, Anthemius's tolerance for diverse Christian sects in Rome did lead to certain tensions with the then bishop of Rome, Hilary (November 461–29 February 468). We hear that Anthemius had allowed a certain Philotheus, an adherent of the Christian sect known as the Macedonians, to hold new public assemblies (*conciliabuta nova*) in the city. Hilary had protested to the emperor at St. Peter's, according to *a Letter* of the late fifth-century bishop Gelasius (494–96). Gelasius asserted that Hilary had been successful in getting Anthemius to stop the sect from

---

[33] See Fl. Messius Phoebus Severus 19, *PLRE* 2, pp. 1005–6.

[34] Sid. Ap. *Carm.* 2. Sidonius's reporting of a document calling Anthemius a Greek emperor, did not hinder his career. On the term, see note 25 above.

[35] Dam. *Epit. Phot.* 108 = Phot. Bibl. 242 (p. 343b). Translation by Fowden 1999, p. 199. For Severus, see note 33 above.

[36] *Chron. Paschale* s.a. 454 records the construction, at his own expense, of a church dedicated to St. Thomas.

holding public meetings in the city.[37] Even if this statement is true, there is no evidence that Anthemius exiled this or any other group from Rome, an expression of tolerance that would have been appealing to certain senatorial elites who held traditional attitudes toward religion.

Bishop Hilary, on the other hand, had openly opposed what he deemed heretical Christian sects in Rome and abroad, but he had had limited success.[38] Rome was still filled with several such sects, including Eutychians and Nestorians. Moreover, Arians were present in large enough numbers to have their own recognized places of worship in the city. As noted in Chapter 4, Ricimer's donation of a mosaic for the apse of the Church of St. Agatha of the Goths was a public statement about the status of Arian worship in Rome (see Map 1).[39] Other Arians, senatorial ranking military as well as non-elites, remained in the city into the sixth century. The Church of St. Agatha continued to be used, presumably by Arians, until Pope Gregory at the end of the sixth century rededicated it to Christian – that is, Nicene – use.[40] The prominent position of this Arian church further underscores the limits of the bishops of Rome.[41] Certainly, Arians had powerful patrons such as the general and patrician Ricimer, who had spent his entire career at the top echelons of late Roman aristocratic society. It is not surprising, then, that Ricimer would adopt the same patterns of patronage that his senatorial peers practiced to the discomfort of Rome's bishops.[42] No wonder that Anthemius's religious as well as dynastic policies irritated Rome's bishops for they also demonstrated the limits of papal authority.

---

[37] Gelasius, *Ep.* 26.11 *ad Episcopos Dardaniae*, ed. Thiel, p. 408: *Sanctae memoriae quoque papa Hilarius Anthemium imperatorem quum Philotheus Macedonianus eius familiaritate suffultus diversarum conciliabuta nova sectarum in Urbem vellet inducere, apud beatum Petrum apostolum palam ne id fieret clara voce constrinxit, in tantum ut non ea facienda cum interpositione sacramenti idem promitteret imperator.* Gelasius's assertion that these emperors bowed to papal preeminence includes Bishop Simplicius's censure of the emperor Zeno, which famously did not at all prevent Zeno from advancing his *Henotikon.* For the limits of these assertions by Gelasius to the bishops of the region of Dardania in the Balkans, a liminal area, see Demacopoulos 2013, pp. 95–99.

[38] *Lib. Pont.* 48, ed. Duchesne 1981, p. 242: *et damnavit Eutychem et Nestorium vel omnes sequaces eorum et vel omnes hereses.*

[39] For Ricimer's dedication, see *ILS* 1294 and Chapter 4, notes 176 and 204.

[40] Pope Gregory mentions the church at *Ep.* 4.19 and *Dial.* 3.30. *Lib. Pont.* 66, ed. Duchesne 1981, p. 312, locates the church in the Suburra, on the Quirinal Hill.

[41] See Chapter 4, note 207 on the very different situation in Milan that Bishop Ambrose confronted.

[42] For this high-profile donation, see too Machado 2019, p. 192.

The Failure of the Vandal and Gallic Expeditions. In contrast to the hopeful atmosphere in Rome at the time of the marriage of Ricimer and Alypia in 467, in Carthage the Vandal king Geiseric fumed at the arrival of the new emperor, Anthemius. Geiseric had hoped the eastern emperor would designate as his colleague the Roman senator Anicius Olybrius. Olybrius was the husband of Valentinian III's youngest daughter, Placidia, whose sister, Eudocia, had been taken from Rome and was now married (as prearranged) to Geiseric's son, Huneric.[43] If Anicius Olybrius were emperor, Geiseric could claim a family tie to the western emperor, a relationship that would thus elevate his position over others within Vandal society and above other kings in the Roman world. Money and land were also incitements; Geiseric had expected Olybrius to give Huneric Eudocia's dowry, a treasure and lands that Geiseric had demanded from the eastern emperor, Leo.[44] Instead, Leo and Anthemius were now attacking Geiseric, who would therefore have to prepare for war.

It was fortunate for Geiseric that the Roman naval expedition in 468 had been a failure. Although most scholars blame the sluggish response of the eastern general Basiliscus for the fiasco, the repercussions for Anthemius were significant.[45] Once Geiseric had managed to outmaneuver Basiliscus in Africa, the eastern emperor Leo, faced with the massive loss of his troops as well as civic conflict in Constantinople, signed a treaty with Geiseric in 468, leaving the West to fend for itself.[46] Anthemius's reputation was further damaged by military losses in Gaul. His son Anthemiolus, whom he had sent to Gaul in 471 to beat back the expansionist efforts of the king of the Visigoths, Euric, had failed to preserve the Roman hold on the Auvergne. The death of Anthemiolus along with the loss of troops in southern Gaul further fueled Ricimer's dissatisfaction with his father-in-law, Anthemius.[47] Even the marriage of Ricimer to Alypia failed to satisfy; there were no attested offspring.

The Outbreak of Civil War in 470

It is a sign of the deteriorating relationship between Ricimer and Anthemius that conspiracy theories and allegations of sorcery emerge in our sources. Anthemius's sudden illness was attributed to both sorcery and a conspiracy, thus justifying this emperor's hasty execution of several Romans, including

---

[43] For Anicius Olybrius, see Olybrius 6, *PLRE*, pp. 796–98; and notes 29 above and 60 below.
[44] Priscus, *Frag.* 38.1, ed. Blockley 1983, pp. 340–41.   [45] MacGeorge 2002 pp. 237–45.
[46] Blockley 1992, p. 76; Conant 2012, p. 32; Merrills and Miles 2010, pp. 121–22.
[47] MacGeorge 2002, pp. 240–42.

Romanus, the master of the imperial household (*magister officiorum*).[48] Romanus was a powerful official indeed, in charge of the various bureaus that served the emperor and also of the imperial post and weapons deposits. The murder – not exile – of this patrician (whom the seventh-century John of Antioch asserts was a friend of Ricimer) was also interpreted as an attack on Ricimer, although hostile eastern sources portrayed Ricimer as the aggressor. Angered by Romanus's execution, "Ricimer left Rome and summoned six thousand men who were under his command for the war against the Vandals."[49] He went north to Milan with his supporters and took over control of northern Italy. Anthemius remained in Rome, in control of Campania and southern Italy.

The peninsula was thus set for a civil war. According to Bishop Ennodius of Pavia, whose life of St. Epiphanius provides a hagiographical account of the saint's intervention in negotiations at this point, Anthemius's and Ricimer's hostility was the result of "that envy [that] divides rulers," a natural produce of that "quality of power [that] became a cause of discord."[50] Some Ligurian nobles tried to avert the upcoming civil war. Ricimer dismissed the prospect of arbitration, asking, who can stop "a Galatian, quick to anger and an emperor (*princeps*)?" Yet as Ennodius makes clear, Ricimer, too, lacked control, being "a very fierce Goth" (*ferocissimus Geta*).[51] In Ennodius's view, this all-too-human flaw afflicted both men, whom he calls *principes* – emperors – without any distinction.[52] The sharing of this title – *princeps*, or "Augustus" – is noteworthy. Of course, in Ennodius's account, only the sainted bishop of Pavia, Epiphanius, can mediate their feud. Epiphanius's successful intervention is recorded, to the amazement of Ricimer (*attonito*), in the spring of 471. Unfortunately, the peace did not last.[53] We are not told why, for the only other insight offered by Ennodius is that Epiphanius's modesty and the

---

[48] John of Antioch *Frag.* 207 = Priscus, *Frag.* 62, ed. Blockley 1983, p. 370, alleged sorcery. Cass. *Chron.* s.a. 470: *Romanus patricius affectans imperium capitaliter est punitus*; Paul. Diac. *Hist. rom.* 15.2: *Romanus patricius imperatoriam fraudulenter satagens arripere dignitatem praecipente Anthemio capite caesus est.*

[49] John of Antioch *Frag.* 207 = Priscus, *Frag.* 62, ed. Blockley 1983, p. 370.

[50] Ennod., *Vita Epiph.* 51–52: *nam imperatore Romae posito seminarium inter eos iecit scandali illa quae dominantes sequestrat invidia et par dignitas causa discordiae.* Text from ed. Cesa 1988, p. 51.

[51] For this criticism of Anthemius, see Ennod., *Vita Epiph.* 53: *quis est qui Galatam concitatum revocare possit et principem? Nam semper, cum rogatur, exuperat qui iram maturali moderatione non terminat.* Text from ed. Cesa 1988, p. 52. Ricimer was similarly criticized; see Ennod. *Vita Epiph.* 60 (by Anthemius); 64, by Epiphanius.

[52] Ennod., *Vita Epiph.* 63–75.

[53] Ennod. *Vita Epiph.* 63–75 for the intervention, with Ricimer's response in 73.

coming preparations for Easter prevented the saint from returning to Milan to accept the gratitude that all felt for his intervention.[54]

Ennodius's focus is hagiography, so unfortunately we do not understand why this arbitration failed to bring a more lasting settlement. Ennodius disrupts the political narrative to recount the miracles of Epiphanius and then returns to the politics with only this bare statement: "In time, Anthemius and Ricimer died."[55] But John of Antioch, as an eastern chronicler, blamed Ricimer for the war and for breaking his bonds to his father-in-law, and he provides some key details of the civil war that overtook Rome.

Siege of Rome. Ricimer marched to Rome and laid siege to Anthemius within the city for at least five months, likely starting in October 471 and continuing through July 472 or perhaps into November.[56] Once more a besieged emperor, this time Anthemius had to rely on the walls of the city. But he also had the support of those "in authority" (οἵ τε εν τέλει); for John of Antioch, this term includes not only officeholders and magistrates but also whoever of the Roman senators and their retainers remained.[57] John does not record the number of men who supported Anthemius, but he does add that the populace at large also supported the emperor.[58] Senatorial aristocratic families had retainers and bodyguards whom they could employ to supplement the soldiers who had come with Anthemius from the East.

Ricimer brought together a coalition of western kings and soldiers against Anthemius. In addition to some named barbarian leaders like Odoacer, Ricimer added his nephew Gundobad, the son of his sister's marriage to the Burgundian king.[59] Some Roman senators sided with Ricimer, including those who were happy with the prospect of the elevation of the senator Anicius Olybrius to the throne. Anicius Olybrius had been sent by the emperor Leo I to Italy to make peace between Ricimer and Anthemius. Instead, in the negotiations with Ricimer, we find Olybrius proclaimed emperor, although his official accession, according to Priscus, happened only after the death of Anthemius, dated by most scholars to April 472.[60]

---

[54] Ennod. *Vita Epiph.* 73.   [55] Ennod. *Vita Epiph.* 79.

[56] John of Antioch, *Frag.* 209.1 = Priscus, *Frag.* 64.1, ed. Blockley, p. 372. John states that the fighting lasted for nine months but at the end of the same passage asserts the siege lasted five months.

[57] For this as a reference to magistrates and to the clients of these administrators, see Roberto 2012, p. 181. For this as a common term also for those in the military, see *LSJ*, A. 2 and 10.

[58] Roberto 2012, pp. 180–81. Roberto sees in this an allusion to the circus factions, armed supporters who could be called upon to fight in Constantinople, but there is no evidence for that sort of armed force in Rome.

[59] For Gundobad, see Gundobadus 1, *PLRE* 2, pp. 524–25.

[60] John of Antioch, *Frag.* 209.1 = Priscus, *Frag.* 64.1, ed. Blockley 1983, p. 372 for this tradition. Nonetheless, negotiations had started well before, and this may explain the alternative tradition,

Senatorial aristocrats had been divided in what all our sources consistently call a civil war.[61] Some scholars, Giuseppe Zecchini and Umberto Roberto in particular, have argued that this division reflected the policies of Rome's two most prominent families – the Anicii and Decii; the Anicii were probarbarian, pro-Christian, and anti-eastern, whereas the Decii took opposing positions on these contemporary matters.[62] The consulship of Flavius Rufius Postumius Festus, a member of the Roman family of the Rufii under Anthemius in 472, indicates his ongoing senatorial support in this troubled time.[63] But there were also those who sided with Ricimer, likely including some members of the Decii; Flavius Caecina Decius Basilius, who had been consul and praetorian prefect under Libius Severus between 463 and 465, apparently continued his ties with Ricimer, for we hear of his family thriving later under Odoacer and Theoderic (see Tables 5.4.1 and 5.4.2, and Chapter 6 for members of the Decii family).[64] His family, the Decii, had returned to Rome and to their house on the Aventine Hill, no doubt lavishly refurnished in the later fifth century, whatever its fate during the 472 civil war. Ricimer also had attracted the backing of some members of the Anicii, especially once he let it be known that he supported Anicius Olybrius to succeed Anthemius as emperor.

But these well-known elite families did not divide so neatly for or against Anthemius. In an important article published in 2012, the late Alan Cameron argued against what he called "Anician Myths." He forcefully asserted that "there is not a shred of solid evidence for rivalry of any sort at any time between the Anicii and the Decii."[65] Rather, as Cameron has demonstrated, these families squabbled with each other and with themselves, and they did not follow a consistent political line. They were not factions with set policies

recorded by Paul the Deacon, that Olybrius's accession took place while Anthemius was alive. Paul Diac. 15.4: *Divisa itaque Roma est et quidam favebant Anthemio, quidam vero Ricimeris perficiam sequebantuur. Inter haec Olibrius a Leone Augusto missus ad Urbam venit vivoque adhuc Anthemio regiam adeptus est potestatem.* See too note 91 below.

[61] For the language here echoing references to these recent events as a civil war, see the *Fasti Vindobonenses Priores*, s.a. 472: *bellum civile*; Bishop Gelasius, in his *Letter to Andromachus* about the Lupercalia, 25A, = *CA* 100, Guenther, Part I, p. 461, call this *civilis furor*; *Paschale Campanus* 2–3: s.a. 472 and the *Chron. Gallica DXI* 650 use the term, *bellum civile*; John of Antioch Frag. 209.1 = Priscus 64, ed. Blockley 1983, p. 372 uses it too, ἐμφύλιος πόλεμος. For discussion, Roberto 2012, p. 187, note 44.

[62] See Roberto 2012, pp. 180–81 and Zecchini 1981, pp. 123–38; and Zecchini 2011, p. 185.

[63] Flavius Rufius Postumius Festus = Festus 5, *PLRE* 2, p. 467; and Orlandi 2020, pp. 195–97.

[64] Fl. Caecina Decius Basilius = Basilius 11, *PLRE* 2, pp. 216–17 is probably the father of Fl. Caecina Decius Maximus Basilius iunior 12 = Basilius 12, *PLRE* 2, pp. 217–18. On the success of the family of the Decii under Theoderic, see also Moorhead 1984, pp. 107–15.

[65] Cameron 2012, pp. 134.

in the fifth-century city.[66] This situation was certainly the case in the events
of the 470s, for there is no evidence that in the civil war of 472, these family
loyalties divided so neatly.

Nonetheless, it is important to emphasize that unlike several other "falls"
of Rome in the fifth century, this civil war pitted Romans against Romans,
with aristocratic supporters on both sides.[67] This division made this siege
costly. Indeed, both sides relied on paid troops, as was the norm in late
Roman warfare. Anthemius still had the troops, including the Goths and
Sueves, that had accompanied him from Constantinople. Umberto Roberto
estimated that there were between ten thousand and twenty thousand men,
including Ricimer's trusted military escort (*bucellari*) and excluding the
Burgundians. They fought against an unknown number of defenders who
relied on the protection of the walls of Rome and expected reinforcements
from Gaul.[68]

The fighting in 472 was even more destructive to the urban fabric, with
more damage done to structures than in the more famous sack of Rome in
410. Then, the Gothic leader Alaric had entered the city without a fight after
a brief siege. As an Arian, Alaric had not slaughtered the inhabitants or
destroyed buildings in large numbers. He sought plunder and captives to
ransom or sell. But in 472 the city became a battlefield. Both sides had armed
soldiers and used buildings and monuments for their own defense.
Moreover, Ricimer camped across the Tiber River in Trastevere, the
Janiculum, and the Vatican. He took control of supplies and starved the
city for five months (see Map 1). The emperor's troops were so hungry that
they allegedly ate hides and other "unwonted" foods.[69] Anthemius and his
supporters, including his bodyguard, dug in and chose to defend themselves
in the palace on the Palatine Hill (see Map 1).

The Romans fought each other in a series of pitched battles, and the
losses were high, especially on Anthemius's side, when many were killed.[70]
Paul the Deacon describes the location of Ricimer's troops as *apud
Anicionis pontem* (near the Anician Bridge).[71] The exact location of that
bridge is not certain, but if it was the Milvian Bridge as Roberto Umberto

---

[66] Cameron 2012, pp. 133–71 argues against this view, articulated by G. Zecchini and U. Roberto
(note 62 above).

[67] For the documentation, see notes 57, 61, and 64 above.

[68] Roberto 2012, p. 181. For the reinforcements from Gaul brought by Bilimer to Rome, see Paul
Diac. *Hist. rom.* XV.4 and Bilimer, *PLRE* 2, p. 230.

[69] John of Antioch, *Frag.* 209.1, ed. Blockley 1983, p. 372. For the starvation of Anthemius's forces,
see Theophanes, *Chron.* Am. 5964 = Priscus, *Frag.* 64, ed. Blockley 1983, p. 372.

[70] John of Antioch, *Frag.* 209.1 = Priscus, *Frag.* 64.1, ed. Blockley 1983, p. 372.

[71] Paul Diac. *Hist. rom.* 15.4.

suggests, then when barbarian troops for Anthemius under Bilimer, *rector Galliarum*, arrived from the north, the decisive battle would have taken place near the Aelian (or Hadrianic) Bridge and the Mausoleum of Hadrian, which Ricimer had used as a fortress – as it remains today, as Castel St. Angelo (see Map 1).[72] The fighting was fierce. According to John of Antioch, Ricimer won only through some unspecified act of treachery.[73] This allusion may be a reference to how Ricimer and his troops actually got inside the city. If the sack of 410 provides a guide, someone – moved by starvation or bribery or both – opened a gate. In the rout that followed, Anthemius tried to flee by blending in with the supplicants in the Church of St. Chrysogonus in modern-day Trastevere (see Map 1), but he was discovered and beheaded by Gundobad in a brutal – and sacrilegious – murder.[74]

The victorious troops then took control of the city, but unlike the situation in 410 or 455, there were no restraints. Either Ricimer lost control of his troops, or he gave way to his own desire for revenge. Nor had the then Bishop Simplicius intervened in any way to mitigate the destruction that unfolded. Cassiodorus records that there was "a terrible devastation of the city."[75] Paul the Deacon sums up the damage:

> Not only was Rome devastated by the hunger and disease which afflicted it in this time, but it was also gravely ravaged, except the two regions in which Ricimer was with his own men. All the rest of the city was devastated by the greed of the looters.[76]

Unfortunately, the archaeological evidence for the impact of this war is quite limited. A hoard of gold coins from a room of the Atrium Vestae near the Palatine, the region where the Vestal Virgins used to live into the early fifth century (see Map 1), can be tied to this event. In one room, 397 gold solidi were discovered in excavations in 1899. These solidi are all from

---

[72] Paul Diac. *Hist. rom.* 15.4: *Bilimer Galliarum rector. . . Romam properavit. Is cum Ricimere aud Adriani pontem proelium committens, continuo ab eo superatus atque occisus est.* See Roberto 2012, pp. 184–85.

[73] John of Antioch, *Frag.* 209.1 = Priscus, *Frag.* 64.1, ed. Blockley 1983, p. 372.

[74] John of Antioch, *Frag.* 209.1 = Priscus, *Frag.* 64.1, ed. Blockley 1983, p. 372, explicitly notes the site of his murder inside the church. John mistakenly calls Gundobad Ricimer's brother. Blockley 1983, p. 400, note 203 attributes this to his reliance on two different sources, but Gundobad was the nephew of Ricimer.

[75] Cass. *Chron.* 1293 s.a. 472: *cum gravi clade civitatis.*

[76] Paul. Diac. *Hist. rom.* 15.4: *Praeter famis denique morbique penuriam quibus eo tempore Roma affligebatur, insuper etiam gravissime depraedata est et excepto duabus regionibus, in quibus Ricimer cum suis manebat, coetera omnia praedatorum sunt aviditate vastata.* For translation and seeing this as a hostile Byzantine view, see MacGeorge 2002, pp. 253–54.

the mint of Rome and date until the death of Anthemius in 472.[77] They may well have been part of an imperial donative that had been buried prior to the fighting by one of Anthemius's supporters. Indeed, Anthemius had arrived from the East with much gold, some of which he struck as solidi for distribution at his accession and, as Richard Burgess suggests, to pay mercenaries and soldiers.[78] This conjecture seems more likely since after the disestablishment of the cult of Vesta, the many bedrooms and central garden in this area near the Palatine and the Senate House may have been used for visiting dignitaries.[79] What is certain is that neither Anthemius nor the person who buried this hoard survived to reclaim it.

The hoard and our texts suggest that the Palatine and central areas nearby suffered greatly during this attack. Indeed, the imperial complex on the Palatine was one *locus* of the most intense fighting. It was, however, also one of the areas that would be the focus of repairs by Roman senators and generals in the coming decades. By the year 500, when King Theoderic visited Rome, he lived on the Palatine comfortably for his six-month stay.[80]

Rome Resilient: From "Civic Madness" to "The Happiness of the Age"

In the aftermath of what the late fifth-century bishop Gelasius called "civic madness" (*civilis furor*), senatorial and military elites faced a formidable task – determining how to restore Rome and their own relations. The general Ricimer soon signaled that he was ready to work with all senators. Neither he nor the man whom he had designated western emperor, the aristocrat Anicius Olybrius, took any action against those aristocrats or officials who had sided with Anthemius.[81] Moreover, Anthemius was granted a royal burial, and in an action that showed respect for tradition, according to John of Antioch, Anicius Olybrius did not take possession of the Palatine Palace until after the funeral of his predecessor.[82] Ricimer and Olybrius thus

---

[77] Ungaro 1985, pp. 47–160.

[78] Burgess, in an unpublished study of the solidi of Anthemius which he generously sent me, points to the unusually high level of solidi from the Roman mint for Anthemius. It is one key to the support that he had from Roman senators as well.

[79] Roberto 2012, pp. 186–87; Filippi 2001, pp. 599–601.

[80] Filippi 2001, p. 601. For more on the Palatine as an imperial residence into the middle of the fifth century, see Wulf-Rheidt 2017, pp. 127–48. For its use under Theoderic, see Maskarinec 2018, pp. 55–56 with bibliography, note 16.

[81] John of Antioch, *Frag.* 209.1 = Priscus, *Frag.* 64.1, ed. Blockley 1983, p. 372 emphasizes the division between Ricimer and his barbarians, versus Anthemius, the senators, and the populace.

[82] John of Antioch, *Frag.* 209.2 = Priscus, *Frag.* 65, ed. Blockley 1983, pp. 372–74.

demonstrated that the reintegration of the senatorial aristocracy behind the new government, not revenge, was their primary goal.

Ricimer's choice of Anicius Olybrius as the next emperor also provided reassurance to civic elites. Olybrius was a leading senator from Rome whose family, the Anicii, had influence and properties across the empire. Even by conservative estimates, they could be considered the third or fourth most powerful family in Rome in the 460s.[83] Olybrius himself appears to have gone to Constantinople, where he, now married to Placidia, the younger daughter of Valentinian III, had set up house.[84] He had a large palace in an area of the city named after it, the "Quarters of Olybrius." He had been honored as the eastern consul in 464.[85] Because of his connections to western senators, however, he had been selected by the eastern emperor Leo to mediate the war between Anthemius and Ricimer.[86]

Our eastern sources make clear that Olybrius was forced into assuming the throne. The sixth-century Greek chronicler Malalas weaves into his account the detail that Emperor Leo had written a secret letter to Anthemius, carried by an unsuspecting Olybrius, that urged the former to murder Olybrius.[87] However, Ricimer intercepted the letter and showed it to Olybrius, thus persuading him to accept the title of emperor, as the Senate then also did. Folktale motif as it is, Malalas's narrative underscores the prestige of this senator whom the eastern emperor had wished to have removed.[88] Olybrius's elevation was not intended by Emperor Leo, who appointed Julius Nepos, the former general of Anthemius, to be the new emperor in Italy.[89]

---

[83] Cameron 2012, p. 153, gives a conservative estimate of their status in Rome in 467. By the mid-470s, their status had risen rather than fallen, based in part on the activities of the women of the Anicii in the East but also on the consulship and activities of Olybrius.

[84] Placidia, taken hostage by Geiseric in the Vandal Sack of 455, was released, with her mother, and sent to Constantinople, likely in 461; see Priscus, *Frag.* 38, ed. Blockley 1983, pp. 340–41. See too Placidia 1, *PLRE* 2, p. 887 for all the sources.

[85] Clover 1978, p. 195 discusses the importation of western senatorial patronage in the eastern capital. Olybrius's patronage of the Church of St. Eufemia, tied closely to the dynasty of Theodosius II, has been seen as one component of his increasing influence on the imperial house in the East. His marriage to Placidia connected him to the western branch of the Theodosian dynasty.

[86] Malalas, *Chron.* 14.45. See note 60 above.   [87] Malalas, *Chron.* 14.45.

[88] Cameron 2012, p. 165, note 156, dismisses Olybrius's influence and this account as a mere folktale motif, but I remain convinced by the arguments of Clover 1978, pp. 169–96, that Olybrius's influence, as manifested by his consulship and his role as envoy, made him a powerful senator. Leo's decision to remove any potential usurpers from Constantinople at this juncture also served his political interests.

[89] Malchus, *Frag.* 14, ed. Blockley 1983, pp. 418–21.

Ricimer's choice of Olybrius was nonetheless politically astute. Olybrius had ties to the former western emperor Valentinian III through his marriage to his daughter Placidia, and through this relationship he could smooth the way for better relations with the Vandals. King Geiseric, as noted previously, had wanted Olybrius to be emperor instead of Anthemius. At the same time, Olybrius's elevation lent legitimacy to this new regime. Olybrius's family ties to western senatorial aristocrats would have gone far to ease tensions among the senatorial aristocracy and encouraged several senators to return to Rome to compete for positions in the new regime rather than to retreat to their estates in Italy or the East. Many had survived earlier crises: Just fifteen years earlier, senators who had returned quickly to Rome after the sack of 455 to support Majorian as emperor and then returned again in 465 after Majorian's demise to support Ricimer's candidate, the senator Libius Severus (461–65), as emperor, had been rewarded with government positions (see Chapter 4). Ricimer's practice of elevating senators to be emperors who would not engage in military affairs had long been acceptable to Rome's senatorial aristocrats, with whom he had worked for more than two decades. The Anicii were not the only aristocratic family willing to make alliances with strong "barbarian" generals.

After Ricimer's unexpected death – he vomited up blood in August 472 – just thirty days after the accession of Olybrius, the senators continued their support for Ricimer's plans. They pledged loyalty to Gundobad, Ricimer's Burgundian nephew who had been a general in Gaul.[90] Olybrius bestowed on Gundobad the title of *patrician*. But of key import, and very much underappreciated, is the fact that the senatorial aristocracy continued its support of Gundobad's government even after the sudden death of Olybrius in November 472. The Senate then proceeded to confirm Gundobad's candidate, Glycerius, as emperor. This new emperor, whose origins are unknown, had been commander of the imperial bodyguard (*comes domesticorum*) before being elevated to the throne in Ravenna or Rome in March 473.[91] In the face of these sudden turnovers, the Senate, newly returned, allied with the military and began the work of restoring the city.

The Senate United. An inscription from the Roman Forum in the area identified as the *atrium Minervae* (also called the *chalcidicum*) supplies important evidence for the resilience of Roman elites in the aftermath of 472. The restoration efforts took place in an area pregnant with political and

---

[90] Priscus, *Frag.* 65 = John of Antioch, *Frag.* 209.2, ed. Blockley 1983, pp. 372–75.

[91] Priscus, *Frag.* 65 = John of Antioch, *Frag.* 209.2, ed. Blockley 1983, pp. 372–74. For the title of *patricius*, see *Fast. Vind. Prior.* s.a. 472. This took place between August 19, 472, when Ricimer died, and November 2, 472, when Olybrius died. See too Gundobadus 1, *PLRE* 2, p. 524.

symbolic meaning; the atrium Minerva, a *porticus*, or vestibule, in front of the Senate House, which housed a gilded statue of the goddess, had originally been dedicated by Augustus.[92] The inscription records the restoration by the urban prefect, who advertised the return to "the happiness of the age" in an inscription dated to 472–73 most likely under the emperor Olybrius (see Table 5.1).[93] The inscription no longer survives – nor does the statue – but it can be confidently reconstructed:

> The statue [*simulacrum*] of Minerva, broken by a falling roof destroyed by fire during a civic conflict [*tumultus civilis*], was restored by Anicius Acilius Agina[n]tius Faustus, of senatorial status [and] aristocrat of the highest rank [*inlustris*], a judge hearing imperial appeals, providing improvements, and completing the work for the happiness of the age.[94]

The restoration of a pagan statue by a man otherwise assumed to have been a Christian attests to the widespread senatorial reverence for the site and for the gilded statue of the patron deity of Rome. Inscribing on a statue base the name of the deity to whom it was dedicated was standard practice, as also evidenced in a third-century restoration of a statue of Silvanus; the inclusion of the name of Minerva thus speaks to traditionalism and veneration of the past.[95] Like Machado, I want to emphasize the complex emotions that likely led to the prefect's decision to restore this statue in a formula that follows conventional pagan expressions of sanctity.[96]

---

[92] Kalas 2015, pp. 101–2; 155.

[93] For the inscription, see note 94 below. For dating it to 471–73, see Roberto 2012, p. 187 and note 44, and the arguments of Fraschetti 1999, pp. 173–74. Faustus was consul in 483, but the date of his urban prefecture is nowhere recorded; see Faustus 8, *PLRE* 2, pp. 451–52. Since his consulship is not mentioned in this inscription, the *terminus ante quem* must be 482, the only civil conflict in Rome that fits with Faustus' career is the one between Anthemius and Ricimer in 472. Fraschetti convincingly argued for a date immediately after the conflict, when the *atrium Minervae* was destroyed with the statue of the goddess. Hence, Faustus's prefecture should be dated to 472–73, since the prefect of the city in 474 is known to have been Castalius Innocentius Audax; see Table 5.3.

[94] *CIL* 6.526=1664 = *ILS* 3132: *simulacrum Minerbae | abolendo incendio|tumultus civilis igni|tecto cadente confractum|Anicius Acilius Agina[n]tius Faustus v.c. et inl. praef. urbi|vic. sac. idu. in melius|integro proviso pro|beatitudine temporis restituit.* Translation adapted from Kalas 2015, p. 101. See *LSA* 791 for discussion. See too Orlandi 2004, pp. 475–76.

[95] There are no less than thirteen inscriptions from the *EDR* that include the term *simulacrum*; for one with the expressed name of the deity, noted here from 231/270 CE and found in Rome in the Church of St. Stephen in the Round, see *EDR*003001: *Aemilius Alcimus | princeps peregr(inorum) simulacrum Silvani | addito pronao | incendio consumptum | restituit.*

[96] Here I concur with Machado 2009, pp. 331–54. For Faustus's later exchange of letters with the bishop Ennodius, see Faustus 8, *PLRE* 2, pp. 451–52. For the references to difficult times increasing in late antique inscriptions, see Alföldy 2001, pp. 3–24.

Some who paused to read this inscription may well have felt that this restoration would appease the divine power that had been alienated by this recent "civil uprising" (*civilis tumultus*), a phrase that echoes other references to the events of 472 as a civil war unlike the earlier crises that had overtaken the city.[97] Seeing this as a civil war allowed for its resolution, and the expression of its resolution leading to "good fortune in this age" (*pro beatitudine temporis*) is very much the theme that Glycerius asserted in the copy of the law that was posted in Rome by the praetorian prefect Himelco, who also emphasized "the happiness of a better age" (*pro beatitudine saeculi melioris*).[98] This distinct phrase reinforces arguments for the dating of the Minerva statue to the hopeful period right after the civil war.[99] Certainly, the desire to appease an angry goddess speaks to a very traditional Mediterranean and pagan understanding of disastrous events.[100]

The prefect who undertook this work, Anicius Acilius Aginantius Faustus, also belonged to the family of the Anicii; he would have a long illustrious career under the barbarian rulers of the late fifth century (see Table 5.1).[101] His restoration also made a strong statement in favor of winning divine favor for the Senate, now unified, as a means of ensuring a "happy age." Moreover, his rise does not mean that other Roman families had disappeared from the political scene in the aftermath of this war.[102] If the dating is accepted, the senator Petronius Perpenna Magnus Quadratianus, a member of the Roman family of the Petronii, repaired the Baths of Constantine, which were similarly damaged at this time – in the "devastation of a deadly calamity" (*feralis cladis vastatione*).[103]

During this period of restoration, however, upwardly mobile elites seized the opportunity for advancement. Based on his nomenclature, the man chosen as the praetorian prefect of Italy, Felix Himelco, was most likely new to the aristocracy (see Table 5.2). And among the new men who were

---

[97] For viewing these events as a civil war, see note 61 above.

[98] Haenel 1879, p. 260: *Quemadmodum Dominus noster invictissimus princeps Glycerius pro beatitudine saeculi melioris et suorum correctione mortalium, ne quine in supernae maiestatis deinceps ex sacerdotali ordinatione tentaretur iniuriam, ac … Datum III. Kal. Mai. Romae.*

[99] There are eleven inscriptions which use some formulation of *beatitudo* in the 87,853 recorded inscriptions on the *EDR*, including the one example cited here. Seven other inscriptions of these eleven use the formula: *beatitudine temporis | temporum*, and one uses the formula *beatitudine saeculi*, but the variations all point to the same idea of a "happy age/time or times" as the result of the donation of the dedicant.

[100] Toner 2013, pp. 153–70.

[101] See Table 5.1, Anicius Acilius Aginantius Faustus iunior (Albus), who is Faustus 4, *PLRE* 2, p. 451; and Orlandi 2010, pp. 475–76.

[102] On this problem, see notes 62 and 66, with my discussion above.

[103] This man was likely related to the praetorian prefect Quadratianus who was PPO Italiae in 443; see Henning 1999, p. 98.

welcomed into aristocratic society was the barbarian general Fl. Valila (who was also called "Theodovius"). He was honored with a seat in the Colosseum, a location generally reserved for senatorial aristocratic families. Indeed, Valila emulated Roman senators in his religious life as well, and regardless of his barbarian origin, he adopted Nicene Christianity, as evidenced by his patronage of the Christian church in Rome.[104]

Elite Contestation for Influence in the Aftermath of 472: Limits on Bishops and Clerics

The sole law to survive from Emperor Glycerius, passed just days after he took office on March 11, 473, published restrictions on the sale of church office.[105] In taking this action, Glycerius was following the guidance of church councils, which had explicitly forbidden simony, the sale of church office, although the first council to have done so was the ecumenical Council of Chalcedon in 451.[106] Glycerius was also following an earlier law of 469 passed by the emperors Anthemius and Leo, who had jointly condemned the sale of church office in vehement terms: "Let the profane ardor of avarice cease to threaten our altars, and let this disgraceful crime [sale of offices] be banished from our holy sanctuaries."[107] Although the sale of civic office was a common occurrence, emperors and churchmen wanted to make church practice distinct from this secular one.[108]

Nonetheless, imperial restrictions on church finances, even the sale of church office, were not necessarily welcomed by the clergy, for such actions meant that emperors were assuming the disciplinary role of the bishop. Indeed, Anthemius's law may well have further strained this emperor's relations with the papacy, which, as noted earlier, had led to a confrontation with

---

[104] For Valilia's seat, see Chapter 4, note 156. His career continued under Odoacer. For the donation of the basilica of Iunius Bassus to the Christian Church in Rome dated likely after his death and then consecrated by Bishop Simplicius (483–92), see Chapter 4, note 157. For the church on property donated near Tibur, Chapter 4, note 164.

[105] For the text, see note 107 below.   [106] Bogaert 1976, p. 871; Jones 1964, pp. 909–10.

[107] *C. Iust.* 1.3.30[31]. 469: *Impp. Leo et Anthemius AA. 3 Cesset altaribus imminere profanus ardor avaritiae et a sacris adytis repellatur piaculare flagitium. The law continues: Ita castus et humilis nostris temporibus eligatur episcopus, ut, locorum quocumque pervenerit, omnia vitae propriae integritate purificet. 4. Non pretio, sed precibus ordinetur antistes ... D. viii id. Mart. Constantinopoli Zenone et Marciano Conss.* ("Therefore, in our times, let chaste and humble bishops be chosen, so that, wherever they may go, they will purify everything with the morality of their own lives. Let the priest be ordained not with money but with prayers.")

[108] Kelly 2004, pp. 162–63, and on *suffragium* in general as an ambiguous term. In 470, another law by these same emperors mandated that no patriarch or steward could transfer any property owned by or given or sold or bequeathed to the Constantinopolitan Church; see *CI* 1.2.14.

the then bishop of Rome, Hilary, due to his religious tolerance. It is also noteworthy that during the siege and fighting, Bishop Simplicius (468–83) had not intervened in any way. In contrast, in other cities and even in Rome earlier in the century, bishops had mediated to seek clemency for the population (see, for example, the role of the Bishop of Rome Leo in Chapter 4). Anthemius's strained relationships with the papacy may provide another reason for Simplicius's silence during the civil war.

However, secular elites, as well as emperors, supported greater control over the financial practices of the clergy. Wealthy donors, among whom were many senatorial aristocrats, were concerned that their gifts to the church remain uncorrupted.[109] The sacred nature of charitable gifts of liturgical vessels was a particular problem, for their sale could alienate the salvation of those who had donated them (as we learn from church councils in the West as early as that of Arles in 314).[110] Of course, the clergy as well as ascetics had also attacked financial abuses by church officials.[111] But they wanted to control such activities and could well have regarded the passage of imperial laws against simony as unwanted state interference. Therefore, such laws were not necessarily a sign of the shared orthodoxy of imperial and civic elites, as some scholars have argued.[112] Rather, imperial interventions in church finances were signs of secular and imperial concern about how the church was being funded.

Glycerius's law, the last law issued by a western Roman emperor, has to be understood against this background. The law reiterated earlier restrictions on the sale of church office in moralizing language, following the same objectives as the earlier law of Anthemius and Leo. Glycerius's righteous indignation is asserted especially against bishops:

> From this practice it has developed that secular power is valued more than reverence for the clergy, and those who were called priests prefer to be "tyrants over citizens" (*tyrannopolitas*); and with religion neglected, having been chosen by the bribery of men, the clergy care more for public matters than divine ones, because they rejoice in impunity in their own violations

---

[109] See, for example, Ambr. *De Off.* 2.15.70, and especially 2.28.136: *Melius est enim pro Misericordia causas praestare vel invidiam perpeti quam praetendere inclementiam, ut nos aliquando in invidiam incidimus, quod confregimus vasa mystica ut captivos redimeremus, quod arianis displicere potuerat.* Possidius, *Vit. Aug.* 24.15 calls them *vasa dominica.*

[110] Munier 1963, *Concilia Galliae* a. 314–506, *CCSL* 148 B, pp. 12, 42–51.

[111] For a good discussion of attempts by the church and the state, see De Salvo 1995, pp. 367–92. This may help explain why this law of Glycerius is preserved in a collection of canon law. The text is known from a single manuscript of an early canonical collection (Vaticanus Reg. Lat. 1997; Kéry 1999, p. 24).

[112] Gusso 1992, pp. 168–93, and at p. 180: "l'editto aveva, per il Nuovo imperatore, intenti di politica interna più che esterna, volto com'era ad ingraziarsi la Chiesa di Roma, per averla alleata contro i propri avversari."

by this very privilege of perpetuity, and they, as if with the zeal of a certain management, steal the church's resources [that] they, by covering the disgraceful deeds of their dastardly design, say are the riches of the poor, by giving rewards to some at court, by obligating themselves to others by financial bond, and by selling for the gain of the debtor what ought to be preserved for needy persons.[113]

This law asserted that the bishops were buying their offices, thus taking what did not rightfully belong to them. Hence, the bishops lived as tyrants, unlawfully ruling over citizens, for that is the meaning of bishops as *tyrannopolitas*, a strong statement indeed.[114] Moreover, the payment to those at court to acquire bishoprics is singled out as a particular cause for concern.

Roman secular elites would have been similarly concerned that such abuses would tarnish the spiritual authority of the church. This notion is expressed by Glycerius, who condemned this practice as *indecora cupiditas* – "dishonorable greed." But Glycerius's indignation also had a contemporary focus, for this law indicated that simony had incurred the divine anger that had led to the recent ills of the civil war:

> Wherefore we believe that it has happened that the Divinity has been offended, which we recognize because we have experienced so many evils, and the Divinity has averted his Majesty's favor and vexed the Roman people with such great misfortunes as have come to pass.[115]

Indeed, for the Christian faithful living in the city who were similarly concerned that divine anger lay at the root of this strife, this action taken to curb these moral abuses by the clergy represented by simony would be reassuring. Attacking simony would also serve a good political purpose since it removed blame from the human civic arena and located it on the divine

---

[113] Haenel 1857, 260: *Hinc natum est, ut antistitum reverentia magis potestas saeculi putaretur, ut tyrannopolitas esse se malint, qui vocabantur antistes; ac religione neglecta sub hominum patrociniis constituti, publica magis quam divina curarent hoc ipso perpetuitatis privilegio delictorum suorum impunitate gaudentes, ecclesiarumque opes, quas mali propositi dedecora protegentes, pauperum dicunt esse divititas, studio veluti cuiusdam administrationis auferrent, aliis in praesenti dando praemia, nonnullis se chyrographis obligando, vendendoque in quaestum debitoris quod oportebat egentibus prorogari.*

[114] Here I do not agree with the view of Coleman-Norton 1966, p. 906, note 5, that *tyrannopolitas* refers to bishops as tyrant-ridden citizens, i.e. living under the tyranny of secular power. Rather, I think that this case, as in Sid. Ap. *Ep.* 5.8.3, the only other instance of this word, is a reference to a tyranny that controls its citizens, having come into power illicitly, i.e. their own willingness to buy and sell offices, theirs and others. The bishops are thus acting as tyrants, because they "rejoice in their own delicts." I thank Rita Lizzi Testa for this suggestion.

[115] Haenel 1857, 260: *Unde factum credimus, ut offensa divinitas, quod tot malis probamus experti, favorem suae maiestatis avertere, et Romanam gentem tantis, quae transacta sunt, infortuniis fatigaret.* I agree with Roberto 2014, pp. 167–82, that this is a reference to contemporary events.

one instead. Moreover, this action fit the moment because Glycerius claimed to be passing this law "for the happiness of a better time" – an appropriate idea for a law posted in Rome, where the nearby restored statue of Minerva spoke of such action as being undertaken for "the happiness of the age."[116]

External imperial attempts to control financial abuses by the clergy as represented by simony may have been one other consideration that had led Simplicius to respond forcefully to complaints by bishops of Italy about another bishop, Gaudentius, in a letter dated to this same period. In November 475 Bishop Simplicius articulated, for the first time in the fifth-century church records of Rome, how the revenues to the church should be divided. His fourfold division of funds – split equally among bishop, clergy, churches or workers, and the poor – was a clear attempt to restrict the abuses of clergy and bishops.[117] Simplicius's position also would have been welcomed by wealthy and aristocratic donors, who were similarly concerned about the misuse of church funds. These same concerns about the sale of charitable goods by bishops and priests were expressed openly by this bishop in the *Scriptura of 483*, which became official policy upon the death of Simplicius. Suffice it to say here that the inclusion of the prefect of Italy, Basilius, and likely other lay elites in the papal elections of his successor, Felix, and the stipulations about using church finances appropriately were natural developments of this post-472 elite concern about the misuse of church funds.[118]

Roman Senatorial and Germanic Military Elites: Rebuilding a Relationship with the East

After 472, Roman senators in alliance with barbarian military generals worked to ensure the restoration of Rome and initially supported weak

---

[116] Haenel 1857, 260: Received at Rome: Datum III. Kal. Maii. Romae: *Quemadmodum Dominus noster invictissimus princeps Glycerius pro beatitudine saeculi melioris et suorum correctione mortalium, ne quid in supernae maiestatis deinceps ex sacerdotali ordinatione tentaretur iniuriam.* ("How our Lord the unconquered prince Glycerius for the happiness of a better age and the correction of its morals, lest someone should attempt an injustice from a priestly ordination then.")

[117] Simplicius *Ep.* 1.2, ed. Thiel, p. 176: *Simul etiam de reditibus ecclesiae vel oblatione fidelium quid deceat nescienti, nihil licere permittat, sed sola ei ex his quarta portio remittatur. Duae ecclesiasticis fabricis et erogationi peregrinorum et pauperum profuturae, a Bonago presbytero sub periculo sui ordinis ministrentur; ultimam inter se clerici pro singulorum meritis dividant.*

[118] We see this emerge fully in the early sixth century when, in 530, at the urging of the then King of Italy, Theoderic, the Senate passed a *consultum* outlawing the sale of church office, an action that Cassiodorus saw as fully in their power since they had so acted under the Bishop of Rome, Boniface I; they did so, moreover, as Cassiodorus described in a letter of 533, because they were "mindful of their nobility"; Cass. *Var.* 9.15.3.

senatorial aristocrats as emperors. But problems in this solution set the stage for the complete demise of imperial office in the West while simultaneously giving greater influence to the Senate and individual senators. Indeed, when Gundobad, Glycerius's commander in chief and patrician, left Italy with his troops and retainers to return to his home in Gaul, he left Glycerius in a weakened position. The death of the Burgundian king Gundioc had left a power vacuum into which Gundobad stepped. Fresh from Rome, and honored with his new title of *patrician*, Gundobad took control of the Burgundians and continued to rule there as king for the next four decades, choosing to forego any attempt to return to Italy.[119] Therefore, it is it is not surprising that when faced with the arrival of Nepos as the new contender for the western throne, Glycerius fled Rome without a fight. Some sources say Glycerius turned to a life in the church, becoming bishop of Salona (modern Split) in Pannonia. This was a major episcopal seat, and clearly, in his view the imperial throne was not worth dying for.

Nepos was then proclaimed western emperor by the Senate.[120] Just as when Anthemius had arrived, so too did Nepos bring a new military force, funding, and the recognition of the newly elevated eastern emperor, Zeno. Like earlier eastern emperors, Zeno desired to have the honor of placing an emperor on the western throne as one further sign of his authority over a unified empire. Nepos, the patrician commander in chief of Dalmatia, was a good choice; since he was experienced in warfare and married to a relative of Empress Verina, wife of Emperor Leo, his appointment would also remove a potential threat to the eastern emperor.[121]

Unfortunately, Nepos made several crucial errors from the perspective of the senatorial aristocrats of Rome. First, he failed to build ties with them. Their influence had grown significantly, and their support was critical if Nepos were to succeed. Second, Nepos chose to rule from Ravenna, a location that would not allow him to establish close ties to senators in Rome. Third, Nepos did not control his forces well. His general, Orestes, revolted in Ravenna in 476. When Orestes then made Romulus, his fourteen-year-old son, emperor, the Senate did not open Rome's doors to Nepos, who had fled from Ravenna and subsequently went into exile in Dalmatia. He

---

[119] For Gundobad's sudden return to Burgundy, see Malalas, *Chron.* 14.44–45, and note 91 above.

[120] Nepos was proclaimed on June 19 or 24, 474; see *Anon. Val.* 7 (36); John of Antioch, *Frag.* 209 = Priscus, *Frag.* 65, ed. Blockley 1983, pp. 374–75; Ennod. *Vita Epiph.* 80; and Nepos 3, *PLRE* 2, p. 777. Nepos was in Italy from June 474–August 475.

[121] For his marriage to a relative of Verina, wife of the emperor Leo, see Malchus, *Frag.* 14, ed. Blockley 1983, pp. 420–21.

continued to claim to rule Italy from there for the next five years. Nor did the Senate support Romulus after his father, Orestes, was subsequently murdered by his forces. Our sources focus on the troops' dissatisfaction with Orestes's arrangements for their recompense in Italy. The military instead turned to the commander Odoacer. He had played a key role in the civil war between Ricimer and Anthemius, and was commander of the imperial bodyguard, having been appointed by Nepos.[122] Odoacer's ethnic background was ambiguous, but his non-Roman identity was no hindrance to the Senate, which also supported Odoacer since they regarded him as a capable general and partner, one whom the continuator of Prosper's *Chronicle* described as a "man experienced in age and wisdom and well trained in the arts of war."[123] The fact that he had spent time in Rome as a supporter of Ricimer meant that he was probably known to many senators as well.

The words of the fifth-century eastern historian Malchus, preserved in a Byzantine account that has been heavily reworked, record that already at this early date in 476, "Augustus, the son of Orestes, having heard that Zeno was back on the throne . . . *compelled* [ἠνάγκασε, italics mine] the Senate to send an embassy to the eastern emperor Zeno proposing that there was no need of a divided rule and that one, shared emperor was sufficient for both territories."[124] The notion that this young augustus, after his father Orestes had been murdered, could force the Senate to take this step is so problematic that an earlier editor of this text suggested that this statement was an error in the compilation of the text and that the text should instead read "Odoacer."[125] The constitutional difficulties of who could send an embassy are not the point here. Rather, it seems to me, the Senate clearly had undertaken this task and that they had clearly done so after working in league with Odoacer, who very soon after this had no compunctions about sending an embassy to Zeno, as a fragment of the Greek historian Candidus's writing indicates.[126] But more importantly for this study is

---

[122] See Odoacer, *PLRE* 2, pp. 791–93. For the imperial bodyguard, see Procop. *Wars* 5.1.6.

[123] *Auct. Havniensis Ordo Prior* a. 476, ed Mommsen, MGH AA, p. 309: *hominem et aetate et sapientia gravem et bellicis rebus instructum*. Although Marcellinus *comes*, in the epigraph to this chapter, calls the kings Goths, Odoacer's ethnicity is a matter of debate; see Arnold 2017, p. 113, note 4, who cites the view that the fluidity of his identity may have been designed to appeal to his polyethnic army.

[124] Malchus, *Frag.* 14 = Blockley 1983, pp. 418–19. Cessi 1916, I, 345, note 2, has argued that Malchus's account here has been reworked to incorporate elements from the *Fasti*. Caliri 2017, p. 53, also favors this view of Malchus's text as a revision, rather than simple transcription. I agree. For the Greek text, see note 127 below.

[125] Niebuhr made this suggestion, as discussed by Caliri 2017, pp. 56–57.

[126] Candidus, *Frag.* 1 = Blockley 1983, p. 469: "After the assassination of Nepos and the expulsion of Augustulus, Odovacar in his own person ruled Italy and Rome. When the Gauls of the West

Malchus's explanation of the Senate's motivation for this request, as articulated by the senatorial ambassador:

> [T]hey [the Senate/βουλὴ] had chosen Odoacer, a man of military and political experience, to safeguard their own affairs [πράγματα] and [had determined] that Zeno should confer upon him the rank of patrician and entrust him with the government of Italy.[127]

These senatorial envoys had been chosen for this delicate political mission because the Senate wanted Odoacer to rule Italy neither as emperor nor as king, as his troops had proclaimed him, but as patrician in order to protect not just their affairs but also their property (πράγματα). The Senate's designation of Odoacer as the result of their choice underscores their ongoing political role in negotiating power between Odoacer and the eastern court.

Significantly, the Senate did not mention Nepos at all. By denying Nepos's existence, the senatorial envoys negated his legitimacy. They did, however, restate their allegiance to the eastern emperor in an effort to forestall intervention. Clearly, the Senate had been working behind the scenes to facilitate the exile of one emperor and the retirement of another, even as it was now working with Odoacer to keep imperial oversight at a safe distance.[128] The eastern emperor Zeno, himself only recently back in control of Constantinople, pointed out that the Romans had already been sent an emperor, Nepos, and that they should "welcome him in return." Moreover, Zeno explained, Nepos was the one to grant Odoacer's request for patrician status. However, the passage ends with notice of Zeno's letter of congratulations to Odoacer, as if Nepos had given Odoacer the patrician status he sought. At the same time, Zeno commended Odoacer for "preserving the

revolted against Odovacer, both they and Odovacer sent an embassy to Zeno. He preferred to support Odovacer." There is no mention of the senate in Candidus, however, nor does this Gallic attack seem to fit the 476 circumstances, so I follow Blockley 1983, p. 472 note 12, in interpreting this fragment of Candidus as not referring to the events of 476.

[127] Malchus, *Frag.* 14 = Blockley 1983, p. 418–19. I cite here the opening of the passage: Ὅτι ὁ Αὔγουστος ὁ τοῦ Ὀρέστου υἱὸς ἀκούσας Ζήνωνα πάλιν τὴν βασιλείαν ἀνακεκτῆσθαι τῆς ἕω τὸν Βασιλίσκον ἐλάσαντα, ἠνάγκασε τὴν βουλὴν ἀποστεῖλαι πρεσβείαν Ζήνωνι σημαίνουσαν, ὡς ἰδίας μὲν αὐτοῖς βασιλείας οὐ δέοι, κοινὸς δὲ ἀποχρήσει μόνος ὢν αὐτοκράτωρ ἐπ' ἀμφοτέροις τοῖς πέρασι. τὸν μέντοι Ὀδόαχον ὑπ' αὐτῶν προβεβλῆσθαι ἱκανὸν ὄντα σώζειν τὰ παρ' αὐτοῖς πράγματα, πολιτικὴν' ἔχοντα σύνεσιν ὁμοῦ καὶ μάχιμον· καὶ δεῖσθαι τοῦ Ζήνωνος πατρικίου τε αὐτῷ ἀποστεῖλαι ἀξίαν καὶ τὴν τῶν Ἰταλῶν τούτῳ ἐφεῖναι διοίκησιν. See too Radtki 2016, 126–27.

[128] For fuller discussion, see Caliri 2017, pp. 56–58.

order of government appropriate for the Romans."[129] Nonetheless, neither Odoacer nor the Senate abided by Zeno's recommendation to bring back Nepos. The Senate's willing support of Odoacer meant the demise of the shared imperial model that Zeno had tried to preserve. Odoacer sent Romulus off to an estate in Campania and returned the western imperial paraphernalia to the Eastern emperor, including the diadem and cloak.[130] The Senate now sought a new *modus operandi* with the new patrician and general, Odoacer, whom the military recognized as king.[131]

Odoacer and the Senatorial Aristocracy: A Match Made in Rome

Odoacer's rule benefited from his collaboration with the ruling Roman elites. His appointments to high civic office, as we shall see, included a good number of men from wealthy established senatorial aristocratic families from Rome and elsewhere in Italy. However, his regime also attracted a number of new men – that is, men from Italy or the provinces – who were the first of their families to attain senatorial rank. The willingness of these men, old and new alike, to return to Rome and to support Odoacer led to their successful careers in government in a newly pacified Italy. Many of these senators and their families continued to thrive into the sixth century (see Chapter 6).

Importantly, Odoacer continued the same administrative structure and offices that had existed up to this date (see Tables 5.4.1 and 5.4.2). Moreover, he, not the eastern emperor, chose senatorial aristocrats to fill high civic offices in Rome and Italy. He appointed men to the position of praetorian prefect of Italy, urban prefect of Rome, quaestor of the sacred palace (*quaestor sacri palatii*, the senior legal authority), count of the private estates of the emperor (*comes rei privatae*, for estates now under the control of Odoacer), and the count of the imperial treasury (*comes sacrarium largitionum*, the chief official for revenue now given to Odoacer). These positions brought senators into closer contact with Odoacer, with all but the urban prefect traditionally part of the advisory council (*consistorium*) of the emperor. After the death of Nepos, Odoacer also appointed western consuls from 480 until

---

[129] Malchus, *Frag.* 14 = Blockley 1983, p. 420–21. I follow Blockley's interpretation of this passage, p. 421, note 21.

[130] See Romulus Augustus, *PLRE* 2, pp. 949–50. Cass. *Chron.* s.a. 476: *cum tamen nec purpura nec regalibus uteretur insignibus.*

[131] For Odoacer's elevation to the kingship, see *Fast. Vind. Prior.* s.a. 476 and Odoacer, *PLRE* 2, p. 792.

489, an honor but an office unlike the five offices noted above since the consul had no real responsibilities.[132]

During the fourteen years that Odoacer ruled Italy as king (476–90), he could have made seventy to seventy-eight appointments, plus appointing the ten consuls (assuming the last was made by Odoacer in 489), for a total of some eighty to eighty-eight possible officeholders since most men held their positions for a year. However, the number of men attested in office is much smaller than that. Sixteen of the possible eighty or more high civic officeholders, or approximately one-fifth of the total, can be securely dated to the reign of Odoacer.[133] The men who held these positions shared certain characteristics, and taken as a group, they point to some significant developments.

Established Roman senatorial aristocratic families are most visible: of the sixteen men with high civic positions or consulships securely attested under Odoacer, nine are from six established Roman families – including the Decii, Anicii, Symmachi, Petronii, Acilii Glabriones, and Boethii (see Tables 5.4.1 and 5.4.2). Although the number of families attested among the high civic officeholders – six – is small, the competition for office must have been keen. But given that most attested officeholders were from established Roman senatorial families, Odoacer's government clearly had relied on these wealthy senators, who, in turn, benefitted from holding high civic office.

Indeed, some families did better than others. The Decii, as several scholars have observed, fared particularly well during this decade, with three of their members holding three high offices in addition to three of the consulships. Other families, including the Anicii, held only one office or at most, in the case of the Petronii, two.[134] But the presence of Anicius Acilius Aginantius

---

[132] Odoacer named consuls from the death of Nepos in 480 down through 489, even if rebels invaded in 486–87. The effective end of his rule was 489, even if Theoderic did not take up the official position of King of Italy until 493. See Vitiello 2005, pp. 39–55; and Orlandi 2010, p. 336.

[133] This group is smaller than in recent studies because I omitted twelve men whom many scholars have included in discussions of Odoacer's rule based on dating several key inscriptions from the Colosseum to the reign of Odoacer by Chastagnol 1966. Orlandi 2004 and 2010, pp. 331–38 has demonstrated that this dating cannot be assumed. See Tables 5.4.1 and 5.4.2. Caliri 2017, p. 116, noted Orlandi's work but strangely she still cites the statistics used by Chastagnol 1966, pp. 149 ff. My number is higher than Sundwall's for the second half of the fifth century. He sees only between twenty and twenty-five *illustres*; that is far too small, since the numbers I have omitted should date to the second half of the century, and there are still others under Theoderic; see Sundwall 1915, p. 152.

[134] I assume that Fl. Anicius Probus Faustus iunior Niger, Faustus 9, *PLRE* 2, pp. 454–56 was appointed consul in 490 by Theoderic; he certainly served the latter as envoy to convince the eastern emperor to appoint the latter. For the view that the election of Olybrius and Petronius Maximus was a triumph of the Anicii, while that of Majorian and presumably Odoacer reflects the successful intervention of the Decii, see especially Zecchini 1981, pp. 128 ff; Max 1979, pp. 225–37.

Faustus iunior as consul in 483 argues against the notion that the Anicii were benefiting from a consistently pro-barbarian view or suffering from a pro-eastern position as opposed to those of their rivals, the family of the Decii.[135] As in earlier periods of the fifth century, under Odoacer there is no good evidence for a consistent position held by one family firmly against those of the other.

The restoration of peace and the reestablishment of a new governing coalition under Odoacer had also attracted many upwardly mobile men new to senatorial status from all over Italy to Rome and Ravenna. Exemplary of these men are such able administrators as Cassiodorus, father of the more famous letter writer of the same name who served Theoderic (king of Italy, 493–526), and whose family had resided in Bruttium in southern Italy. Cassiodorus's grandfather had retired after serving as *tribunus* and *notarius* under Aetius, preferring a title rather than pursuing the rank of *illustris*.[136] But his son was ambitious. The elder Cassiodorus served Odoacer in two of the state's chief financial posts, as count of the private estates and then as count of the imperial treasury. These positions, held at the beginning of his career (see Table 5.4.1), required good financial, administrative, and personnel management skills since the staff of the latter position, for instance, probably still numbered in the hundreds in the West.[137]

Men new to senatorial status were desirable in many ways because they owed their positions to Odoacer. The eminently capable Petrus Marcellinus Felix Liberius, who served Odoacer in some official capacity but whose precise office, like his origins, is not known, is striking (see Table 5.4.1). Liberius worked diligently and effectively to settle Germanic troops in Italy in the early part of Odoacer's reign. When Theoderic succeeded to control of Italy, he appreciated Liberius's administrative skills and his loyalty to Odoacer, so he subsequently elevated him to the office of praetorian prefect of Italy for an unprecedentedly long period.[138] Liberius's career trajectory provides a good example of the upward mobility of some new elites, although his success did not translate into senatorial status for his family, at least as far

---

[135] Caliri 2017, pp. 116–17 discusses some of these ideas only to sensibly dismiss them as reductionist. For this consul, see Table 5.4.1.

[136] Cass. *Var.* 1.4.10–11.13; and Cassiodorus 2, *PLRE* 2, p. 264.

[137] We can only suggest this figure based on a law of 384, *C. Th.* 6.30.7 (384 CE), which was modified in the *C. Iust.* 12.23.7 by a 490 law of Anastasius. Although the two texts should not be conflated and the situation in the West in the late fifth century is obviously different from that in the East by the time of Anastasius's law of 490, the overall structure under Odoacer remained intact. See Kelly 2004, p. 42, note 49. Even if only a third of the 443 positions were still in place, that would be a significant number who provided critical financial services to the new regime.

[138] Cass. *Var.* 2.16.67–68; and Caliri 2017, pp. 112–13. See Table 5.4.1.

as we can see. This was also the case for other seemingly new men under Odoacer, including the powerful praetorian prefect of Italy, Pelagius, and the count of the imperial treasury, Opilio, neither of whom left families that we can trace in the historical record (see Table 5.4.1).

Senatorial supporters of Odoacer remained faithful into the last part of the decade. None are recorded as supporting the rebellion in Ravenna of Brachila, the German military count who seemingly opposed Odoacer's decision to rule without a Roman emperor in 477, or that of Adaric, a German who rebelled against Odoacer in 478; both men were subsequently killed by Odoacer.[139] Respect for Odoacer remained high among provincial elites as well as among Roman senatorial aristocrats, judging from the praise that the nobles expressed for him after he had defeated a neighboring Germanic band, the Rugi. They happily accepted the news that St. Severinus had accurately predicted that Odoacer would rule safely for thirteen or fourteen years.[140]

What Kind of Power Did Senators and the Senate Have? The senatorial aristocracy that supported Odoacer was a smaller body than it had been at the beginning of the fifth century (see Tables 5.4.1 and 5.4.2 as compared with the tables in Chapter 4). But its political influence was real and arguably increased. The 476 senatorial embassy to the eastern emperor Zeno discussed previously indicates the role that they so often fulfilled in negotiating political events. In the complex arrangements that took place between the military commanders and the eastern imperial court – and, as we will see, in negotiations between the bishop of Rome and the eastern patriarch – senators served as indispensable brokers in the networks of power. Senatorial aristocrats also had the right skills – training in literature, administration, and law – to not only serve diplomatically but also to govern in support of their new military partners. They were also seen as socially predominant and these "highborn scions of Roman nobility" attracted, as Rutilius Namatianus put it, new men, the "seeds of virtues" to the Senate House to serve Rome.[141]

In addition, the financial support of senators, as administrators of empire, was key to Odoacer's easy entry into power in another, less discussed way.

---

[139] Jord. *Get.* 243, *MGH AA* 5.1.120; *Auct. Havniensis Ordo Prior* a 477; 478, ed. Mommsen, *MGH AA* 9, p. 311. See also Caliri 2017, p. 119. I follow the dates in *PLRE* 2 for Brachila, p. 241, and for Adaric, p. 7.

[140] *Anon. Val.* 10 (48); and Radtki 2016, p. 127, who also cites Eugippus, *Vita Sancti Severini* 32, ed. Sauppe, who mistakenly locates the nobles talking to St. Severinus in Rome. This event happened after Odoacer had defeated the Rugi, a tribe in modern Austria, and St. Severinus did not travel to Rome.

[141] Rut. Nam. *De red. suo*, lines 7–9.

Procopius is the only source to also suggest the economic reasons why the troops chose Odoacer over Orestes as their king and why the Roman senators would have gone along with him as ruler. According to Procopius, "When the Romans had been weakened in war, they had entered into an alliance with the barbarians" – a mixed group of Germans, Alans, Sciri, and Sueves. But by 475, these troops had become so much stronger than the Roman troops and had so tyrannized and oppressed the Romans that they "finally demanded that they [the Romans] should distribute among them all the lands in Italy."[142] Orestes had refused to accede to these demands or even to the request for a third of the Italian territory, something that had happened in Spain, Africa, and Gaul. Procopius informs us that Odoacer succeeded to power by "giving the third of the land to the barbarians, and in this way, gaining their [the barbarian troops'] allegiance most securely."[143] Which lands Odoacer distributed and how much came from state properties is hard to say, but the absence of complaints from senators suggests their support for this resolution. After all, Odoacer's promise to maintain safe control over their properties – and here the actual properties ceded by senators are unknown – nonetheless ensured that they would receive enough of their continued rents and enjoy financial equilibrium after a period of civil war and economic upheaval.[144] Given that most of Odoacer's troops were in northern Italy, it is also reasonable to surmise that the "one-third" of the lands came from areas in northern or central Italy and that wealthier senators were less affected than others by these losses. Finally, Odoacer did live up to his promise to restore peace and security. He negotiated with the Vandals and protected Sicily, an area where many Roman aristocrats had long had large estates.[145]

Under Odoacer, as before, the Senate remained the primary body representing the wealthy landowning senatorial aristocrats of Rome. As such, it sought to protect senatorial wealth and political influence and oversaw the continuation of traditional administrative and ceremonial functions that legitimated the new government. As the sole continuing political institution

---

[142] Procop. *Wars* 5.1.4, translation by Kaldellis 2014, p. 251.

[143] Procop. *Wars* 5.1.8, translation by Kaldellis 2014, p. 251. Procop. *Wars* 5.1.28, confirms that when the Goths took over, they seized the portion of land that Odoacer had given to his troops, thereby again reassuring aristocrats income from the two-thirds of their lands still under their control.

[144] For a good discussion these issues, see Caliri 2017, pp. 85–95, who underscores that there is no convincing evidence to support Goffart's thesis that money, not land, was given to the troops. Procopius is clear that a third of the land was given to the troops demanding recompense.

[145] For the settlement, see especially Clover 1999, p. 237. For senatorial estates in Sicily, see Salzman 2002, pp. 25–26 for the fourth century; and for recent excavations of estates in Sicily from 300 to 700 CE, and in particular, the Villa Philosophiana, see Vaccaro 2013, pp. 259–313.

in the West, the Senate claimed a particular place in the government of Italy. Many of its traditional activities continued under the new order and were regarded by its members and the military as critical for ensuring the authority of the state and its Roman identity. The Senate House was the place where the acclamation of the new city prefect took place, where imperial legislation was read aloud and the acclamations of the senators recorded for the official record that was sent to the eastern emperor, where trials of senators took place, and where edicts or ordinances were issued.[146] As King Odoacer moved away from Rome to Ravenna, the Senate was increasingly called upon to intervene in affairs pertaining to the city of Rome, a development that would continue into the sixth century (see Chapter 6). As part of the "order of government" that he preserved, Odoacer consciously courted the good will of the Senate. Some scholars have also seen this same desire in the minting of bronze coins with the phrase *Gloria Romanorum* or *Invicta Roma* and the letters *SC* in the field, a reference – the first authorized since the mid third century – to the *S(enatus) C(onsulto)*.[147]

Restoring the Roman Amphitheater. Perhaps the most potent indicator of Odoacer's concerns to honor Roman traditions and institutions, and thus at least formally and ideally to legitimate his own regime, are the senatorial inscriptions in the Colosseum.[148] Considered as a group by Silvia Orlandi in a brilliant study, the inscriptions document the importance Odoacer conferred on these traditional areas of senatorial activity.[149] The names of senators active in repairing and having seats in this location include the most illustrious of the aristocracy, with representatives from the Decii, Symmachi, Rufii, and Anicii so recorded (see Tables 5.4.1 and 5.4.2). Although the number of men active under Odoacer is less than once argued, senatorial concern to demonstrate their wealth and to continue the games had Odoacer's full support (see Table 5.4.1 note 4).

These senators were also concerned about the public buildings in Rome, particularly those tied to the traditional world of the games. Thus, we find

---

[146] For the Senate House as the site of acclamation of the new urban prefect, see Chastagnol 1960, pp. 192–93; and as the site of trials, as that of Arvandus in 468, see Sid. Ap. *Ep.* 1.7.9. For the speech of a new urban prefect in the Senate House in 509–10 CE, see Cass. *Var.* 1.43 and 3.12. For the acclamations to laws as part of the record, we are best informed about the response to the promulgation of the Theodosian Code in 438, see the Minutes of the Senate of the City of Rome, trans. Pharr 1952, pp. 3–7.

[147] Jones 1964, p. 254 is somewhat dubious, but others are more positive; see Orlandi 2004, p. 561; Chastagnol 1966, p. 53. For the coins, see *RIC* 10: 3665–7

[148] Orlandi 2004, with conclusions pp. 545–63; see too La Rocca and Oppedisano 2016, pp. 187–89.

[149] Orlandi 2004, cat. no. 34 and p. 561. The repair of the *Ludus Magnus* is identified with the work of Decius Marius Venantius Basilius, consul of 484.

an inscription relative to renewed activity in the *Ludus Magnus*, the place
for gladiatorial training combat, at the time of Odoacer. Another inscription records the intervention in the podium of the Colosseum by the same
man, Decius Marius Venantius Basilius, assumed to be the consul of 484
and not that of 508.[150] Senatorial traditions of competitive patronage
should be seen as part of the restoration of civic life enjoyed by aristocrats
and residents alike. Odoacer's rule encouraged civic officials to return to
this traditional activity that had been such a fundamental part of their
identity for centuries.

The Parting of the Ways: Senators and Bishops between the East and the West

With the removal of a western emperor, lay senatorial aristocrats and the
Senate of Rome increasingly were influential brokers of relations between
the eastern imperial court and the western government of Odoacer.[151] Thus,
it is not surprising, perhaps, that the bishops of Rome also increasingly
turned to lay senatorial aristocrats in ecclesiastical politics. Indeed,
bishops, priests, and lay senatorial aristocrats had been interacting and
adapting to each other for more than a century in what Charles Pietri has
described as a complex of reciprocal exchanges.[152] But we see a new level of
aristocratic involvement in papal politics in response to the changes that
overtook Rome in the 470s.

Aristocratic Support, the Scriptura *of 483, and the Accession of Bishop Felix III of Rome (483–92)*

When Felix became the bishop of Rome in 483, he had the support of several
Roman aristocratic families. As I have argued, his daughter likely married
a member of the Anicii and hence through her he would have had personal
ties to one key Roman aristocratic family.[153] Felix also had the backing of at

---

[150] Orlandi 2004, cat. no. 5 for the podium of the Colosseum inscription. For the *Ludus Magnus* see
note 149 above.

[151] For the increasing influence of lay aristocrats and the Senate, see Radtki, 2016, pp. 126–27. Of
special note is Malchus, *Frag.* 14, Blockley 1983, pp. 418–21, discussed above.

[152] Pietri 1981, p. 418.

[153] Sections of what follows have been adapted from what first appeared in Salzman, 2019A,
pp. 465–89. They have been excerpted here with permission from John Hopkins University
Press.

least one very prominent member of the Decii.[154] Indeed, the accession of Felix and his willingness to implement policies that were favorable to wealthy lay donors, of which senatorial aristocrats were prominent, are attested by a remarkable document today known as the *Scriptura of 483*. The *Scriptura* likely originated as a testamentary will by the bishop of Rome, Simplicius, but it was preserved in the Acts of the Church Council of Rome in 502 as a record of still-valid papal policy.[155]

The *Scriptura* provides key information about the role of lay elites and the state in the accession of Felix:

> When they sat down in the mausoleum, which is on the site of the Church of Saint Peter's, Basilius, the lofty and most eminent praetorian prefect and patrician, acting on behalf of the most excellent King Odoacer, said:
>
> "Notwithstanding the fact that there is a distinction between our desire and our religion [*religio*] in order that most importantly, in the election of a bishop, the concord of the church be preserved and the condition of civil order not be disturbed by any chance of sedition, nevertheless, at the urging of our most blessed pope, Simplicius, whom we always hold before our eyes, remember that this was mandated to us under a solemn charge before God in order that without any commotion and damage to the venerable Church, if he (Simplicius) should go from this light, no election should be proclaimed without our consultation."[156]

Flavius Caecina Decius Maximus Basilius iunior was praetorian prefect of Italy and deputy (*agens vices*) of Odoacer. He was part of the deliberations over the election of a successor for the ailing bishop, Simplicius.[157] At Simplicius's request, a group met in what the text called a mausoleum near St. Peter's to arrange for a peaceful succession.[158]

---

[154] Flavius Caecina Decius Maximus Basilius iunior, the praetorian prefect, was present to smooth the transition; for his career, see Table 5.4.1.

[155] This document is preserved in the *Acta synhodi A. DII* [sic] *MGH AA* 12, ed. Mommsen, pp. 438–55. For the *Scriptura of 483* originating as a testamentary will, see Sessa 2012, pp. 222–25. For the Council in Rome of 502 in the midst of the Laurentian Schism, see Salzman 2019A, pp. 465–89.

[156] *Acta syn. DII* [sic] *MGH AA* 12, ed Mommsen, p. 445. *Cum in mausoleo, quod est apud beatum Petrum apostolum, resedissent, sublimis et eminentissimus vir praefectus praetorio atque patricius, agens etiam vices praecellentissimi Regis Odovacris Basilius dixit: 'Quamquam studii nostri et religionis intersit, ut in episcopatus electione concordia principaliter servetur ecclesiae nec per occasionem seditionis status civilitatis vocetur in dubium, tamen admonitione beatissimi viri papae nostri Simplicii, quam ante oculos semper habere debemus, hoc nobis meministis sub dei obtestatione fuisse mandatum, ut praeter ullum strepitum et venerabilis ecclesiae detrimentum, si eum de hac luce transire contigerit, non sine nostra consultatione cuiuslibet celebratur electio.'*

[157] For Flavius Caecina Decius Maximus Basilius iunior's career, see Table 5.4.1 and note 165 below.

[158] Their meeting place can be identified as the now-destroyed Rotunda of Saint Petronilla, site of the tomb of Maria, who was a member of the Theodosian dynasty and an empress as the first

The *Scriptura* represents Simplicius's dying wish that the election of the next bishop of Rome consider the opinion of this group that came together; the plural verbs (they sat together, *resedissent*; you [all] remember, *meministis*) are key. There were several men, clergy as well as the laity. Moreover, the *Scriptura* stipulates that his successor's "election not be celebrated without our consultation" (*non sine nostra consultatione cuiuslibet celebratur electio*). Furthermore, the text uses a technical legal term – *consultatio* – meaning a general inquiry or consideration of a subject at hand – in this case, the election of a successor.[159] But the *Scriptura* does not specifically state who was present for this proclamation, and that omission has led to much scholarly discussion.

Several scholars, following Charles Pietri, have argued that this was an official meeting of the Senate and that the *Scriptura* was an official document of the Senate in what they regard as an effort to establish direct senatorial control over papal elections.[160] But there is no evidence that the Senate was present in 483 or that this document was a decree of the Senate.[161] Basilius was present because he was, as the *Scriptura* noted, the representative of Odoacer in Rome. He was not there as "Head of the Senate" (*caput/prior Senatus*), as is often erroneously stated.[162] This clarification is a key point for understanding the political context of Felix's accession. Because Basilius proclaimed the *Scriptura* (*Basilius dixit*), it became an official document. Thus, the *Scriptura* documents the willingness of the dying bishop Simplicius to engage Basilius, Odoacer's deputy, and other lay elite as well as clergy to shape his succession plans. The laity are not specifically named, nor, for that matter, are any other clergy. But as this document shows, in 483 Simplicius

---

wife of the western emperor Honorius, and hence a site associated with imperial authority. For the location, see Liverani 2005, pp. 75–76.

[159] *Acta syn. DII* [sic] *MGH AA* 12, ed. Mommsen, p. 445. For *consultatio* in legal and rhetorical usage, see Lewis and Short 1975, s.v. *consultatio*, I.B. 1 and 2.

[160] Pietri 1981, pp. 451–53 and note 214; and Moorhead 1992a, 120. But Pietri 1981, p. 419, note 7, cited evidence for the role of the Senate from the later period under king Theoderic, and so retrojects a later practice onto the events of 483. Indeed, this was precisely how this action was later viewed because in the 502 Acts of the Council, the bishop of Todi, Cresconius, interrupted the reading of the *Scriptura* and voiced the opinion that this procedure went against church canons because it allowed lay people to intervene in papal elections: *Acta syn. DII* [sic] *MGH AA* 12, ed. Mommsen, p. 445: *Hic perpendat sancta synhodus, ut praetermissas personas religiosas, quibus maxime cura est de creando pontifice, in suam redegerint potestatem, quod contra canones esse manifestum est.*

[161] Sessa 2012, pp. 222–25.

[162] This term – *caput/prior Senatus* – is only first attested under Theoderic in 490 in the *Anonymus Valesianus*, 11.53, but Stein 1920, p. 236, and others assume that it developed probably under Odoacer. It is not used in the *Scriptura* and hence there is no reason to assume that Basilius is acting on behalf of the Senate at this juncture. *PLRE* 2, s.v. Basilius 12, p. 217, erroneously calls him *caput Senatus*. See further Porena 2019, pp. 25–50.

and the unnamed laity and clergy – including, no doubt, the then deacon and future bishop of Rome Felix – were willing to support such a procedure in order to prevent civic uprising (*seditionis status civilitatis*) or any harm (*detrimentum*) to the church.[163]

To accomplish these ends – that is, to protect the city and the church – the choice of a successor was one that required "our consultation." Indeed, Odoacer's representative, Flavius Caecina Decius Maximus Basilius iunior, was an important person to consider, for he was one of the most prominent members of the powerful senatorial Decii family.[164] As I noted earlier, this family had aligned itself early on with Odoacer, and its political influence had increased under Odoacer's long reign (476–89/93). During the nine years of Felix's papacy, four of the highest offices – two praetorian prefectures of Italy and one or two urban prefectures of Rome – were bestowed on family members (see Tables 5.4.1 and 5.4.2).[165]

Given Simplicius's and Felix's desire to maintain good ties with Roman lay aristocrats, it is understandable why the *Scriptura of 483* also included stipulations about donations to the church that would have pleased wealthy donors. Up until this time, the policy had been one articulated by Leo I, Bishop of Rome. In a letter of October 20, 447, to the bishops of Sicily, Leo had limited the sale or transference of ecclesiastical property to allow it only if the bishop had consulted with the whole clergy and justified such a sale would be to the advantage of the church.[166] The bishop of Rome in 475, Simplicius, advanced Leo's policy by stipulating how revenues to the church were to be divided; he stipulated equal shares going to the bishop, to the clergy, to the upkeep of the churches, and to the poor.[167] Felix continued Simplicius's famous fourfold "Roman" division of the revenues, but he added restraints on the bishops regarding the sale or distribution of property and funds from urban or rural estates. These matters could not be alienated by the future bishop or by his successors. Limited sales of gems, furniture, and clothing were allowed if the money was to be used for the poor.[168]

---

[163] Sessa 2012, pp. 222–25; *Acta syn. DII* [sic] *MGH AA* 12, ed. Mommsen, p. 445.

[164] See note 162 above and Table 5.4.1.

[165] For the praetorian prefects of Italy, see Fl. Caecina Decius Maximus Basilius iunior, = Basilius 12, *PLRE* 2, p. 217, PPO in 483; and Caecina Mavortius Basilius Decius = Decius 2, *PLRE* 2, p. 349, PPO in 486 or before. For the urban prefect in 484, see Decius Marius Venantius Basilius = Basilius 13, *PLRE* 2, p. 218; and for a possible urban prefecture before 486, see Caecina Mavortius Basilius Decius = Decius 2, *PLRE* 2, p. 349.

[166] Leo, *Ep.* 17, *PL* 54, 704–6. See Sessa 2012, p. 227.

[167] Simplicius, *Ep.* 1.2, ed. Thiel, p. 176. See too Brown 2012, pp. 488–89.

[168] *Acta syn. DII* [sic] *MGH AA* 12, ed. Mommsen, pp. 445–46.

Simplicius was concerned about the salvation of the donor, as the *Scriptura* goes on to explain:

> For it is unjust and a form of sacrilege that those things [that] someone will have offered or left behind with certainty to help the venerable church's poor for the salvation or the repose of their souls would be transferred to another by those who are supposed to protect them most of all.[169]

The kinds of donations specified – lands or rents from urban or rural estates, along with gems, gold or silver objects, and precious clothes – indicate that these were gifts from wealthy donors. Certainly, such protections would have pleased senatorial aristocrats since they were concerned that their charitable gifts would be alienated and hence would reduce their salvific potential.[170]

The provisions of the *Scriptura of 483* – articulated by Simplicius and continued under Felix's papacy – show papal concern to reassure wealthy patrons about the uses of their gifts and to set additional restrictions on the financial dealings of bishops.[171] Simplicius had also been concerned about including lay elites in his succession plans. And like his predecessor, Felix turned to aristocratic supporters as he faced the demands of the eastern emperor Zeno and the patriarch of Constantinople, Acacius.

Aristocrats, Bishop Felix III, and the Acacian Schism

The immediate problem that Felix faced as he took office was pressure from the East to agree to a new formulation of Christology. As the controversy unfolded, Felix turned to lay aristocrats not only to serve as letter carriers but also to promote his position in the East as well as in the West.[172] Felix's reliance on aristocrats to explain his views to the laity and clergy in Rome and

---

[169] *Acta syn. DII* [sic] *MGH AA* 12, ed. Mommsen, pp. 445–446: *Iniquum est enim et sacrilegii instar, ut quae vel pro salute vel requie animarum suarum unusquisque venerabili ecclesiae pauperum causa contulerit aut certe reliquerit, ab his, quos hoc maxime servare convenerat, in alterum transferantur.* See too Symmachus, *Ep.* 6.2, ed. Thiel, p. 685.

[170] See Brown 2012, pp. 475–77, for fifth-century Rome.

[171] *Acta syn. DII* [sic] *MGH AA* 12, ed. Mommsen, p. 447. It is precisely these financial restrictions on bishops and the possible intervention of lay people in such determinations that aroused the concern articulated by bishop Laurentius of Milan at the Council of 502: *Cumque lecta fuissent, Laurentius episcopus Mediolanensis ecclesiae dixit: laico statuendi in ecclesia praeter papam Romanum habere aliquam potestatem.* And when those things were read, Laurence the bishop of the church of Milan said: "No one of the laity has any power to decide such matters concerning the church except the Roman pope."

[172] For a lucid description of the issues, see Moorhead 1992A, p. 36, and 35–39. The Council of Chalcedon has been the object of much scholarship, some of it cited by Moorhead, but see too Sotinel 2005, pp. 267–90, for a lucid discussion.

Italy, to Odoacer's court in Ravenna, and to the eastern court in Constantinople altered the balance of power between lay aristocrats and the clergy in Rome, further delaying the entry of aristocrats into episcopal office and limiting the influence of the clergy in civic matters.[173]

Felix's Response to the *Henotikon*. Because the bishop of Rome, Simplicius, had been ill for some time before his death in March 483, it fell to Felix to respond to the *Henotikon*, which had been drawn up by the patriarch of Constantinople, Acacius, but promulgated by the eastern emperor Zeno in July 482. The document, named "oneness," aimed to unify Christians who disagreed about the nature of Christ as promulgated in 451 by the ecumenical Council of Chalcedon. This council had argued for the two natures of Christ as human and divine, united within one hypostasis, or underlying reality, of the Divine Word, or *Logos*, which perfectly subsists in these natures. However, Christians had been divided in disagreement about this formulation after 451. The *Henotikon* had tried to bridge these differences, but the bishop of Rome was not comfortable with it for several reasons. First, the *Henotikon* carried with it an implicit condemnation of the views taken by the Council of Chalcedon by failing to take a position on whether Christ had one or two natures. Nor did this document mention Bishop Leo's famous defense of the Chalcedonians' view conveyed by his letter, known as the "Tome." On the contrary, the *Henotikon* condemned what is described as "other views," an assertion that seemed to condemn the 451 Council of Chalcedon's formulation about the nature of Christ. As Claire Sotinel has remarked, "It must have looked to the western church as an imperial attempt to change the faith without going through a church council."[174]

But the challenge to the papacy went beyond theology, for the emperor and the patriarch were seen as making a direct attack on papal disciplinary authority. Bishop Simplicius of Rome had recognized the pro-Chalcedonian John Talaia as Alexandrian patriarch and regarded as "perfidy" Acacius's support for Talaia's rival, Peter Mongus, who had been accused of horrible persecutions of pro-Chalcedonian Christians in Egypt.[175] With no permanent papal *apocrisiarius* in Constantinople to clarify matters, Simplicius had sent two angry letters to the patriarch Acacius and the emperor Zeno in protest before his death.[176]

---

[173] For the relations between the bishops of Rome and the court and patriarch in Constantinople, see Sotinel 2005, pp. 267–90.

[174] Sotinel 2005, pp. 269 and 267–290.

[175] For John Talaia's influence, see *PCBE* 2, 1062, Johannes Talaia, Johannes 9.

[176] Simplicius, *Ep.* 18 (to Acacius) and *Ep.* 19 (to Zeno), ed. Jaffé, Wittenbach, et al., *Regesta pontificum Romanorum*, 1956, pp. 586–89.

After his accession, Felix III sent letters to announce the event to the emperor Zeno and to assert his loyalty to the empire: "Let not your piety conceive that anyone loves you more sincerely than he who wishes that you have perpetual peace with God."[177] With this letter, Felix sent an embassy consisting of bishops to Constantinople to urge Zeno to respect the Chalcedonian settlement.[178] The embassy also carried copies to the patriarch Acacius, summoning him to appear before a synod in Rome to answer charges.[179] This was a forceful statement of papal rhetoric that was met with no response.

What happened to these bishops deterred Felix from relying on clergy as ambassadors again. The bishops Vitalis of Turentum and Misenus of Cumae were arrested, threatened, and then under force made to take communion with Acacius and the legates of the anti-Chalcedonian Alexandrian patriarch, Peter Mongus.[180] From the perspective of the bishop of Rome, this action corrupted his papal legates and negated their mission. But without a permanent papal representative in Constantinople, it took some time for Felix to even discover what had happened. He had to rely on questionable witnesses, in this case a group of pious monks, the so-called "Sleepless Monks" of Constantinople (*Akoimetai*), as his informants.[181] As soon as this embassy had returned to Rome, Felix convened a council of Italian bishops who in July 484 excommunicated Vitalis and Misenus and then excommunicated Acacius, patriarch of Constantinople, a condemnation that was soon reciprocated by Acacius.[182] It was a sign of how little the bishop of Rome could trust his own clergy that he sent the letter of excommunication with a church manager, a *defensor ecclesiae*, Tutus. But that approach failed since Tutus, like the bishops Vitalis and Misenus, was allegedly similarly corrupted, deposed, and excommunicated by a synod held in October 485 after he had returned to Rome.[183]

The schism continued through the eleven-year reign of Felix. Although Felix's extant letters to the eastern emperor show a gradual hardening of

---

[177] Felix III, *Ep.* 1.1 ed. Thiel, p. 223: *Nec existimet pietas tua, quod quisquam magis sincera mente te diligat, quam qui te pacem cum Deo vult habere perpetuam.* For this chapter, it matters little if the letters of Felix were penned by the bishop himself or by his deacon, the future bishop of Rome, Gelasius, as has been argued by others, including Ullmann, *Gelasius* 1981, pp. 135–41. There is no good reason to doubt Felix's abilities in this regard, and in any case, the letters represent Felix's official position whether he penned it personally or not.

[178] Felix III, *Ep.* 1, ed. Thiel, pp. 222–32.   [179] Felix III, *Ep.* 2, ed. Thiel, pp. 232–39.

[180] For an excellent discussion of the limits of communication and of the issues, see Blaudeau 2012, pp. 235–82.

[181] Evagrius, *HE* 3.21.   [182] Felix III, *Ep.* 6, 7, 10, ed. Thiel, pp. 243–47, 251–2.

[183] Felix III, *Ep.* 11, 12, ed. Thiel, pp. 252–59. On the position of the *defensor ecclesiae*, see Frakes 2001, p. 184; and Jones, 1964, p. 911.

feeling, the bishop continued to write to the emperor to take a stand in favor of the apostle Peter instead of the "perfidious" Peter Mongus.[184] Of the eighteen extant letters of Felix, four were written to Emperor Zeno directly, dating from 483 through early 490 (*Letters* 1, 4, 8, and 15). Felix also wrote a letter, not extant, to the new emperor Anastasius upon his accession in 491.[185] This correspondence shows Felix seeking avenues to maintain lines of communication with the eastern court. However, he persisted in his position and told the new emperor that he should "learn the holy teachings from the stewards [of the Church], not to teach them [the holy teachings]"; Felix was polite but forceful in his recommendation that the emperor "bow in pious devotion."[186]

Felix's restraint demonstrated in his letters to the emperor is strikingly different from his biting, harsh stance in his correspondence with the patriarch of Constantinople, Acacius, to whom he directed four letters and three edicts.[187] For example, in *Letter* 6, Felix recounts Acacius's many transgressions and condemns his "haughty pride" (*superbia*).[188] Felix's hostility toward the patriarch revolved in part around the disciplinary threat to his own authority over his bishops. Felix had been scandalized by the corruption of his bishops Misenus and Vitalis because, as he had written to the emperor, they were not just the bearers of papal letters but also were to be regarded as taking the place of the bishop of Rome as if he himself were present.[189] Because Felix viewed the corruption of his legates as a direct attack by Acacius on the person and authority of the bishop of Rome, his anger was intensely personal. The severity of this transgression is underscored as well by the propapal *Book of the Popes*; in the *Life of Felix*, the outrageous attack on papal legates is given prominence by

---

[184] Felix III, *Ep.* 8, ed. Thiel, 250, pp. 247–50.

[185] Gelasius, *Ep.* 10, ed. Thiel, cited as Felix III, *Ep.* 21, ed. Thiel, p. 284.

[186] Felix III, *Ep.* 8, ed. Thiel, p. 250: *et sacrosancta per eorum praesules discere potius quam docere . . . Deus voluit clementiam tuam piae devotionis colla submittere.* I do not concur with Meier 2015, 28, that Felix is here making an "absolute demand for the superiority of the bishop over the secular ruler." Rather, Felix's letter is limited to the theological issue at hand.

[187] Felix III, *Ep.* 2, 3, 6, 7, ed. Thiel, pp. 232–40, 243–47; and three edicts/*libelli* directed against Acacius (*Ep.* 4, ed. Thiel, pp. 240–42, directed to Zeno; *Ep.* 7, ed. Thiel, p. 247 = Edict of 481; *Ep.* 13, ed. Thiel, pp. 259–66 = *Exemplar gestorum*, of 487 CE).

[188] Felix III, *Ep.* 6, ed. Thiel, p. 243.

[189] Felix III, *Ep.* 1.1, ed. Thiel, p. 223: *legatio mitteretur, qui non tam bajuli specie ista deferent, quam meam vicem peragentes me quodammodo vobis facerent esse praesentem. Per hos, igitur velut cominus honorificentiae tuae junctus coloquiis precor, ut supplicationem meam benignus auribus sicut princeps Christianus accipias.* ("A legation was sent, which carried those letters, appearing not so much as letter carriers as much as executing my part in such a way as to make me present to you. Through these men, therefore, as if I am nearby joined to your honor, I beseech you in these conversations so that you, as a Christian emperor, listen favorably and accept my supplication.")

granting it and the Acacian Schism some eleven of the seventeen lines of this bishop's life in the text published by Louis Duchesne.[190]

Aristocrats as Papal Ambassadors. The failure of his bishops and his *defensor ecclesiae* to remain faithful, along with the loss of a permanent papal *apocrisiarius* in Constantinople, convinced Felix to turn to lay aristocrats to advance his position before the eastern court. Other bishops may have used aristocrats for such missions, but the circumstances here made Felix rely on them not only as carriers but also as advocates.[191] In 489, Felix turned to the Roman senator Andromachus, a *vir illustris*, who was going on a mission to Constantinople.[192] As we are later told in a letter by the then bishop of Rome, Gelasius, Andromachus [in 489] had been "copiously instructed by us [Gelasius, then deacon to Felix] to encourage Acacius once he had laid aside his inflexibility."[193] Upon his return to Rome, Andromachus was made to bear witness under oath that he had delivered this message without being corrupted.[194] He passed the test.

But Andromachus's role had not ended, for he must have brought to Rome the arguments of the emperor and the patriarch. We know that he did because a very precise refutation of these arguments has survived in the *Avellana Collection* of papal and imperial letters, the *Gesta de nomine Acacii*. As Philippe Blaudeau demonstrated well, the unknown authors of this document – of which sections survive in other papal letter collections – most likely prepared this reply within the papal establishment under Felix to respond to the charges made by Constantinople in 489.[195] The *Gesta* underscores the importance that the papacy placed on persuading the eastern emperor and the patriarch of the validity of Rome's position. Rather than its eastern audience, however, I want here to highlight the political context in which such a document had likely been prepared. The *Gesta* also had a local audience; clergy as well as lay aristocrats had to be persuaded of the validity of papal opposition to the emperor and the patriarch of Constantinople. Indeed, since the lay aristocrats were acting as ambassadors for the bishop of Rome, their support for his position was critical. And since lay aristocrats were also the administrators of Italy, they played a critical role in ensuring

---

[190] *Lib. Pont.* 50, ed. Duchesne, 1981, p. 252, line 4–14 of 17 lines.

[191] It is indicative of the political situation that Felix also relied on lay aristocrats to send messages to bishops in the West; for example, Felix sent a letter for the bishop of Merida with a Spanish *clarissimus*, Terentianus. See Felix III, *Ep.* 5, Thiel, p. 242. For Terentianus, see *PLRE* 2, p. 1058.

[192] The ruler on behalf of whom Andromachus intervened in 489 was Odoacer; see *PLRE* 2, 89, Andromachus 3, and Moorhead 1992A, 200.

[193] Gelasius, *Ep.* 10.7, ed. Thiel, p. 346. Translation by Neil and Allen, 2014, p. 113.

[194] Gelasius, *Ep.* 10.7, ed. Thiel, pp. 346–47.

[195] Blaudeau 2012, pp. 45–49. The *Gesta de nomine Acacii* is CA 99, Guenther, Part I, pp. 440–53.

papal independence. Hence, aristocrats were key to the relationship between the papacy and the Constantinopolitan court.

As the schism wore on, Bishop Felix and his successors "had to find new ways to legitimate their disagreement with the religious policy of the East and to uphold the authority of the Roman See."[196] The focus on local support may explain why the *Gesta* was augmented and used for a subsequent senatorial embassy headed by the former consul Flavius Anicius Probus Faustus Niger that included the *vir illustris* Irenaeus; this embassy was most likely sent in the early months of the papacy of Gelasius, in 492–93, on behalf of the new king of Italy, Theoderic.[197] This same embassy was given a formal set of instructions, a *commonitorium*, by the then Bishop of Rome, Gelasius, to explain his position to the new emperor, Anastasius, and carried instructions from Theoderic to reopen discussions about legitimating his rule. However, it failed on both counts.[198]

Bishop Gelasius of Rome and the Aristocracy. At the beginning of his papacy under King Theoderic, Gelasius (492–96) continued to strongly oppose Acacius, even demanding that Acacius's name be removed from church records.[199] He, like Felix, relied on lay aristocrats as political advocates and involved them in ecclesiastical politics. Those practices likely explain not only the composition of the embassy noted above but also why in 495 Gelasius allowed a lay aristocratic contingent to sit alongside the clergy at the council that pardoned Bishop Misenus and to sign the decision. The document includes the names along with ranks of such important men as the highly ranked illustrious senator Amandianus and the outstanding senator (*vir spectabilis*) Diogenianus.[200]

Gelasius's acquiescence to the decision to pardon Bishop Misenus and his action to go against his predecessor's excommunication of this man has perplexed several scholars. Since Gelasius had taken a strong stand against Acacius and had been one of Felix's deacons, it is assumed that he must have agreed with Felix's earlier excommunication of this bishop.[201] Gelasius's

---

[196] Sotinel 2005, p. 269.

[197] Gelasius, *Ep.* 12, ed. Thiel, p. 312. For Flavius Anicius Probus Faustus iunior Niger, see Faustus 9, *PLRE* 2, pp. 454–56. For Irenaeus, see Irenaeus 4, *PLRE* 2, p. 625. For the reuse of the *Gesta de nomine Acacii*, see Blaudeau 2012, pp. 46–49. For this embassy, see Moorhead 1992A, pp. 35–39.

[198] Gelasius, *Ep.* 10, ed. Thiel, pp. 341–48, is a formal *commonitorium*. See too Anon. Val. 12.5.7: *Theodericus enim in legationem direxerat Faustum Nigrum ad Zenonem* (sic); the emperor was in fact Anastasius (491–518).

[199] Gelasius, *Ep.* 12.9, ed. Thiel, pp. 356–57.

[200] Gelasius, *Ep.* 30, ed. Thiel, p. 437 = *CA* 103, Guenther, Part I, p. 474. See Amandianus 1, *PLRE* 2, p. 66, and Diogenianus 3, *PLRE* 2, p. 36.

[201] Demacopoulos 2013, pp. 80–82.

pardon points again to friction on a local level. Felix's excommunication of Misenus had not been acceptable to most of the Italian bishops and suggests a growing dissatisfaction within the clergy and the aristocracy with the papal separation from the eastern court and patriarch. The bishop's pardon underscores how, as George Demacopoulos has argued, Gelasius, despite his rhetorical bluster, was in a relatively weak position. Bishop Gelasius may have had no choice but to acquiesce to the decision of this council, composed as it was of powerful lay aristocrats and Italian bishops.[202]

Gelasius, Felix's former deacon, was not as successful in maintaining the support of senatorial aristocrats as Felix had been. Gelasius had alienated a certain number of them with his attack on traditional Roman practices.[203] He famously tried to stop the celebration of the Roman holiday of the Lupercalia, a pagan celebration in honor of the origins of Rome. In taking this action, the bishop faced opposition from Christian Roman senators, including the same senator noted above who had served as envoy, Andromachus, now seen as patron of the celebration that was defended as a Roman tradition.[204] Gelasius's letter may have even been provoked by some adulterous priest involved with an aristocratic woman, for the scandal had made the rounds of those Romans who sat in judgment "at home"; his letter attacked lay Christians who saw the continued celebration of the Lupercalia as part of Roman tradition.[205] But we have no idea if Bishop Gelasius was actually able to stop this celebration, another sign of the limits of papal authority.[206] His failure to ensure a peaceful papal succession is a further sign that ecclesiastical elites should concern themselves with maintaining good relations with the aristocracy. Indeed, Gelasius, like Felix, could maintain his autonomy from the eastern emperor and patriarch due, in no small part, to the ongoing support of Christian senatorial aristocrats and the willingness of Arian military kings, first Odoacer and then Theoderic, to remain removed from papal theological disputes.

---

[202] Demacopoulos 2013, pp. 80–82.

[203] For his high-handed remarks that alienated the Senate and senators, see Gelasius, *Ep.* 10.2, which Neil and Allen 2014, p. 110, capture beautifully in their translation: "However, it is up to the Senate of Rome to see that the commemoration of the faith, which it is mindful of having received from its ancestors, should shun the infection of communion with outsiders, lest it be put outside communion with this apostolic see (heaven forbid!)."

[204] See the discussion by Neil and Allen 2014, p. 209, for bibliography.

[205] Neil and Allen 2014, p. 211; for the Latin, see *CA* 100, ed. Guenther, Part I, pp. 453–64. Demacopoulos 2013, pp. 74–80, suggests that Gelasius was focusing on the clergy, but the opening clearly addresses Andromachus and Romans, even in their homes.

[206] This has been observed by several scholars, including Demacopulos 2013, pp. 74–80 and Cameron 2011 p. 170.

472: What Difference Did It Make?

The resilience of senatorial aristocrats in alliance with the military had allowed Romans to restore their city and reconstitute their world in the last decades of the fifth century. But political change had been necessary. In the wake of 472, many senatorial aristocrats had become aware that it was no longer desirable to have a resident western emperor. The shared rulership model was no longer effective in securing their "things." Long periods without a resident western emperor had demonstrated that the Senate and its senators could oversee Rome and Italy. What aristocrats needed was a strong military with whom to work to provide protection from other, predominantly Germanic, military forces and from unwanted eastern imperial interference. Nonetheless, many western senatorial aristocrats sought to maintain contact with the eastern court in Constantinople. They were even willing to express their allegiance to the emperor – at a distance. Thus, the removal of a resident western emperor did not signal the "decline and fall of the Roman Empire" to the inhabitants of Rome.

In the wake of the civil war of 472, senatorial aristocrats were able to retain and even augment their hold on high civic office. And acting as envoys on behalf of new military generals, they played pivotal political roles in negotiating a new order without competition from eastern imperial officials. New senators, also eager for civic office, were again attracted to Rome in these years. The city and the new political order offered opportunities for established senatorial aristocrats to restore their familial and patronage networks that had been disrupted by the civil war. A decade of peace under Odoacer also allowed these old families the opportunity to recover their economic losses.

Rome's population had declined after 472, but it certainly did not vanish in 476, as Edward Gibbon was well aware. When the western emperor Nepos died in exile in 480, the senators had already been at work rebuilding Rome for some eight years. Odoacer, who chose to remove himself and his court to Ravenna, acknowledged the dominant role of the senatorial aristocracy in the city. In the absence of a resident western emperor, senatorial aristocrats rose to increased political prominence not only in the city but also in service to Odoacer's government and as intermediaries to the eastern court.

Bishop Felix's attempts to maintain the support of senatorial aristocrats reflected the new political realities in Italy. Like Odoacer, Felix turned to Roman senatorial aristocrats in his struggles with the eastern emperor and patriarch as well as with local clergy. This strategy had worked well for this bishop since he had strong personal ties to several elite families to whom he turned. Felix's willingness to engage lay aristocrats so directly in ecclesiastical politics provided an important avenue for them to influence the church without taking up clerical careers, as had happened earlier elsewhere in the West.[207]

This alliance between senatorial aristocrats and the clergy in Rome, and between senatorial aristocrats and the military elites located in Ravenna – all at a distance from the Eastern emperor and the patriarch – resulted in more than a decade of recovery. Senators returned to their traditional modes of life, competing for office and honor during this period of restoration in the late fifth century. The challenge of another military contender for control of Italy would lead to a change in government, but it would not undermine the equilibrium that Roman aristocrats had found. Only the direct intervention of the eastern emperor Justinian would bring on the next major crisis that would threaten the survival of Rome.

[207] See my discussion in Chapter 6.

6

The Fall of Ostrogothic Rome and the Justinianic Reconstruction

[Fulgentius saw] the noble appearance of the Roman Senate and the varied ranks of the aristocracy, each with its own distinctive insignia. Hearing with his inexperienced ears the acclamations of a free people, he recognized the nature of the glories of this world. But he was not willing to recognize anything worthwhile in the spectacle, nor did he let himself be tempted by the useless seduction of earthly frivolity. Rather, he was inspired mostly by the aspiration to possess the happiness of the celestial Jerusalem. To his companions, who were standing near him, [Fulgentius] exclaimed the following words: "How beautiful must be the heavenly Jerusalem if the earthly Rome thus shines. And if in this world one can accord so much honor to those who love vanity, then how much this honor and glory and peace will be elevated to the saints who live contemplating truth."

—Ferrandus, *Life of Fulgentius*, dated to Theoderic's Entry into Rome in 500.[1]

The holy man Fulgentius was impressed, as his biographer Ferrandus observed in the epigraph to this chapter, by "how much honor and glory and peace" were manifested by the Senate and Rome's senatorial aristocracy in 500. The "Indian Summer" that the Italo-Roman elite and Senate had enjoyed under Odoacer (476–89/93) continued during the reign of his

---

[1] Ferrandus, *Vita S. Fulgentii* 9, ed. Lapeyre, p. 79: *Romanae curiae nobilitatem, decus ordinemque distinctis decoratam gradibus exspectaret, et favores liberi populi castis auribus audiens, qualis esset huius saeculi gloriosa pompa cognosceret. Neque tamen in hoc spectaculo aliquid libenter intuitur, nec nugis illis saecularibus superflua illectus delectatione consensit: sed inde potius ad illam supernae civitatis Hierusalem desiderandam felicitatem vehementer exarsit, salubri disputatione praesentes sic admonens: Fratres, quam speciosa potest Hierusalem coelestis, si sic fulget Roma terrestris. Et si in hoc saeculo datur tanti honoris dignitas diligentibus vanitatem, qualis honor et gloria et pax praestabitur sanctis contemplantibus veritatem?* Translation adapted from Eno, p. 25.

successor, the Ostrogothic king Theoderic (489/93–526).[2] Senators were honored in a city that was thriving under the regime of this king who, like his predecessor, relied on the Senate and individual senators not merely to validate but also to administer the government of Rome and Italy.

This peaceful prosperity had been disrupted by the warfare that had led to the fall of Odoacer. Theoderic arrived in Italy to remove Odoacer from power at the direction of the eastern emperor Zeno (474–75, 476–91).[3] After Odoacer's two defeats in battles in northern Italy near the River Sontius and again near Verona in late September 489, Rome's senators refused Odoacer safe harbor when he attempted to return to the city.[4] Theoderic's victories, coupled with his threats to seize their properties and remove their legal rights, had persuaded them to abandon Odoacer.[5] After another major defeat in 490 near the Adda River in modern Lombardy, Odoacer retreated to Ravenna, where he withstood a siege for the next three years.[6] A negotiated settlement in 493 with the promise of shared rule did not last. Theoderic accused Odoacer of treachery and murdered him, allegedly with his own hands, within weeks of Odoacer's surrender.[7]

---

[2] For the reign of Theoderic as an "Indian Summer" for the Italo-Roman senatorial aristocracy, see La Rocca 1993, pp. 454–55; Marazzi 2016, p. 106. I thank Hendrik Dey for calling to my attention this source for this metaphor.

[3] This was the arrangement made in 488 CE; see *Anon. Val.* 11 (49); Jord. *Get.* 290 ff.; Procop. *Wars* 5.1.10–11. For the agreement between Zeno and Theoderic, see Moorhead 1992A, pp. 17–19. Zeno had two primary reasons for his actions; he had never recognized Odoacer's rule in Italy and tensions were increasing in 488 with the western ruler's claims to territory. In addition, by sending Theoderic's Ostrogothic army from the Balkans, Zeno put an end to his demands for more land and money.

[4] Paul the Deacon, *Hist. rom.* 15.16: *Theodoricus uero dum ipso impetu subsequitur fugientes, Veronam ilico pauore ciuibus consternatis inuadit. Odouacer autem cum his qui euaserant fugiens Romam contendit, sed obseratis continuo portis exclusus est. Qui dum sibi denegari introitum cerneret, omnia quaeque adtingere potuit gladio flammisque consumpsit.* As far as I am aware, Paul is our only source for this Roman moment in the war. For these events, see Caliri 2017, pp. 153–55.

[5] Enn. *Vita Epiph.* 122: *Interea subita animum praestantissimi regis Theoderici deliberatio occupa-vit, ut illis tantum Romanae libertatis ius tribueret, quos partibus ipsius fides examinata inuxisset; illos vero, quos aliqua necessitas diuiserat, ab omni iussit et testandi et ordinationum suarum ac voluntatum licentia submoueri. Qua sententia promulgata et legibus circa plurimos tali lege calcatis universa Italia lamentabili iustitio subiacebat.* Cesa 1988, p. 189 points out that only this text and the *Ancedoton Holderi* transmit the information that Theoderic had threatened this action against those property owners and senators who supported Odoacer.

[6] *Anon. Val.* 11 (50–53); Jord. *Get.* 292 ff; Enn. *Vita Epiph.* 109–11. For a detailed account with summary of movements, see Theoderic 7, *PLRE* 2, p. 1082.

[7] *Anon. Val.* 11 (55), wrongly dates this to 491.

The demise of Odoacer, although bloody, had not greatly harmed Roman senatorial aristocrats. Most had thrown their support to Theoderic early on. In 490, the eminent Roman senatorial aristocrat Flavius Rufius Postumius Festus had traveled to Constantinople as part of a senatorial embassy to the emperor Zeno to request full recognition of Theoderic's rule in Italy. Unfortunately, Zeno died before Festus and the other senators were able to fulfill their task, and Zeno's successor, the new eastern emperor Anastasius (491–518), was reluctant to grant this request. But that mattered little when, upon the death of Odoacer in 493, Theoderic's army proclaimed him "king of Italy."[8] Only in 497 did Anastasius finally agree to the request of the senatorial envoy Flavius Anicius Probus Faustus iunior Niger to fully recognize Theoderic's "presumption of rule" (*praesumptio regni*). Anastasius sent back with Niger "all the ornaments of the palace which Odoacer had sent to Constantinople."[9] Although the beginning date and the precise status of Theoderic's position remain open to some scholarly debate, there is general consensus that Theoderic exercised his rule over the inhabitants of Italy, dating either to his defeat of Odoacer in 489 or to his election as king by his Gothic army in 493, and received full recognition of his authority by the eastern emperor after 498.[10]

Theoderic's visit to Rome in 500 was thus a significant event that demonstrated this king's good relations with Roman senatorial aristocrats and the Senate.[11] As an Arian Christian, Theoderic's visit also offered him the opportunity to advertise his good relations with the papacy. Until the end of his rule, he maintained this relationship by pursuing a broad policy of religious toleration.[12] The peaceful prosperity of Rome and Italy during these decades was possible because of the equilibrium Theoderic reached with the Senate and the church. However, key to maintaining this balance was the Italo-Roman senatorial aristocracy.

Rome under the Ostrogothic Kings Theoderic and Athalaric
(489/93–534)

Like his predecessor Odoacer, Theoderic turned to the Senate and to individual senatorial aristocrats to oversee the civic administration of Rome and

---

[8] *Anon. Val.* 12 (57). For Flavius Rufius Postumius Festus, see Festus 5, *PLRE* 2, pp. 467–69.

[9] *Anon. Val.* 12 (64). Presumably, Odoacer had sent them back to Constantinople when he assumed control of Italy in 476. For this senator as Flavius Anicius Probus Faustus iunior Niger, see Faustus 9, *PLRE* 2, pp. 454–56 and not Festus 5, as did *PLRE* 2, pp. 467–69. On this, see Radtki 2016, p. 131.

[10] For discussion of the scholarship on this, see Heydemann 2016, pp. 21–22.

[11] Arnold 2017, pp. 113–26; and for a positive view of his reign, Arnold 2014.

[12] On the King's religious tolerance see Cohen 2016, pp. 510–21.

Italy, to implement his policies, and to negotiate with the eastern court. In return, Theoderic protected the estates of Roman senatorial aristocrats, brought peace to the peninsula, and offered Roman aristocrats prestigious civic offices not only in Rome and Italy but also at the king's court in Ravenna. Over the three decades of Theoderic's rule (489/93–526) and in the subsequent decade under his successors, Athalaric and Theodahad (526–36), Roman senatorial aristocrats thus dominated the city of Rome and reaped the rewards of peace. The church, too, was influenced by their interventions.

Appointments to High Office and the Senate under the Ostrogothic Kings

Theoderic followed the practices of earlier Roman emperors in using appointments to high civic office to secure loyalty. Indeed, as one anonymous late Roman author observed, "Theoderic ordered that the civil service should function as under the emperors."[13] This policy was exactly what the senatorial aristocracy of Italy desired, for they wanted now, as earlier, to attain the highest offices that would bring them the status of *illustris*. This rank bestowed not just the greatest prestige but also real privileges that had economic as well as legal and political consequences, such as protection from certain forms of taxation and physical punishment.[14] Under the Ostrogoths the same titles designating specific offices granted the status of illustrious senator (*illustris*) as they had under Odoacer: consul, praetorian prefect, urban prefect of Rome, quaestor of the sacred palace (*quaestor sacrii palatii*), master of the household (*magister officiorum*), count of the imperial treasury (*comes sacrarum largitionum*), and count of the private fortune (*comes rei privatae*), and count of patrimony (*comes patrimonii nostri*).[15] Although most of the titles remained the same, M. Shane Bjornlie is right to observe that "there [was] a tendency for high ministers of the Palatine bureaucracy to exercise broader administrative powers than might have been the case in a traditional Roman administration."[16] For example, although the master of the household (*magister officiorum*) formally held authority over the public post (the *cursus publicus*), the praetorian prefect and a Gothic official called a *saio* often assumed this duty in practice.[17] Moreover, under the Ostrogothic regime, the praetorian

---

[13] *Anon. Val.* 12 (60): *militiam sicut sub principes esse praecepit.* See too Brown 1984, pp. 25–27.

[14] On the benefits of senatorial status, and especially *illustris* status, see also Chapter 2, especially notes 164 and 238, and my discussion below, notes 27, 28, and 30.

[15] Schäfer 1991; Henning 1999; Radtki 2016, p. 128.   [16] Bjornlie 2016, p. 63.

[17] For the *magister officiorum* see Cass. *Var.* 6.6; for the *cursus publicus*, see *Var.* 4–47; 5.5; 11.2; 11.14; 12.15, 12.18.

prefect had broad control over legal and financial personnel, so he oversaw tasks that would have earlier fallen to other officials. For example, the praetorian prefect directed his assistants to administer the grain supply in Rome more directly, a responsibility that had previously been largely under the purview of the urban prefect.[18]

There were also new opportunities for ambitious senators to serve at the Ostrogothic court in Ravenna. In fact, all but the offices of consul, praetorian prefect, and urban prefect required a senator's presence there. This condition meant that established senatorial aristocrats as well as upwardly mobile Italo-Roman civic elites would be engaged at court in Ravenna, developing personal ties with the Gothic elites in these cities. This situation as well as the declining size of empire and contracted economy would have naturally also had some impact on the Senate, which was no doubt smaller than it had been in the early fifth century. Nonetheless, although a few Goths and Gauls are known as *illustres* and members of the Senate, and there may have been others whom we do not know by name, the Senate remained the central institutionalized focus of Italo-Romans and their aristocratic political life in the early sixth century.[19]

Theoderic's continued reliance on Italo-Roman senatorial aristocrats to govern Italy, including them as well in high civic positions at the Amal court, seems to have pleased many men and women. Aspiring senators could even aim for the consulship or the lofty title of *patrician* under his watch. In 498, when the emperor Anastasius officially recognized Theoderic, he granted the imperial right to nominate one of the two annual consuls and to grant the title of *patrician* (which was by and large given to men of *illustris* rank).[20] The system for holding office that evolved under Theoderic still allowed Italo-Roman elites to retain power and prestige and to compete for honor without facing eastern imperial officials as rivals, as had been true in the past. But the situation was complicated. Fortunately, we have an excellent guide to these changes.

---

[18] Cass. *Var.* 6.18.

[19] Radtki 2016, p. 217 note 41 sees a far smaller number of senators because she relies on Schäfer 1991, pp. 9–117, who counts 110 names of *illustres* senators for the period 490–540. Unfortunately, Schäfer includes men whose dates are no longer secure in light of the redating of the Colosseum inscriptions by Orlandi 2004, especially pp. 545–50. There is simply not enough epigraphic evidence to provide a reliable quantitative answer to how many senators there were in Ostrogothic Rome, as observed as well by La Rocca and Oppedisano 2016, pp. 187–88.

[20] Heather 2018, p. 22; and Heather 1996, pp. 215–21. Miller and Sarris 2018, p. 688 assert that this was the right of the Senate to appoint the western consul, but the norm was for the Senate to validate the recommendation of the King; see La Rocca and Oppedisano 2016, pp. 111–17.

The *Variae* of Cassiodorus and the Role of the Senate in Appointments.
We are well informed about the workings of the Senate of Rome, about the
roles of individual senators, and a great deal more about the court of
Theoderic and his successor Athalaric in large part due to the evidence
provided by Cassiodorus's published letters, the *Variae*. Cassiodorus, who
himself was from an established Italo-Roman senatorial family with large
estates in Bruttium, served as quaestor of the sacred palace (*quaestor sacri
Palatii*) from 507 to 511. His legal duties entailed the drafting of edicts and
laws and ultimately led him to the position of master of the household
(*magister officiorum*) beginning in 524 at the court of Theoderic in
Ravenna.[21] Cassiodorus continued in that role until 528 for Theoderic's
successor, King Athalaric (526–34), before attaining the position of praetorian prefect of Italy (533–40).[22] He published a selection of his letters from his
time in office, although scholars continue to debate the exact date of their
publication, favoring the period between 537 and 540, before the fall of
Ravenna to the Byzantines, or the period after 540, when Cassiodorus was
in exile in Constantinople.[23] Regardless of the precise date of publication, the
collection was a product of the first stage of the war between the Ostrogoths
and Byzantines that dragged on from 535 to 554.

The *Variae* offer a direct commentary on sixth-century elite society from
an insider's perspective. But this unique position can itself cause problems of
interpretation. For example, Cassiodorus does not explain what he knows his
contemporary readers knew about the processes of senatorial election. More
importantly, he shaped the collection to suit his aims. Cassiodorus's *Variae*,
for instance, emphasize how much the Ostrogothic kings respected the
Senate's prestige and authority. He advertised their good relations with the
Senate to demonstrate that Theoderic and Athalaric possessed the traditional
virtues of a good ruler – prudence, restraint, and *civilitas*.[24] As such,
Cassiodorus showed how Theoderic followed the advice of the eastern
emperor Anastasius (491–518) "to love the Senate" (Cass. *Var.* 1.1.3: *ut diligam
senatum*). Consequently, it should not be surprising that most of the letters
to the Senate show Theoderic and Athalaric seeking approval for their
nominees to high office. Although there is no evidence in Cassiodorus's
letters that the Senate denied any candidates, they still possessed the right to

[21] Cass. *Var.* 1.12 and Bjornlie 2016, p. 60.

[22] For the career of Cassiodorus, see Cassiodorus 4, *PLRE* 2, pp. 265–69.

[23] For the dating but arguing for a date after 540, see Bjornlie 2017, pp. 533–48, and Giardina 2006,
pp. 15–25. I will use the term Byzantine to describe the Eastern Romans, following the arguments
of Amory 1997, pp. XV–XVI.

[24] Radtki 2016, p. 130; Bjornlie 2013, pp. 147–59.

do so, and they could also delay approval. The relative infrequency of conflict over nominations in the *Variae* is no doubt indicative of the information that Cassiodorus selected to publish.[25] The appointment process outlined by the *Variae* shows kings and the Senate working together harmoniously on the whole. On the other hand, the fact that the names of candidates had to be approved by the Senate meant that this body exercised real influence on the king. And certainly, many of the names advanced for appointment were the result of private negotiations and recommendations that senators as well as Gothic intermediaries had conveyed to the king.[26]

Ranking Senators. Unlike the Senate in Constantinople, which was so tied to the emperor that it came to function as part of the imperial advisory council (the consistory), the Senate in Rome under the Ostrogoths, as the *Variae* make clear, maintained a certain degree of independence from the king. We see this, for instance, in their avoidance of paying taxes, in their abovementioned role in approving the admission of men and the children of senators into the Senate, and in their resistance to certain royal initiatives.[27] Moreover, since in Rome, unlike Constantinople, the Senate's members all had the right to speak, we can see another reason why this body allowed more room for political negotiations and the exercise of power.[28]

As Adolfo LaRocca and Fabrizio Oppedisano have demonstrated, we can identify at least five ways in which senators came to be active in the western Senate at the time of the Ostrogothic kings: the "most outstanding" (*clarissimi*) and "respectable" (*spectabiles*) of senatorial birth, who entered the Senate when they had reached adulthood; new men of these ranks brought into the Senate by the king through a *relatio in senatu*, or request of the king; men new to *spectabilis* rank, who had attained that rank by holding those few offices that gave them direct access into the Senate; *illustres* of senatorial birth, who had entered the Senate as *clarissimi* and then were elevated to

---

[25] Cass. *Var.* 4.29 and 3.33 are rare instances where the king had to intervene directly to bring about his appointment of Armentarius and his son.

[26] La Rocca and Oppedisano 2016, pp. 63–92; Moorhead 1992, pp. 144–58.

[27] Cass. *Var.* 2.24 on taxation. I thank Shane Bjornlie for this suggestion. See Cass. *Var.* 4.29 for resistance to appointment, and 3.31 on resistance over the spoliation of buildings. On the approval of the children of senators based likely on census information, see the arguments of La Rocca and Oppedisano 2016, pp. 145–68.

[28] For the Constantinopolitan senate, see Dagron 1974, pp. 119–46, based on the *Digest* 1.9.12; and see Burgarella 2001, pp. 121–75, both of whom think the Senate in Constantinople and Rome only had *illustres,* as do many scholars, including Jones 1964, p. 529. But La Rocca and Oppedisano 2016, pp. 63–92 demonstrate that the Senate in Rome had men of all ranks, as did the Senate in Constantinople.

illustres by holding high office or by being granted an honorary appointment; and finally, new men who entered the Senate directly by virtue of having attained an office that bestowed *illustris* rank. And just as in the second half of the fifth century, these men had their fiscal residence in Rome.[29]

Nonetheless, in this hierarchal institution, there were distinctions even among the most powerful senators. A wealthy, established senatorial family gave an aspiring senator distinct advantages. Sons of prominent senatorial aristocratic families were able to advance to high office quickly at a young age and could more easily rise to lead the Senate and the state, while others received honorary appointments and were not as politically engaged as their peers. After them were senators of more recent senatorial rank; here we find the offspring of officials who had served Odoacer and Theoderic faithfully and had thus attained *illustris* rank. The lower level of the *illustres* were new men who had served the king at court in Ravenna and who generally entered the Senate later in life. Although these status distinctions among senators are not always clear to the modern eye, they nonetheless were relevant to contemporaries. They also strengthened the Senate's sense of corporate identity that so impressed the holy man Fulgentius, as observed by his biographer in the epigraph to this chapter.

One attested manifestation of senatorial influence in this hierarchical institution was the order of speaking in the Senate. Those of the highest rank spoke first, a privilege that had real consequences and was often decisive in senatorial decision making.[30] The *Variae* indicate that the urban prefect had the right to speak first (*Var.* 6.4.14), even if this same magistracy was also the presiding head of the Senate (*Var.* 1.42.15). From the Ostrogothic period on we have evidence of a second leading senator, the *caput Senatus*, or *prior Senatus*, whom we can consider the "most illustrious" member of the Senate. He was entitled to speak next, after the urban prefect.[31] This order is clear, too, as Pierfrancesco Porena has recently shown, because the *caput Senatus* was listed first in the ranks of senators in the official senatorial record.[32] After him, other *illustres* spoke, followed by the senators in lower ranks and years; thus, the oldest of *spectabile* rank, the *rector decuriarum*, would go first, then

---

[29] La Rocca and Oppedisano 2016, p. 181, and Cass. *Var.* 2.15,2.16, 6.10, 6.11.

[30] See, for example, Symm. *Rel.* 23.12.13; Chastagnol 1960, p. 69; and La Rocca and Oppedisano 2016, pp. 182–83.

[31] *Anon. Val.* 11 (53) and 15 (92); *Lib. Pont.* 53.5, ed. Duchesne 1981, p. 260 (*caput Senatus*); Ennod. *Conc. Didasc.* 19 (*curiae principatus*). Stein 1920, pp. 235–38 suggests that this office had more extended authority in this period, but that is not evidenced by our sources. See Chapter 4, note 222 and La Rocca and Oppedisano 2016, pp. 181–82.

[32] Porena 2019, pp. 25–50.

other *spectabiles*.[33] That even a *clarissimus* like Armentarius or a *spectabilis* like Capuanus could speak in the Senate, although both had the king's direct support, indicates the ways in which even those of low senatorial rank could exercise political influence.[34]

Birth was another key to status. Those who were senatorial by birth, the "seedbed of the senatorial order," as it were – belonging to the old Roman senatorial aristocracy – were often among the wealthiest and most powerful men in the Senate. Their families, whose members we have been discussing over the course of this study, had accrued means and clients over the centuries. Their sons were born into senatorial status.[35] Although some of these families had died out, and those that were not politically active may have simply retreated to their estates, the active members of these families had to claim fiscal residence in Rome and they also retained their ties to the city of Rome, as evidenced in such public monuments as the seating inscriptions in the Colosseum. These established families – the Decii, the Anicii, and the Symmachi – could trace their roots to the later third or fourth century. They took leading roles in Rome and Italy, working closely with the Ostrogothic king, and are thus attested best in our sources. After them were more recent senatorial families, as that of Cassiodorus himself, whose senatorial standing can be traced back to the mid fifth-century emperor Valentinian III.[36] They, too, willingly offered their services to the Ostrogothic king and court in Ravenna. Yet many of these men, too, were rooted in Rome and had homes and properties there.

The *Variae* show that the traditions and laws that created cohesion among senators in Rome and maintained the status of the Roman Senate had survived the fifth century and flourished under the Ostrogothic kings in the sixth-century city. The fact that so many of Cassiodorus's letters are about the senatorial prerogative to accept candidates for membership underscores the ongoing political influence that he attributed to the Senate and its members. It also demonstrates that these positions were still attractive to newcomers as well as to established elites who maintained residency in the city.

Governing Rome. The *Variae* also provide unique insights into how the Senate exercised an increased influence over the city of Rome under the

---

[33] La Rocca and Oppedisano 2016, p. 183, noting Cass. *Var.* 6.21.12, in which those who are *maiores natu* are understood as being older in age.

[34] For Armentarius, see Cass. *Var.* 3.33. For Capuanus, see Cass. *Var.* 5.21.3.

[35] For the terminology, see Cass. *Var.* 4.52.17, *germen sanatorium*; and 8.19.9, *seminarum senatus*: and La Rocca and Oppedisano 2016, p. 183, note 12.

[36] For the *vir illustris* who was great-grandfather of the Cassiodorus who was author of the *Variae*, see Cassiodorus 1, *PLRE* 2, pp. 263–64.

Ostrogoths. For instance, following the *Novella* of the emperor Majorian in 458, Theoderic expected the Senate to take seriously its role in the preservation of public buildings. *Variae* 3.31, directed to the Senate, expresses the king's dismay concerning their inadequate care of the public fabric of the city. The misuse of aqueduct funds, the appropriation of building materials from public works, and the destruction of monuments led the king to send his own agent, Johannes, to prepare a detailed report. The king did not explicitly blame the Senate, but his intervention demonstrates his grave concern for the monuments and infrastructure of the city.

Nevertheless, Theoderic's praiseworthy preservation of Rome's patrimony had its limits. He did grant certain senators the right to use some abandoned granaries (*Variae* 3.29). In an interesting letter that also attests to senators' personal investments in the city, Theoderic (*Variae* 4.30) gave the powerful patrician senator Albinus, consul of 493 and praetorian prefect of Italy between 500 and 503, the right to expand his palace by occupying part of a previous public space, the *Portico of Curva* in the Forum of Trajan. Theoderic thus secured the goodwill of this powerful senator at the expense of a public building.[37] Similarly, he granted the right to reclaim land from the Pomptine marshes to some senators who benefitted by thereafter holding it as private property free of tax obligations.[38] These acts encouraged reuse of public spaces by wealthy senators, who could use these investments for personal gain.

Several of the *Variae* point to the traditional role played by the Senate's chief officer, the urban prefect, in the administration of the city.[39] The urban prefect was still charged with the maintenance of food, water, and entertainment for the city's population. But when the urban prefect failed to resolve a problem concerning the management of the sewers, the king dispatched his own agent (*Variae* 3.30). If a senator, acting in his capacity as urban prefect, performed well, he might be offered another position at court. For instance, as noted in *Variae* 3.22, the urban prefect, Artemidorus, was invited to join the king's *comitatus* at Ravenna after finishing his service. This letter indicates a change in senatorial office-holding patterns, for although the office of urban prefect was still a high point in a senatorial career, as it is described at length in Argolicus's appointment to it in 510–11 (*Variae* 3.11 and 3.12), it could also be a stepping-stone to higher service and influence at the Ostrogothic court.

Although the Senate was charged with maintaining civic order in Rome, especially when religious conflicts broke out into fighting, the urban prefect

---

[37] For more on building in Rome under Theoderic, see Fauvinet-Ranson 2006, pp. 226–98.
[38] Cass. *Var.* 2.32, 33.   [39] La Rocca and Oppedisano 2016, p. 181 and Cass. *Var.* 1.42.15; 6.4.14.

had only cohorts of lightly armed police forces with which to enforce peace (see Chapter 2). Individual senators did possess slaves, clients, and guards who could protect them or their property when needed. And the Senate could investigate and bring to trial those responsible for urban violence. As *Variae* 4.43 (509–11) relates, Theoderic charged the Senate with undertaking an inquiry of those found guilty of burning down a synagogue in Rome in the wake of violence by Christian slaves against their Jewish owners. Theatrical performances by pantomimes that took place along with the circus games were often the time when riots broke out. When there were brawls, individual senators and the Senate were held responsible. Senators did not personally face physical punishment, but they were forced to turn over their slaves involved in urban violence to the urban prefect for disciplinary action.[40]

The Papacy, Senatorial Aristocrats, and the Senate under Ostrogothic Rule

Senators and the Senate were also increasingly involved in the religious life of the city under the Ostrogoths. We see senatorial influence most often in the conflicts that emerged over the elections of popes, with senators supporting one candidate over another. But the Senate as a corporate body was frequently involved in such matters as well, for it, too, was charged with maintaining civil order. For example, the Senate issued an edict (*consultum*) prohibiting bribery in clerical elections in 533 in an attempt to reduce conflict.[41] One of the most notorious contested papal election took place after the death of Pope Anastasius II in 498. Two different men, with two different groups of supporters, were ordained as bishop of Rome. One candidate, the priest Laurentius, had the backing of certain senators as well as that of many priests, while his rival, Symmachus, counted on other senators, including Cassiodorus and Liberius, along with a number of high-ranking clergy.[42] This rivalry, today known as the Laurentian Schism, demonstrates well how Roman senatorial aristocrats increasingly influenced religious matters under the Ostrogothic kings.

The Laurentian Schism. Because the contested papal election of 498 had led to street fighting in Rome, King Theoderic had been called to intervene to resolve the issue. In doing so, he was following imperial precedent to restore

---

[40] We hear about the use of slaves and local tenants during the Gothic War; see note 201 below. For slaves protecting masters at the games, see Cass. *Var.* 1.30–32.

[41] For the edict, see Cass. *Var.* 9.15.3. And see Lizzi Testa (in press), pp. 44–61.

[42] Radtki 2016, p. 131; Gasparri 2002, p. 61.

civic order. After inquiry, he cast the deciding vote for Symmachus.[43] However, charges of continuing papal misdeeds, including financial mismanagement, led to ongoing outbursts of violence in the city.[44] Theoderic then summoned Symmachus to Ravenna for questioning, and he subsequently encouraged the bishops to hold a council in Rome to resolve these allegations. The council met and ended by supporting Symmachus as pope in November 502. At that council, a copy of the will of the previous bishop of Rome, Simplicius, the *Scriptura of 483* (discussed in Chapter 5), was read out loud, and it demonstrated how Symmachus was following papal precedent.[45] However, at this same council, some procedures were condemned, including the involvement of secular elites in papal elections, although that had been the procedure followed upon the accession of Bishop Felix III. Unfortunately, physical attacks on Symmachus and his clergy continued.[46] These actions led the Senate and clergy to travel to Ravenna in August 502 to again request the intervention of King Theoderic, who once more lent his support to Symmachus.[47] Theoderic also again made it clear that it was the duty of the Senate to restore peace "through the Senate's persuasion" (*suadente senatu*).[48]

When complaints about Symmachus arose again some years later, the king again intervened; in 506–07 he directed the patrician senator Festus, a fierce opponent of Pope Symmachus, to restore to the pope's authority all Catholic churches in Rome.[49] By this date, as conflicts continued, the Senate turned to the king again to resolve another contested papal election. As Cassiodorus's *Variae* 8.15, directed to the Senate in 526 by King Athalaric, recounts, senators had turned to Theoderic in the disputed papal election of the next pope, Felix IV (526–30). As an Arian outsider, King Theoderic was seen by the Senate and its members as an unbiased actor who could help resolve this conflict "of a religion foreign to him."[50]

---

[43] Sessa 2016, p. 442 and note 81.

[44] For an excellent discussion and bibliography of the Laurentian schism but with a focus on property not politics, see Sessa 2012, pp. 212–45. For the charges of financial mismanagement by Symmachus rebuffed at the Council of 502, see note 45 below.

[45] On this Council and the evidence for 502 dating, see Moorhead 1992A, pp. 114–21, and his Appendix I, 259–60. For the charges, see the *Frag. laur.*, in *Lib. Pont.* ed. Duchesne 1981, pp. 44–46.

[46] *Acta syn.* DII [sic] *MGH AA* 12, ed. Mommsen, p. 420.3 and p. 421.3. Attacks continued even after another council in May 502.

[47] In this controversy, the *tertia Praeceptio* of August 8, 502 was produced by the king, *secundum petitionem senatus et cleri*; see *Acta syn.* DII [sic] *MGH AA* 12, ed. Mommsen, p. 420.3 and p. 421.7. Lizzi Testa in press, p. 50.

[48] *Frag. laur.*, in *Lib. Pont.* ed. Duchesne 1981, vol. I, pp. 43–46 at p. 45.

[49] Moorhead 105, p. 57, citing *Laur. Frag.* 12 ff; *MGH AA* 12, ed. Mommsen, p. 392.

[50] Cass. *Var.* 8. 15.1.

The End of the Acacian Schism. Perhaps one of the more intriguing documents that demonstrates the Senate's influence in what Philippe Blaudeau has aptly described as *geo-ecclesiology* is dated to 516, when the eastern emperor Anastasius directed a letter to the Senate asking it to intercede on his behalf to convince the pope to end the ongoing Acacian Schism between the popes of Rome and the bishops in Constantinople.[51] As noted in Chapter 5, the Acacian Schism had grown out of theological differences about the nature of Christ and the authority of the Church Council of Chalcedon (451). Bishop Leo I (440–61), along with many Christian bishops in the West, had upheld the council's definition of *Christ* as having two natures "in one person." However, this formulation had been rejected by many Christians, especially in the East. In the 480s, the eastern emperor Zeno, with the assistance of Bishop Acacius of Constantinople, had tried to force the Bishops Simplicius and Felix to agree to a compromise doctrine of unity, the *Henotikon*. In 484, Felix had refused and excommunicated the patriarch Acacius. Acacius had responded in kind. Although the popes had not broken ties to the eastern emperor, the schism had continued.

In 516 the eastern emperor Anastasius had decided to appeal directly to the Senate in Rome. He sent a letter to "the proconsuls, consuls, praetors, tribunes of the plebs, and *his Senate* (emphasis my own)" that urged its members to pressure the then pope Hormisdas (514–23) to compromise.[52] This act was a confident assertion of the emperor's ties to the Roman Senate and an explicit attempt to engage its assistance. Anastasius felt the Senate had real political influence in the Ostrogothic state. Indeed, the emperor regarded the Senate's unique role as that of a mediator that possessed "propitious good will for each part of the State."[53] That is, he saw the Senate's role as pivotal in uniting the emperor and the church.[54] Perhaps Anastasius had sent this letter because he also knew that some senators had been in favor of ending the Acacian Schism during the period of the contested papal elections at the time of the Laurentian Schism (498–508).[55] But Anastasius's efforts failed. The Senate's polite – but firm – refusal to side with the emperor and patriarch gave the pope additional support to maintain his independence. The Senate, as a corporate body, wrote a letter back to the

---

[51] *CA* 113, ed. Guenther, Part II, pp. 506–7, by Emperor Anastasius (= Thiel, p. 765); *CA* 114 ed. Guenther, Part II, pp. 508–9, is the response of the Senate. On this exchange, see Salzman 2019, pp. 138–58. For Blaudeau's terminology, see Blaudeau 2012.

[52] *CA* 113,1, ed. Guenther, Part II, p. 506, by Anastasius (= Hormisdas, *Ep.* 112, Thiel, p. 765): . . . *proconsulibus, consulibus, praetoribus, tribunis plebis senatuique suo salutem dicit.*

[53] *CA* 113, ed. Guenther, Part II, pp. 506.26–27: *quotiens utrisque publicis rebus prospera uoluntate consulitur.*

[54] *CA* 113, ed. Guenther, Part II, p. 507.17–20.   [55] Kruse 2019, p. 209, with dates, p. 225.

emperor after first reassuring King Theoderic of its loyalty.[56] The Senate asserted that it supported the pope and his position, in defiance of the emperor Anastasius, but couched its response in religious terms. The Senate's letter quoted a passage from Matthew about the need to resist and cut off sinful members of one's body rather than to sin in order to justify their support of the pope's refusal to end the schism.[57] This letter displayed considerable political tact as well as independence in the face of unwanted eastern pressure.

The Arian king Theoderic backed up the bishop and the Senate in their continuing resistance to eastern pressure.[58] Theoderic had made it known that he would exercise religious toleration at the beginning of his reign.[59] The king had no interest in bringing a rapprochement of the papacy with Constantinople. However, if religious conflict threatened the public order, Theoderic could and did intervene, as he had during the Laurentian Schism. Because of his avowed toleration, Theoderic did not intervene when new negotiations led to the resolution of the Acacian Schism after the accession of the new emperor, Justin II (518–27). Pope Hormisdas's doctrinal formulation, the *libellus Hormisdae*, allowed for official communion between the eastern and western churches in 519, even if, as Claire Sotinel has observed, both sides had different understandings of the theology in the signed documents.[60] Moreover, as Kristina Sessa has observed, Hormisdas had limited authority to enforce this agreement, for when the bishop of Thessalonica, Dorotheus, refused to back this formulation, neither Hormisdas nor the emperor Justin II could force Dorotheus to stand trial in Rome.[61] But the cessation of the schism opened the way for more cordial relations between the eastern court, the papacy, and the Senate.

The Last Years of the Reign of Theoderic (522–26). Nevertheless, the positive relationship of senatorial aristocrats and the king portrayed in Cassiodorus's letters papered over some of the tensions that had existed not only among the established families of the Italo-Roman senatorial aristocracy, but also between senatorial aristocrats from Rome and the "new men" who had risen to senatorial status through their service to the

---

[56] *CA* 114, ed. Guenther, Part II, pp. 508–9 (= Hormisdas, *Ep.* 14, ed. Thiel p. 769). Theoderic's name is included along with the appropriate honorific: *domini nostri inuictissimi regis Theoderici filii uestri* (*CA* 114, ed. Guenther, Part. II, p. 508.8–9).

[57] Matthew 18.8: *Vae mundo ab scandalis, et <absc>idere oportere homines scandalizantem partem membrorum, quam ut in ignem non renuntiando scandalis mittantur aeternum*, in *CA* 114, ed. Guenther, Part II, pp. 508.18–21.

[58] *Anon. Val.* 12 (60): *tamen nihil contra religionem catholicam temptans.*

[59] See Moorhead 2015, pp. 51–54; and Sessa 2012, pp. 212–45.   [60] Sotinel 2005, pp. 267–90.

[61] Sessa 2016, p. 445.

Ostrogothic king. Established Italo-Roman aristocratic families had enjoyed the economic and social benefits of peace that came from their properties, for they owned estates not only in the regions of Rome and Campania but also in Sicily and throughout southern Italy, with some also holding properties in the eastern Mediterranean and even in southern Gaul.[62] The newer senators who had arisen through service to the king in his court or administration were largely from northern Italy, with properties concentrated in Liguria. But both sets of men were competing for the same offices, and this rivalry created some frictions.

Such internal tensions among senatorial elites were exacerbated by the power struggles that emerged in the last years of Theoderic's rule.[63] In my view, the shifting politics behind dynastic succession among the Ostrogoths were the key to the events that unfolded in the years 522 to 524 and led to changes in the balance of power among Italo-Roman senators.[64] During the last years of Theoderic's rule, a number of court officials were appointed to offices like that of the urban prefect that had traditionally fallen to the older Rome-based senatorial families.[65] Consequently, suspicions were aroused on both sides, Ostrogothic and Roman. When the senators Albinus, Boethius, and Symmachus were accused of secretly sending letters to the eastern court in a plot against King Theoderic, some senators stood up to support them. Boethius, master of the household, came to the defense of Albinus, a member of the Decii family. Boethius asserted that he had been upholding senatorial liberty since he had earlier saved a certain former consul and patrician, Paulinus, from the "Palatine dogs."[66] It is not entirely clear to whom this slur referred, but this statement was a clear attack on courtiers of the king. Interestingly, Boethius took an open stand in this against his own father-in-law, the senator Symmachus. Symmachus rose to Boethius's defense. Both men had no doubt assumed that their status would protect them and that the

---

[62] See my discussion of property holdings in Chapter 4; and for the fourth-century example of Symmachus, see Vera 1986, pp. 231–76.

[63] Radtki 2016, pp. 132–34; following Schäfer 1991, pp. 170 ff.; Cracco Ruggini 1986, pp. 245–61; Bjornlie 2013, pp. 127–34.

[64] Heather 2016, pp. 15–37.

[65] Moorhead 1992, pp. 148–55; and more recently in support of this view, see Bjornlie 2013, pp. 127–67.

[66] Boethius, *De cons. Phil.* 1.4.16–21; for the slur about the "Palatine dogs." See 1.4.34–75. The senator Paulinus whom he had saved had also been accused by his father-in-law, along with Festus, so the divisions here are not simply of old senatorial versus new court agents. What had changed was Theoderic's willingness to intervene directly in senatorial disputes rather than appointing commissions to resolve them; see Cass. *Var.* 1.23. I concur with Heather 2016, pp. 15–37, that dynastic succession struggles were the key factor in this change. For Paulinus, consul in 498 and patrician in 510, see Paulinus 11, *PLRE* 2, p. 847.

king would not allow the case to be prosecuted. They were wrong. Boethius and his father-in-law were condemned to death by the Senate, with the support of Theoderic, on charges of colluding with the eastern court.[67] The Greek historian Procopius singles out their murders as the sole unjust acts in Theoderic's otherwise unblemished rule.[68] Certainly, their deaths benefitted some senators as well as some at the Amal court who had been jockeying for power during this time of transition.[69]

Not only senators but also bishops fell in the dynastic infighting that played out at the end of Theoderic's rule. In 526, King Theoderic had sent Pope John I (523–26) to Constantinople with four senatorial aristocrats, along with the bishop of Ravenna, to suspend a recent seizure of Arian churches and/or certain worshippers and to return these churches to their original owners. However, John failed to win any concessions. The *Book of the Popes* alleges that upon John's return to Ravenna, King Theoderic jailed him and the other ambassadors on charges of collusion with the eastern emperor Justin II and then, allegedly, so maltreated them that they died in prison.[70] Some have doubted this narrative since the king returned the pope's body to St. Peter's for burial.[71] Nonetheless, given Theoderic's recent actions, the popes of Rome now had reason to be dissatisfied with Ostrogothic rule.

Ostrogothic Succession Struggles. The death of Theoderic in 526 and the appointment of his daughter, Amalasuntha (526–35), as queen regent for her ten-year-old son, Athalaric, brought a brief restoration of the status quo. The Senate and the leading Italo-Roman senatorial families, along with Italian court officials like Cassiodorus, continued to support the Amal family. However, the death of eighteen-year-old Athalaric from "a wasting disease" in 534 forced Amalasuntha to appoint her kinsman Theodahad (534–36) as her coruler.[72] But Theodahad was not trustworthy. Instead of ruling with her, he imprisoned the queen until his agents murdered her in April 535. The eastern emperor Justinian (527–65) claimed that Amalasuntha had been under his protection and that he thus was forced to send troops to Italy to cast off the "foreign domination" of the Ostrogoths and restore "Sicily, Rome, and Italy to their ancient way

---

[67] For the murder of Boethius, *Anon. Val.* 15 (87) and Procop. *Wars* 5.1.32–39; for the murder of Symmachus, *Anon. Val.* 15 (92). Radtki 2016, pp. 137–40; Bjornlie 2013, pp. 138–42. Procop. *Wars* 5.1.32–39.

[68] Procop. *Wars* 5.1.39.   [69] Heather 2016, pp. 15–37; Moorhead 1992, pp. 219–26.

[70] *Lib. Pont.* 55.4–6, ed. Duchesne 1981, pp. 275–78.

[71] For the alleged murder of Pope John I, see *Anon. Val.* 15 (93) and Moorhead 2015, pp. 55–68; Moorhead 1992, pp. 212–45.

[72] Procop. *Wars* 5.3.10; 5.4.4–10.

of life."[73] Justinian may have hoped to take control of Italy through negotiations with Theodahad in the winter of 535–36, but the Ostrogoths did not capitulate so quickly.[74]

The Gothic War and Its Impact on Roman Elites

Justinian's general Belisarius invaded Ostrogothic Sicily in 535 and entered Rome in victory a year later.[75] Belisarius's troops now faced determined Ostrogothic opposition from the then king Witigis and, later in the war, from his Ostrogothic successors, Totila and Teia. The arrival of the Byzantines had divided the Roman senatorial aristocracy. Some welcomed Belisarius as a liberator, but others had remained loyal to the Amal regime.[76] As the war dragged on until 554, Gothic losses and Byzantine overtures led many to change their loyalties, some more than once.[77] Because the fighting unfolded in Italy over a twenty-year period, few areas of the peninsula were spared. The city of Rome suffered several spectacular assaults. Its fate is emblematic of the impact of the war on Italy in general, but it is critical for understanding the responses of the elites who survived the Gothic War and chose to return to try to restore Rome.

The City of Rome

Between 535 and 552, the city of Rome was sieged three times and sacked twice: first taken by Belisarius without a fight in 536; sieged by Witigis, 537–38; sieged and sacked by Totila, 545–46; then sieged and sacked again by Totila, 549–50. By the end of the war in 554, the Byzantines claimed victory. Procopius, our most reliable source for the war since he had interviewed its survivors and served in the Byzantine military, claimed that "Rome then again became [subject to the Romans]."[78] This is the view of events from the Justinianic court in Constantinople. How Romans in the city viewed this

---

[73] The machinations that took place against Amalasuntha by Theodahad have received a very detailed account by Vitiello 2017 and 2014. For the assertion that Justinian was "casting off foreign (i.e. Gothic) domination," see Agathias, *Histories*, Preface 30. For this version of events, see too Sarris 2011, pp. 112–19 and Procop. *Wars* 5.4.4.10–30.

[74] Procop. *Wars* 5.6.1–11; and 5.7. See too Kruse 2019, pp. 150–52.

[75] Procop. *Wars* 5.5.17–19; and for entry into Rome, *Wars* 5.14.14.

[76] Bjornlie 2013, p. 143. Procop. *Wars* 5.14.4.

[77] Schäfer 1991, pp. 263 ff., sees the majority of Italo-Roman senators as pro-Byzantine, but it took twenty-five years to "break the resistance of the politically enfranchised caste of the Gothic population of Italy," as Heather 1996, p. 275, observed.

[78] Procop. *Wars* 5.14.14, with the missing section provided on the basis of Evagrios, *HE* 4.19. I follow here Kaldellis 2014, p. 287, note 521.

transition after the war ended and having lived through twenty years of fighting was quite different.

The Siege of Witigis, February 537–March 538. Of the five sieges of the city, Witigis's siege of Rome (February 537–March 538) was perhaps the costliest because it came after sixty years of peace and prosperity. Although the Senate and the people had gone over to supporting Belisarius, fearing the same punishment as that suffered by the Neapolitans for resisting the Byzantines in 536, they had no say in preventing Belisarius from turning Rome into an armed camp. Belisarius restored the city's walls and prepared for what turned out to be Rome's longest siege during the war. Witigis blockaded Rome for thirteen months, beginning on February 17, 537, and lasting until March 538.[79]

Belisarius took action against Witigis by closing a number of the city's aqueducts. To feed the city, Belisarius cleverly devised mills for grinding grain that floated on the Tiber River. Fortunately, the population had access to water from private wells in the city, and the sewers continued to function.[80] But the great public bath complexes, so much a part of daily life in the city, stopped functioning.[81] The suffering that followed led the senators to urge Belisarius to leave, but their arguments fell on deaf ears.[82] One sign of the breakdown of public norms in these trying conditions is narrated by Procopius, who tells us that at the initiative of the patricians – that is, the senators – there was an inspection of the Sibylline Books, which were incorrectly read to predict, among other things, the end of the siege of the city in the fifth month, meaning July. The willingness of Christian senators to resort to pre-Christian rituals is reminiscent of the desperate attempt undertaken by senators during the siege of 410.[83] Similarly, they tried to open the Temple of Peace, but to no avail.[84]

When there was a break in the fighting, Belisarius ordered all the women and children to leave Rome for Naples. This evacuation saved many residents since a "great majority were able to depart from Rome, and some went to Campania, some to Sicily, and others wherever they thought it was easier or better to go."[85] The men who remained were drafted to guard the wall.[86] However, even those who stayed in the city were not safe from suspicion of colluding with the Goths. According to Procopius and the *Book of the Popes*, Pope Silverius was accused of having conspired with the Goths to relieve the

---

[79] Bjornlie 2013, p. 143. Procop. *Wars* 5.14.4–6 for handing over the city; 5.14.15–17; 5.19 for the blockade; and see Roberto 2012, p. 218.

[80] Procop. *Wars* 5.19.13–29. Roberto 2012, p. 218 and note 26 for the aqueducts.

[81] Procop. *Wars* 5.19.27.   [82] Procop. *Wars* 5.20.5–20.   [83] Procop. *Wars* 5.24.28–37.

[84] Procop. *Wars* 5.25.22–25.   [85] Procop. *Wars* 5.25.10.   [86] Procop. *Wars* 5.25.11–13.

suffering in the city.[87] Silverius may have been trying to mediate some sort of truce, as Leo had done in 455 (see Chapter 4). But Belisarius did not believe the pope, or, as Procopius recounts in his *Secret History*, he may have acted to please Justinian's wife, Theodora (who was angry at the pope for condemning the bishop of Constantinople).[88] Belisarius condemned the pope to exile and ordered the apocrisiarius, or papal envoy, Vigilius (soon to be pope with Belisarius's support) to defrock him. When Silverius was returned to Rome, he was starved to death, a lesson that not even the pope was beyond the reach of the Byzantine military.[89]

Several Roman senators were also banished from Rome on the same suspicion of treason, although after the siege was over, several of them were allowed to return.[90] Among these was the former consul of 523, Flavius Maximus, a descendant of the mid fifth-century usurper Petronius Maximus and a member of the Anicii who had married an Ostrogothic princess. Flavius Maximus was one of the Anicii who had thrived under the Amal regime. He would suffer the consequences of his loyalty later in the war, for the Goths killed him as he was returning to Rome in 552, and Justinian confiscated part of Maximus's property, which the emperor gave, in 554 to those Italo-Romans who had supported the Byzantines during the war.[91] Maximus's fate is representative of the problems facing Italo-Roman senators whose successful careers under the Ostrogoths had put them in danger. When pressing his siege of Rome, Witigis had sent orders to Ravenna to kill all the Roman senators whom he had taken there at the beginning of the war; he failed in this effort only because some senators had gotten wind of this order and fled Ravenna to avoid being captured and killed.[92]

By 540, Belisarius had succeeded in turning the tide. The first phase of the war ended with the defeat and capture of Witigis, who, along with his court, had surrendered to Belisarius in 540.[93] The capture of Theoderic's treasury helped offset the cost of the war, but the departure of Belisarius to fight against the

---

[87] Procop. *Wars* 5.25.13.

[88] Procop. *Secret History* 1.14; and 1.27. Liberatus, *Breviarium* 22, claims that a letter of Silverius to the Goths was forged to make him look guilty. Procopius and the *Lib. Pont.* 60.6–9, ed. Duchesne 1981, pp. 293–94, *Life of Silverius*, assert that the empress Theodora and Belisarius's wife were involved in the plot against Pope Silverius. Sotinel 2005, pp. 279–84 is right to see the troubled sources as a reflection of the times.

[89] See Moorhead 2015, pp. 79–81 for discussion of the incident; Roberto 2012, p. 219; and Sotinel 2005, pp. 279–80.

[90] Procop. *Wars* 5.25.14–15.

[91] See note 161 below. For Maximus's murder, see Procop. *Wars* 8.34.6.

[92] Procop. *Wars* 5.26.1–2.   [93] Procop. *Wars* 6.29–7.1.

Persians allowed the Ostrogoths to regroup under a new king, Totila, so the warfare resumed in 541.

The Sack of Rome by Totila, December 17, 546. Totila was able to regain territory through a combination of military force and publicized clemency for those cities that had returned peacefully to Gothic rule. Thus, after taking the fortress at Cumae and finding the wives of senators there, he ostentatiously released them and hence "won a great name for wisdom and humanity among the Romans."[94] Nevertheless, in 546 he once more was at the gates of Rome. Months of siege had created a severe famine that had been exacerbated by the corrupt practices of the Byzantine commander Bessas, who had sold grain to the populace at a profit and had reduced the senators to begging for food and clothing.[95] In desperation, many had left Rome even before the Byzantine commander opened the gates to allow them to depart.[96]

Totila's well-advertised willingness to reward those who crossed sides worked again. He encouraged four Isaurian guards fighting for Belisarius to betray the city.[97] As in the more famous sack of 410, Totila's men entered the city through the Porta Asinaria, but after months of siege, they found a depopulated city on December 17, 546.[98] Procopius cites the names of the most eminent senators (patricians) who escaped, including the high-ranking senators Decius and Basilius.[99] Other patricians of high rank, also named by Procopius – Orestes, Olybrius, and Maximus – fled for safety to St. Peter's in the Vatican (see Map 1 at the beginning of the book).[100] Since Pope Vigilius was outside the city, the deacon Pelagius, the next bishop, begged Totila to spare the lives of the remaining Romans, carrying the scriptures from St. Peter's to soften the anger of the Goths.[101] Totila complied and prevented murder, but he allowed the plundering of the city without any restrictions.

It is worth underscoring that Rome still had much wealth to attract looters, for there was still much valuable booty in the city, not only in the house of the wealthy, corrupt Byzantine commander Bessas.[102] Seizing captives to sell into slavery was also always an option, and women were easy targets. Some Goths blamed the aristocrat Rusticiana, wife of Boethius and daughter of Symmachus, for her charity to impoverished Roman senators and intended to do her harm. She had remained in the city during this siege when Totila, to

---

[94] Procop. *Wars* 7.6.4.   [95] Procop. *Wars* 7.20.27.   [96] Procop. *Wars* 7.17.23–24.
[97] Procop. *Wars* 7.20.4.   [98] Procop. *Wars* 7.20.4–20. See too Roberto 2012, pp. 220–21.
[99] Procop. *Wars* 7.20.18 See Decius 1, consul in 529, *PLRE* 3A, p. 391; see Basilius 3, *PLRE* 3A, pp. 174–75, the last nonimperial holder of the consulship in 541.
[100] See Procop. *Wars* 7.20.19. See Orestes, *PLRE* 3B, p. 956; for Olybrius as the consul of 526, see Olybrius 2, *PLRE* 3B, p. 953; and Flavius Maximus, consul of 523 see Maximus 20, *PLRE* 2, pp. 748–49.
[101] Procop. *Wars* 7.20.22–25.   [102] Procop. *Wars* 7.20.26–28.

his credit, prevented her rape and saved several other, unnamed elite women from violence.[103] Once more, clemency won Totila acclaim, but the difficulty of restraining the anger of soldiers after a long siege was a familiar situation; it was a problem that Ricimer had also faced after the civil war of 472 (see Chapter 5).

Procopius asserts that Totila had sent the priest Pelagius and an orator to Justinian to end the war and save the city of Rome.[104] But when Justinian deferred negotiations with Totila to Belisarius, Totila was so infuriated that he at first decided to raze the city to the ground. He had allegedly torn down one-third of its fortifications including several gates.[105] Only a letter from Belisarius, according to Procopius, convinced the Ostrogothic king to spare Rome.[106] The letter, a trope of ancient historiography, nonetheless represents the kinds of considerations that may have swayed Totila. Moreover, physically destroying a city does take a good deal of time and effort. The displacement of the human population was even more damaging, for Totila did not let anyone return to Rome. He kept the Roman senators he found in the city with him and deported all other men and women to Campania, leaving the city deserted.[107] Now the fighting took on the appearance of a social war. The senators, forced by Totila, wrote their tenants and slaves to stop serving the Byzantines; promised land instead by Totila, some of them turned away from their former Roman lords to fight for the Ostrogoths.[108]

The Final Stages of the War. The recapture of Rome by Belisarius in February 547 was short-lived; the city had to face one more siege by Totila in 549 through 550. Then, we are told, Totila resettled Rome with senators and Goths and rebuilt the walls of the city.[109] Hence, Rome was once more inhabited as the final stages of the war played out under the direction of the general Narses. The Byzantines defeated the Goths at a major battle near Tadinae (Taginae), at a place called Busta Gallorum in July 552 (see Map 5).[110] The deaths of Totila and his successor, Teia, at the Battle of *Mons Lactarius* in Campania in this same year forced the Goths to come to terms with Narses.[111] Narses directed his troops to enter Rome, probably in July of 552, and sent the keys of its gates to the emperor.[112] But the war was not over yet, for the Goths regrouped with the

---

[103] Procop. *Wars* 7.20.29–31; Roberto 2013, p. 221, note 30 for differing views of Totila's actions after the siege.

[104] Procop. *Wars* 7.21.18–24.   [105] Procop, *Wars* 7.22.7 and note 109 below.

[106] Procop. *Wars* 7.22.6–19.   [107] Procop. *Wars* 7.22.19.

[108] Procop. *Wars* 7.22.20–21. For senators using bands of private retainers even in the fifth century, see Mathisen 2019, pp. 147–48.

[109] Procop. *Wars* 7.24.8–34 for Belisarius's retaking of Rome; Procop. *Wars* 7.36 for Totila's siege and capture.

[110] Procop. *Wars* 8.29.3–32.21.   [111] Agathias, *Histories* 1.1; Procop. *Wars* 8.32.22–35.29.5.

[112] Procop. *Wars* 8.33.1–27, and 27 for the keys to the gates. Narses celebrated a triumph in Rome in 554, according to Agathias, *Histories* 2.7.

support of the Franks to renew the fighting in Italy for three more years.[113] Mercifully, their last efforts bypassed Rome. The Goths' final defeat took place in 555 at Casilinum near Capua.[114] After that, imperial control was reestablished in Liguria, Histria, and most of Venetia, with the defeat of a Gothic count named Widin in Brixia (modern Brescia) in 561 marking the final end of Gothic resistance (see Map 5).[115]

Where to Begin to Rebuild Rome?

When Narses entered Rome in 552, he found a city that had been badly damaged by the war. The aqueducts needed repair, and the baths were no longer functioning. The city wall and several of its gates had been damaged. Many buildings had been plundered, and others simply destroyed or abandoned. Some of Rome's most celebrated public works of art had been ruined. Procopius graphically describes the toll the fighting had taken. He relates how, when the Goths had attacked the city gate near the Aelian Bridge and attempted to storm the Mausoleum of Hadrian (see Map 1 in the beginning of the book), which the Byzantines had used as a fortress, the soldiers then destroyed the ornamentation of the building in self-protection:

> By common agreement they [the Byzantines] broke in pieces most of the statues, which were very large, and taking up the great number of stones thus secured, threw them with both hands down upon the heads of the enemy, who gave way before this shower of missiles.[116]

The Mausoleum of Hadrian survived in its ruined state, however, for it is attested as a fortress in later times.[117] More destructive than the plundering were the fires that followed; we hear of a terrible one that Procopius says devastated Trastevere, a key commercial area of the city (see Map 1).[118] Bridges needed to be rebuilt, and the Tiber River channel was in need of repair.[119]

---

[113] For the continued fighting, see Agathias, *Histories* 1.5–2.8; 10.7; Procop. *Wars* 8.35.37 for the Gothic leader Indulf at Pavia; 8.34.19–20 for the Gothic general Aligern at Cumae; and Agathias, *Histories* 2.13–14 for Ragnaris at Cona della Campania.

[114] Agathias, *Histories* 1.22.8–2.1; 2.10.7, and 2.1–14.

[115] For the final defeat of Widin, see Paul the Deacon, *History of the Lombards* 2.2 and Narses, *PLRE* 3B, p. 924.

[116] Procop. *Wars* 5.22.12–25. For the need for repair, see the *PS.* Constitution 25, Miller and Sarris 2018, p. 1128.

[117] See *LTUR*, s.v. P. Aelii Hadriani Sepulcrum in *LTUR Suburbium* v.1, 2001, pp. 15–22; pp. 15–19 by P. Liverani and pp. 19–22 by M. A. Tomei.

[118] Procop. *Wars* 8.22.3.   [119] For restorations undertaken by Narses, see notes 232–234 below.

Map 5 Justinianic Italy in 565.

Procopius's allegation that there were no more than five hundred men surviving among the "common people" in the city when Totila took it in 546 is not to be taken as fact. Some of the city's inhabitants had endured. The senators, including Decius and Basilius, "with some others," had escaped, while the senators Maximus, Olybrius, Orestes, and some unspecified number had fled to the Church of St. Peter's. Nonetheless, the population was at a low point then, for, as Procopius says, many had "departed to other lands" or died from famine.[120] Scholars suggest that before the Gothic War began in 535, the city had revived and had reached a population estimated at its highest, between 100,000 and 140,000, and at its smallest, at 50,000. By the 550s, after the war had ended, Rome likely lost at least half of its population, if not more. That would mean that the population had declined to anywhere from 25,000 to 50,000, although it is possible that there may have been even fewer residents. But these are guesses. The actual numbers are simply not known. Similarly, although we see in our sources, textual and material, that people returned to Rome after the war in the late sixth century, we can do no more than estimate the city's size because we lack firm evidence. A population at the end of the sixth century of between 50,000 and 90,000 is plausible but not demonstrable.[121]

Twenty years of fighting on Italian soil had diminished, if not destroyed, not only the administration but also an entire generation of Italo-Romans along with the Ostrogoths. All classes of society had suffered the traumatic and violent loss of life and property. Dislocations of the population had occurred at all levels of society. Senatorial aristocrats had been targeted by both sides during the wars as Byzantine and Ostrogothic generals sought to use them to break the will of the other side.[122] Witigis had ordered the murder of all of the Italo-Roman senators in Ravenna, but he did not succeed, as Procopius tells us, because news of his plot came out. The most well-known elites who survived this attack, notably Reparatus, soon to be

---

[120] Procop. *Wars* 7.17.17–19; 7.20.18–21.

[121] Roberto 2013, p. 223 for a population estimate of 50,000 for the late sixth century, based on Santangeli Valenzani 2004B, pp. 22–24, who discusses the population reductions of the late sixth century. Delogu 1993, pp. 7–29, at p. 13, note 7, thinks, following Krautheimer 1980, p. 62, and based on migrations due to the Lombard invasions, that the population by the time of Gregory swelled to around 90,000. For the early-sixth-century estimate of 100,000, see Cosentino 2005, pp. 411–13. For an argument that the city's population in 535 was no more than 100,000, though possibly as low as 50,000, Lo Cascio 2013, pp. 417–18. The early-sixth-century calculations rely heavily on Cass., *Var.* 11.39, on which see also Barnish 1987, esp. pp. 160–61, and my discussion in Chapters 1 and 4.

[122] Procop. *Wars* 5.26.1, Witigis's order to kill Roman senators in Ravenna; cf. *Wars* 6.21.40 for the later murder of Reparatus, the pretorian prefect. Byzantine forces also took revenge on Goths, as did Goths on alleged Italo-Roman collaborators; see, for example, Procop. *Wars* 8.34.1–8 and note 131 below.

praetorian prefect of Italy in 538–39 and brother of Pope Vigilius, along with Bergantinus, who led the resistance against the Goths, remained in Liguria to fight on. But after the fall of Milan to the Goths, Bergantinus joined the increasing number of Italo-Roman expatriates who went to Constantinople and were welcomed by Justinian at his court.[123] Later, under Totila's siege of Rome in 549, we are told of the safe flight of several senators to Constantinople, where Justinian welcomed them.[124] Those Romans and senators who remained in Rome sought and received sanctuary in St. Peter's Basilica at the Vatican. Although angry Goths had murdered some sixty unnamed people, Totila, persuaded by the future bishop Pelagius, prevented further murders while allowing the plunder of Romans' property.[125] And after taking Rome again in 551, Totila had "placed a part of the Romans and some of the members of the Senate in Rome, leaving the rest in Campania. And he commanded them to look after the city."[126] However, we are told that these Romans were so impoverished that they could not do that.

Like Bergantinus, several senatorial families had fled from Italy to Constantinople. Their departure, along with the forced emigration of King Witigis and his courtiers to Constantinople in 540, ruptured Italy's legislative and administrative structures. Cassiodorus, the *magister officiorum* and praetorian prefect of Italy, who had remained loyal to the Ostrogoths after Belisarius's landing in Italy, also had departed for Constantinople, likely soon after 540, taking with him the kind of experience and the records that the Ostrogothic government had relied upon. Cassiodorus, like other Italo-Roman senators, was given safe harbor in Constantinople and by 550 had devoted himself to a religious life.[127] Others were honored with the title of *patrician*, a "conciliatory gesture" on the part of Justinian to win support during the war.[128]

The war had destroyed the norms and fortunes of many Italo-Roman senatorial aristocrats, but it did not eradicate them entirely. As noted earlier,

---

[123] Procop. *Wars* 5.26.2. For Bergantinus in Constantinople, see *Wars* 6.21.41.

[124] *Lib. Pont.* 55.7, ed. Duchesne 1981, p. 298, records the names of the prominent senators Cethegus, Albinus, and Basilius who escaped, reached Constantinople, and were presented before the emperor Justinian.

[125] Procop. *Wars* 7.20.25–20.31.   [126] Procop. *Wars* 8.22.2–22.4.4.

[127] Vigilius, *Ep.* 14 = *PL* 69.43 says that Cassiodorus had already turned to religion by then, addressing the senator as *religiosus vir item filius noster Senator*. See too Giardina 2006, pp. 15–25.

[128] Bjornlie 2019, p. 8, thinks that Cassiodorus was granted patrician status by Justinian after 540, but the date of his patriciate is not certain. His patriciate is only attested in later sources, as Vigilius, *Ep.* 14 in 550 and Jord. *Get.* praef. 1; see too O'Donnell 1979, pp. 131–36. For Justinian's use of the patriciate, see, for example, his award to Theodahad's son-in-law, Procop. *Wars* 5.8.3–4; and also his award to Witigis in Constantinople, Jord. *Get.* 313.

when Totila took Rome, he allowed a number of Italo-Romans to flee, and the others who remained were spared.[129] As T.S. Brown observed, although Procopius's dramatic account of the slaughter of patricians found in Campania by King Teia in 552 is a moving and bitterly ironic commentary on the vagaries of the war, it runs counter to Procopius's own statement that John in 550 had evacuated a number of senators from Campania to Sicily.[130] So, too, the horrific episode of Teia's slaughter of three hundred Roman children who had been taken as hostages north of the Po had destroyed the offspring of those "loyal – [that is], high – Romans" – meaning local notables as well as senators.[131] Totila had placed a number of Roman senators in Rome, though Procopius tells us that at this point in the war, "stripped of their money, [they] were not only unable to lay claim to the public funds . . . but [also] could not even secure those which belonged to them personally."[132]

A number of senatorial aristocrats, including those in Constantinople, survived the war and were intent on reclaiming their property, especially their estates outside of war-damaged Rome.[133] The eminent Cethegus, a consul and leader of the Senate, had gone to Constantinople in the 540s and had returned to reside in Sicily, for we hear of his son or grandson living in Rome in the late sixth century.[134] A member of the illustrious Symmachi was also attested in Rome at that time.[135] A Boethius and a Dominica appear to have returned to Rome (see my discussion below). As well, the family of the patrician Liberius thrived into the late sixth century in Rome, assuming that a senator titled *magnificus*, or "magnificent," by the name of Liberius, with property in Genoa and a residence in Rome in 593 was his son.[136] A member of the Decii was also attested; he became a patrician and may have been the first official holder of the office of exarch of Italy in 584.[137]

Italo-Roman senatorial aristocrats were eager for imperial assistance to recover their estates. Those in Constantinople would have sought to influence the emperor directly. The set of constitutions passed by Justinian and

---

[129] See note 125 above.   [130] Brown 1984, p. 32; Procop. *Wars* 8.34.6 is counter to *Wars* 7.26.14.

[131] Procop. *Wars* 8.34.7–8: δοκίμων Ῥωμαίων τοὺσ παῖδας.   [132] Procop. *Wars* 8.22.1–4.

[133] Brown 1984, p. 143; Burgarella 1998, pp. 121–75, especially pp. 157–63; and Cracco Ruggini 1981, especially pp. 157–93.

[134] For Cethegus resident in late sixth-century Rome, see *PLRE* 3B, p. 279 and Gregory, *Ep.* 9.72, 598 CE.

[135] Symmachus 4, *PLRE* 3B, p. 1213.

[136] Liberius, *PLRE* 3B, pp. 791–92; Gregory, *Dialog* 4.55. The connection to Liberius 3, *PLRE* 2, pp. 677–81, is plausible. The family burial site was in Ariminum: *CIL* 11.382.

[137] Decius 2, *PLRE* 3A, p. 391. For his possible identification as the first recorded *exarchus Italiae*, also called Decius, see note 208 below.

today known as the *Pragmatic Sanction* (discussed below) included stipulations that aimed to satisfy the landed senatorial aristocrats and to make their economic recovery easier by, among other remedies, removing travel restrictions to Italy.

The church, too, needed imperial support, for it had also suffered tremendous losses. Clergy had fled and needed to be replaced. The war had ravaged the agricultural estates of the church as well as those of individual landowners. Alongside these very real economic losses, the church, like wealthy landowners, faced a population emotionally scarred by two decades of fighting. A weakened papacy confronted the need to restore the faith of its adherents as well as its authority in Italy, and it, too, looked to the emperor for assistance in these tasks.

The Justinianic Reconstruction: The *Pragmatic Sanction*

Almost two years after the defeat and death of the last Gothic king, Teia, Justinian asserted his control over Italy in legal enactments or constitutions that are dated to August 13, 554. These are today known as the *Pragmatic Sanction* (*PS* hereafter).[138] The *PS* that has come down to us in three manuscripts includes some twenty-seven constitutions. Most scholars consider that the *PS* took the form of a general law since its content, as Justinian asserted, mattered to "all those who live in the West."[139] These constitutions outline the administration of law, justice, taxation, and security in the areas under Byzantine control. Even if enforcement of the *PS* was imperfect, the outlines of provincial society and government articulated in it elucidate why Justinian's reconstruction of Italy and the western provinces was, ironically, so destructive to the Senate and senatorial aristocrats, even as bishops and military administrators rose to prominence in Italy after the Gothic War.

The Addressees of the *Pragmatic Sanction*: The Bishop, the Senate, and the Byzantine Administrators of Italy

The first constitution of the *PS* is granted in response to a now-lost petition by "the venerable Vigilius of the elder Rome" and to a request from the

---

[138] Just. *Nov., Appendix VII*, eds. Schoell and Kroll 1954, iii, pp. 799–802. It is also included at *Iuliani Epitome Latina Novellarum Iustiniani*, ed. Hänel, 1873, pp. 185–91. *PS.* constitution 27 (hereafter c.) mentions that this is a *divinam pragmaticam sanctionem*. All translations of the *PS* in this chapter are adapted from Miller and Sarris 2018, pp. 1116–30.

[139] Kearley 2010, 379, note 8 follows Wenger 1953, pp. 434–38; as does Miller and Sarris 2018, p. 1116, note 4.

"Romans or their Senate."[140] Vigilius is usually identified as the Bishop of Rome (537–55) who had been summoned to Constantinople and been in the city since December 546.[141] Since *venerabilis* is an epithet often attached to the bishop of Rome, it is more than likely that this is the person to whom this first constitution was directed.[142] Yet the omission of the formal title – *episcopus* or *archiepiscopus* – from this first constitution calls for comment.

In the only other constitution that mentions the bishop of Rome directly, 19, the emperor does not mention Vigilius by name but refers to "the most blessed pope (*beatissimus papa*)." This use of *papa* – pope – fits with the growing sixth-century habit seen among the clergy of Rome and among Christians abroad to employ *papa*/pope as a title to refer to the person holding this office, which is why I use "pope" to refer to the sixth-century bishops of Rome in this book as well. [143] But in other laws, as in an earlier novel to Pope John (533–35) on the eve of the reconquest of Sicily and Italy, the emperor addresses bishops by their official titles – "the most blessed and most holy John, archbishop and patriarch of Old Rome" (*archiepiscopus et patriarcha*) – and refers to this bishop's "holiness" (*sanctitas*) twice.[144] It is possible that the *PS* had addressed the bishop more formally in the now-lost heading or title.[145] However, the lack of a title reinforces the idea that at the time of passing this constitution, Justinian was still displeased with Vigilius, whom he soon dismissed in spring 555 to return to Rome.[146]

Vigilius owed his position as pope to the Byzantines. The general Belisarius had supported his election as pope in 537, and as early as 540, Vigilius had supported Justinian's side in the war as had several western Italo-Roman aristocrats.[147] In fact, unlike earlier popes, Vigilius was from a senatorial aristocratic family. As the son of a consul, he was experienced in

---

[140] *PS.* c.1, ed. Schoell and Kroll, 1954,iii, pp. 799–800; ed. Hänel, 1873, p. 185: *Romanis vel senatu poscente.*

[141] *Lib. Pont.* 61.4, ed. Duchesne 1981, p. 297.

[142] *Venerabilis* was used for popes, bishops and clergy, but also for laymen, see Martin 1930, pp. 122–24, and, for example, Ennodius, *Ep.* 22.73.19. But when a bishop was called *venerabilis*, his title was also usually included, as, for example: *Sanctus et venerabilis vir episcopus sanctae ecclesiae catholicae Ravennatis*, Tjäder 1954–55, I, pap. 4–5 A-B, B V, rr. 7–8.

[143] On "papa" in the sixth century for the bishop of Rome, see Moorhead 1986, p. 350.

[144] Just. *Nov.* 9.: *Iohanni viro beatissimo et sanctissimo archiepiscopo et patriarchae veteris Romae.* For the pope's "holiness" (*sanctitas*), see *Nov.* 9.2. 5.

[145] On the transmission of the *PS*, see my discussion and notes 156–58 below.

[146] Moorhead 2015, p. 92 suggested this based on the Byzantine writer Theophanes, *Chron.* 6045. However, the petition is a standard one, not showing junior status, as Morehead had argued, p. 93, note 85.

[147] For Belisarius's support for Vigilius, see *Lib. Pont.* 60.6; 61.4, ed. Duchesne 1981, pp. 291–92; and p. 297. For the plot involving the removal of Silverius, see notes 88 and 89 above.

politics and the ways of the eastern court, for he had also been a papal envoy there prior to his accession.[148] But after he became bishop of Rome, he faced increasing pressures to support the emperor's theological position in what is today called the "Three Chapters Controversy" (see below). By February 554, Vigilius had capitulated to the imperial will.

Assuming that Pope Vigilius was the instigator of this petition, the infrequent mention of issues concerning the church is striking. In contrast, the other addressees of this first constitution, the Senate and the Romans, and the contents of the *PS* more broadly, suggest that Justinian saw the primary audience for these constitutions as the wealthy, aristocratic property owners in Italy and the West. The first seven of the twenty-seven constitutions that make up the *PS* deal with the restoration of land and property, and another three deal with the restoration of goods, including slaves (13, 14, and 16). Only two of the twenty-seven constitutions (12 and 19) explicitly mention the church or bishops. This coverage contrasts with the *PS* for Africa, which, in the aftermath of defeating the Arian Vandals in 535, Justinian used to condemn heretical, or schismatic, groups and to proclaim the restoration of property to the Catholic churches.[149] For Italy, as far as we know, it is not until two years after the 554 dating of the *PS* that we have evidence that Justinian, in reference to Ravenna, had returned Arian churches to orthodox bishops.[150] If the same thing had happened in Rome, as is likely, it was not attested until thirty years later.[151]

Generally speaking, however, the *PS* did ensure some degree of financial well-being for the church in Italy and made certain changes that augmented the influence of the bishop in society. The constitutions that affirmed that property would be protected and that its ownership would revert to pre-Totila status would have been a relief to the bishops of Italy who, like their

---

[148] For Vigilius's career, see *Lib. Pont.* 61, ed. Duchesne 1981, pp. 296–302; *PCBE, Italiae*, s.v. Vigilus I. For Vigilius's letter of 540, see *CA* 92, ed. Guenther, Part II, pp. 349–54.

[149] Just. *Nov.* 37, 535 CE.

[150] Agnellus Ravennatis, *Lib. Pont. Eccl. Rav.*, ed. Deliyannis 2006, 85, pp. 252–53. *Temporibus istius Iustinianus rectae fidei augustus omnes Gothorum substantias huic ecclesiae et beato Agnello episcopo habere concessit, non solum in urbibus sed et in surburbanis villis et viculis, etiam, et templa et aras, servos, et ancillas, quicquid ad eorum ius vel ritum paganorum pertinere potuit, omnia condonavit et concessit et per privilegia confirmavit et corporaliter per epistolam tradi fecit, ex parte ita continentem: "Sancta mater ecclesia Ravennae, vera mater, vera orthodoxa, nam ceterae multae ecclesiae falsam propter metum et terrores principum superinduxerunt doctrinam, haec vero et veram et unicam sanctam catholicam tenuit fidem, numquam mutavit, fluctuationem sustinuit, et tempestate quassata immobilis permansit."*

[151] Gregory, *Ep.* 3.19; and see Tjäder 1954–55, vol. 1, p. 180, note 4. on rededicating the Arian church in Rome in the city's third region to St. Severinus in 593; and Gregory, *Ep.* 4.19 on the return of the Arian church of St. Agatha of the Goths in 594.

aristocratic contemporaries, were in control of large, landed estates whose incomes were critical for the restoration of their communities. However, Justinian's reconstruction of the administration of Italy also included a new role for the bishops that reflected his general reliance on them as his "ears and eyes" in order to increase central supervision over provincial governors (see discussion of Constitution 12).[152]

Along with a more prominent administrative role for bishops, Justinian's reconstruction relied heavily on Byzantine military commanders. This change is signaled in the *PS* by, among other things, the fact that the emperor addressed this general law to the commander in chief of the Byzantine forces in Italy, Narses, as well as to the praetorian prefect of Italy, Antiochus (for more on the Byzantine military elite, see below).[153] The praetorian prefects, however, as the highest civic officials in Italy, were increasingly involved in military matters. Indeed, the Byzantine forces in 553 refused to follow their commander back to Parma without the praetorian prefect Antiochus's assurance that he would feed and pay them.[154]

The Publication of the Pragmatic Sanction *and Its Survival*

The *PS*, as other imperial laws, was posted in public locations such as the Senate House. Following what had become normative practice after 535 (*Novel* 8), the *PS* would have also been posted in churches in Italy and read aloud.[155] But, as noted, the document itself does not survive. Most scholars ascribe to the view that what has come down to us in three separate manuscripts is a mid sixth-century summary version of Justinian's 554 enactments.[156] The common opinion is that the copy we have, which was appended to the *Epitome* of Julian, was drawn up by this same Julian, a professor of law in Constantinople, for teaching purposes.[157]

---

[152] *Just. Nov.* 8 included a section to that effect in 535, as did *Just. Nov.* 15. For this view of Justinian's utilization of bishops, see Miller and Sarris 2018, p. 42.

[153] For the general Narses, a Persarmenian by origin and a eunuch, famous for his beauty and for the final pacification of Italy, see Narses 1, *PLRE* 3B, pp. 912–28. For Antiochus, see note 154 below.

[154] Antiochus 2, *PLRE* 3A, p. 90. For his role provisioning the army, see Agathias, *History* 1.18.1–2. PPO of Italy, 552–54 CE.

[155] Humfress 2006, pp. 161–84.

[156] The *PS* survives in three manuscripts that were appended to the *Epitome* of Julian; on these see Hänel 1873, p. 185. For these manuscripts, see Archi 1978, p. 18, and also Hänel, pp. XLVII–XLVIII.

[157] Corcoran 2016, p. 172, asserts that its survival in this manuscript is not, unusual, for "most of the post-codification imperial novels that became known in Italy in fact circulated as two sets of Justinianic materials, the *Epitome* of Julian being one of them."

Unfortunately, the preamble of the *PS*, where the emperor would have more fully articulated his intent, is missing.

Some scholars have pointed to the limited transmission of the *PS* and to irregularities in the constitutions themselves – for example, at the end of every constitution is found the same date and subscription – to question whether all twenty-seven constitutions in the *PS* were issued in 554 by Justinian as the first three constitutions were. Hypothetically, some of the twenty-four constitutions that lack a heading could have been issued either earlier or later than 554 by Justinian or his successor.[158] This explanation would address some of the anomalies in the manuscripts.

Given the secure 554 date of the first three constitutions, however, along with its association in the manuscripts with the *Epitome* of the sixth-century professor of law Julian – a work that itself was regarded as authoritative by the seventh-century historian Paul the Deacon – I follow the consensus view of the *PS* as a sixth-century collection of Byzantine enactments, beginning with Justinian's first constitution in 554 and perhaps extending into the reign of Justin II (565–74). As such, the constitutions in the *PS* were directed to Italy and claimed broad application to "all known inhabitants in the West."[159] Thus, Constitutions 4 through 27 of the *PS* reflect a sixth-century Byzantine vision of rule for Italy in response to the particular circumstances beginning in 554 and extending not much later, given the early association of the *PS* with the sixth-century *Epitome* of Julian.

The Opening of the PS

The *PS* makes a strong claim that Justinian is continuing the government and the policies established by the legitimate rule of the Amals and of the Senate. The first constitution (1) forcefully asserts continuity with the former regime before restating the validity of Justinian's and his wife's grants and gifts not just for Rome but also for all those living in the western provinces:

---

[158] Archi 1978, pp. 11–36 raises doubts about the dates of the later constitutions. Battistella 2017, pp. 52–53, with bibliography in note 156, follows Archi to argue that only the first three constitutions were issued in 554, and that the remaining constitutions may reflect the influence of Pope Pelagius I (556–61) or earlier. If so, then they could have been gathered for reissuing with the 554 constitutions.

[159] *PS*. c. 1, Sarris and Miller 2018, p. 1116. For the importance of the *Epitome* of Julian, which was taken as authoritative no later than Paul the Deacon in the seventh century, see especially Kearley 2010, pp. 383–85, and more broadly on the promulgation of Justinianic Law in Italy, Corcoran 2016, pp. 163–97.

c.1. All concessions granted by Amalasuntha or Athalaric or Theodahad to
be confirmed.

Pursuant to the petition of the venerable Vigilius of the elder Rome,[160] we
have deemed it necessary to make certain dispositions pertinent to the
advantage of all known inhabitants of the West.

First, then, we command that all concessions granted by Athalaric, his
royal mother Amalasuntha, or Theodahad, at the request of the Romans or
after their Senate had asked for it, shall be preserved inviolably; we also wish
to be kept intact those conferred by ourselves or by our late consort
Theodora Augusta, of pious memory. No license is to be granted to anyone
to oppose grants or concessions known to have been made by the abovementioned persons, on any matters or heads whatsoever. There is an
exception; the grant of the property of Marcianus made by Theodahad to
Maximus. We bear in mind that we granted a half share of that to the Most
Illustrious Liberius, leaving the magnificent Maximus the other half; these
are to be confirmed as remaining with each of them.[161]

However, despite the assertion of imperial concern for the economic and
political well-being of the propertied classes, Justinian's claims to continuity
cannot be taken at face value; he had used such declarations in the past to
mask innovations in law and in the administration of the provinces.[162]

But the absence of any rhetoric of victory is similarly striking. Given the cost
and length of the war, Justinian may have seen it as more politic to omit claims
that the reconquest proved divine favor, although some of this sort of tri-
umphalism may have been included in the missing preamble. Rather, in this
554 constitution Justinian emphasized that the Amal regime had ruled with his
support, having received formal recognition as a legitimate Roman state.[163]

---

[160] I have here omitted the insertion of "bishop" after Vigilius's name found in the Sarris and
Miller 2018, p. 1116, since this is an assumption not in the text.

[161] Miller and Sarris 2018, pp. 1116–17. *Just. Nov.*, ed. Shoell and Kroll, 1954, c. 1, ed. p. 799: *Ut omnia
firma sint, quae Amalasuinta vel Atalaricus vel Theodatus concesserunt. Pro petitione Vigilii
venerabilis antiquioris Romae <episcopi> quaedam disponenda esse censuimus ad utilitalem
omnium pertinentia, qui per occidentales partes habitare noscuntur. Inprimis itaque iubemus, ut
omnia quae Atalaricus vel Amalasuinta regia mater eius vel etiam Theodatus Romanis vel senatu
poscente concesserunt, inviolabiliter conserventur. Sed et ea quae a nobis vel a piae memoriae
Theodora Augusta quondam coniuge nostra conlata sunt, volumus illibata servari, nulla cuicumque danda licentia contra ea venire, quae a praedictis personis pro quibuscumque rebus vel
titulis data vel concessa esse noscuntur; excepta videlicet donatione a Theodato in Maximum pro
rebus habita Marciani, ex quibus dimidiam portionem Liberio viro gloriosissmo dedisse memi-
nimus, reliqua dimidia Maximo viro magnifico relicta; quas apud utrumque firmiter manere
censemus.*

[162] Maas 1986, pp. 17–31 with bibliography.

[163] As early as 497 or 498, Theoderic had certain imperial prerogatives, such as the right to appoint
one of the two consuls for each year; Heather 2018, p. 22 and Heather 1996, pp. 215–21.

Loyalty to the Amals and to Justinian was rewarded. Liberius had served the Amals and then changed allegiance prior to Totila's rise, successfully executing Justinianic diplomatic as well as military missions in Sicily and Spain. He lived and worked into a remarkably old age, into his late 80s.[164] Justinian's gift of property to Liberius for fighting against Totila advertised the value of loyalty to the new regime, demonstrating graphically how the emperor would act "for the advantage of all known inhabitants in the West."[165]

As many of the constitutions in the *PS* emphasized, Justinian strove to reassure the Italo-Romans that no retribution would be taken against those who had supported the Amal family. The blame rests entirely on Totila, who took over the Gothic War effort from 540 until 552, followed by Teia, 552–53. Consequently, Justinian voided all gifts, contracts, and offices held under the "usurper" – in Latin, *tyrannus* – Totila.[166] This word is found in only one other of Justinian's *Novels*, and there it is used in reference to the history of a province.[167] Labeling the reign of Totila as the "period of the usurper" underscores the eastern interpretation of the war.[168] In fact, Totila, a great-nephew of King Theudis of the Visigoths, was invited to be King by the Ostrogoths to lead the war effort.[169] Certainly, this massaging of history to rationalize Justinian's actions is not a new strategy for this emperor.[170] It served Justinian well again here, for it justified the recovery of possessions and lands from the defeated enemy and his supporters.[171]

---

[164] Liberius 3, *PLRE* 2, pp. 677–81.

[165] *PS.* c.1, Miller and Sarris 2018, p. 1116. This indicates that now Justinian is legislating for the former Roman territories of the West as a whole.

[166] *PS.* c.2., eds. Shoell and Kroll, 1954, p. 799: *Ut per Totilanem factae donationes omnes irritae sint. Si quid a Totilane tyranno factum vel donatum esse invenitur cuicumque Romano seu cuicumque alio, servari vel in sua firmitate manere nullo modo concedimus, sed res ablatas ab huiusmodi detentatoribus antiquis dominis reformari praecipimus. Quod enim per illum tyrannidis eius tempore factum esse invenitur, hoc legitima nostra notare tempora non concedimus.* Translation by Miller and Sarris 2018, pp. 1117–18: c. 2. "All gifts made by Totila to be inoperative. In no way do we permit any act of the usurper Totila, or grant found to have been made by him to any Roman, or to anyone else, to be upheld or to remain in its own force; we instruct that property is to be taken away from such holders and restored to its original owners. We do not allow an act found to have been made by him during his usurpation to leave its mark on our law-abiding times." See note 168 below for Totila as a usurper.

[167] *Just. Nov.* 28. 1, 535 CE refers to an ancient tyrant, Polemon, of Pontus. On this, see Archi 1978, pp. 22–24.

[168] *PS* c. 2 labels Totila a usurper, in Latin *tyrannus*, and c. 12 talks of the period of the usurpers [*tyranni*]," meaning Totila (540–52 CE), and his successor, Teia (552–53 CE).

[169] Procop. *Wars* 7.2.18, and 7.3.1; Jord. *Rom.* 379; *Lib. Pont.* 61.7, ed. Duchesne 1981, p. 298. For other sources on Totila's elevation, see Totila, *PLRE* 3B, p. 1329.

[170] On this as typical Justinianic strategy, see Maas 1986, pp. 17–31.

[171] There may have been more of this eastern interpretation in the now lost preface to the *PS*; see my discussion above and note 156 above.

The Constitutions of the *PS*. The twenty-seven enactments, or constitutions, of the *PS* that applied to Italy and the West fall under three broad categories: the restoration of property and people, the tax system, and the administration of Italy. As well, the *PS* supplies specific information about the restoration of the capital after the Gothic War and the growing militarization of Byzantine Italy.

Property and People Restored. Most of the *PS* is devoted to the restoration of property and goods. These enactments would assuage the concerns of landowners and others who had suffered property losses as a result of the Gothic War. As befits Roman law, the constitutions are quite specific about the nature and mechanics of the goods to be returned: Constitution 3 stipulates that the loss of documents does not hinder the return of property; Constitutions 4 and 5 stipulate the return of properties – such as flocks or lands – even if that property had been sold out of fear; Constitution 7 records that deeds are not to be revoked; Constitution 8 covers the return of all movable and immovable property; Constitution 13 reiterates the restoration of flocks that may have been accidentally found to have wandered into another person's lands; Constitution 14 stipulates that restitution must be made for any stolen goods; Constitution 16 stipulates the return of slaves or farmers (*coloni*)[172] detained by others; and Constitution 21 requires that even those who have taken some building material and incorporated it into another construction must return it. For, as Justinian states in Constitution 7.5, "We think it not unlikely that at that period [under Totila] fear, or violence, was responsible for much being done that the justice of our time demands should be rescinded."[173]

Given the emphasis on the return of properties and goods, it is reasonable to think that many who were seeking this law were Italo-Roman senators who had been among those who had fled to Constantinople to seek refuge during the war, especially in the final phases of the fighting under Totila or Teia. Indeed, "the Most Illustrious and Glorious Senators" (*viros etiam gloriosissimos ac magnificos senatores*) are singled out in the final constitution, 27, as receiving the right to travel freely to and from the court in Constantinople and to go and stay as long as they like in any province of Italy "for the purpose of recovering their lands, as it is difficult for holdings to

---

[172] The *coloni*, the farmers, in Ostrogothic Italy were tied to their lands, but their precise status is still disputed. See Miller and Sarris 2018, p. 1124, note 30 for bibliography.

[173] *PS* c. 5, Miller and Sarris 2018, p. 1119. Just. *Nov. App. VII*, ed. Schoell and Kroll, 1954, iii, p. 802: *cum non absque ratione esse putamus, multa tunc temporis per metum vel violentiam facta esse, quae nostris temporibus rescindi exposcit iustitia.*

be revived, or given their proper cultivation, in the absence of their masters."[174] Totila had deliberately targeted and confiscated the lands of senators, and the properties of absentee senators were particularly vulnerable. This constitution also encouraged continuing interaction between the court and western senators, whose support the Byzantine state needed for the payment of taxes; the opening section makes this explicit by calling these men both "our senators and taxpayers" (*senatoribus nostris vel collatoribus*).[175] The other large landholder in Italy who would benefit from this emphatic restoration of property was the church, whose reliance on Byzantine administrators to facilitate the recovery of its properties will be discussed later in this chapter in the context of the papacy of Pelagius.

Taxes. The restoration of property and the changes to the administration of Italy stipulated in the *PS* were intended to ensure that the collection of taxes continued without interruption, even as the emperor asserted his desire to protect taxpayers from fiscal abuse. Tax collection was essential from the eastern imperial perspective in order to finance a military presence and hence retain control of Italy. A number of constitutions – 9, 10, 12, and 18 – address the restoration of a Roman system of taxation that had been weakened and in places destroyed by twenty years of fighting.[176] In an attempt to reassert preexisting practices, Justinian asserted that taxes be collected "regularly, at the usual times and places" and in the usual manner.[177] This ruling presupposed that these administrative practices were even still remembered by local communities despite the displacements of the war years. The desired return to prewar practices emerges as well from the amounts stipulated for tax collection; these were to be the same as before the war, with the burden of collection and making up any shortages falling on provincial governors and their staffs.[178] Procopius singled out Justinian's agent, Alexander the Logothete, as an example of how greedy and cutthroat Byzantine tax collectors in Italy could be.[179]

---

[174] Just. *Nov. App.* VII, ed. Schoell and Kroll, 1954, iii, p. 802 states: *Sed etiam in Italiae provinciam eundi eis et ibi quantum voluerint tempus commorandi pro reparandis possessionibus aperimus licentiam, cum dominis absentibus recreari possessionibus aut competentem mereri culturam difficile sit.*

[175] Justinian, *Nov. App.* VIII, ed, Schoell and Kroll, 1954, iii, p. 802. Constitution 27 begins: *Viros etiam gloriosissimos ac magnificos senatores ad nostrum accedere comitatum volentes sine quocumque impedimento venire concedimus, nemine prohibendi eos habituro licentiam, ne senatoribus nostris vel collatoribus debitus introitus quodammodo videatur excludi.*

[176] On this, see Sarris 2015, pp. 126–36, and more broadly, Tedesco 2015.

[177] *Just. Nov. App. VII* eds. Schoell and Kroll, 1954., iii, p. 800, c. 10.

[178] *Just. Nov. App. VII*, eds. Schoell and Kroll, 1954 iii, p. 800, c. 9.

[179] Procop. *Secret History* 26.27–30. For Totila's harangue, see Procop. *Wars* 7.9.9 and also 7.1.32–.33.

Justinian professed concern for protecting taxpayers not only from his own administrators but also from aristocratic landowners who were customarily well placed to avoid taxes or to extract the funds from their clients or tenants. Such concerns justified the inclusion in Constitution 12 of provincial landed gentry and bishops in the choice of provincial governors "from the actual provinces that they are going to govern."[180] This innovation, as it turns out, did little to protect the non-elites from their wealthy landowning neighbors, for its implementation relied on these same rich property owners. Indeed, this system was quite flawed in terms of protecting taxpayers, as several scholars have observed.[181] Moreover, Justinian's optimism about a "return to usual" tax collection soon ran up against the reality of ongoing warfare in Italy. Byzantine forces continued to fight Ostrogothic soldiers until 556, and they also faced a Frankish assault on Italy in 553–55. In response, in 555 Justinian directed another law, addressed to Narses, the general in charge of Italy, to Pamphronius, the urban prefect of Rome, and to the Senate. Justinian acknowledged that the recent attacks had been harmful and so he deferred the payment of debts for those in Italy and Sicily for five years.[182] The landed aristocracy and the church certainly benefited from this law.

The administration of tax collection under Byzantine rule gave additional incentives to landowning senators to remain involved in the choice of provincial governors on a local level, but it weakened the motivation for senators to hold office in the civic administration of Rome or Italy, the traditional means to power and prestige that had continued under the Ostrogoths. Indeed, as Totila had pointed out when he had lectured the senators after he took back the city of Rome, Byzantine administrators had been hard on Italo-Roman senators, stripping them of practically all of their offices and taxing them without mercy; in contrast, the senators had enjoyed honors, high office, wealth, and peace under the Ostrogoths.[183] Totila's warning was prophetic, for the system put in place during the period of reconstruction would reinforce the burden of Byzantine taxes and deprive

---

[180] *Just. Nov. App. VII*, eds. Schoell and Kroll, 1954, iii, pp. 800–01, c. 12.

[181] Heather 2018, pp. 64–68, on these changes on a local and empire-wide level prior to Justinian. For the problems under Justinian, see Sarris 2011, pp. 130–31.

[182] *Just. Nov. App. VIII* ed. Schoell and Kroll, 1954, iii, p. 803. This law was directed to Narses, Pan(m)fronius, and the Senate of Rome. Pan(m)fronius was most likely the urban prefect of Rome; see Lounghis, et al., 2005, p. 337, and Pamphronius, *PLRE* 3B, pp. 962–63, which suggests that he is descended from the *vir illustris Pamphronius*, correspondent of Ennodius (*PLRE* 2, p. 825).

[183] Procop. *Wars* 7.21.12–17.

senators of access to high office. It is no wonder that Procopius safely inserted this criticism into the mouth of King Totila.

Administration. The *PS* contained some significant changes to the administration of Italy that would, in essence, bring this province more in line with Justinian's treatment of other provinces, such as North Africa.[184] Although Justinian had promulgated some changes in earlier laws in his *Code* in the first and second editions of 533 and 534, it is unlikely that these had been applied in Italy by the Ostrogothic rulers, who, especially after the death of Amalasuntha in 535, would not have accepted many of these laws "so redolent of claims at once imperial and Catholic."[185] Belisarius's invasion in late spring 536 and the ongoing warfare in Italy made the application of the *Code* and newer laws, the *Novellae*, dependent upon whether or not the Byzantines controlled an area, and that control had shifted during the course of the Gothic War.[186] The one *Novella* directed to the pope in Rome in 535 was part of an imperial effort to win the clergy over to Justinian's war effort, but its application in Italy was not likely.[187] Thus, the *PS* represents, for the first time, a full statement about the application of Justinian's law to Italy.[188]

Constitution 12: *Bishops and Landowners in the Administration of Italy.*
Constitution 12 is of key importance in the Justinianic reorganization of Italy. This enactment brought the bishops and local landowners into the process of determining provincial *iudices* – that is, provincial governors – for the first time in Italy. Governors were responsible for determining tax payments and adjudicating disputes. Because Justinian had wanted to ensure the independence of these provincial governors, he removed the payments, known as *suffragium*, typically required for one to attain civic office. Because this was a noteworthy change, the constitution is worth citing in full:

---

[184] Maas 1986, p. 21, observed that Justinian's reforms were part of his "all-embracing effort to impose good order and unity through the empire thereby earning the divine favor necessary to maintain his throne."

[185] Corcoran 2016, p. 169 and pp. 169–75 for an excellent survey of the bibliography on the Justinianic *Code*.

[186] The *Novels* were never officially codified by Justinian, who continued to legislate. Unofficial collections of his laws circulated. For this, see Corcoran 2016, pp. 169–75. For *Novels* dated from 535 and after; see Kruse 2019, pp. 223–24.

[187] *Just. Nov.* 9, 535, was directed to "archbishop and patriarch of Old Rome"; see Sarris and Miller 2018, p. 1116, note 1. This law extended to the bishops of Italy a right granted to the eastern churches in 530, to claim property owned in the last 100 years. The emperor rescinded this law in 541, in part due to complaints by property owners, and reverted to the previous policy of granting possession up to a period of forty years; *Just. Nov.* 111 in 541 CE and *Nov.* 131, c. 6, 545 CE.

[188] I agree with Liebs 1987, p. 126, who rejects with good reason any suggestion that the *PS* refers back to the original promulgating constitutions of 533 and 534. Similarly, Corcoran, 2016, p. 170, rejects this idea. For the PS as an attempt to restore social and economic order through law, see also Miller and Sarris 2018, p. 1116, note 1.

c.12. *Suffragium* [= payment for office] from taxpayers. We command that the appointment of provincial governors is to be made from the actual provinces which they are going to govern, suitable men who are capable of governing the place. The appointment is to be without *suffragium*; and the customary codicils are to be issued to them through the office-holder concerned, with the condition that should they be found to have inflicted any injury on the taxpayers, to have exacted anything in excess of the set taxes, or to have caused loss to landowners over compulsory purchases by using excessively heavy weights, by other prejudicial or burdensome acts, or by using *solidi* below the true weight, they are to give compensation out of their own resources. Also, if any administrator or tax-official [*actionariis*] is found to have been acting this way during the period of the abominable usurpers [*tyrannorum*], we command that he is to make restitution out of his own resources to the person from whom he has stolen. We wish the freedom of our subjects from loss to be ensured at all points.[189]

Although an earlier precedent for the inclusion of bishops and local notables in the selection of a local official existed in an early sixth-century law concerning the designation of *defensores* in the eastern parts of the empire, or legal advocates, assigned to cities to restrain the abuses of the imperial administration, the inclusion of bishops and local notables in the designation of a provincial governor was a new development for Italy.[190] Like the early sixth-century law, Constitution 12 was intended to increase the civic influence of bishops and local elites at the expense of the administrators or senators who held these offices.[191] Now the local bishop and large landowner

---

[189] *Just. Nov. App. VII*, ed. Schoell and Kroll, 1954, iii, p. 802, c. 12. *De suffragio collatorum. Provinciarum etiam judices ab episcopis et primatibus uniuscuiusque regionis idoneos eligendos et sufficientes ad locorum administrationem ex ipsis videlicet iubemus fieri provinciis, quas administraturi sunt, sine suffragio, solitis etiam codicillis per competentem iudicem eis praestandis ita videlicet, ut si aliquam collatoribus laesionem intulisse inveniantur aut supra statuta tributa aliquid exegisse, vel in coëmptionibus mensuris enormibus aliisque praeiudiciis vel gravaminibus aut iniquis solidorum ponderibus possessores damnificasse, ex suis satisfaciant facultatibus. Quod etiam si quis de administratoribus aut actionariis de praeteritorum nefandorum tyrannorum tempore fecisse invenitur, ex suis facultatibus ei, a quo abstulit, restituere iubemus, cum nos indemnitatem subiectorum undique volumus procurari.*

[190] The choice of the *defensores* of cities in an earlier law, *C. Just.* 1.55.8, is correctly dated to the sixth-century easterm empire; see Brown 2012, p. 347, and note 47. On the importance and novelty of Constitution 12, see too Lizzi Testa 2018, pp. 149–62.

[191] Schmidt-Hofner 2014, pp. 487–523, has argued that the growing power of the office of the *defensor* led to political resistance on the part of local elites against the more powerful imperial government officials or senators who held this office. Miller and Sarris 2018, p. 185, note 1, on *Nov.* 15, observe that by the time of Justinian, the holders of this post had failed to protect the populace because they relied on imperial and senatorial aristocrats. For the reassignment of these duties to the bishops, see my discussion of Constitution 12 below.

would choose the provincial governors who would collect their taxes and administer their local laws.[192]

The inclusion of bishops in the choice of provincial governors as a means of countering the influence of the local landed elites is also consistent with Justinian's tendency, as outlined by Roger Scott, to "make the bishop the point of contact between the imperial government and local authorities."[193] Thus, in 553 the emperor gave the local bishops a number of the responsibilities previously delegated to the *defensor civitatis* (see *Nov.* 145 of 553). However, Constitution 12, like other of Justinian's reforms, was flawed insofar as it relied on the cooperation of the local notables, including members of the senatorial aristocracy, to restrain the locally powerful men – that is, themselves![194] Therefore, I do not see this as an effective restriction on the abuses of powerful officials, though it may have been so intended.[195] Nor do I see it as a burden, as some scholars have argued; rather, it opened up possibilities for increased political influence for the bishops and local elites in the late sixth century, as the appeals of Pope Pelagius I to provincial governors suggest (see discussion below).[196]

There is one other outcome from Constitution 12 that I want to emphasize, because it undermined the attraction of traditional civic senatorial office for wealthy landowners. With this new law, senatorial aristocrats could themselves become or could delegate their clients as provincial governors and thus control on a local level the men who made key determinations about their own tax burdens as well as the enforcement of law. None of these powers required the local landowner to take office. This situation even contrasts with the one in the East, where there was incentive for local elites to take on office and to enter the Constantinopolitan Senate to avoid financial responsibilities.[197] In Italy, Constitution 12 allowed elites on a local level to limit their financial burdens.

This system was so satisfactory to local landowning elites that Justin II extended it to all the provinces in 569 after Justinian's death. It is noteworthy that Justin asserted that he had acted out of his desire to diminish complaints

---

[192] Malalas, *Chron.* 16.12 claims that Anastasius dismissed all members of the city councils and in their place creates *vindices* in cities. Cf. John Lydos, *de Magistratibus* 3.49, ed. Wuensch 1967, p. 208 and Evagrius, *HE* 3.42. Scott 2012, pp. 18–19, supports this view. The imperial officials, known as *vindices*, appear as early as the reign of Anastasius (491–518 CE). On notables, see Laniado 2002, pp. 27–40.

[193] See Scott 2012, pp. 18–19.   [194] On this I agree with Miller and Sarris 2018, p. 185, note 1.

[195] Brown 1984, p. 12, arguing against earlier scholarship.

[196] See my discussion and notes 273–277 below.

[197] Sarris 2011, pp. 130–31 sees this as a development between the reigns of the emperors Theodosius II and Anastasius where accommodations were reached with the "owners of the expanding estates."

from provincials about taxes.[198] But as Peter Sarris has argued convincingly, in fact, during his rule Justin II gave greater power to landowning elites – that is, to men who were leading city councillors as well as to locally based senatorial landowners – a policy that went against many of Justinian's reforms.[199] The ability of local landed elites to designate their own provincial governors, as attested first for Italy by Constitution 12 after the war, suited the needs of the landowning senatorial aristocrats, but it also discouraged them from holding high civic office in Italy and, as I discuss in Chapter 7, removed some of the financial incentive to take an active role in the Senate in Rome.

The Growing Militarization of Italy. The presence of Byzantine troops in Italy was a mixed blessing. On the one hand, they offered Italo-Romans protection from invading forces. Byzantine soldiers would be useful even for those landowners who had developed their own armed forces during the war, as had, for example, the brothers Tullianus and Deopheron, who had employed peasants, slaves, and mercenaries to protect estates in Bruttium and Lucania.[200] Landowners needed their slaves and farmers (*coloni*) to work on their estates.[201] Yet the price for having protective forces in Italy was increasing Byzantine taxation and control, economic as well as political.

The Byzantine administration of Italy took a decidedly military turn in the later sixth century. As T.S. Brown observed:

> It would be wrong to see the end of the Gothic War as marking a full-scale return to civilian rule. There is a striking absence of references to a strict division between civil and military authority. The *Pragmatic Sanction of 554* cannot be taken as a blueprint for a return to civilian government since only one clause [Constitution 23] points to a division between civil and military authority by specifying that cases involving civilians should be tried by civil

---

[198] *Just. Nov.* 149.1, trans. Miller and Sarris 2018, p. 962: "Accordingly to spare the provinces from unlawful actions by intruders from abroad, and ourselves from the trouble of frequent suits against them, we enjoin them to holy bishops of each province, and those among its landowners and inhabitants who play the leading roles to submit to our Majesty and those who occupy the first rank among the land-owners and inhabitants, to report to us by a common petition the names of those whom they deem competent to administer the province."

[199] Miller and Sarris 2018, p. 960, note 1 emphasize how Justin II's rule brought "a rapprochement between the imperial government and members of the imperial and provincial aristocracy." These policies aided members of the senatorial aristocracy, who benefited from his rule by gaining, for example, tax relief (*Just. Nov.* 148).

[200] For Tullianus, see Procop. *Wars* 7.18.20–22, 7.22.1–5; for Deopheron, ibid. 7.30.6. For this phenomenon, see Brown 1984, pp. 194–97; and note 108 above.

[201] Procop. *Wars* 7.22.20–21 relates how Totila forced senators to order their slaves and farmers to go back to work on the farms instead of fighting in the war so that they could have their masters' property. This did not take place, so the landowners still needed farm workers.

judges; however, this procedure remained customary well into the period of recognized military dominance.[202]

Constitution 23 aimed to reverse the practice that had developed under the Ostrogoths of including an Ostrogothic military official along with a Roman (i.e., civilian) official to solve civic disputes.[203] Military judges had continued to be involved in legal disputes in areas under Byzantine rule during and after the war. In a fascinating land dispute that spanned the period of the Gothic War and concluded after the *PS* was promulgated, we find the Goth Gundila turning to the Catholic bishop, the Arian bishop, and the patrician and general Belisarius to resolve his claims to land. Only in its final stage in 557, right before the papyri break off, do we see Gundila once again pleading before the bishop of Rome.[204] In this case, it was the bishop's intervention that was last recorded, but in the letters of Pope Pelagius I, we see their involvement in administering justice.[205]

The lack of division between civil and military duties in the *PS* is in line with the changed nature of provincial government after Justinian's reforms of 535–39; the emperor had appointed several provincial administrators who combined civil and military functions.[206] This change had happened earlier in Italy as well; in 542 Justinian had appointed Maximinus as prefect of Italy and had given him authority over military personnel at a critical moment in the war (see Table 6.1).[207] Justinian continued to appoint officials who combined civic and military responsibilities. By 584, the supreme military commander of Italy was identified with the title of *exarch*, a position that combined civic and military power.[208]

Certainly, the Byzantine civic administration continued to function in Italy after the Gothic War, with the emperor appointing praetorian prefects

---

[202] Brown 1984, pp. 8–9.

[203] PS c. 23, eds. Schoell and Kroll 1954, iii. p. 802: *Ut civiliter inter se causas audient. Lites etiam inter duos procedentes Romanos vel ubi Romana persona pulsatur, per civiles iudices exerceri iubemus, cum talibus negotiis vel causis iudices militares immiscere se ordo non patitur.* Cf. Cass. *Var.* 7.3 on the practice of disputes between a Goth (i.e., a soldier) and a Roman (i.e., a civilian) heard jointly by a military (i.e., Gothic) judge and a Roman magistrate. See too Miller and Sarris 2018, p. 1128, note 43.

[204] *PItal* 49, ed. Tjäder 1954–55, vol. 2, p. 299 is an enquiry into Gundila's property. For more discussion of this case, see Amory 1997, pp. 321–22.

[205] *PItal* 49, ed. Tjäder 1954–55, vol. 2, p. 29. Pelagius *Ep.* 31, 73, ed. Gassó and Batlle 1956, pp. 87–88, 185–86.

[206] Brown 1984, p. 9, note 17. See too Maas 1986, pp. 17–31, who notes that Egypt's Augustal Prefect after 539 CE combined civic and military authority. Interestingly, Liberius, recognized in *PS.c.*1, had also held this office in a career that included both military and civic posts.

[207] Maximinus 2, *PLRE* 3B, pp. 865–66; Procop. *Wars* 7.6.9.

[208] The first record of the exarch as a title is in 584; see Jones 1964, p. 312 and Brown 1984, p. 48, note 31. He is identified as the patrician Decius in a letter of Pelagius II, *Ep.* 1; addressed as *Vir gloriosus dominus Decius patricius* and was in Ravenna in 584. He is most likely a member of the Decii of Rome. See too note 137 above.

of Italy and urban prefects of Rome as well as lesser officials known as *vicarii* and the above-discussed provincial governors. During this period of reconstruction, praetorian prefects were charged with publishing and administering the law, overseeing the collection of the land tax, and ensuring that civic officials fulfilled their responsibilities. Nonetheless, the holders of this office in the post-Gothic War period were predominantly easterners; Longinus and Acataphronius were both likely eastern in origin (see Table 6.1). The last known urban prefect, Ioannes, probably also an easterner, was a Byzantine appointee based in Ravenna (see Table 6.2). There is no evidence of the office of urban prefect functioning after 599 since its duties in the city had gradually been assumed by the prefect of Italy.[209]

In light of ongoing threats to their safety, Italo-Roman citizens, along with the papacy, came to rely on the military to undertake tasks that the civil administration had once handled.[210] The *Letters* of Pope Pelagius I (556–61), discussed later in this chapter, amply testify to the bishop's reliance on the Byzantine military. In the recent past, under the Ostrogothic kings, popes had turned to the Senate or the urban prefect for assistance. Now, however, popes turned to the imperial representatives with the most power in Italy, the Byzantine military officials.

The Restoration of the City of Rome and the Role of the Senate. Only a few constitutions in the *PS* were directed at "old Rome" and its Senate. Key to these laws was Justinian's concern to ensure the collection of taxes and the return to Roman – that is, Byzantine – rule. Any rhetoric of praise for the city is missing.

Constitution 19 required that the standard "measures and weights" be delivered not only to the "blessed Pope" to hold in church, a practice that had been the case in the previous legislation, but also now to the "most eminent Senate of Rome."[211] The manipulation of such weights and measures by bishops or individual landowners had allowed elites to avoid the full payment of taxes.[212] By housing these implements with the bishops and the

---

[209] Brown 1984, pp. 10–11. For the praetorian prefect taking over the duties of the urban prefect in Rome, like appointing the curator of the city's aqueducts, see Gregory, *Ep.* 5.36.

[210] See, for example, Pope Pelagius II begging the emperor Maurice in 584 to assign a *dux* or *magister militum* to defend Rome, see Pelagius II, *Ep.* 1 and note 208 above. Jones 1964, p. 1129, note 27, observed that the emperor did not assign an officer on a regular basis since it is absent from the letters of Pope Gregory I.

[211] PS c. 19. eds. Schoell and Kroll 1954, iii, p. 801: *De mensuris et ponderibus. Ut autem nulla fraudis vel laesionis provinciarum nascatur occasio, iubemus in illis mensuris el ponderibus species vel pecunias dari vel suscipi, quae beatissimo papae vel amplissimo senatui nostra pietas in praesenti contradidit.*

[212] For the manipulation of weights on papal estates, see Gregory, *Ep.* 13.37; and Miller and Sarris 2018, p. 1126, note 36.

Senate, Justinian was once more relying on a flawed system since it placed the protection of taxpayers in the hands of those groups that had manipulated the system to their own advantage.

Justinian also wanted to signal the restoration of Roman order by supporting the same groups that had been essential to the city and its government under Theoderic. Hence, the *annona* – the publicly funded food and stipends – was designated to be paid for positions "necessary to the state":

> We order that the *annona,* which Theoderic used to pay, and which we too have granted to Romans, is also to be paid in [the] future. Similarly, we order that the *annonae,* which used customarily to be paid to teachers and rhetoricians, or also to doctors or jurisconsults, are also to be disbursed in [the] future to those of them who are practicing their profession ... so that the young may be educated in liberal studies and may prosper, throughout our realm.[213]

Under Theoderic, however, as Cassiodorus's *Variae* 9.21 tells us, the Senate had been tasked with making sure that candidates for these positions were of high moral quality, and the Senate had been directly involved in overseeing their salaries. As such, the Senate had played a patronage role of some consequence. That role stopped under Justinian. And despite the *PS,* scholars have doubted the extent of the recovery of the schools of rhetoric and law in Rome after the war, especially since Ravenna was the primary seat of the Byzantine government.[214] Indeed, the poet Venantius Fortunatus, for one, moved to Ravenna, not Rome, in the 550s and 560s in search of a rhetorical education.[215]

This reference to salaries is the only time that Justinian notes the *annona* – the publicly funded stipends or funds – in the *PS.* There is no mention of the supply of free public grain to the city, a system of privileges that had been praised by Cassiodorus and that had continued in some form under the

---

[213] Translation by Miller and Sarris 2018, c. 22, eds. Schoell and Kroll 1954, iii, p. 802: *Ut annona ministretur medicis et diversis. Annonam etiam, quam et Theodoricus dare solitus erat et nos etiam Romanis indulsimus, in posterum etiam dari praecipimus, sicut etiam annonas, quae grammaticism ac oratoribus vel etiam medicis vel iurisperitis antea dari solitum erat. et in posterum per nostram rempublicam floreant.*

[214] Procop. *Secret History* 26.27–30 suggests Justinian undermined the rhetorical and legal system in the Greek East. Doubts about the recovery of legal and rhetorical schools in Rome are cast by Guillou, 1978, p. 294 and Loschiavo 2015, pp. 91–93. Liebs 1987, pp. 124–29, 195–220, and 246, has argued for the revival of the law schools in Rome after 554 until 620/630 CE.

[215] For Fortunatus, see George 1992, pp. 18–26. On pp. 23–24, George notes that Ravenna also failed to provide adequate support, for Fortunatus left that city in the 550s/560s to try his fortunes in Gaul, where in 566 he found patrons at the court of Sigibert and Brunhild.

Ostrogoths.[216] We have some evidence that some free grain distribution system continued even into the late sixth century because Pope Gregory reminded a Byzantine administrator of his duty to supply grain for the city.[217] The silence about the grain supply in the *PS* suggests a lack of imperial concern for this key component of the recovery of the city and contrasts markedly with the imperial concern for rebuilding the infrastructure necessary for its defense.

State Expenditures on the Urban Fabric of Rome. Constitution 25 allocated the maintenance of the public workshops (*fabricae publicae*) and the "customary payments and privileges of the Roman state" for the "repair of public workshops for the channel of the Tiber, the Forum, the port of Rome or for repair of the aqueducts," with the proviso that they should be paid for "solely from the actual tax-schedules that were assigned as their source."[218] These workshops produced items essential for the defense of Rome and its recovery, such as bricks.[219] However, the funds were to come from ordinary taxes. This lack of generosity is striking when we compare it with the attention paid to the city by traditionalist emperors like Majorian, who in the aftermath of an earlier occupation of the city had manifested his concern for the physical fabric of Rome in his first law in office directed to the Roman Senate (see Chapter 4). By contrast, in Constantinople Justinian had rebuilt grandly after the city had been damaged after the Nike riots; he had sponsored or rebuilt a number of palaces, the Senate and other government buildings, public squares, markets, colonnaded streets, public baths, cisterns, harbors, churches, and other charitable institutions to demonstrate his concern for the city and its population.[220] Estimates for the rebuilding of St. Sophia alone range to more than 30,000 pounds of gold solidi.[221] But in "old Rome," after two decades of war and facing demands for an ongoing military presence in Italy and new fighting in the East, there is no evidence of the emperor undertaking the restoration of a single building in his name, nor did he set

---

[216] Cass. *Var.* 6.18.2 praises the prefect of the grain supply, for instance. The system of free grain and pork was apparently functioning under the Ostrogoths.

[217] For the system of *annona* functioning still, albeit in a more limited and uneven way, at the time of Pope Gregory, see Salzman 2017, pp. 65–85.

[218] PS c. 25, eds. Schoell and Kroll 1954, iii, p. 802: *Ut fabricae publicae serventur. Consuetudines etiam et privilegia Romanae civitatis vel publicarum fabricarum reparationi vel alveo Tiberino vel foro aut portui Romano sive reparationi formarum concessa servari praecipimus, ita videlicet, ut ex isdem tantummodo titulis, ex quibus delegata fuerunt, praestentur.*

[219] Cass. *Var.* 1.25 mentions these brickworks in Rome's harbor specifically.

[220] For Justinian's rebuilding efforts in Constantinople after the Nike riots in a broad survey, see Alchermes 2005, p. 355.

[221] For the estimate, see Moorhead 2015, pp. 81–82.

aside special funds for the reconstruction of Rome, although Narses, the military head of Italy, is attested as having undertaken such work on the city's infrastructure (see discussion below).

Strikingly absent, too, is any rhetoric in the constitution that would recognize that "old Rome" deserved any special consideration. The impression that emerges from the *PS* is that the city and its Senate would be treated little differently than any other large city in any province would. The Byzantine administrators who would direct the city's restoration were to use the monies of Rome and its cities, with little outside financial help from the eastern emperor.

Travel Privileges and High Office. Constitution 12 had diminished the attraction of civic office in Italy for western senatorial aristocrats. Constitution 27 went further, for it removed any obstacles for elites who sought honors and office – not in Rome or Ravenna, but in Constantinople. This constitution allowed for travel to the imperial court in Constantinople by "our senators or taxpayers" on the grounds that this privilege would allow "Most Illustrious and magnificent senators, who wish to attend, to come to it without any impediment." In the next clause, Justinian explained that his primary motivation for this ruling was economic; landowners concerned about their properties in Italy desired to have imperial permission to travel to Italy and so could now stay "for as long as they may wish, for the purpose of recovering their lands." And the constitution goes on to explain that "it is difficult for holdings to be revived or given their proper cultivation . . . in the absence of their masters."[222] Indeed, many western senatorial aristocrats were concerned about their estates in Italy because Totila had deliberately confiscated senatorial properties as part of his attempt to break the Byzantine war effort.[223] Not only western senators but also a number of eastern elites desired this concession, for, as David D. J. Miller and Peter Sarris point out, senators in Constantinople were "also likely to have owned or inherited claims to land in Italy."[224]

If the primary intention of this constitution was economic, its social and political implications were equally consequential. We hear of a certain number of westerners who stayed on in Constantinople. Some sent agents or

---

[222] PS c. 27, ed. Schoell and Kroll 1954, iii, p. 802: *Ut qui voluerint ad praesentiam imperatoris navigare, non impediantur. Viros etiam gloriosissimos ac magnificos senatores ad nostrum accedere comitatum volentes sine quocumque impedimento venire concedimus, nemine prohibendi eos habituro licentiam, ne senatoribus nostris vel collatoribus debitus introitus quodammodo videatur excludi. Sed etiam ad Italiae provinciam eundi eis et ibi quantum voluerint tempus commorandi pro reparandis possessionibus aperimus licentiam, cum dominis absentibus recreari possessiones aut competentem mereri culturam difficile sit.*
[223] Procop. *Wars* 7.22.20–22.   [224] Miller and Sarris 2018, p. 1130, note 51.

relatives to oversee their estates in Italy. At the end of the sixth century, for example, the wealthy heiress Rusticiana, who had lived in Rome and belonged to the influential western Roman aristocratic families of the Symmachi and the Boethii, sent her brother, Symmachus, back to oversee her western estates (for discussion of Rusticiana's family, see Chapter 7).[225] Some westerners had already established themselves in Constantinople. As early as 536, a Symmachus, likely a western aristocratic senator had gone from Constantinople to Africa as a prefect.[226] Another western aristocrat, Boethius, who had been consul in 522 and was likely the son of the murdered philosopher Boethius, was active in Constantinople after the execution of his father. He attained the office of praetorian prefect of Africa after the fighting stopped and the *PS* had been promulgated (c. 556–61; see Table 6.3). The appointment of a westerner at this juncture was atypical and likely a reflection of Justinian's desire to justify his war as revenge for the elder Boethius's murder. Nonetheless, the son Boethius seems to have remained in the East, assuming that he is tied to the Anicii who are attested in the early seventh century in Constantinople and Egypt.[227]

The movement of westerners to Constantinople or to Italian estates, encouraged by this constitution, had certain advantages for emperors and senators. On the one hand, it allowed the emperor to attract wealthy western landowners to the eastern Senate and ensured their loyalty. Admittedly, this development undermined the preexisting practice that senators stayed in Rome and left only with special permission (*commeatalis*), which Theoderic had granted for certain circumstances but with the stipulation that, as in the case of the former official seeking leave from Rome in Lucania, he return to Rome: "When those days have been spent, and with the anticipation of many people, hasten to return to your Roman home. You must return to the assembly of nobles and to a concourse worthy of your character."[228] Returning to Rome was not a necessity after the Gothic War.

Justinian had also wanted to inspire loyalty to his new regime, so he advertised its rewards in the first constitution of the *PS*, which recounted the lands

---

[225] See Rusticiana 2, *PLRE* 3B, pp. 1101–2. Her brother is likely Symmachus 4, *PLRE* 3B, p. 1213. He conveyed at least one letter, 11.26 (601 CE), to Pope Gregory for her. For her estates in Sicily and Italy, see Gregory, *Ep.* 9.83 (an estate near Syracuse) and 13.26.

[226] Symmachus 2, *PLRE* 3B, p. 1213 may be of western origin, possibly tied to the Symmachus cited in note 225.

[227] See Boethius 1, *PLRE* 3A, pp. 236–7 and Table 6.3. For a branch off the Anicii in the east, see Chapter 7, note 88.

[228] King Theoderic to Eusebius, the future urban prefect of Rome, in Cass. *Var.* 4.48, 507–11: *Quibus peractis multorum desiderio, ad Romanas sedes venire festina, conventui nobilium et Digna tuis moribus conversatione reddendus.* Cf. Cass. *Var.* 7.36 on another senatorial leave from Rome.

given to Liberius for his service to the emperor. Although Liberius's family had remained in Italy, other westerners, as noted earlier, were free to pursue careers and fortunes in Constantinople.[229] Indeed, the possibilities for attaining a high civic office in Rome or Italy had significantly narrowed after the Gothic War, in large part due to the Justinianic reconstruction of the administration of Italy. After 554, most of the men who served the Byzantine government in Ravenna were from the East (see Tables 6.1–6.7).[230] Moreover, the civic offices that had granted senators political influence under the Ostrogoths, along with a concept of an elite with prestigious, autonomous Roman senatorial traditions, were challenged by the increased influence held by Byzantine administrators and the military in Italy in the decades after the Gothic War.

Rebuilding Rome after 554: The Impact of the *PS*

If we look at the rebuilding in Rome, there is evidence that the *PS* was implemented by the Byzantine administrators of Italy who had sought to restore the functions of the city. At the same time, the diminished role of western Italo-Roman senatorial aristocrats in the public civic spaces in the city is striking. As the prestige of and funding for the office of urban prefect declined and its responsibilities were gradually taken over by the praetorian prefect of Italy, who was housed in Ravenna near the military and the Byzantine administration, we should not be surprised that the last known Byzantine appointee of urban prefect, attested in 599 and a resident of Ravenna, was himself likely of eastern origin. This appointment is just one sign of the diminishing number of public roles left for Italo-Roman senatorial aristocrats after the Justinianic reconstruction, when the Byzantine administrators oversaw even the rebuilding of Rome's infrastructure.[231]

Evidence for Rebuilding by Byzantine Officials. Scholars have called attention to a vault inscription on the gate leading out of the city on the Via Appia that supports texts that attribute much of the work of restoring the walls of Rome from 554 and continuing over the subsequent twelve years to

<hr>

[229] See note 136 above.

[230] Even in Ravenna, most of the important bureaucratic positions were filled with officials sent from Constantinople; see among others Cracco Ruggini 1985, pp. 204–7; Falkenhausen 1985, pp. 86–88 especially.

[231] See Ioannes 109 in Table 6.2.

the Byzantine general Narses (see Map 1 in the beginning of the book).[232] Narses also claimed credit for the reconstruction of the Salarian Bridge in 565 and for the dredging of the Tiber.[233] Other archaeologists point to works along the rivers, notably the restoration of a number of bridges along the Anio – including the Nomentano, Mammolo, and Lucano Bridges – and connect them with Narses's rebuilding efforts.[234] And there is textual evidence that the aqueducts were similarly swiftly repaired and that they continued to be maintained through the eleventh century, although their number had been reduced. By the time of Pope Hadrian I (772–79), only four of the fourteen aqueducts had been repaired; that reduction may have been made by the Byzantine administration right after the Gothic War.[235] Pope Gregory makes it clear that it was the duty of an official in the office of the praetorian prefect in Ravenna to repair and maintain the aqueducts, even if they no longer supplied water to the public bath complexes.[236] This change in bathing habits would have reduced the per capita need for water, making the available supply adequate for a smaller population.

As Robert Coates-Stephens observed based on the *Book of the Popes*, beyond supplying water for drinking, water in post–Gothic War Rome was needed for baptisteries, mills, and small-scale baths, so four working aqueducts would have been quite adequate. The oversight of these repairs fell, again, to the Byzantine administration. The popes may have made sure that branch water supplies to major churches, notably St. Peter's, were working, but they, too, relied on Byzantine officials to oversee the maintenance of Rome's aqueducts. Thus, in 602 Gregory wrote to a subdeacon to ensure that the praetorian prefect would dispatch an official to repair the city's aqueducts that, the pope complained, were falling into disrepair.[237]

Byzantine administrators were also charged with the maintenance Auct. of Rome's many statues and monuments. In the fourth and fifth centuries, the urban prefect was tasked with that responsibility. But in the immediate aftermath of the Gothic War, this task also fell to the praetorian prefect in Ravenna or to the general Narses. For example, we know that Narses set up statues on the Capitoline and Palatine Hills and also likely in the Palatine Palace, where he could stay, as did later Byzantine officials who resided there into the eighth century.[238]

---

[232] Coates-Stephens 2006, pp. 149–66; Dey 2011, pp. 294–307. Auctarii Hauniensis Extrema, ed. Mommsen, *MGH AA IX*, p. 337: *Narses patricius cum Italiam florentissime administraret et urbes atque moenia ad pristinum decorem per XII annos restauraret.*

[233] The inscription on the Salarian Bridge was copied in the *Silloge of Einsiedeln*, *CIL* 6.1199 a–b.

[234] Coates-Stephens 2004, p. 300, note 2.   [235] Coates-Stephens 2006, pp. 151–2 and 165–66.

[236] Gregory, *Ep.* 16.6, 602 CE.   [237] Gregory, *Ep.* 12.6. See too Dey 2011, pp. 241–50.

[238] *Excerpta Sangallensia, MGH AA IX*, ed. Mommsen, p. 336: *Narsis ingressus Romam et deposuit palatii eius statuam et Capitolium.* Agnellus Ravennatis, *Lib. Pont. Eccl. Rav.* 95. See too

As the *PS* stipulated and the evidence on the ground demonstrates, "the monumental patrimony of Rome remained in the ... titular possession of the emperor, who was represented locally by officials attached to the Byzantine civil service, among whom [were] local officials in charge of the water supply and of the Palatine."[239] Therefore, when Pope Boniface IV wanted to transform the Pantheon into a church, he had to get permission from the Byzantine emperor Phocas (602–10) to do so. Similarly, when Pope Honorius (625–38) wanted to take the bronze roof tiles from the Temple of Venus and Rome to use for repairs for St. Peter's, he first needed the approval of Emperor Heraclius (610–41).[240] After the Gothic War, no major rebuilding project with imperial funding was recorded for Rome, nor do we have evidence that Justinian (527–65) or his successor, Justin II (565–74), planned to adorn "Old Rome" at their own expense.

The *PS* and St. Peter's: Bishops under Byzantine Rule

Although Justinian and his Byzantine administrators sought the involvement of the bishops of Rome and Italy to secure control of the peninsula, only one enactment, Constitution 12, discussed above, specifically tasked the bishops – along with local provincial landowners and *potentes* – to assist the state by helping to choose provincial governors. Aside from a stipulation that the church, along with the Senate, guarantee weights, there is no other stipulation directed to the bishop of Rome or the church in the *PS*. In contrast to his assertion of a religious motivation for attacking the Vandals in North Africa, Justinian does not indicate that he had any religious motivation for his war on Totila and the Ostrogoths. Justinian could have taken action in support of the Catholic Church, however, by transferring the churches of the now-defeated Arian Ostrogoths to Catholic bishops in the cities of Italy. But such motivation was not stated as reason for his actions in the surviving enactments. And as I noted earlier, such a transfer was so attested in Ravenna after the final defeat of the Ostrogothic forces in northern

Coates-Stephens 2006, p. 152. The Byzantine administrator responsible for the Palace, the *curator palatii Urbis Romae*, is attested into the late seventh century when the emperor Constans II (641–68) came to Rome and likely stayed there. Dey 2011, p. 62, note 107 cites the epitaph of Plato, father of the future pope John VII, who died in 686 as the last known holder of this office: *ICUR* 2/1, p. 442, 152, anno 687; and p. 244.

[239] Dey 2011, p. 244.

[240] *Lib. Pont.* 69, ed. Duchesne 1981, p. 317 for Boniface IV, and 72.2, p. 312 for Honorius. See too Coates-Stephens 2006, pp. 154–65.

Italy in 556.[241] Only decades later do we hear of the request of the then pope Gregory (590–603) that two Arian churches be placed under his control.[242]

Although there is no mention of funding for church restoration or building in the *PS*, churches in the city of Rome and in Italy needed repair and restoration. Yet the finances of the bishops of Rome and Italy had been greatly diminished. The bishops relied in part on rents from church properties, and these, like rents due from senatorial landowners, had been significantly reduced over the course of the war. Charitable donations were also down. Financial losses hampered the efforts of bishops to rebuild churches and their communities. The *Book of the Popes* notes only one modest church begun by Pope Pelagius (556–61), which had to be completed by his successor.[243] The only other church construction in Rome during the immediate period after the war was a rather modest transformation of a preexisting oratory in the Roman Forum, St. Maria Antiqua, which is likely dated to the reign of Justin II (565–74). We do not have any evidence of who paid for this reconstruction.[244] In contrast, in Ravenna during the Gothic War, new church buildings arose, as St. Vitale, with its splendid mosaics of Justinian and Theodora.[245]

In the aftermath of the Gothic War, Pope Pelagius sought Byzantine assistance to reconstitute the clergy and rebuild Christian communities in Rome and Italy, physically as well as spiritually. Justinian had early on advertised his willingness to bestow favors and land on the church.[246] It is understandable, then, that after the war Pelagius and other bishops increasingly turned to Byzantine military and civic figures for assistance, whereas earlier, when under Ostrogothic rule, they would have turned to senatorial aristocrats and institutions that were now, like the papacy, struggling to rebuild and restore their roles in society.

The Letters *of Pope Pelagius (556–61)*

We can see at close hand how Pelagius marshalled his resources to rebuild Christian communities and assert his authority immediately after the war. Not only have some ninety-six of his letters survived from these years, but

---

[241] See note 150 above.   [242] See note 151 above.

[243] *Lib. Pont.* 53, ed. Duchesne 1981, p. 306, note 2 cites the inscription that was on the lintel of the door for the basilica of SS. Philip and Jacob: *Pelagius coepit; complevit papa Iohannes; |unum opus amborum, par miscat et meritum.* The Church is now known as the Church of the Holy Apostles.

[244] Bordi, 2014, pp. 285–90 gives an overview of recent discussions of the dating, but it is not a settled issue by any means.

[245] For church-building in Ravenna, see Deliyannis 2010, pp. 219–76. For the mosaics in San Vitale dated to before 545 and after 540, and a second phase from 546 to 549, see her discussion, p. 137.

[246] See note 187 above; and Miller and Sarris 2018, pp. 157–59 and note 1.

unlike the letters of his papal predecessors, which, as Neil has rightly observed, were cherry-picked and heavily doctored to focus on papal primacy, disciplinary, and doctrinal issues, those of Pelagius record the earthly responsibilities of a pope dealing with the management of the church and its property as well as with the temporal needs of the clergy, the poor, and those in need.[247] Perhaps because Pelagius was himself the son of a *vicarianus* – a deputy to the praetorian prefect of a civic diocese, or a civic official on the staff of the *vicarius* and hence at least of the senatorial *spectabilis* grade – this pope was more open to detailing his mundane responsibilities. His family's aristocratic status would have made him familiar with estate management as he faced the challenges of reviving revenues from church properties that had suffered significant damage after a twenty-year war.[248] Pelagius's attention to the details of estate management is impressive; in one letter, for example, he reminds Count Gurdimer about pruning trees within five or six days before they drop seeds.[249]

In another age Pelagius would likely have put his various skills to work in a senatorial civic career path, as his father had done. As the *Book of the Popes* notes, Pelagius was, like his predecessor, Vigilius, from a senatorial aristocratic family.[250] But in the unsettled times of the Gothic War, his education and ambition had led him to the papacy and to use his skills to negotiate for Rome with the Byzantine administration.

Pelagius and Constantinople: The Three Chapters Controversy. Pelagius owed his position to his Byzantine supporters. Indeed, he had been engaged with the eastern court for some twenty years. As early as 535, Pelagius had been part of a delegation to Constantinople sent by the Ostrogothic ruler Theodahad to try to deter Justinian's invasion.[251] He then had stayed on in Constantinople as the papal representative, the *apocrisiarius*, of Vigilius. Pelagius went back to Rome during the Gothic War and is recorded as having generously given money to help feed those in need. When Totila took Rome in 546, Pelagius, as deacon, negotiated for the lives of its inhabitants.[252] Totila then sent Pelagius back to Justinian's court to advocate on his behalf.[253] Although Pelagius failed to win any concessions, he

---

[247] For an excellent summary of the survival of Pelagius's letter collections, see Neil 2015, pp. 206–20.

[248] For his status, see *Lib. Pont.* 62 ed. Duchesne 1981, p. 303. For a *vicarianus*, see Davis 2010, p. 141.

[249] Pelagius I, *Ep.* 76, ed. Gassó and Batlle, 1956, p. 191.

[250] On Vigilius's elite background, see Salzman 2019A, pp. 465–89.

[251] Caspar 1930–33, vol 2, pp. 227ff.   [252] Liberatus, *Brev.* 22, 23; and Procop. *Wars* 7.16.5–27.

[253] Procop. *Wars* 7.21.18.

remained in Constantinople, where he assisted Pope Vigilius in a conflict today known as the "Three Chapters Controversy."

In an attempt to reconcile the opponents of the 451 Council of Chalcedon and those who supported it (discussed earlier in this chapter), Justinian had issued an edict in 543 or 544 that condemned the writings or chapters of three theologians – Theodoret of Cyrrhus, Ibas of Edessa, and Theodore of Mopsuestia. Justinian had intended to end ongoing arguments about the nature of Christ between Chalcedonians, who supported the council's view of Christ as having two natures "in one person," and those who opposed this view and defined Christ as a single divine nature, the position now associated with the terms Miaphysite or Monophysite. But signing this agreement presented problems for Pope Vigilius and the western bishops because the first two theologians had been deemed acceptable at the 451 Council of Chalcedon, which had also supported Pope Leo's (440–61) formulation of the nature of Christ. Hence, to agree to Justinian's edict was anathema to western bishops.

Justinian had pressured the patriarchs of Constantinople, Alexandria, Antioch, and Jerusalem to accept his edict, but Pope Vigilius made no official statement in what appears an attempt to find another solution.[254] In 545, Vigilius was taken to Sicily by Byzantine soldiers, and was then summoned to Constantinople. Vigilius's unwillingness to condemn "The Three Chapters" led to his refusal to attend the 553 Council in Constantinople. Instead, Vigilius wrote the *Constitutum*.[255] But six months later, after being deposed by the 553 Council and facing ongoing imperial pressure, Vigilius capitulated. He wrote a letter that condemned the "Three Chapters." His deacon, the future pope Pelagius, similarly compromised. In 554 Pelagius wrote a work against the "Three Chapters," endearing himself to the emperor in what some see as a prearranged means for Pelagius's accession.[256]

When Vigilius died in Sicily on his way back to Rome in 554, as did Mareas, the priest and potential papal successor, Pelagius, back in Rome, was ordained as the next pope. He had another key Byzantine backer, for the general Narses had supported him even in the face of widespread western hostility about his condemning the "Three Chapters." Only two bishops instead of the usual

---

[254] Vigilius perhaps tried to craft a middle ground, which may explain his unwillingness to take an active stand in opposition or to break with the East: see Sotinel 2005, pp. 280–81.

[255] This is a brief summary of a much contested time period. On the "Three Chapters" and Vigilius's changing positions, see Moorhead 2015, pp. 87–92; Sotinel 1992, pp. 439–63. For Vigilius's *Constitutum de tribus capitulis*, see CA 83, ed. Guenther, Part I, pp. 230–322.

[256] Vigilius, *Ep. ex tribus capitulis, Acts of the Council of Chalcedon*, ed. Schwarz, 1940, vol. 4, part 2, pp. 138–68. For Pelagius's work, see *In Defensione trium capitulorum*, ed. Devreese 1932, 67.14 ff, and 53.25–28 on Vigilius; and pages xviii–xx for the date of this work. Procop. *Wars* 7.16.5 calls Pelagius "a close friend of the emperor Justinian."

three could be found to agree to Pelagius's ordination.[257] The *Book of the Popes* states that neither the nobility nor the clergy of Rome would enter into communion with Pelagius, and rumors surfaced that he had been involved in the death of the previous pope, Vigilius.[258] At the suggestion of Narses, Pelagius made a public vow of his innocence before the entire population at the Church of St. Pancras in modern Trastevere. This was a well-chosen location since it was believed that those who swore false oaths at St. Pancras came to a bad end.[259] Pelagius also reversed himself on the "Three Chapters." In an attempt to appease the dissatisfied western bishops and people of Rome, Pelagius wrote an open letter in late 557 to "all the people of God" professing his acceptance of the four councils and whatever his predecessors, especially Leo, had done; thus, he held Theodoret and Ibas as orthodox.[260] Nevertheless, concerns about his being under the control of Justinian persisted among the bishops in northern Italy and Gaul.[261] Pelagius was also still under suspicion from the clergy in Rome, a situation that explains why, as John Moorhead has observed, Pelagius appointed only forty-nine bishops in his five years as pope, as compared with Vigilius's eighty-one.[262] Nonetheless, Pelagius strove to restore faith through his actions in rebuilding the church in Rome and Italy.

Restoration of Liturgical Plate. In light of the resistance to Pelagius's papacy, it is noteworthy that the very next item in the "Life of Pelagius" in the *Book of the Popes* is the replacement of "all the gold and silver vessels and *pallia*" in all the churches in Rome. As we saw in Chapters 4 and 5, this was the foundational symbolic act by any bishop trying to rebuild the community of the faithful after a crisis. The importance of this act is heightened when we consider how strapped the papacy was to meet the basic needs of food and clothing for its clergy and the poor, to be discussed below. It seems likely, then, that some of the money for the replenishment of liturgical silver had come from wealthy Byzantine donors such as Narses, Pelagius's patron.

Papal Requests for Assistance. Inspired by a pastoral concern for living conditions in Rome, Pope Pelagius I often requested assistance from Byzantine officials to meet the basic needs of the clergy and the poor in the city and in Suburbicarian Italy. In an early letter of 556, Pelagius turned to

---

[257] *Lib. Pont.* 62, ed. Duchesne, 1981 ed., pp. 303–4. See too Neil 2015, pp. 212–13; and Moorhead 2015, p. 102.

[258] *Lib. Pont.* 62, ed. Duchesne 1981, pp. 303–4.   [259] Moorhead 2015, p. 103.

[260] Pelagius, *Ep.* 11, ed. Gassó and Batlle, 1956, pp. 35–40.

[261] See Pelagius, *Ep.* 7, ed. Gassó and Batlle, 1956, pp. 20–25. He reached out to King Childebert to try to win over the Gallic bishops who were opposed to him.

[262] Moorhead 2015, p. 141, note 7, cites this number in *Lib. Pont.* 62.4, ed. Duchesne 1981, p. 303, in comparison to Pope Vigilius, who appointed eighty-one bishops in *Lib. Pont.* 61.9, ed. Duchesne 1981, p. 299.

Sapaudus, bishop of Arles, and requested that he ask his father, the patrician governor of Provence, to use the rents of the properties of the church in Gaul to purchase clothing to be sent to Italy. In this letter Pelagius describes the sad economic state of Italy: "The fields of Italy are so desolate that no one occupies themselves with their recovery."[263] But rather than asking for food, Pelagius asked Sapaudus to use some of the *solidi* from the rents to buy clothing that was available in Provence – Gallic woolen cloaks or white tunics, hooded capes, and undergarments – and send it to be distributed to the poor in Rome. Pelagius wrote Sapaudus again in April 557 to send clothing, for "such great need and nudity exists in the city [Rome] that we cannot look without sadness and a pained heart on those men whom individually we know were born in honorable positions."[264] Those who had lost their status in society received the pope's personal sympathy, for indeed, he had been of senatorial status himself.

The church in Rome was financially strapped when in 560 the pope wrote to Boethius, the praetorian prefect of Africa, to send the *stipendia* – the income – of the church from foreign islands or places in Africa for the benefit of the "the clergy and the poor" because Italy was still suffering from the devastation caused by the war.[265] Pelagius indicates that this money would be used to buy food, which appeared to be available for cash. Pelagius also wanted Boethius to protect the shipment of the funds, presumably because he feared robbery or attack. He was sensitive to financial matters and tried to tamp down on the mismanagement of church funds by the clergy as well.[266] Pelagius applied his senatorial management skills to overseeing church properties, an effort now all the more critical due to the exigencies of the recent war.[267] And he was adamant about rooting out graft, writing the patrician John, *comes patrimonii*, in 559 that no one deserved any reward for anything obtained

---

[263] For Sapaudus, see Pelagius I, *Ep.* 1, Gassó and Batlle 1956, p. 1. Sapaudus was not appointed bishop until the return of Pelagius to Rome. They had close ties; see Klingshirn 2004, pp. 264–67. Pelagius I, *Ep.* 4.4, Gassó and Batlle 1956, p. 12: *quia Italiae ita desolata, ut ad recuperationem earum nemo sufficiat.*

[264] Pelagius *Ep.* 9, Gassó and Batlle 1956, pp. 30: *quia tanta egestas et nuditas in civitate ista est, ut sine dolore et angustia cordis nostri homines quos honesto loco natos idoneos noveramus, non possumus aspicere.*

[265] Pelagius, *Ep.* 85, Gassó and Batlle 1956, pp. 207–8.

[266] Pelagius, *Epp.* 65, 66, and 67, pp. 171–76 on the fraudulent papal administrator Maximilian and other schismatic bishops. See too Pelagius, *Ep.* 84, ed. Gassó and Batlle 1956, pp. 205–6 on the proper treatment of workers.

[267] The argument of Pietri 2000, p. 262, that this is a sign of the breakdown of the old system of senatorial management is not compelling, based on the letters themselves.

fraudulently.[268] Pelagius also admonished his patron, the patrician Narses, to only give money to men who were truly in need.[269]

As is clear, Pelagius did not have direct control of municipal monies, nor did he control essential services tied to the infrastructure of Rome or Italy.[270] He saw it as his responsibility to make sure that the Byzantine officials fulfilled their roles and assisted the church in its role of feeding the clergy and the poor. "Rather than as an independent authority, the pope appears here [in Rome] as an accomplice of the civil bureaucratic apparatus," and in that role he was, as Hendrik Dey observed, led "to advise and admonish more than to command."[271] Pelagius also saw it as his duty to remind Byzantine officials of their responsibilities in restoring Rome by making sure to repair its walls, statues, bridges, aqueducts, as these were necessary for city life.[272]

Disciplining Errant Clergy. Like other popes, Pelagius sought to assert his authority by disciplining errant clergy. But now Pelagius turned to Byzantine officials to assist him in this task. For example, Pelagius wrote to the Byzantine general Narses in 559, urging him to punish the bishop Paulinus of Fossombrone for financial dishonesty and for being one of a group of schismatics who opposed the "Three Chapters" and had thus broken off relations with Pelagius.[273] Frustrated by Narses's delay in responding, Pelagius then wrote to the Byzantine commander John to put Paulinus in chains "for the sake of the church."[274] Pelagius also asked for the use of force to repress another bishop, Maximilian, and sent a priest named Peter and the secretarial assistant (*notarius*) Proiectus to admonish the Byzantine general Carellus to take this action in 559.[275] Pelagius had no compunctions about instructing these officials (*defensores*) to arrest priests in northern Italy and Gaul, charging them with disobeying and disrupting the peace of the church because they doubted the orthodoxy of the Roman See.[276]

---

[268] Pelagius *Ep.* 75, ed. Gassó and Batlle, 1956, pp. 189–90.

[269] Pelagius *Ep.* 90, ed. Gassó and Batlle, 1956, p. 216.

[270] For this view, see Brown 1984, pp. 9–10 citing bishops in control of aqueducts, corn supply, etc. This view is also found in more recent scholarship, as, for example, on the annona of Rome; for a critique, see Salzman 2017, pp. 65–85.

[271] Dey 2011, p. 244.   [272] Coates-Stephens 2004, pp. 299–316; and 2006, pp. 149–66.

[273] Pelagius I, *Ep.* 60, ed. Gassó and Batlle 1956, pp. 159–61, end of March–April 16, 559 to Narses the patrician. See too Allen and Neil 2013, pp. 186–91. Pelagius's *Epp.* 69, 70, 71, ed. Gassó and Batlle 1956, pp. 178–84, asks for assistance against Paulinus.

[274] Pelagius I, *Ep.* 71, to John *magister militum*, ed. Gassó and Batlle, p. 182, dated April 559.

[275] Pelagius I, *Ep.* 65, ed. Gassó and Batlle, 1956, pp. 171–72.

[276] Pelagius I, *Ep.* 91, Gassó and Batlle 1956, pp. 217–18; Pelagius I, *Ep.* 70, Gassó and Batlle 1956, pp. 180–81; Pelagius I, *Ep.* 31, to *Sindu<l>ae Magistro Militum*, ed. Gassó and Batlle 1956, pp. 87–88, turned to the *magister militum* to resolve a case in the absence of a witness; *Ep.* 73 ed. Gassó and

Pelagius's willingness to use Byzantine administrators and generals to discipline errant clergy underscores how much resistance persisted in Italy in opposition to the "Three Chapters"; schism with Rome persisted until 573 in the church in Milan and until the beginning of the seventh century in the ecclesiastical province of Aquileia. Apparently, Byzantine administrators in northern Italy did not force dissident clergy in these areas to take communion with Rome because they needed local support in facing the Lombard invasion of Italy in 568. Although there were limits to what Byzantine officials would do against Northern clergy, nonetheless Pelagius and his successors relied on them for regaining and expanding papal authority.[277]

The Failure of the Justinianic Reconquest: Italy in Pieces

Twenty years of guerilla fighting on Italian soil may have caused many an Italo-Roman to regret his or her early support for the return of Byzantine rule. Certainly, the last decade of the war was particularly deadly, causing huge economic and population losses and massive displacements of people. After the fighting had ground to a halt, a weary Senate and surviving senators, along with the pope and clergy of Rome, could look forward to a period of reconstruction. The Byzantines had styled themselves as "liberators" of the state from tyranny, and Italo-Romans did not challenge this view as they positioned themselves to restore their city and their roles in Italo-Roman society.[278]

There are no indications that the senatorial aristocracy or the papacy had any real concerns about Justinian's government after the end of the war in 554. They had returned to Rome after crises in the past, and their resilience was a point of pride. Though a generation of Italo-Romans had suffered, and many had died during the long war, their numbers could be replenished. Aristocrats and clergy who had received favors during the war for supporting Justinian expected that the restoration of Roman rule would enable them to recover their social positions and economic fortunes. Those aristocrats who owned properties in Sicily, Sardinia, and the East were especially well positioned to reclaim their status and wealth. A number had spent the war

Batlle 1956, pp. 185–86, to the same Sindula, about one Montinianus. For Sindula, see *PLRE* 3B, pp. 1154–55. Pelagius's willingness to use force in disciplinary matters is not, I believe, as Allen and Neil 2013, p. 189, have said "the last resource," but follows upon his position. It is also, as Battistella 2017, p. 190, notes, an attempt to expand papal authority into northern Italy and Gaul.

[277] For Byzantine reliance on local communities, see Pelagius I, *Ep.* 75, ed. Gassó and Batlle 1956, pp 189–90. See too Sotinel 2005, pp. 286–87.

[278] For the war as a liberation from a tyrant, see. note 168 above.

years in safety in Constantinople or in Sicily, which had been little affected by the fighting.[279] In light of Justinian's *Pragmatic Sanction*, senatorial aristocrats and their families could look forward to the recovery not just of their property but also of their traditional leadership roles in Rome and Italy. The church, too, could anticipate assistance in reclaiming its properties, as had happened in Africa after Justinian's defeat of the Vandals in that province.

But the hoped-for restoration of senatorial power in the West did not happen. The political, economic, and social changes wrought not just by the Gothic War but, most importantly, also by the Justinianic reconstruction of the administration of Italy in the decades immediately after the resolution of the war removed the structural supports that had allowed the Italo-Roman senatorial aristocracy to retain power in late Roman society and politics. The traditional civic, senatorial aristocracy and the Senate declined rapidly in prestige and influence. The full impact of these changes that affected the senatorial aristocracy emerged most clearly at the end of the sixth and in the early seventh centuries, the subject of Chapter 7 of this book.

In contrast, the position and influence of the pope had risen significantly. As noted, during the Gothic War we find for the first time in Rome bishops from senatorial aristocratic families; Popes Vigilius and Pelagius I are emblematic of this development. Now, service to the church attracted established senatorial families. During the period of Justinianic reconstruction, the bishops of Rome secured the recovery of the church and the papacy by aligning themselves with the Byzantine administration. The *Letters* of Pelagius I offer insights into how this pope, through frequent requests to Byzantine administrators and generals, marshalled the resources from church properties to rebuild the church in Rome and Italy. Justinian's willingness to incorporate bishops into the management of this new province, a policy that he had used in other areas before, provided additional impetus to the rising status of the pope in Rome.[280] As we shall see in the next and final chapter, the papacy in the late sixth and early seventh centuries emerged as a revitalized presence in the city of Rome and in Italy.

---

[279] For the administration of Sicily and its importance during and after the war, with close ties to Constantinople for administration and its food supply, see Messina 2016, pp. 161–67.

[280] See Scott 2012, pp. 18–19, and my discussion of the *PS*.

7

The Demise of the Senate

For at that time, after the foundation of the church had been laid, all of Italy was shaken by the greatest disturbance. Then in Caesarea, near Ravenna, the prefect Longinus (568–74/75) erected a palisade in the form of a wall because of the peoples's fear [of the Lombards]. From that time, little by little, the Roman Senate grew weak, and afterwards the liberty of the Romans was laid low with the triumph [of the Byzantines].

—Andreas Agnellus (805–46?), author of *The Book of the Popes of Ravenna, 95*[1]

Competition for political favor and social preeminence had time and again stimulated Roman elites to marshal their resources, to return to the city of Rome, and to fund the restoration that allowed for the resumption of their own positions in society. The resilience, adaptability, and resourcefulness of these elites – senators, bishops, kings, emperors, and generals – over three centuries of daunting political and military crises were central components to this process. Admittedly, elites did not always respond to crises in ways that advanced the best interests of the populace or society at large. Nonetheless, their return had enabled the recovery of Rome over the *longue dureé*. And through these centuries, the Senate had survived as an autonomous political institution, enduring through and after the Gothic War. Hence, the demise of the Senate by the early seventh century is a fitting epilog to this study. Its passing is documented on the ground by the transformation of the *Curia* (Senate House) in the Roman Forum into the Church of St. Hadrian, the eastern martyr, by the Bishop of Rome, Honorius, during his pontificate (625–38). This act was rendered still

---

[1] Agnellus Ravennatis, *Lib. Pont. Eccl. Rav.* 95, p. 260 ed. Deliyannis, 2006: *Eo namque tempore, post fundamentum ecclesiae positum, tota Italia vexatione maxima exagitata est. Tunc illis temporibus in Caesarea iuxta Ravennam a Longino praefecto palocopia in modum muri propter metum gentis exstructa est. Deinde paulatim Romanus defecit senatus, et post Romanorum libertas cum triumpho sublata est.* Translation by author.

more meaningful because Honorius was from one of the last of the Roman senatorial aristocratic families, as the *Book of the Popes* proudly proclaimed.[2]

To my mind, the end of the Senate represents the final fall of Rome as an ancient city – that is, one in which the ideal of civic society inspired senatorial aristocrats and ambitious men new to senatorial status to serve the state. Therefore, I will use this chapter to discuss what I regard as the most compelling explanations for the disappearance of the Italo-Roman senatorial aristocracy and the Senate of Rome even as the Byzantine government put in place a military elite that supported the rise of the bishop's civic role in what many refer to, for simplicity's sake, as "papal Rome."

The Fall of the Italo-Roman Senatorial Aristocracy

It must have seemed to contemporaries who had survived the Gothic War that the Senate and its senatorial aristocratic members would also lead Rome's recovery as it had in the past. Indeed, the senatorial aristocracy had survived the fall of the republic "to evolve into the dominant social and economic status group in the Roman state, whose position, based on extensive landownership and reinforced by a near monopoly of key government offices, was transmitted from generation to generation through the inheritance of both landed wealth and senatorial titles."[3] As I discussed in Chapter 2, the Senate and the Roman senatorial aristocracy had gained political and social influence in late antiquity, fueled in part by Constantine, who had sought its members to serve in his new regime. Established senatorial families along with men new to political office competed for recently augmented offices and honors that were opened to them after the civil war of 312. The expansion of senatorial ranks in the later fourth century was also accompanied by increased privileges and power for the illustrious senators at the apex of power, and the *illustres* were still tied to the Senates in Rome and Constantinople.[4]

---

[2] *Lib. Pont.* 72.1, ed. Duchesne 1981, p. 323: *Honorius, natione Campanus, ex patre Petronio consule, sedit ann. XII mens. XI dies XVII*; 72.6, ed. Duchesne 1981, p. 324: *Fecit ecclesiam beati Adriani in tribus Fatis, quem et dedicavit, et dona multa optulit.* ("Honorius, born in Campania, whose father was the consul Petronius, was bishop of Rome for twelve years, eleven months, and twelve days. . . . In the areas of the Three Fates, he made the Basilica of Saint Hadrian, which he also dedicated and to which he gave many gifts.")

[3] Haldon 2004, p. 184.

[4] See my discussion in Chapter 2. For the ties of highest ranked senators to Rome but the relaxation of such requirements for *clarissimi* and *spectabiles*, see the laws on new men of curial status who attain senatorial rank, from 386 CE and then expanded between 426 and 442, *C. Th.* 12.1.111; 12.1.122 and *C. Iust.* 12.1.5. Although some *illustres* are attested as residing in the provinces, their ties to Rome were critical to participating in the Senate. See La Rocca and Oppedisano 2016, pp. 26–31 and 185–87 and Chapter 3, note 228.

A fourth-century senatorial resurgence was fitting given that the locus of senatorial action, the Senate House in the Roman Forum, had been recently rebuilt after a fire in the 280s (see Map 1 at the beginning of the book). This tall structure of red brick faced with opulent marble revetments reflected the contemporary ideals of luxury and prestige (see Figure 7).[5] Senators relished

Figure 7 Senate House in Roman Forum. Jeff Bondono. IMG_3459–20121028 (www.jeffbondono.com).

[5] For the *Curia* and its history, see among others Bond 2015, pp. 84–102.

their traditions there, as is evidenced by one of the most celebrated incidents of senatorial resistance to imperial policy that we know about from the late fourth-century city. A majority of Roman senators at that time empowered the urban prefect Symmachus to protest the Christian emperor Gratian's order to remove the Altar of Victory from the Senate House as well as the imperial seizure of funding for pagan cults.[6] Though the senators did not succeed, their willingness to take a public stand in opposition to imperial policy on this issue speaks to the importance of the Senate House and its traditions to Roman elite identity.

Adherence to a senatorial set of values in service to the state continued even after many senators had converted to Christianity by the early fifth century. The ideals and the careers that allowed senators to realize traditional honors, wealth, and status continued to attract senatorial aristocrats to civic rather than spiritual or military service, although the church and the army did also expand. In the city of Rome, for instance, we do not find large numbers of senators entering the church to seek clerical careers until the Gothic War.[7] The bishop of Rome and the clergy certainly had gained status and prestige in late Roman society, and the church had accrued wealth over time. But in Rome, the bishop faced a strong, conservative Italo-Roman senatorial aristocracy that had a significant impact on the religious life of the city as patrons and as magistrates. The bishops of Rome thus had to compete for influence in a city still run by a resilient, albeit tradition-bound civic senatorial elite well into the sixth century.

Italo-Roman senators had successfully defended their positions in society through the turbulent crises of the fifth and sixth centuries. In fact, the Senate, as the sole continuing, functioning political body, took on a newly important role as intermediary between the eastern court in Constantinople and the Ostrogothic king Theoderic. As I explained in Chapter 6, the Italo-Roman senators and the Senate enjoyed, to a degree, a revival of their political power by assisting the Ostrogothic military leaders in ruling Italy, even as the Amal court's choice of residence in Ravenna allowed for greater autonomy for senatorial aristocrats in Rome. Like the senators, the bishops of Rome benefited from Ostrogothic rule, for they, too, enjoyed increased independence from the eastern court, even as they also relied on senatorial aristocratic support to assert their views in the face of eastern imperial or patriarchal pressure to conform.[8]

---

[6] For the Altar of Victory Controversy, see Symm. *Rel.* 3; and Chenault 2016, pp. 46–63.

[7] Salzman 2019A, pp. 465–89. As I have argued, the first pope from a senatorial family was Pope Vigilius, 537–55.

[8] On this, see especially 2019A, pp. 456–89.

However, the Gothic War forced a renegotiation of Roman social and religious as well as political relations among elites. During the war, we find for the first time bishops from senatorial families.[9] After the war, bishops and senators strove to restore Rome and Italy and sought to recover their positions under a Byzantine administration. However, as I argued in Chapter 6, the changes to society and the government of Italy in the aftermath of the war – some of which were outlined in Justinian's *Pragmatic Sanction* – greatly reduced the prospect that civic senatorial aristocrats could regain political influence through their traditional avenues. Now, for example, landed gentry and bishops chose their own provincial governors. Byzantine administrators in Ravenna or Byzantine generals like Narses oversaw the food supply and infrastructure of the city of Rome, and Sicily was under the direct economic and judicial control of the eastern emperor.[10] The possibilities for competing for office were in fact further diminished as Byzantine administrators replaced Italo-Romans in positions of authority, such as praetorian prefects of Italy (see Table 6.1). Under this reconstituted government, the bishops of Rome relied heavily on imperial representatives to reinforce their authority over the clergy and population at large.

Ongoing warfare with the Franks in Italy after 554 and Lombard military successes in Italy compounded the impact of the structural changes made by the Byzantine administrators of Italy that had undermined the social and political roles of the senatorial civic aristocracy and favored the military elite. Beginning in 568, the Lombards had attacked and taken a number of northern Italian cities, including Milan in 569 and Ticinum (modern Pavia) in 572. Rome itself suffered famine and a siege in 579, but the Lombards were successfully deflected.[11] By 584, the Lombard king Authari (584–90) had established himself in the Po Valley as ruler, and Lombard dukes had taken over areas to the south at Spoletium and Beneventum[12] (see Map 6). The need for military action against the Lombards in northern and central Italy reinforced the influence of the Byzantine military. As the power of Byzantine generals and administrators in Italy grew during the last decades of the sixth and in the first years of the seventh centuries, the political influence of the Italo-Roman senatorial aristocrats declined.

---

[9] See my discussion in Chapter 6, and also Salzman 2019A, pp. 465–89.

[10] See my discussion in Chapter 6. For Sicily, see also Justinian's *Novel 75*, dated to 537, ed. Miller and Sarris 2018, pp. 553–54.

[11] The only source for the 579 attack on Rome is the *Lib. Pont.* 65.1, *Life of Pelagius II*, ed. Duchesne 1981, p. 309.

[12] For the Lombard conquests as undermining the Justinianic reconstitution of Italy, see also Moorhead 2015, pp. 106–07; Brown 1984, passim. For the Lombard invasions in general, see Zanini 1996, pp. 51–63.

Map 6 Lombard and Roman Italy in 600.

As this chapter argues, the rising power and prestige of the Byzantine military coincided with a decrease in the number of opportunities and incentives for Italo-Roman senatorial aristocrats to strive to attain positions of political leadership within the state. With the diminished viability of a civic career, participation in the Senate similarly declined. The Senate lost its role as an autonomous political institution in the last decades of the sixth and the first decades of the seventh centuries.

Given the impact of Byzantine rule on Italy, I cannot agree with those scholars who see the demise of the Senate as the result of its having been weakened irrevocably by the loss of a western emperor or as the price paid for the Gothic War.[13] Nor do I regard the end of the Senate as largely a cultural and religious response in the wake of the spread of Christianity and its values. In his pathbreaking 1984 study of senators and bureaucrats in Italy from 554 to 800, T.S. Brown concluded by attributing the demise of the Senate "most of all" to the Christianization of the empire:

> More important is the broader question of morale. In the last analysis the Senate was defined by Roman secular values as much as by birth or wealth, and the increasing authority of Christian and other worldly values could only in the long term erode its identity as a self-conscious choice.[14]

However, Brown's view fails to adequately acknowledge that Christianity had supported Roman senatorial elites with their "secular values" for more than three centuries. Nor am I convinced by what could be termed a continuist view. Maya Maskarinec, for one, sees the implantation of a Christian cult in the seat of the former Senate as "a dedication that ... affirmed the role of Rome's senatorial elite in steering the empire" because Bishop Honorius gave this church an "administrator-turned-martyr" fitting to its senatorial past.[15] To my mind, the continued symbolic role rings hollow. The cult and church of St. Hadrian did not preserve the aristocratic values of service to state, even if some of the "secular" values of Italo-Roman senatorial aristocrats – birth and wealth, along with an appreciation of classical learning – continued. With the demise of the Senate House, its role as the locus of competition for political power that had stimulated senators to fund the recovery of the city for centuries had ended. Wealthy Italo-Roman senatorial aristocrats by and large retreated to their estates in Sicily and Campania or to cities with a strong Byzantine presence in Italy or the East.

---

[13] Brown 1984, pp. 21 and 25 in reference to the work of Wes 1967.   [14] Brown 1984, p. 35.
[15] Maskarinec 2018, p. 47.

The Bishops of Rome and the Byzantine Administrators of the Late Sixth and Early Seventh Centuries

By contrast, the bishops of Rome took an increasingly active role in the city, even as they relied more and more on the Byzantine administrators of Italy, who had largely replaced Italo-Roman senatorial aristocrats. The emperor Maurice (582–602) granted military and civic authority over Italy to the governor, now called the *exarch*, who was based in Ravenna. The exarch was assisted by the praetorian prefect of Italy in civic administrative matters. The praetorian prefect, in turn, had authority over Rome and the city's urban prefect, the office that had previously been a pinnacle of a senatorial career. However, under the Byzantines, the powers and duties of the urban prefect were greatly diminished, and the position's disappearance in the early seventh century (the last attested holder is dated to 599) reflects the degeneration of civic life, as does the demise of the Senate.

When the exarch Smaragdus wanted to honor the Byzantine emperor Phocas (602–10) in 608, he alone, not the urban prefect, and without any reference to the senators or Senate of Rome, placed a gilded statue of the ruler and dedicated it with an inscription on a preexisting column with reused reliefs in front of the Senate House in the Roman Forum (see Map 1 at the beginning of the book for the Senate House).[16] Although the raising of this monument speaks to the conservation of the Roman Forum as a site for political action, the exarch's assertion of his control over the city by elevating this statue of the emperor well above all others in this location was a stark statement about whose authority ruled over the political life of Rome.

As symbolized by the Column of Phocas, the growing dominance of the military in Italy led the exarch to assert greater control over its civic administration. Even the office of praetorian prefect of Italy disappeared, with the last appointment attested in 639. By then, the exarch was administering Italy and Rome through his own civic officials and directing the defense of the city of Rome through a commander in chief with the title *magister militum*.[17]

---

[16] For the Column of Phocas, see Kalas 2015, pp. 96–99 and 2017, pp. 173–90. For the inscription dated to August 1 608, see *CIL* 6.1200. Coates-Stephens 2003, pp. 168–86, and 2006, pp. 150–51, rightly emphasizes the Byzantine attention to the maintenance of the Roman Forum, as the Column indicates.

[17] Brown 1984 is the best treatment still of the political and social structures of Byzantine Italy. The military and political developments from 554–751 are well summarized by Zanini 1998, pp. 33–104; Guillou 1988; and in brief by Dey 2011, pp. 241–48. For the praetorian prefects of Italy, see *PLRE* 3B, pp. 1474–75. Brown 1984, p. 55 rightly notes that there was no *dux* attested in Rome in 584, but there was a *magister militum*, Castus, *PLRE* 3A, p. 275 and Gregory *Ep.* 3.51. Castus was in command of troops in Rome from 593–95, with the title of *magister militum*. The earliest attestation of a *dux* in Rome is Christoforus in 713; see Brown 1984, p. 55, note 32.

Given these changes to the administration of the city of Rome and the continuing military conflicts in Italy, it is not surprising that the bishops turned to Byzantine military administrators for assistance. Indeed, Bishop Pelagius I, as I discussed in Chapter 6, had done so during the Justinianic reconstruction period. He established a pattern in which we see the growing ties between the bishops and Byzantine generals and governors. In the last decades of the sixth century and into the seventh, the bishops turned to Byzantine military administrators not only to meet the civic needs of their communities for security and for the protection of their food supply and urban infrastructure but also to ensure their own doctrinal and disciplinary authority over the church clergy in Rome.

The increasing influence of the bishops in the late sixth and early seventh centuries did not, in and of itself, undermine the power of senatorial civic elites. On the contrary, Rome's bishops worked hard to restore senatorial aristocratic landowners to their traditional role in society. At the end of the sixth century, the bishop of Rome, Gregory (590–604), for one, intervened on behalf of impoverished aristocrats, including orphans and his own aunt, using relatively small sums of money to allow for the recovery of their senatorial status.[18] Gregory favored a well-ordered society and regarded traditional senatorial grades and ranks as signs of divine dispensation.[19] Nonetheless, the growing civic role played by bishops and their deepening reliance on the Byzantine military state are indicative of a city without a strong, present senatorial aristocracy.

For their part, the Byzantine emperors and administrators of Rome and Italy did little to restore the political roles formerly enacted by the senatorial elite and the Senate. Byzantine emperors instead turned primarily to easterners to govern Italy and Rome. Hence the possibilities for obtaining senatorial rank were greatly reduced in the late sixth and early seventh centuries. Byzantine emperors enlisted bishops to assist the exarch and his representative in Rome and Italy. Byzantine rulers could have relied more on senators and the Senate in Rome in the later decades of the sixth and the early seventh centuries, but they did not. The reasons for this choice bear additional scrutiny.

The Importance of Senatorial Status in Byzantine Italy. It is worth emphasizing that still, in the last decades of the sixth century, senatorial

---

[18] Brown 1984, p. 31. Gregory's aunt, Pateria, received 40 solidi and 300 modii of wheat; see Gregory, *Ep.* 1.37. Gregory asked the praetorian prefect George to give a position to an orphaned young man, Armenius, *PLRE* 3A, p. 121. His office would allow him to recover his wealth, since his parents had donated monies to the church, so it seemed a fair solution to Gregory, *Ep.* 3.28.

[19] Gregory, *Ep.* 5.59.

rank continued to offer financial, social, economic, and legal privileges.[20] So, too, the association of high rank, nobility of birth, and praiseworthy character remained under Byzantine rule. It was still the case then, as it had been from the time of Constantine, that the sons and daughters of senatorial aristocrats were *clarissimi* or *clarissimae*, the lowest senatorial rank (see Chapter 2). Not surprisingly, family strategies for maintaining and transmitting status and property included the marriages of aristocratic women along with those of men. Indeed, women wanted to marry a senatorial aristocrat to ensure that their children would inherit senatorial status, which depended on the husband. And *illustris* senatorial status gave these children – and their parents – more privileges and protections. For example, only senators of the *illustris* rank could avoid financial burdens connected with local town councils.[21] *Illustres* could also plead legal cases in person or through representatives in all circumstances and could demand a trial of their peers.[22] The men who reached the highest senatorial rank of *illustris* thus reaped the full economic, legal, political, and social benefits of their status, advantages that were still relevant in Byzantine Italy.

Attaining Highest Senatorial Rank through Office Holding. As before the war, an Italo-Roman aristocrat could attain the highest rank of *illustris* by holding a high office – civic or military – or by being granted an honorary title.[23] However, even before the Gothic War, the opportunities to attain the highest civic offices that bestowed *illustris* rank in the western empire had declined. This situation would have led to a shrinking of the size of the Senate in Rome, with some scholars estimating that even under the Ostrogothic kings, the membership was probably closer to a few hundred rather than the six hundred to a thousand reckoned for the early fourth century.[24] But regardless of size, the Senate of Rome had exercised real political, economic, social and religious influence under the Ostrogothic kings. Its role in government, its prestige, and that of its senators had been useful supplements to

---

[20] On this, see especially Jones 1964, pp. 529–35.

[21] On freedom from curial burdens, see Jones 1964, pp. 535–36, and *Just. Nov.* 45, 537 CE and 70, 538 CE, talks of curial duties for others, not those of senatorial rank. See also note 4 above.

[22] *Just. Nov.* 71, 538 CE on the rights of *illustres* to plead through representatives in all circumstances. On the prerogatives of senators to judge each other, see *C. Th.* 9.1.3, 376 CE, and still in place for the trial of Boethius, discussed in Chapter 6, note 67.

[23] Justinian, *Digest* 4.2.23; *C. Iust.* 1.82; Jones 1964, pp. 544–45. See my discussion of the *illustris* rank in Chapters 2 and 6; and also Cass. *Var.* 3.6. See too Schoolman 2017, pp. 6–13.

[24] Secure statistics for both periods are lacking Chastagnol 1966, pp. 45–47, estimates a maximum of 60–80 *illustres* in the late fifth century, but this estimate is based on dating a number of the senators attested by seating inscriptions from the Coliseum to the age of Odoacer and not earlier or later, as indeed they should be based on more recent work; see Cameron 2012A, pp. 513–30, and Chapter 5.

Gothic rule, especially in negotiating ongoing conflicts with the Byzantine court in Constantinople.[25]

Senatorial landowners had expected to continue playing a leading political role in the newly formed government in Italy by holding high civic office. But now the offices that bestowed senatorial status were granted by the emperor in Constantinople, whose preference for easterners was easily observed. Moreover, the competition for these offices was intense. On the one hand, the Byzantines had reduced the sheer number of offices a western senator could hold to attain *illustris* rank in the period of reconstruction, and this situation continued into the later sixth and seventh centuries. As I observed in Chapter 6, there were only three civic offices that bestowed *illustris* rank in the West: praetorian prefect of Africa (attested down through 641), praetorian prefect of Italy (attested into the seventh century), and urban prefect of Rome (attested down through 599).[26] A number of posts that granted *illustris* status that a man could have attained before the Gothic War by service at the Ostrogothic court in Ravenna, such as count of the imperial treasury or count of the private estates of the emperor (or king), had disappeared. Even the office of western consul that Theoderic had controlled was no longer available; no western consul was appointed after 534, and no private citizen was appointed consul in the East after the westerner Basilius held it in 541.[27] When Justin II revived the office of consul on January 1, 566, out of reverence for its traditions, he held it himself and did not grant it to private individuals, a practice that his successors continued.[28]

Moreover, Italo-Roman elites who sought administrative office had to compete for advancement in Ravenna, where they faced competition not just from their Italo-Roman peers but also from Byzantine officials. As is clear from the appointments they made, Byzantine emperors preferred loyal easterners for these positions, as they also did for the praetorian prefects of Italy and Africa.[29]

---

[25] See my discussion in Chapter 6. Certainly, the sources – Cassiodorus, Marcellinus *comes*, the Anonymus Valesianus, and Jordanes – are pro-senatorial, but that does not diminish the political role of senators and the Senate in the Ostrogothic regime. See also La Rocca and Oppedisano, 2016; Arnold 2014; and Bjornlie 2013.

[26] See Tables 6.1–6.3. For later praetorian prefects, see *PLRE* 3B, pp. 1474–75; and for later urban prefects, see *PLRE* 3B, p. 1481.

[27] Meier 2002, pp. 277–79; Miller and Sarris 2018, p. 688 on *Just. Nov.* 107. Justinian had removed the consulship from private individuals, likely out of concern for any one person gaining too much prestige and hence threatening his regime, as he suspected had happened with Belisarius's consulship; see Bagnall, Cameron, Schwarz, and Warp 1987, p. 10.

[28] For his revival, see Stichel and Stichel 2015, pp. 827–44. For the context for his granting this office to himself, see Cameron (Averil) 1979, pp. 13–15.

[29] See Tables 6.1 and 6.3. For a list of names of praetorian prefects in the years afterward, see the *PLRE* 3B, pp. 1474–75.

Also making these offices more difficult for westerners to attain during the period of reconstruction was the fact that Justinian tended to keep men in the highest offices for extended periods of time. So, for example, the praetorian prefects of Italy, Aurelianus (554–68) and Longinus (568–74/75), men sent from the East and of uncertain origin, were each in office for longer than five years (see Table 6.1). This pattern did not change in the later sixth century.

Even the holders of the office of urban prefect, once the preserve of Italo-Roman senators, indicate the Byzantine preference for easterners. Pamphronius, likely the urban prefect in 559 (see Table 6.2), was the last attested sixth-century western senator to hold this office. The last recorded urban prefect, Iohannis (597–99), was probably an easterner chosen by the exarch in Ravenna.[30] Ambitious western senators could now make their way to the emperor's court and Senate in Constantinople or go north to Ravenna rather than attempt to gain office in Rome.[31]

Elevation among Officeholders (Adlectio inter agentes). The Byzantine emperors could have simply elevated men to the highest senatorial rank had they wanted to expand the senatorial class and restore the Senate of Rome.[32] But neither Justinian nor his successors evidently deemed it desirable to do so. In keeping with his policies in the East, Justinian wanted greater control over aristocratic landowners, and he did not want to cede greater political power to them. Thus, as *PS* Constitution 12 indicates (discussed in Chapter 6), he removed incentives for senatorial aristocrats to take political positions in the state by allowing powerful local landowners to have greater influence in choosing those who would oversee their taxes, a condition immensely important for their survival.[33]

Elevating Provincial Governors to Illustris Status. Alternatively, emperors could have expanded the senatorial order in the West by elevating some provincial governorships to high senatorial rank. Constantine had done that to great effect, as I described in Chapter 2. And Justinian had granted some holders of provincial offices as well as *curiales* (town council members) the title of *illustris* but not all of the fiscal privileges associated with the rank. Indeed, this elevation has been seen as part of an attempt to undermine the the *illustris*

---

[30] See Ioannes 109, *PLRE* 3B, p. 683, who was urban prefect from 597 to 599; his wife, Dominica 3, *PLRE* 3A, p. 410, feared Lombard attacks on the road from Ravenna. Pope Gregory wrote letters to persuade her (*Ep.* 7.34) and to ensure her safe travel to Rome (*Ep.* 9.117 and 9.118).

[31] On the drift of senators to Constantinople during the Gothic War and after, see Brown 1984, p. 28, and my discussion below.

[32] Brown, p. 26, note 10 on *illustres inter agentes.*

[33] For Justinian's attempts to control landowning elites in the East, policies that he apparently adapted in the West, see Sarris 2006, pp. 194–99; and pp. 219–27 on Justin II's attempt to renew ties with the senatorial aristocracy. See too Chapter 6, notes 198 and 199.

status.[34] But neither Justinian nor his late sixth-century successors granted such titles in large numbers to western provincials.

Honorary Titles. One other way to achieve high senatorial rank was to attain an honorary title, again a designation bestowed by the emperor. In effect, a man then held not the office but only the honor of this title. These were lesser honors than the ones bestowed on active officeholders, who were carefully distinguished from those men who held these offices and honors in name only.[35] Nonetheless, a westerner could hope to obtain from the emperor an honorary office that would also bestow some of the benefits of *illustris* rank. There are honorary prefects recorded during this period, but again, the bulk of men, judging from their names, appear to be easterners.[36] That westerners rarely held these honors appears most clearly if we look at the two positions that bestowed *illustris* rank at the top of the social hierarchy, honorary consul and patrician.

Honorary Consul. The office of honorary consul was used often in the late fifth-century East; the emperor Zeno had greatly increased the use of this honorific, in part to raise funds for the imperial treasury since the successful candidate had to pay one hundred pounds of gold.[37] Of seventeen honorary consuls dated between 554 and 616, not one of them can be said to have been a western senator, and all the known dated honorary consuls were easterners. A number were linked to the imperial family, while one Germanus may have been of Germanic origins, but his was a military, not a civic, career (see Table 7.1). In addition to these dated honorary consulships, there are also sixty-five undated honorary consuls listed in the *Prosopography of the Later Roman Empire* who could have been appointed in the mid-sixth or mid-seventh century and another sixty-nine who are simply listed as seventh century. Of these, only a few may have been Italo-Roman western senators, and most were appointed earlier than the post–Gothic War reconstruction period.[38] These men were predominantly eastern, judging from their names – such as Arsaphius,

---

[34] Haldon 2004, p. 189, citing *Just. Nov.* 70, 538.

[35] Haldon 2004, pp. 189–90. He analyzes the key text, the 425 law of Theodosius II, *C. Th.* 6.22.8 that lays out the different orders; first and highest are those who held actual posts with *illustris* rank; second are those who receive a titular post while at court (described as *vacans*); third are those who receive such an office in *absentia*; fourth, those who received an honorary office while at court; fifth, those awarded such an office in *absentia*.

[36] *PLRE* 3B, pp. 1475–79 for a convenient list.

[37] *C. Iust.* 12.3.3. For Zeno's financial motivations, see Mathisen 1991B, pp. 209–13.

[38] One honorary consul was Asterius 1, *PLRE* 3A, pp. 138–39. But his western origin rests on his identification with the aristocratic consul of 494, Turcius Rufius Apronianus, and this is based on the somewhat unreliable testimony for Asterius in the *Lib. Pont.* 61.4, ed. Duchesne 1981, p. 297.

Demetrius, Stephanus, Theophylactis, and Zacharias. Hence, it is clear that this honor continued to be accorded during this period, just not with much frequency to westerners.

One reason why westerners were not often attested for this honor was likely the high cost of this office, which the appointee paid into the aqueduct fund.[39] This was a sum that many western senators would have had a hard time raising after the war. Nor would they have been strongly motivated to do so, since this was an honor that held few possibilities for recouping the cost of gaining the office. That the money required to attain this honor was a problem for some is indicated by one well-documented case. The western senator Venantius, from Sicily and grandson of the patrician Venantius Opilio, offered a price of thirty pounds of gold for the honorary consulship instead of the standard one hundred. Bishop Gregory, in a letter dated 592, charged his *apocrisiarius* in Constantinople to intervene with Emperor Maurice on behalf of Venantius. We do not know if Venantius's bid was accepted.[40] After 603, the attestations for honorary consul in the West are rare.[41] Among them is Petronius, the father of Pope Honorius.[42] Petronius's payment for office is thus a sign of the wealth his son inherited and that he, as bishop of Rome, contributed toward building churches in Rome. Most of the other holders of this honor in Italy were Byzantines.[43]

Patrician Honors. The emperor could also bestow the honor of the patriciate, which had been used since the time of Constantine for the purpose of rewarding one's friends and encouraging service to the state. After his accession in 467, for example, the newly arrived emperor from the East, Anthemius, had granted patrician status to influential western senators who were not part of the imperial family in order to build support for his regime.[44] Subsequent emperors, including Justinian, continued these grants of patrician status. However, as I have noted, Justinian's "successors seem to have been much more reluctant to issue this most elevated, noninheritable dignity."[45]

---

[39] *C. Iust.* 12.3.3.1.

[40] Stein, 1939, p. 320. See Venantius 3, *PLRE* 3B, p. 1368. For the request, see Gregory, *Ep.* 2.36.

[41] Brown 1984, pp. 137–38 and note 20 suggests that this honor went mostly to landowners without official positions. But Brown does not note the rarity of the honor in Italy in contrast to its continued use in the East until 681.

[42] See note 2 above.

[43] See Table 7.1. I take into account nomenclature, although it is an imperfect indicator of origin; see note 127 below. I also include social factors, such as career path and family ties.

[44] Mathisen 1991B, pp. 194–99 especially.

[45] Brown 1984, p. 26. Stein 1968, p. 316–18. See Chapter 6 note 128 for the liberal use of patrician status during the Gothic Wars.

The title of *patrician* added prestige to a person who had already distinguished himself in his service to the state. It was not an office in its own right but rather an honor. My study of ninety-four men listed as patricians in *PLRE* 3 who date from the mid sixth to the early seventh centuries indicates that when Justinian and his successors bestowed this honor, they generally granted it to men who were already of the highest senatorial rank – that is, *illustris* (see Table 7.2).[46] This practice was in line with a 537 law of Justinian that stipulated that the *patriciate* should be granted only to those who already held the rank of *illustris*.[47] After the Gothic War and continuing into the later sixth century, the men honored as patricians were largely the same as those evidenced earlier, even in the fifth century; masters of the soldiers, imperial family members, and influential senators from the East predominated, and of the latter, many were so honored in order that they would be better able to serve as envoys as they performed their diplomatic missions abroad.[48] However, even among the group who attained patrician honors in order to go on diplomatic missions, only a handful appear not to have already held an office that conferred *illustris* rank. Those listed who are not attested as holding *illustris* rank prior to receiving their patriciates may well have had this rank but appear without it as the result of gaps in our knowledge. High senatorial rank remained one of the qualifications for the ideal ambassador.[49]

Another indicator of the limits on the granting of patrician status to western senators is provided by an overview of the origins of patricians after the Gothic Wars. The great preponderance of the ninety-four named patricians from the late sixth and early seventh centuries were easterners; only some seven or eight of the ninety-four were westerners, a tally again largely ascertained from a review of social factors including nomenclature (see Table 7.2).[50] This handful of patricians who were westerners included a few men from old senatorial families who likely already held *illustris* rank

---

[46] I considered men listed as patricians in *PLRE* 3B, pp. 1466–70 but restricted the dates to the mid-sixth century. I omitted those men whose patriciate was granted before the end of the war in 554, and those eighteen men who were simply listed as undated beyond belonging to the sixth century. There are new patricians found after this list, but the trend is so clearly in favor of easterners that a few added names will not offset this pattern.

[47] Just. *Nov.* 62.2.5, drops Zeno's requirement (note 37 above) that the candidates be *illustres* based on consular or prefectorial office.

[48] Mathisen 1986B, pp. 35–49 focuses primarily on the diplomatic activities of patricians. Barnish 2006, p. 186, notes that this is a nonhereditary honor granted by the Ostrogothic rulers to leading senators and habitually to the commander in chief in waiting (*magister utriusque militia praesentalis*).

[49] Mathisen 1986B, pp. 38–40 for a list of ambassadors.

[50] I considered men listed as patricians in *PLRE* 3B, pp. 1466–70 For the limits of nomenclature, see note 127 below.

when they were honored with the patriciate. Pamphronius was probably urban prefect directly after the war ended, about 555, and was attested as holding the patriciate in 561 at the earliest, presumably having been rewarded for his loyalty to Justinian.[51] Another senator, Olybrius, was likely a patrician under the Ostrogoths, assuming that he was the man of the same name who had been consul.[52] I have already noted Decius, whose name suggests that he was a member of an old senatorial family, as the first attested exarch.[53] If this assumption is correct, Decius would have been one of the few western patricians to also have been appointed to high office.[54] However, it is worth emphasizing that Decius had military as well as civic authority. Two patricians from the eminent Italo-Roman family of the Venantii are also known, and both were active in Sicily, not Rome. These examples also suggest the movement of senatorial aristocrats away from Rome, as noted earlier.[55] Finally, the patrician Decoratus may have been from an established senatorial family, a conjecture again based on his name.[56]

The Vanishing of Western Senatorial Rank. I have gone into these details of senatorial careers to demonstrate that Byzantine emperors could have found a number of ways to elevate western aristocrats to the highest senatorial rank – that is, *illustris* – to replenish the western senatorial aristocracy, to strengthen the Senate in Rome, and to maintain the system of rank and honor that still existed in the East into the late sixth and later seventh centuries. However, the extant evidence of honorary consuls and patricians (Tables 7.1 and 7.2) indicates that such appointments were not a priority for the Byzantine rulers of Italy. Although some westerners are so attested, they are few. And as I noted earlier, Byzantine emperors favored easterners in their appointments of the praetorian prefects of Italy and Africa and the urban prefect of Rome.

---

[51] Pamphronius, *PLRE* 3B, pp. 962–63 dates his patriciate to c. 561 the earliest. He may be the *vir illustris* Pamphronius who corresponded with Ennodius, *PLRE* 2, p. 825. See Table 6.2; and my discussion below, with notes 134–35.

[52] Olybrius is Olybrius 2, *PLRE* 3B, p. 953. Olybrius was in Rome when it fell to Totila in 546, and is called a patrician by Procop. *Wars* 7.20.18–19.

[53] Decius 2, *PLRE* 3A, p. 391. See Chapter 6, note 208 for his identification as the exarch.

[54] Brown 1984, p. 222 and note 2 cites the eighth-century poem, *Ex gestis sancti Bonifati martyris archiepiscopi legati Roman ecclesiae*, for the reference to "the warlike Decii." It may be a bridge too far to think that his family survived into the eighth century.

[55] For the Venantii, see Venantius 2, *PLRE* 3B, pp. 1367–68 and Venantius 4, *PLRE* 3B, p. 1369. Both received letters from Pope Gregory.

[56] Decoratus, *PLRE* 3A, pp. 391–92. He may be the son of the quaestor Decoratus 1, *PLRE* 2, pp. 350–51. See Pelagius I, *Ep.* 30, ed. Gassó and Batlle, 1956, p. 86. Although his office is not known, he was involved in adjudicating a legal case at the request of Pope Pelagius.

Some scholars see the Byzantine failure to maintain the system of rank and status in late sixth- and early seventh-century Italy as an indication of the loss of value of senatorial rank. They regard the proliferation of honorific language in contemporary documents as evidence of the system's debasement. However, this argument is not compelling. The proliferation of honorific language goes back to the fourth and early fifth centuries, when the system of rank and honor was secure in the West. Admittedly, the existence of so many honors and titles made it hard even for those trained in the nuances of their usage to keep these distinctions straight, but that situation is quite different from denying that these distinctions still carried weight. An examination of the letters of Bishop Gregory, written by a man from a senatorial family who had been trained in proper usage and reflecting contemporary legal as well as ecclesiastical protocol, confirms the continuing relevance of status and rank distinctions in the last decade of the sixth century.[57]

The Evidence for Senatorial Rank in the Letters of the Bishop of Rome, Gregory. In the letters of Gregory, Bishop of Rome from 590–604, we find men of the *illustris* rank described as *gloriosi* or *magnifici*; these include Callinicus, the patrician and exarch of Italy from 596/97 to 602/03, a man who clearly deserved this rank based on his office. One man who was honored as an *illustris*, Reccaredus, king of the Visigoths, did not hold the requisite office, but his royal stature indicates that this honorific was a sign of his status.[58] Similarly, the two legates to the Burgundian queen, who had Germanic names, Burgowald and Warmaricar, do not fit easily into a traditional rank system.[59] But these clearly were highly important political figures. The other seven male senators or women with senatorial titles explicitly attested as *illustris* in Gregory's letters were likewise privileged figures. For example, the *illustris* Eutychus claimed certain honors based on his rank as a former prefect.[60] As well, Gregory draws further distinctions

---

[57] I disagree with Haldon 2004, p. 189 and Haldon 2005, pp. 28–59, that the profusion of honorary language diminished the value of *illustris* as a rank and title.

[58] Callinicus 10, *PLRE* 3A, pp. 264–65. For Reccaredus I, see *PLRE* 3A, pp. 1079–80 and Gregory, *Ep.* 9.228 and 9.229. For *gloriosus* used for men and women in the letters of Gregory, I note Aldio, Apollonius, Appio, Callinius, Comitiolus, Domnica, Eusebia, Gregorius ex praefect, Justinus praeter, Leontius ex conss., Maria, Maurentius ex praef., Romanus, exarch, Rusticiana, Sebastianus, Smaragdus, Venantius, Berta, Iohannes.

[59] Gregory, *Ep.* 13.7.

[60] The eight men and women called *illustris* in Gregory's *Letters* are Adeodata, *Ep.* 8.34 and 11.5; John, *Ep.* 9.14; Iovinus, *Ep.* 9.15; Isidorus, *Ep.* 9.35; Rustica, Ep. 9.164; Eutychus, *Ep.* 9.115; and the two legates to the Queen of the Franks, Burgowald and Warmaricar, *Ep.* 13.7. Eutychus asserted that he was an "*illustris* and a former prefect." He is not otherwise attested as a prefect, and so it is conjectured by *PLRE* 3A, p. 476, that his was an honorary title.

within the rank of *illustris* for those *illustres* at the highest levels – notably, honorary consuls, patricians, and praetorian or urban prefects – who were distinguished by the superlative honorific *gloriossisimi*. Men and women referred to by Gregory simply with the adjectives *gloriosi* and *magnifici* were honorific officeholders, either ex-honorary consuls or praetors.[61] Thus, the *Letters* of Gregory illustrate systematic uses of titles and rank, even as they also record new offices in Italy, civic and military, that conveyed senatorial status. Of the fifty-nine instances of men or women who held senatorial rank – *clarissimus*, *illustris*, or *spectabilis* – men of the lowest senatorial rank, *clarissimi*, were often imperial officials or military tribunes.[62] These men had not been born into senatorial status. Rather, they, like others since the age of Constantine, had attained senatorial rank through service in the military or the imperial or civic administration. That fact does not mean, however, that the system was no longer relevant to elites in Byzantine Italy.

What Happened to the Italo-Roman Senatorial Aristocracy?

Difficulties in attaining high political office encouraged the movement of senatorial families away from Rome. The members of established Italo-Roman senatorial families who survived the Gothic War and the Justinianic reconstruction appear only infrequently in our late sixth- and early seventh-century sources.[63] And when we do find them, the senators were, by and large, no longer residing in Rome or engaged in an active political life there. We can see this movement if we consider the men and women who were addressed as holding senatorial rank – that is, as *gloriosi*, *magnifici*, *illustres*, or patrician – in the *Letters* and *Dialogues* of Bishop Gregory.

Letters of Pope Gregory. By examining the more than eight hundred and fifty letters written during the fourteen years of Gregory's papacy, we can discern some thirty-six senatorial elites.[64] Of these, only three are recorded as

---

[61] Men referred to as *gloriosissimus* in the letters of Gregory include Leontius the ex-consul honorary, *Ep.* 9.182; Maurentius the *magister militum*, *Ep.* 9.133; Peter the praetorian prefect, *Ep.* 13.50; John, the urban prefect, *Ep.* 9.117; Faustus *Ep.* 9.146; and Venantius, the patrician, *Ep.* 9.119. See too Haldon 2004, p. 189; Stein 1949, vol. 2, pp. 429–32; Jones 1964, pp. 529–35. See *CJ* 12.1.11; 16.1 = *C. Th.* 6.23.1, 415; Just. *Nov.* 62.1, 537, and 70, 538.

[62] Schoolman 2017, p. 13.   [63] Brown 1984, p. 23.

[64] They had the high ranks just noted (i.e., addressed as *gloriosi*, *magnifici*, *illustres*, or patrician).

having resided in Rome. Fourteen were located in Sicily, twelve in Campania, two in southern Italy, and three or four in Ravenna and northern Italy.[65] These were their principal areas of domicile when Gregory wrote them letters, although some men clearly moved about, as, for instance, Gregory's brother, Palatinus, who had been active in southern Italy, Rome, and likely Ravenna.

Two people mentioned by Gregory as residing in Rome belonged to established senatorial families, but neither had held important political office. The first is the senator Cethegus, whose father, also named Cethegus, had been consul and leader of the Senate in Rome before fleeing to Constantinople in the 540s. His father had returned to his estates in Sicily after the war.[66] The son had spent some time in Rome with his wife, Flora, although, like many of his peers, he had also been actively engaged in managing his properties in Sicily, was a donor of a monastery in Campania, and had close contacts in Constantinople.[67] The second man attested in Gregory's letters to have been in Rome was a member of the powerful family of the Symmachi. This Symmachus had come to Rome from Constantinople to give Gregory a gift from his sister, Rusticiana. Symmachus stayed in Rome long enough for the bishop to recover from an illness in order to personally deliver the gift.[68]

---

[65] Brown 1984, p. 23 and note 5 records thirty-five names, and I have added one more, Faustus 4. The numbers refer to the identifications of these people in *PLRE* 3A and 3B where they are known, or the letter from Gregory that cited this person. From Sicily: Adeodata *illustris, PLRE* 3A, p. 15, Alexander 10 *v.m. PLRE* 3A, p. 45 (although he was from Palermo, he had a large house in Rome too); Faustus 4, *PLRE* 3A, p. 480; Felix 11 *v.g. PLRE* 3A, p. 483; Florus *v.m. PLRE* 3A, pp. 490–91; Iohannes 112 *v.i. PLRE* 3A, p. 684; Iovinus 3 *v.g. PLRE* 3A, p. 71; Iuli(a)nus 38 *v.g. PLRE* 3A, p. 741, Iulius *patricius*, Gregory, *Ep.* 2.26; Pascasinus *v.m. PLRE* 3B, p. 968; Petrus 2 *v.g. PLRE* 3B, p. 1004; Placidus 2 *v.m. PLRE* 3B, p. 1043; Venantius 2 *v.e. PLRE* 3B, pp. 1367–68; Venantius 4 *v.e. PLRE* 3B, p. 1369. From Campania: Aetia *gloriosa PLRE* 3A, p. 22; Alexandria 2 *magnifica PLRE* 3A, p. 47; Clementina *patricia PLRE* 3A, pp. 317–18; Faustus 3 *v.g. PLRE* 3A, p. 480; Felix 12 *v.m. PLRE* 3A, p. 483; Herene *gloriosa PLRE* 3A, p. 589; Palatina 2 *illustris PLRE* 3B, p. 960; Pateria *donna? PLRE* 3B, p. 970; Romanus 9 *v. sp. PLRE* 3B, p. 1093; Rustica *illustris PLRE* 3B, p. 1100; Stephanus 10 *v.m.* (= Stephanus 21, *PLRE* 3 B, p. 1188); Viviana *domna PLRE* 3B, p. 1387. Southern Italy: Petronella *nobilis, PLRE* 3B, p. 992; Gregory's brother (likely Palatinus, *PLRE* 3B, p. 960, although he was also active in Rome). For Ravenna and North Italy: Andreas 15 *v.m. PLRE* 3A, p. 78, Armenius *v.m. PLRE* 3A, p. 593; Mastalo (?) *PLRE* 3B, p. 850; Themotea *illustris PLRE* 3B, p. 1224. From Rome: Campana *patricia, PLRE* 3A, p. 269; Cethegus 2 *patricius, PLRE* 3A, p. 279; Symmachus 4 *v.m. PLRE* 3B, p. 121.

[66] The father is identified as Fl. Rufius Petronius Nicomachus Cethegus, cos. 504, *patricius* 512–c. 558, *PLRE* 2, pp. 281–82. If so, he lived an extraordinarily long life.

[67] For Cethegus as a possible resident in Rome, see Cethegus 2, *PLRE* 3A, p. 279 and Gregory, *Ep.* 9.72, 598 CE. Cethegus and his wife Flora sent Maximus 7, *PLRE* 3B, p. 867, a *palatinus rerum privatarum*, to collect the revenues of the *res privata* in Sicily. Since this was a Constantinopolitan official, it is also possible that Cethegus had also stayed on for some time in the East.

[68] Symmachus 4, *PLRE* 3B, p. 1213. His sister was Rusticiana 2, *PLRE* 3B. pp. 1101–02. On his sister, see Chapter 6, note 225.

Another man, Campana, owner of a large house in Rome, was not from any known family.[69]

In contrast, of the twenty-six named and ranked men and women from Sicily and Campania, more than five were from older senatorial families, including the two Venantii and the senator Placidus in Sicily, and Faustus and Rusticus in Campania.[70] These senatorial families focused their political and social attentions on the cities near their estates, notably Naples and Panormus (modern Palermo). Admittedly, Gregory may have had less reason to write letters to senators who resided in Rome. But a consideration of Gregory's popular work, the *Dialogues*, does not change the impression that the highest ranked men and women resided outside of Rome, even if they traveled to Rome for business or to simply to consult with him.

***Dialogues* of Pope Gregory.** The most popular of Gregory's writings were his *Dialogues*, four books of some two hundred stories of holy men working miracles. Gregory narrated these stories in alleged conversations with his deacon Peter, presumably in Rome.[71] Although the number of highly ranked senators in this work is small, it does indicate that some senators still resided in Rome; however, among these, those from established Rome-based families do not predominate. Of the seven men noted with rank and attested in Rome in the *Dialogues*, only Symmachus and Liberius are from old established senatorial families. Symmachus, as noted previously, had come from Constantinople to Rome to give a gift to Gregory and remained there for some time, while Liberius's residence was more likely in Genoa.[72] However, residency is sometimes difficult to verify. The death of a senatorial *illustris* named Stephanus in Rome did not mean that he had resided there; the narrative indicates that he traveled widely.[73] Two other senators called "noble," Tertullus and Eutychius (Euthicicus), are said to have been from Rome, but neither was from an established senatorial aristocratic family, nor do we know what, if any, office they held. Interestingly, their sons did not remain in Rome, if the son of Tertullus was the same Placidus who had properties

---

[69] Campana, *PLRE* 3B, p. 269.

[70] Fausti 1, 2, 3, and 4, *PLRE* 3A, p. 480; and Rusticus 5, *PLRE* 3B, p. 1104; Placidus 2, *PLRE* 3B, p. 1043; see *PLRE* 3B, p. 1367–68 for Venantius 2, *patricius*, who lived in Syracuse; and p. 1369 for Venantius 4 *v.g.*, who lived in Palermo. Venantius 3 *v.c. PLRE* 3B, p. 1368, is attested as being in Rome, but his residence is uncertain.

[71] Moorhead 2005, 14–16 on this work in general.

[72] Liberius 2, Gregory, *Dial.* 4.55. For Symmachus, see note 68 above.

[73] Stephanus in *Dial.* 4.37 = Stephanus 21, *PLRE* 3B, p. 1188. According to Gregory, Stephanus died twice from the plague, once in Constantinople and then afterward in Rome. He could have been a resident of either city.

in Sicily.[74] Certainly, the son of Eutychius left Rome for the monastery of St. Benedict in Subiaco.[75] The other five ranked senatorial men and women in the *Dialogues* appear to have been living away from Rome. Armentarius, the grandfather of Mascator, had been residing in Campania.[76] Venantius, the senator, lived in Samnium.[77] Similarly, three senatorial women mentioned in the *Dialogues* – Galla, Columba, and Savinella – had been living in Africa, where they were commemorated for their charitable acts, thereby demonstrating the Christian virtue so often associated with wealthy aristocratic females.[78]

The Disappearance of Senatorial Names. The gradual removal of senators from Rome is also suggested by the disappearance of the names of Italo-Roman senatorial families from our extant documents and texts. One Basilius, one Decius, and three Venantii are mentioned in texts, including the letters of Gregory. The references to these senatorial family names suggest that the influential and wealthy senatorial family of the Decii continued into the seventh century.[79] Two aristocratic Fausti and a late sixth-century woman named Rustica may also be identified with established senatorial families on the basis of their nomenclature.[80] Most perplexing is the disappearance of the western senatorial Anicii family. Some scholars have linked the last known members of that family with the Bishop of Rome, Gregory, but the evidence for that association cannot be substantiated.[81] The father of Pope Honorius, Petronius, belonged to an old noble family from Campania, and the father of Pope Severinus, Avienus, may have been a descendant from the fifth-century Avienii.[82]

The decline in the mention of senatorial family names unfolded alongside general changes in patterns of nomenclature. In the sixth century we still find senatorial families with the distinctive Roman habit of including three or

---

[74] Placidus was the son of Tertullus, noted in Gregory, *Dial.* 2.6. The Placidus 2, *PLRE* 3B, p. 1043 noted in Gregory, *Ep.* 10.32 is dated to 601, so the two men may or may not be connected.

[75] Eutychius's son, Maurus 1, *PLRE* 3B, p. 863, is noted in Gregory, *Dial.* 2.3.6.

[76] Armentarius I, in Gregory, *Dial.* 3.16, is an *illustris*, but he lived in the early sixth century, for his grandson, Mascator, *PLRE* 3B, p. 850, is likely dated to the mid sixth century.

[77] Venantius noted in Gregory, *Dial.* 1.1. He seems distinct from the Venantii noted in the letters, but perhaps may be either the father or a relative.

[78] Columba, *PLRE* 3A, p. 321; Galla, *PLRE* 3A, p. 501 and Savinella, *PLRE* 3B. p. 1116.

[79] See Basilius 6, *PLRE* 3A, pp. 175–76; Decius 2, *PLRE* 3A, p. 391; and Venantius 2, 3, and 4, *PLRE* 3B, pp. 1367–69. See note 54 above for a mention of an eighth-century Decius.

[80] See Faustus 3 and 4, *PLRE* 3A, pp. 480; and Rustica *PLRE* 3B, pp. 1100–02, who died in 578.

[81] On Gregory as a member of the Anicii, see note 96 below. On the fluidity of the Anicii even in the early sixth century, see Cameron 2012, pp. 133–71. On their demise after the Gothic War, see Wickham 2005, p. 160, and pp. 206–7.

[82] See Petronius 2, *PLRE* 3B, p. 993; and Avienus, *PLRE* 3A, p. 155.

four names – praenomen, nomen, plus cognomen and/or agnomen – such as Rufius Magnus Faustus Avienus iunior.[83] But even in the later sixth and increasingly in the seventh century the use of single or double names can be documented in our texts and in the papyri, with the second name sometimes being an honorific or qualifier like "the younger (iunior)," as in the name Melminius Iohannes iunior. More typical is the single name, as for the patrician Pamphronius and for the senator of *spectabilis* rank known from a papyrus fragment only as Dulcitius.[84] Although these changing patterns of nomenclature make it harder to trace senatorial families into the later sixth century, even those few senatorial names with simplified formulae (one or two names) associated with the established Italo-Roman aristocratic families fade out by the middle of the seventh century.[85]

The waning of the occurrence of names of senatorial families in Italy, along with the evidence for the relocation of senators to their estates in Sicily and Campania, suggests that wealthy senatorial families merged into the local provincial landowning elites in the West over the course of the seventh century. The trajectory of the senatorial family of the patrician Venantius and his wife Italica speaks to these changes. Their daughters, Barbara and Antonina, are mentioned by Gregory, who desired to see them in Rome with their husbands. If they did marry husbands in their home town of Syracuse, one suspects that they blended into local provincial families.[86] Even if Venantius's daughters had had children, they did not keep their family names, as far we know. The demise of family names is, in and of itself, a significant indicator of a changing social system that devalued secular senatorial identity and family.

Similarly, western senatorial aristocratic families who had remained in Constantinople are not attested as having survived much later than the early seventh century. For example, Dominica, a western elite woman who had

[83] For this man, see Avienus 2, *PLRE* 2, pp. 192–93. He was a native of Rome: Ennod. *Ep.* 9.32: *habet de origine eius Roma iactantiam.* He was consul in 502, and praetorian prefect of Italy in 527–58, for Athalaric.

[84] For Pamphronius, see note 51 above, and notes 134–35 below. For Dulcitius, see Brown 1984, Dulcitius 3, p. 258.

[85] Brown 1984, p. 24 makes this observation about these changing naming patterns. More recent work has not overturned this analysis. We see a similar trend toward single or double names in the Ravenna papyri; see Schoolman, forthcoming 2021. Schoolman noted that there are no trinomina in the Ravenna Papyri of the Tjader editions. Only the family of the Melminii, both known as *clarissimi*, had two names, Melminius Andreas 6, *PLRE* 3A, p. 75, and Melminius Cassianus iunior, *PLRE* 3A, p. 274.

[86] Barbara, *PLRE* 3A, p. 170, and Antonina 3, *PLRE* 3A, p. 93 profess a desire to visit Gregory and St. Peter's Basilica; see Gregory, *Ep.* 11.23, 59. Their father is Venantius 2, *PLRE* 3B, pp. 1367–68.

been at court in the late sixth century, left no family to follow her.[87] The heiress Rusticiana, from the Italo-Roman aristocratic families of the Symmachi and the Boethii, also had remained in Constantinople. She lived to see her daughter Eusebia marry into the wealthy eastern family of the Apiones. Their children and the eastern Apiones thrived into the seventh century, but the western senatorial Symmachi disappeared with the brother of Rusticiana.[88] Rusticiana herself fell out of favor in Constantinople, becoming one of the western senatorial aristocrats who left no traces after the assassination of Emperor Maurice (582–602) and his family (see discussion below).[89]

Senatorial Aristocrats in the Church: The Rising Status of the Papacy

Petronius, the honorary consul who was the father of the Bishop of Rome, Honorius (625–38), was one of the last attested Italo-Roman senatorial aristocrats.[90] His son's ecclesiastical career is emblematic of the path that several Italo-Roman senators chose. Indeed, from the Gothic War on, opportunities for senatorial aristocrats to gain prestige and influence had increased greatly through service in the clergy. Certainly, well before the invasion of Italy by Justinian, senators had been concerned about and had taken active roles in the religious life of Rome. As wealthy donors, landowners, and leaders of late Roman society, senatorial aristocrats had supported for the papacy particular candidates whose theological views aligned with their own. As well, the Senate had repeatedly intervened to try to resolve conflicts within the church. For example, the Senate had issued a *senatus consultum* to regulate a controversial papal election in 529, and as I noted before, the Emperor Anastasius had directed a letter to the Senate to use its

---

[87] Dominica 2, *PLRE* 3A, p. 410.

[88] Rusticiana 2, *PLRE* 3B, pp. 1101–2 and Chapter 6, note 225. Eusebia 2, *PLRE* 3A, p. 467 may also have been the mother of Eudoxius 2 and lived to see her grandson, Strategius, and granddaughters. Her granddaughter Eusebia 2, *PLRE* 3A, p. 467 married into the wealthy Apion family of Egypt. Gregory met a number of these western expatriates when he was apocrisiarius in Constantinople prior to his elevation in 590; see Averil Cameron 1979, pp. 225–27. On the Anicii, see Bjornlie 2013, p. 149; Brown 1984, pp. 28–29; Sarris 2006, pp. 21–22.

[89] For the impact of the coup of Phocas on expatriate western aristocrats, see Brown 1984, p. 29. For Maurice's intention to revive a western imperial courts, see note 141 below.

[90] Petronius = Petronius 2, *PLRE* 3B, p. 993. For Petronius as consul, see *Lib. Pont.* 72, ed. Duchesne 1981, pp. 324–25. For the text, see note 2 above. Petronius's successor, Severinus (640), is not noted as senatorial by the *Book of the Popes*, although his name may be tied to a senatorial family; see Brown 1984, p. 24, note 7, and Avienus, *PLRE* 3A, p. 155.

influence to persuade Pope Felix to relent in the Acacian Schism (see Chapter 5).[91] But senators had not become bishops in Rome until the Gothic War. This is noteworthy because the integration of the senatorial aristocracy into the clergy is often seen as a critical part of the process whereby the church came to dominate Roman society.[92]

In Rome the rise of senatorial bishops coincided with the Gothic War and continued under Byzantine administrators of Italy, who had intentionally elided the ecclesiastical and civic authority of the bishop. This development had led to the increasing identification of the church with the empire and the patronage of the bishop over his city, as Claudia Rapp has argued had already happened in the East.[93] Similarly, in Italy after the Gothic War, the Byzantine officials regarded bishops as their assistants in administering this province. And some clergy were well equipped for the task. For example, the senatorial noble Agnellus had had a secular career prior to his becoming the bishop of Ravenna from 557 to 570.[94]

Under the Byzantines, the bishops of Rome were expected not just to oversee their clergy and the worshippers in their congregation but also to take responsibility for the citizens and the city more broadly. As I discussed in Chapter 6, Vigilius (537–55), the first of Rome's senatorial aristocratic bishops, had petitioned Justinian to restore order to Rome and the West, as evidenced by the *Pragmatic Sanction of 554*. The senatorial bishops of Rome who followed him – notably Pelagius I (556–61), John III (561–74), and Gregory (590–604) – took on several civic duties that senatorial aristocratic officeholders had once fulfilled. In fact, their aristocratic backgrounds – educated, socially connected, and generally endowed with some wealth – suited them well for the increasing number of civic responsibilities placed on them by Byzantine officials.[95] As Italo-Roman bishops strove to cooperate with Byzantine administrators, these officials came to rely more heavily on the bishops in return. The ties between the church and the Byzantine officials in Italy deepened and allowed for the integration of the latter into Italian society.

---

[91] Council of 529, *CCSL* 148A: 644 ff. See too the discussion by Moorhead 2015, p. 93. For Anastasius's interactions with the Senate, see Salzman 2019B, pp. 138–58.

[92] On this phenomenon, see Salzman 2019A, pp. 465–66.

[93] Rapp 2005, pp. 183–97, and passim on their authority more broadly.

[94] Agnellus 1, *PLRE* 3A, p. 30.

[95] For Vigilius, see *Lib. Pont.* 61, ed. Duchesne 1981, p. 296; the text calls his father, John, a consul. *Lib. Pont.* 62, p. 303 describes Pelagius's father John as a *vicarianus*. *Lib. Pont.* 63, p. 305, calls Pope John a son of the *illustris* Anastasius. The omission of any information about Gregory's social status or the occupation of his father Gordianus may reflect biases in the composition of this life; see *Lib. Pont.* I, ed. Duchesne 1981, p. 312, note 1,; and Llewellyn 1974, pp. 363–80. For Gregory, see note 96 below.

The Growing Civic Role of the Bishop of Rome: Gregory I (590–604). By the time that Gregory became bishop in 590, the Byzantine administration of Italy had already solidified its relations with the church. The imperial government, centered in Ravenna, was directed by the exarch, who was appointed by the emperor in Constantinople. The praetorian prefects of Italy remained in place for civic matters, although the urban prefects who reported to them were predominantly Easterners (see Table 6.2). When Gregory became bishop, his prior experience in government made him the perfect candidate to work with Rome's Byzantine rulers.

Gregory's family, as noted earlier, was wealthy. His father, Gordianus, had held a position, likely as a *regionarius*, a subdeacon, in the church hierarchy in Rome.[96] His brother, Palatinus, had attained the patriciate, although Palatinus's office, if he had had one, is not certain.[97] Gregory himself had held a civic office in 573, that of the urban praetor, an honor traditionally entailing the donation of money for games, which were now no longer given in Rome, as best as we can tell.[98] It was perhaps from personal knowledge of the challenges of the praetorship that Gregory later discouraged an applicant for this office in Sicily by emphasizing the "sorrows and tribulations" the office had brought to its past occupants.[99] Nonetheless, Gregory was well acquainted with the demands of a political life since, after beginning life as a monk, he later served as the papal

---

[96] Gregory's father was Gordianus, *PLRE* 3A, p. 544. John the Deacon, *Sancti Gregorii Magni Vita* 4.83, *PL* 75, cites Gordianus's office as *regionarius*. If correct, this was an office within the church, perhaps a subdeacon, as was the John mentioned in *Lib. Pont.* 60.8, ed. Duchesne 1981, p. 293. Gregory's ties to the Anicii are not attested in antiquity. The bishop of Rome that Gregory mentions is either Felix III (483–92) or Felix IV (526–30). If Felix III, that bishop was not himself a member of the Anicii; see Salzman 2019A, pp. 475–76. If Gregory referred to Felix IV as his ancestor, he did not have Anician ties since Felix IV (526–30) was from Samnium, Italy. For further doubts, see Pietri 1981, pp. 434–36, and Maskarinec 2020, unpublished paper. But his family connections do suggest his was a an old, well-established and wealthy, aristocratic family.

[97] For Gregory's brother, see Palatinus, *PLRE* 3B, p. 960. Gregory of Tours, *HF* 10.1, relays a story of the soon-to-be-made bishop of Rome Gregory being offered and then refusing the office of urban prefect in 590, and then it being held by a man called Germanus. This story confused some details of Gregory's life; see note 98 below. Nor is it likely that this is a reference to Gregory's brother, Palatinus, as some have thought since there there was an urban prefect named Germanus; see Table 6.2.

[98] Gregory, *Ep.* 4.1, dated 593: *ego quoque tunc urbanam praeturam gerens pariter subscripsi.* Through the Ostrogothic period, this office would have involved the giving of circus games. What responsibilities it entailed by the time Gregory held it are not clear. However, there is no evidence that he held the urban prefectureship. Only one variant manuscript used the word *praefectura.* John the Deacon, *Sancti Gregorii Magni Vita* 1.4, *PL* 75, also called him a *praetor* (*sub praetoris urbani habitu*). For these officials under the Ostrogoths, see Jones 1964, p. 542, and Boethius, *Cons.* 3.4.

[99] Gregory, *Ep.* 9.6.

envoy (*apocrisiarius*) in the eastern court in Constantinople. He had come to the office of bishop with a wide network of friends and clients in the Byzantine administration, in civic society, and in the church hierarchy.[100]

Gregory thought that the church and the state should work together for the common good. But I underscore that Gregory, like bishop Pelagius I thirty years earlier, felt that only when the imperial authorities were unwilling or unable to undertake their civic responsibilities did it fall to the bishop of Rome to take on these tasks. In earlier periods the Senate and its senators had assumed civic responsibilities for administering Rome and for restoring the city after crises. Now the administration of the city and responses to the political and military crises that befell its inhabitants fell to the Byzantine administrators. Only if those officials could not undertake those responsibilities did the pope take action for the whole city. We can see this development if we consider three areas of civic responsibility that were central to the survival of Rome – the feeding, maintenance, and defense of the city.

Feeding Rome. In his *Pragmatic Sanction* from the year 554 (discussed in Chapter 6), Justinian had asserted that he would continue the *annona* system that Theoderic had maintained. The *PS* does not discuss the nature of support for the grain supply for the city, which is one meaning of *annona*, but rather uses this word in reference to the publicly funded stipends and allowances paid to teachers, rhetoricians, doctors, and lawyers.[101] But Theoderic, in a conspicuous act of charity, had also supported Rome's populace with free grain, the other meaning of *annona*.[102] When Rome's food supply had been threatened after the Gothic War, the Byzantine emperors continued to intervene to help. For example, during the period of reconstruction, Justin II (565–74) had sent grain to Rome from Egypt because the city had been under attack by the Lombards (578?).[103] As well, in a letter of 590, Pope Gregory used his influence on the praetor Justin to ensure that the public granary in Sicily was stocked for Rome. A certain agent, Citonatus, had alerted Gregory to potential shortages.[104] Gregory had also been concerned about

---

[100] For his career, see Demacopoulos 2015, pp. 1–4 and especially pp. 104–7. Paul. Diac. *Vita S. Gregorii* 29 (*PL* 85.58); cf. *Lib. Pont.* 66, ed. Duchesne 1981, pp. 312–14.

[101] For the *Annona* in the *PS*, see c. 22, ed. Miller and Sarris, 2018, p. 1127.

[102] See Chapter 4, and notes 52 and 54.

[103] *Lib. Pont.* 64, ed. Duchesne, 1981, p. 308, from the *Life of Benedict* (575–79).

[104] Gregory, *Ep.* 1.2: *De frumentis autem quae scribitis, longe aliter vir magnificus Citonatus asserit, quia solummodo tanta transmissa sunt, quae pro transactae indictionis debito ad replendum sitonicum redderentur. De qua re curam gerite, quia si quid minus hic transmittitur non unus quilibet homo, sed cunctus simul populus trucidatur.* ("But concerning the grain which you write about, that magnificent gentleman Citonatus asserts, very differently, that only so much has been sent across as should be supplied to replenish the public granary, in proportion to the

feeding Rome during the Lombard siege of the city in 595.[105] Gregory saw it as his responsibility to ensure food for the city as well as for southern Italy and Sicily by getting the Byzantine administrators to do their job. Indeed, these areas were under his control as part of Suburbicarian Italy (on this, see Chapter 2). So Gregory wrote to the Byzantine administrator Cyridianus, who had been sent by the emperor to secure the grain supply of Sicily, to ensure that he work closely with the church *defensor*.[106] In an interesting letter dated to 599 to the prefect of Italy, John, Gregory used the traditional ideals of social prestige as well as divine reward to encourage the prefect to maintain the state grain supply for the poor in Naples so "that the administration of this office may provide praise for you before your fellow men . . . and prepare a reward for you before almighty God."[107]

Although the church had its own granaries that it could use to feed the population in a shortage or crisis, Gregory did not regard it as the role of the bishop to do so since the state should fulfill that responsibility. Admittedly, the bishop also had significant resources at his disposal. The accumulation of land, money, and rents from wealthy donors had made the church the largest landholder in Italy by the late sixth century. Thus, the bishop's perceived ability to feed Rome and those others in need had increased pressure on him to undertake this formerly entirely civic responsibility. And in times of food shortages during the early seventh century, the populace expected the bishop to do this *gratis*. When Gregory's successor, Pope Sabinian (604–6), sold corn from papal granaries rather than distributing it for free, he incurred such undying hatred that his funeral procession had to be diverted outside the city to avoid the enraged crowds.[108]

---

debt from the past fifteen-year period. Concerning this matter, take care in case, if any lesser amount is sent over here, not just one person but the whole population may be destroyed simultaneously.") Translation by Martyn, 2004, vol. 1, p. 120 and note 7. Martyn explains the Greek word *sitonicum* as derived from *sitos* (grain), suggesting an annual measure of wheat, or a public granary, as here. See too Delogu 2001, pp. 3–40.

[105] Gregory, *Ep.* 5.36, defends himself against charges after the corn ran out in the city during the Lombard siege.

[106] Gregory, *Ep.* 9.16, 598 CE; 9.31, 599 CE.

[107] Gregory, *Ep.* 10.8, dated 600. I disagree with Demacopoulos 2015, p. 104, that the state supply was replaced by the Roman Church's stock on a regular basis under Gregory. Rather, I am convinced about its continuation by the arguments of Richards 1980, p. 88 and notes 9–11 on the basis of Gregory, *Ep.* 5.36, 9.10, and 10.8, dated 600; and *Ep.* 9.31 about the continuation of the *annona*, albeit in attenuated form. See also Delogu, 2001, pp. 3–40; and Delogu and Paroli, eds. 1993, pp. 11–29

[108] *Lib. Pont.* 67, ed. Duchesne 1981, p. 315.

Infrastructure. As with the food supply, maintenance of the public buildings of Rome remained the responsibility of the emperor and his administrators in the late sixth and early seventh centuries. For example, Pope Boniface IV had to get permission to convert the Pantheon into the Church of St. Mary and All the Martyrs from the emperor Phocas in 609.[109] But the maintenance of Rome's buildings and infrastructure – roads, bridges, and aqueducts – was not the highest priority of the Byzantine exarch. Once again, the pope saw it as his duty to remind the state of its responsibilities and to complain when its efforts had been insufficient. In 602 Gregory wrote to a subdeacon to pressure the praetorian prefect of Italy, John, to dispatch a certain Augustus to oversee the repairs of Rome's aqueducts, since it was not the pope's responsibility to fix them.[110]

Defense. Gregory, like his predecessors, was also concerned that Rome be adequately defended. According to the *Book of the Popes*, Gregory's predecessor, Pope John (561–74), had personally gone to Naples to request the return of the general Narses to Rome to help in the city's defense against Lombard attacks and to avoid alienating the imperial representative.[111] The Lombards had been attacking Italy from 568 on, even besieging Rome in 579.[112] When the Lombard duke of Spoletum, Ariulf, made plans to invade the south of Italy in 591, Pope Gregory rose to the defense of the city, urging the efforts of three Byzantine generals.[113] Gregory had admonished the Byzantine military commanders to send more soldiers to protect Rome and to guard not only the Flaminian Way, the route between Ravenna and Rome.[114] When the exarch Romanus failed to provide the requisite military protection for the city, and the pope saw Roman prisoners paraded before the walls of a starved populace under assault from the Lombard king Agilulf, he intervened more directly. Pope Gregory had already negotiated with the Lombard duke of Spoletum, Ariulf, and now he used money from the church, perhaps as much as five hundred pounds, to pay off the Lombard king to leave Rome in

---

[109] *Lib. Pont.* 69.2, ed. Duchesne 1981, p. 317.

[110] Gregory, *Ep.* 12.6; see too Dey 2011, pp. 241–50.

[111] *Lib. Pont.* 63.2–5, ed. Duchesne 1981, p. 305.

[112] *Lib. Pont.* 64.1, ed. Duchesne 1981, p. 308, under Bishop Benedict. The only source for this siege of Rome is the *Liber Pontificalis*, as Zanini 1998, p. 52, observed.

[113] Gregory, *Ep.* 2.4, 2.10, 2.27, and 2.28. Demacopoulos 2015, pp. 106–7, goes too far when he asserts that Gregory actually coordinated their efforts. He may have tried to, but he lacked the authority to intervene so directly.

[114] Gregory, *Ep.* 2.27, 2.28, and 5.34.

peace.[115] This payment, a standard means of defense, seems to have worked well. The Lombards were not a direct threat to the city after 593, even though they continued to remain a threat to the Byzantines for the remainder of Gregory's papacy. Their control of much of northern Italy was a continuing source of conflict (see Map 6).

The pope's independent defense of the city and his leadership in this crisis led, however, to tense relations with the exarch Romanus. In a letter of 595, Gregory acknowledged that Romanus had complained to the emperor, Maurice, about his actions and that Romanus had even called Gregory's negotiated settlement with the Lombards "treachery."[116] Yet Gregory wanted the Byzantine exarch to reach a settlement for Italy. He continued to urge that the exarch Romanus make a treaty and also take on the defense of Rome and Italy, even threatening to excommunicate those who got in the way.[117]

In sum, a pope like Gregory – from a wealthy family, well educated, and well connected – could use the prestige of his office and the finances of the church as well as his own monies to take on a number of civic functions that had earlier been the responsibility of senatorial magistrates and administrators of Italy. Admittedly, Gregory was pope during unusually turbulent times. After his death in 605, the Byzantines came to a resolution with the invading Lombards and established a more permanent peace. The Byzantine secular administrators resumed control of Rome's infrastructure for the next century.[118] Italy was partitioned, with Byzantine control over Ravenna, Rome, and Naples and with the Lombards in the north of Italy and parts of central Italy (see Map 6). Only after the last Byzantine exarch fell in 751 would popes again take on the administration of civic responsibilities such as repairing the aqueducts and feeding the city with regularity.[119] Nonetheless, the popes could, indeed, assume control of Rome in a crisis.

---

[115] For Gregory's payments, first to the duke of Spoleto, in 592, and then to the Lombard king Agilulf in 593, see Gregory, *Ep.* 5.36, dated to 595 in which the pope states that he had made peace with no cost to the imperial treasury. The document that attests to this purchase is a Lombard chronicle, dated around 625, known as the *Continuatio Hauniensis Prosperi*, ed. Mommsen, MGH AA 9, rept. 1981, p. 339. See Demacopoulos 2015, pp. 106–9.

[116] Gregory, *Ep.* 5.36; 6.34; and Richards 1980, pp. 188–91.

[117] Gregory, *Ep.* 5.34 for his efforts to assist the exarch's advisers; 5.36 for his defense of his actions; and 6.34 for the treaty, as Demacoupolos 2015, p. 209 observed.

[118] For this argument see Humphries 2007, and Dey 2011, pp. 243–44. For a succinct history of this century, see Wickham 1981, pp. 28–46.

[119] Coates-Stephens 2003, pp. 168–85.

In addition, we should not be surprised to learn that Gregory was the first pope to organize processional liturgies in Rome, a kind of rite that had, until his day, been controlled by senatorial aristocrats and used only for civic ceremonials.[120] Gregory's appropriation of ritual processions underscores how the balance of social prestige and civic life had shifted in favor of ecclesiastical rather than senatorial elites.

Because I have been focused here on civic life, I have not devoted much attention to the senators who turned to the church through asceticism. But the ascetic life, too, led to positions of leadership for some aristocrats. I cite but one instance from Italy. Eutychius, one of the *Romanae Urbis nobiles et religiosi* (noble and devout men of the city of Rome), had sent his son, Maurus, to St. Benedict for training rather than to the Senate in Rome or to the imperial center in Ravenna for a civic career. Maurus, as a monk, rose to prominence in his new community to become the assistant of Benedict in his monastery in Subiaco.[121] And unlike in an earlier period when many senators chose to turn to asceticism or a bishopric after a secular career, Maurus lived his entire life within a monastic setting.[122] This option was also one that some senatorial daughters followed. For example, the noble woman Petronella fled from Lucania to Sicily to live in a convent in 593.[123]

The Rise of the Military in the Late Sixth Century

Even as the church offered senators new options for prestige and civic influence, the ongoing warfare in Italy, first with the Franks and then from 568 on with the Lombards, meant that the Byzantine military played an ever more important role in Italy. If an Italo-Roman senator were eager for prestige, status, and power, the other path to advancement, theoretically, was to enter the Byzantine army. Decius, who has been identified as the first to hold the title of exarch of Italy in 584 – a position with civic as well as military duties – may have been a member of one of the most powerful,

---

[120] Latham 2012, pp. 298–327.

[121] Eutychius (Euthicius) 1, *PLRE* 3A, p. 476. For the discussion of his choice, see Gregory, *Dial.* 2.3. For the career of Maurus as *magistri adiutor*, see Gregory, *Dial.* 2.4, 6, 7, 8 and Maurus 1, *PLRE* 3B, p. 863.

[122] For the more usual path of secular office prior to asceticism, see Rapp 2005, passim, and pp. 183–201

[123] For Petronella, see *PLRE* 3B, p. 992. Gregory, *Ep.* 4.6, tells us that she was seduced by the bishop Agnellus's son and fled her convent in Sicily. Gregory, in 593, ordered that she be returned along with her property. We do not know if she obeyed him.

established senatorial families of Rome, the Decii.[124] Yet if that assumption is true, it is also the case that at the time that he assumed the position of exarch, he also had civic duties. And more importantly for this chapter, Decius was not typical of the men chosen by the eastern emperors for this position or to be generals in Italy.

Almost all of the leading generals in Italy whose origins are known were either of Eastern or German origin. Those for whom we cannot attest origin suggest upward mobility. We saw this pattern for the *magistri militum* in the period after the war from 550 until 570; the highest military officers (*magistri militum*) active in Italy after the war were non-Western. For example, Narses, the patrician sent out to replace Belisarius, was from the East, as was Valerianus, the *magister militum* credited with restoring northern Italy, who was from Thrace.[125] After the war, some of these eastern generals continued to remain in office or settle in Italy. For example, the general Maurentius, who had property in Sicily, appears to have settled there.[126] And this pattern continued for leading generals who had been sent from the East in the late sixth and the early seventh centuries, even though, as T.S. Brown has observed, identifying ethnicity solely on the basis of Greek-sounding names is not a reliable method.[127]

The exarchs who ruled after Decius were generally experienced military men who had been sent from the East, even if we cannot know their origins for certain in all cases. The exarch Romanus, who had been active in Italy against the Lombards between 590 and 596 and with whom Pope Gregory had corresponded, was likely the son of a general active in the East.[128] The one mid seventh-century exarch of Italy with possible Roman roots in Ravenna was Theodore Calliopa, whose origin rests on the weak assumption that because he held property in Ravenna, he was of local extraction.[129] Certainly, military officials had owned land in Italy since the mid fifth century, when Valentinian III had changed the laws to allow officials to hold property in the areas in which they served.[130] But equally plausible is the suggestion that

---

[124] On the militarization of the administration, see Brown 1984, pp. 46–56. For the identification, see Decius 2, *PLRE* 3A, p. 391, and Chapter 6, note. 208.

[125] Valerianus 1, *PLRE* 3B, pp. 1355–61. See too Table 6.7.

[126] Maurentius 3, *PLRE* 3B, p. 853. His property in Sicily does not mean he was from an old Roman family, for generals often purchased land as well; see note 130 below. On this I disagree with Brown 1984, p. 78.

[127] Brown 1984, p. 78; see also p. 64 on trends; pp. 67–68 on Greek names as unreliable evidence for ethnicity.

[128] See Romanus 7, *PLRE* 3B, pp. 1092–93. His father has been identified as the general Anagastes who served under Justin II and Tiberius in war against Persia.

[129] For Theodore Calliopa, see Brown 1984, p. 277. Theodorus was *patricius exarchus* 643–ca. 645 and 653–66, *Lib. Pont.* 75, ed. Duchesne, 1981, p. 332.

[130] See *N. Val.* 32.1, 451 CE.

Theodore Calliopa was a recent arrival in northern Italy. Nor can we assume that the military who owned estates in Sicily, Apulia, Bruttium, Calabria, and Campania – the areas that had been the sources of senatorial wealth for centuries – were from old senatorial families, either; they, too, could have acquired estates there during their service in these areas.[131]

By the second half of the seventh century and clearly in the eighth century, a new military elite centered in Ravenna had emerged.[132] If some of these men had come from formerly wealthy Italo-Roman senatorial families, we cannot trace them. Not only do changes in the location and possession of properties make tracking these families difficult, but also the fact that the use of Roman *trinomina*, a practice indicative of Roman senatorial traditions, had disappeared, as noted earlier, means that we cannot follow these families. At the same time, the Roman epigraphic practice of inscribing the titles of one's offices on stone had disappeared, as had so many identifying documents in the West. The lack of comparable sources in the East makes it hard to assess the careers of western senatorial family members who may have moved to Constantinople in the early seventh century.[133] So while it is plausible that former senatorial Italo-Roman aristocrats may have moved into the Byzantine military or to Constantinople, we do not have the evidence to demonstrate the accuracy of that supposition. But we can be certain that by the seventh century, the opportunities for obtaining high senatorial office in Italy had greatly diminished. In their place were opportunities for advancement in the army and the church. Against these social and political changes, the decline of the senatorial aristocracy brought with it the end of the Senate.

The Last Acts of the Senate of Rome

The last recorded functions of the Senate of Rome as a corporate body are emblematic of the shifts in late Roman society that I have been describing. The Senate sent two embassies to the emperor Tiberius II in Constantinople in the years 578 and 579–80 to request aid to fight the Lombards. The first embassy had included the former urban prefect, the patrician Pamphronius, who was

---

[131] We cannot say if the praetorian prefect of Ravenna in 595, Gregory, identified with Gregorius 6, *PLRE* 3A, pp. 551–52, who had large estates in Bruttium, was from an older, established senatorial origin based simply on landownership. Nor do we know if the former praetor Romanus, who had estates in Bruttium, Campania, Apulia, Calabria, and Sicily, was of Italo-Roman senatorial status; see Romanus 6, *PLRE* 3A, p. 1092.

[132] Brown 1984, 46–60; 101–25.

[133] Brown 1984, p. 133 on documents vanishing in the West; p. 68 on the demise of epigraphic evidence from the late sixth century on.

most likely a member of an established Italo-Roman senatorial aristocratic family.[134] According to the contemporary eastern historian Menander the Guardsman, Pamphronius had returned from Constantinople with three thousand pounds of gold but not the men that he had requested; Tiberius II was involved in the Persian War and would not send the men, but he did offer a quite considerable sum. Moreover, he urged that the prefect use it to win over the leaders of the Lombards or, if that failed, to bribe the Franks.[135] The Lombard siege of Rome forced a second embassy to the emperor in 579–80 that included not only men "from the Senate of old Rome" but also "priests dispatched by the archbishop of Rome." These men came to Tiberius II to ask him to defend Italy. Again, war with Persia hampered Tiberius's ability to lend support. Instead, he sent a small contingent of men and undertook some diplomatic initiatives "to win over the leaders of the Lombards by approaching them with gifts." Again according to Menander the Guardsman, "very many of the leaders [of the Lombards] (πλεῖστοι τῶν δυνατῶν) did accept the emperor's generosity and came over to the Romans."[136] Thus, paying the Lombards to not attack provided a successful defense of Rome (see Map 6).

The Senate survived the Lombard attacks of the 570s and early 580s. The historian Agnellus of Ravenna, writing in the ninth century, who is quoted in the epigraph to this chapter, claimed that only sometime after the praetorian prefectureship of Longinus (568–74/75) did the Senate disappear "gradually and after the freedom of the Romans had been carried off in triumph [by the Byzantines]."[137] He may have been repeating a fragment of an earlier *Chronicle*, and surely the coupling of the demise of the Senate with the loss of freedom is based on earlier Roman literary topoi.[138] Gregory's famous lament in a *Homily* delivered in Rome in 593 was rhetorical rather than actual fact when he asked, "Where is the Senate; where are the people?" and proclaimed, "The Senate is gone; the people are

---

[134] For Pamphronius, see note 51 above; Table 6.2 and Table 7.2.

[135] *History of Menander the Guardsman*, ed. Blockley, 1985, *Frag.* 22 = *Exc. De Leg. Gent.* 25, pp. 196–97. Contrary to what Brown 1984, p. 33 says, there is no evidence that this was money raised by the Senate to give to the emperor. Rather, Menander's text indicates that the money was offered to the embassy as a sign of Tiberius's concern for Rome.

[136] *History of Menander the Guardsman*, ed. Blockley 1985, *Frag.* 24 = *Exc. De Leg. Gent.* 29, pp. 216–17. I follow Blockley (who follows Stein 1968), that the embassy arrived in Constantinople in 579, not 580 CE.

[137] Agnellus Ravennatis, *Lib. Pont. Eccl. Rav.* 95, p. 260 ed. Deliyannis, 2006. The first lines appear in the epigram to this chapter. After this, Agnellus goes on: *A Basilii namque tempore consulatum agentis usque ad Narsetem Patricium provinciales Romani ubique ad nichilum redacti sunt. Post haec vero exierunt Langobardi et invaserunt Tusciam usque ad Romam.*

[138] For the great possibility that Agnellus was using an earlier Chronicle, see Humphries 2007, p. 24, note 15.

gone." The circumstances – being in the midst of a crisis that Gregory himself acknowledged as an emotional challenge when the Lombard king Agilulf laid siege to Rome – called for excess, not accuracy.[139] Nonetheless, it is also true that there was no explicit mention of the Senate in the 580s or 590s in any texts, even as the exarch, pope, and Lombard king maneuvered for control of Italy. When the Lombard king Agilulf went to negotiate with Pope Gregory, he met him on the steps of St. Peter's. The pope paid him to desist with monies from the church treasury. The king then agreed to lift his siege of Rome, returning to Milan without consulting with a senatorial embassy or a single senator.[140]

The assassination of Emperor Maurice brought in the antisenatorial Byzantine emperor Phocas, and under his rule we have the last securely attested reference to the Senate in Rome.[141] Pope Gregory, in a letter describing the ceremonial acclamation of the icons of the Byzantine emperor Phocas and his wife, Leontia, in the Lateran Basilica in Rome on May 7 (or April 25) 603, relayed the cries of all the clergy and Senate: "Hear Christ! Life to the Augustus Phocas and the Augusta Leontia."[142] The ninth-century priest John the Deacon reiterated the details of this scene, also noting the presence of the pope, people, and Senate.[143] Mark Humphries has argued that the ceremony that took place in the Lateran Basilica demonstrated the traditional formal role of the Senate in imperial

---

[139] For the poetic convention behind Gregory's statement, *Hom in Ezech.* 2.6.22; *PL* 76, 1010 C-D *Ubi enim senatus? Ubi iam populus? … senatus deest, populus interiit*, see Moorhead 2015, pp. 93–94, who cites Boethius, *Cons. Phil.* 2.6.22. See the lucid discussion by Humphries 2007, pp. 23–24, of Gregory's use of apocalyptic imagery. For the immediate crisis, see Paul the Deacon, *Hist. Lang.* 4.7 and Gregory, Preface to *Hom. in Exech.* 2.

[140] *Continuatio Hauniensis Prosperi*, ed. Mommsen, MGH AA 9, at p. 339, for the meeting at St. Peter's. For Agilulf's movement toward Rome dated to 593, see Agilulfus, *PLRE* 3A, p. 28 and Paul the Deacon, *Hist. Lang.* 4.8; Gregory, *Hom. in Exech.* 2, preface 5.36.

[141] For Maurice as being favorably disposed toward aristocrats, as manifested by his intention to send one son to be emperor in Rome, see Theophylact Simocatta, *Historia* 8.11.9–10, ed. Whitby, p. 228; and Kalas 2017, p. 13.

[142] Gregory, *Ep.* 13.1, ed. Norberg, p. 1101: *Venit autem icona suprascriptorum Focae et Leontiae Augustorum Romae septimo Kalendarum Maiarum, et acclamatum est eis in Lateranis in basilica Iulii ab omni clero vel senatu: "Exaudi Christe! Focae Augusto et Leontiae Augustae vita!" Tunc iussit ipsam iconam domnus beatissimus et apostolicus Gregorius papa reponi eam in oratorio sancti Cesarii intra palatio.* Translation as Appendix 8 by Martyn, 2004, vol. 3, p. 886. For this letter as a subtly disguised indictment of Phocas, see Martyn 2002, pp. 5–38, especially 23–28. Contra, see Kalas 2017, p. 13. For this scene, see Humphries 2007, pp. 21–58; and Arnaldi 1982, pp. 5–56.

[143] John the Deacon, *Sancti Gregorii Magni Vita* 4.20, PL 75, 59–242, p. 183: *imago Phocae et Leontiae, augustorum, cum eorumdem favorabilibus litteris Romam delata est.[136]. Et postquam a clero et senatu acclamatum est eis in basilica Iulii, jussu Gregorii in oratorio sancti Caesarii Lateranensi palatio constituto reponitur.*

acclamations.[144] That statement is true, but it was nonetheless a significant shift in the status of the Senate and the papacy that this ceremony took place not in the Senate House, as would have been normative, nor on the Palatine Hill in the palace, but in the Lateran Basilica, the seat of the pope. Moreover, both Gregory and Paul the Deacon note that the icons of the emperor and his empress were deposited in the Oratory of St. Caesarius in the Palatine Palace at the command of Pope Gregory; the new emperor and empress are associated with imperial and senatorial traditions in Rome through the pope.[145] The rise in the status of the papacy and the decline of senatorial prestige could not have been better demonstrated.

After 603, no actions or interventions are recorded by the Senate, nor are senators noted in positions of leadership. The authority to make decisions devolved on the Byzantine military officials representing the exarch, the *iudices*. Even a formal role is not attested for the Senate after 603. The Senate is not noted in the ceremonies and elections described in the contemporary *Liber Diurnus*, as Ernst Stein pointed out long ago.[146] In a city controlled by an aristocrat turned pope, with an ever smaller number of resident senatorial aristocrats and with a Byzantine ruler known for his hostility toward aristocrats, as Phocas was (he had his troops murder Emperor Maurice along with a number of Maurice's western and eastern senatorial supporters at the Constantinopolitan court), we can see why the Senate makes no further appearance in our documents.[147]

The End of the Senate: The Fall of Rome

The demise of the Roman Senate after thirteen hundred years in existence was an important turning point in the history of Rome. It is unfortunate that our evidence for its end is so spotty. Nonetheless, its disappearance was the logical result of the failure of the western Italo-Roman senatorial aristocracy to revive after the Justinianic reconstruction of Italy. In the past, senatorial aristocrats had been spurred to return to Rome and its Senate to compete with each other to "reconstitute the world," as Adrienne Rich had said in the epigraph to Chapter 1. After each crisis, as outlined in this book, Roman senatorial aristocrats had turned their resources and their will toward restoring the city and their positions in society. But under

---

[144] Humphries 2007, pp. 23–24.   [145] See Maskarinec 2018, pp. 55–61.
[146] Stein 1968, pp. 308–22.
[147] For his murder, see Gregory, *Ep.* 13.1; Paul the Deacon, *Hist. Lang.* 4.26, and Mauricius 4, *PLRE* 3B, p. 860.

Byzantine rule, the resilience that had marked the political life of the Roman senatorial aristocracy and had motivated individuals to return to the city to compete for office and to take up civic leadership dissipated.

As the political and social influence of its members disappeared from civic life in Rome, the functions of the Senate declined. Although Justinian had entrusted to the Senate, as well as to the bishop of Rome, the protection of imperial weights and measures in 554 and had included the Senate in a subsequent law concerning debtors in 555, the implementation of these and other functions devolved onto the church and Byzantine administrators.[148] The bishops, who had gained power, responsibility, and financial security under Justinian thus stepped into civic leadership in the absence of a strong Senate or a vibrant senatorial aristocratic presence in Rome.

When Byzantine emperors after Justinian thought of the Senate, they did so in terms of the Senate of Constantinople. It remained only for the emperor to dispose of the meeting hall of the Senate (see Figure 7). Around 630, Pope Honorius, whose father was remembered by the papal writers of the *Book of the Popes* as a consul (honorary), received permission from the Byzantine emperor Heraclius to transform the Senate House in the Roman Forum into the Church of St. Hadrian.[149] Dedicating the church to this saint, who was worshipped in Constantinople, was a fitting homage to the emperor. Hadrian had been an eastern administrator who had converted to Christianity while seeing Christians tortured for their faith in the persecutions under the emperor Maximian (286–305); he was subsequently martyred in Nicomedia. His life thus speaks to the former status, responsibilities, and independence that the senators who once met in this space had enjoyed.[150] But his glory was now mediated through the authority of the pope in Rome.

The church that would bear Hadrian's name would be only slightly modified from its original status as the Senate House with the addition of an apse and an altar to Christ, not to the traditional ideals of military victory that Symmachus had defended so eloquently in the late fourth century.[151] Whatever independent political valence the Senate House, or the Senate, once had was now no more than symbolic. It was the memory of this once-vibrant political institution that inspired the revival of the term *Senate* in the

---

[148] For the weights and measures in *PS* c.19, see Chapter 6, note 211. For the law on forgiveness of debt, see *Just. Nov.* Appendix 8, eds. Miller and Sarris 2018, pp. 1131–33.

[149] *Lib. Pont.* 72., see note 2 above.   [150] Maskarinec 2018, pp. 47–49.

[151] On the modifications, see Maskarinec 2018, pp. 46–49.

eighth century by a quite different military elite in Rome. At that time it was adopted as a token of the Roman political past, not as a sign of any continuity with it.[152] When the eighth-century *Donation of Constantine* granted the Roman clergy the privilege of wearing senatorial insignia such as the black silk slippers and white stockings, they had no competition from living senators. Rather, these were simply fitting reminders of the senatorial power that had once existed in this city now firmly under papal control.[153]

[152] Stein 1968, pp. 320–22 is quite compelling on this. For a different view, contra, see Kalas 2015, p. 263.

[153] See Brown 1984, p. 35, note 24 for the *mappulae*, ecclesiastical robes, and the *udones*, slippers.

Tables

Table 2.1 *Urban Prefects of Rome from Maxentius through Constantine (306–37)*

Urban Prefects of Rome, 306–37	Dates	Religion	Evidence for Religion	Highest Office and Year	Family and Origin
C. Annius Anullinus (3) (*PLRE* 1, p. 79)	3/19/306–8/27/ 307 (1st)	Pagan	Zos. 2.10.1. Called *impius iudex*: Optatian, *Carm.* 3.8.	cos. 295	Probably son of Anullinus (1), and native of Africa
Attius Insteius Tertullus (6) (*PLRE* 1, pp. 883–84)	8/27/307–4/ 13/308	Unknown[1]			Probably descended from L. Insteius Tertullus, third-century senator of Thuburbo
Statius Rufinus (22) (*PLRE* 1, p. 781)	4/13/308–10/ 30/309	Unknown			Rufini
Aur. Hermogenes (8) (*PLRE* 1, p. 424)	10/30/309–10/ 28/310	Unknown			proc. Asiae 286/305 before being urban prefect suggests noble descent to Moser 2018, p. 20.
C. C(a)eionius Rufius Volusianus (4) (*PLRE* 1, pp. 976–78)	10/28/310–10/ 28/311	Pagan	*CIL* VI.2153.5: *XVVIR SACRIS FACIVNDIS*; *Not. Scav.* 1917, 22.	cos. 311. (Maxentius) cos. 314. (Const.)	Father of Ceionius Rufius Albinus (14); Claimed old patrician descent; Rut. Nam. *De red. suo I.* 168; tied to Rufii, Numii, Fulvii, Gavii, and C(a)eionii.
Iunius Flavianus (10) (*PLRE* 1, p. 344)	10/28/311–2/ 9/312	Unknown			

Name	Date	Religion	Inscription	Consulate	Notes
Aradius Rufinus (10) (*PLRE* 1, p. 775)	2/9/312–10/27/312 (2nd)	Probably pagan	Probably the dedicator (*CIL* VIII.14688–9)	cos. 311. (Maxentius)	Aradii / Rufini. Probably descended from old Roman families.
Anonymus (11) (*PLRE* 1 p. 1006)	306/312	Unknown			
C. Annius Anullinus (3) (*PLRE* 1, p. 79)	10/27/312–11/29/312 (2nd)	Pagan	See above.	cos. 295	Probably son of Anullinus 1, who was a native of Africa
Aradius Rufinus (10) (*PLRE* 1, p. 775)	11/29/312–10/8/313 (3rd)	Probably pagan	See above.	cos. 311. (Maxentius)	Aradii / Rufini. Probably descended from old Roman families.
C. C(a)eionius Rufius Volusianus (4) (*PLRE* 1, pp. 976–78)	10/8/313–8/20/315 (2nd)	Pagan	See above.	cos. 311. (Maxentius) cos. 314. (Const.)	Father of C(a)eionius Rufius Albinus (14); Claimed old patrician descent see Volusianus (4) above.
C. Vettius Cossinius Rufinus (15) (*PLRE* 1, p. 777)	8/20/315–8/4/316	Pagan	*CIL VI.32040: Pontifici Dei Solis, Avgvri, Salio Palatino*	cos. 316	Rufini. Aradii / Rufini. Probably descended from old Roman families.
Ovinius Gallicanus (3) (*PLRE* 1, p. 383)	8/4/316–5/15/317	Possibly Christian	Possibly the dedicant of a basilica: *Lib.*	cos. 317	Unknown

Table 2.1 *(cont.)*

Urban Prefects of Rome, 306–37	Dates	Religion	Evidence for Religion	Highest Office and Year	Family and Origin
Septimius Bassus (19) (*PLRE* 1, p. 157)	5/15/317–9/1/319	Unknown	*Pont.* 34.29 and *CIL* 830 = D 1280		First attested member of Roman family of the Septimii Bassi.
Valerius Maximus (48) Basilius (*PLRE* 1, p. 590)	9/1/319–9/13/323	Probably Pagan	*CTh* XVI.10.1		Possibly from a Roman senatorial family if descendant of the cos. of 256, Valerius Publicola Balbinus Maximus.
Locrius Verinus (2)[2]= Verinus (1) (*PLRE* 1, pp. 950–52)	9/13/323–1/4/325	Unknown			Identified with governor in Syria in 305; perhaps of Italic origin given his nomenclature.[3]
Acilius Severus (16) (*PLRE* 1, p. 834)	1/4/325–11/13/326	Probably Christian	Corresponded with Lactantius; ancestor of Severus (17): Jer. *De vir. ill.* 111	cos. 323	Senatorial from the early fourth century.[4]
Amnius Anicius Iulianus (23) (*PLRE* 1, pp. 473–74)	11/13/326–9/7/329	Unknown		cos. 322	Anicii. Father of Paulinus (14), noted below. Probably

Name	Dates	Religion		Office	Notes
					proc. of Africa in 300/303: *CIL* VI.1682 = D 1220.
Publilius Optatianus (3) Porphyrius (*PLRE* 1, p. 649)	9/7/329–10/8/329	Christian	Wrote poem (*Carm.* 8) to Constantine praising Christ.		Perhaps married to family of M. C(a)eionii.[5]
Petronius Probianus (3) (*PLRE* 1, pp. 733–34)	10/8/329–4/12/331	Unknown		cos. 322	For his family, see his entry under proconsul of Africa, 315–16, Table. 2.3.1. Uncertain family origin; see Salzman 2010; 2015, p. 17.
Sex. Anicius Paulinus (15) (*PLRE* 1, pp. 679–80)	4/12/331–4/7/333	Unknown		cos. 325	Anicii
Publilius Optatianus (3) Porphyrius (*PLRE* 1, p. 649)	4/7/333–5/10/333 (2nd)	Christian	See above.		Perhaps married to family of M. C(a)eionii, but family origin is not attested.[6]
M. Ceionius Iulianus (26) Kamenius (*PLRE* 1, p. 476)	5/10/333–4/27/334	Unknown			Family of the C(a)eionii; perhaps married to Optatianus (3) Porphyrius
Amnius Manius Caesonius Nicomachus Anicius Paulinus (14) Honorius (*PLRE* 1, p. 679)	4/27/334–12/30/335	Unknown		cos. 334	Anicii. Son of Iulianus (23), above. Possibly father of Anicius Auchenius Bassus (11), PUR 382–3.

Table 2.1 *(cont.)*

Urban Prefects of Rome, 306–37	Dates	Religion	Evidence for Religion	Highest Office and Year	Family and Origin
Ceionius Rufius Albinus (14) (*PLRE* 1, p. 37) + Anonymus (12) (*PLRE* 1, pp. 1006–8)	12/30/335–3/10/337	Probably pagan	A *philosophus: CIL* VI.1708. Subject of a horoscope cited by Firm. Mat. (*Math.* II.29.10–20). Identified with Albinus (14)[7]	cos. 335	Son of C. C(a)eionius Rufius Volusianus (4), above.
L. Aradius Valerius Proculus (11) Populonius (*PLRE* 1, pp. 747–49)	Sometime between 326–37 3/10/337–1/13/338	Pagan	*CIL* VI.1690 = D 1240 and VI.1691 and others: *AUGUR, PONTIFEX MAIOR . . .*	cos. 340	Aradii/ Rufini, Probably the son of Aradius Rufinus (10), a pagan and a member of the Aradii / Rufini, Roman families.

[1] In this table, those prefects noted as "Unknown" under religion are men for whom we cannot ascribe probable or possible religious affiliation because of a lack of secure documentation. Urban prefects from 306 to 312 are appointed by Maxentius; those from 312 to 337 are appointed by Constantine.

[2] On Locrius Verinus, see too Salzman and Roberts 2015, pp. 14–17; and Moser 2018, pp. 26–27. See too Verinus 1, *PLRE* 1, p. 950 = Locrius Verinus 2, *PLRE* 1, p. 951.

[3] Salzman and Roberts 2015, pp. 14–17.

[4] For the inscriptions, see Groag 1924–7, pp. 102–9. For this urban prefect as the son, see Wienand 2017, pp. 121–63.

[5] Wienand 2017, pp. 141–48.

[6] Wienand 2017, pp. 141–48, and note 147 in text.

[7] Barnes 1975, pp. 40–49; Moser 2018, p. 37 note 106.

Table 2.2 *Praetorian Prefects Appointed by Constantine (312–37)*[1]

Praetorian Prefects of Constantine 312–37	Dates	Place	Highest Office and Year	Family and Origin	Social Ties/Religion
Iunius Bassus (14) (*PLRE* 1, p. 154)[2]	317/8–322 326–333/34	Illyricum? Illyricum	cos. 331	His son is Iunius Bassus signo Theotecnius (15) (*PLRE* 1, p. 155). Of uncertain origin.	His son was buried in St. Peter's basilica in 359. Possibly identical to the Bassus who was the dedicatee of Optatian, *Carm.* 21.14.
Petronius Annianus (2) *PLRE* 1, p. 68	4/28/315–3/1/317		cos. 314		
Fl. Constantius (5) (*PLRE* 1, p. 225)	324–26 8/22/326–6/24/327	East East	cos. 327	Possibly a relative of Constantine	Imperial ties on the basis of his nomenclature.
Evagrius (2) (*PLRE* 1, p. 284)	326–31 8/22/336–37, death of Constantine 5 or 6/332–5/5/ 333–12/29/328,	Africa? Africa? Gaul? Gaul? Illyricum? Gaul?	PPO	His son is possibly Plutarchus (2) (*PLRE* 1, p. 707). Likely from the East.	
Val. Maximus (49) (*PLRE* 1, p. 590)	1/21/327–33/336/337	Gaul?	cos. 327	His father or uncle is possibly Valerius Maximus signo. Basilius 48 (*PLRE*	His prior office as vicarius Orientis in 325 suggests he was already of senatorial rank.[3]

				1, p. 590). His son is possibly Basilius 2 (*PLRE* 2, p. 148).	
Fl. Ablabius (4) (*PLRE* 1, p. 3), possibly identified with the historian Ablabius (3) (*PLRE* 1, p. 2).[4]	328/9[5] – 336–337 late summer	East East	cos. 331	Native of Crete (Lib. *Or.* XLII 23). Humble origins. His children are Olympias 1 (*PLRE* 1, p. 642) and possibly Seleucus I *ex comitibus* (*PLRE* 1 p. 818).	Wrote verses on Constantine (Sid. Ap. *Ep.* 5. 8.2). He owned a house in Constantinople (Symm. *Ep.* 61) and estates in Bithynia, where he was assassinated (Eun. *V. Soph.* 6.3.10).
L. Papius Pacatianus (2) (*PLRE* 1, p. 656)	4/12/332–33/337 336–37	Italy	cos. 332 PPO		
C. Caelius Saturninus signo Dogmatius (9) (*PLRE* 1, p. 806).	334–35	Illyricum		Holder of several equestrian offices. His son is C. Fl. Caelius Urbanus 4 (*PLRE* 1, p. 983).	He was adlected into the Senate in Rome among the consulars (*CIL* 6.1704 = *ILS* 1214, line 3). He had a home in Rome; *LTUR* 2, (1995), p. 174.
C. Annius Tiberianus (4) (*PLRE* 1, p. 911), possibly identified with the poet = Tiberianus 1 (*PLRE* 1, p. 911)	7/21/335–2/4/337	Gaul	PPO	His ancestors are possibly the Iunii Tiberiani and/or the Anni Anullini, based solely on his name.[6]	A highly educated man (Jer. *Chron.* s.a. 336)

Table 2.2 *(cont.)*

Praetorian Prefects of Constantine 312–37	Dates	Place	Highest Office and Year	Family and Origin	Social Ties/Religion
Felix (2) (*PLRE* 1, pp. 331–32)	4/18/333–3/9/336	Africa	PPO	Possibly senatorial since he was likely the *vicarius* cited in *C. Th.* 7.4.1, 325–26.	
Gregorius (3) (*PLRE* 1, p. 403)	7/21/336–2/4/337	Africa	PPO		Took action against the Donatists (Optatian 3.3.10)
Nestorius Timonianus (*PLRE* 1, p. 915)	335–37	Italy	PPO		
Aemilianus (3) (*PLRE* 1, p. 22)	5/9/328	Italy	PPO		

[1] Dates follow those in *PLRE* 1, by and large. But unlike the *PLRE*, I follow the arguments for the praetorian prefects advanced by Porena 2003, 2006, and 2007. Until 324, I assume that there was only one praetorian prefect for each Augustus. The Caesars did not have their own praetorian prefects. After 324, probably in 326, Constantine multiplied the praetorian prefects to five and sent them to seats far from his court. They thus supervised the civil administration of large administrative areas or dioceses apart from the presence of the emperor or Caesar. The places associated with their action are so listed following Porena 2003 and 2007, pp. 237–62.

[2] Moser 2018, pp. 296–97.

[3] Moser 2018, p. 21, n. 35.

[4] Moser 2018, pp. 65–69, 92, 150, 152, 247.

[5] Moser 2018, p. 66.

[6] See Moser 2018, p. 74, on his possible Roman family associations. Porena 2006, p. 352 doubts this association.

Table 2.3.1 *Proconsuls of Africa under Constantine (312–37)*

Proconsuls of Africa under Constantine (312–37)	Dates	Highest Office and Year	Family and Origin
Anullinus (2) (*PLRE* 1, p. 78)	4/15/313–10/313	proc. 313	His father is possibly Anullinus (3) (*PLRE* 1, p. 79), cos. 295, PUR 306–07, PUR II 312.
Aelianus (2) (*PLRE* 1, p. 17)	10/01/314–4/26/315	proc.	
Petronius Probianus (3) (*PLRE* 1, p. 733–34)	8/25/315–8/13/316	cos. 322	His son is possibly Petronius Probinus (2) (*PLRE* 1, p. 735) / grandson: Sex. Claudius Petronius Probus (5) (*PLRE* 1, p. 736).
Aco Catullinus (2) (*PLRE* 1, p. 187)	4/17/317–12/12/318	proc.	His son is possibly Aco Catullinus signo Philomathius (3) (*PLRE* 1, p. 187).
Proculus (3) (*PLRE* 1, p. 745)	4/24/319–12/26/319	proc. or cos. (?) 325[1]	His nephew is possibly Proculus (11) (*PLRE* 1, p. 747); see *stemma* 30 (*PLRE* 1, p. 1147).
Domitius Latronianus (2) (*PLRE* 1, p. 496)	? 314/24	proc.	His is a possible ancestor of Latronianus 1 (*PLRE* 1, p. 496), which would make him a Spaniard.
Maecilius Hilarianus (5) (*PLRE* 1, p. 433)	7/9/324	cos. 332	He is an ancestor of Maecilius Hilarianus (4) (*PLRE* 2, p. 562).
Sex. Anicius Paulinus (15) (*PLRE* 1, p. 679)	before 325	cos. 325	His father is possibly Anicius Faustus (6) (*PLRE* 1, p. 329) / His brother is possibly Amnius Anicius Iulianus (23) (*PLRE* 1, p. 473) / His son or grandson is Anicius Paulinus (12) (*PLRE* 1, p. 678), see *stemma* 7 (*PLRE* 1, p. 1133).

Table 2.3.1 (cont.)

Proconsuls of Africa under Constantine (312–37)	Dates	Highest Office and Year	Family and Origin
Tertullus (1) (*PLRE* 1, p. 882)	7/6/326	proc.	His father is possibly Attius Insteius Tertullus (6) (*PLRE* 1, p. 883) / His son is possibly Tertullus 2 (*PLRE* 1, p. 882).
Domitius Zenophilus (*PLRE* 1, p. 993) + Anonymus (37) (*PLRE* 1, p. 1012)[2]	328–33	cos. 333	From a senatorial family from North Africa: his brother, Domitius Latronianus (2) (*PLRE* 1, p. 496) was also a proc. in Africa in 321/324.
M. Ceionius Iulianus (26) (*PLRE* 1, p. 476)	326/33	PUR 333	His son is possibly P. Publilius C(a)eionius Iulianus (27) (*PLRE* 1, p. 476) / His grandson is Alfenius Ceionius Iulianus signo Kamenius (25) (*PLRE* 1, p. 474).
L. Aradius Valerius Proculus signo Populonius (11) (*PLRE* 1, p. 747)	before 333	cos. 340	He is possibly related to Val. Maximus (49) (*PLRE* 1, p. 590) / His father is possibly Aradius Rufinus (10) (*PLRE* 1, p. 775) / His brother is possibly Q. Aradius Rufinus Valerius Proculus signo Populonius (12) (*PLRE* 1, p. 749). His sons are possibly Proculus (4) (*PLRE* 1, p. 742) and Aradius Rufinus (11) (*PLRE* 1, p. 775).
Anonymus (42) (*PLRE* 1, p. 1013)	?334	proc.	

Q. Fl. Maesius Egnatius Lollianus signo Mavortius (5) (*PLRE* 1, pp. 512–14)	334/7	cos. 355	He is possibly related to L. Egnatius Victor Lollianus. His sons are Placidus Severus (*PLRE* 1, pp. 836–37) and Q. Flavius Maesius Cornelius Egnatius Severus Lollianus (6) (*PLRE* 1, p. 514).
Cezeus Largus Maternianus (*PLRE* 1, p. 567)		proc.	
Aurelius Celsinus (4) (*PLRE* 1, p. 192)	6/12/338–1/08/339	PUR 341 and 351	His relative is possibly Fabius Titianus (6) (*PLRE* 1, p. 918). His son is possibly Celsinus Titianus (5) (*PLRE* 1, p. 917).

[1] Salway 2015, p. 211.

[2] For the identification of Domitius Zenophilus with Anonymus 37 and the dates of his proconsulship, I follow Moser 2018, p. 31, note 78.

Table 2.3.2 *Proconsuls of Achaia under Constantine (312–37)*

Proconsuls of Achaia under Constantine (312–37)	Dates	Highest Office and Year	Family and Origin
C. Vettius Cossinius Rufinus (15) (*PLRE* 1, p. 777)	?305/6 or 312/15	cos. 316	Rufinus (10) (*PLRE* 1, p. 775) and possibly Rufinus (25) (*PLRE* 1, p. 782).
Domitius Zenophilus (*PLRE* 1, p. 993) + Anonymus (37) (*PLRE* 1, p. 1012)[1]	321/325[2]	cos. 333	From a senatorial family from North Africa: his brother Domitius Latronianus 2 (*PLRE* 1, p. 496) was also a proc. in Africa in 321/324.
Publilius Optatianus signo Porphyrius (3) (*PLRE* 1, p. 649)	325/9 or 326/329[3]	PUR 329, 333	Perhaps a client of Iunius Bassus (14) (*PLRE* 1, p. 154). Exiled but recalled by Constantine. See my discussion in chapter 2.
Ceionius Rufius Albinus (14) (*PLRE* 1, p. 37) + Anonymus (12) (*PLRE* 1, p. 1006)[4]	328/333[5]	cos. 335	Exiled but recalled by Constantine. His father is Volusianus (4) (*PLRE* 1, p. 976), PUR 310–11, cos. 311, PUR (II) 313–5, cos. II 314; see *stemma* 13 in (*PLRE* 1, p. 1138).

[1] Moser 2018, p. 31, note 78.
[2] Moser 2018, p. 31.
[3] Moser 2018, p. 24.
[4] Moser 2018, p. 37, note 106 and p. 283. This table identifies Albinus (14) with Anonymus (12) whose proconsulship is identified by Firmicus Maternus, *Mathesis*, 2.29.10–20.
[5] Moser 2018, p. 338.

Table 3.1 *Urban Prefects of Rome under Honorius (410-23)*

	Year of Office	Highest Office and Year	Other Offices/ Honors	Origin	Social Connections
Bonosianus (*PLRE* 2, p. 240)	9/25/410–11/ 28/411	PUR, 410–11			
Palmatus (1) (*PLRE* 2, p. 824)	3/29/412	PUR, 412		Italian?	
Fl. Annius Eucharius Epiphanius (7) (*PLRE* 2, p. 399)	10/15/412–5/ 27/414	PUR, 412–14			Perhaps related to Eucharius (1), proconsul of Africa in 412.
Rutilius Claudius Namatianus (*PLRE* 2, pp. 770–71)	Summer 414	PUR, 414	mag. off. 412	Gallic, Toulouse?	Author of *De reditu suo*; son of Lachanius (PLRE 1, p. 491), likely urban prefect.
Caecina Decius Acinatius Albinus (7) (*PLRE* 2, pp. 50–51)	9/17/414	PUR, 414		Italian, Rome	Roman noble family, connected to the Ceionii and the Decii. Probably father of Fl. Caecina Decius Basilius (11), cos. 463. Probably the son of Caecina Decius

Table 3.1 *(cont.)*

	Year of Office	Highest Office and Year	Other Offices/ Honors	Origin	Social Connections
					Albinus (10, *PLRE* 1, pp. 35–6), and grandson of the senator Aginatius (*PLRE* 1, pp. 29–30).
Gracchus (*PLRE* 2, p. 518)	7/25/415	PUR, 415	cons. Campaniae, 397.	Italian, Campania?	Presumably a descendant of Furius Maecius Gracchus and Gracchus PUR 376–77 (both in *PLRE* 1).
Probianus (1) (*PLRE* 2, p. 908)	12/12/416	PUR, 416			A Probianus was on a senatorial mission with Caecilianus (1) in 400, mentioned by Symm. *Ep.* 8.14.
Rufius Antonius Agrypnius Volusianus (6) (*PLRE* 2, pp. 1184–85)	11/417– mid-418	PPO *Italiae et Africae*, 428–29	proc. Africae, before 412; QSP, before 412	Italian, Rome	Son of Ceionius Rufius Albinus 15 (*PLRE* 1), urban prefect in 389–91; friend of Rutilius Namatianus

Aurelius Anicius Symmachus (6) (*PLRE* 2, pp. 1043–44)	12/24/ 418–1/420	PUR, 418–20	proc. Africae, 415	Italian, Rome	A relative of the orator Symmachus. Married into the Roman family of the Anicii.
Petronius Maximus (22) (*PLRE* 2, pp. 749–51)	1 or 2/420–8 or 9/421 and a second time 421/439	cos. 433, 443 Augustus 455	?Praetor, c. 411; trib. et not. c. 415; CSL, ?416–19; PPO 421/439; PPO *Italiae* (II) 439–41; pat. 445		From a noble family whose origins are not attested; see Chapter 2, note 208. He had ties to the Anicii and Petronii; see Chapter 4, note 17.
Iunius Valerius Bellicius (*PLRE* 2, p. 223)	408/423	PUR, 408/423			Probably identical with or related to Bellicius, the correspondent of bishop Ambrose, *Epp.* 79–80. Possible correspondent of Symmachus, *Epp.* 8.47, 57
Anicius Acilius Glabrio Faustus (8) (*PLRE* 2, pp. 452–54)	421/423[1]	cos. 438	*quaestor candidatus; praetor tutilaris; comes intra consistorium*	Italian, Rome	From a Roman noble family

Table 3.1 *(cont.)*

	Year of Office	Highest Office and Year	Other Offices/ Honors	Origin	Social Connections
			PUR (III) 408/ 423, 425, 425/ 437; PPO (*Italiae, Africae et Illyrici*) 437–38; PPO (II) *Italiae* 442		

[1] Orlandi 2013, p. 342 and note 127 in Chapter 3.

Table 3.2 *Counts of the Imperial Treasury* (Comites sacrarum largitionum) *of Honorius in the West (410–23)*

	Year of Office	Highest Office and Year	Other Offices/Honors	Origin	Social Connections
Gaiso (*PLRE* 2, p. 490)	9/28/409	mag. off. 410	com. 410	Germanic?	
Probus (1) (*PLRE* 2, p. 910)	2/29/412–6/ 11/414	cos. 406 if is Probus (11) (*PLRE* 2, pp. 913– 14).	CRP 412	Italian, Rome?	Possibly identified with Fl. Anicius Petronius Probus (11), son of Sextus Petronius Probus
Lucillus (*PLRE* 2, p. 691)	Before 417?	CSL, Before 417?		Italian?	Father of Decius (1), *consularis Tusciae et Umbriae*, 417/(Rut. Nam. *De red. suo* 1.598–600)
Anonymus 30 (*PLRE* 2, p. 1224)	Before 418	CSL, Before 418			
Petronius Maximus (22) (*PLRE* 2, pp. 749–51)	?416–19	ccs. 433, 443 Augustus 455 [see Table 3.1]	?Praetor, c. 411; trib. et not. c. 415; PUR 420–21; PUR (II) 421/ 439; PPO 421/439; PPO Italiae (II) 439–41; pat. 445		From a noble family whose origins are not attested; see Chapter 2, note 208. He had ties to the Anicii and Petronii; see Chapter 4, note 217.
Rufinus (6) (*PLRE* 2, p. 952)	2/8/423	CSL, 423			

Table 3.3 *Counts of the Imperial Estates (*Comites rei privatae*) of Honorius (410–23)*

	Year of Office	Highest Office and Year	Other Offices/Honors	Origin	Social Connections
Macedonius (2) (*PLRE* 2, p. 697)	2/8/411	CRP, 411			
Claudius Lepidus (*PLRE* 2, p. 675)	?E V	CRP, ?E V	com.; cons. Germaniae Primae; mag. mem.		Brother of Cl. Postumus Dardanus; see Table 3.4
Fl. Peregrinus Saturninus (7) (*PLRE* 2, pp. 980–81)	?E/M V	PUR (II), ? E/M V	*tribunus militum*; trib. et notarius; *comiti ordinis primi.*		Gilded statue displayed in Forum of Trajan suggests Roman ties
(H)osius (2) (*PLRE* 2, p. 572)	E/M V	?CRP/ CSL/pat.	?CRP/CSL/pat.	Italian, Milan	Perhaps the dedicatee of a translation and commentary of Plato's *Timaeus* by Calcidius (*PLRE* 1)

Ursacius (1) (*PLRE* 2, p. 1191)	8/8/414–5/14/417	CRP, 414–17		
Venantius (1) (*PLRE* 2, p. 1152)	2/20/422	PPO ?Italiae et Africae, 423		
Proculus (1) (*PLRE* 2, p. 923)	8/25/422	PPO ?Italiae et Africae, 423		
Trygetius (1) (*PLRE* 2, p. 1129)	5/19/423	ex PPO or PUR, 452	*vir praefectorius* 452	Probably father of Memmius Aemilius Trygetius (3)

Table 3.4 *Praetorian Prefects Appointed by Honorius in the West (410–23)*

	Year of Office	Highest Office and Year	Other Offices/Honors	Origin	Social Connections
Melitius (*PLRE* 2, p. 753)	11/16/410–3/19/412	PPO Italiae, 410–12			
Claudius Postumus Dardanus (*PLRE* 2, pp. 346–47)	12/7/412–Spring–413	PPO (II) Gall., 412–13	pat.; cons. Viennensis; mag. lib.; QSP; PPO (I) Gall.		Correspondent of Jerome, and referenced by Augustine, *Ep.* 129.1
Seleucus (*PLRE* 2, pp. 987–88)	4/3/414–12/11/415	PPO (II) *Italiae et Africae,* 414–15	PPO (I) Africae, 412		.
Agricola (1) (*PLRE* 2, pp. 36–37)	4/17/418–5/23/418 PPO (II) Gall.	cos. 421	PPO? West, before 418	Gallic, Narbo?	Possible kinship with family of the Augustus Avitus (5)
Ioannes (4) (*PLRE* 2, p. 594)	7/11/422	PPO (II) *Italiae,* 422	notarius, 394; *primicerius notariorum,* 408; PPO (I) *Italiae et Africae,* 412–13		

Hadrianus (*PLRE* 2, p. 527)	8/3/413–3/3/414	PPO (II) *Italiae et Africae*, 413–14	CSL 395; mag. off., 397–99; PPO I *Italiae et Africae*, 401–05 [Before 410]		
Fl. Iunius Quartus Palladius (19) (*PLRE* 2, pp. 822–24)	1/7/416–7/28/421: PPO *Italiae*; [PPO *per annos sex Illyrici Italiae et Africae*][1]	cos. 416	*praetor et quaestor kandidatus*; trib.; not.; CSL, 408–09.	From Rome? Italian?; owned house on the Aventine Hill	Noble; sent on four senatorial embassies.
Fl. Avitus Marinianus (3) (*PLRE* 2, pp. 723–24)	11/3/422, PPO ? *Italiae*	cos. 423	?pat.		
Venantius (1) (*PLRE* 2, p. 1152)	3/9/423	PPO ? *Italiae*, 423	CRP, 422		
Proculus (1) (*PLRE* 2, p. 923)	5/18/423	PPO *Africae et* ?*Italiae*, 423	CRP, 422		

[1] The inscription with his *cursus* notes these offices, and his noble family as being of "outstanding nobility," *nobilitate conspicuus*, *AE* 1928, p. 80.

Table 3.5 *Master of the Offices (Magister Officiorum) of Honorius in the West (410–23)*

	Year of Office	Highest Office and Year	Other Offices/ Honors	Origin	Social Connections
Olympius (2) (*PLRE* 2, pp. 801–2)	?408–09; and a second time ? 409/410	mag. off. 408–09; 409/410	mag. scrinii, 408	Native of the Black Sea region	Correspondent of Augustine and aligned with anti-Stilicho faction
Gaiso (*PLRE* 2, p. 490)	2/12/410–6/12/410	mag. off. 410	CSL, 409; com. 410	Germanic?	
Rutilius Claudius Namatianus (*PLRE* 2, pp. 770–71)	12/7/412	PUR, 414		Gallic, Toulouse?	See Table 3.1

Table 4.1 *All Civic Officeholders in the Western Court or in Italy Appointed by Avitus (455–56)*

Appointee	Year of Highest Office	Highest Office	Office Held under Avitus	Other Offices and Honors	Origin	Social Connections
Paeonius (2) (*PLRE* 2, p. 817)	456–457	PPO Gall.	vic. *Septem Provinciarum*[1]		Likely Gallic, not from an aristocratic family.	Cited at a dinner party by Sidonius Apollinaris, below; *Ep.* 1.11.
… ius Iunius Valentinus (5) (*PLRE* 2, p. 1140)	455/476?	PUR	PUR		Italian, from Rome	Identified as a member of the Symmachi.
Consentius (2) (*PLRE* 2, pp. 308–9)	455/456	cura palatii	cura palatii	trib. et not. 437/450	Gallic	Friend of Sidonius Apollinaris; *Carm.* 23 and received *Ep.* 8.4.
Magnus (2) (*PLRE* 2, pp. 700–1)	460	cos.	mag. off. in Spain 458?[2]	PPO Gall. 458 (under Majorian)	Gallic, Narbonne	Friend of Sidonius Apollinaris.
Hesychius (10 and 11)[3] (*PLRE* 2, pp. 554–55)	456	trib. et not., if identified with Hesychius 10.	trib. et not.		Gallic	Identified as married to Audentia, the sister of Sidonius Apollinaris. Bishop of Vienne after 474.
Turpio (*PLRE* 2, p. 1133)	456?	trib. et not.?	trib. et not.?		Gallic	Noted by Sidonius Apollinaris *Ep.*

Table 4.1 *(cont.)*

Appointee	Year of Highest Office	Highest Office	Office Held under Avitus	Other Offices and Honors	Origin	Social Connections
						4.24; he seems to have come to Rome with Avitus.[4]
G. Sollius Apollinaris (6) Sidonius (*PLRE* 2, pp. 115–18)	468	PUR	trib. et not.? 456/461[5]	com. 461.	Gallic, Lyon	Poet and son-in-law of the Aug. Eparchius Avitus. Bishop of Clermont-Ferrand from 469.
Avitus (1) (*PLRE* 2, pp. 194–95)	455–56?	trib. et not.?	trib. et not.?		Gallic	Friend of Sidonius Apollinaris (6) above; seems to have come to Rome with Sidonius.[6]
Fronto (*PLRE* 2, p. 486)	452–55	com.	com.		Gallic, Clermont-Ferrand?	Friend of Sidonius Apollinaris, see Sid. Ap. *Ep.* 4.21.4.

[1] Mathisen 1979, p. 603.

[2] Henning 1999, p. 76 and note 26 makes the reasonable argument for his position as *magister officiorum* falling under Avitus.

[3] Henning 1999, p. 77.

[4] Henning 1999, p. 77 suggests that he was one of the men who accompanied Sidonius to Rome with Avitus, Sid. Ap. *Ep.* 4.24.1. I include him as a possible officeholder under Avitus.

[5] The date is based on Sidonius Apollinaris, *Ep.* 3.1.1. No specific office is mentioned, but as he received a statue in the forum, he was in Rome likely with an office.

[6] Likely in Rome in an official capacity with Sidonius Apollinaris; Sid. Ap. *Ep.* 3.1.1.

Table 4.2 *All Civic Officeholders in the Western Court or in Italy Appointed by Majorian (457–61)*

Appointee	Year of Highest Office	Highest Office	Offices Held under Majorian	Other Offices and Honors	Origin	Social Connections
Aemilianus (3) (*PLRE* 2, p. 15)	7/11/458	PUR	PUR		Likely Italian, if identified with the Aemilianus recorded in Colosseum seat inscription.[1]	Received *Novella* 4 from Majorian.
Ennodius (1) (*PLRE* 2, pp. 392–93)	9/4/458	CRP	CRP		Gallic?	Perhaps related to Ennodius (3).
Fl. Iulius Valerius Maiorianus Augustus (*PLRE* 2, pp. 702–03)	458	cos.		MUM, 457; com. dom. under Aetius and Valentinian III in Gaul.	Pannonian?	Emperor, 457–461.
F. Rusticius Helpidius Domnulus (1)[2] (*PLRE* 2, p. 374)	458?	QSP	QSP		African; resident of Gaul.	Correspondent with Sidonius Apollinaris, *Ep.* 4.25 and *Ep.* 9.15.1.
Petrus (10) (*PLRE* 2, p. 866)	458	mag. epist.	mag. epist.	Commanded troops to retake Lyon.	Italian	Friend of Sidonius Apollinaris, *Ep.* 9.13.5, below.

Table 4.2 *(cont.)*

Appointee	Year of Highest Office	Highest Office	Offices Held under Majorian	Other Offices and Honors	Origin	Social Connections
Magnus (2) (*PLRE* 2, pp. 700–1)	460	cos.	mag. off., PPO Galliarum, 458.		Gallic, Narbonne	Friend of Sidonius Apollinaris.
Fulgentius (1) (*PLRE* 2, p. 487)	Before 461?	QSP	QSP			Cited by Sidonius Apollinaris (6) for an anecdote, *Ep.* 2.13.5.
Fl. Severinus (5) (*PLRE* 2, p. 1001)	461	cos.	cos.			At banquet at Arles, noted by Sidonius Apollinaris *Ep.* 1.11.10–11, 16.
Philoxenus (3) (*PLRE* 2, p. 878)	458–60	*agens in rebus*	*agens in rebus*			Not known if he served in the east or the west, but he carried letters of Bishop Leo to Constantinople.
Fl. Caecina Decius Basilius (11) (*PLRE* 2, pp. 216–17)	463	cos.		PPO (I) Italiae, 458. pat. 463; PPO (II) Italiae, 463–65	Italian	Probably the father of Caecina Decius Maximus Basilius (12), Decius Marius Venantius Basilius (13), below, and Caecina Mavortius Basilius Decius (2).

G. Sollius Apollinaris (6) Sidonius (*PLRE* 2, pp. 115–18)	468	PUR	trib. et not. 458/461; com. 461.	trib. et not. 455/456?	Gallic, Lyon	Poet and son-in-law the Augustus. Eparchius Avitus. Bishop of Clermont-Ferrand from 469.
Rogatianus (*PLRE* 2, p. 946)	4/17/459	cons. *Tusciae suburbicariae*	cons. *Tusciae suburbicariae,* 459.			
Suniericus (*PLRE* 2, p. 1040)	459–60	com. (Hispaniarum?)	com. (Hispaniarum?) 459–60			Visigothic general 459–61
Catullinus (2) (*PLRE* 2, pp. 272–73)	Before 461 . . .	trib. et not.?	trib. et not.?	*Illustris* rank later attested, likely had another higher office.	Gallic, Clermont-Ferrand	Friend of Sidonius Apollinaris; Sid. Ap. *Ep.* 1.11.3.

[1] Henning 1999, p. 79, identified Aemilianus, urban prefect in 458 and the recipient of four *Novels* of Majorian, with an old Roman family, with no evidence. If this urban prefect can be identified with the seat holder from the Colosseum named Aemilianus, his Italian identity is more than likely; see Orlandi 2004, p. 454, number 5.

[2] May be identical with Helpidius (7). *Consularis Tusciae suburbicariae.*

Table 4.3 *All Civic Officeholders in the Western Court or in Italy Appointed by Libius Severus (461–65)*

Appointee	Year of Highest Office	Highest Office	Offices Held under Severus	Other Offices and Honors	Origin	Social Connections
Arvandus (*PLRE* 2, pp. 157–58)	464–68	PPO Gall.	PPO Gall.		Gallic	Sid Ap. *Ep.* 1.7.1–13 (469), discusses his arrest and trial in Rome.
Fl. Synesius Gennadius Paulus (36) (*PLRE* 2, p. 855)	Before 467	PUR	PUR?		Italian, Rome	Related to Rufius Synesius Hadrianus and Gennadius Avienus (4). He was called *praefectorius* by Sidonius Apollinaris who stayed at his house in Rome in 467; *Ep.* 1.9.2–4.
Caelius Aconius Probianus (4) (*PLRE* 2, p. 908)	471	cos.	PPO Italiae, 461/463		Italian, Rome	Probably related to the Aconii and the Fabii.[1]
Fl. Caecina Decius Basilius (11) (*PLRE* 2, pp. 216–17)	463	cos.	PPO (II) Italiae, 463–65; pat. 463	PPO (I) Italiae, 458	Italian	Probably the father of Caecina Decius Maximus Basilius (12), Decius Marius Venantius Basilius (13), and Caecina Mavortius Basilius Decius (2).

| Macrobius Plotinus Eustathius (13) (*PLRE* 2, p. 436) | 457–72, but most likely 461–65[2] | PUR | PUR, 461–65? | Italian | Identified with Eustathius, son of the writer Macrobius.[3] |

---

[1] *PLRE* 2, p. 908.

[2] I date his urban prefecture to the reign of Libius Severus based on the arguments of Cameron 2011, p. 238. He may be identical with Eustathius 4, *PLRE* 2, p. 435.

[3] Cameron 2011, p. 238; and Panciera 1982, pp. 658–60.

Table 5.1 *All Civic Officeholders Appointed by Anicius Olybrius (472)*

Appointee	Year of Office under Olybrius[1]	Office under Olybrius	Highest Office	Origin	Social Connections
Anicius Acilius Aginantius Faustus iunior (Albus) (Faustus 4)[2] (*PLRE* 2, pp. 451–52)	472/473; or before 482.[3]	PUR	cos. 483, under Odoacer PUR II? 502–3, under Theoderic	Italian, Rome	A friend of Magnus Felix Ennodius (3), bishop of Ticinum; named on seats in the Flavian Amphitheater. He restored a statue of Minerva (*CIL* 6.526 = *ILS* 3132) in Rome.
Polemius (2) (*PLRE* 2, p. 895)	?471–72	PPO Gall.	PPO Gall. under ? Anthemius ? Olybrius	Gallic	From a noble family; philosopher with interest in Neoplatonism. He married Araneola, who was from a leading Gallic family and sister of Magnus Felix (21).

[1] Henning 1999, p. 98 and p. 114, dates the urban prefect Petronius Perpenna Magnus Quadratianus = Quadratianus 2, *PLRE* 2, pp. 931–32, to the rule of Olybrius. He argues that the inscription that attested his work when he restored the baths of Constantine was similar to that of the work on the *simulacrum of Minerva* restored by Faustus iunior (4), urban prefect in 472/473. But more recent analysis of the blocks from the baths of Constantine by Grossi 2019, pp. 61–64 indicates an earlier date for this Quadratianus, as urban prefect in 433 or 439–41, and praetorian prefect in 443. This would mean that Quadratianus 1 and 2 in *PLRE* 2, pp. 931–32 are the same person, and hence not officeholders under Olybrius.

[2] Following Henning, I suggest that this Anician senator was appointed by his relative, the emperor Anicius Olybrius, *PLRE* 2, pp. 796–98. The date is not secure however.

[3] Faustus was consul in 483; see Faustus 8, *PLRE* 2, pp. 451–52. For the date of his PUR, see note 93 in this chapter.

Table 5.2 *All Civic Officeholders Appointed by Glycerius (473–74)*

Appointee	Year of Office under Glycerius[1]	Highest Office	Origin	Social Connections
Felix Himelco (*PLRE* 2, p. 565)	3/11/473–4/29/473	PPO Italiae		Attested by a *Novella* of Glycerius, March 11, 473; *Corp. leg.* 1226, p. 260.
Aurelianus (5) (*PLRE* 2, p. 199)	4/29/473	PPO Gall. or Ill.?	Gallic?	Attested by a *Novella* of Glycerius, March 11, 473; *Corp. leg.* 1226, p. 260. Possibly to be identified with the patrician Aurelianus of Marseille noted by Gregory of Tours, *Glor. Mart.* 76.
Protadius (2) (*PLRE* 2, p. 927)	4/29/473	PPO Gall. or Ill.?	Gallic?	Attested by a *Novella* of Glycerius, March 11, 473; *Corp. leg.* 1226, p. 260.

[1] For the argument that Petronius Perpenra Magnus Quadratianus 2 was the praetorian prefect of Glycerius in 472, see Henning 1999, pp. 98 and 114. But this has been disproved by Grossi 2019, pp. 61–64.

Table 5.3 *All Civic Officeholders Appointed by Iulius Nepos (474/5–480)*

Appointee	Year of Office under Nepos	Office under Nepos	Highest Office	Social Connections
Castalius Innocentius Audax (3) (*PLRE* 2, pp. 184–85)	7/474–8/475[1]	PUR	PUR	Of distinguished family; addressee of a letter by Sidonius Apollinaris on his appointment, *Ep.* 9.7. Named on an inscription, for a repair in Rome;[2] and named on two bronze tablets.[3]
Agricola (2) (*PLRE* 2, p. 37)	Not dated	Perhaps PPO Gall.?[4]	Perhaps PPO Gall.?	If identified with Agricola 2, he was brother of Ecdicius (3) who was MUM under Nepos; brother-in-law of Sidonius Apollinaris; and son of the Emperor Avitus.
Licinianus (1) (*PLRE* 2, p. 682)		QSP	QSP	Envoy to the Visigothic king Euric in 474 from Ravenna.

[1] *ILS* 814 (1) = *CIL* 15, 07110a (2); and Elvers 2011, pp. 213–14.

[2] Wheeler 1988, p. 82, interpreted a reference to a "restoration after a sudden barbarian attack" (*CIL* 6.1663 = *ILS* 814: *barbarica incursione| sublata restitutit*) as referring to the Vandal raid of 455. The repair, however, is dated to when Audax was urban prefect under Julius Nepos. See Orlandi 1997, "Salvo Domino Nostri," *MEFRA* 109, 1997, pp. 31–40, and at p. 39.

[3] Kulikowski 2017, pp. 11–12.

[4] Henning 1999, p. 101 and n. 168 argues that his title was attained in Gaul earlier than its attestation in 485–506 as *vir illustris* by Ruricius, *Ep.* 2.32.

Table 5.4.1 *Civic Officeholders Appointed by Odoacer (476–93)*

Appointee	Year of Highest Office under Odoacer	Highest Office under Odoacer	Other Offices under Odoacer	Origin	Social Connections
Pelagius (1) (*PLRE* 2, p. 857)	c. 477	PPO Italiae	PPO Italiae		Ennod. *Vita. Epiph.* 107; active in Liguria.
Fl. Caecina Decius Maximus Basilius iunior (12) (*PLRE* 2, p. 217)	480	cos.	PPO Italiae 483; pat.	Italian, Rome	From the aristocratic family of the Decii. Patron of the Greens at Rome, he also owned a house on the Aventine. Praetorian prefect mentioned in the *Scriptura* *of 483.*
Caecina Mavortius Basilius Decius (2) (*PLRE* 2, p. 349)	486	cos.	?PUR before 486; PPO? Italiae before 486; pat.	Italian, Rome	From the aristocratic family of the Decii; probably son of Fl. Caecina Decius Basilius (11) and brother of Basilius (12) and Basilius (13). He undertook drainage activities in Campania under Theoderic in 507/11.
Fl. Nar. Manl(ius) Boethius (4). (*PLRE* 2, pp. 232–33)	487	cos.[1]	PPO? Italiae 480/486; pat.	Italian, Rome? Grand-father from Milan	Probably son of Boethius (1), who was PPO Italiae under Valentinian III in 454.

Table 5.4.1 *(cont.)*

Appointee	Year of Highest Office under Odoacer	Highest Office under Odoacer	Other Offices under Odoacer	Origin	Social Connections
Anicius Acilius Aginantius Faustus iunior (albus) (4) (*PLRE* 2, pp. 451–52)	483	cos.	PUR? 472/473[2]	Italian, Rome	From the aristocratic family of the Anicii. A friend of Ennodius (3), bishop of Ticinum. Named on seats in the Flavian Amphitheater. As urban prefect, restored a statue of Minerva in the Atrium of Minerva (*CIL* 6.526 = *ILS* 3132).
Quintus Aurelius Memmius Symmachus iunior (9) (*PLRE* 2, pp. 1044–46)	485	cos.	PUR 476/ 485[3]; pat.	Italian, Rome	From the aristocratic family of the Symmachi; father-in-law of Boethius (5); addressee of Magnus Felix Ennodius (3). Supporter of Bishop Symmachus in Rome (Avit. *Ep.* 34). In Rome, he repaired the Theater of Pompey (Cass. *Var.* 4.51). "caput Senatus" (*Anon. Val.* 15 (92)).

Name	Date	Office	Office	Origin	Notes
Decius Marius Venantius Basilius (13) (*PLRE* 2, p. 218)	484	cos.	PUR 484; pat.	Italian, Rome	From the aristocratic family of the Decii, probably son of Basilius (11), brother of Decius (2) and Basilius (12). Made repairs in the Flavian Amphitheater.
Andromachus (3) (*PLRE* 2, p. 89)	489	mag. off.?	mag. off.?		Sent by Odoacer and Bishop Felix III to Constantinople in 488/89.
Opilio (3) (*PLRE* 2, pp. 807–8)	476/490	CSL	CSL		
Cassiodorus (3) (*PLRE* 2, pp. 264–65)	476/490	CRP then CSL (West)	*consularis Siciliae*, 490/493, perhaps began under Odoacer?	Italian, born in Bruttium, where his father and grandfather had resided, and hence Italian.	From the aristocratic family of the Cassiodori. Father of Fl. Magnus Aurelius Cassiodorus Senator (4); abandoned Odoacer in favor of Theoderic c. 490; subsequently well connected at the court of Theoderic. He was PPO Italiae and patrician (under Theoderic, c. 503/507)
Petrus Marcellinus Felix Liberius (3) (*PLRE* 2, pp. 677–81)	Specific Office under Odoacer not attested			Italian? Ligurian?	No attested family. Praised for his loyalty to Odoacer even when Theoderic had taken control of Italy (Cass. *Var.* 2.16). PPO Ital, 493–500 under Theoderic; PPO Gall, ca. 510–534; patrician 500–54.

Table 5.4.1 *(cont.)*

Appointee	Year of Highest Office under Odoacer	Highest Office under Odoacer	Other Offices under Odoacer	Origin	Social Connections
Total: Ten men with specific offices and one unattested officeholder.[4]					*Total: Six of eleven men from aristocratic families from Rome (Decii, Anicii, Symmachi, Boethii/Severini or Anicii); and one from Italy, the Cassiodori.*

[1] His consulship was not recognized in the East, as was true of the consuls appointed by Odoacer from 480–86 or 489; see Orlandi 2010, p. 336 and n. 27; Vitiello 2005, p. 39–55.

[2] Henning 1999, p. 97.

[3] Elvers 2011, pp. 217–18; Kulikowski 2017, pp. 11–12.

[4] I removed from consideration Fabius Felix Passifilus Paulinus (13) based on Orlandi 2010 and 2004; and Coates-Stephens 2012, p. 326. The following men cannot be securely dated as holding office under Odoacer: Aggerius (*PLRE* 2, pp. 33–34); Venantius Severinus Faustus (10) (*PLRE* 2, pp. 456–57); (Glabr?)io Venantius Faustus (11) (*PLRE* 2, p. 457); Rufius Synesius Hadirianus (*PLRE* 2, p. 527); Rufius Valerius Messala (4) (*PLRE* 2, p. 761); Tito Haditanus Secundus (3) (*PLRE* 2, p. 986); Memmius Aemilius Trygetius (3) (*PLRE* 2, pp. 1129–30); Sev(erus?) Ant(oni[n?]us) (2) (*PLRE* 2, p. 107); Anonymus 33 (*PLRE* 2, p. 1225); Victorius M … (*PLRE* 2, p. 696); Fl. Turcius Rufius Apronianus Asterius (11) (*PLRE* 2, pp. 173–74); and Fl. Basilius? (*CRP* according to Henning 1999, p. 109).

Table 5.4.2 *Men Attested Only as Consuls under Odoacer (476–89)*[1]

Rufius Achilius Maecius Placidus (6) (*PLRE* 2, p.891)	481	cos.[2]	cos. 481, under Odoacer. No colleague in East or West.	Italian, Rome	Probably from the aristocratic family of the Petronii.[3] Father of consul of 489, Petronius Probinus (2).
Severinus iunior (3) (*PLRE* 2, p. 1001)	482	cos.[4]		Noricum? but tied to Roman families.	Probably son of Fl. Severinus, consul, 461, and probably tied to the aristocratic family of Boethius later in the century.[5]
Claudius Iulius Eclesius Dynamius (2) (*PLRE* 2, p. 382)	488	ccs.	PUR c. ?488		
Rufius Achilius Sividus (*PLRE* 2, pp. 1017–18)	488	cos.	QSP? before 483; PUR (II) before 488; pat.	Italian, Rome?	Probably from the aristocratic family of the Achilii Glabriones; son or uncle to Anicius Acilius Glabrio Faustus, cos. 438.[6]

Table 5.4.2 *(cont.)*

Petronius Probinus (2) (*PLRE* 2, pp. 909–10)	489	cos.		Italian, Rome	From the aristocratic family of the Petronii. Son of Placidus (6), cos. 481; father of Cethegus, consul of 504. He and Festus (5) led opposition to Bishop Symmachus. Patrician, 511–12
Total: Five men					*Total: Three men from two Roman aristocratic families (Acilii Glabriones; Petroni).*

[1] I removed the consul of 490, Fl. Anicius Probus Faustus iunior Niger (9) because I am convinced by the arguments of Vitiello 2005, pp. 48–55 that Theoderic was in control of Rome by this date and hence, Faustus's consulship should be attributed to Theoderic.
[2] Orlandi 2010, p. 331 n. 3.
[3] Henning 1999, p. 104.
[4] Orlandi 2010, p. 331, n. 3.
[5] Henning 1999, p. 104.
[6] Henning 1999, p. 105.

Table 6.1 *Praetorian Prefects of Italy Appointed by Justinian or Justin II (542–75)*

Praetorian Prefects	Year of Office	Highest Office	Origin	Social Connections
Maximinus (2) (*PLRE* 3B, pp. 865–66)	542	PPO Italiae	Procop. *Wars* 2.29.1 indicates that he was in the Senate of Constantinople.	He and Fl. Domnicus 3 were sent by Justinian as envoys to King Witigis in Italy in early 540 to arrange for peace and the partition of Italy.
Antiochus (2) (*PLRE* 3A, p. 90)	(?late) 552–54	PPO Italiae	Likely Eastern	Addressee with Narses 1 of the *PS*. He restored the city of Forum Cornelii (Imola) as prefect.
Fl. Marianus Micahelius Gabrihelius Petrus Iohannis Narses Aurelianus Limenius Stefanus Aurelianus (1) (*PLRE* 3A, p. 156)	554–68	PPO Italiae	Likely Eastern	Presided over hearings held by representatives of the church of Ravenna.[1]

Table 6.1 *(cont.)*

Praetorian Prefects	Year of Office	Highest Office	Origin	Social Connections
Longinus (5) (*PLRE* 3B, p. 797)	568–574/5	PPO Italiae	Likely Eastern	Sent to Italy as prefect by the Emperor Justin II to replace Narses 1.
Anonymus (133) (*PLRE* 3B, p. 1451)	VI	*Praefectus Italiae*		
Acataphronius (*PLRE* 3A, p. 10)	VI/early VII	PPO Italiae	Likely Eastern	

[1] Tjäder 1954–55, I, p. 419.

Table 6.2 *Urban Prefects of Rome, 550–99*

Urban Prefects	Year of Office	Highest Office	Other Offices or Honors	Origin	Social Connections
Pamphronius (*PLRE* 3B, pp. 962–63)	c. 555	? PUR	pat. 561–78	Italian, Rome?	Perhaps descended from the *illustris* Pamphronius (*PLRE* 2, p. 825). A law reducing debt was addressed to him, Narses, and the Senate by Justinian, *Nou. App.* 8. See Lounghis et al., 2005, p. 337. Leader of the senatorial embassy that traveled in 578 to Constantinople to seek military assistance from the Emperor Tiberius Caesar to fight against the Lombards; Men. Prot. *Frag.* 22, ed. Blockley, 1985, p. 196.
Germanus (7) (*PLRE* 3A, p. 530)	590	PUR			
Ioannes (109) (*PLRE* 3A, p. 683)	597–99	PUR		Probably Eastern because he was based in Ravenna and because of his name.	Pope Gregory (*Ep.* 7.34; 9.116, 117) had to persuade his wife, Dominica 3, *PLRE* 3A, p. 410, to leave Ravenna to join her husband in Rome. Presumably, they both had lived together in Ravenna.

Table 6.3 *Praetorian Prefects of Africa, 550–70*

Praetorian Prefects	Year of Office	Highest Office	Other Offices or Honors	Origin	Social Connections
Athanasius (1) (*PLRE* 3A, pp. 142–44)	545–48 (–?549)	PPO Africae	PPO Italiae, 539-542	Eastern	Brother of the senator and *uir illustris* Alexander 1 and father-in-law of the senator and *uir illustris* Leontius 5; sent with Petrus 6 as an envoy to Theodahad in Italy by the Emperor Justinian.
Paulus (17) (*PLRE* 3B, p. 979)	9/6/552	PPO Africae			Addressee of the Emperor (Just. *Nov. App.* 6).
Boethius (1) (*PLRE* 3A, pp. 236–37)	556/561	PPO Africae		Rome	Likely identical with the son of the philosopher Boethius (*PLRE* 2, Boethius 3, p. 232).
Ioannes (69) (*PLRE* 3A, p. 668)	9/22/558	PPO Africae			Addressee of the Emperor (Just. *Nov. App.* 9).

Ioannes (75) (*qui et* Rogathinus) (*PLRE* 3A, p. 670)	1/563	PPO (or MUM) Africae		
Thomas (15) (*PLRE* 3B, pp. 1317–19)	563/5, 574?–578	PPO Africae	Eastern?	Perhaps sent to Africa with Marcianus 7 by the Emperor Justinian; addressee of the African grammarian and poet Fl. Cresconius Corippus.
Theodorus (30) (*PLRE* 3B, p. 1254)	3/1/570	PPO Africae		Addressee of a constitution of the Emperor Justin II.

Table 6.4 *Masters of Offices (Magistri Officiorum), 550–70*

Masters of Offices	Year of Office	Highest Office	Other Offices or Honors	Origin	Social Connections
Petrus (6) (*PLRE* 3B, pp. 994–98)	539–65	*ex consule*, 1/28/552	Envoy to Italy, late 534–35; pat. c. 542; envoy to Persian king Chosroes, 550, 561; *iudex*, 551–53.	Native of Solachon, near Dara in Mesopotamia but born at Thessalonica	Father of Theodorus 34 and possibly related to Petrus 17; interacted with Pope Vigilius; high official of the Emperor Justinian.
Anastasius (14) (*PLRE* 3A, pp. 64–66)	565/566	QSP, 565/6–c. 572		Native of Samaria	Subject of a panegyric by the grammarian and poet Fl. Cresconius Corippus; supporter and high official of the Emperor Justin II; cooperated with Patriarch John Scholasticus.

| Theodorus (34) (*PLRE* 3B, pp. 1255–56) | 566-?/576 | CSL, 576 | Official in Thrace, 3/562; pat. 576; Envoy to Persia, 576 | Native of Solachon, near Dara in Mesopotamia | Son of Petrus 6; a Monophysite and supporter of Paul of Antioch; high official of the Emperor Justin II. |
| Anonymus (21) (*PLRE* 3B, p. 1431) | ? mag. off. or MUM, 565/578 | ? mag. off. or MUM, 565/578 | | Eastern? | High official and companion of the Emperor Justin II. |

Table 6.5 *Quaestors of the Sacred Palace and Honorary Quaestors of the Sacred Palace* (Quaestores Sacri Palatii and Quaestores Sacri Palatii Honorati), *550–70*

Quaestors	Year of Office	Other Offices or Honors	Origin	Social Connections
Constantinus (4) (*PLRE* 3A, pp. 342–43)	548/9–562 (–? 565/6)	A *iudex* with Petrus 6.	Eastern?	A close friend of the Emperor Justinian. Engaged with Pope Vigilius on behalf of the emperor.
Anastasius (14) (*PLRE* 3A, pp. 64–66)	565/6–c. 572	mag. off. 565/6	Samarian	Subject of a panegyric by the grammarian and poet Fl. Cresconius Corippus; supporter and high official of the Emperor Justin II.

Table 6.6 *Counts in Charge of Imperial Estates (Comites Rei Privatae), 550–70*

Counts	Year of Office	Highest Office	Other Offices or Honors	Origin	Social Connections
Marthanes (2) (*PLRE* 3B, p. 837)	11/17/558	CRP		Likely Eastern?	Perhaps related to Marthanes 1, MUM; addressee of the Emperor Justinian (*Nou.* 142).
Petrus (14) (*PLRE* 3B, p. 1003)	1/1/566	CRP		Likely Eastern?	Addressee of the Emperor Justin II.

Table 6.7 *Commanders in Chief* (Magistri Militum) *554–70 on Active Service in Italy*

Commanders in Chief	Year of Office	Highest Office	Other Offices or Honors	Origin	Social Connections
Narses (1) (*PLRE* 3B, pp. 912–28)	551–554?/562?– effectively MUM	pat. ?559–573; *ex consule* 565	*sacellarius, (sacellarius et)* PSC 537/ 538–558/559	Native of Persar- menia	Eunuch. He was sent from Constantinople by Justinian to Italy in 538 to assist with the war. In 551, he was appointed commander in chief of the war in Italy. He stayed on to direct war against the Heruls and Lombards; died ca. 574 in Rome; *Lib. Pont. Eccl. Rav.* 95.
Sindual (*PLRE* 3B, pp. 1154- 1155)	(?554–) 559 (–556?)	MUM		Heruli.	Herul Leader
Aemilianus (3) (*PLRE* 3A, p. 19)	559	*mag. mil. Italiae*			Addressed as *filius noster vir magnificus Aemilianus magister militum* by Pope Pelagius I, Feb. 559, *Ep.* 29. He was active in Apulia.

Name	Date	Office	Title	Origin	Notes
Armentarius (2) (*PLRE* 3A, p. 121)	559	*mag. mil. Italiae*			Addressed as *Gloria vestra* by Pope Pelagius I, *Ep.* 55.
Carellus (1) (*PLRE* 3A, p. 272)	559	*mag. mil. Italiae*		Probably Eastern	Addressed as *Gloria vestra* by Pope Pelagius I, *Ep.* 65. Attested by Greek seals that may suggest an eastern origin. Possibly identified with the *gloriosus magister militum* Carellus whose wife and son were killed in Moesia Secunda.
Ioannes (71) (*PLRE* 3A, pp. 669–70)	559	MUM Italiae	pat. 559; Honorary Consul?	Perhaps Eastern?	Addressee of letters from Pope Pelagius I, *Ep.* 53.
Ioannes (72) (*PLRE* 3A, 670)	559	MUM Italiae	Honorary consul?;	Eastern?	Addressee of letters from Pelagius I. Active in Flaminia and Picenum.

Table 6.7 (cont.)

Commanders in Chief	Year of Office	Highest Office	Other Offices or Honors	Origin	Social Connections
Valerianus (1) (*PLRE* 3B, pp. 1355–61)	559	MUM	MUM *per Armeniam*, 541–47	Thracian	
Francio (1) (*PLRE* 3A, pp. 492–93)	c. 568– c. 588	MUM Italiae		Germanic?	
Sisinnius (1) (*PLRE* 3B, p. 1159)	574	MUM Italiae		Probably eastern, arrived with Narses.	Probably one of the *mag. mil.* left by Narses to guard the northern boundaries of Italy. Stationed in Susa (Segusio in the Alpes Cottiae) when the Lombards arrived.

Table 7.1 *Dated Honorary Consuls 554–616*

Honorary Consuls	Year of Office	Other Offices or Honors	Locations of Other Offices or Honors	Origin[1]	Social Connections
Iustinus (5) (*PLRE* 3A, pp. 754–56)	552 or 553(–65) Honorary consul	Augustus, 565–78; *cura palatii*, 552–65	Constanti-nople	Thracian	Son of sister of Justinian.
Petrus (6) (*PLRE* 3B, pp. 994–98)	552–65	mag. off. 539–65; pat. 542	Constanti-nople	Native of Mesopotamia; born in Thessalonica	Famous for his learning; practiced law and advocacy. Sent by Justinian as envoy to Amalasuntha, 534: Procop. *Wars* 5.3.30.
Anatolius (7) (*PLRE* 3A, p. 72)	557	*curator domus divinae*		Resident of Constantinople; likely Eastern.	Killed in earthquake at Constantinople; Agath. 5.4.2–3.
Eusebius (4) (*PLRE* 3A, p. 468)	562	*comes foederatum*	Constanti-nople	Likely Eastern; active in Constantinople	Active in Constantinople; revealed plot against Justinian in 562; Mal. 493.
Ioannes (90) (*PLRE* 3A, pp. 676–77)	562–77	? pat.	Constanti-nople	Eastern	Member of the family of emperor Anastasius; grandson of the empress Theodora: John Eph. *HE* 3.2.11.

Table 7.1 *(cont.)*

Honorary Consuls	Year of Office	Other Offices or Honors	Locations of Other Offices or Honors	Origin[1]	Social Connections
Narses (1) (*PLRE* 3B, pp. 912–28)	565 (–73?)	PSC? 537/38–54; pat.; *sacellarius*, 530–31; *primicerius sacri cubiculi*, 530–31	Constantinople	Native of Persarmenia: Proc. *Wars* 1.15.31	Eunuch who took over the war in Italy, and was victorious over the Goths and Franks.
Petrus (17) (*PLRE* 3B, pp. 1003–04)	576	*curator Augustae*;? pat.	Constantinople	Eastern	Sent as envoy to Persia in 576. Member of the family of emperor Anastasius, likely also tied to the patrician Petrus 6.
Magnus (2) (*PLRE* 3B, pp. 805–07)	581	com. dom.; *curator domus divinae rerum Hormisdae*; CSL, 565/66–73; v.glor. when *curator* in Syria.	Constantinople; Syria	Native of Syria	Active in the east.

Georgius (10) (*PLRE* 3A, p. 515)	586/87			Eastern; lands in Egypt, but also a home in Constantinople	Landowner at Oxyrhynchus; addressee of accounts from the Apion estates. He, Fl. Praeiecta (his mother?), and Apion (his brother) were the surviving heirs of Apion 3.
Apion (4) (*PLRE* 3, pp. 98–99)	586–619/23	pat.	Constanti-nople	Eastern; estates in Egypt, but also in Constantinople	Leading member of the Apion family of Oxyrynchus
Leo (5) (*PLRE* 3B, p. 769)	590–91				In Sicily in 590 and expected to visit Rome; Gregory, *Ep.* 1.3.
Ioannes (105) (*PLRE* 3A, p. 682)	591	QSP; pat.	Constanti-nople	Likely Eastern	Acquaintance of Gregory in Constantinople before 590; he recommended him to become pope; Gregory *Ep.* 1.30.
Leontius (11) (*PLRE* 3B, pp. 776–77)	598–600	v.glor; imperial commissioner in Sicily	Sicily	Likely Eastern	Active in Sicily. Sent by the emperor Maurice to examine accounts of fraud and misconduct by officials: Gregory *Ep.* 9.4.

Table 7.1 *(cont.)*

Honorary Consuls	Year of Office	Other Offices or Honors	Locations of Other Offices or Honors	Origin[1]	Social Connections
Germanus (13) (*PLRE* 3A, pp. 532–33)	602–04	MUM (vacans), 602	Dara	? German?	Replaced Narses 10 in command of the fort of Dara; possibly identical with Germanus 6 (*PLRE* 3A, pp. 529–30).
Bonosus (2) (*PLRE* 3A, pp. 239–240)	609	com. Or. 609–10	Palestine, Antioch		
Olympius (6) (*PLRE* 3B, p. 954)	615/16	pat.; PPO	Constanti-nople, Persia with Leontius 31	Likely Eastern	Envoy of Heraclius to Chrosroes
Leontius (31) (*PLRE* 3B, p. 780)	615/16	pat.; PUC	Constanti-nople, Persia with Olympius 6	Likely Eastern	Envoy of Heraclius to Chrosroes

[1] For criteria of origin, see Chapter 7, note 43.

Table 7.2 *Patricians Mid Sixth Century to 641 (PLRE 3B: pp. 1466–72)***

Patricians	Year Patriciate Attested	Origin (Italo-Romans are in Bold)[1]
Addaeus	566	Syrian
Aetherius (2)	566	Leading member of the senate of Constantinople; Eastern
Alamundarus	578–80	Phylarch of the Ghassanids Arabs
Anagastes	M VI	Gothic?
Apion (3)	547/48–577/79	Eastern Senator
Areobindus (2)	M VI	Eastern/Germanic
Arethas	c. 528–69	Ghassanids Arabs
Athanasius (3)	563–68	Theban?
Baduarius (2)	565–?76	Dux Scythiae. German?
Bassus (2)	M VI	Resident in Constantinople
Belisarius (1)	(?532)536–65	German? Thracian?
Callinicus (2)	565	Eastern; Constantinopolitan
Carianus	Before L VI	Constantinopolitan
Constantianus (2)	562	Eastern/Military
Constantinus (12)	L VI	Governor of Alexandria under Maurice, from Constantinople
Damianus (6)	M/L VI	Greek seal suggests Eastern origin
Decius (2)	584	**Italian, Rome. Pope Pelagius, *Ep.* 1, mentions him. Possibly descended from Italo-Roman senatorial family of the Decii.**

Table 7.2 *(cont.)*

Patricians	Year Patriciate Attested	Origin (Italo-Romans are in Bold)[1]
Decoratus	559	**Possible descendant of Decoratus 1, *PLRE* II, pp. 350–51. Possibly Italian, Rome.**
Dulcitius (2)	558/59	**Western: *vir gloriosus*. Wrote to bishop Pelagius I about a dispute; Pelagius I, *Ep.* 22.**
Elpidius (1)	583/84	Senator from Constantinople but served as praetor of Sicily.
Epiphanes	M/L VI	Greek Seal suggests Eastern origin.
Eubulus	E/M VI	Resident in Constantinople
Eusebius (6)	565/578	Resident in Constantinople
Felix (6)	M/L VI	**Husband and heir of Rustica. He did not complete the monastery that she had asked him to build; Gregory, *Ep.* 9.164. Likely Italian**
Germanus (5)	582	Eastern/Constantinopolitan
Germanus (9)	?M/L VI	Probably Jerusalem
Ioannes (36) (*qui et* Troglita)	M VI	Probably Thrace
Ioannes (52)	M VI	Egyptian
Ioannes (59)	M VI	Egyptian
Ioannes (71)	559	MUM in Italy? Origin unknown
Ioannes (81)	567	Eastern
Ioannes (90)	576/77	Eastern/Imperial family

Table 7.2 *(cont.)*

Patricians	Year Patriciate Attested	Origin (Italo-Romans are in Bold)[1]
Ioannes (101) / Mystacon	589–91(?)	Thracian
Ioannes (105)	591	Acquaintance and patron of Gregory in Constantinople before 590. He helped Gregory obtain the bishopric. QSP in Constantinople; his name and residence suggest an Eastern origin.
Ioannes (85)	M/L VI	Patriarch of Alexandria
Iulianus (10)	M VI	Law professor in Constantinople
Iustinianus (3)	572–77	Eastern/Military
Longinus (4)	M VI	Cappadocian, Caesarea
Mamianus	M VI	Seleucia, resident in Constantinople
Manasses	M VI	Status is not certain; possibly resident in Constantinople
Marcellus (5)	565	Nephew of Justinian
Marcianus (7)	572	MUM *per Orientem* Nephew of Justinian
Mauricius (4)	577/578–82	Emperor; Cappadocian
Megas (2)	L VI	High official in Constantinople
Narses (1)	559–?73	Persarmenian
Narses (3)	565/78	Resident in Constantinople
Narses (5)	M/L VI	**Resident in ROME**
Narses (6)	M/L VI	Monophysite in African
Nordulfuls	590(–?95)	Lombard Noble

Table 7.2 *(cont.)*

Patricians	Year Patriciate Attested		Origin (Italo-Romans are in Bold)[1]
Olybrius (2)	M VI		**In Rome when it fell to Totila. Perhaps identified with the Olybrius who was consul in 526, and Italian from Rome.**
Pamphronius	c.561–78		**Italian, Rome? See Table 6.2.**
Paulus (23)	?582–93		Cappadocian; father of emperor Maurice
Petrus (6)	542–65		Mesopotamian
Petrus (9) (*qui et* Barsymes)	542–65		Syrian
Petrus (17)?	? 576		Family member of Anastasius
Romanus (7)	589/90–595/ 97	Exarch of Italy	Exarch of Italy. Accused of accepting a bribe to make Maximus bishop of Salona; Gregory, *Ep.* 5.6
Se …	M VI		
Sergius (4)	559		Mesopotamian, Dara
Strategius (3)	557		Son of Apion 3; Egyptian landowners; active in Constantinople
Syagrius (2)	587		a Gallo-Roman; *comes* and envoy in the Burgundian kingdom under Guntram.
Theodorus (34)	576		Mesopotamian, Solachon (near Dara)
Theodorus (78)	M/L VI		Greek Seal suggests Eastern origin
Theodorus (79)	M/L VI		Greek Seal suggests Eastern origin

Table 7.2 *(cont.)*

Patricians	Year Patriciate Attested		Origin (Italo-Romans are in Bold)[1]
Traianus (3)	575		Senator from Constantinople; envoy to Persia
Valerianus (1)	559		Died and buried in Brixia; uncle of Damianus (2). A Thracian who came west to fight and stayed.
Anonymus (7)	565/578		
..itius	M VI		
VI or VI century (*PLRE 3B*: pp. 1469–72)			
Athanasius (6)	M VI/M VII		Greek Seal suggests Eastern origin
Bonus (8)	VI/VII		Greek Seal suggests Eastern origin
Callinicus (10)	596/97–602/ 03		? Exarch of Italy
Comentiolus (1)	(585)–602	MUM	Thracian
Demetrius (8)	M VI/M VII		Greek Seal suggests Eastern origin
Georgius (36)	VI/ VII		Greek Seal suggests Eastern origin
Gregoras (2)	VI/ VII		Greek Seal suggests Eastern origin
Ioannes (181)	VI/ VII		Greek Seal suggests Eastern origin
Ioannes (205)	VI/ VII		Greek Seal suggests Eastern origin
Marcus (10)	M VI/M VII		Greek Seal suggests Eastern origin
Mauricius (7)	M VI/M VII		Greek Seal suggests Eastern origin

Table 7.2 *(cont.)*

Patricians	Year Patriciate Attested	Origin (Italo-Romans are in Bold)[1]
Olympius (4)	M VI/M VII	Greek Seal suggests Eastern origin
Petrus (45)	M VI/M VII	Greek Seal suggests Eastern origin
Philippicus (3)	L VI/E VII	Married to sister of emperor Maurice; urged Gregory to become pope. Eastern
Priscus (6)	593–602	Married to daughter of Phocas
Probus (6)	M VI/M VII	Greek Seal suggests Eastern origin
Procopius (7)	?VI/VII	Greek Seal suggests Eastern origin
Smaragdus (2)	c. 585–608	Exarch of Italy, 603–8
Stephanus (44)	VI/VII	Greek Seal suggests Eastern origin
Theodorus (120)	M VI/M VII	Greek Seal suggests Eastern origin
Theodorus (121)	M VI/M VII	Greek Seal suggests Eastern origin
Theodorus (122)	M VI/M VII	Greek Seal suggests Eastern origin
Theodosius (33)	VI/ VII	Greek Seal suggests Eastern origin
Thomas (29)	M VI/M VII	Greek Seal suggests Eastern origin
Valentinus (4)	VI/VII	Greek Seal suggests Eastern origin
Venantius (2)	587/88–601	**Husband of Italica; lived in Syracuse. Father of Antonina (3) and Barbara. In Sicily 587/88–601. He had a house in Rome.**

Table 7.2 *(cont.)*

Patricians	Year Patriciate Attested	Origin (Italo-Romans are in Bold)[1]
Venantius (4)	598–602	**Lived in Palermo.**
Anonymus (1)	L VI/E VII	
105 Names Total		

[1] For criteria of origin, see Chapter 7, note 50.

** I counted some 105 names in total. I omitted some men listed in *PLRE* 3B, pp. 1466–69 since they could not be dated to the period of this study. I also omitted the names of seventh-century patricians in *PLRE* 3 B. The men noted as VI (sixth century) who were omitted for lack of specific dates are:

Abramius (2)
Anastasius (23)
Carinus (2)
Constantinus (17)
Ebrimuth
Gennadius (1)
Iulianus (26)
Genethlius (1)
Marianus (3)
Patricius (8)
Philippicus (1)
Hotius (3)
Probus (4)?
Procopius (3)
Senuthius (1)
Solomon (6)
Theodorus (80)
Theodorus (81)

Bibliography

Aguilera Martín, A. *El Monte Testaccio y la llanura subaventina: topografía extram portam Trigeminam*, Rome, 2002.

Aiello, V. "Costantino e I vescovi di Roma. Momenti di un problematico incontro," in *Enciclopedia Costantiniana*, 2013, pp. 203–18.

Alchermes, J. "Petrine Politics: Pope Symmachus and the Rotunda of Andrew and Old Saint Peter's," *Catholic Historical Review* 81, 1995, pp. 1–40.

Alchermes, J. "Art and Architecture in the Age of Justinian," in *The Cambridge Companion to the Age of Justinian*, ed. M. Maas, Cambridge, 2005, pp. 343–75.

Alföldi, A. *The Conversion of Constantine and Pagan Rome*. Translation by H. Mattingly. Oxford, UK, 1948.

Alföldi, G. "*Difficillima tempora*: Urban Life, Inscriptions, and Mentality in Late Antique Rome," in *Urban Centers and Rural Contexts in Late Antiquity*, ed. T. Burns and J. Eadie, East Lansing, 2001, pp. 3–24.

Allen, P. and B. Neil, *Crisis Management in Late Antiquity (410–590 CE)*. Leiden, 2013.

Ambrogi, A. "Documentazione sulla statuaria a Roma nel' V secolo," in *Roma e il sacco del 410: Realtà, interpretazione, mito*, ed. A. Di Berardino, G. Pilara, and L. Spera, Roma, 2012, pp. 157–218.

Amory, P. *People and Identity in Ostrogothic Italy*. Cambridge, 1997.

Anders, F. *Flavius Ricimer. Macht und Ohnmacht des weströmischen Heermeisters in der zweiten Hälfte des 5. Jahrunderts*. Frankfurt a.M., Berlin, 2010.

Anderson, W.B. *Sidonius. Poems and Letters*, with an English Translation, Cambridge, Mass. 2 volumes, 1996–1997 rept., = *LCL* 296 and 420.

Angelelli, C. and F. Guidobaldi. '*I primi* tituli *della chiesa romana: una possibile istituzione di età costantiniana?*', in *Costantino e i costantinidi. L'innovazione cost-antiniana, le sue radici e i suoi sviluppi*, ed. O. Brandt and V. Fiocchi Nicolai, Acta XVI Congressus Internationalis Archaeologiae Christianae, *Roma 22–28 settembre 2013*, Città del Vaticano, 2016, pp. 353–60.

Archi, G. G. "*Pragmatica sanctio* pro petitione Vigilii," in *Festschrift für Franz Wieacker zum 70 Geburtstag*, ed. O. Gehrends et al., Göttingen, 1978, pp. 11–36.

Arnaldi, G. "Rinascita, fine, reincarnazione e successive metamorfosi del Senato romano (secoli V–XIII)," *Archivio della Società Romana di Storia Patria* 105, 1982, pp. 5–56.

Arnheim, M. T. W. *The Senatorial Aristocracy in the Later Roman Empire*. New York, 1972.

Arnold, J. "Theoderic and Rome: Conquered but Unconquered," *Antiquité Tardive* 25, 2017, pp. 113–26.

Arnold, J. *Theoderic and the Roman Imperial Restoration*. New York, 2014.

Bagnall, R., A. Cameron, S. Schwarz, and K. A. Warp, *Consuls of the Later Roman Empire*. Philadelphia 1987.

Baldassarri, P. "Indagini archeologiche a Palazzo Valentini: domus di età imperiale ai margini del Foro di Traiano," *Rendiconti della Pontificia Accademia Romana di Archeologia* LXXXI, 2008–09, pp. 343–84.

Baldassarri P. "Archaeological Excavations at Palazzo Valentini. A Residential Area in the Shade of the Trajan's Forum," in *XIth International Colloquium on Ancient Mosaics*, Bursa, October 16–20, 2009, ed. M. Şahin, Istanbul, 2011, pp. 43–67.

Baldassarri, P. "Lusso privato nella tarda antichità: le piccole terme di Palazzo Valentini e un pavimento in *Opus Sectile* con motivi complessi," *Arch. Class.* 68, 2017, pp. 245–88.

Baldovin, J. S. J. *The Urban Character of Christian Worship*. Rome, 1987.

Baldwin, B. "Some Addenda to the Prosopography of the Later Roman Empire," *Historia* 25, 1976, pp. 118–21.

Baldwin, B. "Some Addenda to the Prosopography of the Later Roman Empire," *Historia* 31, 1982, pp. 97–111.

Bardill, J. *Divine Emperor of the Christian Golden Age*. Cambridge, UK, 2012.

Barnes, T. D. "Who Were the Nobility of the Roman Empire?" *Phoenix* 28, 1974, pp. 444–49.

Barnes, T. D. "Two Senators under Constantine," *JRS* 65, 1975, pp. 40–49.

Barnes, T. D. *Constantine and Eusebius*. Cambridge, MA, London, 1981.

Barnes, T. D. *The New Empire of Diocletian and Constantine*. Cambridge, London, 1982.

Barnes, T. D. "Late Roman Prosopography between Theodosius and Justinian," *Phoenix* 37, 1983, pp. 248–70.

Barnes, T. D. "Statistics and the Conversion of the Roman Aristocracy," *JRS* 85, 1995, pp. 135–47.

Barnes, T. D. *Constantine. Dynasty, Religion and Power*. Chichester, 2011.

Barnish, S. J. B. "Pigs, Plebeians and *Potentes*: Rome's Economic Hinterland, c. 350–600 A.D.," *Papers of the British School at Rome* 55, 1987, pp. 157–86.

Barnish, S. J. B. "Transformation and Survival in the Western Senatorial Aristocracy, c. AD 400–700," *PBSR*, 1988, vol. 56, pp. 120–55.

Barnish, S. J. B. "A Note on the *collatio glebalis*," *Historia*, 38 (2), 1989, pp. 254–56.

Barnish, S. J. B. *Selected "Variae" of Magnus Aurelius Cassiodorus Senator*. Liverpool, UK, 2006, rept. of 1992 ed.

Barnwell, P. S. *Emperors, Prefects and Kings. The Roman West, 395–565*. London, 1992.

Battistella, F. *Pelagius I. und der Primat Roms*. Hamburg, 2017.

Bauer, A. "Saint Peter's as a Place of Collective Memory in Late Antiquity," in *Rom in der Spätantike. Historische Erinnerung im städtischen Raum*, eds. R. Behwald and C. Witschel, Stuttgart, 2012, pp. 155–70.

Baynes, N. H. "The Decline of the Roman Empire in Western Europe: Some Modern Explanation," *JRS* 33 (1943), pp. 29–35.

Begass, C. *Die Senatoraristokratie des oströmischen Reiches, ca. 457–518. Vestigia* 71, Munich, 2018.

Bidez, J. and C. Parmentier, ed. *Evagrius. Historia Ecclesiastica.* London, 1898, rept., Amsterdam, 1964.

Bileta, V. "The *venatio* in the Emperor's Presence? The *consistorium* and the Military Men of the Late Roman Empire in the West," in *Gaining and Losing Imperial Favor in Late Antiquity. Representation and Reality,* eds. K. Cyprian Choda, M. Sterk de Leeuw, and F. Schulz, Leiden, Boston, 2020, pp. 73-104.

Bjornlie, M. S. *Politics and Tradition between Rome, Ravenna and Constantinople.* Cambridge, UK, 2013.

Bjornlie, M. S. "Governmental Administration," in *A Companion to Ostrogothic Italy,* eds. J. Arnold, M. S. Bjornlie, and K. Sessa, Leiden, Boston, 2016, pp. 47–72.

Bjornlie, M. S. "The Letter Collection of Cassiodorus," in *A Critical Introduction and Reference Guide to Letter Collections in Late Antiquity,* eds. C. Sogno, B. Storin, and E. Watts, Oakland, CA, 2017, pp. 533–48.

Bjornlie, M. S. *Cassiodorus. The Variae. The Complete Translation.* Oakland, CA, 2019.

Bjornlie, M. S. "The Sack of Rome in 410: The Anatomy of a Late Antique Debate," in *Leadership and Community in Late Antiquity: Essays in Honour of Raymond Van Dam,* eds. Y. R. Kim and A. E. T. McLaughlin, Turnhout, 2020, pp. 249–79.

Blair-Dixon, K. "Memory and Authority in Sixth-Century Rome: The *Liber Pontificalis* and the *Collectio Avellana,*" *Religion, Dynasty, and Patronage in Early Christian Rome, 300–900,* eds. K. Cooper and J. Hillner, Cambridge, UK, New York, 2007, pp. 59–76.

Blaudeau, P. *Le siège de Rome et l'Orient 448–536: étude géo-ecclésiologique.* Rome, École française de Rome, 2012.

Blockley, R. C. (ed.) *The Fragmentary Classicizing Historians of the Later Roman Empire,* 2 vols., Liverpool, UK, vol. I, 1981; vol. II, 1983.

Blockley, R. C. *The History of Menander the Guardsman.* Liverpool, UK, 1985.

Blockley, R. C. *East Roman Foreign Policy: Formation and Conduct from Diocletian to Anastasius,* ARCA Classical and Medieval Texts, Papers and Monographs 30, Leeds, 1992.

Blume, G. H. *Annotated Justinianic Code,* 1943, www.uwyo.edu/lawlib/blume-justinian /ajc-edition-2/novels/. Accessed December 5, 2018.

Bogaert, R. "Geld," *Reallexikon für Antike und Christentum* 9, 1976, pp. 798–907.

Bonamente, G. "Dall'imperatore divinizzato all'imperatore santo," in Pagans and Christians in the Roman Empire: The Breaking of a Dialogue (IVth–Vth Century A.D.): Proceedings of the International Conference at the Monastery of Bose (October 2008), eds. P. Brown and R. Lizzi Testa, Vienna, Zurich, Berlin, Muenster, New Brunswick, London, 2011.

Bond, S. "Curial Communique: Memory, Propaganda, and the Roman Senate House," *Aspects of Ancient Institutions and Geography. Studies in Honor of Richard J. A. Talbert,* eds. L. L. Brice and D. Slootjes, Leiden, Boston, 2015, pp. 84–102.

Bond, S. *Trade and Taboo. Disreputable Professions in the Ancient Mediterranean.* Ann Arbor, MI, 2016.

Bonin F. "Costantino, i barbari e la riforma della prefettura del pretorio," in *LIMES: spazio di divisione e di contatto. Profiles from the late antique period* (Acts AST Parma, March 2015), in *Cultura Giuridica e Diritto Vivente* 3, 2016, pp. 20–30.

Bonnet, C. and E. Sanzi. *Roma, la città degli dei. La capitale dell'Impero come laboratorio religioso*. Roma, 2018.

Bordi, G. "Santa Maria Antiqua. Prima di Maria Regina," in *L'Officina dello Sguardo. Scritti in honore di. Maria Andaloro*, eds. G. Bordi, I. Carlettini, M. L. Fobelli, M. R. Menna, P. Pogliani, vol. 1, Rome 2014, pp. 285–90.

Bowes, K. *Private Worship, Public Values and Religious Change in Late Antiquity*. New York, 2008.

Brandenburg, H. *Ancient Churches of Rome from the Fourth to the Seventh Century*. Turnhout, Belgium, 2005.

Brandt, H. *Konstantin der Grosse. Der erst christliche Kaiser*. Munich, 2006; 2nd ed., 2007.

Brent, A. *Hippolytus and the Roman Church in the Third Century: Communities in Tension before the Emergence of a Monarch-Bishop* (Supplements to Vigiliae Christianae volume 31), Leiden, 1995.

Brogiolo, G. P. "Immigration and Urban Transformation in the Capitals of the West in the 5th Century," in *Le trasformazioni del V secolo, l'Italia, I barbari e l'Occidente romano*: atti del seminario di Poggibonsi, 18–20 Ottobre 2007, eds. P. Delogu and S. Gasparri, Turnhout, Belgium, 2010, pp. 215–36.

Brogiolo, G. P. and Bryan Ward-Perkins. "Introduction," in *The Idea and Ideal of the Town between Late Antiquity and the Early Middle Ages* eds. G.P. Brogiolo and B. Ward-Perkins, (The Transformation of the Roman World 4), Leiden, 1999.

Brown, P. *The World of Late Antiquity: from Marcus Aurelius to Muhammad*. London, 1971.

Brown, P. *Power and Persuasion in Late Antiquity*. Madison, WI. 1992.

Brown, P. *Poverty and Leadership in the Later Roman Empire*. Hanover and London, 2002.

Brown, P. *Through the Eye of a Needle. Wealth, the Fall of Rome, and the Making of Christianity in the West, 350–550 AD*. Princeton, 2012.

Brown, T. S. *Gentlemen and Officers. Imperial Administration and Aristocratic Power in Byzantine Italy A.D. 554–800*. Rome, 1984.

Bruun, P. *Studies in Constantinian Chronology*. New York, 1961.

Bruun, P. "The Consecration Coins of Constantine the Great," *Arctos* 1, 1954, pp. 19–31.

Burckhardt, J. *The Age of Constantine*, translation by M. Hadas, New York, 1949.

Burgarella, F. "Il senato di Costantinopoli," in *Il Senato nella storia 1. Il Senato nell' età romana*, ed. E. Gabba, Rome 1988, pp. 399–442.

Burgarella, F. "Il senato," *Roma nell'alto medioevo. Settimane di studio del centro italiano di studii sull'alto medioevo* 48, vol. 1, Spoleto, Italy, 2001, pp. 121–75.

Burgess, R. "The Third Regnal Year of Eparchius Avitus: a Reply," in *Chronicles, Consuls and Coins: Historiography and History in the Later Roman Empire*, ed. R. Burgess, Farnham 2011 (reprinted from *Classical Philology* 82 [1987], pp. 335–45).

Burgess, R. *The Chronicle of Hydatius and the Consularia Constantinopolitana*. Oxford, 1993.

Burgess, R. "The Gallic Chronicle of 452: A New Critical Edition with a Brief Introduction," in *Society and Culture in Late Antique Gaul. Revisiting the Sources*, eds. R. W. Mathisen and D. Shanzer, Aldershot, 2001, pp. 52–84.

Burgess, R. "The Gallic Chronicle of 511: A New Critical Edition with a Brief Introduction," in *Society and Culture in Late Antique Gaul. Revisiting the Sources*, eds. R. W. Mathisen and D. Shanzer, Aldershot, 2001A, pp. 85–100.

Cabié, R. *La lettre du pape Innocent Ier à Décentius de Gubbio (19 Mars 416): Texte critique, traduction et commentaire*, Leuven, 1973.

Calderone, S. *Costantino e il cattolicesimo*. Florence, 1962.

Caliri, E. *Aspettando I barbari: la Sicilia nel V secolo tra Genserico e Odoacre*. Catania, 2012.

Caliri, E. *Praecellentissimus rex. Odoacre tra storia e storiografia*. Messina, 2017.

Cameron, Al. "Boethius's Father's Name," *ZPE* 44, 1981, pp. 181–83.

Cameron, Al. "The Date and the Owners of the Esquiline Treasure," *American Journal of Archaeology*, vol. 89, No. 1, Centennial Issue, Jan. 1985, pp. 135–45.

Cameron, Al. *The Last Pagans of Rome*. New York, 2011.

Cameron, Al. "Anician Myths," *JRS* 102, 2012, pp. 133–71.

Cameron, Al. "Basilius and His Diptych Again: Career Titles, Seats in the Colosseum, and Issues of Stylistic Dating," *JRA* 25, 2012A, pp. 513–30.

Cameron, Averil and S. Hall, *Eusebius, Life of Constantine*. Translation with introduction and commentary, Oxford, UK, 1999.

Cameron, Averil. "A Nativity Poem of the Sixth Century A.D.", *Classical Philology* 74 (1979), pp. 222–32.

Cameron, Averil. "Images of Authority: Elites and Icons in Late Sixth-Century Byzantium," *Past and Present* 84, 1979, pp. 3–35 = 1979A.

Canella, T. "Gli *Actus Silvestri* tra Oriente e Occidente. Storia e diffusione di una leggenda costantiniana," in *Costantino I, Enciclopedia Costantiniana sulla figura e l'immagine dell'imperatore del cosidetto Editto de Milano, 312–2013*, Rome, 2013, vol. II, pp. 241–58.

Carmassi, P. "La prima redazione del *Liber Pontificalis* nel quadro delle fonti contemporanee: Osservazioni in margine alla *vita* di Simmaco," in *Atti del colloquio international: Il Liber Pontificale e la storia materiale*, 21–22 febbraio 2002, ed. H. Geertman, Rome, Netherlands Institute in Rome, 2003, pp. 235–66.

Carney, T. F. *Bureaucracy in Traditional Society, Book One: A Survey of Roman and Byzantine Bureaucracies; Book Two: Byzantine Bureaucracy from Within; Book Three: John the Lydian on the Magistracies of the Roman Constitution, Coronado Press, Winnipeg, 1971.*

Caspar, E. *Geschichte des Papstums (von den Anfängen bis zur Höhe der Weltherrshaft)*, 2 vols. Tübingen, 1930–33.

Cecconi, G. A. *Governo imperiale e élites dirigenti nell'Italia toardoantica*. Como, Italy, 1994.

Cecconi, G. A. "Gruppi di potere, indirizzi politici, rapport tra goti e romani. La vicenda di Prisco Attalo, in *Potere e politica nell'età teodosiana (395–455). I linguaggi dell'impero, le identità dei barbari* ed. S. Cosentino, Romania-Gothica I. Atti del convegno internazionale di Ravenna, 24 e 25 settembre 2010, 2013, pp. 141–62.

Cesa, M. (ed.) *Ennodio. Vita del beatisissimo Epifanio vescovo della chiesa pavese*. Como, Italy, 1988.

Cessi, R. "Studi sulle fonti del'età gotica e longobarda I. *I Fasti Vindobonenses*," in *Archivio Muratoriano. Sudi e Riverche della Nuova Edizione dei* Rerum Italicarum Scriptores *di L.A. Muratori*, Città di Castello, 1916, pp. 17–18.

Chadwick, H. *The Church in Ancient Society: From Galilee to Gregory the Great*. Oxford, 2001.

Champlin, E. J. "Saint Gallicanus (Consul 317)," *Phoenix* 36, 1983, pp. 71–76.

Chastagnol, A. *La préfecture urbaine à Rome sous le Bas-Empire*. Paris, 1960.

Chastagnol, A. *Les fastes de la préfecture urbaine de Rome au Bas-Empire*. Paris, 1962.

Chastagnol, A. *Le sénat sous le règne d'Odoacre: recherches sur l'épigraphie du Colisée au Ve siècle*, Bonn, 1966.

Chastagnol, A. "Les années régnale de Maximien Hercule en Egypte et les fêtes vicennales du 20 novembre 303," *RN* 6.9, 1967, pp. 54–81.

Chastagnol, A. "Constantin et le sénat," in *Atti dell'Accademia Romanistica costantiniana II*, Perugia, 1976, pp. 51–69.

Chastagnol, A. *Le sénat romain à l'époque impériale*. Paris, 1992.

Chavasse, A. *Sancti Leonis Magni Romani pontificis Tractatus septem et nonaginta*. *CCSL* 138A, Turnhout, Belgium, 1973.

Chenault, R. *Rome without Emperors: The Revival of a Senatorial City*. PhD dissertation, University of Michigan, 2008.

Chenault, R. "Statues of Senators in the Forum of Trajan and the Roman Forum in Late Antiquity," *JRS* 102, 2012, pp. 103–32.

Chenault, R. "Beyond Pagans and Christians: Politics and Intra-Christian Conflict in the Controversy over the Altar of Victory," in *Pagans and Christians in Late Antique Rome*, eds. M. R. Salzman, M. Sághy, and R. Lizzi Testa, New York, Cambridge, UK, 2016, pp. 46–63.

Chiocci, Pia Federica and Rossella Zaccagnini. "Mausoleo C, la tomba di Marco Nonio Macrino: descrizione e interpretazione delle evidenze," in *Sulla via flaminia. Il mausoleo di Marco Nonio Macrino*, ed. D. Rossi, Rome, 2012.

Christie, N. *From Constantine to Charlemagne. An Archaeology of Italy, AD 300–800*. Aldershot, UK, 2006.

Christie, N. *The Fall of the Western Roman Empire. An Archaeological and Historical Perspective*. London, New York, 2011.

Claridge, A. *Rome. An Oxford Archaeological Guide*. Oxford, 2010, 2nd edition.

Clemente, G. "Il Senato e il governo dell' impero tra IV e VI secolo: la religione e la politica," *in Costantino prima e dopo costantino*, ed. G. Bonamente, R. Lizzi Testa, and N. Lenski, Edipuglia, 2012, pp. 321–31.

Clover, F. M. "The Family and Early Career of Anicius Olybrius," *Historia* 27, 1978, pp. 169–96.

Clover, F. M. *Merobaudes: A Translation and Historical Commentary*. Philadelphia, 1971.

Clover, F. M. *Gaiseric the Statesman: A Study of Vandal Foreign Policy*, PhD dissertation, University of Chicago, 1966.

Clover, F. M. "A Game of Bluff: The Fate of Sicily after A.D. 476," *Historia* 45.1, 1999, pp. 235–44.

Coarelli, F. "L'urbs e il suburbia," in *Società Romana e impero tardantico. Roma politica economia paesaggio urbano II*, ed. A. Giardina, Rome, Bari, 1986, pp. 47–48.

Coates-Stephens, R. "Dark Age Architecture in Rome," in *PBSR* 65, 1997, pp. 177–232.

Coates-Stephens, R. "La committenza edilizia bizantina à Roma dopo la riconquista," in *La città italiane tra la tarda antichità e l'alto Medioevo, Convegno sulle città dell'alto Medioevo*, ed. A. Augenti, Ravenna, Italy, 2004, pp. 299–316.

Coates-Stephens, R. "The Water-Supply of Rome from Late Antiquity to the Early Middle Ages," in *Acta ad Archaeologiam et Artium Historiam Petinentia*, 17, 2003, pp. 165–86.

Coates-Stephens, R. "Byzantine Building Patronage in Post-Reconquest Rome," in *Les cités de l'Italie tardo-antique, IV–VI siècles: institutions, économie, société, culture et religion*, ed. M. Ghirlardi et al., Rome: École française de Rome, 2006, pp. 149–66.

Coates-Stephens, R. "Review of Excavations," *PBSR* 2012, p. 326.

Coates-Stephens, R. "Statue Museums in Late Antique Rome," *Arch. Class.* 68, 2017, pp. 309–42.

Cohen, S. "Religious Diversity," in *A Companion to Ostrogothic Italy*, eds. J. Arnold, M. S. Bjornlie, and K. Sessa, Leiden, Boston, 2016, pp. 503–32.

Coleman-Norton, P. R. *Roman State and Christian Church. A Collection of Legal Documents to A.D. 535*, London, 1966, 3 vols.

Conant, J. *Staying Roman: Conquest and Identity in Africa and the Mediterranean, 439–700. Cambridge Studies in Medieval Life and Thought: Fourth Series, 82*, Cambridge, UK, New York, 2012.

Consolino, F. E. "Panegiristi e creazione del consenso nell'Occidente latino," in *Dicere Laudes. Elogio, comunicazione, creazione del consenso*. Atti del convegno internazionale (Cividale del Friuli, 23–25 settembre 2010), ed. G. Urso, Cividale del Friuli, Italy, 2011, pp. 299–336.

Cooper, K. and J. Hilner (eds.) *Religion, Dynasty and Patronage in Early Christian Rome, 300–900*, Cambridge, UK, 2007.

Corcoran, S. "Roman Law in Ravenna," in *Ravenna: Its Role in Earlier Medieval Change and Exchange*, ed. J. Herrin and J. Nelson, London, 2016, pp. 163–97.

Cosentino, S. *Prosopografia dell'Italia Bizantina (493–804)*, 2 vols., Bologna, 1996–2000.

Cosentino, S. "L'approvvigionamento annonario di Ravenna dal V all'VIII secolo: l'"organizzazione e i riflessi socio-economici," in *Ravenna da capitale imperiale a capitale esarcale*, I, Spoleto, Italy, 2005, pp. 405–34.

Courcelle, P. *Histoire littéraire des grands invasions germaniques*. 3rd ed. Paris, 1964.

Coustant, P. (ed.) *Epistolae romanorum pontificum et quae ad eos scriptae sunt a S. Clemente I usque ad Innocentum III*, t. 1, Paris, 1721; Farnborough, Hant, 1967 rept.

Cracco Ruggini, L. *Economia e società nell'Italia annonaria*. Milan, 1961.

Cracco Ruggini, L. "Nobiltà romana e potere nell'età di Boezio," in *Atti del Congresso Internazionale di Studi boeziani*, ed. L. Obertello, Rome, 1981, pp. 73–96.

Cracco Ruggini, L. "Giustiniano e la società italica," in *Il mondo del diritto nell'epoca giustinianea. Caratteri e problematiche*, ed. G. C. Archi, Ravenna, 1985, pp. 173–207.

Cracco Ruggini, L. "Società provinciale, società romana, società bizantina in Cassiodoro," in *Atti della Settimana di studi su Flavio Magno Aurelio Cassiodoro*, ed. S. Leanza, Rubettino, Italy, 1986, pp. 245–61.

Cracco Ruggini, L. "Gli Anicii a Roma e in provincia," in *MEFRM* 100, 1988, pp. 69–85.

Cracco Ruggini, L. "Il senato fra due crisi [III/VI sec.]," in *Il senato nella storia 1. Il senato nell'età romana*, F. De Martino, Rome, 1998, pp. 223–398.

Cracco Ruggini, L. "L'Ordine naturale sconvolto e la morte di un mondo nella storiografia tardoantica," *Rivista Storica Italiana* 114, 2002, pp. 820–50.

Croke, B. "A.D. 476: The Manufacture of a Turning Point," *Chiron* 13, 1983, pp. 81–119.

Croke, B. *Count Marcellinus and His Chronicle*. Oxford, UK, 2001.

Croke, B. "Dynasty and Aristocracy in the Fifth Century," in *The Cambridge Companion to Attila the Hun*, ed. M. Maas, Cambridge, MA, London, 2015, pp. 98–124.

Curran, J. *Pagan City and Christian Capital. Rome in the Fourth Century*. Oxford, 2000.

Dagron, G. *Naissance d'une capitale. Constantinople et ses institutions de 330–451. Bibliothèque byzantines*, Études 7, ed. Paris, 1974.

Davenport, C. *A History of the Roman Equestrian Order*. Cambridge, UK, New York, 2019.

de Blaauw, S. *Cultus et Décor. Liturgia e Architettura nella Roma tardoantica e medievale*. Vatican City, 1994.

De Bruyn, T. "Ambivalence within a 'Totalizing Discourse': Augustine's Sermons on the Sack of Rome," *JECS* 1.4, 1993, pp. 405–21.

De Giorgio, D. "Caesario di Arles e la 'redemptio' dei 'captivi infideles': *Vita Caesarii* I, 32–33," *Cristianesimo nella Storia* 26.3, 2005, pp. 671–82.

De Salvo, L. "Simonie e malversazioni nell'organizzazione ecclesiastica IV–V secolo," in *Corruzione, Repressione e rivolta morale nella tarda antichità*, ed. R. Soraci, Catania, 1995, pp. 367–92.

De Salvo, L. "I commerci mediterranei in età vandala," in *Guerrieri, mercanti e profughi nel Mare dei Vandali* ed. V. Aiello, (Atti del Convegno Internazionale, Messina 7–8 settembre 2009), Messina, 2014, pp. 73–84.

Del Chicca, F. "La presunta restituzione al Senato dell'*auctoritas* di nominare i magistrati minori," *ZPE* 204 (2017), pp. 280–86.

Deliyannis, D. (ed.). *Liber Pontificalis Ecclesiae Ravennatis*, Turnhout, 2006.

Deliyannis, D. *Ravenna in Late Antiquity*. Cambridge, UK, 2010.

Delmaire, R. *Les responsables des finances impériales au Bas-Empire romain (IVe-VIIe s.)*. Études prosopographiques, Brussels, 1989.

Delogu, P. "Il passaggio dall'antichità al medioevo," in *Roma medievale*, ed. A. Vauchez, Rome and Bari, 2001, pp. 3–40.

Delogu, P. and L. Paroli (eds.) *La storia economica di Roma nell'alto medioevo alle luce dei recenti scavi archeologici: Atti del seminario, Rome, 2–3 Aprile, 1992*. Rome, 1993.

Demacopoulos, G. D. *The Invention of Peter: Apostolic Discourse and Papal Authority in Late Antiquity*. Philadelphia: University of Pennsylvania, 2013.

Demacopoulos, G. D. *Gregory the Great: Ascetic, Pastor and First Man of Rome*. Notre Dame, IN, 2015.

Demougeot, E. "A propos des interventions du Pape Innocent I dans la politique séculiere," *Révue Historique* 212, 1954, pp. 23–38.

Denzey Lewis, N. *The Early Modern Invention of Late Antique Rome*. Cambridge, 2020.

Destephen, S., B. Dumézil, and H. Inglebert. (eds.) *Le prince chrétien de Constantin au royautes (barbares) (IVe – VIII siècle)*. Paris, 2018.

Devreese, R. (ed.) *Pelagii diaconi In defensione trium capitulorum*, Vatican City, 1932.

Dey, H. *The Aurelian Wall and the Refashioning of Imperial Rome, AD 271–855*. Cambridge, 2011.

Dey, H. *The Afterlife of the Roman City. Architecture and Ceremony in Late Antiquity and the Early Middle Ages*. Cambridge, 2015.

Di Berardino, A. "Milziade, santo," in *Enciclopedia dei Papi*, Rome 2000, I, pp. 317–21.

Digeser, E. "Crisis as Opportunity: Urban Renewal and the Christianisation in Constantine's Gaul," *RRE* 5, 2019, pp. 103–24.

Dillon, J. "The Inflation of Rank and Privilege. Regulating Precedence in the Fourth Century AD," in *Contested Monarchy: Integrating the Roman Empire in the Fourth Century AD*, ed. J. Wienand, Oxford, 2015, pp. 42–66.

Doyle, C. *Honorius. The Fight for the Roman West AD 395–423*. Abingdon, Oxon and New York, 2019.

Drake, H. A. *Constantine and the Bishops: The Politics of Intolerance*. Baltimore, 2000.

Drake, H. A. "The Impact of Constantine on Christianity," in *The Cambridge Companion to the Age of Constantine*, ed. N. Lenski, Cambridge, revised ed. 2012, pp. 111–36.

Drake, H. A. *A Century of Miracles. Christians, Pagans, Jews and the Supernatural, 312–410*. New York, 2017.

Drijvers, H. J. *Helena Augusta. The Mother of Constantine the Great and the Legend of the Finding the True Cross*. Leiden, 1992.

Dunn, G. "The Validity of Marriage in Cases of Captivity: The Letter of Innocent I to Probus," *Ephemerides Theologicae Lovanienses* 83.1, 2007, pp. 107–21.

Dunn, G. "The Care of the Poor in Rome and Alaric's Sieges," in *Prayer and Spirituality in the Early Church, vol. 5: Poverty and Riches*, eds. G. Dunn, D. Luckensmeyer, and L. Cross, Strathfield, 2009, pp. 319–33.

Dunn, G. "Innocent I, Alaric, and Honorius. Church and State in Early Fifth-Century Rome," in *Studies of Religion and Politics in the Early Christian Centuries*, eds. D. Luckensmeyer and P. Allen, Brisbane, Australia, 2010, pp. 243–62.

Dunn, G. "Innocent I and the First Synod of Toledo," in *The Bishop of Rome in Late Antiquity*, ed G. Dunn, Surrey, UK/Burlington, VT, 2015, pp. 89–108.

Durliat, J. *De la ville antique à la ville byzantine: Le problème des subsistances (CEFR 136)*, Rome, 1990.

Eck, W. "Eine historische Zeitenwende: Kaiser Constantins Hinwendung zum Christentum und die gallischen Bischöfe," in *Konstantin der Grosse. Kaiser einer Epochenwende*, eds. F. Schuller and H. Wolff, Lindenberg, 2007, pp. 69–94.

Ekonomou, A. *Byzantine Rome and the Greek Popes. Eastern Influences on Rome and the Papacy from Gregory the Great to Zacharias, A.D. 590–752*. Lanham, MD, 2007.

Elia, F. *Valentiniano III*. Catania, 1999.

Ellis, S. "Middle Class Houses in Late Antiquity," in *Social and Political Life in Late Antiquity. Late Antique Archaeology 3.1*, eds. W. Bowden, A. Gutteridge, and C. Machado, Leidien/Boston, 2006, pp. 413–40.

Elsner, J. *Art and the Roman Viewer: The Transformation of Art from the Pagan World to Christianity*. Cambridge, UK, 1995.

Elton, H. "Military Developments in the Fifth Century," in *The Cambridge Companion to Attila the Hun*, ed. M. Maas, Cambridge, MA, London, 2015, pp. 125–39.

Elvers, Karl-Ludwig. "Zwei neue sog. tesserae monumentorum im Archäologischen Museum der Westfälischem Wilhelms-Universität Münster und in westfälischem Privatbesitz: Mit einem Katalog der bekannten Exemplare," *Boreas: Münstersche Beiträge zur Archäologie* 34, 2011, pp. 203–14.

Erdkamp, P. "The Food Supply of the Capital," in *The Cambridge Companion to Ancient Rome*, ed. P. Erdkamp Cambridge, UK, New York, 2013, pp. 262–77.

Esders, S. *Römische Rechtstradition und merowingisches Königtum: Zum Rechtscharakter politischer Herrschaft in Burgund im 6. und 7 Jahrhundert.* Göttingen 1997.

Falkenhausen, V. von. "I rapporti di ceti dirigenti romani con Costantinopoli dalla fine del V alla fine del VI secolo," in *Il mondo del diritto nell'epoca giustinianea. Caratteri e problematiche*, ed. G. C. Archi, Ravenna, 1985, pp. 59–90.

Faust, S. "Original und Spolie. Interaktive Strategien im Bildprogramm des Konstantinsbogens," *MDARI* 117, 2011, pp. 377–408.

Fauvinet-Ranson, V. *'Decor Civitatis, Decor Italiae.' Monuments, trauvaux publics et spectacles au VIe siècle d'après les 'Variae' d Cassiodore.* Bari, 2006.

Ferrandus. *Vita S. Fulgentii 9 (Vie de Saint Fulgence de Ruspe)*, ed. G. Lapeyre, Paris, 1929. Translation by R. B. Eno, Washington, DC, Catholic University of America, 1997.

Filippi, D. "*L'Atrium Vestae* in età tardoantica," in *Roma d'all'antichità al medioevo. Archeologia e storia*, eds. M. Stella Arena, P. Delogu, L. Paroli, M. Ricci, L. Saguì, and L. Vendittelli, Rome 2001, pp. 599–601.

Flower, H. *Ancestor Masks and Aristocratic Power in Roman Culture.* Oxford, UK, 1996.

Folke, C. "Resilience: The Emergence of a Perspective for Social-Ecological Systems Analyses," *Global Environmental Change* 16 (2006), pp. 253–367.

Fowden, P. *Damascius. The Philosophical History.* Text with translation and notes, Oxbow Books, Oxford, 1999.

Frakes, R. M. *Contra Potentium Iniurias: The Defensor Civitatis and Late Roman Justice.* Munich, 2001.

Fraschetti, A. *La Conversione. Da Roma pagana a Roma cristiana.* Bari, 1999.

Frendo, J.D. *Agathias. The Histories.* Translation with an introduction and notes. Berlin, 1975.

Fuhrmann, H. "Studien zu den Consulardiptychen verwandten Denkmälern I. Eine Glasschale von der Vicennalienfeier Constantins des Grossen zu Rom im Jahre 326 Nach Chr.," *RM* 54, 1939, pp. 161–75.

Garbarino, P. *Ricerche sulla procedura di ammissione al Senato nel tardo impero romano.* Milan, 1988.

Gaspari, S. "The aristocracy," in *Italy in the Early Middle Ages*, ed. C. La Rocca, Oxford, UK, 2002, pp. 59–84.

Gassó, P.M. and C. M. Battle. (eds.) *Pelagii I Papae. Epistulae quae supersunt (556-561)*, Monserrat, 1956.

Gaudemet, J. (ed.) *Conciles Gaulois du IVe siècle.* SC 241. Paris, 1977.

Geertman, H. "Documenti, redattori e la formazione del testo del *Liber Pontificalis*," in H. Geertman ed., *Atti del colloquio international: Il Liber Pontificalise la storia materiale*, 21–22 febbraio 2002. Rome, Netherlands Institute in Rome, 2003, pp. 267–355.

George, J. *Venantius Fortunatus: A Latin Poet in Merovingian Gaul.* Oxford. 1992.

Gerontius. *Life of Melania the Younger = Vie de Sainte Mélanie*, SC 90, ed. D. Gorce, Paris, 1962.

Gianandrea, M. "The Artistic Patronage of the Popes in Fifth-Century Rome," in *The Fifth Century in Rome. Art, Liturgy, Patronage*, eds. I. Foletti and M. Gianandrea, Rome, 2017, pp. 183–216.

Giardina, A. "La formazione dell'Italia provinciale," in *Storia di Roma III, 1 (Crisi e trasformazione)*, eds. A. Carandini, L. Cracco Ruggini, and A. Giardina, Turin, 1993, pp. 51–68.

Giardina, A. *Cassiodoro Politico*. Rome, 2006.

Gibbon, E. *The Decline and Fall of the Roman Empire*, ed. J. B. Bury, vol. 4, London, 1897.

Gillett, A. "Rome, Ravenna and the Last Christian Emperors," *Papers of the British School at Rome*, 59, 2001, pp. 137–67.

Gillett, A. *Envoys and Political Communication in the Late Antique West, 411–533*. Cambridge, New York, 2003.

Giovannini, F. "Le trasformazioni demografiche in Italia tra IV e V secolo," in *Le trasformazioni del V secolo: Italia, i barbari e l'Occidente romano*, eds. P. Delogu and S. Gasparra, Tournhout, Belgium, 2010, pp. 431–54.

Girardet, K. M. "Die Petition der Donatisten an Kaiser Konstantin (Frühjahr 313). Historische Voraussetzungen und Folgen," *Chiron*, 19 (1989), pp. 185–206.

Girardet, K. M. "Gericht über den Bischof von Rom. Ein Problem der kirchlichen und der staatlichen Justiz in der Spätantike (4–6 Jahrhundert)," HZ 259, 1994, pp. 1–38 = reprint in K. M. Girardet, *Kaisertum, Religionspolitik und das Recht von Staat und Kirche in der Spätantike* [Antiquitas 56] Bonn, 2009, pp. 455–89.

Girardet, K. M. "Konstantin d. gr. und das Reichskonzil von Arles (314). Historisches problem und methodologische Aspekte," in *Oecumenica et Patristica. Festschrift für Wilhelm Schneemelcher zum 75 Geburtstag*, eds. D. Papandreou, W. A. Bierner, and K. Schäferdiek, Stuttgart, pp. 151–74 (reprint in K. M. Girardet, *Kaisertum, Religionspolitik und das Recht von Staat und Kirche in der Spätantike* [Antiquitas 56] Bonn, 2009, pp. 43–72).

Girardet, K. M. *Der Kaiser und sein Gott: Das Christentum im Denken und in der Relgiionspolitik Konstantins des Grossen*. Berlin, 2010.

Goldsworthy, A. *How Rome Fell: Death of a Superpower*. New Haven, 2009.

Goody, J. *The Theft of History*, Cambridge, UK, 2006.

Goody, J. *The Eurasian Miracle*. Cambridge, UK, 2020.

Graen, D. *Sepultus in villa: Die Grabbauten römischer Villenbesitzer. Studien zu Ursprung und Entwicklung von den Anfängen bis zum Ende des 4. Jahrhunderts nach Christus*. Hamburg, 2008.

Green, B. *The Soteriology of Leo the Great*. Oxford, 2008.

Green, R. "The Sadness of Eparchius Avitus," *CQ* 66, 2016, pp. 821–25.

Grig, L. "Throwing Parties for the Poor: Poverty and Splendour in the Late Antique Church," in *Poverty in the Roman World*, eds.M. E. Atkins and R. Osborne, Cambridge, UK, 2006, pp. 145–61.

Grig, L. "Deconstructing the Symbolic City: Jerome as a Guide to Late Antique Rome," *PBSR* 80, 2012, pp. 126–43.

Grig, L. and G. Kelly. Introduction to *Two Romes. Rome and Constantinople in Late Antiquity*, eds. L. Grig and G. Kelly, Oxford, 2013, pp. 3–30.

Groag, E. "Der Dichter Porfyrius in einer stadtrömischen Inschrift," *Wiener Studien* 44–45, 1924–7, pp. 102–09.

Grossi, I. "Appendix A. Valentinus," pp. 256–59 to Salzman 2017 C.

Grossi, I. *I prefetti urbani di Roma tra il 423 ed il 599 d.C.: un analisi prosopografica. I prefetti urbani dell' età di Valentiniano III (425-455)*. University of Rome, La Sapienza, 2019. https://iris.uniroma1.it/handle/11573/1293495#.XROH5ugzbIU

Guidobaldi, F. "L'edilizia abitativa unifamiliare nella Roma tardoantica," in *Società romana e impero tardo antico II. Roma: politica economia paesaggio urbano*, ed. A. Giardina, Roma-Bari, 1986, pp. 165–237.

Guidobaldi, F. "L'inserimento delle chiese titolari di Roma nel tessuto urbano preesistente: osservazioni ed implicazioni," in *Quaeritur inventus colitur: miscellanea in onore de padre U. M. Fasola*, eds. P. Pergola and F. Bisconti, Vatican City, 1989, pp. 381–96.

Guidobaldi, F. "Le domus tardoantiche di Roma come 'sensori' delle trasformazioni culturali e sociali," in *The Transformations of Urbs Roma in Late Antiquity*, ed. W. V. Harris, *JRA* Supplementary Series 33, 1999, pp. 53–68.

Guidobaldi, F. *La fondazione delle basiliche titolari di Roma nel IV e V secolo. Assenze e presenze nel* Liber Pontificalis, in *Il* Liber Pontificalis *e la storia materiale, ed. H. Geertman, Atti del Colloquio Internazionale, Roma 21–22 febbraio 2002, in Mededelingen van het Nederlands Instituut te Rome – Antiquity*, LX/ LXI, 2001–2002 (2003), pp. 5–12.

Guillou, A. *Culture et Société en Italie Byzantine, (VIe–XIe s.)*, London, 1978.

Guillou, A. "L'Italia bizantina dall'invasione longobarda alla caduta di Ravenna," in *L'I'talia bizantina. Dall esarcato di Ravenna al tema di Sicilia*, ed. A. Guillou and F. Burgarella Turin, 1988, pp. 3–122.

Gusso, M. "Sull'imperatore Glycerio (473–474)," in *SDHI* 58, 1992, pp. 168–93.

Haldon, J. "The Fate of the Later Roman Senatorial Elite: Extinction or Transformation," *The Byzantine and Early Islamic Near East*. VI, eds. J. Haldon and L. I. Conrad, Princeton, 2004, pp. 179–234.

Haldon, J. "Economy and Administration: How Did the Empire Work?" in *The Cambridge Companion to the Age of Justinian*, ed. M. Maas, Cambridge, UK, New York, 2005, pp. 28–59.

Hanaghan, M. "Latent Criticism of Anthemius and Ricimer in Sidonius Apollinaris's *Epistulae* 1.5," *CQ* 67.2, 2018, pp. 631–49.

Handley, M. "One Hundred and Fifty-Two Addenda to *PLRE* from Gaul, Spain and Britain," *Historia* 54/1, 2005, pp. 93–105.

Hänel, G. (ed.) *Corpus Legum ab Imperatoribus Romanis ante Iustinianum latarum quae extra Constitutionum Codices supersunt*, Leipzig, 1857.

Hänel, G. (ed.) *Iuliani Epitome Latina Novellarum Iustiniani*, Leipzig, 1873.

Harper, K. *The Fate of Rome*. Princeton, 2017.

Harries, J. *Sidonius Apollinaris and the Fall of Rome, 407–485*. Oxford, 1994.

Haynes, I. et al., "The Lateran Project: Interim Reports," in *Papers of the British School in Rome*, 85, 2017–2018, pp. 320–25.

Heather, P. "The Historical Culture of Ostrogothic Italy," in *Teoderico il Grande e i Goti d'Italia. Atti del 13 Congresso internazionale di studi sull'Alto Medioevo*, Spoleto, 1993, pp. 317–53.

Heather, P. *The Goths*. Oxford, 1996.

Heather, P. "Senators and Senates," in *The Cambridge Ancient History*, vol. 13; *The Late Empire, AD 337–425*, ed. A. Cameron and P. Garnsey, Cambridge, 1998, pp. 184–210.

Heather, P. *The Fall of the Roman Empire*. Oxford, 2006.

Heather, P. "A Tale of Two Cities: Rome and Ravenna under Gothic Rule," in *Ravenna: Its Role in Earlier Medieval Change and Exchange*, eds. J. Herring and J. Nelson, London, 2016, pp. 15–37.

Heather, P. *Rome Resurgent*. Oxford, 2018.

Hedrick, C. *History and Silence. Purge and Rehabilitation of Memory in Late Antiquity*, Austin, TX, 2000.

Heinzelmann, M. "Gallische Prosopographie 260–527," *Francia* 10, 1982, pp. 531–718.

Hellström, M. "On the Form and Function of Constantine's Circiform Funerary Basilicas in Rome," in (eds.) *Pagans and Christians in Late Antique Rome*, eds. M. R. Salzman, M. Sághy, and R. Lizzi Testa, New York, Cambridge, 2016, pp. 291–313.

Henning, D. "*CIL* VI 32005 und die rostra Vandalica," *ZPE* 110, 1996, pp. 259–64.

Henning, D. *Periclitans res publica: Kaisertum une Eliten in der Krise des Weströmischen Reiches 454/5–493 N.Chr. = Historia Einzelschriften* Heft 133, Stuttgart, 1999.

Heydemann, G. "The Ostrogothic Kingdom: Ideologies and Transitions," in *A Companion to Ostrogothic Italy*, eds. J. Arnold, M.S. Bjornlie, and K. Sessa, Leiden, Boston, 2016, pp. 17–46.

Hijmans, S. "Temples and Priests of Sol in the City of Rome," *Mouseion*, 10.3 (2010), 381–427.

Hillner, J. "Clerics, Property and Patronage: The Case of the Roman Titular Churches," *Ant. Tard.* 14, 2006, pp. 59–68.

Hillner, J. "Families, Patronage and the Titular Churches of Rome," in *Religion, Dynasty and Patronage in Early Christian Rome*, eds. K. Cooper and J. Hilner, 2007, pp. 225–61.

Hillner, J. "A Woman's Place: Imperial Women in Late Antique Rome," *Ant. Tard.* 25, 2017, pp. 75–94.

Honoré, T. *Law and the Crisis of Empire 379–455*. Oxford, 1998.

Humfress, C. "Law and Legal Practice in the Age of Justinian," in *The Cambridge Companion to the Age of Justinian*, ed. M. Maas, 2006, pp. 161–84.

Humphries, M. "Roman Senators and Absent Emperors in Late Antiquity," in *Institutum Romanum Norvegiae, Acta ad Archaeologiam et Artium Historiam Pertinentia XVII (N.S. 3), = Rome AD 300-800. Power and Symbol - Image and Reality*, ed. J. Rasmus Brandt, Rome, 2003, pp. 13–26.

Humphries, M. "From Emperor to Pope? Ceremonial, Space and Authority at Rome from Constantine to Gregory the Great," in *Religion Dynasty and Patronage in Early Christian Rome, 300-900*, eds. K. Cooper and J. Hillner, Cambridge, 2007, pp. 21–58.

Humphries, M. "From Usurper to Emperor: The Politics of Legitimation in the Age of Constantine," *JLA* 1.1, 2008, pp. 82–100.

Humphries, M. "Valentinian III and the City of Rome (425–55). Patronage, Politics, Power," in *Two Romes. Rome and Constantinople*, eds. L. Grig and G. Kelly, Oxford, 2012, pp. 161–82.

Humphries, M. "Late Antiquity and World History: Challenging Conventional Narratives and Analyses," *Studies in Late Antiquity: A Journal* 1.1 (2017), pp. 8–37.

Humphries, M. *Cities and the Meanings of Late Antiquity*. Leiden, Boston, 2019.

Hunter, D. "Rivalry between Presbyters and Deacons in the Roman Church," *Vigiliae Christianae* 71, 2017, pp. 496–510.

Huxley, A. *Texts and Pretexts: An Anthology with Commentaries*. New York, London, 1933.

Insalco, A. *La città dell'acqua. Archeologia sotteranea a Fontana di Trevi*, Milan, 2002.

Izdebski, A., L. Mordechai, and S. White. "The Social Burden of Resilience: A Historical Perspective," *Human Ecology* 46 (2018), pp. 291–303.

Jaffé, P, W. Wittenbach, et al. eds. *Regesta pontificum Romanorum ab condita ecclesia ad annum post Christum natum MCXCVIII. Ed. secundam correctam et auctam. I. II.*

Ab A. MCXLLII ad A. MCXCVIII. Addenda et corrigenda, Graz: Akademische Druck- u. Verlagsanstalt, 1956.

Jeffreys, E., M. Jeffreys, and R. Scott. *The Chronicle of Malalas. A Translation,* Melbourne, 1986.

John the Deacon. *Sancti Gregorii Magni Vita, PL* 75, Paris, 1849, pp. 59–242.

Johnson, M. "On the Burial Places of the Theodosian Dynasty," *Byzantion* 61, 1991, pp. 330–38.

Johnson, M. "Architecture of Empire," in *The Cambridge Companion to the Age of Constantine,* ed. N. Lenski, Cambridge, 2012 revised ed., pp. 278–97.

Jones, A. H. M. *The Later Roman Empire, 284–602,* 2 vols., Baltimore, MD and London, 1964. Reprint ed. 1986.

Kahzdan, A. and A. Cutler (eds.) *Oxford Dictionary of Byzantium.* Oxford, 2005.

Kaiser, W. "Justinian and the *Corpus Iuris Civilis,*" in *Cambridge Companion to Roman Law,* ed. D. Johnston, Cambridge, 2015, pp. 119–50.

Kalas, G. "Writing and Restoration in Rome: Inscriptions, Statues and the Late Antique Preservation of Buildings," in *Cities, Texts and Social Networks, 400–1500,* eds. C. Goodson, A. E. Lester, and C. Symes, Surrey, UK/Burlington, VA, 2010, pp. 21–43.

Kalas, G. *The Restoration of the Roman Forum in Late Antiquity: Transforming Public Space.* Austin, TX, 2015.

Kalas, G. "The Divisive Politics of Phocas (602–610) and the Last Imperial Monument in Rome," *Ant. Tard.* 25, 2017, pp. 173–90.

Kearley, T. G. "The Creation and Transmission of Justinian's Novels," *Law Library Journal* 102, 2010, pp. 377–97.

Kelly, C. *Ruling the Later Roman Empire.* Cambridge and London, UK, 2004.

Kéry, L. *Canonical Collections of the Early Middle Ages (ca 400–1140).* Washington, DC, 1999.

Kinney, D. "Expanding the Christian Footprint: Church Building in the City and the *Suburbium,*" in *The Fifth Century in Rome. Art, Liturgy, Patronage,* eds. I. Foletti and M. Gianandrea, Rome, 2017, pp. 65–98.

Klingshirn, W. "Charity and Power. Caesarius of Arles and the Ransoming of Captives in Sub-Roman Gaul," *JRS* 75, 1985, pp. 183–203.

Klingshirn, W. *The Making of a Christian Community in Late Antique Gaul.* Cambridge, UK, 2004.

Kneale, M. *Rome. A History in Seven Sackings.* New York, 2017.

Koch, P. *Die Byzantinischen Beamtentitel von 400 bis 700.* Jena, 1903.

Koortbojian, M. *Crossing of the Pomerium. The Boundaries of Political, Military and Political Institutions from Caesar to Constantine.* Princeton, NJ, 2020.

Kraft, H. "Das Silbermedaillon Constantins des Grossen mit dem Christusmonogramm auf dem Helm," *JNG* (1954), pp. 151–78.

Krautheimer, R. *Profile of a City. 312–1308.* Princeton, 1980.

Krautheimer, R. *Three Christian Capitals: Topography and Politics.* Berkeley and Los Angeles, CA, 1983.

Krautschick, S. "Bemerkungen zu *PLRE* II," in *Historia* 35, 1986, pp. 121–24.

Kriegbaum, B. "Die Religionspolitik des Kaisers Maxentius," *Archivum historiae pontificiae* 30, 1992, pp. 7–54.

Kruse, M. *The Politics of Roman Memory. From the Fall of the Western Empire to the Age of Justinian.* Philadelphia, PA, 2019.

Kulikowski, M. *Rome's Gothic Wars: From the Third Century to Alaric.* New York, 2007.

Kulikowski, M. "Urban Prefects in Bronze," *JLA* 10.1, 2017, pp. 3–41.

Lactantius. *De mortibus persecutorum*, ed. J. L. Creed, Oxford, 1984.

Landelle, M. "À propos de la création des 'magistri militum' par Constantin Ier," in *REA* 118/2, 2016, pp. 493–509.

Laniado, A. "Some Addenda to the 'Prosopography of the Later Roman Empire' (vol. II, 395–527)," *Historia* 44, 1995, pp. 121–28.

Laniado, A. *Recherches sur les notables municipaux dans l'empire protobyzantin.* TM Monographies 13, Paris, 2002.

La Rocca, A. and F. Oppedisano. *Il senato romano nell'Italia Ostrogota.* Rome, 2016.

La Rocca, C. "Una prudente maschera 'antiqua.' La politica edilizia di Teoderico," in *Teoderico il Grande e i Goti d'Italia. Atti del 13 Congresso internazionale di studi sull'Alto Medioevo*, Spoleto, 1993, pp. 451–515.

Latham, J. "From Literal to Spiritual Soldiers of Christ," *Church History* 81:12, June 2012, pp. 298–327.

Leader Newby, R. E. *Silver and Society in Late Antiquity.* Aldershott, 2004.

Lenski, N. "Evoking the Pagan Past: *Instinctu divinitas* and Constantine's Capture of Rome," *JLA* 1.2, 2008, pp. 204–57.

Lenski, N. "The Reign of Constantine," in *The Cambridge Companion to the Age of Constantine*, ed. N. Lenski, Cambridge, rev. ed. 2012, pp. 59–90.

Lenski, N. "The Sun and the Senate: The Inspiration for the Arch of Constantine," in *Costantino il Grande. Alle radici dell'Europa*, ed. E. Dal Cavo and G. Sfameni Gasparro., Atti del Convegno Internazionale di Studio in occasione del 1700' anniversario della Battaglia di Ponte Milvio e della conversione di Costantino. Vatican City, 2014, pp. 155–96.

Lenski, N. "Constantine and the Donatists. Exploring the Limits of Religious Toleration," in *Religiöse Toleranz, 1700 Jahre nach dem Edikt von Mailand*, ed. M. Wallraff, Berlin/Boston, 2016, pp. 101–39.

Lenski, N. *Constantine and the Cities.* Philadelphia, 2016 = 2016A.

Lepelley, C. "Fine dell'ordine equestre: le tappe dell'unificazione della classe dirigente Romana nel IV secolo," in *Società roman e impero tardoantico, vol. 1: istituzioni, ceti, economie*, ed. A. Giardina, Rome, 1986, pp. 229–31.

Leppin, H. *Justinian. Das Christliche Experiment.* Stuttgart, 2011.

Leppin, H. and H. Ziemssen. *Maxentius. Der letzte Kaiser in Rom.* Mainz, 2007.

Lewis, C. T., and Short, C. *A Latin Dictionary.* Oxford, 1975.

Liebeschuetz, J. H. W. G. *The Decline and Fall of the Roman City.* Oxford, 2003.

Liebs, D. *Die Iurisprudenz im spätantiken Italien (260–640 n. Chr).* Berlin, 1987.

Linn, J. "The Roman Grain Supply, 442–455," *JLA* 5.2, 2013, pp. 298–321.

Lipps, J., Machado, C., and von Rummel, P. (eds.) *The Sack of Rome in 410 A.D.*, Wiesbaden, 2013.

Liverani, P. "Note di topografia lateranense: le strutture di via Amba Aradam. A proposito di una recente pubblicazione," *Bull. Com.* 95, 1993, pp. 143–52.

Liverani, P. "The Evolution of the Lateran: From the Domus to the Episcopal Complex," in L. Bosman, I. Haynes, and P. Liverani, *The Basilia of Saint John Lateran to 1600* (Cambridge, UK, 2000), pp. 6–24.

Liverani, P. "L'area lateranense in età tardoantica e le origini del Patriarchio," *MEFRA* 116, 2004, pp. 17–49.

Liverani, P. "Honorii et Mariae mausoleum, sepulcrum," in *Lexicon Topographicum Urbis Romae*, Suburbium III, Rome, 2005, pp. 75–76.

Liverani, P. "Saint Peter's and the City of Rome between Late Antiquity and the Early Middle Ages," in *Old Saint Peter's, Rome*, ed. R. McKitterick, J. Osborne, C. M. Richardson, and J. Story, Cambridge, 2013, pp. 21–34.

Liverani, P. "Composite Constantine", in *The Past as Present. Essays in Honour of Guido Clemente*, eds. G.A. Cecconi, R. Lizzi Testa, and A. Marcone, Turnhout 2019 (Brepols, Studi e Testi tardoantichi 17), pp. 385–404 = 2019A.

Liverani, P. "Osservazioni sul *Libellus* delle Donazioni Costantiniane nel *Liber Pontificalis*," *Athenaeum* 107.1, 2019, pp. 169–204.

Lizzi Testa, R. *Vescovi e strutture ecclesiastiche nella città tardoantica (L'Italia Annonaria nel IV–V secolo d.C.)*. Como, 1989.

Lizzi Testa, R. "Paganesimo politico e politica edilizia: la 'cura Urbis' nella tarda antichità," *AARC* XIII, Naples, 2001, pp. 671–707.

Lizzi Testa, R. *Senatori, popolo, papi. Il governo di Roma al tempo dei Valentiniani*, Munera 21, Bari, 2004.

Lizzi Testa, R. "Il sacco di Rome e l'aristocrazia romana, tra crisi politica e turbamento religioso," in *Rome e il sacco del 410. Realtà, interpretazione, mitos*, eds. A. Di Berardino, G. Pilara, and L. Spera, Rome, 2012, pp. 1–32.

Lizzi Testa, R. *Costantino e le chiese cristiane all'indomani del 312* in *Costantino il Grande alle radici dell'Europa* eds. E. Dal Covolo and G. Sfameni Gasparro, Vatican City, 2014, pp. 251–72.

Lizzi Testa, R. "Tolerance for the Gentiles, Intolerance of Heretics: The First Interventions of Constantine in the Life of the Catholic Church and of the Pagan Priests," in *Serdica Edict (311 A.D.). Concepts and Realizations of the Idea of Religious Toleration*, ed. V. Vachkova and D. Dimitrov, Sofia, Bulgaria, 2014, pp. 87–106 = 2014A.

Lizzi Testa, R. "Costantino e Ossio," in *Ossio e Costantino*, in *Fra Costantino e i Vandali. Atti del Convegno Internazionale di Studi per Enzo Aiello (1957–2013) (Messina 29–30 ottobre 2014)* ed. L. De Salvo, E. Caliri, and M. Casella, Bari 2016, pp. 183–96.

Lizzi Testa, R. "I Vescovi e il governo della città (IV–VI secolo d.C)," *Ant. tard* 26, 2018, pp. 149–62.

Lizzi Testa, R. "Rome Elects Her Bishop: The *Collectio Avellana* and Cassiodorus's *Variae* Compared," in *Religion, Power and Politics in Late Antiquity: Bishops, Emperors and Senators in the Collectio Avellana 367–553 AD*, eds. A. Evers and B. Stolte (in press).

Lizzi Testa, R. *Christian Emperor, Roman Senate and Its Aristocracy. The Roman Empire in Late Antiquity*. (Unpublished manuscript).

Lizzi Testa, R., and G. Marconi. (eds.) *The "Collectio Avellana" and Its Revival*, Cambridge, UK, 2019.

Lizzi Testa, R., M. R. Salzman, and M. Sághy, "Introduction," in *Pagans and Christians in Late Antique Rome*, eds. M.R. Salzman, M. Sághy, and R. Lizzi Testa, New York, Cambridge, UK, 2016, pp. 1–8.

Llewellyn, P. "The Roman Church in the Seventh Century: The Legacy of Gregory I," *Journal of Ecclesiastical History* 25, 1974, pp. 363–80.

Lloyd, J. B., "Sixth-Century Art and Architecture in 'Old Rome': End or Beginning?' *Byzantina Australiensia* 10, Brisbane, 1996, pp. 224–35.

Lo Cascio, E. "Canon frumentarius, suarius, vinarius: stato e privati nell'approvvigionamento dell' *Urbs*," in *The Transformations of Urbs Roma in Late Antiquity*, ed. W. Harris, Portsmouth, RI, 1999, pp. 163–82.

Lo Cascio, E. "La popolazione," in *Roma imperiale. Una metropoli antica*, ed. E. Lo Cascio, Florence, 2000, pp. 17–69.

Lo Cascio, E. *Crescita e declino. Studi di storia dell'economia Romana*. Rome, 2009.

Lo Cascio, E. "La popolazione di Roma prima e dopo il 410," in *The Sack of Rome in 410 A.D.*, ed. J. Lipps, C. Machado, and P. von Rummel, Wiesbaden, 2013, pp. 411–21.

Löhken, H. *Ordines Dignitatum. Untersuchungen zur formalen Konsitutierung der spätantiken Führungsschicht*. Cologne/Vienna, 1982.

Loschiavo, L. "Was Rome Still a Centre of Legal Culture between the 6th and 8th Centuries? Chasing the Manuscripts," *Rechtsgeschichte* 23, 2015, pp. 83–108.

Lounghis, T. C. et al., *Regesten der Kaiserurkunden des oströmischen Reiches von 476 bis 565*, Nicosia, 2005.

Maas, M. "Roman History and Christian Ideology in Justinianic Reform Legislation," *DOP* 40, 1986, pp. 17–31.

Maas, M. "Reversals of Fortune: An Overview of the Age of Attila," in *The Cambridge Companion to Attila the Hun*, ed. M. Maas, Cambridge, MA, London, 2015, pp. 3–25.

MacCormack, S. *Art and Ceremony in Late Antiquity*, Berkeley, Los Angeles, 1981.

MacGeorge, P. *Late Roman Warlords*, Oxford, UK, 2002.

Machado, C. "Building the Past: Monuments and Memory in the *Forum Romanum*," in *Social and Political Life in Late Antiquity*, eds. W. Bowden, A. Gutteridge, L. Lavan, and C. Machado, Leiden, 2006, pp. 157–82.

Machado, C. "Religion as Antiquarianism: Pagan Dedications in Late Antique Rome," in *Didache sacre nel mondo Greco-romano. Diffusione, funzioni, tipologie*, eds. J. Bodel and M. Kajava, Rome, 2009, pp. 331–54.

Machado, C. "Aristocratic Houses and the Making of Late Antique Rome and Constantinople," in *Two Romes. Rome and Constantinople in Late Antiquity*, eds. L. Grig and G. Kelly, New York, 2012, pp. 136–58 = 2012A.

Machado, C. "Between Memory and Oblivion: The End of the Roman *domus*," in *Rom in der Spätantike. Historische Erinnerung im städtischen Raum*, eds. R. Behrwald and C. Witschel, 2012, pp. 111–38 = 2012B.

Machado, C. "The Roman Aristocracy and the Imperial Court, before and after the Sack," in *The Sack of Rome in 410 AD*, eds. J. Lipps, C. Machado, and P. von Rummel, *Palilia* 28, 2013, pp. 49–76.

Machado, C. *Urban Space and Aristocratic Power in Late Antique Rome*. Oxford, UK, 2019.

Machado, C. and J. Lenaghan, "Rome," in *The Last Statues of Antiquity*, eds. R. R. Smith and B. Ward-Perkins, Oxford, UK, 2016, pp. 121–35.

MacMullen, R. *Christianizing the Roman Empire*, New Haven, CT, 1984.

MacMullen, R. *Voting about God in Early Church Councils*, New Haven, CT, 2006.

MacMullen, R. *The Second Church. Popular Christianity A.D. 200–400*, Society for Biblical Literatures, Atlanta, GA, 2009.

MacMullen, R. "The End of Ancestor Worship: Affect and Class," *Historia* 63, 2014, pp. 487–513.

MacMullen, R. "Roman Religion: The Best Attested Practice," *Historia* 66, 2017, pp. 111–27.

Mahoney, J. "Path Dependence in Historical Sociology," *Theory and Society*, 29.4, 2000, pp. 507–48.

Maier, H. "Leo the Great and the Orthodox Panopticon," *JECS* 4.4, 1996, pp. 440–61.

Maier, J. L. *Le Dossier du Donatisme*, 2 vols., Berlin, 1987–9.

Malmberg, S. "'Ships Are Seen Gliding Swiftly along the Sacred Tiber': The River as an Artery of Urban Movement and Development," in *The Moving City. Processions, Passages and Promenades in Ancient Rome*, eds. I. Östenberg, S. Malmberg, and J. Bjornbye, London and New York, 2015, pp. 187–202.

Mango, M. M. *Silver from Early Byzantium. The Kaper Koraon and Related Treasures*, Baltimore, MD, 1986.

Mansi, J. D. (1759–98), *Sacrorum Conciliorum Nova et Amplissima Collectio*, 1759–98.

Marazzi, F. "The Last Rome: From the End of the Fifth to the End of the Sixth Century," in *The Ostrogoths from the Migration Period to the Sixth Century: An Ethnographic Perspective*, eds. S. J. B. Barnish and F. Marazzi, Woodbridge, UK, 2007, pp. 279–316.

Marazzi, F. "Ostrogothic cities," in *A Companion to Ostrogothic Italy*, eds. J. Arnold, M. S. Bjornlie, and K. Sessa, Leiden, Boston, 2016, pp. 98–120.

Marcos, M. "Papal Authority, Local Autonomy and Imperial Control: Pope Zosimus and the Western Churches," in *The Role of the Bishop in Late Antiquity* eds. A. Fear, J. Fernández Ubiña, and M. Marcos, London, 2013, pp. 145–66.

Markus, R. *Saeculum: History and Society in the Theology of St. Augustine*, Cambridge, UK, 1970.

Marlowe, E. "*Liberator urbis suae*. Constantine and the Ghost of Maxentius," in *The Emperor and Rome. Space, Representation and Ritual*, eds. B. C. Ewald and C. F. Norena, Cambridge, UK, 2010.

Marlowe, E. "Framing the Sun: The Arch of Constantine and the Roman Cityscape," *Art Bulletin* 88, 2006, pp. 223–42.

Martin, M. A. *The Use of Indirect Discourse in the Works of St. Ambrose*, PhD dissertation, Catholic University of America, Washington, DC, 1930.

Martyn, J. C. "Four Notes on the *Registrum* of Gregory the Great," *Parergon* 19.2, 2002, pp. 5–38.

Maskarinec, M. *City of Saints. Rebuilding Rome in the Early Middle Ages*, Philadelphia, 2018.

Maskarinec, M. "Saintly Genealogies: The Frangipani and Gregory the Great," Unpublished paper at the Huntington Library, Pasadena, CA, May 2020.

Mathisen, R. "Resistance and Reconciliation: Majorian and the Gallic Aristocracy after the Fall of Avitus," *Francia* 7, 1979, pp. 597–627.

Mathisen, R. "Avitus, Italy and the East in A.D. 455–456," *Byzantion* 51, 1981, pp. 232–47.

Mathisen, R. "*PLRE II*. Suggested Addenda et Corrigenda," *Historia* 31, 1982, pp. 364–86.

Mathisen, R. "Ten Office Holders. A Few Addenda and Corrigenda to PLRE," *Historia* 35, 1986, pp. 125–27 = 1986A.

Mathisen, R. "Patricians as Diplomats in Late Antiquity," *Byzantinische Zeitschrift* 79.1, 1986, pp. 35–49 = 1986B.

Mathisen, R. "Some Hagiographical Addenda to *PLRE*," *Historia* 36, 1987, pp. 448–61.

Mathisen, R. *Ecclesiastical Factionalism and Religious Controversy in Fifth-Century Gaul*. Washington, DC, 1989.

Mathisen, R. "The Third Regnal Year of Eparchius Avitus. The Interpretation of the Evidence," *Studies in the History, Literature and Society of Late Antiquity*, Amsterdam, 1991, pp. 163–66.

Mathisen, R. "Emperors, Consuls and Patricians: Some Problems of Personal Preference, Precedence and Protocol," *Byzantinische Forschungen* 17, 1991, pp. 173–90 = 1991A.

Mathisen, R. "Leo, Anthemius, Zeno and Extraordinary Senatorial Status in the Late Fifth Century," *Byzantinische Forschungen* 17, 1991, pp. 191–222 = 1991B.

Mathisen, R. *Roman Aristocrats in Barbarian Gaul: Strategies for Survival in an Age of Transition*, Austin, TX, 1993.

Mathisen, R. "Ricimer's Church in Rome: How an Arian General Prospered in a Nicene World," in *The Power of Religion in Late Antiquity*, ed. A. Cain, Surrey, UK/ Burlington, VT, 2009, pp. 307–26.

Mathisen, R. "Barbarian Arian Clergy, Church Organization, and Church Practices," in *Arianism: Roman Heresy and Barbarian Creed*, eds. G. Berndt and R. Steinach, Surrey, UK/Burlington, VT, 2014, pp. 145–92.

Matthews, J. "Anicius Manlius Severinus Boethius," in *Boethius, His Life, Thought and Influence*, ed. M. Gibson, Oxford, 1981, pp. 17–43.

Matthews, J. *Western Aristocracies and Imperial Court A.D. 364–425*. Oxford, 1975; expanded, 1990.

Max, G. E. "Political Intrigue during the Reigns of the Western Roman Emperors Avitus and Majorianus," *Historia* 28, 1979, pp. 225–37.

Mazza, M. "I vandali, la Sicilia e il Mediterraneo nella tarda antichità," *Kokalos* 43–44, 1997–1998, pp. 107–38.

Mazzarino, S. *Serena e le due Eudossie*. Rome, 1946.

Mazzarino, S. "Problemi e aspetti del basso impero, in tardo antico e alto medioevo. La forma artistica nel passaggio dall antichità al medioevo," in *Antico, tardoantico ed èra constantiniana*, ed. S. Mazzarino, vol. 1, Rome, 1974, pp. 183–96.

McCormick, M. *Eternal Victory: Triumphal Rulership in Late Antiquity, Byzantium and the Early Medieval West*, Cambridge, UK, 1986.

McEvoy, M. "Shadow Emperors and the Choice of Rome (455–476 AD)," *Ant. Tard.* 25, 2017, pp. 95–112.

McEvoy, M. *Child Emperor Rule in the Late Roman West, 367–455*, Oxford, 2013.

McEvoy, M. "Rome and the Transformation of the Imperial Office in the Late Fourth-mid-Fifth Centuries A.D.," *Papers of the British School at Rome* 78, 2010, pp. 151–92.

McKitterick, R. "Roman Texts and Roman History in the Early Middle Ages," in *Rome across Time and Space: Cultural Transmission and the Exchange of Ideas c. 400–1400*, eds. C. Bolgia, R. McKitterick, and J. Osborne, Cambridge, 2011, pp. 19–34.

McKitterick, R. "The Constantinian Basilica in the Early Medieval *Liber* Pontificalis," in *The Basilica of St. John Lateran to 1600*, Cambridge, UK, 2020, eds. L. Bosman, I. Haynes, and P. Liverani, pp. 197–220.

McLynn, N. "The Transformations of Imperial Churchgoing in the Fourth Century," in *Approaching Late Antiquity*, eds. M. Edwards and S. Swain, Oxford, 2004, pp. 235–70.

Mecella, L. and L. Rossi (eds.,) *Scuole e maestri dall età antica al medioevo in Atti dell'età antica al medioevo 2015*, Rome, 2017.

Meier, M. "Das End de Konsulats im Jahr 541/2," *ZPE* 138 (2002), pp. 277–79.

Meier, M. "Rethinking *Rulership*: The Significance of the Year A.D. 476," in *Politische Fragmentierung und kulturelle Kohärenz in der Spätantike*, ed. D. Boschung, M. Danner, and C. Radtki. Paderborn, 2015, pp. 15–68 (= *Morphomata*, Band 26).

Meneghini, R. and R. Santangeli Valenzani "Fase tarde di occupazione dell'isolato E con domus e balnea," in *Antiche stanze. Un quartiere de Roma imperiale nella zona di termini*, eds. R. Paris and M. Rosaria Barbera, Milan, 1996, pp. 172–77.

Mennen, I. *Power and Status in the Roman Empire*, Leiden, 2011.

Merrills, A. H. and R. Miles. *The Vandals*, Chichester, 2010.

Merrony, M. *The Plight of Rome in the Fifth Century*, London and New York, 2017.

Messina, R. Gentile. "La Sicilia tra Roma e Costantinopoli (secoli VI–VII)," in *Silenziose Rivoluzioni. La Sicilia dalla tarda antichità al primo medioevo*, eds. C. Giuffrida and M. Cassia, Catania-Rome, 2016, pp. 161–90.

Miller, D. J. D. and P. Sarris. *The Novels of Justinian. A Complete Annotated English Translation*, 2 vols. Cambridge, 2018.

Modéran, M. *Les Vandales et l'Empire Romain*, Paris, 2014.

Molinari, A. "La Produzione artigianale a Roma tra V e XV secolo. Reflessioni sui risultati di uno studio archeologico sistematico e comparativo," in *L'Archéologia della produzione à Roma (secoli V–XV)*, eds. A. Molinari, R. Santangeli Valenzani, and L. Spera, *Atti del Convegno Internazionale di Studi Roma 27–29 marzo, 2014* (Collection de l'École de Française de Rome, 516), 2015, pp. 613–35.

Momigliano, A. "Cassiodorus and the Italian Culture of His Age," *Proceedings of the British Academy* 41, 1955, pp. 207–45.

Mommsen, T. (ed.) *Acta synhodi A. DII [sic] MGH AA* 12. Berlin, Weidmann, 1961, pp. 438–55.

Mommsen, T. *Römisches Staatsrecht, Vol. 3. Bürgerschaft und Senat*, 3rd ed, Leipzig 1887.

Mommsen, T. "Ostgotische Studien," Neues Archiv der Gesellschaft für ältere deutsche Geschichtskunde XIV, 1889, 445 = *Gesammelte Schriften* 6, 1907, pp. 428–30.

Mommsen, T. (ed.), *Chronica Minora*, vol. 1. *MGH AA* 9, Berlin, 1892, Munich rept., 1981.

Mommsen, T. (ed.), *Chronica Minora* Vol. 3. MGH AA 11, Berlin, 1894, Munich rept., 1981.

Montanari, E. "Nota sulla storia del testo dei sermoni," in *I Sermoni di Leone Magno Fra Storia e Teologia*, 3 vols., ed. M. Naldini, Florence, 1997, vol. 1, pp. 171–214.

Moorhead, J. "The Last Years of Theoderic," *Historia* 32, 1983, pp. 106–20.

Moorhead, J. "Theoderic, Zeno and Odovacer," *Byzantinische Zeitschrift* 77, 1984A, pp. 261–66.

Moorhead, J. "The Decii under Theoderic," *Historia* 33, 1984, pp. 107–15.

Moorhead, J. "Papa as 'Bishop of Rome,'" *The Journal of Ecclesiastical History* 36, 1986, pp. 337–50.

Moorhead, J. *Theoderic in Italy*. Oxford, 1992A.

Moorhead, J. *Victor of Vita: History of the Vandal Persecution*, Liverpool University Press, 1992.

Moorhead, J. "On Becoming Pope in Late Antiquity," *Journal of Religious History* 30, 2006, pp. 279–93.

Moorhead, J. *The Popes and the Church of Rome in Late Antiquity*, New York, Abingdon, UK, 2015.

Moorhead, S. and D. Stuttard. *AD 410. The Year That Shook Rome*. The J. Paul Getty Museum, Los Angeles, 2010.

Moralee, J. "Commemorating Defeat: Cultural Memory and the Vandal Sack of Rome in 455," in *The Fifth Century: Age of Transformation* eds. J.W. Drijvers and N. Lenski, Proceedings of the 12th biennial Shifting Frontiers in Late Antiquity Conference, Bari, Italy, 2019, pp. 307–20.

Moralee, J. *Rome's Holy Mountain. The Capitoline Hill in Late Antiquity*, Oxford, 2018.

Moralee, J. and K. Moe. "What Francesco di Giorgio Saw on the Capitoline Hill *c.* 1470," *Papers of the British School at Rome* 83, 2015, pp. 149–73.

Morley, N. "Population Size and Social Structure," in *The Cambridge Companion to Ancient Rome*, ed. P. Erdkamp, Cambridge, UK, New York, 2013, pp. 29–44.

Morley, N. *Metropolis and Hinterland*. Cambridge, UK, 1996.

Moser, M. *Emperor and Senators in the Reign of Constantius II*. Cambridge, UK, 2018.

Mueller, L. (ed.) *Publilii Optatiani Porfyrii, Carmina*. Leipzig, 1877.

Müller, C. (ed.) *Fragmenta Historicorum Graecorum, Paris 1951, volume IV*: Menander Protector; volume V, 1870.

Munier, C. (ed.) *Concilia Galliae a. 314–506*, in *CCSL* 148B, Turnhout, 1963.

Nagy, L. "Myth and Salvation in the Fourth Century: Representations of Hercules in Christian Contexts," in *Pagans and Christians in Late Antique Rome*, eds. M. R. Salzman, M. Sághy, and R. Lizzi Testa, New York, Cambridge, 2016, pp. 11–45.

Nash, E. "Secretarium Senatus," in *In Memoriam Otto J. Brendel: Essays in Archaeology and the Humanities*, eds. L. Bonfante and H. von Heintze, Mainz, 1976, pp. 191–206.

Neil, B. *Leo the Great*. Oxon, UK, New York, 2009.

Neil, B. "*De Profundis*. The Letters and Archives of Pelagius I of Rome (556–561)," in *Collecting Early Christian Letters. From the Apostle Paul to Late Antiquity*, eds. B. Neil and P. Allen, Cambridge, UK, 2015, pp. 206–20.

Neil, B. "Papal Letters and Letter Collections," in C. Sogno, B. Storin, and E. Watts (eds.), *A Critical Introduction and Reference Guide to Letter Collections in Late Antiquity*, Oakland, CA, 2017, pp. 449–66.

Neil, B. "Imperial Benefactions in the Fifth-Century Roman Church," in G. Nathan and L. Garland (eds.), *Basileia. Essays in Honour of E. M. and M. J. Jeffreys* (Byzantina Australiaensia 17), 2017, pp. 55–66 = 2017A.

Neil, B. and P. Allen. *The Letters of Gelasius I (492–496): Pastor and Micro-Manager of the Church of Rome. Introduction, Translation and Notes*, Turnhout, 2014.

Neri, V. "Aurelio Vittore e la tradizione pagan su Costantino," in *La storiografia tardoantica. Bilcanci e prospettive*, ed. V. Neri and B. Girott, Milan, 2017, pp. 13–35.

Nixon, C. E. V. and B. S. Rodgers. *In Praise of Later Emperors*, Berkeley, Los Angeles, 1994.

Novak, D. M. "Constantine and the Senate," in *Ancient Society* 10, 1979, pp. 271–310.

Novak, D. M. "The Early History of the Anician Family," *Studies in Latin Literature and Roman History* 1, 1979, pp. 119–65 = 1979A.

O'Dahl, C. "Review of J. Bardill, *Constantine. The Divine Emperor of the Roman World*," *The Ancient World*, 44 2, 2013, pp. 199–202.

O'Donnell, J. *Cassiodorus*. Berkeley and London, 1979.

Oulton, J. E. L. with H. J. Lawlor, *Eusebius. Ecclesiastical History and Martyrs of Palestine*. Translated with introduction and notes, London 1927–28.

Oost, S. "D. N. Libius Severus P. F. Aug.," *Classical Philology* 65, 1970, pp. 228–40.

Oppedisano, F. *Impero d'occidente negli anni di Maiorano*. Rome, 2013.

Oppedisano, F. "Social Profile and Authority of the Senate between the end of the Roman Empire and the Ostrogothic Period," in P. Buongiorno, N. Lenski, and U. Roberto (eds.), *Fonti tardoantiche per lo studio dei senatus consulta: percorsi fra giurisprudenza e storiografia*. Stuttgart, forthcoming.

Oppedisano, F. "Introduzione," in F. Oppedisano (ed.), *Procopio Antemio. Imperatore di Roma*. Bari, 2020, pp. 5–9.

Oppedisano, F. "Sidonio, Antemio e il Senato di Roma," in *Procopio Antemio. Imperatore di Roma* ed. F. Oppedisano, Bari, 2020A, pp. 100–19.

Oppedisano, F. "Santo Mazzarino e il Senato tardoantico," *Studi Storici* 1, 2020B, pp. 27–39.

Orlandi, S. "Salvo Domino Nostri," *MEFRA* 109, 1997, pp. 31–40.

Orlandi, S. *Epigrafia anfiteatrale dell'Occidente Romano. VI. Roma. Anfirteatri e strutture annesse con una nuova edizione e commento dell' iscrizioni del Colosseo*, Rome, 2004.

Orlandi, S. "L'epigrafia sotto il regno di Odoacre," in *carismi ed esercizio del potere (IV-VI secolo d.C.)*, eds. G. Bonamente and R. Lizzi Testa, Bari, 2010, pp. 331–38.

Orlandi, S. "Le tracce del passaggio di Alarico nelle fonti epigrafiche," in *The Sack of Rome in 410 AD*, eds. J. Lipps, C. Machado, and P. von Rummel, *Palilia* 28, 2013, pp. 335–52.

Orlandi, S. "Urban Prefects and the Epigraphic Evidence of Late-Antique, Rome," *Ant. Tard.* 25, 2017, pp. 213–22.

Orlandi, S. "L'epigrafia sotto il regno di Antemio," in *Procopio Antemio. Imperatore di Roma*, ed. F. Oppedisano, Bari, 2020, pp. 177–97.

Panciera, S. *Tituli* 4 (1982), pp. 658–60.

Panciera, S. "Il precettore di Valentiniano III," in *Studi in Onore di Albino Garzetti*, eds. C. Stella and A. Valvo, Brescia, 1996, pp. 277–97.

Panella C., L. Saguì, M. Casalini, and F. Coletti. "Contesti tardoantichi di Roma: una rilettura alle luce di nuovi dati," in *LRCW 3. Late Roman Coarse Wares, Cooking Wares and Amphorae in the Mediterranean: Archaeology and Archaeometry. Comparison between Eastern and Western Mediterranean*, eds. S. Menchelli, S. Santoro, M. Pasquinucci, and G. Guiducci (BAR-IS 2185), Oxford 2010, pp. 57–78.

Paschoud, F. *Histoire Auguste. Vies d'Aurélien et Tacite*, Paris, 1996.

Paschoud, F. "Zosime 2,29 et la version païenne de la conversion de Constantine," *Historia* 2, 1971, pp. 334–53.

Patterson, H. "The Middle Tiber Valley in the Late Antique and Early Medieval Periods," in *Mercator Placidissimus: The Tiber Valley in Antiquity, New Research in the Upper and Middle River Valley*, eds. H. Patterson and F. Coarelli, Rome, 2008, pp. 499–532.

Patterson, H. "The Tiber Valley Project: Archaeology, Comparative Survey and History," in *General Issues in the Study of Medieval Logistics. Sources, Problems and Methodologies*, ed. J. Haldon, Leiden, Boston, 2006, pp. 93–117.

Pavolini, C. "Nuove indagini sul Celio (secoli V–IX)," in *Roma dall' antichità al medioveo. Archeologia e storia nel Museo Nazionale Romano Crypta Balbi*, ed. M. S. Arena, P. Delogu, L. Paroli, M. Ricci, L. Saguì, and L. Vendittelli, Milan, 2001, pp. 616–18.

Pavolini, C. "Le consequenze del Sacco di Alarico sul Celio," in *The Sack of Rome in 410 AD*, eds. J. Lipps, C. Machado, and P. von Rummel, *Palilia* 28, 2013, pp. 163–83.

Pierson, P. "Increasing Returns, Path Dependence, and the Study of Politics," *The American Political Science Review*, 94 2, June 2000, pp. 251–67.

Pietri, C. *Roma christiana. Recherches sur l'Églises de Rome; Son organisation, sa politique, son idéologie de Militiade à Sixte III (311–440)*, Rome, 1976, 172–78.

Pietri, C. "Evergétisme et richesses eccléstiques dans l'Italie du Ive à la fin du Ve siècle: l'exemple romain," *Ktema* 2, 1978, pp. 317–37.

Pietri, C. "Aristocratie et société cléricale dans l'Italie chrétienne au temps d'Odoacre e de Théoderic," *Mélanges de l'École française de Rome Antiquité* 93 1, 1981, pp. 417–67.

Pietri, C. "Evergétisme chrétien et fondations privées dans l'Italie de l'antiquité tardive," in *Humana sapit. Études d'antiquité tardive offerts à Lellia Cracco Ruggini*, ed. J. M. Carrié and R. L. Testa, Turnhout, 2000, pp. 253–63.

Pocock, J. G. A. *Barbarism and Religion. Volume I. The Enlightenments of Edward Gibbon, 1737–1764*. Cambridge, UK, 1999.

Pollmann K. and H. Harich-Schwarzbauer (eds.) *Der Fall Roms und seine Wiederauferstehungen in Antike und Mittelalter*, Berlin, 2012.

Porena. P. *Le origini della prefettura del pretorio tardoantica*. Rome, 2003.

Porena, P. "Problemi cronologia costantiniana. L'Imperatore, Vettius Rufinus e il senatore," *Ant. Tard.* 13, 2005, pp. 205–46.

Porena, P. "Trasformazioni istituzionali e assetti sociali: I prefetti del pretorio tra III e IV secolo," in *Le Trasformazioni delle élites in età tardoantica*, ed. R. Lizzi Testa, 2006, Rome, pp. 325–56.

Porena, P. "À l'ombre de la pourpre.' L'évolution de la prefecture du prétoire entre le IIIe e le IV siècle," *Cahiers du Centre Gustave Glotz* 18, 2007, pp. 237–62.

Porena, P. "I dignitari di Costantino: dinamiche di selezione e di ascesa durante la crisi del sistema tetrarchio," in G. Bonamente, N. Lenski, and R. Lizzi Testa (eds.), *Costantino prima e dopo Costantino/Constantine before and after Constantine*, 2012, Bari, pp. 293–320.

Porena, P. "À l'ombre de la pourpre.' L'évolution de la prefecture du prétoire entre le IIIe e le IV siècle," *Cahiers du Centre Gustave Glotz* 18, 2017, pp. 237–62.

Porena, P. "La riorganizzazione amministrativa dell'Italia. Costantino, Rom, il Senato e gli equilibii dell'Italia romana," in *Enciclopedia Costantiniana sulla figura e l'immagine dell'Imperatore del coisdetto editto de Milano*, 313–2013, vol. II, Rome, 2013, pp. 329–49.

Porena, P. "Il *Prior/Caput Senatus* in Occidente: Aspetti del primato dell'aristocrazia di Roma dopo il 478," *Latinitas* 7, 2019, pp. 25–50.

Potter, D. *The Roman Empire at Bay: AD 180–396*. London, 2004.

Potter, D. *Constantine the Emperor*. New York, 2013.

Presicce, Parisi. "L'abbandono della moderazione. I ritratti di Costantino e della sua progenie," in *Costantino Il Grande: La civiltà antica al bivio tra Occidente e Oriente*, eds. A. Donati and G. Gentili, Milan, 2005, pp. 138–55.

Presicce, Parisi. "Konstantin als Iuppiter: Die Kolossalstatue des Kaisers aus der Basilika an der Via Sacra," in *Imperator Caesar Flavius Constantinus. Konstantin der Grosse. Austellungskatalog*, ed. A. Demandt and J. Engemann, Mainz, 2007, pp. 117–31.

Purcell, N. "The Populace of Rome in Late Antiquity: Problems of Classification and Historical Description," in *The Transformations of Urbs Roma in Late Antiquity*, ed. W. Harris, Portsmouth, RI, 1999, pp. 135–62.

Purcell, N. "'Romans, Play On!' City of the Games," in *The Cambridge Companion to Ancient Rome*, ed. P. Erdkamp, Cambridge, UK, New York, 2013, pp. 441–60.

Radtki, C. "The Senate at Rome in Ostrogothic Italy," in *A Companion to Ostrogothic Italy*, eds. J. Arnold, M. S. Bjornlie, and K. Sessa, Leiden, Boston, 2016, pp. 121–45.

Ramskold, L. and N. Lenski. "Constantinople's Medallions and the Maintenance of Civic Traditions," *Numismatische Zeitschrift* 119 (2012), pp. 59–92.

Rapp, C. *Holy Bishops in Late Antiquity*. Berkeley, CA, 2005.

Rea, R. "L'Anfiteatro dal 411–526: da Onorio e Teodosi II a Teoderico," in *Rota Colisei. La Valle del Colosseo attraverso I secoli*, ed. R. Rea, Milan, 2002, pp. 126–39.

Rees, B. R. *Pelagius. Life and Letters*. Woodbridge, Suffolk, UK, and Rochester, NY, 1998.

Rich, Adrienne. *The Dream of a Common Language*, New York, 1978.

Richards, J. *The Popes and the Papacy in the Early Middle Ages, 476–572*. London, 1979.

Richards, J. *Consul of God: Life and Times of Gregory the Great*. London, 1980.

Rickman, G. *The Corn Supply of Ancient Rome*. Oxford, 1980.

Ridley, R.T. *Zosimus. A New History. A Translation with Commentary*, Canberra, 1982.

Roberto, U. *Roma capta. Il Sacco della città dai Galli ai Lanzichenecchi*. Bari, 2012.

Roberto, U. "Il senato di Roma tra Antemio e Glicerio. Per una rilettura di *CIL*, VI 526 = 1664 = *ILS* 3132," in *Epigrafia e ordine senatorio*, 30 anni dopo, eds. M. L. Caldelli and G. Gregori, Rome, 2014, pp. 167–82.

Roberto, U. "Le Corte di Antemio e i Rapporti con l'Oriente," in *Procopio Antemio. Imperatore di Roma* ed. F. Oppedisano, Bari, 2020, pp. 141–76.

Rogers, A. *Late Roman Towns in Britain: Rethinking Change and Decline*. New York, 2011.

Rolfe, J. C. *Ammianus Marcellinus*, Cambridge, MA, and London, 1986, 3 vols.

Rose, B. "Reconsidering the Frieze on the Arch of Constantine," *Journal of Roman Archaeology* 34.1, 2021 doi:10.1017/S1047759421000015

Rüpke, J. *Fasti Sacerdotum. A Prosopography of Pagan, Jewish, and Christian Religious Officials in the City of Rome, 300 BC to 499 AD*. Oxford, 2008.

Saguì, L. "Roma, I centri privilegiati e la lunga durata della tarda antichità," *Archeologia Medievale* 29, 2002, pp. 7–42.

Salway, B. "Redefining the Roman Imperial Elite in the Fourth Century AD," in *Elites in the Ancient World*, eds. D. Okon and P. Briks, Szezecink Praca Zbiorowa, 2015, pp. 189–220.

Salway, B. "Late Antique Epigraphy," in *The Oxford Handbook to Roman Epigraphy*,. Edmundson and C. Bruun, Oxford, 2015, pp. 364–96 = 2015A.

Salzman, M. R. *On Roman Time. The Codex-Calendar of 354 and the Rhythms of Urban Life in Late Antiquity*, Berkeley, London, 1990.

Salzman, M. R. *The Making of a Christian Aristocracy*. Cambridge, MA, 2002.

Salzman, M. R. "Symmachus and the 'Barbarian' Generals," *Historia* 55.3 (2006), pp. 352–67.

Salzman, M. R. "Apocalypse Then? Jerome and the Fall of Rome in 410," in *Maxima Debetur Magistro Reverentia. Essays on Rome and the Roman Tradition in Honor of Russell T. Scott*, eds. P. B. Harvey, Jr., and C. Conybeare, *Biblioteca di Athenaeum* 54, 2009, pp. 175–92.

Salzman M. R. "Why Rome?" Review of *AD 410. The Year That Shook Rome*. Sam Moorhead and David Stuttard, Los Angeles, 2010, pp. 947–50.

Salzman, M. R. "Leo's Liturgical Topography: Contestations for Space in Fifth-Century Rome," *JRS* 103, 2013, pp. 208–32.

Salzman, M. R. "Leo the Great: Responses to Crisis and the Shaping of a Christian Cosmopolis," in *The Transformation of City and Citizenship in the Classical World: From the Fifth Century BCE to the Fifth Century CE*, eds. H. Drake and C. Rapp, Cambridge, MA, New York, 2014, pp. 183–201 = 2014A.

Salzman, M. R. "Christian Sermons against Pagans: The Evidence from Augustine's Sermons on the New Year and on the Sack of Rome in 410," in *The Cambridge Companion to Attila the Hun*, ed. M. Maas, Cambridge, MA, London, 2015, pp. 346–59.

Salzman, M. R. "Constantine and the Roman Senate: Conflict, Cooperation, and Concealed Resistance," in *Pagans and Christians in Late Antique Rome*, eds. M. R. Salzman, M. Sághy, and R. Lizzi Testa, New York, Cambridge, UK, 2016, pp. 11–45.

Salzman, M. R. "Aurelian and the Cult of the Unconquered Sun: The Institutionalization of Christmas, Solar Worship and Imperial Cult," in *Expressions of Cult in the Southern Levant in the Greco-Roman Period: Manifestations in Texts and Material Culture*, eds. O. Tal and Z. Weiss, Turnhout, 2017, pp. 37–50 = 2017A.

Salzman, M. R. "From a Classical to a Christian City: Civic Euergetism and Christian Charity in Late Antique Rome," *Studies in Late Antiquity: A Journal*, 1.1, 2017, pp. 65–85 = 2017B.

Salzman, M. R. "Emperors and Elites in Rome after the Vandal Sack of 455," *Ant. Tard.* 25, 2017, pp. 243–62 = 2017C.

Salzman, M. R. "Symmachus's Varro: Latin Letters in Late Antiquity," *Bulletin of the Institute for Classical Studies* 61.2, 2018.2, pp. 92–105.

Salzman, M. R. "New Light on the Papacy of Felix III (483–492) and the Acacian Schism after the Fall of the Western Roman Emperor," *Journal of Early Christian Studies* 27.3, 2019, pp. 465–89 = Salzman 2019A.

Salzman, M. R. "Contestations between Elites: Italo-Roman Senatorial Aristocrats and the Senate in the *Collectio Avellana*," in *The "Collectio Avellana" and Its Revival*, eds. R. Lizzi Testa and G. Marconi, Cambridge, 2019, pp. 138–158 = Salzman 2019B.

Salzman, M. R. "The Religious Economics of Crisis: The Papal Use of Liturgical Vessels as Symbolic Capital in Late Antiquity," *Religion in the Roman Empire* 5.2, 2019, pp. 125–41 = 2019C.

Salzman, M. R. "Senate I," in *Reallexikon Für Antike und Christentum*, Band 30, eds. C. Hornung, H. Brakmann, S. De Blaauw, T. Fuhrer, H. Leppin, W. Löhr, H. Nesselrath, M Niehoff, G. Schöllgen, and I. Tanaseanu-Döbler, Stuttgart, 2020, pp. 251–94.

Salzman, M. R. "A New 'Topography of Devotion.' Aurelian and Solar Worship in Rome," in *Urban Religion in Late Antiquity*, ed. A. Lätzer-Lasar and E. Urciolo, Berlin, 2020, pp. 149–67= 2020A.

Salzman, M. R. and M. Roberts Transl. *Letters of Symmachus. Book 1.* Introduction and commentary by Michele Renee Salzman. Atlanta, 2015 revised ed. of 2010.

Santangeli Valenzani, R. "I quartieri residenziali. Depressamento, crisi e mutamenti proprietari delle domus aristocratiche," in *Roma e il sacco del 410. Realtà, interpretazione, mito*, eds. A. Di Berardino, G. Pilara, and L. Pera, Rome, 2012, pp. 219–27.

Santangeli Valenzani, R. *Edilizia residenziale in Italia nell'altomedioevo*, Rome, 2011.

Santangeli Valenzani, R. "Strutture demografiche, economiche e sociali," in *Roma nell'altomedioevo. Topografia e urbanistica della città dal V à X secolo*, ed. R. Meneghini and R. Santangeli Valenzani, Rome, 2004, pp. 21–27 = 2004B.

Santangeli Valenzani, R. "Abitare a Roma nell'alto medioevo," in *Roma dall'antichità al medioevo II. Contesti tardo antichi e altomedievali*, eds. L. Paroli and L. Vendittelli, Milan, 2004, pp. 41 = 2004A.

Santangeli Valenzani, R. "Public and Private Space in Rome during Late Antiquity and the Early Middle Ages," *Fragmenta* 1, 2007, pp. 63–82.

Sarris, P. *Economy and Society in the Age of Justinian*, Cambridge, 2006.

Sarris, P. *Empires of Faith. The Fall of Rome to the Rise of Islam, 500–700*, Cambridge, 2011.

Sarris, P. "The Formation of the Post-Roman Economy and the Cultural Legacy of Rome," in *Politische Fragmentierung und Kulturell Kohärenz in der Spätantike*, eds. D. Boschung, M. Danner, and C. Radtki, Paderborn, 2015, pp. 123–36.

Savino, E. "La conquista vandola dell' Africa e la popolazione di Roman nel V secolo," *Athenaeum* 107, 2019, pp. 156–68.

Saxer, V. "L'utilisation par la liturgie de l'espace urbain et surburbain: L'exemple de Rome dans l'Antiquité et le haut Moyen Âge," in *Actes du Xie Congrès international d'archéologie chrétienne: Lyons, Vienne, Grenoble, Genéve et Aoste (21–28 septembre 1986)*, CEFR 123, Studi di antichità cristiana 42, 3 vols., eds. N. Duval, F. Baritel, and P. Pergola, 1989, vol. II pp. 917–1033.

Schäfer, C. *Der weströmische Senat als Träger anitker Kontinuität unter den Ostgotenkönnigen (490–540 n. Chr)*, St. Katharinen, 1991.

Scharf, R. "Der Stadtpräfekt Iulius Felix Campanianus," *ZPE* 94 (1992), pp. 274–78.

Scheidel, W. *Escape from Rome: The Failure of Empire and the Road to Prosperity*, Princeton, 2019.

Schmidt-Hofner, S. "Der *defensor civitatis* und die Enstehung des Notan regiments in den spätrömischen Städten," in *Chlodwigs Welt. Organisation vom Herrschaft um 500*, ed. M. Meier and S. Patzold, Stuttgart, 2014, pp. 487–523.

Schoolman, E. "*Vir Clarissimus* and Roman Titles in the Early Middle Ages: Survival and Continuity in Ravenna and the Latin West," *Medieval Prosopography. History and Collective Biography*, 32, 2017, pp. 1–39.

Schoolman, E. "Dux to Episcopus: From Controlling Cities to Sees in Byzantine Italy, 554–900," in *Italy and the East Roman World in the Medieval Mediterranean: Empire, Cities and Elites, 476–1204*, eds. T. Macmaster and N. Matheu, Birmingham Byzantine and Ottoman Studies, London, Forthcoming 2021.

Schoolman, E. "Aristocracies in early medieval Italy, ca. 500–1000 CE," *History Compass.* 2018; DOI: 10:1111/hic3.12499, pp. 1–13.

Schwarz, E. (ed.) *Acts of the Council of Chalcedon, 1914-40*, 4 vols. Concilium Universale Chalcedense, ACO 2, Berlin, 1914–40.

Scott, R. "Chronicles versus Classicizing History: Justinian's West and East," in *Byzantine Chronicles and the Sixth Century*, ed. R. Scott, Farnham, Surrey, UK/ Burlington, VT 2012, Selection VI, pp. 1–25.

Scott, R. "Interpreting the Late Fifth and Early Sixth Centuries from Byzantine Chronicle Trivia," republished from *Basileia: Essays on Imperium and Culture in Honour of E. M. and M. J. Jeffreys*, eds. G. Nathan and L. Garland, *Byzantina Australiensia* 17, Brisbane, 2011, pp. 83–93, = R. Scott, *Byzantine Chronicles and the Sixth Century*, Farnham, Surrey, UK and Burlington, VT, 2012, Chapter XVIII = 2012A.

Sessa, K. *The Formation of Papal Authority in Late Antique Italy. Roman Bishops and the Domestic Sphere*. New York, 2012.

Sessa, K. "The Roman Church and Its Bishops," in *A Companion to Ostrogothic Italy*, eds. J. Arnold, M. S. Bjornlie, and K. Sessa, Leiden, Boston, 2016, pp. 425–50.

Sessa, K. "Constantine and Silvester in the *Actus Silvestri*," in *The Life and Legacy of Constantine Traditions through the Ages*, ed. M. S. Bjornlie, London, New York, 2017, pp. 77–91.

Sessa, K. *Daily Life in Late Antiquity*, New York, Cambridge, 2018.

Sessa K. "The New Environmental Fall of Rome: A Methodological Consideration," *Journal of Late Antiquity* 12.1, 2019, pp. 211–55.

Shaw, B. *Sacred Violence. African Christians and Sectarian Hatred in the Age of Augustine*. Cambridge, UK, New York, 2011.

Shelton, K. J. *The Esquiline Treasure*. London, 1981.

Sirks, B. *Food for Rome*. The Legal Structure of the Transportation and Processing of Supplies for the Imperial Distributions in Rome and Constantinople = Volume 31, Studia Amstelodamensia ad epigraphicam, ius antiquum et papyrologicam pertinentia, Amsterdam, 1991.

Sivan, H. "Sidonius Apollinaris, Theodericus II and Gothic-Roman Politics from Avitus to Anthemius," *Hermes* 17, 1989, pp. 85–94.

Sogno, C., B. Storin, and E. Watts (eds.) *A Critical Introduction and Reference Guide to Letter Collections in Late Antiquity*. Oakland, CA, 2017.

Sotinel, C. "Autorité pontificale et pouvoir impérial sous le règne de Justinien: le pape Virgilius," *MEFR Antiquité* 104, 1992, pp. 439–63.

Sotinel, C. "Emperors and Popes in the Sixth Century: The Western View," in *The Age of Justinian*, ed. M. Maas, Cambridge, 2005, pp. 267–90.

Sotinel, C. "Les évêques italiens dans la société de l'Antiquité tardive: l'émergence d'une nouvelle élite?" in *Le trasformazioni delle élites in età tardoantica*, ed. R. Lizzi Testa, Rome, 2006, pp. 377–404.

Sotinel, C. "Pontifical Authority and Imperial Power in the Reign of Justinian," in *Church and Authority in Late Antique Italy and Beyond*, ed. C. Sotinel, Surrey, UK/ Burlington, VT, 2010, I, pp. 1–25.

Sotinel, C. "Vigilius in the *Liber Pontificalis*: a Memory Lost, or Manipulated?" in *Church and Authority in Late Antique Italy and Beyond*, ed. C. Sotinel, Surrey, UK/ Burlington, VT, 2010, III, pp. 1–21.

Speidel, M. P. "Maxentius and His *Equites Singulares* in the Battle at the Milvian Bridge," *CA* 5, 1986, pp. 253–62.

Spera, L. "La realtà archeologica: restauro degli edifici pubblici e riassetto urbano dopo il sacco," in *Roma e il Sacco del 410. Realtà, interpretatione, mito*, eds. A. Di Berardino, G. Pilara, and L. Spera, Rome, 2012, pp. 113–55.

Spinola, G. *La domus di Gaudentius*, in *Aurea Roma. Dalla città pagana alla città cristiana*, eds. S. Ensoli and E. La Rocca, Rome, 2000, pp. 152–55.

Stein, E. "Untersuchungen zum Staatsrecht des Bas-Empire," in *Zeitschrift der Savigny-Stiftung für Rechtsgeschichte, Romanist. Abt.* 41, 1920, pp. 195–251.

Stein, E. "La disparition du Sénat de Rome à la fin du VIe siécle," reprt. of 1937 publication in E. Stein, *Opera minora selecta*, Amsterdam, 1968, pp. 308–22.

Stein, E. *Histoire du Bas-Empire, De l'état romain à l'état byzantin, Tome I; De la disparition de l'empire d'Occident à la mort de Justinien (476–569), Tome II*, Paris-Brussels-Amsterdam, 1949.

Stichel, D. and R. H. W. Stichel "Kaiser Justin II [565–578] als Konsul auf Folles," *Byzantinische Zeitschrift* 108, 2015, pp. 827–44.

Straub, J. "Konstantins Verzicht auf dem Gang zum Kapitol," *Historia* 4, 1955, pp. 100–118 (=*Regeneratio imperii*, Darmstadt, 1972, pp. 100–18).

Sundwall, J. *Weströmische Studien*, Berlin, 1915.

Sundwall, J. *Abhandlungen zur Geschichte des Ausgehenden Römertums*, Helsingfors, 1919.

Tedesco, P. "Late Roman Italy: Taxation, Settlement and Economy, AD 300–700," PhD dissertation, University of Vienna, 2015.

Tedesco, P. "Exploring the Economy of Byzantine Italy," *Journal of European Economic History* 45, 2016, pp. 179–93.

Thacker, A. "Rome of the Martyrs. Saints, Cults and Relics, Fourth to Seventh Centuries," in *Roma Felix-Formation and Reflections of Medieval Rome*, eds. É. Ó. Carragáin and C. Neuman de Vegvar, Hampshire, 2007, pp. 13–50.

Thiel, A. (ed.) *Epistolae romanorum pontificum genuinae et quae ad eos scriptae sunt a S. Hilario usque ad Pelagium II*. 2nd ed. Braunsberg, 1868.

Thompson, G. "The *Pax Constantiniana* and the Roman Episcopate," in *The Bishop of Rome in Late Antiquity*, ed. G. Dunn, Surrey, UK/Burlington, VT, 2015, pp. 17–36.

Tjäder, J. *Die nichtliterarischen lateinischen Papyri Italiens aus der Zeit 445–700*, 2 vols. Uppsala, 1954–55.

Toner, J. *Roman Disasters*, Cambridge, UK/Malden, MA, 2013.

Trevor-Roper. H. *Edward Gibbon, The Decline and Fall of the Roman Empire*, New York, 1994, introduction to volume IV, pp. iv–lxviii.

Trout, D. *Damasus of Rome. The Epigraphic Poetry. Introduction, Text, Translations and Commentary*. Oxford, UK, New York. 2015.

Turcan, R. "Le délit des monétaires rebellés contre Aurélien," *Latomus* 28 (1969), pp. 948–59.

Twyman, B. "Aetius and the Aristocracy," *Historia* 19, 1987, pp. 480–503.

Ullmann. W. *Gelasius I. (492–496): Das Papsttum an der Wende der Spätantike zum Mittelalter*. Stuttgart, 1981.

Ungaro, L. "Il Ripostiglio della casa delle Vestali," Rome, 1899; now in *Bollettino di Numismatica* 4, 1985, pp. 47–160.

Vaccaro, E. "Patterning the Late Antique Economies of Inland Sicily in a Mediterranean Context," *Late Antique Archaeology* 10 (2013), pp. 259–313.

Van Dam, R. *The Roman Revolution of Constantine*, Cambridge, UK, and New York, 2007.

Van Dam, R. "Bishops and Clerics during the Fourth Century. Numbers and Their Implications," in *Episcopal Elections in Late Antiquity*, ed. J. Leemans,

P. Van Nuffelen, S. W. J. Keought, and C. Nicolaye, Berlin and Boston, 2011, pp. 217–42 = 2011A.

Van Dam, R. *Remembering Constantine at the Milvian Bridge*, Cambridge, UK, New York, 2011.

Van Dam, R. "Constantine's First Visit to Rome with Diocletian in 303," *JLA* 11.1 (2018), pp. 6–41.

Van Dam, R. "A Lost Panegyric: The Source for Eusebius of Caesarea's Description of Constantine's Victory and Arrival at Rome in 312," *JECS* 27.2, 2019, pp. 211–40.

Vannesse, M. "La reconstruction de Rome après le sac de 410. Entre mythe et réalité," *Latomus* 69, 2010, pp. 539–41.

Vassili, A. "La cultura di Anthemio," *Athenaeum* 16, 1938, pp. 38–45.

Vera, D. "Simmaco e le sue proprietà, Stuttura e funzionamento di un patrimonio aristocratico del quarto secolo d.C." in *Colloque genevois sur Symmaque: Àl'occasion du mille six centième anniversaire du conflit de l'autel de la Victoire*, ed. F. Paschoud, Paris, 1986, pp. 231–76.

Vera, D. "I paesaggi rurali del Meridione tardoantico: bilancio consuntivo e preventivo," in *Paesaggi e insediamenti rurali in Italia meridionale fra tardoantico e alto medioevo*, eds. G. Volpe and M. Turchiano, Bari, 2005, pp. 23–38.

Vera, D. "Questioni di storia agraria tardoromana: schiavi, coloni, 'villae'," *Ant. Tard.* 20, 2012, pp. 115–22.

Verardi, A. *La memoria legittimante: Il "Liber Pontificalis" e La chiesa di Roma del secolo VI*, Rome, 2016.

Ville, G. "Les jeux de gladiateurs dans l'empire chrétien," *MEFRA* 72 (1960), pp. 228–32.

Virlouvet, C. Tessera frumentaria. *Les procédures de distribution du blé à Rome à la fin de la Républic et au début de l'empire*. Rome, 1995.

Virlouvet, C. "L'approvvigionamento di Roma imperiale: una sfida quotidiana," in *Rome imperiale. Una metropoli antica*, ed. E. Lo Casio, Rome, 2000, pp. 103–35.

Vitiello, M. *Momenti di Roma ostrogota: adventus, feste, politica*. Stuttgart, 2005.

Vitiello, M. *Theodahad: A Platonic King at the Collapse of Ostrogothic Italy*. Toronto, 2014.

Vitiello, M. *Amalasuntha. The Transformation of Queenship in the Post-Roman World*. Philadelphia, 2017.

Von Schoenebeck, H. "Beiträge zur Religionspolitik des Maxentius und Constantin," *Klio* 43, NF 30, 1939, pp. 5–6.

Ward-Perkins, B. *From Classical Antiquity to the Middle Ages: Urban Public Building in Northern and Central Italy, AD 300-850*. Oxford, 1984.

Ward-Perkins, B. *The Fall of Rome and the End of Civilization*. Oxford, 2005.

Ward-Perkins, B. and C. Machado, "410 and the End of New Statuary in Italy," in *The Sack of Rome in 410 AD, Palilia* 28, eds. J. Lipps, C. Machado, and P. von Rummel, 2013, pp. 353–63.

Wenger, L. von, *Die Quellen des Römischen Rechts*, Vienna, 1953.

Weiss, P. "The Vision of Constantine," translation by A. R. Birley, in *JRA* 16, 2003, pp. 237–59.

Weisweiler, J. "The Roman Aristocracy between East and West: Divine Monarchy, State-Building and the Transformation of the Roman Senatorial Order (c. 25 BCE–425 CE)," in *New Approaches to the Later Roman Empire: Proceedings of a Conference*

Held at Kyoto University on 8 March 2014, ed. Takashi Minamikawa, Kyoto, pp. 31–52 = Weisweiler 2015A.

Weisweiler, J. "Domesticating the Senatorial Elite. Universal Monarch and Transregional Aristocracy in the Fourth Century AD," in *Contested Monarchy*, ed. J. Wienand. Oxford, New York, pp. 17–41 = Weisweiler 2015B.

Weisweiller, J. "Inscribing Imperial Power: Letters from Emperors in Late Antique Rome," in *Historische Erinnerung im städtischen Raum: Rom in der Spätantike*, eds. C. Witschell and R. Behrwald, Stuttgart, 2012, pp. 309–30.

Weisweiler, J. Society of Classical Studies, Panel Abstract, Published for the Annual Meeting, 2019.

Weisweiler, J. "The Heredity of Senatorial Status in the Principate," *JRS* 110, 2020, pp. 29–56.

Wermelinger. O. *Röm und Pelagius. Die theologische Position der römischen Bischöfe im pelagianischen Streit in den Jahren 411–432, Päpste und Papsttum*, Bd. 17. Stuttgart, 1975.

Wes, M. A. *Das Ende des Kaisertums im Western des römischen Reiches*. Gravenhage, 1967.

Wessel, S. "Religious Doctrine and Ecclesiastical Change in the Time of Leo the Great," in *The Age of Attila the Hun*, ed. M. Maas, Cambridge, New York, 2015, pp. 327–43.

Wheeler, E. *Stratagem and the Vocabulary of Military Trickery*, Mnemosyne Supp. 108, Leiden, 1988.

Whitby, M. *The Emperor Maurice and His Historian: Theophylact Simocatta on Persian and Balkan Warfare*. Oxford, 1988.

Wickham, C. *Early Medieval Italy. Central Power and Local Society. 400–1000*. Ann Arbor, MI, 1981.

Wickham, C. *Framing the Early Middle Ages*. Oxford, 2005.

Wiemer, H. U. "Libanios und Zosimus über den Rom-Besuch Konstantins I. im Jahre 326," in *Historia* 43, 1994, pp. 469–94.

Wiemer, H. U. "Libanius on Constantine," *CQ* 44 (1994), pp. 511–24.

Wienand, J. *Der Kaiser als Sieger*. Berlin, 2012.

Wienand, J. "Deo et domino. Aurelian, Serdica und die Restitutio orbis," *Jahrbuch für Numismatik und Geldgeschichte*, 85 (2015), pp. 63–99.

Wienand, J. "Publilius Optatianus Porfyrius. The Man and His Book," in *Morphogrammata: The Lettered Art of Optatian. Figuring Cultural Transformation in the Age of Constantine*, eds. M. Squire and J. Wienand, Paderborn, 2017, pp. 121–63.

Wilkinson, K. "Palladas and the Age of Constantine," *JRS* 99, 2009, pp. 36–60.

Wilkinson, K. "On Alan Cameron," *JLA* 10.1, 2017, pp. 270–77.

Williams, M. S. "No Arians in Milan? Ambrose on the Basilica Crisis of 385–386," *Historia* 67.3, 2018, pp. 346–65.

Wood, I. "Sidonius and the Burgundians," in *"Academica Libertas": Essais en l'honneur du professeur Javier Arce*, 2020, pp. 365–72.

Woods, D. "Some Addenda to *PLRE*," in *Historia* 42, 1993, pp. 122–25.

Woods, D. "A Misunderstood Monogram: Ricimer or Severus?" *Hermathena*: A Trinity College Dublin Review 172, 2002, pp. 5–22.

Wormald, P. "Review. The Decline of the Western Empire and the Survival of Its Aristocracy," *JRS* 66, 1976, pp. 217–26.

Wuensch, R. ed. *John Lydos, de Magistratibus*, Leipzig, 1903, rept. Stuttgart, 1967.

Wulf-Rheidt, U. "Die schwierige Frage der Nutzung des römischen Kaiserpalastes auf dem Palatini in Rom in der Spätantike," *Ant. Tard.* 25 (2017), pp. 127–48.

Yasin, A. M. *Saints and Church Spaces in the Late Antique Mediterranean. Architecture, Cult, and Community.* Cambridge, UK, New York, 2009.

Zanini, E. *Le Italie bizantine.* Bari, 1998.

Zecchini, G. "'Gesta de Xysti purgatione' e le fazioni aristocratiche a Roma alla metà del V secolo, *Rivista di Storia della Chiesa in Italia,*" 34, 1980, pp. 60–74, reprinted in *Ricerche di storiografia latina tardoantica*, II, Rome, 2011, pp. 185–99.

Zecchini, G. "La politica degli Anicii nel V secolo," in *Atti del Congresso Internazionale di Studi Boeziani*, ed. L. Obertello, Rome, 1981, pp. 121–38.

Zecchini, G. "I papi e i Lupercalia," in *Tolleranza religiosa in età tardoantica (IV–V secolo)*, eds. A. Marcone, U. Roberto and I. Tantillo, Cassino, 2014, pp. 267–82.

Zuckerman, C. "Two Reforms in the 370s. Recruiting Soldiers and Senators in the Divided Empire," *Rev. Ét. Byz.* 56 (1998), pp. 79–139.

Index

For EU product safety concerns, contact us at Calle de José Abascal, 56–1°,
28003 Madrid, Spain or eugpsr@cambridge.org.